CIVIL WAR *in the*
SOUTHWEST BORDERLANDS, 1861–1867

CIVIL WAR
in the
SOUTHWEST
BORDERLANDS
1861–1867

Andrew E. Masich

University of Oklahoma Press : Norman

For Deb

Library of Congress Cataloging-in-Publication Data

Names: Masich, Andrew Edward, author.
Title: Civil War in the southwest borderlands, 1861–1867 / Andrew E. Masich.
Description: Norman : University of Oklahoma Press, 2016. | Includes
    bibliographical references and index.
Identifiers: LCCN 2016023966 | ISBN 978-0-8061-5572-2 (cloth) |
    ISBN 978-0-8061-6096-2 (paper)
Subjects: LCSH: Southwest, New—History—Civil War, 1861-1865. | Indians of
    North America—History—Civil War, 1861-1865. | Mexican-American Border
    Region—History—19th century.
Classification: LCC E470.9 .M37 2016 | DDC 979/.02—dc23
LC record available at https://lccn.loc.gov/2016023966

The paper in this book meets the guidelines for permanence and durability of the
Committee on Production Guidelines for Book Longevity of the Council on Library
Resources, Inc. ∞

Contents

Illustrations

Acknowledgments

Growing up in the East while the Centennial of the Civil War was in full swing, I became fascinated by the diverse cast of characters engaged in America's deadliest and most defining conflict. My family moved west, and I completed my high school education in Tucson, Arizona. So, naturally, I examined the history of the Southwest Borderlands through a Civil War lens, attempting to understand the lasting impact of the war on the region and its people. Many people have assisted and inspired me along the way. Family, friends, teachers, students, colleagues, curators, archivists, editors, and historians have given generously of their time and talent, unselfishly sharing their ideas and insights. Traveling in Mexico and throughout the Southwest—on foot and horseback, by automobile and airplane—I have seen the places where history was made and heard the stories of the people who have called the mountains, deserts, and river valleys home for generations. They have all helped me better appreciate the challenges and joys of life in the borderlands. I have endeavored to glean what could be found in private collections, libraries, archives, museums, and archaeological sites. Everywhere, there were people willing and able to guide me.

Among those deserving special recognition are friends and colleagues: David F. Halaas, Harwood Hinton, James F. Brooks, Bruce Dinges, Jay Van Orden, Carol Brooks, Dawn Santiago, Cameron Laughlin, Tonia Rose, Breanna Smith, Betty Arenth, Lauren Uhl, Cody Boemig, Joe

Trotter, Paul Eiss, Van Beck Hall, Scott Sandage, and the University of Oklahoma Press team: Byron Price, Chuck Rankin, Steven Baker, and Kerin Tate. My wife, Debbie, has been with me every step of the way and has kept me on the straight and narrow. My children, Matthew, Molly, and Max, all contributed in their own ways. Gone but not forgotten are Don Bufkin, Steve Brady, Patricia Callahan, Mildred Cleghorn, Laird and Colleen Cometsevah, and Harvey Johnson.

Still, I have much to learn. And while this work will not satisfy all of my friends, it is at least a place to begin a serious discussion of the civil wars of the 1860s. My debt of gratitude is too large to pay with these few words in this small space. Thanks to all for your understanding, support, and encouragement. Please know that I have done my best to listen to and echo, with the deepest respect, the important stories of the peoples of the Southwest Borderlands.

CIVIL WAR *in the* SOUTHWEST BORDERLANDS, 1861–1867

Introduction

From 1861 to 1867 the diverse peoples—Indian, Hispano, and Anglo—of the Southwest Borderlands struggled for survival and dominance in civil wars, quite apart from the Civil War of the Southern rebellion that raged in the eastern United States. Successful adaptation to the changing conditions in the borderlands required accommodation, compromise, and alliances as much as it did martial prowess and the capacity to wage war. The warrior cultures of each of the antagonistic groups bore many similarities, but each brought to the conflict its traditional means of fighting while adapting to the rapidly evolving political and social landscape. At the beginning of the Civil War, Navajos, Apaches, and Comanches held the reins of power in the borderlands while sedentary Indian tribes, Hispanos, and Anglos maintained strongholds in fortified communities, mining settlements, and outposts.

By 1867 the last of the volunteer soldiers of the Civil War era mustered out of service, and Benito Juárez's Republicans had ousted French invaders, executed puppet emperor Maximilian, and reclaimed Mexico. In the border states of Chihuahua and Sonora, Republican troops began relocating tribes and reestablishing settlements devastated by Apache raiders, while in the newly configured U.S. territories of Arizona and New Mexico, the captivity- and slavery-based economic and social system was doomed to extinction. A new military, political, and economic order arose, with Anglos and Hispanos at the top of the hierarchy and the raiding tribes at the bottom. As the violence following the Civil War abated, a more centralized and powerful federal government exerted control over reservation-bound Indians and new territorial boundaries. International relations also changed; a more closely guarded and restrictive border between Mexico and the United States emerged from the war-torn borderlands, and Hispano and Anglo citizens uneasily shared an American political and economic model for survival in the Southwest.[1]

While historians have addressed the Union and Confederate conflict in the Southwest, none has focused on the importance of the Civil War as the spark that ignited a powder keg of civil wars related to preexisting ethnic tensions in the borderlands. I contend that cultural groups fought civil wars in the Southwest Borderlands concurrent with and connected to the American Civil War and that such wars often occur when two or more ethnically or culturally distinct peoples occupy the same space and vie for survival and dominance. In the borderlands of the 1860s, the dominant or militarily stronger party might characterize the conflict as civil war, while the insurgent faction might recognize it as an international or interethnic struggle. These conflicts resulted in new social hierarchies. As with most civil wars, the fighting in the Southwest pitted family members against one another, as adversaries were often related by blood, a result of years of captive-taking, adoption, slavery, and intermarriage.[2]

A culturally rooted sense of martial manhood triggered or intensified the violence in the Southwest. The warring peoples all shared aspects of this philosophy, but they differed in the ways they manifested it in their codes of honor, traditions, and modes of fighting. Although the role of women as both agents and victims of violence is not the focus of this work, women's actions and attitudes profoundly influenced their communities' conceptions of manhood.[3] Expanding on the idea advanced by other borderlands scholars that there existed a fundamental difference between "raiding" for gain and status and "warfare" for revenge and honor, I examine in detail the military doctrine or warrior traditions—tactics, logistics, weapons, martial customs, treatment of enemy captives—of the communities in conflict to demonstrate how the preparation for and practice of warfare set in motion actions that resulted in violence and played a significant role in the causes and outcomes of the wars for the borderlands.[4]

War reveals much about human nature—our loves and hates, our beliefs and superstitions, and our penchant and capacity for violence. Only in recent years, however, with advances in social history, new western history, and more specifically, new Southwest Borderlands studies, have scholars attempted to understand the Civil War's full impact and multicultural dimensions.[5] Employing interdisciplinary, microhistorical, and narrative approaches, historians are beginning to look westward—far from the eastern "seat of rebellion"—and are advancing a broader understanding of the conflict. In the Southwest Borderlands of the 1860s, violent conflict resulted from each community's desire for security and cultural preservation.[6]

As the Civil War raged in the eastern United States, Indian, Hispano, and Anglo peoples fought other civil wars in the Far West along the U.S.-Mexico border.[7] Building on the work of borderlands scholars and employing some previously untapped Indian Depredation Claims records discovered at the National Archives—as well as military and government documents, newspapers, ethnographies, museum collections, and other primary source materials—this book examines the types of warfare engaged in by the diverse peoples of the Southwest. It also reveals the role this violence played in the civil wars spawned by the American Civil War and how the resulting conflicts led to a shift in the delicate balance of power in the Southwest Borderlands.

The American Civil War created conditions that resulted in or expanded violent conflict between and among peoples of different communities (bands, tribes, races, ethnicities, and nations) and led to multiple concurrent civil wars in the Southwest Borderlands between 1861 and 1867. Before the Civil War, intercultural tension and a hostile but interdependent raid-and-reprisal relationship existed between the Indian, Hispano, and Anglo peoples. This conflict was most often characterized by raiding and captive-taking but rarely "war to the death" resulting in the total destruction or extermination of an enemy. The Navajos, Apaches, and Comanches often bested their Hispano, Anglo, and agrarian Indian adversaries and were at the top of the power hierarchy in the territories when the war began. The initial withdrawal of regular U.S. troops in 1861 led to a temporary power vacuum that opportunistic warriors rushed to fill. The subsequent invasion of the territories by Anglos—Union and Confederate—resulted in alliances among Anglo soldiers, Hispanos, and sedentary Indian tribes, allowing them, collectively, to wage a relentless war on the raiding tribes. The wars north of the international border also served to re-inflame a smoldering civil war in Mexico and enabled European intervention that vastly enlarged that conflict and brought it to new levels of violence.[8]

This work is at once a microhistory of the American Civil War in the borderlands and an examination of warrior traditions in civil wars. It focuses on the clash of cultures and the transnational aspects of the U.S.-Mexico borderlands during the Civil War years. While concentrating generally on the American Southwest, I emphasize New Mexico and Arizona Territories (the latter carved out of the former in 1863) and portions of California, Texas, and the Mexican border states of Sonora and Chihuahua. The history of the nations, states, tribes, and ethnic communities is transnational and cannot be confined to the borders established by governments and drawn on maps. In the borderlands, human populations interacted across political boundaries, sometimes in spite of them and at times because of them. Whereas others have explored captivity and slavery as conceptual frameworks, I look more closely at warfare and violence as organizing themes. In the tradition of earlier borderlands historians, I have adopted a chronological narrative approach while presenting, whenever possible, illustrative material and detailed analysis on a micro level. There is significance in microcosm often lost in grand historical theories. In my search for large lessons in small worlds, I have merged archaeological, anthropological, ethnographic, and documentary sources to chronicle the Southwestern Borderlands during the Civil War years. The narrative of the civil wars is necessarily complicated because it involves so many cultures and communities. At the same time, the stories behind individual actors in a diverse cast of characters are rich and varied. While studying the grand scheme of things, one must not overlook the idiosyncratic behavior of idealistic and self-interested individuals. The microhistorical approach enables a better understanding of the complex and nuanced lives of the peoples and individuals of the Southwest Borderlands during this turbulent period.[9]

A shared understanding of the often contentious terms used to describe relationships among and between peoples and communities of the borderlands during the Civil War era is essential if my arguments are to make sense. Toward this end, I have appended a glossary intended to reflect recent scholarship in borderlands history. The reader will also find my own interpretations of sometimes controversial ideas. Included are definitions of obscure and archaic words as well as Spanish, Apache, and Navajo terms. For the purpose of this study I will define "raid" (an extension of hunting traditions based on resource acquisition for survival), "war" (socially or politically motivated violence), "civil war" (war within a polity or region considered unified by one or both antagonists), "revolution/rebellion" (civil war resulting from an ideological change or a desire to maintain traditionally held values, depending on the perspective of the antagonists), "nation" (a community with geographic boundaries imagined and defined by one or more peoples), "tribe" (a linguistically and culturally related group that is inclined to cooperate especially when faced with external threats), and "community" (a real or imagined group of people with common interests) and demonstrate the cultural imperatives behind these meaning-freighted terms.

The Spanish, Mexicans, and Americans declared and defined their "imagined communities" (nations) in the Southwest without the consent of the other peoples encompassed within the boundaries.[10] By the 1860s, more than three hundred years after the Spanish *entrada,* the descendants of the Euro-Americans considered Indian resistance to be rebellion while the indigenous groups (bands and tribes) saw it as war against outside invaders—a transnational war. The warfare waged by the Yuman-speaking Colorado River tribes against the Yuman-speaking Maricopas and allied Uto-Aztecan Pimas was at once a civil war and an international conflict. Similarly, conflicts between the U.S.-Anglo-Hispano alliance and Apache bands, as well as between various Navajo and Apache bands (both raiding-pastoral Athabaskan peoples), might be considered civil wars and international struggles. Ópatas fought Ópatas in Mexico as the American Civil War created conditions that exacerbated the civil war south of the border. From the U.S. perspective, the fact that tribal representatives had entered into treaties that swore allegiance and subordination to the federal government meant that warfare represented civil unrest rather than international conflict. This domestic dependent relationship between the tribes and the United States became the basis for the record number of claims made against the government, which accepted a measure of responsibility for losses resulting from attacks by tribal members, during this period.

Socially constructed notions of race and ethnicity are also fundamental to understanding the civil wars of the Southwest. For these

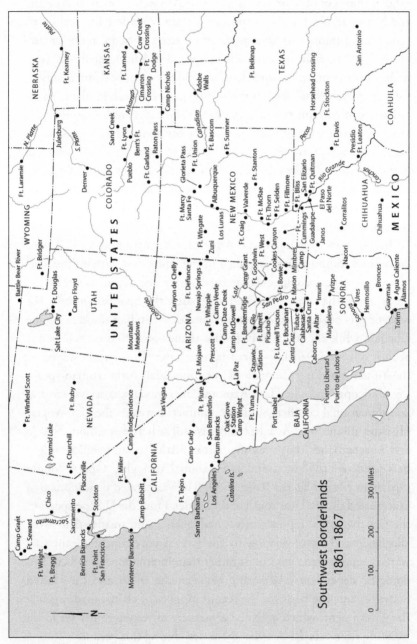

Southwest Borderlands
1861–1867

N

0   100   200   300 Miles

NEBRASKA

Platte

Ft. Kearney

KANSAS

Cow Creek
Crossing

Ft. Larned

Arkansas
Cimarron
Crossing   Dodge

Adobe
Walls

Camp Nichols

Julesburg

W. Platte

S. Platte

Sand Creek

Ft. Lyon

Bent's Ft.

Raton Pass

Canadian

Ft. Bascom

Ft. Sumner

TEXAS

Ft. Belknap

San Antonio

COLORADO

Denver

Pueblo

Ft. Garland

Glorieta Pass

Ft. Union

Pecos

Horsehead Crossing

Ft. Stockton

WYOMING

Ft. Laramie

Battle Bear River

Ft. Bridger

UTAH

Salt Lake City

Camp Floyd

Mountain
Meadows

Colorado

Ft. Marcy
Santa Fe

Albuquerque

Los Lunas

NEW MEXICO

Ft. Stanton

Valverde

Ft. Craig

Ft. McRae

Ft. Thorn

Ft. Selden

Ft. Fillmore

Ft. Bliss

San Elizario

Ft. Quitman

Ft. Davis

Presidio
Ft. Leaton

Rio Grande

El Paso
del Norte

Guadalupe

Janos

Corralitos

CHIHUAHUA

Chihuahua

Conchos

M E X I C O

COAHUILA

United States

Ft. Defiance

Canyon de Chelly

Ft. Wingate

Zuni

Navajo Springs

Camp Verde

Ft. Whipple

Prescott

Camp Date Creek

ARIZONA

Ft. Mojave

La Paz

Salt

Gila

Camp McDowell

Stanwix
Station

Ft. Breckenridge

San Pedro

Ft. Goodwin

Camp Grant

Ft. West

Cookes Canyon

Ft. Bowie

Ft. Mason

Picacho

Ft. Lowell Tucson

Ft. Barrett

Ft. Buchanan

Tubac

Calabasas

Santa Cruz

Cummings

Camp
Mimbres

Nacori

SONORA

Ures

Arizpe

Hermosillo

Bronces

Guaymas

Agua Caliente

Torim

Alamos

Magdalena

Santa Cruz

Caborca   Altar

Imuris

Sonora

NEVADA

Pyramid Lake

Ft. Churchill

Ft. Ruby

Camp Independence

Ft. Winfield Scott

Las Vegas

Ft. Piute

San Bernardino

Oak Grove
Station
Camp Wright

Ft. Yuma

Port Isabel

Puerto Libertad

Puerto de Lobos

BAJA
CALIFORNIA

Camp Cady

Drum Barracks

Ft. Miller

CALIFORNIA

Ft. Tejon

Los Angeles

Catalina Is.

Santa Barbara

Camp Babbitt

Camp Grant
Ft. Seward

Ft. Wright

Ft. Bragg

Chico

Placerville

Sacramento

Stockton

Benicia Barracks

Ft. Point
San Francisco

Monterey Barracks

controversial terms I rely on interpretations advanced by scholars who believe that "race" is often used to refer to "others" while "ethnicity" is how a group defines itself. Even though these ideas are artificial historical or social constructs, race and ethnicity matter in understanding the civil wars of the Southwest Borderlands because the people involved in the struggles believed these distinctions to be important. The relationships between the ethnic groups of the Southwest today are still colored by these differences in perception of what constitutes a community, a nation, and a people. It is hoped that this study will foster a better understanding of these differing and often conflicting perceptions.[11]

A wide array of U.S. and Mexican primary sources including military records, newspapers, census reports, and manuscript collections complement a largely unresearched body of government documents—the Indian Depredation Claims, housed with related United States Court of Claims records (Record Group [RG] 75, 123, 205) at the National Archives (NARA) in Washington. U.S. military records are especially rich in information relating to the peoples of the territories. Officers' reports (in RG 94, 98, 393) including Letters Sent and Received, Post Returns, Ordnance Returns, Records of Courts Martial, and Records of Continental Commands (General, Special, and Post Orders) provide insights into groups the government considered enemies and allies, detailing strengths, weakness, motivations, and methods of warfare. Rich collections of well-organized Mexican archival material relating to the period of the War of the Reform and French Intervention were found in Mexico City at the Centro de Estudios de Historia de México CARSO, and Centro Cultural, Archivo Histórico de APAN.

Newspaper accounts submitted by soldier correspondents and other eyewitnesses are also valuable sources of uncensored observations and candid information about the activities of combatants, civil and military, in the borderlands. Though newspapers from Arizona, New Mexico, Texas, and California, as well as periodicals from Mexican states and the Imperial government of Maximilian, must be carefully evaluated for their editorial agendas, many articles are simply verbatim reprints of private correspondence from soldiers and citizen participants in the border wars. These accounts complement the letters and diaries, including those of U.S. Volunteer troops and Confederates serving in the territories as well as those of Anglo and Hispano civilians living in or traveling through the Southwest.

Continuing in the tradition of borderlands studies, I have employed anthropological materials, including archaeological reports on forts, camps, villages, and massacre and battle sites, which are located at the Smithsonian National Anthropological Archives, University of Arizona, Colorado Historical Society (now History Colorado), and other state and local repositories. Ethnographic accounts in the form of oral histories of the Indian peoples of the borderlands are essential to a balanced study of this subject. The best of these sources, recorded by Smithsonian and other ethnographers in the late nineteenth century, relate directly to matters of raiding and warfare and delve into the motivations for intertribal, intratribal, and interethnic conflict. I surveyed museum collections for ethnographic materials, art, and artifacts that shed light on the technologies, traditions, and modes of warfare employed by the antagonists. Most helpful were collections at the New Mexico History Museum, Arizona Historical Society, and the Smithsonian Institution, as well as the National Museums of Mexico, especially the Museo del Virreinato, the Museo Nacional de Historia, and the Instituto Nacional de Antropología e Historia, Museo Nacional de las Intervenciones.

The Indian Depredation Claims are an especially valuable resource. These records contain eyewitness testimony, rich in detail, describing attacks, stock raids, captivity, and other types of conflict that, when combined with other primary source accounts and materials, provide insights into the civil wars in the borderlands. Researchers will find more than ten thousand depredation claim cases filed between 1796 and 1920, many still bundled and securely tied with their original red tape. Of these claims, nearly seven hundred relate to Arizona and New Mexico during the period 1861–67. The case files contain depositions, testimony, cross-examinations, and other evidence detailing the nature of raids and warfare in the Southwest. This wealth of information sheds light on the groups initiating the attacks, the number of depredations over time, the magnitude of violence, and the patterns of conflict and tactics employed. When examined with other primary sources, the testimonies of Indian, Hispano, and Anglo antagonists present a complex yet compelling picture of the culturally distinct methods of conflict, accommodation, cooperation, and other survival strategies employed by the peoples of the borderlands during the Civil War years.[12]

Prologue

Captain Melchior Díaz had time to reflect on the adventures and misadventures of his life as he lay dying on the Arizona desert trail the Spanish would name El Camino del Diablo, the Devil's Road. Díaz's martial skills with sword and lance and his natural gifts as a leader of men had advanced him quickly through the ranks of New Spain's military establishment. In July 1540, Governor Francisco Vázquez de Coronado trusted him to guide the way north to the extreme edge of Spain's American empire for the final assault on the Zuni Indian village of Hawikuh, the key to the fabled golden cities of Cíbola. The cities of gold had turned out to be no more than the fictional ravings of the now-despised priest, Fray Marcos de Niza, whom Coronado later placed in Díaz's protective custody so the beguiled and embittered Spanish soldiers would not murder the cleric before he could answer to the viceroy. The slung stones and arrows of the Zuni warriors, however, had turned out to be all too real. Díaz had witnessed Coronado himself, conspicuous in his gilded armor and plumed helm, knocked senseless from his horse during the fighting in the narrow streets of the fortified Indian city. The natives, who possessed no gold to speak of, had zealously resisted the Spanish invaders from centuries-old, compactly built stone structures terraced atop imposing mesas which overlooked fields of corn and beans in the green valleys below. Coronado's force of some 1,300 cavalry, infantry, and Indian auxiliaries from the south could not subsist on the Zunis' meager supplies, so the governor sent Díaz westward to rendezvous with Captain Hernando Alarcón's ships dispatched by the viceroy to support the overland expedition.

After many days of hard riding, more than ten days southwest of Coronado's position, Díaz discovered the Quechan, Cocopah, and Maricopa peoples living near the confluence of the Gila and Colorado Rivers, fishing and growing crops in lowlands wetted by seasonal floodwaters. Comfortably housed in thatched dwellings, these exceptionally tall and powerfully built river people impressed the Spaniards. The Quechans obligingly showed the strangely bearded and cleverly armored white men where Alarcón's boatmen had buried a letter and supplies. Díaz knew the fact this tempting cache had remained intact, even though Alarcón's worm-eaten ships had been forced to depart weeks earlier, was as much a tribute to the good nature of their Indian hosts as it was to the sea captain's diplomacy. In truth, Díaz liked and trusted these Yuman-speaking peoples, who shared their food and seemed genuinely eager to make friends and forge alliances. But the ride to the west had been another disappointment. Instead of the Pacific Ocean, Díaz and Alarcón discovered that California was not an island, as had been supposed but, rather, a peninsula defined on its upper, eastern boundary by the muddy Colorado River. In any case, the water lay too far distant from Cíbola to serve as a convenient port for Coronado's inland operations.

Now Díaz lay dying, the jarring of his horse-drawn litter paining him as his men slowly bore him away from the river toward the City of Mexico, the greatest bastion of Spanish civilization in the New World. He had been ingloriously felled by his own lance. Thrown in a fit of pique at a hungry dog, an unruly herder's whippet, the point had stuck fast in the ground and, as Díaz was unable to rein in his charging horse, the iron-ferruled butt of the lance pierced his thigh and groin. As infection spread, he knew he had only days to live and would never see Spain again. Perhaps he recalled the peoples he had encountered in this northern frontier of New Spain. Some had been accommodating, while others had proved fierce foes. It would not be so easy a task to subdue and enslave them as he had once believed.[1]

Chapter 1

Peoples of the Southwest Borderlands

During the 1860s, Indians, Hispanos, and Anglos struggled for power in the area now known as the Southwest Borderlands of the United States. Each group brought to the conflict its own ideas of war. While there were significant differences in the way they sought power through violence, there were also many similarities. All the peoples of the borderlands embraced some form of martial credo. In every group the men spent an inordinate amount of time developing warrior traditions, weapons, strategies, and tactics intended to give them an advantage over rival communities while demonstrating their value to the women and other members of their society. The men's sense of worth was inextricably tied to the way they were viewed by their own group. Social status and the acquisition of mates depended on their ability to dominate or exert power over others inhabiting or passing through the territory they considered their domain.[1]

All the peoples of the Southwest understood the concept of conquest by force of arms, yet the rules of war differed for each group, and the strategies and tactics employed varied. The antagonists all adopted elaborate war rituals, costumes, and weaponry designed to achieve tactical advantage and calculated to awe their enemies. All the groups that vied for power and dominance in the borderlands believed in some form of vengeance warfare and practiced some form of captivity and slavery. The peoples who came into conflict in the borderlands of the 1860s all shared a belief in an afterlife and had religious and spiritual traditions that guided their behavior in the corporeal world.

Though each tribe or band had its distinctive characteristics, the indigenous Indian peoples of the Southwest all felt a deep connection to the land they inhabited. Whether they adopted sedentary, seminomadic, or nomadic-pastoral survival strategies, they differed significantly from their Hispano and Anglo counterparts in their ideas of land ownership. The Indian warriors especially valued independent initiative and action and only followed chiefs or war leaders in whom they had confidence. These positions were not hereditary. When it came to war, leaders changed often, and individual warriors or bands followed their own course. Leaders influenced followers or led by example, rather than demanding compliance based on rank. This leadership model made cooperative strategic operations against enemies difficult to plan and execute. Groups of like-minded men within a band or tribe typically congregated in warrior societies, which became both social and fighting units. Their weapons varied depending on the men's physical abilities, the environment, and the motives for violent conflict.

The pedestrian Yumans of the Colorado River generally preferred close combat with war clubs while the mounted warriors of the southern plains employed lances and other weapons suited for fighting on horseback. The mountain-born Apaches mastered surprise, ambush, and fighting-retreat tactics—rarely attacking head-on in the open—loosing arrows and slung stones with extraordinary skill. All the indigenous peoples quickly adapted to weapons and war materials introduced by Hispano and Anglo newcomers. Most of the Indian peoples of the borderlands recognized sharp distinctions between "raiding" and "warfare." The raid for enemy property was an extension of time-honored hunting and gathering traditions, while war was motivated by revenge for losses or offenses suffered at the hands of enemies. Women and children captives were an essential feature of the raid-war complex. Men took captive women for wives, and families desired male children to replace losses resulting from war and natural attrition. Raiding and warfare were often seasonal activities, closely related to the availability of food and forage.

Hispano warriors exhibited a merging of Indian and European martial traditions. A racially hierarchical and, often, hereditary system of leadership emerged from the Spanish conquest of the Americas. In war, officers exerted control over soldiers—both regulars and militia—and

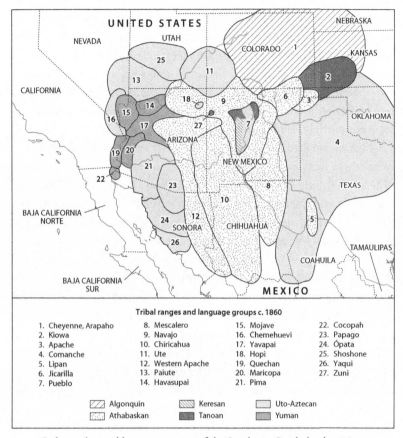

Indian tribes and language groups of the Southwest Borderlands, 1860s.

civilian auxiliaries. Leaders generally came from the upper classes, while fighting men came from the lower classes of *mestizos* and assimilated or subject Indian peoples. Internecine fighting characterized the borderlands of the 1860s, and political and class rivalries often hampered concerted or strategic action against enemies. Hispanos highly valued individual courage and honor, and abhorred the *vergüenza*, or shame, that attached to cowardly misconduct. Their weapons and tactics reflected the mixture of ethnicities seen in the men themselves. Lances and short swords were often the weapons of choice for mounted warriors, while footmen employed a wide variety of arms depending on terrain and availability. Over time, firearms became increasingly important. Slavery and peonage were deeply rooted in the Hispano tradition, and captive-taking often became the primary motive for raiding and the cause of retaliatory warfare. Women captives were desired as *criadas* (servants) and boys as herders; these were quickly assimilated into the Hispanos' sedentary agricultural or pastoral settlements. Raids, punitive expeditions, and campaigns related to the growing seasons but were not entirely dependent on them.

Anglos brought a highly militarized society to the borderlands. They were by no means a homogeneous group—Texas rebels, for example, differed culturally and temperamentally from Anglo Unionists, from California and the territories, and from regular army soldiers. Among the Anglos were small numbers of African Americans who, in the late 1860s, fought with regular U.S. Army units and were, from the Indians' point of view, virtually indistinguishable from their white counterparts in terms of tactics and martial culture. The Indian peoples of the southern plains called them "black whitemen" and, by the end of the decade, referred to them as "Buffalo Soldiers."[2] In general, the combative Anglo-Americans exhibited European ideas of strategic warfare and military doctrine, adhering to highly stylized tactics that evolved from the Napoleonic tradition. The soldiers organized themselves around an officer corps composed largely of trained professionals. A rigidly hierarchical system of leadership left little room for independent action in the standing professional army, but during wartime, volunteer troops demonstrated a willingness and capacity for innovation that often surprised the regulars.[3]

The concepts of "total war" and "war of extermination" introduced by the Anglos escalated the violence in the borderlands to new levels of lethality. Combined with industrial mass production of sophisticated firearms and logistical technologies, the Anglos sustained campaigns and operations on tactical and strategic levels during all seasons of the year and in all conditions. In the borderlands of the 1860s, their practice of capturing "prisoners of war" was a kind of captive-taking generally seen as a temporary war measure, never the raison d'être for fighting. At the same time, their evolving attitudes toward slavery and race became the root cause of cultural difference and internecine conflict. Loyalties, North or South, were generally determined by state of origin, though individual conscience and circumstance often influenced decisions related to which army a man would join. The Anglos, led by professional military men, sought to subdue other peoples by armed force and then regulate all aspects of civil life.

Indigenous Peoples and the Spanish

Hundreds of years prior to the arrival of Spanish conquistadors in the sixteenth century, people descended from ice age migrants, who had come to North America twenty thousand years earlier, settled along the tributaries of the Colorado and Rio Grande Rivers of the arid Southwest.[4] The Indian peoples and cultures that evolved in the Americas were by no means a monolithic group, but, rather, diverse tribes and bands with distinct languages, survival strategies, traditions, and customs.[5] By the time Europeans arrived in the Americas, Yuman- and Uto-Aztecan–speaking peoples lived in permanent villages along rivers or fortified stone and adobe structures atop high mesas and subsisted by means of intensive agriculture supplemented by hunting and foraging.[6] Pressured by Comanche, Kiowa, Arapaho, and Cheyenne peoples of the central and southern plains,[7] Athabaskan-speaking Navajos and Apaches migrated into the region from the north and east as the Spanish *entrada* developed from the south.[8]

By the early eighteenth century, the Navajo clans sheltered in the deep canyons of the upper Colorado River, growing crops and hunting, while diverse Apache bands subsisted primarily by foraging, hunting, and seasonally cultivating crops along the mountain rivers and high desert streams to the south. These people became adept at supplementing their supplies by raiding the more sedentary agrarian tribes in search of food, captives, and other useful or fungible commodities. Over the next hundred years, this tradition of raiding increasingly targeted the Spanish arrivals who lived in small, isolated villages and possessed herds of domesticated animals—cattle, sheep, goats, and horses.

The horses brought to the Americas by the Spanish radically changed the survival strategies and lifestyles of the first peoples to inhabit the Southwest. The availability of the easily domesticated quadrupeds revolutionized transportation and band mobility on the southern plains, where true horse cultures evolved within only a few generations of the animal's introduction. The peoples of the plains began to follow the great buffalo herds as they migrated across the vast grasslands. Prior to the adoption of the horse, hunters on foot found it difficult to kill the powerful American bison and, when successful, to transport the hundreds of pounds of perishable meat. Horses enabled the hunters to ride alongside a running buffalo and slay it with a lance or arrows, then pack meat, hide, and other useful parts of the animal back to a village. In time, the Comanches and other Plains Indians learned to move their villages with the wide-ranging herds, carrying buffalo hide tipis, camp equipment, and children on pole-drag travois pulled by ponies bred for their stamina.

The mobility of the villages greatly expanded the reach of the horse peoples and increasingly brought them into conflict with others. Employing many of the same skills used in buffalo hunting, the Comanches and Kiowas became expert mounted fighters. Wars of conquest and retaliation escalated as did raiding for captives and profit. The Plains warriors drove most of the neighboring Apache bands from the open grasslands of the Staked Plains (Llano Estacado) to the mountains and deserts to the south and west. More than thirty related and cooperating Comanche and Kiowa bands kept the Arapahos and Cheyennes well to the north toward the Arkansas River and away from the southern herds. The people inhabiting the northernmost Mexican outposts and Pueblo Indian villages feared and paid tribute to the warriors of the plains and did not stray far from the protection of settlements on the Rio Grande.

In the eighteenth and early nineteenth centuries, the influence of the ever-expanding Comanche empire rippled westward toward the Rio Grande. By trade and raid the river and mountain peoples of the Southwest also adopted horses, but the effect of these animals on their tribes was not as profound as it was on the nomadic Plains tribes. The sedentary peoples remained in their villages close to dependable crops, foraging ranges, and hunting grounds. The seminomadic Athabaskan Navajos and Apaches, however, lived in seasonal *rancherías* and increasingly relied on horses for hunting and for raiding neighboring tribes, sometimes even venturing onto the plains and ranging deep into Mexico. Their horse herds remained relatively small when compared to the Comanches, Kiowas, and Cheyennes, and the animals sometimes served as a supplementary food source, an unthinkable dietary taboo for the horse people of the plains.[9] Still, even in the Southwest Borderlands, horses began to take hold as the principal medium of wealth and economic exchange.[10]

Spain's northern frontier in New Mexico lay far from the seat of government in Mexico City. The 1,600-mile-journey on the Camino

Real, either on foot or by ox-drawn *carreta*, from the capital to Santa Fe and the *provincias internas* (interior provinces), might take two to three months, if all went well. The far-flung presidios and settlements suffered attacks by Indian raiders as well as internal strife in the form of uprisings by conquered *indios bárbaros* (barbarous Indians) and occasionally even the captive *indios mansos* (tame Indians). The bloody Pueblo Revolt of 1680 left hundreds of Spanish settlers dead and thousands captured or displaced. The Spanish regained their northernmost settlements after nearly two decades of *reconquista* (reconquest) and many concessions to the Pueblo peoples, including guarantees of more tolerance for traditional ways and local autonomy. In 1751, nearly fifteen thousand Pimas attempted to throw off the Spanish yoke in a loosely coordinated uprising that left hundreds dead in Sonora. New Spain's viceroy, Carlos Francisco de Croix, marqués de Croix, eventually forgave the Pimas and expelled the Jesuit missionaries in 1767 for abusing their native charges. But the seed of rebellion had taken root, and in 1781 the Quechan uprising at Yuma Crossing destroyed the Spanish garrison and missions on the lower Colorado, effectively closing the royal road connecting Mexico City to California and ending Spanish influence in that portion of Pimería Alta (upper Pima territory).[11]

When the Mexican War of Independence from Spain erupted in 1810 with the rallying cry of Father Miguel Hidalgo y Costilla at Dolores, near Guanajuato in central Mexico, many Hispanos in the already militarized northern settlements embraced the call to arms and the promise of a new and more responsive regime. Pueblo peoples, Comanches, Apaches, and Navajos (whom the Spanish called Apaches del Navahu) had to choose sides as well, and the civil war in New Spain resulted in fighting that saw loyalties tested and changed.[12]

By 1821, more than a decade of fighting had depleted the Spanish treasury and made monarch Ferdinand VII vulnerable to a European coup. The conservative Mexican *criollos* (Mexico-born Spaniards), led by Augustín Iturbide, united with Hidalgo's radical *mestizo* (mixed Spanish and Indian blood) forces, who had borne the brunt of the fierce *guerrilla* war waged against the Spanish. If successful, the rebellion would guarantee independence from Spain; equal rights for *criollos* and *peninsulares* (Spanish-born) alike; recognition of the Roman Catholic Church, with all its privileges, as the official religion; and the establishment of a new monarchy headed by a suitable European royal.

This Plan de Iguala became the centerpiece of the Treaty of Córdoba, which brought the war to a close in August 1821 and led eventually to Iturbide's installation as emperor of Mexico.

United States of Mexico

Conditions did not improve, however, for the Mexicans of the northern frontier. In 1824, the people of Mexico dissolved Iturbide's empire and adopted a new constitution, which defined the nation as a federal republic with nineteen states and five territories. The United States of Mexico (Estados Unidos de Mexico) abolished slavery, recognized Roman Catholicism as the state religion, and elected its first president. The northern territories of Alta California and Nuevo Mexico and the newly created state of Texas (Coahuila y Tejas) with its capital in Saltillo, hundreds of miles from the former Texas capital (San Antonio de Bexar), constituted the borderlands with the United States. Mexico's bankrupt and distracted central government and war-weary military focused little attention on the distant outposts in Sonora, Chihuahua, California, New Mexico, and Texas. In need of a buffer against raiding Comanches and Apaches, the Mexican government invited enterprising Americans to occupy the Indian frontier. It seemed a logical solution to the unstable borderlands situation. The settlers were encouraged to create their own citizen *milicias* (militias) for protection against the tribes considered hostile. Soon the people of the sparsely populated frontier, with its liberalized immigration policies and independent armed forces, began to think and fend for themselves.

Mexican officials saw to it that the newly arrived Anglos took oaths of allegiance to the republic and the Catholic Church, and for a time it seemed as though the borderlands buffer strategy was working. But both Anglos and Hispanos in the north resented taxation without the benefits of military protection and full political participation. By 1830, American settlers outnumbered the Hispano residents in Texas. To address this ethnic imbalance, Mexico's president, Anastásio Bustamante, prohibited further immigration from the United States into the borderlands, though American citizens were allowed to settle in other parts of Mexico. Furthermore, the Mexican government rescinded the property tax law, intended to exempt immigrants from paying taxes for 10 years, and increased tariffs on goods shipped from the United States.

Bustamante also ordered all Texas settlers to comply with the federal prohibition against slavery or face military intervention. The Americans from Tennessee, Kentucky, and other Southern states found ways to circumvent or simply ignore the new laws.

As significant numbers of Americans settled in Texas, the horse-rich and militarily powerful Comanches had become the masters of the southern plains. By 1835 more than 30,000 Comanches lived in Coahuila y Tejas, along with 30,000 Anglos and only 7,800 Hispano Tejanos. While both the Mexicans and Comanches held captives as slaves, the Americans emigrating to Texas from the southern states and territories also brought in bondage approximately 5,000 enslaved Africans and African Americans (born in the United States).[13] The Anglo Texans from Kentucky and Tennessee were a fiercely independent people descended from Scots-Irish immigrants who evolved on the American frontier a warrior tradition that originated in ancient Celtic tribalism. Quick to resort to virile violence, dueling for honor and killing for revenge were common practices. These warlike Anglo and allied native Hispano Texans developed a violent competition with the Comanches. The efforts of the warring cultures to dominate the southern plains were characterized by brutal attacks and retaliatory raids that left hundreds dead and firmly established fierce warrior cultures in the Hispano, Anglo, and Indian communities of the borderlands.[14]

Rebellion once again ignited and spread in the northern states of Mexico, with the heart of the conflict clearly centered in Texas, fueled by Anglos with a sense of entitlement and destiny that bordered on religious fervor. General Sam Houston's Texian forces, composed of both Anglos and Hispanos disaffected by the constitutional changes and lack of communication and support from the central government of Mexico, battled General Antonio López de Santa Anna's well-equipped but poorly led army. An isolated command of Texians, joined by notable adventurers including Davy Crockett and Jim Bowie, was overwhelmed and killed to a man at the old San Antonio mission known to history as the Alamo. After months of fighting that resulted in battles, guerilla attacks, and massacres—committed by both sides—Houston forced the surrender of the Mexican army at San Jacinto. On May 14, 1836, the captured Santa Anna signed under duress the Treaties of Velasco, formally bringing the war to a close. The independent Republic of Texas became a reality, at least in the imaginations of the Anglo-Americans.[15]

The mere existence of the Republic of Texas galled Mexican pride and remained a source of *vergüenza* for President Santa Anna, who struggled to maintain his power and prestige after his ignominious defeat and surrender. Mexico's Congress never ratified the treaties and did not recognize the independent Texas republic. To save face, the Mexican president made it clear to his people that Texas should be restored, and armed clashes along the new border continued incessantly after the signing of the 1836 treaties. The Texans took the offensive twice, in 1841 and 1843, intent on the conquest of New Mexico, which they claimed as part of their republic, hoping to capitalize on its lucrative trading opportunities. These invasions were twice repelled before the armed battalions of Texas rangers could reach Santa Fe.[16]

By mid-decade, full-scale war erupted anew. In 1845 the United States annexed the Republic of Texas as the Union's twenty-eighth state, following heated congressional debate between Democrats and Whigs over the morality and necessity of conflict with Mexico, which further exposed the growing sectional schism between slave and free states and foreshadowed civil war. President James K. Polk then deliberately provoked Mexico, ostensibly over the international boundary line, and the war came. Many Americans saw Polk's military action and declaration of war as a usurpation of congressional authority, but the president's vision of Manifest Destiny coupled with a general belief in Anglo-Saxon racial superiority captured sufficient votes in Congress and the popular imagination. The U.S. Senate formally declared war against Mexico on May 13, 1846, and the struggle for Texas and northern Mexico resumed.

Mexico's people experienced unprecedented violence during the 1846–48 conflict with the United States, but the New Mexico settlements survived the war relatively unscathed. New Mexicans had developed a mutually beneficial relationship with American trappers and traders in the decade prior to the war. Still, Governor Manuel Armijo, who had twice repelled the Texans' attempts to take Santa Fe, marched an army of some 3,000 volunteers to confront Stephen Watts Kearny's 1,600-man Army of the West. Kearny, an experienced frontier regular, had earned a reputation as a disciplinarian and the best long-distance marching field officer in the army following an unequaled two-thousand-mile tramp along the Platte to South Pass just a year earlier. Now his command of U.S. Dragoons and Missouri Volunteers marched steadily down the Santa Fe Trail, approaching the New Mexican capital from the northeast through Raton Pass in the Sangre de Cristo Mountains. Armijo positioned his men in the narrow Apache Canyon at Glorieta Pass, just twelve miles from New Mexico's capital. But after negotiating with the Americans, Armijo disbanded his army without firing a shot, much to the dismay of his subordinates. As he approached Santa Fe, Kearny warmed to the role of benevolent conqueror. He attempted to assure the New Mexicans that the all-powerful U.S. government would intercede on their behalf and could be depended upon for protection, as he proclaimed:

> From the Mexican government you have never received protection. The Apaches and Navajoes come down from the mountains and carry off your sheep, and even your women, whenever they please. My government will correct all this. It will keep off the Indians, protect you and your persons and property; and I repeat again, will protect you in your religion.[17]

Once he entered Santa Fe on August 19, 1846, Kearny played on the popular belief that Armijo and other government officials had betrayed the people, and he boasted that the Americans had taken possession of New Mexico "without firing a gun or spilling a single drop of blood." Though spared bloodshed and suffering, many Hispanos and Pueblo Indians loyal to the old Mexican regime found the occupation of Santa Fe and Taos shameful. Most New Mexicans, however, accepted the Americans and their promises of respect for religious beliefs and protection against Indian raiders. The Anglos and Hispanos had much to learn about each other. After Kearny read his proclamation at the Palace of the Governors, he demanded that Mexican officers look him in the eye as they swore oaths of allegiance to the United States, the American little comprehending that their bowed heads and downcast eyes were not signs of sullen resistance but, rather, obeisance to their new governor.[18]

South of the Rio Grande and in the border states of Chihuahua and Sonora, Mexican citizens and tribes suffered much more violence as an indirect result of the war. Mexico's central government had been forced to further reduce its already depleted northern garrisons in an effort to rally enough soldiers to combat invading American armies, which came by land and sea to converge on Mexico City. Taking advantage of the power vacuum on the northern frontier, Comanche and Apache warriors boldly attacked the vulnerable settlements and brought devastation that depopulated entire communities and turned once-productive farms into deserts. Survivors sought shelter in Mexico's southern cities and rural pueblos or joined friendly tribes. Some hardy souls fled northward across the Colorado River to Alta California or up the Rio Grande to the relatively secure New Mexico settlements.[19]

The American public may have considered the conquest of the Southwest Borderlands to be an inevitable chapter in their republic's Manifest Destiny, but during the summer of 1846 the undertaking was no sure thing in the minds of the military men charged with the task. Under the direction of John C. Frémont, with his Bear Flag army of frontiersmen, and Commodore Robert Stockton's Pacific naval squadron, the conquest of California seemed at first almost too easy. Mexican forces at Monterey, San Diego, and Los Angeles either surrendered or simply disbanded in the face of the American invaders, but although California appeared to have quickly fallen, an angry resistance movement simmered. Before the conquest was fairly settled, the famed mountain man Christopher "Kit" Carson set out on a sixty-day ride to Washington bearing dispatches containing news of the victory for President Polk.

Carson had been instrumental in safely guiding the celebrated "Pathfinder" Frémont's thinly disguised "exploring party" to the Pacific, and then served as chief scout and lieutenant in the California coup de main. Frémont believed Carson deserved the honor of personally delivering the news of the conquest, and now leading a party of fifteen trappers and Delaware Indian scouts, Carson headed his mule eastward along the Gila and across the Sonoran Desert. The party rode 850 hard miles through the lands of the Quechans, Pimas, Papagos, Chiricahuas, and Mescalero Apaches until finally reaching the Rio Grande settlements. There at a river ford called Valverde they chanced upon General Kearny's column of three hundred U.S. Dragoons, the vanguard of the Army of the West, en route to California. Kearny had already led his command more than one thousand miles and occupied Santa Fe and other New Mexican pueblos without firing a shot, but as he set out across the unmapped and arid borderlands, he could only hope the rest of the journey to California would go as well. His luck held. In 1846 Carson was arguably the most experienced and gifted Anglo scout in the West—the best man imaginable for the task at hand.[20]

Carson had been continuously in the saddle for weeks and was then only a few days south of Taos, where his wife and family, whom he had not seen in more than a year, anxiously awaited his return. Kearny's powers of persuasion were considerable, however, and he somehow prevailed upon the patriotic frontiersman to turn about and recross the Sonoran Desert. With only one hundred picked troopers, the general would continue to California, mop up any pockets of Mexican insurgents, and secure the extensive Pacific empire. Carson dutifully led Kearny's dragoons down through the Rio Grande villages and westward through Chiricahua Apache country past the Santa Rita Copper Mines and Cooke's Canyon. On the headwaters of the Gila they met with and received assurances of friendship from the Chiricahua chief Mangas Coloradas, the best-known headman among the southern Apache bands, before pushing on and taking possession of the old pueblo of Tucson on the Santa Cruz River.[21]

Following the Gila to the Colorado River, which the command forded south of the Quechan villages at Yuma Crossing, the expedition met virtually no resistance on the hard ride across the thousand-mile breadth of Mexico's northern frontier. But the exhausting desert march took its toll on men and animals. The soldiers now wore only ragged remnants of their blue wool uniforms, once gaily trimmed with brass buttons and gaudy yellow lace, and rode broken-down mules and jaded horses toward San Diego. Still, Kearny believed his confident Americans, with their sabers, pistols, breech-loading carbines, and mountain howitzers, more than a match for any force the Mexicans could muster. He was wrong. At San Pasqual on December 6, 1846, the dragoons fought for their lives against *caballeros* commanded by Captain Andrés Pico. Expert with lariat (*la reata*) and lance, Pico's men felt honor-bound to resist the arrogant Anglos. Shouting "*viva California*," the Mexicans at first yielded to the charging Americans, but once the Anglos had been sucked into the chase, the Californios wheeled about. The Mexicans literally rode circles around the dazed dragoons and, darting through the broken ranks, lanced twenty-one men to death. None of the soldiers in the leading formation, including Kearny, escaped without a wound. Only Kearny's defensive delaying tactics and the timely arrival of reinforcements from Commodore Stockton's naval contingent on the coast saved the Americans from annihilation.[22]

The Mexican settlements Carson and Kearny passed through en route to California had suffered fewer Indian raids than the states to the south because the people of the northern frontier had long since established a tense but mutually beneficial trade relationship with many of the Apache, Navajo, and Comanche bands that dominated the martial power hierarchy of the borderlands. The headmen of these powerful tribes even made regular trade missions to Santa Fe or went there to accept tribute payments, made willingly by the New Mexicans, in exchange for peace promises. Comanche, Navajo, and Apache raiders had stripped the other *provincias internas* (Mexico's northern provinces) in the years following Mexico's 1821 War of Independence, the civil war that permanently separated the nation from Spain. The losses in horses alone numbered in the hundreds of thousands while Mexicans captured or killed in attacks could be counted in the thousands. But while Comanche and Apache warriors raided nearly to the Gulf of Mexico, and the Sonora and Chihuahua frontier had been significantly depopulated as the result of a strategy of conciliatory accommodations, the New Mexico settlements on the Santa Cruz, Rio Grande, and Pecos rivers emerged comparatively unscathed.[23]

Santa Fe had fallen to the Americans without bloodshed, but one last gasp of resistance shattered the fragile peace. Though Governor Armijo's abdication surrendered New Mexico, many Hispanos and Pueblo Indians seethed with shame over the betrayal and chafed under the new Anglo regime. In March 1847 the Pueblo people of Taos and Mexican loyalists rose up and went on a killing rampage reminiscent of Pueblo revolts more than one hundred years before. Charles Bent, the American Governor of New Mexico, fell victim in the rebellion's first rush. A coalition of trappers, traders, and soldiers ruthlessly crushed the insurrection and soon reestablished American control, at the cost of many Pueblo lives. Though the enraged rebels had scalped then killed and decapitated Bent and other government officials, the governor's New Mexican wife, Ignacia Jaramillo, and his immediate family and servants had been spared. The vengeful Americans were not so generous. Within weeks of the uprising, authorities rounded up known leaders of the rebellion and other suspects and, by spring, had tried and hanged or otherwise executed more than twenty men, both Mexicans and Pueblo Indians.[24]

In the summer of 1847, 1,600 miles to the south, General Winfield Scott's American army battered its way from Veracruz to Mexico City in a series of bloody battles. The American force of 8,500 regulars and volunteers faced off against a Mexican army of 12,000 under the command of President Antonio López de Santa Anna. The Mexicans fought bravely in disciplined, Napoleonic style that won the admiration of their American foes. But Scott outgeneraled Santa Anna, and after the fall of Chapultepec Castle in the heart of the capital city, the Mexican government was forced to capitulate. On February 2, 1848, the Treaty of Guadalupe Hidalgo concluded the U.S.-Mexican War and detailed the surrender terms, including the withdrawal of occupying U.S. troops, new international boundaries, payments for debts and surrendered territory, and guarantees for the rights of Mexicans who chose to remain north of the new borderline. Most of the Mexican people, imbued with a growing sense of national pride since establishing their independence from Spain less than a generation before, had fiercely resisted the American invasion. The terrible battles fought to capture Mexico City resulted in proportionately higher casualties than any other American war. Effective partisan resistance by die-hard Mexican *guerrilleros* had severed unprotected supply and communication lines and killed many straggling or incautious soldiers. But the conflict had been a disaster for the Mexicans, most of whom believed the surrender to the Americans and the cession of territory in exchange for $15 million and payment of debts owed Americans brought only national dishonor and individual shame on its leaders.[25]

United States and Territories of the Southwest

The United States acquired from Mexico most of the region North Americans came to know as the Southwest—including all or portions of the present-day states of California, Nevada, Colorado, Arizona, New Mexico, Texas,[26] Utah, and Wyoming. The Mexican cession, combined with Texas, comprised nearly one million square miles in all—the greatest land-grab in American history. For the people of Mexico, especially the laboring classes, who had suffered most of the sixteen thousand dead resulting from the war, the sense of *vergüenza* ran deep. Americans had been sharply divided on the blatantly imperialistic war. Young Congressman Abraham Lincoln had opposed it, as did many regular army officers, including Ulysses S. Grant, who said, "I do not think there was ever a more wicked war than that waged by the United States on Mexico." The Americans attempted to ease their collective conscience by offering to pay for property taken by conquest, though they offered no compensation for death and suffering.[27]

In the borderlands, many Mexicans saw that the treaty also addressed the problem of cross-border raiding, especially by Comanches, Kiowas, and Apaches, which had left the northern Mexican states financially ruined and partially abandoned. North of the new international border, the Americans tried to understand the implications of their new acquisition. Henry Clay's Compromise of 1850 created New Mexico Territory and preserved the Union for another decade. Texas grudgingly surrendered its tenuous claim to New Mexico in exchange for the federal government's assumption of its enormous war debts. The future of chattel slavery in New Mexico and Utah would be determined by popular sovereignty.

By the early 1850s, small numbers of Anglo-Americans began entering the recently redefined borderlands. The new arrivals soon realized that with the territorial acquisition came the legacy of generations of interethnic tension and conflict. Article eleven of the 1848 Treaty of Guadalupe Hidalgo stipulated that responsibility for controlling the "savage tribes" that raided northern Mexico along the newly defined border would be the responsibility of the United States. The governors of Chihuahua and Sonora offered American and Mexican mercenary scalp hunters cash bounties for Apache *piezas* (scalps) in an effort to stop the incessant raiding. These efforts, however, only served to stimulate increasingly violent interaction and perpetuate a cycle of revenge attacks in the borderlands.[28]

The Franklin Pierce administration accepted the challenge of managing the vast new territory and lost little time setting in motion the machinery of government. Initially, the Americans made little attempt to disrupt the existing raid-and-retaliation economy. It soon became apparent, however, that the economic system then in place was entirely incompatible with American-style capitalism, reliant on intensive resource extraction, commerce, and settlement. With little understanding of the Indian cultures of the borderlands, government agents and army officers attempted to identify tribal headmen with whom to treat. In most cases, such chieftains or plenipotentiary representatives did not exist. Nevertheless, U.S. authorities executed formal treaties, all of which were predicated on the idea that the tribes, or nations, were subordinate to the federal government. Through treaty, trade, and a small but active military force, the Anglos at first maintained relatively good relations with both the Indian and Hispano people of the Southwest Borderlands.

In 1856, Mexican presidial soldiers abandoned the last of their adobe forts and rode south from Tucson and other outposts on the northern frontier as companies of U.S. Dragoons finally arrived to establish an American military presence. But peace eluded the borderlands. During the 1850s, Anglo-American mercenaries known as "filibusters," piratical freebooters, invaded Mexico and other countries to the south in search of wealth and empire. North of the border, in the desert Southwest, other Anglos, sanctioned by the U.S. government, improved the Indian-trapper-miner-immigrant trail from Texas across southern New Mexico, including what was already becoming known as Arizona, to establish the San Antonio–San Diego Mail Line to California. The "Jackass" Mail, as it was dubbed by all who saw the rickety mule-drawn mud wagons, opened an essential overland communication link for the Americans. On September 1, 1857, mail company employees traveling from Texas to California along this southern route chanced upon an epic Indian battle—the last of its kind—at the confluence of the Gila and Santa Cruz Rivers, eighty miles north of Tucson.[29]

The "Massacre on the Gila," as the 1857 Quechan-Maricopa-Pima war became known to outsiders, was one of the last great Indian battles to take place in the Southwest without direct interference from Hispano and Anglo newcomers. As the fighting men from allied tribes— Cocopahs, Mojaves, Chemehuevis, Yavapais, and Tonto Apaches—approached from the north, more than one hundred Quechan warriors, on sandaled feet, swiftly traveled 150 miles across the burning desert pavement to attack the western Maricopa and Pima farms and villages clustered along the life-giving waters of the Gila River. The attackers carried traditional weapons including short mesquite-wood war clubs (*kelyaxwai*); willow bows with long-shafted cane arrows tipped with stone, glass, or iron; and knives of metal or fire-hardened wood. Their rawhide shields could deflect an arrow or turn a lance thrust. With guidance from shamans, they painted their bodies for the spiritual protection and supernatural power they would need to defeat their foes. The Quechan men had confidence in their war leaders, who included the most notable men in the tribe. The *kwoxot*, the tribe's moral leader, had dreamed of victory and when he examined the enemy scalps taken in past battles, which were entrusted to his care, he heard a mystical war cry—an omen of success.

The Quechan men hoped a surprise attack at dawn would allow them to close quickly and fight hand-to-hand, believing that their superior size, strength, and fighting ability would give them the advantage over their enemies. The Maricopas and Pimas wielded similar weapons when prepared for battle, but on this day they were unaware of their enemies' approach until they saw the smoke from burning houses and heard the cries of the women. The Quechans' allies left the killing field after overrunning and destroying the first two Maricopa villages, satisfied with the spoils swept up in the initial attack. But the Quechans stayed to finish the job, intent on the total conquest of their foes. The Pimas, many on horseback, rallied swiftly and descended on the remaining attackers, who retreated to a hillside to make their stand. The Quechans now found themselves greatly outnumbered as the enraged Pimas loosed their arrows and then rushed in to club and stab the surrounded warriors, who were killed to a man.[30]

The battle between the Colorado River Yumans and the agrarian Maricopas and Pimas was a microcosmic reflection of American expansionism. Both the battle between Indian peoples on the Gila and the Manifest Destiny–fueled filibustering south of the Mexican border resulted from martial masculinity run amok.[31] The Quechans had established stable communities on the banks of the Colorado River, which provided abundant fish, game, and seasonal floods to water crops. As women performed most of the agricultural work, which provided the bulk of the food needed to support the people, the role of men as hunter-providers became less important. By the middle of the nineteenth century, the men increasingly focused their energies on warrior traditions, martial rituals, and war preparations aimed at enemies, real and imagined. A man's sense of self-worth became inextricably entwined with his role as a warrior and protector of the community. The Quechan men, however, had few external threats upon which to loose their lethal aggression.[32]

Having established truces and treaties with the Mexicans and then the Americans, who were now ensconced at Fort Yuma, it seemed the Quechans had run out of enemies—a situation that threatened the warriors' self-esteem, masculinity, and status within their tribe. The Quechans' devotion to martial virtues and their capacity for war, however, had never been greater—the people were strong and their weapons and warriors were at a high state of readiness. The war launched against the neighboring Maricopas (who had split off from the Colorado tribes a century earlier)[33] and their peaceful Pima allies could not be justified as a defensive action, though the warriors' bellicose rhetoric presented the strike as preemptive. The Quechan offensive, presented as a defensive measure, was merely a pretense intended to demonstrate the worth of the men to their families and communities. The Quechan attack was not just a raid intent on booty, like most confrontations between Indians in the borderlands, but a war intended to destroy or totally dominate their perceived enemy.[34]

Martial Masculinity

The spirit of martial masculinity that animated Indian men of the borderlands was not unique; similar ideas related to ethnic identity and superiority were concurrently evolving in Anglo America. It appears that when competitive societies reach a comfort level with their food acquisition strategies and have more time to spend in less essential pursuits, men desire to expand their territorial domain through conquest. By identifying those outside one's ethnic, tribal, or national group as "others" (those who appear different, speak another language, and possess foreign traditions and technologies), members of a community will cooperate to protect possessions and loved ones through the use or threat of violence. This phenomenon is a fundamental and almost universal cause of war and is especially pronounced in the "middle ground" between cultures, that region sometimes known as borderlands. When people cannot manage their misunderstandings and cultural accommodation fails, the points of contact often become flash points for violence. The Southwest Borderlands on the eve of the American Civil War became a stage upon which martial men assumed roles dictated by their conceptions of manhood, honor, and violence. The drama played out with deadly consequences.[35]

Many ambitious Anglo men of the post–Mexican-American War period, also seeking to demonstrate their value to society, acted on the impulse by raising mercenary armies to invade neighboring peoples in search of empire and glory. Among the best known and most disruptive to peace and harmony in the Southwest Borderlands were the filibustering efforts of William Walker and Henry A. Crabb. In the late 1840s the Tennessee-born Walker studied medicine and law in Philadelphia and then practiced for a time in New Orleans, where the diminutive five-foot-two young man earned a reputation as a cold-blooded duelist. He then emigrated to California where, as a newspaper editor, he promoted the idea that the nation's Manifest Destiny would lead it to expand to its "natural frontiers" in Latin America. His charismatic personality, the audacity of his scheme to establish an American Republic of Sonora in 1853, and his later conquest of Nicaragua—which he ruled briefly in 1856–57—made Walker a much-admired "man of destiny." He inspired a generation of young military-minded Americans who had missed out on the martial glory of the Mexican-American War.[36] His fiery rhetoric rallied young men from factories and fields, North and South, who were drawn to his idealized views of manhood and Anglo-American racial superiority.[37]

Henry A. Crabb, a former California state senator who had failed in his 1856 reelection bid, sought filibustering success in Mexico where Walker had failed.[38] Crabb's Mexican wife and brother-in-law helped connect him with Sonora's liberal reform governor Ignacio Pesqueira, who was then engaged in a power struggle with conservative, prochurch governor Manuel Gándara. With promised support from Pesqueira, who initially believed he would need American help to defeat Gándara and beat back Apache raiders from the north, Crabb raised an army of adventurous young men who set out, ostensibly, to "free" and then "colonize" Sonora. In truth the filibusters intended to create an independent republic that would eventually be admitted, as had Texas, to the growing union of the United States. His actions, Crabb declared, were consistent with "natural law" even if they did not conform to international law.[39] The little "army" of one hundred well-armed men, officered by a number of prominently placed California legislators, marshaled at what became known as Filibusters Camp on the Gila River, between Fort Yuma and the Pima Villages, before marching south through Tucson and into Sonora.[40]

Crabb's *filibusteros* represented Mexico's worst nightmare come true—armed *norte americanos* set on conquering still more of the already diminished nation. When Sonoran officials divined the true nature of the invasion and rallied their countrymen with cries of "liberty or death" and "death to filibusters," Crabb disingenuously wrote to the prefect of Altar that his party was simply exploring mining opportunities and was armed to the teeth only because of the threat of attack from the "savage" Apaches. "I learn with surprise," he complained, that the Mexicans who invited him to Sonora now want to "exterminate me and my companions." Pesqueira himself issued orders to resist the barbarian invaders by any means necessary. "Free Sonorians," he wrote, "to arms all of you!"[41]

By the time Crabb's command reached the town of Caborca, Pesqueira's Reform Army, comprising Mexicans and Papago Indians (Tohono O'odham), had already defeated Gándara's conservatives and so turned its attention to the invading Americans. Mexican pride demanded the blood of the now-despised *yanquis*, whose appetite for empire seemed insatiable. When the smoke of battle cleared, all the Americans had been killed or executed, and nearly twice that number of Mexicans lay dead. A one-hundred-man firing squad riddled Crabb with musket balls then placed his saber-severed head in a jar of alcohol for preservation and transport to Mexico City.[42]

American envoys and government officials had no illusions about Crabb's real mission. Though the illegal escapade embarrassed consular officials and the administration, public opinion generally agreed with the filibuster's premise that enterprising Anglos could make better use of the undeveloped borderlands than the Mexicans could. But what really united American support for the filibusters and ignited indignation directed at the Mexicans were stories of the summary execution of Crabb's party. Congress debated and newspapers reported that the Mexicans had shown a savage side unworthy of a modern nation. The filibusters, they said, however misguided, had died nobly, even heroically, and the cowardly men detailed to the Mexican firing squads could not even bring themselves to look their victims in the face. The captured Americans, it was claimed, were tied embracing their posts, facing away from their executioners, and shot in the back. Coming closely on the heels of the Mexican-American War and the cession of nearly half of Mexico's national territory, the Crabb affair served to deepen the mistrust that had come to characterize relations between the two countries.[43]

In the time since the beginning of the Spanish *entrada* three centuries earlier, the people of Mexico had merged physically and culturally in a process known as *mestizaje*. The mixed race *mestizo* people (*casta*), collectively and individually, had developed a love-hate relationship with their own heritage. In a highly stratified society whose caste-like system placed Spanish-descended whites at the top and dark skinned Indians and Africans at the bottom, the indigenous people at once embraced and resisted the ways of the Spanish invaders. Yet the new culture that emerged from this union of peoples from the old world and new blended religion, art, language, and traditions so seamlessly it seemed difficult to imagine that it had not always been so. Mexico's warrior traditions were no exception.[44]

Spanish notions of war and honor often complemented native ideas. So too, Iberian captive-taking and slave practices seemed compatible with those that evolved in the Americas.[45] In Mexico the people used horses of Spanish descent for work and war. The European idea of heavy cavalry, which emerged in the era of armored knights, quickly transformed in the New World into light cavalry. Fast-moving *compānias volantes* (flying companies) far better suited the broken terrain, vast distances, and hit-and-run tactics of Indian adversaries. Lightweight lances became the weapon of choice for Mexican horse soldiers, who also carried carbines (*escopetas*) and short swords (*espadas anchas*) as secondary armament. With the *espada* came a code of honor. Whether arsenal-made or hand-forged by local smiths, the blades of the swords often bore the bold inscription, *"No me saques sin razón, ni me envaines sin honor"* (Do not draw me without reason, nor sheathe me without honor). Some presidial troops even preferred bows and arrows as more reliable and faster to load and shoot than the notoriously unreliable flintlock firearms then available on the frontier. Like their Indian adversaries, Hispanos viewed wars of conquest and revenge as fundamentally different from raids for slaves and booty. And, as with the natives, Mexican frontiersmen usually preferred peaceful trade to violence as a survival strategy in the middle ground of the borderlands.[46]

While the Mexican government had a standing professional army of full-time fighting men, most frontier settlements were protected by undermanned and undersupplied presidial garrisons. Many of the soldiers at these fortified settlements resorted to native customs in matters of dress and armament, the men often spending more time attending to farms and families than military duties. The militia companies (*milicias*) were even more like their Indian counterparts in that these men were part-time fighters, not professional soldiers, and only responded to the call of duty in emergencies. Like Indian warriors, Mexican soldiers—whether regular or militia—who demonstrated ability in war improved their chances for advancement, wealth, and marriage.

By the 1860s, the ethnically mixed Spanish-speaking Hispano population of the borderlands had developed reciprocal and even symbiotic trade and raid relationships with many of the Indian tribes on both sides of the border that had once been Mexico's northern frontier. Though often avowed enemies, these peoples on the fringes of national and tribal boundaries had come to depend on one another. The Hispanos sought livestock, the basis of the regional economy, and captive women and children for slaves (*criadas*) and concubines. The Indians of the Southwest also captured animals, crops, manufactured goods, and people, especially male children, to replace losses resulting from war, raiding, and other high-risk activities.[47]

Pressured by the Kiowa and Comanche mounted warriors of the southern plains, the Apaches and Navajos had, in turn, pressed the Puebloans and the Hispanos, now well-established along the Rio Grande on the north-south axis of central New Mexico. The Hispanic frontier expanded—in search of grazing, farming, and mineral lands—then recoiled from the warriors who dominated the plains and Comanchería. The New Mexicans, in turn, pressured the Eastern and Western Apaches. Warriors from these bands increasingly sought opportunities for profitable raiding south of the Mexican border in Chihuahua and Sonora. The O'odham peoples of the Gila and Santa Cruz Rivers, the Pimas and related Papagos, also found themselves at odds with the westering Apaches while at the same time suspiciously watching the Colorado River Yuman tribes—especially the Quechans, Mojaves, and Chemehuevis—whose 1857 offensive had unambiguously demonstrated their desire to assert hegemony over the agrarian Uto-Aztecan Pima and Papago peoples (Akimel and Tohono O'odham) and their exiled Yuman-speaking allies, the Maricopas (Piipaash). South of the border, Mexicans and their allied tribes among the Lower Pimas, Papagos, and Ópatas looked both northward, to protect against Apache raiders and American *filibusteros*, and southward, wary of the growing civil unrest from Mexican conservatives who in desperation turned to Europe in search of allies to combat Benito Juárez's liberal government.

In the borderlands of the 1860s, ethnocentrism was endemic. The condition was not peculiar to any one people, but lay at the root of all intercultural relations. Each ethnic group feared, misunderstood, and imagined the worst of the others. The seminomadic Apacheans despised the sedentary Hispano farmers, thinking of them as weak and unmanly and as easy prey for stock raiders. The Anglos they saw as fiendishly clever with their weapons, wagons, and other contraptions but domineering and relentlessly acquisitive, especially when it came to gold and land. The Hispanos viewed the raiding tribes as godless savages, fearsome and cruel in war, and suitable only for enslavement, while the Anglos were arrogant, greedy, and rapacious in their quest for wealth and empire. The Anglos generally categorized the Indians as uncivilized or even subhuman, felt Indians had no legitimate claim to the land, and saw them as possessing neither the genius nor industry to cultivate and exploit the land to its full potential. The Hispanos were also seen as indolent and superstitious, bereft of enterprise and little better than the Indians in taking advantage of the resources of the western wilds that Providence had lain before them. It seemed manifest to the Anglos that it was their destiny to control the peoples and real estate of the American West. At the same time, each group believed in its innate superiority and its inherent right, granted by the highest authority, to control the borderlands.[48]

In 1857 the federal government demonstrated little interest in quelling conflict between the warring Indian tribes on the Colorado and Gila Rivers or even the unrest prompted by filibusters crossing the border into Mexico. The "Mormon War," as it was then known, diverted most of the U.S. Army's budget and western manpower. In September 1857, just a few months after the "Crabb Massacre" at Caborca, fifty miles south of the Arizona border, Brigham Young's highly militarized democratic-theocracy in Utah Territory erupted in violence. Mormon militiamen calling themselves the Nauvoo Legion wiped out a California-bound Arkansas emigrant train of some 120 "Gentiles"—men, women, and children—as its wagons rolled across southwestern Utah about fifty miles north of the Arizona (then New Mexico) border. The "Mountain Meadows Massacre," perpetrated with cooperation from the Mormons' Paiute allies, riveted the nation's attention. Americans were fascinated to learn more about the inner workings of the polygamous Church of Jesus Christ of Latter-day Saints and its eye-for-an-eye doctrine of "blood atonement," which church leaders condoned when performed in response to murderous acts. As Young rallied the considerable military might of his faithful legions and their Indian allies along the California-Oregon Trail, U.S. troops led by General Albert Sidney Johnston invaded Utah. In 1859 Major James H. Carleton's company of the First Dragoons gathered the bones of the slaughtered emigrants and buried them beneath a field stone cairn topped with a twelve-foot cedar cross graven with the words, "Vengeance is mine; I will repay, saith the Lord."[49]

The ethnic rivalries, competition for resources, and deeply rooted warrior traditions of the peoples of the Southwest Borderlands would result in violent conflict and significantly change the alliances and power hierarchy in the region. By 1861 the borderlands seemed a powder keg of competing communities—bands, tribes, and nations. Representing less than 3 percent of the total population, the Anglo-Americans were not yet present in sufficient numbers to make a significant impact on the existing economic or social order. Hispano-Indian trading and raiding for animals, captives, and goods continued much as before. The recently redrawn Mexican-American boundary remained ill-defined and permeable, allowing virtually unrestricted passage by Indians, Hispanos, and Anglos. This would all change with the coming of the American Civil War. Southern Americans sought westward expansion for the extension of their peculiar brand of chattel slavery and to exploit the region's mineral wealth. Similarly, the northern states saw the Southwest not only as a source of wealth but as a vital, year-round, east-west transportation corridor and buffer against both Southern slavery extension and a potentially hostile Mexico, which was gripped in civil unrest and invaded by European princes in search of empires.[50]

Chapter 2

The Civil War

Like a rapidly receding sea before the onrush of a violent tidal wave, the Civil War at first created a great power vacuum. The retreating federal presence and redirection of resources left the Southwest temporarily exposed to opportunistic raiding and conquest, but soon United States government forces overwhelmed the borderlands with irresistible waves of military might. The national conflict in the United States had far-reaching effects north and south of the border, spawning or exacerbating civil wars among the diverse peoples of Arizona, New Mexico, and Mexico itself. These conflicts led to struggles for power and dominance that redefined peoples ethnically and nationally, and ultimately led to new political and social hierarchies in the region. The martial traditions of the warring peoples played a significant role in the violence, alliances, and outcomes of the conflicts that followed.[1]

Immediately following Abraham Lincoln's election in the presidential contest of 1860, southern states began seceding from the Union. This national crisis quickly rippled westward to the Territory of New Mexico, then comprising the present-day states of Arizona, New Mexico, and southern Nevada. Once Confederate guns opened fire on Fort Sumter in Charleston Harbor on April 12, 1861, federal troops abandoned most of the far-flung western forts and began consolidating on the Pacific coast and along the Rio Grande in the eastern portion of New Mexico in anticipation of a rebel invasion from Texas.[2] At the same time, Mexico's internal standoff between conservative and liberal political factions erupted into full-blown civil war as European powers, emboldened by American weakness resulting from the Southern secession crisis, converged on Veracruz in defiance of the now unenforceable Monroe Doctrine. The disruption of U.S. authority in its southwestern territories, and of its international influence in Mexican affairs, pushed the peoples of the borderlands into violent confrontation.[3]

Prior to the American Civil War, the ethnically related Navajos and Apaches (Apacheans) were the dominant military powers in the borderlands north and south of the New Mexico territorial boundary with old Mexico. William Dole, commissioner of Indian affairs, admitted that the Indians now "possess the balance of power in New Mexico."[4] Together, the Apacheans and allied tribes numbered more than forty thousand people. Though they shared a common linguistic heritage, the pastoral and seminomadic Navajos and Apaches now exhibited distinctly different cultures, and the tribes often found themselves at odds with each other and also with the Hispanos and Anglo newcomers who shared the land and competed for its resources. An uneasy peace, characterized by intermittent raiding activity but far short of total war, prevailed while U.S. government authority remained intact, but the American rebellion that began in the East triggered a largely unanticipated and irrepressible response in the Southwest Borderlands.[5]

The prewar regular U.S. Army constituted a small but professional military establishment charged with protecting the nation against external as well as domestic threats. Considering that the 15,000-man force numbered only a quarter as many men as the U.S. Postal Service then had at its disposal, the magnitude of the assignment was absurdly large. The seacoasts and international borders the soldiers guarded exceeded 16,000 miles in length, and the hundreds of forts and stations they manned from the Atlantic to the Pacific often held only skeleton garrisons or corporals' guards barely sufficient to protect the government property in their charge. The War Department did station most of the active regiments of dragoons, mounted rifles, cavalry, and infantry in the Far West, but the general staff deployed these fragmented units as company-sized (one-hundred-man) detachments incapable of large-scale campaigning. The troops dutifully garrisoned forts in the territories and confined their operations to policing main roads, making occasional forays against Indian raiders, and attempting to maintain peace between the natives and the Hispano and Anglo settlers, emigrants, miners, mail carriers, and wagon freighters.

As Lincoln made his way to Washington to be inaugurated in February 1861, seven Confederate Sates had already seceded from the Union, and the fragile peace that existed in the Southwest Borderlands began to unravel. In 1858 the improved Butterfield Overland Mail Company stage line had replaced the old "Jackass" Mail as the government mail contractor on the southern route. The stations that dotted the tortuous trail from St. Louis to San Francisco provided horse-drawn stagecoach teams and drivers with water, forage, and food at twenty-mile intervals along the entire route. The Anglo station men were hardy and resourceful, but largely dependent on the good will of Indians who allowed passage of wagons through their territory and who provided wood, hay, and other subsistence as mail company contractors. The U.S. government viewed these indigenous peoples not as citizens but as "wards" and the tribes as "domestic dependent nations" whose lands were subject to federal control but were not bound by state or territorial laws.[6] Indian people, however, saw things quite differently.

The Chiricahua Apaches under the Chokonen chief Cochise and the Chihenne and Bedonkohe bands of his father-in-law Mangas Coloradas controlled much of the borderlands through which the southern overland trail passed. Though these Apaches raided Hispanos on both sides of the border, they maintained relatively friendly relations with the Anglos. The Chiricahuas did occasionally take possession of stray or unguarded stock as payment for the use of their land, but they did not, as a rule, kill Anglos or take them captive. On January 27, 1861, however, unidentified Apaches raided John Ward's ranch near the Mexican border at Sonoita, Arizona, to steal horses. The warriors also made off with the rancher's ten-year-old Mexican stepson, Félix.[7] Ward alerted the garrison commander at Fort Buchanan, who detailed troops to pursue the raiders. But instead of following the fresh trail, twenty-four-year-old Lieutenant George Bascom, assuming the nearby Chiricahuas had taken the boy, led his infantry company directly to Cochise's *ranchería* near the stage station in Apache Pass, hoping to head off the raiders.[8]

Determined to retrieve the captive boy, the young lieutenant decided that a firm hand would be needed to chastise the Apaches he considered brazen marauders. When Cochise came to the soldiers' camp to parley on February 3, Bascom made prisoners of the chief, his brother, and other family members. Cochise used his knife to slash the canvas of an army tent and make his escape, but Bascom adamantly refused to release the other prisoners until the Chiricahuas surrendered the Ward boy. Neither Cochise's nor Mangas's people, however, had been involved in the raid on Ward's ranch, supposed now to have been committed by Western Apaches living to the northwest of the Chiricahuas' territory. Despite the well-intentioned efforts of the stage station keeper to interpret and correct the misunderstanding, negotiations broke down, and the Apaches responded to the seizure of their people by taking the station keeper prisoner and waylaying overland travelers in an attempt to find enough Anglo captives to trade for the Apache men, women, and children still held by Bascom.

Cochise's band, joined by Mangas's people, tortured and killed all the Hispanos they captured, but the Chiricahua leaders still hoped an exchange or ransom of Anglo prisoners might be possible. During further unsuccessful negotiations and a standoff lasting more than a week, the Apaches captured most of the soldiers' and stage station's stock. Cochise's exasperated Chokonen followers then lanced to death and mutilated the bodies of their Anglo captives, including the erstwhile peace-making station keeper, and decamped for Sonora, seventy miles south, knowing full well the Americans would not cross the Mexican border. Bascom, meanwhile, had been reinforced, and the soldiers in the pass were now commanded by First Lieutenant Isaiah Moore, First Mounted Rifles, who wasted no time in ordering the hanging of Cochise's brother and other male relatives while releasing the captive women and children. The Apache corpses, suspended just high enough to keep them from scavenging coyotes, swung from tall trees on the very spot in the pass where the executed Anglo men had just been buried. The Anglos generally demonstrated a profound ignorance of their Indian enemies, but these soldiers understood enough to know that the Apaches would not attempt to retrieve the bodies of their kin or disturb their enemies' graves for fear of contact with the spirits of the dead. Bascom and Moore did not realize at the time that they had turned what started as a stock raid into a war that would eventually claim hundreds of lives.[9]

The incident at Apache Pass changed the relationship between the united bands of Chiricahua Apaches and Anglos in the borderlands.

While Mangas's bands went north into the mountains at the head-waters of the Gila, Cochise's people crossed the border to Fronteras, Sonora. There Mexican officials warily eyed the Apaches and provided them with rations, a course of action that the Hispanos had come to learn was safer and less costly than fighting. They knew these Apaches well—as traders of livestock and goods raided from the north and as fierce foes who often captured Mexican animals and people to trade on the American side of the border. Though Cochise's people were now safe in Mexico, the blood feud that the soldiers' actions triggered compelled the Chokonens to recross the border to attack any and all Anglos traveling the overland route or working isolated ranches and mines. The required *gegodza* (literally, "to be paid back," a revenge obligation) could be satisfied only when a warrior took a captive or a life. Ideally, Cochise would kill Bascom, but the death of any Anglo, regardless of culpability, would help satisfy the blood debt.[10]

On August 1, 1861, fifty-year-old Felix Grundy Ake's party made its way eastward through the narrow defile of Cooke's Canyon, New Mexico, midway between Tucson and the Rio Grande. He had packed everything he owned or held dear—merchandise, gold, and his wife and five children—into covered wagons and a spring buggy that followed several small herds of horses, cattle, sheep, and goats along the rough road through the heart of Chiricahua Apache country. Around the fire at their camp on the Mimbres River the night before, the men of the party, a group of experienced frontiersmen including mountain man Mose Carson (Kit's brother), Mexican *vaqueros*, and several Arizona ranchers, talked of the dangers they would face. Like Ake, the men were heading east to escape Apache raiders who were seeking revenge for the Bascom affair and emboldened by the departure of U.S. troops withdrawn to fight the Civil War in the East. Ake was determined to press on, but soon regretted his decision when one of the advance riders reported the discovery of scalped and mutilated corpses. Within minutes of this sobering news, gunshots echoed from the high ground overlooking the pass, followed by a rain of arrows.

Nearly two hundred Apache warriors of different bands led by Mangas Coloradas and Cochise closed the trap on the Ake caravan with deadly efficiency, shooting the lead mules and emerging from concealment to pick off outriders at the head and rear of the column. Ake and two others took a defensive position on a high hillside, but when flanking Apaches killed his companions, he scrambled down the rocky slope to the corralled wagons where women and children frantically loaded weapons or huddled out of sight as arrows and bullets thudded into the wagon boxes and dead draft animals. After three hours the fighting degenerated into intermittent sniping, and Ake's survivors realized that their herds had been driven off and only a handful of watchful warriors remained. Mose Carson, who had distinguished himself in the fight, helped load Ake's family along with the wounded herdsmen and other travelers into two stripped-down wagons. He rounded up enough horses and mules to make a run for Pinos Altos, one of the few remaining mining settlements, where a rebel cavalry company had recently arrived to claim Arizona Territory for the Confederacy.

As Ake's exhausted survivors lamented their losses and counted their blessings at Pinos Altos, back at the pass the Apaches scalped their dead enemies and carried off their own killed and wounded. Women and children arrived to help pack the bounty of food, clothing, tools, and weapons on captured mules and horses. But before the Apaches left the scene of battle, they burned the rolling stock and slashed, smashed, and destroyed everything—wagon covers, furniture, dishes, cast iron skillets—abandoned by the whites. Nothing of value remained. This coordinated attack was more than a stock raid—this was war.[11]

The attacks continued into the summer of 1861 when, from the Apache point of view, the most amazing thing happened. Just as the warfare intensified, Dr. Michael Steck, the Apaches' government-appointed Indian agent, headed east and did not return. Even more surprising to Cochise and Mangas, Anglo settlers and miners began pulling out, abandoning their ranches and camps. The Butterfield Overland Mail shuttered its stage stations and ceased operation. Then occurred the most extraordinary development of all. Beginning in early July, the U.S. troops at Forts Davis, McLane, Buchanan, Breckenridge and other military posts—from Texas to California—packed up their supplies and set ablaze everything their overburdened wagons could not carry. The eastbound soldiers from Buchanan and Breckenridge stopped for nothing, and in their panicked retreat even burned their wagonloads of supplies rather than delay, even a day, their march to the Rio Grande. The Chiricahuas had not imagined this unexpected outcome of their brief war against the Americans. Cochise later said, "We were successful and your soldiers were driven away and your people killed and we again possessed our land." It appeared to the Apaches that their attacks and terror tactics had resulted in a signal victory. The whites, it seemed, had little stomach for war.[12]

From the Anglo perspective, the situation was very different. The secession of rebellious Southern states, from Virginia to Texas, resulted in the capture of U.S. forts and property, and the onset of civil war quickly changed military priorities in the Far West. Federal troops boarded transport ships in California to return to the "seat of the rebellion" in the East or consolidated on the Rio Grande in anticipation of Confederate attack from Texas or Mexico. The U.S. Postal Service moved its operations to the central overland route to avoid hostile interference from rebels. One report from the territories indicated, "Navajo Indians obstruct the route from Albuquerque to Los Angeles, now important as the only one on which the daily mail from the states can be carried, that of the north being blocked up with snow; that of the south being in possession of the Rebels at its eastern end and on the Rio Grande." Indian agents in New Mexico attempted to reassure their Apache and Navajo wards, but feared the withdrawal of troops combined with the war that had begun with Cochise's people in Apache Pass might well lead to a general uprising. Major Isaac Lynde, Seventh U.S. Infantry, reported from Fort Fillmore, "The Apaches have commenced operations in our immediate vicinity," resulting in lost stock and dead herders. He complained that he had insufficient troops to deal with the problem while addressing the Confederate threat.

Colonel Edward R. S. Canby, commanding in New Mexico, confirmed that in addition to Mescalero raiders, Navajo, Ute, Kiowa, and Comanche "marauders" had increased their attacks. To make matters worse, in the absence of federal control, Hispano New Mexicans had increased their raiding of peaceful Navajo bands, ramping up the hostilities between those peoples. Elsewhere in the borderlands, from Fort Mojave on the Colorado River to Fort Davis, Texas, Indians observed in wonder the departure of U.S. troops and the abandonment of government property. Unwilling to let supplies and munitions fall into enemy hands, regular federal troops in Arizona destroyed everything they could not haul away before marching for the strong points on the Rio Grande in New Mexico.[13]

The temporary withdrawal of federal troops following the opening shots of the Civil War destabilized the region, leaving overland trails, forts, mines, settlements, herds, and villages unguarded against Indian raiders. A Tucson newspaper editor expressed generally held feelings of abandonment and siege mentality when he wrote, "We are hemmed in on all sides by the unrelenting Apaches. Since the withdrawal of the Overland Mail and the garrison troops the chances of life have reached the maximum height. Within but six months nine-tenths of the whole male population have been killed off, and every ranch, farm and mine in the country have been abandoned in consequence." At the same time, rebelling Confederates from Texas and New Mexico took advantage of vulnerable federal outposts and other targets of opportunity.[14]

South of Tucson, near the old Spanish mission of San Xavier del Bac, Hispano and Anglo ranches and the farming villages of the Papagos were suddenly overrun by more than two hundred Apache raiders from the White Mountains. The boldness of the early-morning attack took the settlements completely by surprise. The warriors, some on horseback and others on foot, ran off hundreds of corralled cattle and some horses and mules. One of the Hispanas caught out in the open clung to her horse and was cut down in the first sweep through the ranches and corrals. Two teenage boys, Apaches *mansos* employed at Fritz Contzen's ranch, confronted the raiders and attempted to shout a warning to the ranchmen, but it was too late. The other *vaqueros* ran for Contzen's adobe house overlooking his fenced yard and corral. There they armed themselves with rifles, shotguns, and pistols and blazed away as some of the Apaches broke open the main corral that sheltered the cows and yearlings while other raiders provided covering fire from the nearby trees and desert scrub.

The ranchers identified their assailants as White Mountain or possibly Tonto Apaches but later admitted that they could not tell the difference between Aravaipas, San Carlos, Tontos, and other Western Apaches. All the survivors of the attack thanked God and the Papagos for their salvation. The native farmers had quickly rallied and come to the defense of their neighbors in time to prevent greater loss of life and property. Contzen later swore that had it not been for the Papagos, "the Apaches would have cleaned us out." Two of the raiders were killed near the corrals, and twenty-five or thirty men—Hispanos, Papagos, and Anglos—gave chase. The pursuers rode fifteen miles but gave up when they discovered that the Indians had broken into small parties each herding a portion of the more than four hundred captured animals now being driven toward the mountains at a killing pace. Many of the ranchers were so unnerved by the scale and ferocity of the assault that they determined to flee the territory, as Ake's party had done, while others sought security in Tucson or Tubac or forted up as best they could at their own ranches while sending desperate pleas for help to the departing troops.[15]

Federal officials feared that the Navajos and Apaches were now undertaking a war of extermination aimed at the "white race" and that a combination with the warriors of the southern plains would give the "red race" the upper hand in such a contest. They believed that the balance of power in the region had begun to tip. In the absence of federal authority, the Apacheans increased their forays against long-standing adversaries, Indian and Hispano, as well as the more recent Anglo arrivals, in search of livestock, merchandise, and captives. The raiders shut down road networks, severed communications, and drove Hispanos and Anglos along with their Papago, Pima, Maricopa, and Pueblo Indian allies to take refuge in fortified towns and villages, setting off civil wars in the southwestern territorial borderlands. This expansion of raiding activities prompted an aggressive response, first by Confederates and then by U.S. troops, who joined forces with Anglo and Hispano territorial citizens. Most of the sedentary tribes would also join the federal government's campaign against their Indian enemies, and Mexican citizens and soldiers eventually contributed to the concerted effort against the raiding tribes.[16]

South of the U.S.-Mexico border, another civil war further unsettled political, economic, and social affairs in the borderlands. Cross-border Indian raiding, requests from Mexican nationals for political asylum, clandestine support of Juárez's government from the United States, and the very visible buildup of U.S. troops on the border contributed to Mexico's political instability. Some observers in the borderlands believed that Mexico's northern states were "*de facto* independent of the central government" and that Sonora had been in a state of civil war since 1860 as Ópatas and Yaquis took sides in the clash between Juárez's liberals and the church-backed conservatives. The American Civil War created the conditions that brought Mexico's smoldering internal conflict into full flame and made possible the external threat of European intervention.[17]

In 1861, with the initial complicity of Britain and Spain, Louis Napoleon (Napoleon III) ordered French forces to invade Mexico ostensibly to collect debts from President Benito Juárez's democratic government as it struggled for survival in a civil war of its own. Mexican conservatives opposed Juárez's "ungodly constitution" with its antichurch, liberal reforms and allied themselves with Napoleon. With brazen disregard for Mexico's sovereignty and the Monroe Doctrine, the French emperor soon made it clear that he intended to reestablish an empire in the Americas while the United States was distracted with its internecine quarrel.[18] As the French intervention in Mexico developed, Confederates from Texas, New Mexico, and Arizona quickly mobilized and, seizing the initiative, began occupying towns and abandoned forts while, at the same time, dispatching diplomats to Mexico in hope of securing international recognition.[19]

The Confederate threat in the remote Southwest Borderlands became more alarming as Lincoln focused his administration's energies on raising armies and suppressing the rebellion in the eastern states. The far western theater could not be ignored, however, as Texas rebels and California Copperheads sprang into action and emboldened Apache and Navajo warriors increased their attacks. The U.S. War Department concentrated its regular troops on the Pacific coast, augmented by rapidly recruited California Volunteer regiments, and on the Rio Grande, with additional volunteer troops from New Mexico and Colorado. As the poorly trained New Mexico territorial troops, mostly Hispano and Pueblo Indian farmers, and Anglo miners from Colorado Territory mustered into federal service, a well-organized brigade of California Volunteers comprising cavalry, infantry, and artillery units began concentrating at Fort Yuma, with significant logistical support from Pima and Maricopa farmers, who provided vital food supplies for the soldiers and forage for their animals.[20]

In July 1861 the U.S. government had called on the State of California and territories of Colorado and New Mexico for volunteer troops. The army needed soldiers to put down the rebellion brewing in southern California and protect the federal property and transcontinental mail routes in the Southwest Borderlands from both secessionists and Indian raiders. Lincoln endorsed the Volunteer Employment Act the day after the Bull Run disaster of July 21. This emergency legislation specified that volunteers would be enlisted for terms of not less than six months and no longer than three years for the purpose of "suppressing rebellion." As battlefield casualties increased, it became clear to all that the country was now engaged in civil war.[21] Later that month Congress amended the law to allow soldiers to enlist for the duration of the war. Following calls in July and August, California enrolled and mustered two regiments of cavalry and five regiments of infantry for federal service. Two mountain-howitzer batteries, trained in Arizona, composed the California artillery complement.[22]

The sixteen thousand volunteers raised by the state of California for service in the West combined with more than three thousand Coloradans and nearly five thousand New Mexicans represented a military force almost twice as large as the entire U.S. Army at the time the Civil War began. These volunteer soldiers would replace the regular troops sent east and provide a bulwark against Confederates in the West while patrolling the territories to ensure the safety of U.S. citizens and overland mail routes. California Volunteer regiments provided the vast majority of the manpower in the Far West, serving as far north as Fort Colville, Washington Territory, and as far east as Fort Leavenworth, Kansas, while also garrisoning New Mexico posts, pursuing rebels in Texas, and even making forays from Arizona deep into French-occupied Sonora and Chihuahua, Mexico.[23]

Texans

While the first regiments of California infantry and cavalry mobilized, news of a Confederate invasion of New Mexico and Arizona reached the San Francisco headquarters of the U.S. Army's Department of the Pacific. On July 27, 1861, before Canby could mass his dispersed forces, Confederate Lieutenant Colonel John R. Baylor's companies of mounted riflemen, recruited in Texas and the territories, captured seven hundred regular troops of Major Isaac Lynde's command—including seven companies of his Seventh U.S. Infantry regiment, a squadron of U.S. Mounted Rifles, and a battery of 12-pounder field howitzers—as it retreated northward from Fort Fillmore, New Mexico.[24] Just days before, the Federals had tentatively attacked Baylor's outnumbered command, which was then holed up at the town of Mesilla awaiting reinforcements. Lynde's assault was no more than a demonstration that lobbed a few howitzer rounds short of the town's adobe dwellings. When the rebels showed fight, the nervous Federals quickly limbered their guns and returned to Fort Fillmore. There they torched the valuable military, subsistence, and medical stores, though the veteran soldiers somehow managed to save some of its whiskey supply, and began to evacuate the place. The strung-out column of troops, government contractors, and panicked civilian camp followers headed northward toward Fort Stanton by way of San Augustin Pass, some twenty miles distant, ill-prepared for the trek through the desert heat. Lynde's soldiers had insufficient water in their three-pint canteens, some of which may have been filled with whiskey. Soon the men began shedding their uniforms and straggling. As the sun grew hotter, the line of march could be easily followed by the cast-off knapsacks and weapons that littered the trail.[25]

Baylor's small advance force of 162 mounted riflemen chased after Lynde's disorganized command, passing nearly 200 dehydrated soldiers who collapsed on the side of the road from heat exhaustion. Not stopping to corral prisoners he was ill-equipped to handle, Baylor caught up with Lynde's entourage and other officers near San Augustin Springs. There he found the Federal major confused and barely able to maintain his saddle. Realizing he was outnumbered and dangerously low on water himself, Baylor pushed the Union men to surrender immediately, but the regular officers of the mounted companies still had some fight in them and urged their commander to resist. Baylor took control of the parley, staring down the junior officers and demanding to know just who was in command. Baylor's bluster won out, and Lynde conditionally surrendered without firing a single shot, believing that "honor did not demand the sacrifice of blood" after the suffering already endured by his men during the retreat. Some of the officers present protested and swore aloud, "The damned old scoundrel has surrendered us!" Fort Fillmore's post surgeon witnessed "old soldiers and strong men weep like children" and attributed Lynde's actions to cowardice, imbecility, and an inability to manage logistics, including the disposition of the inordinate number of camp followers and officers' wives that impeded the retreat and field operations. The Union men had succumbed to the desert heat, enemy bravado, and their own inept commander's loss of heart. Before submitting to Baylor's custody or parole, the men of the Seventh Infantry set ablaze their silken regimental colors rather than surrender them to the rebels.[26]

Though Lynde's regular troops wore splendid brass-buttoned uniforms and brandished burnished weapons with martial élan on the fort's parade ground, Baylor's motley band of Texan volunteers, indifferently attired and armed with a variety of shotguns and revolvers, were battle-hardened, combative, and confident. They knew how to survive in the desert, and most of the enlisted men and officers, including Baylor himself, had previously fought Comanches in military companies organized for that purpose. Only six months earlier, some of these same rangers had defeated the Noconee Comanches at Pease River, Texas, and significantly reduced raiding from that part of the powerful Comanche confederation. The aggressive and warlike Texans exhibited a unique brand of Anglo-Saxon martial masculinity, which evolved from their Kentucky and Tennessee frontier lineages and the hostile environment of the Texas borderlands between the Comanche empire to the north and the often-adversarial Mexico to the south.[27]

On August 1, 1861, Colonel Baylor proclaimed a "Territory of Arizona" for the Confederacy, marking the first time any government officially recognized the area (then considered southern New Mexico Territory) as a separate political unit. In a proclamation dated August 1, 1861, Baylor decreed from Mesilla:

To the People of the Territory of Arizona:

The social and political condition of Arizona being little short of general anarchy, and the people being literally destitute of law, order, and protection, the said Territory, from the date hereof, is hereby declared temporarily organized as a military government until such time as Congress may otherwise provide.

I, John R. Baylor, lieutenant-colonel, commanding the Confederate Army in the Territory of Arizona, hereby take possession of the said Territory in the name and behalf of the Confederate States of America.

For all the purposes herein specified, and until otherwise decreed or provided, the Territory of Arizona shall comprise all that portion of New Mexico lying south of the thirty-fourth parallel of north latitude.

All offices, both civil and military, heretofore existing in this Territory, either under the laws of the late United States or the Territory of New Mexico, are hereby declared vacant, and from the date hereof shall forever cease to exist.

That the people of this Territory may enjoy the full benefits of law, order, and protection and, as far as possible, the blessings and advantages of a free government, it is hereby decreed that

the laws and enactments existing in this Territory prior to the
date of this proclamation, and consistent with the Constitution
and laws of the Confederate States of America and the provisions of this decree, shall continue in full force and effect, without interruption, until such time as the Confederate Congress
may otherwise provide.

In Richmond, Confederate president Jefferson Davis confirmed Baylor's self-proclaimed governorship.[28]

The energetic Baylor wasted no time securing Arizona for the Confederacy. After routing federal forces on the Rio Grande, he focused his
attention on the Apache raiders who had shut down the east-west transportation corridor between Mesilla and Tucson. The allied Chiricahua
Apache bands had driven off miners, ranchers, and other Hispano and
Anglo settlers and traders. Finding the displaced miners of Pinos Altos
and other refugees eager for protection and revenge, he began recruiting
experienced frontiersmen, whom he formed into mounted companies
designated "Arizona Guards" and "Arizona Rangers."[29]

Baylor had come north with his Texans intent on ending federal
authority in the territories and equally determined to kill any and all
Indians he encountered. Prior to secession, Governor Sam Houston
himself had praised the past efforts of independent ranging companies,
urging them to "repel, pursue, and punish every body of Indians coming into the State."[30] Nearly all of Baylor's Texans had lost family and
friends in the struggle for survival and dominance with the Comanches,
and all the rangers believed in "war to the knife."[31] These men had come
of age in a martial culture that valued personal daring and courage in
the face of an enemy. It mattered little to them that they came home
with Apache or Comanche Indian scalps on their belts. Baylor vowed to
do just that, believing an aggressive offensive the best strategy in deal-
ing with the enemy warriors. He openly advocated extermination of the
Apaches and other Indians, whom he viewed as hostile subhumans.[32]

His company commanders received orders to kill Apache men
whenever encountered and to sell any captives into slavery. "You will
therefore use all means to persuade the Apaches or any tribe to come
in for the purpose of making peace," he instructed Arizona Guards
Captain Thomas Helm, "and when you get them together kill all the
grown Indians and take the children prisoners and sell them to defray
the expense of killing the Indians. Buy whisky and such other goods

as may be necessary for the Indians and I will order vouchers given to cover the amount expended. Leave nothing undone to insure success, and have a sufficient number of men around to allow no Indian to escape." Though Comanches, Kiowas, Utes, Navajos, and Apaches typically took captives for sale or ransom to other tribes, or to Mexicans in Chihuahua and Sonora, there was something especially cold-blooded and calculating in Baylor's orders. Perhaps it was the bureaucratic thoroughness or the stated goal of extermination that gave even hard-hearted Indian killers and slaveholders pause.[33]

Baylor's Confederate Arizona Territory stretched from the Texas line westward to Tucson, Arizona's only town of consequence, between Mesilla and Arizona City opposite Fort Yuma on the Colorado River. In August 1861 Mangas Coloradas's and Cochise's allied Chiricahua Apache bands—Bedonkohe, Chihenne, Chokonen—had already captured Ake's valuable wagon train near Cooke's Canyon on the main southern overland trail. Ake knew he had to leave the territories when the federal soldiers pulled out, but based on previous experience, he believed his well-armed men would be enough to safeguard his family and property as they traveled east along the abandoned Butterfield stage road. But the Apache ambush had sent Ake's survivors running for their lives. Captain Thomas Mastin's company of Confederate Mounted Volunteers discovered the bodies of nine Hispano herders and six of Ake's Anglo escorts and immediately galloped off in pursuit of the Indians. The rebel rangers, all experienced Arizona frontiersmen, intercepted the Apaches, slowed down by their plunder, and inflicted many casualties. But the Apaches did not make a run for Mexico nor did they take refuge in the mountains, as the Anglos expected. Instead they retaliated at the Pinos Altos gold mines, killing Mastin and four other men in a close-quarters fight to the death.[34]

While some of Baylor's ranger companies attempted to protect the mines and settlements from the escalating Apache attacks, Captain Sherod Hunter arrived in Tucson with about one hundred men of Company A, Second Texas Mounted Volunteers and elements of other Confederate territorial companies[35] on February 28, 1862. Colonel James Reily, the special envoy of General Henry Hopkins Sibley, now in overall command of Confederate forces in New Mexico, accompanied Hunter's command to Arizona. On March 3, 1862, Reily left Tucson with twenty men under Lieutenant James Tevis for Ures, Sonora, in an attempt to contact Governor Ignacio Pesqueira and secure Mexican recognition of the Confederate government and, if all went well, negotiate for food supplies desperately needed by the overextended Texas regiments pushing up the Rio Grande in New Mexico.[36]

After seeing Reily's diplomatic mission off, Captain Hunter's small but self-reliant command promptly seized the initiative in Arizona. Most of his men had lived and worked in the borderlands prior to the war and were familiar with the people, places, and essential survival skills. No Union forces opposed the arrival of the rebel horse soldiers, and the Anglo residents, it seemed, welcomed them as a means of protection from the increasingly aggressive Apaches. Attacks by Chiricahuas and Western Apaches, as well as the eastern Mescalero bands in southern New Mexico, had taken their toll on civilian miners between Tucson and the Rio Grande. Territorial citizens believed Apache war leaders, encouraged by the earlier withdrawal of U.S. troops, now raided with impunity. They even attacked Hunter's heavily armed rebel rangers, making no distinction between Union and Confederate whites. While Baylor and Hunter began the tasks of occupation and control of the natives considered hostile, they kept an anxious eye on the California Volunteer units already moving across the desert to Fort Yuma on the Colorado River.[37]

At the beginning of the Civil War, the raiding Navajos, Apaches, and other tribes were, together, militarily stronger than any other group in the borderlands. Even though the Anglo-Americans affiliated with the U.S. government then represented only a small minority of the inhabitants of the territories, their presence had been significant as a stabilizing influence. The federal government sought peaceful relations with the native tribes believing it was morally preferable to feed and pacify its "wards" rather than fight them. At the same time the government worked to prevent cross-border Indian raiding, as well as Anglo filibustering, and attempted to limit hostile acts between Hispano, Indian, and Anglo peoples within New Mexico Territory. The disruption and violence resulting from the absence of federal authority demonstrated just how important the U.S. presence had been in steadying the balance of power and maintaining the peace.[38]

Civil wars in the Southwest Borderlands pitted Anglo-Americans and their Hispano and Indian allies against Confederates and Apacheans, while other conflicts north and south of the Mexican border led to warfare between and within ethnic groups and classes. Some of these conflicts had international dimensions as well. U.S. forces confronted Confederates, Apaches, Navajos, Mojaves, Yavapais, Hualapais, Paiutes, Comanches, Kiowas, Ópatas, and Mexican Imperial forces. Alliances were fluid and subject to change, but the principal allies of the Anglos from the United States included Hispano New Mexicans, Pimas, Maricopas, Papagos, Pueblos, and, occasionally, Utes, Apaches, and Juaristas from across the border in Mexico. The ethnically related Navajos and Apaches fought one another, as well as Union and Confederate Anglos, Hispanos north and south of the border, and agrarian tribes including Pimas, Maricopas, Papagos, and Pueblos. Raids, skirmishes, and battles ranged across the border with Mexico, which was also embroiled in civil war. Liberal laboring-class and middle-class Indians and Hispanos faced off against predominantly prochurch, upper-class, and high-caste conservatives and their Indian and Hispano allies as well as European imperialists from France and Austria.

Union Martial Manpower, Logistics, and Mobilization

Anglo-American Unionists from California, Colorado, and New Mexico along with their Hispano and Indian allies faced off against Anglo Confederates from Texas and New Mexico. Though the distinct groups of Anglos were linked by language, shared history, and many traditions, their approaches to war in the borderlands differed significantly. The Union and Confederate westerners who joined military units were above-average physical specimens and had demonstrated a willingness to take risks. These characteristics are typical of groups that survived voluntary migrations under adverse conditions. While nearly all the Anglos believed in the manifest destiny of their "race" to control Indian and Hispano inhabitants of the borderlands, the Southern men were steeped in a culture of martial masculinity, which unabashedly advocated the taking of the territories by force. The Anglos' strategies and tactics were influenced by European traditions, especially the art of war as it had evolved since the time of Napoleon. The logistics required of this type of warfare, combined with the unique conditions, terrain, and alliances in the borderlands, necessitated special preparations and new modes of combat.

The Northern men generally exhibited a more restrained form of the Anglo cultural ideal of manhood and typically advocated the conquest of enemies and "inferiors" in a seemingly more humane way. Union officers forged strategic alliances and made logistics a priority, bringing sophisticated technology to bear whenever possible in order to achieve a military advantage over adversaries. They also sought to win the support of the local citizenry and understood the importance of maintaining or building civil government, infrastructure, and economies in the territories. The Union men also kept a close watch on affairs in Mexico and endeavored to maintain neutrality and avoid foreign intervention. The Confederates demonstrated considerable élan yet often neglected supply lines and relations with Hispano communities. The Texans and other Confederates in the borderlands also took an aggressive posture in response to Indian raiders while investing little energy in establishing alliances with sedentary tribes.

In August 1861 Lincoln and his senior officers at the War Department had debated the practicability of a column from California striking the Confederates in Texas by way of Mexico. Brigadier General Edwin V. Sumner, then commanding the Department of the Pacific, sought and received cooperation from Mexican officials and began planning such an operation. U.S. troops would land at Guaymas or Mazatlán on the Gulf of California, march overland across the states of Sonora and Chihuahua, and strike the rebels along the border in west Texas if not in Mexico itself. Reports of Confederate-sanctioned filibustering with designs on Sonora and the port of Guaymas caused Sonora's anxious Governor Pesqueira to work willingly with U.S. military officials in California to intercept the Texans and eliminate this serious threat to Mexican sovereignty.[39]

Civil unrest in southern California, however, diverted the first of the new California regiments. Federal authorities feared, with some justification, that some twenty thousand Confederate sympathizers would collaborate with disloyal Hispanos—still embittered by the hostile Anglo takeover twelve years earlier—and instigate civil war in the southern counties. Quick and decisive action led to the roundup of agitators and quashed open rebellion by December, just as the alarming news of Confederate victories in New Mexico and the rebel invasion of Arizona reached the Pacific coast. The command of the Department of the Pacific had devolved upon Colonel George Wright, commander of the Ninth U.S. Infantry—the only regular regiment remaining on the West Coast—when General-in-Chief George B. McClellan recalled Sumner to the East.[40] Wright, believing it was too late to protect western ports and territories by preemptively attacking west Texas by way of Mexico, proposed invading the territories more directly with a force of California troops that would cross the Colorado River at Yuma and proceed to New Mexico along the Gila River on the old Butterfield Overland Mail route. Understanding the urgency, McClellan approved the operation.[41]

Wright's promotion to Brigadier General came through without delay, and he quickly selected forty-seven-year-old James Henry Carleton, colonel of the First California Infantry and formerly major of the First U.S. Dragoons, to lead the column into Arizona. Wright wanted an aggressive field commander to find and strike the Confederates as soon as possible. He knew Carleton to be a tough and efficient officer—a protégé of the hard-marching Stephen Watts Kearny—with many years of frontier experience. After more than twenty years in the saddle and considerable time as a commissary of subsistence, Carleton had earned a reputation as both an uncompromising disciplinarian and a stickler for detail. Lean, sharp-featured, and ramrod straight, subordinates believed his steel gray eyes commanded obedience. At the same time he was well-read, articulate, and possessed an artistic bent that he satisfied through creative and historical writing, and natural history and botanical explorations. As a youth and as a frontier officer before the war, he corresponded with naturalist John J. Audubon. Carleton focused his inquiring nature on the study of America's "aboriginal peoples" and even consulted the novelist Charles Dickens on the subject.

As a military man, however, Carleton was a no-nonsense, by-the-book regular, always anticipating logistical needs when organizing, equipping, and deploying troops. As he developed the plan for the Arizona expedition, Wright was made aware of the international implications of war in the borderlands. The War Department, it turned out, had rejected the idea of attacking the Confederates in Texas by way of the northern Mexican states as politically dangerous. He also learned that leaders in Washington had originally intended that Carleton command the soldiers assigned to guard the overland mail on the central route through Nevada, Utah, and Dakota (Wyoming, after 1865) territories. Brigham Young saw the departure of federal troops from Utah as an opportunity to strengthen his independent state of Deseret and quickly made overtures to Shoshones, Paiutes, Utes, and other tribes to prepare for war against emigrating "Gentiles" and U.S.

troops. Carleton seemed the logical choice for the command since he had led his dragoons over this country following the Mormon War, but his original orders were rescinded when the Confederate threat in the Southwest became apparent.[42]

Union authorities reasoned that a thrust from southern California across Arizona and New Mexico to the Rio Grande would serve several strategic purposes: it would block a junction of Texas and California secessionists, reopen the southern overland mail route, provide garrisons for abandoned posts, and furnish protection to the citizens of the territories and the northern states of Mexico. Many of the new Hispano and Anglo inhabitants were miners taking advantage of the tremendous mineral wealth—gold and silver—long evident since Spanish times, as well as new deposits discovered in Colorado, New Mexico and, most recently, Arizona. The Californians would also be in a position to fall upon the flank and rear of Sibley's Texans, who seemed invincible as they captured or pushed past federal forts while marching up the Rio Grande toward Santa Fe and the Colorado goldfields. Wright advised McClellan, "Under the command of Colonel Carleton, an officer of great experience, indefatigable and active, the expedition must be successful."[43]

Carleton's force included ten companies of his own regiment, the First California Infantry; five companies of the First California Cavalry under Lieutenant Colonel Edward E. Eyre; and Light Battery A, Third U.S. Artillery. First Lieutenant John B. Shinn commanded the battery, which consisted of four bronze field pieces (6-pounder guns and 12-pounder field howitzers) manned by regulars. Wright assigned Captain John C. Cremony's Company B, Second California Cavalry to Carleton's contingent before the column set out across the desert. Later Colonel George W. Bowie's ten companies of the Fifth California Infantry and two improvised mountain-howitzer batteries, commanded by Lieutenants Jeremiah Phelan and William A. Thompson, joined Carleton's command, bringing the total force to 2,350 men. Before the war's end, some six thousand additional California soldiers would follow this advance column.[44]

Experienced regular-army officers raised and trained the regiments bound for Arizona. Lieutenant Colonel Benjamin F. Davis, formerly captain of Company K, First U.S. Dragoons, drilled the First California Cavalry into a well-trained and disciplined battalion. But by the time the

Californians marched for the territory in late 1861, Davis and many of the other regular officers had gone east to fight, and civilian appointees led the volunteers. The men benefited greatly from the training provided by their original cadre of officers, and these professionals agreed that no finer material for soldiers could be found anywhere. The first men to answer the call were Anglo-Americans recruited from every part of California. More than half the state's Anglo population was of military age, and these men flocked to enlistment centers at forts and camps.

These volunteer soldiers represented a true cross section of California's Anglo male population. They were a hardy lot, used to working outdoors in the harshest conditions imaginable. Most of them labored in the mines and goldfields of the mother lode country of northern California when the war broke out. In the 1850s they had rushed to California from every state in the Union and many European countries—nearly one in four were born outside the United States. They were risk takers and tended to be bigger and stronger than their stay-at-home eastern brethren. Army quartermasters discovered that the men of the West needed coat, trouser, hat, and shoe sizes considerably larger than those required by their counterparts in the Army of the Potomac. As was the case with most voluntary migrations, the westerners exhibited not only above average stature (five feet, eight inches for federal soldiers) but intelligence and self-reliance as well. As youthful argonauts, they had undertaken the difficult journey to California—by land or sea—and then survived the rough-and-ready miner's life. Other occupations appearing on the regimental descriptive lists include laborer, farmer, mechanic, printer, and seaman. The men ranged in age from eighteen to forty-five, though most were in their early twenties, and had at least some formal education.[45]

The Californians enlisted for a variety of reasons, from a patriotic desire to preserve the Union to the lure of three regular meals a day. Others found the pay of eleven dollars a month a compelling inducement. In the ranks there was little talk of the slavery issue, but occasionally tempers flared between proslavery and antislavery men. Whether or not they approved of slavery, the majority of Californians agreed that the Union must be preserved. Californios, native Californians descended from Spanish and Mexican pioneers, adopted a wait-and-see attitude as the sectional strife between North and South escalated. Most of the Hispanos felt that this was not their war, yet.

In many ways the California Volunteers proved to be superior to the soldiers of the regular army who preceded them in the Southwest Borderlands. Although well officered, the regular ranks were filled with recent immigrants and Americans from the lowest rung of the socioeconomic ladder. They had little or no formal education and most were illiterate. Alcoholism, a 33 percent desertion rate, malingering, and a host of social diseases crippled the strength and effectiveness of the standing army. The regulars lacked the diverse talents of the volunteers, most of whom viewed military service as a temporary break from their civilian occupations. The volunteers were literate, even literary, and quickly adapted to new people, environments, and challenges, while the regulars looked to their officers and the security of military routine. All things considered, the independent Californians seemed ideally suited for the arduous service they would face in the border territories.[46]

Although the newly formed California regiments lost most of their regular officers—who transferred to eastern units—before departing for the territories, able and experienced volunteer officers eagerly took their places. Virtually all the men awarded a major's commission or higher, including Joseph R. West, Edwin A. Rigg, Clarence E. Bennett, and Edward Eyre, had served in California's large and active militia during the 1850s. Others had seen service in volunteer regiments during the Mexican-American War. Oscar M. Brown, William P. Calloway, Charles W. Lewis, John Martin, and Edmond D. Shirland could all claim war experience.[47]

California governor John Downey confirmed commissions for a number of outstanding officer candidates who had served as enlisted men in the regular army before the war. William McCleave had served as Carleton's first sergeant in Company K, First U.S. Dragoons, during the decade preceding the Civil War, and Carleton pushed for his old friend's appointment to command Company A, First California Cavalry. McCleave left the service in 1860 to oversee the army's experimental camel herd at Fort Tejon, California, but now he jumped at the chance to serve as an officer under Carleton. Similarly, Sergeant Emil Fritz received a commission to captain Company B, First California Cavalry. Fritz had previous military training in Germany before arriving in California in 1849 (he succeeded McCleave as first sergeant of Company K, First Dragoons in October 1860). Second Lieutenant James Barrett of Company A, First California Cavalry, also served beside McCleave and Fritz as a corporal in the First Dragoons before the war. Chauncey Wellman, a first sergeant in the First U.S. Cavalry before the war, also won a California Volunteer commission. Cavalry commands were the most sought after in the patriotic rush that followed the opening of hostilities. Carleton made certain that these plum commissions went to men of proven ability.[48]

Although the governor had to approve commissions in the volunteer service, a military board established in the early months of the war reviewed all officer candidates as a safeguard against unqualified appointments. At first the enlisted men of the California companies elected their officers, as was common practice in militia companies. The men usually chose competent officers and practically considered such factors as fairness and general likeability. Oftentimes the men had little opportunity to size up their leaders, other than their physical appearance and stature. The Anglo frontiersmen looked for a leader with a "military bearing" who could command respect. In the rush to recruit and organize units, the amateur soldiers chose volunteer officers as much for their imposing appearance as their military competency. Consequently, the elected officers were often physically impressive and well above average height.[49] Later in the war many veteran volunteers with demonstrated aptitude were promoted from the ranks. A soldier in the First California Infantry lamented, "There has been about 15 or 16 sergeants in our column promoted to Second Lieut. Our sergeant went among the rest." The volunteer army, more so than the regular army, recognized and rewarded ability.[50]

Demands and Supplies

U.S. Army regulations made no special provisions for the volunteer soldiers destined for service in Arizona and New Mexico. The army expected these troops to be organized, uniformed, armed, and equipped the same as the regular regiments they replaced. In practice, however, the availability of matériel, the personal preferences of officers and men, the anticipated enemy, and the desert environment influenced the formation and outfitting of the California regiments. Most of the regular troops returning to the East in 1861 deposited their arms and equipage at government arsenals and forts in California. Ordnance officers inspected and quickly reissued serviceable equipment to the newly formed regiments. Large stocks of unused weapons and accoutrements, some obsolescent, were issued in the rush to arm the volunteers, and armorers and artificers at Benicia Arsenal near San Francisco repaired unserviceable equipment as fast as possible.[51]

Carleton understood that logistics would be the key to success in the arid Southwest. As a former commissary of subsistence on Kearny's 1845 Oregon Trail expedition to South Pass, a grueling ninety-nine-day march across two thousand miles of parched mountains and plains, Carleton recognized that the winner of the war in the borderlands would be the one that controlled the food and water supplies. The campaign in the desert would be successful only if the men could be sheltered, fed, properly equipped in any conditions, and sustained in the field the longest. In 1856 Secretary of War Jefferson Davis had charged Carleton with compiling recent studies by McClellan and others on European tactics and lessons from the Crimean War. Carleton's definitive work, *The Battle of Buena Vista*, which prominently featured the successes of Davis's own Mississippi troops, convinced the Secretary that he was the perfect man to write a new manual on cavalry, the arm most in need of reorganization to successfully combat Indian raiders in the vast new western territories.[52]

The first mounted volunteers to answer the call to arms in California received the weapons turned over by the regulars. These included Sharps carbines, muzzle-loading rifles, Colt's revolving "Dragoon" pistols, and heavy cavalry sabers. Only the most expert horsemen and noncommissioned officers received the sabers when supplies ran low. Anxious about the arms issued to his mounted troops, Carleton knew from experience that uniformity of armament would be critical when it came to supplying ammunition in the field. His ordnance officers would have a hard time keeping track of and supplying ammunition for two different models of Sharps carbines as well as muzzle-loading rifle cartridges.[53]

After more regulars left for the East and the workers at Benicia repaired unserviceable weapons, all the horsemen with Carleton's column and most of the subsequent California cavalry companies serving in the Southwest received the Sharps carbines. This short-barreled rifle shot true at ranges up to one hundred yards. A trained trooper could load a combustible linen cartridge into the open breech, aim, and fire every ten seconds. By comparison, an infantryman with a muzzle-loading rifle musket could fire only three rounds per minute. The carbine, designed for use on horseback, attached to a snap hook on a broad leather strap slung across the trooper's chest. Cavalry officers preferred the short and easily managed carbines over long rifles or muskets, which they considered too unwieldy for mounted service.[54]

Carleton appreciated the need to balance firepower with the horses' capacity and the men's ability to carry the weapons. Accordingly he requested that the commander of Benicia Arsenal provide his cavalry with the lightweight Colt Navy revolver instead of the heavy, four-and-a-half-pound, .44-caliber Dragoon pistol. Although the Navy was only .36 caliber and its smaller powder charge and bullet rendered it effective only at close range, Carleton preferred it because of the weight savings in the weapon itself and the ammunition. His soldiers would wear the gun in a flapped scabbard on the saber belt rather than strapped to the saddle in pommel holsters as regulations prescribed for the heavier pistol. Despite Carleton's insistence, some of the Second California Cavalry companies had to carry the heavy Dragoon pistol when supplies of the Navy revolver ran out.[55]

The Navy revolver also had a reputation for being a natural pointer and was, therefore, more accurate, a decided advantage considering that most of the volunteers were not accomplished pistol shots and little ammunition could be spared for practice. To load their pistols, the men inserted a combustible cartridge containing powder and ball into the front of each of the revolving cylinder's six chambers and compressed the charge by cranking a loading lever. Then thimble-shaped copper percussion caps had to be pinched onto the six steel nipples, which automatically aligned under the hammer when the pistol was cocked. The whole operation took about five minutes—too time-consuming to be done in combat—so most soldiers packed pistol cartridges in their pockets or saddlebags.[56]

Carleton preferred the heavy 1840 cavalry saber to the newer and lighter 1860 pattern for the mounted troops. All his experience had been with the old pattern, and he felt that if the soldiers kept their sabers razor sharp, the heavier blades could more easily cut through the clothing of enemy cavalrymen and inflict serious casualties in close-quarter fighting. Cold steel, he contended, would win out against the pistol in a melee.[57]

Each infantryman destined for service in the borderlands carried a nine-and-a-half-pound, .58-caliber Springfield rifle musket. These single-shot muzzleloaders fired expanding lead bullets, a deadly innovation developed a decade earlier by Captain Claude Minié of the French Army. A paper cylinder contained the bullet and powder until the soldier tore open the tail of the cartridge with his teeth and rammed the contents down the gun barrel in a nine-step process, which took twenty to thirty seconds to complete. Hoping to shave a few seconds off the loading time, the army adopted the Maynard patent tape-priming system, but experience had taught Carleton that the exploding paper caps misfired after being exposed to moisture. He ordered his troops to use the tried-and-true percussion caps in place of the unreliable Maynard primers.[58]

The foot soldier also carried an eighteen-inch triangular steel socket bayonet for his rifle musket, but as the first volunteers were being equipped, a shortage of the proper leather scabbards for this weapon caused supply officers to issue older patterns designed for the 1842 musket. The shorter and wider scabbards resulted in a loose fit and bayonets being dropped and lost on the march. Increased production at Benicia Arsenal corrected the shortage, but only after many heated exchanges between the Ordnance Department and frustrated volunteer officers.[59]

Selected men from infantry regiments and unassigned recruits received training in the use of the bronze 12-pounder mountain howitzers, which constituted the volunteer portion of the California artillery complement. Adopted by the army in 1835, these cannons weighed only five hundred pounds each when fully assembled and could be broken down into two or three loads and packed on mules. Where the desert roads and trails permitted, the little mountain guns could be mounted on wide-axled "prairie carriages" and pulled by horses or mules. Some of the infantrymen-turned-cannoneers retained their rifle muskets, unwilling to enter hostile country without some means of self-defense. These raw volunteer crews contrasted sharply with Captain Shinn's polished regulars of Battery A, Third U.S. Artillery, with their two full-sized 12-pounder field howitzers and two 6-pounder guns, which weighed four times more than the little mountain howitzers.[60]

Newly commissioned California infantry officers eagerly sought to complete their personal equipage, only to discover that arsenal workers could not supply sufficient quantities of the standard 1850 pattern sword, with its ornately etched blade and brass-mounted leather scabbard, prescribed by army regulations. The disappointed officers needed something to serve as a symbol of rank and command, so the ordnance officer in charge at Benicia granted them permission to purchase the model 1840 light artillery saber and belt normally issued to enlisted men of this mounted branch of the service. This brass-hilted horseman's sword, with its dangerous-looking curved blade, came complete with a polished steel scabbard and only cost $5.50, which could be deducted from the purchaser's uniform allowance. Many officers who were not presented swords by friends or civic organizations or could not afford to buy swords from private dealers took advantage of this bargain.[61]

Carleton wanted to ensure that civilian teamsters could defend themselves in case of attack by Confederates or Apaches. They received the heavy Dragoon revolver, deemed unsuitable for cavalry, and the 1849 pattern Rifleman's sheath knives, which had been stored unused for years at Benicia. The teamsters also brought along obsolescent Mississippi Rifles for use in an emergency. This muzzle-loading weapon, adopted in 1841 and made famous by Jefferson Davis's Mississippi troops during the war with Mexico, was not as long as the infantry rifle musket. It fired a .54-caliber ball, though government arsenals had reamed and rerifled many of these older weapons in order to use the standard .58-caliber minié cartridge.[62]

To lighten the wagons drawn by overburdened mules, the troops were ordered to carry much of the ammunition needed for their weapons. For this purpose the depots in California issued two types of leather cartridge boxes. The foot soldiers received large boxes with removable tin compartments holding forty paper cartridges. The men wore these boxes suspended from broad leather shoulder belts. Each cavalryman had a shorter box, worn on the saber belt, containing a wooden block bored through with twenty holes that snugly held the paper or linen cartridges used in the carbines. Both foot and horse soldiers also received small leather pouches, which held the percussion caps needed to fire the carbines, pistols, and muskets they carried.[63]

Although the Californians received both dress and fatigue uniforms while on the West Coast, Carleton ordered the men of his expedition to bring only their fatigue uniforms. Utility won out over looks, and unnecessary items were left behind or packed into escort wagons, two of which followed each company. Carleton itemized every article his soldiers would wear or carry on the march across the formidable

Sonoran Desert.[64] The brigade commander had no use for ornamentation and instructed the men to wear the regulation 1858 pattern black felt uniform hat—a flat-crowned, broad-brimmed affair—without the brass trimmings that designated branch of service, regiment, and company. He also deleted the prescribed black ostrich plume (one for enlisted men, two for officers) and directed that soldiers wear the hat brim folded down rather than looped up on the side according to regulation. The old dragoon knew that his men would need their hats for protection from the burning desert sun.[65]

The wool fatigue uniform consisted of a loose-fitting sack coat of dark blue wool, sky blue kersey trousers, and a forage cap. Undergarments were also woolen, though occasionally the men drew cotton drawers. The burgeoning California wool industry provided much of the raw material for the army clothing produced by busy San Francisco contractors, who augmented their work force with inmates from the military prison on Alcatraz Island. Shipments from eastern manufacturers filled shortages, but especially in the later years of the war, overworked or corrupt government inspectors approved much shoddy clothing produced in New York sweatshops.[66]

Carleton paid particular attention to his men's shoes. He ordered that ankle-high "bootees" be made with sewn rather than pegged soles. The wooden pegs, he knew, had a tendency to shrink in the hot desert sands. When the pegs fell out, the sole detached and the soldier went barefoot. "Once their feet come to the hot ground," he wrote his chief supply officer, "they will suffer immeasurably." Mounted men had the option of drawing calf-high boots as protection against chafing stirrup straps and the rough chaparral, instead of the low-cut bootee. In practice, however, most soldiers accepted whatever the quartermaster had available, pegged or sewn, boots or bootees.[67]

Carleton required both cavalrymen and infantrymen to carry "Green River" sheath knives. Experience had taught him that this versatile tool would be indispensable in the field. Before leaving California, church and temperance organizations provided some volunteer regiments with "butcher knives" and other necessities such as sewing kits, toothbrushes, and shoe blacking.[68]

Horses and horse equipment would prove vital to successful operations in the borderlands. Although the army tried to procure fifteen-and-a-half-hand "American" or Morgan horses, most volunteers found themselves astride smaller "California" horses of Spanish stock. Though these mounts were famed for their endurance, they could not carry the same weight larger horses bore. Several companies of the First California Cavalry reluctantly relinquished their American horses, turned in by the regulars, for use with the artillery batteries and freight wagons. The Americans also prized mules for their strength and endurance in the harsh western environment, and the army had come to rely on these tough crossbreeds rather than horses to carry the 225-pound mountain howitzer barrels on their backs. Mules ate less than horses and, even more importantly, were less susceptible to dehydration. Carleton saw to it that mules did most of the heavy hauling required by the freight trains that would follow his command across the desert. During the war, the army's mules would outnumber horses nearly two to one in the Southwest Borderlands.[69]

Cavalry regiments received three types of saddles. The "Grimsley" dragoon saddle, adopted in 1847, was too wide and flat in design to fit the small California horses; these saddles went back to the arsenal for reissue to the artillery. The volunteers soon learned an ill-fitting saddle would gall and ruin a good horse, so a new pattern, inspired by a popular Mexican style, went into production. The San Francisco firm of Main and Winchester, as well as some smaller contractors, manufactured these "California," or "Ranger," saddles in large numbers. This distinctive western saddle had a horn, like a stock saddle; Mexican hooded stirrups (*tapaderas*); and a leather saddle cover, called a *mochila*. The Californians also used the relatively new 1859 McClellan saddle. With its spare, rawhided wooden seat, the McClellan came in three sizes and proved to be an acceptable alternative for use with the narrow-backed California horses.[70]

Mounted soldiers received wool saddle blankets and bridles, either the old dragoon style or the new 1859 pattern. Picket pins and lariats, hobbles or side lines—all designed to secure horses while camped—completed the trooper's horse equipment. The horsemen carried leather-reinforced canvas nosebags for feeding their mounts measured rations of grain. Carleton also ordered seamless burlap gunny bags, capable of holding one hundred pounds of barley, manufactured expressly for the march to Fort Yuma. He directed officers to make certain the men soaked the grain in water before feeding in order to maintain the animals' strength and hydration during the difficult desert march.[71]

Carleton appeared to be obsessed with horseshoes and nails—after all, "for the want of a nail" the expedition might be lost. He required that only hand-forged iron horseshoes be taken on the expedition. Machine-made steel shoes, he believed, would require too much hand fitting on his "quick thrust" into Arizona. Each soldier carried in his saddlebags two spare shoes, with nails, ready to set, and farriers prepared special steel-toed mule shoes in anticipation of the rocky terrain.[72] Indians did not nail iron shoes to the hooves of their mounts—only Anglos and some Hispanos felt the need to alter nature and modify their animals' feet in this way. While Carleton's attention to these details may have seemed obsessive to some, the shod hooves of the soldiers' horses can be viewed as a metaphor for the Anglo philosophy of war and conquest.[73]

The U.S. Army bred big horses and mules to carry heavy loads—from heavily armed soldiers to packed cannons—while the Indians traveled and fought as light cavalry. Before going into battle, warriors often stripped off their saddles and other impedimenta to reduce the burden on their animals and ensure swiftness, which they prized over strength. Anglos expected their often-overburdened animals to traverse terrain, including rocky mountain trails and lava beds, which unshod horses could not travel without splitting hooves or incurring other crippling injuries. Indians would make rawhide moccasins for horses suffering from cuts, bruises, or split hooves, but this was not intended as a preventative treatment and did not enable their animals to carry heavier burdens. The Anglos and Indian people of the borderlands had fundamentally different approaches toward nature and survival. The seminomadic tribes carried little in the way of camp equipage and learned to live off the land while the Anglo soldiers packed everything they needed to survive in the desert.[74]

Carleton would not risk a repeat of Lynde's disgraceful surrender of his dehydrated command and made certain that all the officers under his command understood that water was their first priority. Little space could be spared in the company wagons for creature comforts, and every enlisted man would have to carry fifty to sixty pounds of clothing, arms, supplies, and equipage. Each one-hundred-man company was issued only two tipi-shaped Sibley tents for hospital use.[75] Always, water was the most important cargo. Each company wagon packed two six-gallon water kegs from which the men could refill their three-pint tin canteens. "Have the men drink heartily before setting out on a march," Carleton ordered, "and husband their canteens of water." Theoretically the company wagon carried enough water to enable one hundred men to travel eighty miles—a real possibility if a well were found poisoned or dry. Before leaving Fort Yuma, coopers fashioned huge six-hundred-gallon rolling water tanks to supply Carleton's column. The expedition could not wait for zinc lining material from San Francisco, so the enterprising soldiers stripped the tin linings from arms and ammunition boxes and soldered them together to make the tanks watertight.[76]

Advance units of the expedition began the difficult march from southern California's Camp Wright, at Oak Grove, and Camp Latham, at Wilmington, to Fort Yuma on the California side of the Colorado River in late October 1861. One of Carleton's ablest subordinates, Lieutenant Colonel Joseph R. West, commanded the 180-mile tramp across the desolate basin and sandy dunes of the Colorado Desert. West carefully planned the movement, requisitioning supplies for men and animals and deploying advanced guards to clean out wells and collect the precious water. He staggered the departure of his command—no more than one hundred men moved at a time—to avoid overtaxing the capacities of the wells. The dry desert, however, was not the only obstacle in the path of the Californians.[77]

There seemed to be no happy medium when it came to water during the winter of 1861. Rains drenched southern California and the lower Colorado River region. Roads became mud bogs, making the movement of men and supplies virtually impossible. Soon after West's command reached the Colorado, the river overflowed its banks. Torrents of muddy water swept a new channel around Fort Yuma, making it an island, and washed away tons of stockpiled supplies. Despite these conditions, by February 1862, oceangoing vessels and river steamers had delivered all the expedition's supplies, now safely stored on high ground at Fort Yuma.[78]

Situated on a bluff overlooking the confluence of the Gila and Colorado rivers, Fort Yuma guarded that strategic crossing on the southern overland route. Carleton remained in southern California to expedite the movement of troops and supplies. Expresses left his headquarters nearly every day carried by cameleers Hi Jolly (Hadji Ali) or Greek George, both of whom had come to America with the camels imported by Secretary of War Jefferson Davis in 1857. Although the War Department had discontinued the camel experiment, Carleton relied on the animals and their able handlers for the frequent desert crossings. The colonel sent detailed instructions for the proper placement of field and siege artillery to command all river and land approaches to Fort Yuma. His men sank, or brought within range of the guns, the ferries at the crossings above and below the fort. Carleton ordered his officers to watch the steamboat men for signs of treachery. No one would be allowed to cross the river in either direction without the knowledge and approval of the army.[79]

Carleton insisted that the officers "drill, drill, drill, until your men become perfect as soldiers, as skirmishers, as marksmen." When the first California infantry companies arrived at Fort Yuma, Major Edwin Rigg began drilling the men in earnest. They loaded their muskets with blanks and practiced firing by company and battalion—by rank, by file, and in double-ranked "line-of-battle" all at once in crashing volleys. Late into the night the officers memorized the pages of William Hardee's *Infantry Tactics*, and the mounted officers studied the drill commands from the old cavalry manual. Carleton forwarded additional instructions to Rigg. Each night after taps, the officers were to recite passages by rote. Every morning they would drill their companies in compact linear formations, then in the afternoon they would practice dispersed as skirmishers.[80]

Carleton left little to chance. He knew that the arid land could be as fierce a foe as any rebel legion or Indian adversary the California men might encounter and that superior logistics would conquer the desert and win the war. Winning the war meant keeping the peace with the citizens and the indigenous peoples on both sides of the Mexican border and seeking out strategic alliances whenever possible. Carleton's confidence in his men and his own abilities was bolstered by a staunch Yankee patriotism and the conviction not only that God was on his side, but also that he himself was an instrument of the republic's destiny who would transform and civilize the Southwest Borderlands.

Prelude to Invasion

In March 1862, as Carleton consolidated his forces at Fort Yuma, scouts rode toward Tucson to learn the strength of the enemy there. Rumors filtered back that Confederate cavalry would soon be riding down the

Gila in force. Both Carleton and Rigg had spies in Tucson. These men traveled via Sonora to avoid suspicion and carried a secret code, the key to which Rigg kept safely locked at Fort Yuma. Writing under the pseudonym "George Peters," Peter Brady, the former post interpreter at Fort Mojave, sent Rigg information concerning the rebels. One of Carleton's agents, Frederick C. Buckner, made the five-hundred-mile round trip from Yuma to Tucson in twenty-two days. He returned with a letter from merchant Solomon Warner reporting that attacks by Apache bands around Tucson grew bolder and more frequent with each passing day. "Protection," he pleaded, "would be favourably received here from any quarter," even from the rebels.[81]

Rigg worried about the rumors of Confederate raiders. He particularly feared for the safety of Ammi White, a loyal Union man who operated a flour mill at the Pima Villages along the Gila River, about ninety miles northwest of Tucson. White had stockpiled 1,500 sacks of wheat at his mill for the subsistence of the California troops. The major also fretted about the piles of hay that volunteer parties from Fort Yuma had cut and stacked along the Gila River, knowing that lack of forage for horses and mules would stall Carleton's supply trains and doom the expedition from the start.[82]

Captain McCleave took action to deal with these concerns. His dragoon service with Carleton before the war had earned him the commander's fullest confidence; over the years the two men had become close. McCleave's Company A, First California Cavalry, rode to Fort Yuma in two sections, and the captain must have breathed a sigh of relief upon seeing the adobe fort perched on the Colorado River bluffs, realizing that he had made the first leg of the desert crossing without incident. Eager to leave Yuma behind,[83] McCleave did not wait for the second detachment of his company to catch up. He knew that Carleton had selected his men for the advance because they possessed "first-rate dash and good pluck." The commander had confidentially advised his friend that taking Hunter and his company by surprise at Tucson "would be a coup that would last you all your life," but also added some fatherly caution: "You should have spies ahead to keep you warned of danger of ambushes, &c., en route, and to let you know all about the enemy."[84]

McCleave crossed the river and started up the north bank of the Gila with an escort of only nine men, heading for the Pima Villages and White's Mill. The riders urged their horses on as they rode through the dense cottonwood stands along the sandy Gila bottoms, but the party moved with greater caution as it neared the villages of the Maricopa and Pima Indians. Of course, these industrious farmers posed no threat; in fact they were the best allies the soldiers had in combating their common enemy—Apaches. Some miles back, near Burke's Station, the Californians had paused to stare at the desiccated body of an Apache warrior bristling with Pima arrows and hanging by a horsehair rope from the limb of a mesquite tree—a warning to enemy raiders.[85]

Perhaps the captain was too eager and not nearly cautious enough. He had galloped ahead with his small force to see whether he could locate a civilian scout, John W. Jones, who may have sought shelter at Ammi White's flour mill near the Pima Villages. Weeks before, Carleton had ordered Jones to ride unescorted from Yuma to spy on the rebels in Tucson. Not having heard from him, McCleave feared the scout had run into trouble.[86] At midnight, the captain halted to water and rest his horses at the Butterfield stage station known as the Tanks, just twenty miles short of White's Mill. Behind his back the boys had taken to calling him "Uncle Billy," but as they entered enemy country he was confident they would do anything he asked of them.[87] On March 6, determined to press on, he allowed six troopers to stay behind at the Tanks to eat and sleep while he continued on with three others. Four hours later, as McCleave and his companions spurred their tired horses into the corral at White's, a startled sentinel shouted a challenge from the darkness. "We're Americans," McCleave called out in his distinctive Irish brogue.[88]

McCleave, Carleton's most trusted officer, had unwittingly ridden into a trap. The resourceful Confederate Captain Sherod Hunter had scouts of his own, and they had learned that the California troops were crossing the Colorado and marching up the Gila. Soon after Colonel Reily left on his mission to Sonora, Hunter rode to the Pima Villages, took White prisoner, and disabled the mill. Hunter did not have enough wagons to haul off all the captured wheat, so he distributed it to the Pimas, from whom it originally came, figuring he would need all the friends he could get as the Californians approached. When McCleave boldly walked up to White's house and pounded on the door, one of Hunter's men greeted him. None of the Confederates lounging about the house wore recognizable uniforms. His hosts put him at ease, and McCleave introduced himself to Hunter, who represented himself as

White. After gleaning what intelligence he could from the unwary officer, Hunter suddenly revealed his true identity as his men leveled cocked
revolvers on the astonished captain. McCleave was outraged by the
rebel captain's brazen deception and grabbed for his pistol, but Hunter
threatened, "If you make a single motion I'll blow your brains out.
You are in my power—surrender immediately."[89] His pride wounded
but otherwise unhurt, the California captain gave up without further
resistance, and within a matter of hours the Confederates surprised his
six men waiting at the Tanks. The rebels had won the first engagement
in Arizona, much to McCleave's humiliation and Carleton's disbelief.[90]

Hunter followed this initial success by sending a platoon of his
mounted rangers down the Gila to intercept Union supply wagons and
burn the forage stockpiled by government contractors along the route.
He understood that he could defeat his enemies more easily and without combat by denying them subsistence for the mules that pulled the
wagons that fed the troops. Meeting no opposition, they successfully
fired the haystacks at six stations. On March 29 at Stanwix Station,
some eighty miles east of Fort Yuma, the Confederates encountered
two California cavalrymen on patrol. The rebel riders opened fire, hit-
ting Private William Semmelrogge of Company A in the shoulder. The
wounded man and his comrade rode for help without returning fire,
and Hunter's men wheeled and rode for Tucson after realizing that they
had engaged the advance guard of Carleton's column.[91]

Although the forward units had suffered at the hands of the Arizona Confederates, the Californians at Fort Yuma eagerly awaited an
opportunity to prove themselves in battle. While the soldiers anxiously
anticipated skirmishes with rebels and possibly Indians, their company
commanders worried about logistics and the difficulties of getting their
men across the Arizona desert. The march would tax them all to the
limits of endurance.

Chapter 3

Anglo Invasion

The war between Union and Confederate forces in the Southwest Borderlands reflected the martial traditions of the Anglo-American antagonists. It also triggered multiple, concurrent, and frequently interethnic civil wars resulting from the federal government's preoccupation with its rebellious Southern states. The distinctive warrior and martial traditions of the combatants dictated the nature and outcome of the struggles, but in all cases, alliances, accommodation, and compromises characterized the survival strategies of each cultural community. The fighting between the warring Anglo factions, Union and Confederate, reflected their common heritage and especially the European martial tradition. The borderlands of the 1860s saw battles of massed armies, isolated skirmishes, and broken small-unit actions as well as terror tactics and guerilla warfare prompted by both the environment and the warrior traditions of the indigenous peoples. The Union men better managed logistics and alliances, while the Confederates excelled in the boldness of their attacks, which in many instances carried the day. Though the rebel Anglos often succeeded tactically, their victories were not sustainable, allowing the Union men and their allies to prevail strategically.[1]

On the morning of March 22, 1862, the men of Captain William P. Calloway's Company I, First California Infantry, saw the distant Gila Mountain peaks silhouetted against the cloudless blue sky as they

73

marched in column, four abreast, down the winding road from the Fort Yuma bluffs to the Colorado River ferry crossing at the narrows below. Regimental musicians shrilled and beat their fife-and-drum version of "The Girl I Left Behind Me," a lilting Irish tune traditionally played when a command left a military station for the field. The river rushed a muddy torrent as officers herded their men onto the ferry, taking care to balance the load to prevent capsizing. As they were equipped in heavy marching order with full packs and weapons, a tumble into the water would mean certain death. The flatboat yawed across the river as the ferrymen hauled on the stout hemp rope lowered from the high masts planted at the landings on the east and west riverbanks. Everyone involved in the expedition—soldiers, surgeons, teamsters, contractors—thrilled at the day's activity, understanding that the crossing into Arizona meant their war was about to begin in earnest.[2]

When he learned that Hunter's Confederates had captured Captain McCleave, Carleton appointed Captain Calloway to command the advance into Arizona. This vanguard totaled 272 men and included Calloway's own company and Captain McCleave's and Nathaniel Pishon's companies, A and D, of the First California Cavalry. Young Lieutenant James Barrett commanded McCleave's men now, and Second Lieutenant Jeremiah Phelan had drilled his own detachment of unassigned recruits until they could service the two mule-packed 12-pounder mountain howitzers the Californians dubbed the "Jackass Battery."

Hoping to mislead Confederate spies, Carleton announced that his Arizona invasion aimed to chastise Indian raiders. He instructed the advance guard, "When you leave Fort Yuma, you are to say you go and campaign against the Tontos."[3] It was true that Western Apache bands (Gila, Aravaipa, and Tonto Apaches, as well as neighboring Yavapais) had stepped up their attacks on overland travelers and the farms of the Pimas and Maricopas on the Gila River, but Carleton had no intention of allowing these native warriors to distract him from his primary mission—the destruction of Confederate forces in the Southwest territories. In fact, Calloway and all the other company commanders received specific instructions *not* to engage any Indians on the road to Tucson. Confused and frustrated soldiers held their fire when they stumbled upon war-painted warriors.[4] Fearing Carleton's wrath more than the Indians, the troops gave the tribesmen an opportunity to fire first. One soldier wrote of such an encounter between an Apache warrior and Private David Carver, a member of Carleton's escort, near Grinnel's Ranch on the Gila River:

> Just as he reached the river, an Apache sprang from the bushes, gun in hand, and the muzzle directed full upon Carver, who, fortunately, saw him at the same moment, and brought his Colt to bear upon the savage. The latter stood ready for a few seconds, Carver likewise, both with weapons leveled and both, doubtless, anxious to fire; But the Indian seemed to think the odds too great, at the short distance between them, some twelve feet, and Carver had positive orders not to fire first. The savage, who was in his full panoply of war paint, then dropped his muzzle and said, "How de do?" "How do you do?" replied Carver. "You Captain?" asked the Indian. "No," answered Carver, "Are you a Chief?" "No," growled the ring-streaked and spotted Apache, and without further parley he plunged into the river and swam across, bearing his gun up out of the water as he went. The temptation to shoot was a sore one for Carver, but he would not disobey his orders.[5]

Sam Hughes, a Tucson citizen traveling with the column, thought Carleton's policy absurd. Hughes refused to respect the ceasefire with regard to Apaches and bet the colonel a new pair of boots that raiders would run off at least one-third of the command's horses before it reached Tucson. But Carleton was nobody's fool. His "Tonto campaign" was only intended to confuse the rebels in Arizona and New Mexico as his column marched toward the Rio Grande.[6]

The colonel kept his own counsel and demanded the same of others. From the time he accepted command of the Arizona expedition, he had attempted to mask the movements and intentions of his troops. He strictly forbade soldiers to correspond with newspapers, though this prohibition was largely ignored. To ensure secrecy, he wrote messages to Fort Yuma in code or occasionally in Greek. He even sent some dispatches on tissue paper for easy concealment and, if necessary, destruction. Trusted couriers, including the camel rider Greek George and expressman John W. Jones, often carried fake correspondence in addition to genuine dispatches. If captured, the messenger would be expected to eat the real thing and turn the phony papers over to the enemy. Carleton intended to deceive the Confederates for as long as possible about the expedition's true purpose, hoping to surprise them in Tucson or pitch into Sibley's rear somewhere along the Rio Grande.[7]

Calloway's advance troops prepared well for the long desert trek to Tucson. The march across the sandy scrub and dunes of the desert to Fort Yuma, where some of the California soldiers waited and acclimated for as many as five months, served to toughen the men for the still more arduous journey ahead. Both officers and enlisted men benefited from this first leg of the expedition and the experience of living in the arid environs of Fort Yuma while the command slowly grew one company at a time. They began the march across Arizona using the same survival skills learned while crossing the Colorado Desert. Small parties went out to fill water tanks and cut hay at the abandoned stage stations in advance of the column. It made sense to follow the old Butterfield Overland Mail route so that soldiers and draft animals could water at the way station wells. The rough wagon road followed the Gila trail across the Sonoran Desert where the annual rainfall averaged only five or ten inches, yet the soldiers discovered an amazing variety of life. Scorpions and rattlesnakes taught them to watch their steps and shake out their bedrolls; coyotes dogged their trail in search of scraps; and antelope fell to their rifle muskets. The Californians began to appreciate the desert flora too—barrel cacti with fishhook thorns, prickly pears topped with colorful flowers, and the impressive giant saguaros. The men marched with tarred canvas knapsacks and carried ten days' rations in their haversacks. Company commanders made certain their wagons had full water kegs and sufficient forage to travel without having to resupply at one of the stations.

Carleton hoped that Calloway's command would move rapidly up the Gila, surprise Hunter's company at Tucson, and recapture McCleave and his party. The advance companies moved along cautiously with civilian scouts, including half-Indian mountain man Powell Weaver and scout John Jones in the lead. When the two vedettes from Company A ran into Hunter's rangers at Stanwix Station, Captain Pishon gave chase with his cavalry, but the well-mounted rebels made good their escape.[8]

On April 12, 1862, Calloway's command reached the Pima Villages, where the stage road left the Gila to follow the broad valley of the Santa Cruz River south into Tucson. The Pimas gladly resold the wheat given back to them by Hunter, trading for bolts of "manta," a cotton cloth that had become their principal medium of exchange, and handkerchiefs that Carleton had wisely ordered taken along. Here Calloway learned of a Confederate outpost in Picacho Pass, about forty miles southeast on the road to Tucson. Picacho, a volcanic plug of red rock rising nearly one thousand feet from the valley floor, stood alone at the end of a range of rugged mountains.[9] Just west of the peak, the river sank beneath its sandy bed, leaving only a dry wash to mark its path to the Gila. A ten-man rebel picket post guarded the pass, while Hunter sent Lieutenant Jack Swilling, with another detachment, east to Mesilla to escort Ammi White and Captain McCleave to Confederate authorities at the Rio Grande.[10]

Originally ordered to push on to Tucson by way of abandoned Fort Breckenridge, Calloway diverted his whole command to Picacho instead. If he could capture the rebel outpost there, the shorter stage road to Tucson would give him a better chance of rescuing the hapless McCleave. On April 15 he ordered the white canvas covers stripped from his supply wagons to make his column of infantry and the mountain howitzer battery less visible as it tramped down the dusty stage road to Tucson. At the same time, Lieutenant Ephraim Baldwin's cavalry would circle Picacho from the west while Barrett's platoon would ride wide to the east. By reining in their horses to keep the dust down and walking as much as possible, Calloway hoped the rebels would not observe their approach. According to the plan drawn up the night before, the captain intended the mounted flankers to coordinate their attack, dashing in and cutting off the rebels' retreat to Tucson—and possibly grabbing McCleave, if he was there. The plan seemed simple enough, but timing was everything.

Barrett's men got into position first, their blue uniforms and equipment thoroughly powdered with the fine alkali dust that inevitably coated travelers in this country. The troopers were eager for a fight. Most were in their twenties but strong and tough beyond their years, hardened by labor in the California gold fields. Compared to his men, Barrett seemed an old hand. Although only twenty-eight, he had served as an enlisted man in the First Dragoons ever since his ship arrived at New York City from County Mayo, Ireland. As a dragoon he had taken orders from the likes of McCleave, a tough first sergeant then. As captain of the First California Cavalry's Company A, McCleave was now Barrett's commanding officer, and it was Barrett's job to get him back from the rebels.

Having taken the shorter route, Barrett's platoon arrived at the rendezvous point south of the peak long before Baldwin's men. Just days before, Barrett's superiors had described his men as "pawing for the advance."[11] Perhaps sensing Barrett's eagerness, Calloway had taken the precaution of assigning John Jones to accompany the young officer. Jones knew the country and possessed survival skills honed by numerous close calls in Apache territory. He sensed danger and urged caution. But as noon passed, the young troopers waited impatiently. They found little relief from the Arizona sun, which burned with searing intensity, even in April. The tangled mesquite thickets offered little shade as the thirsty men drained the last of the water from their canteens and stood to their horses. Barrett worried the rebels must be aware of his little command by now—if the pickets escaped, the Confederate garrison in Tucson would be warned and McCleave would be lost. Jones counseled patience, but Barrett could wait no longer for Baldwin and Calloway.

He ordered the men to mount and move toward Picacho station. Then he saw them—rebel rangers playing cards and resting in a small clearing not far from the old Butterfield stage corral. They wore no uniforms—just broad-brimmed hats and the practical garb of the frontier—but were armed to the teeth with revolvers, rifles or shotguns, and bowie knives. Without warning, and before Jones could interfere, Barrett drew his revolver and fired a shot in the air while shouting a demand that the rebels throw down their arms and surrender.[12]

The Confederates caught in the open obeyed immediately, but as Barrett and his men rushed into the clearing, a close-range volley boomed from the surrounding chaparral, knocking four of the Californians from their saddles. Barrett's troopers wasted no time returning fire with their carbines and revolvers, shooting wildly at phantom puffs of gun smoke. The lieutenant dismounted to help tie one of three captured rebels who had thrown down their arms at the first fire. Intent on flushing the remaining rangers, he quickly remounted and called out an order, cut short by a rifle blast. A ball smashed through the back of Barrett's neck, breaking it and killing him instantly. Cat-and-mouse skirmishing continued for more than an hour, but ended abruptly when the rebels worked their way through the underbrush to their picketed horses, quickly mounted, and rode for Tucson. When the smoke finally cleared, two of Barrett's men, Privates George Johnson and William

Leonard, lay dead or dying, and three others were wounded. The Confederates suffered no casualties other than the three prisoners taken early in the fight.[13]

By late afternoon Calloway's entire command reached the scene of the fight, too late to overtake Hunter's well-mounted rangers, now well on their way to Tucson. The captain soon came to understand that when his two cavalry units failed to link up, the impetuous Barrett's unsupported detachment had engaged Captain Hunter's picket consisting of a sergeant and nine privates. Before the light of day began to fade, Lieutenant Phelan selected some high ground near the base of "Picacho Mountain" and unpacked his howitzers to protect the column against a possible counterattack, but the rebel prisoners, which included the sergeant in command, confirmed that the pickets were expecting no reinforcements and that McCleave was no longer in Tucson.[14]

This news added to the despondency of the Californians, who had been bested once again by the Confederates. Dark and early the following morning, Private Leonard succumbed to an agonizing neck wound, which had left him moaning throughout the night. Now the only sounds were the howling coyotes and the metallic clank and scrape of picks and shovels on the rocky earth. Calloway's men solemnly wrapped Barrett, Johnson, and Leonard in their woolen blankets and buried them alongside the stage road where they had fallen. In the moonlight the burial detail used cracker-box boards to mark the cactus-covered mounds of earth and stone.[15] Unnerved by the ordeal and worried his supplies would not be sufficient if the rebels in Tucson held their ground, Calloway ordered his men to retreat to the Pima Villages, against the wishes of his subordinates and much to the consternation of the men.[16] Old Powell Weaver, disgusted by the inept handling of the affair, took leave of the outfit at White's Mill, remarking as he rode west to prospect on the Colorado, "If you fellers can't find the road from here to Tucson, you can go to hell!"[17]

Two weeks later, when Colonel West arrived at the Pima Villages with the second contingent of the expedition, he found Calloway's men already dug in.[18] West ordered the construction of a more substantial earthen fortification and named it in honor of Lieutenant Barrett. From Fort Yuma, Carleton attempted to boost morale by memorializing those who had fallen "in defense of the colors." He ordered that "until the end of the war [the names Johnson and Leonard] be called at every stated roll-call of their respective companies, and a comrade shall always respond, 'He died for his country!'" Carleton later designated Camp Barrett a sub-depot, the only source of supply between Yuma and Tucson. On the march the men ate jerked beef, hardtack, and pemmican packed in tin cans. This last item, intended to serve as a high-energy campaign ration, was formulated by the commander himself. Made of pounded dried beef and lard, it was much despised by the men, who complained it could kill rats and even claimed that a hungry dog would not eat it. The horses and draft animals fed on barley soaked in water and the native grama and galleta grasses that grew wild along the Gila. With the exception of their skirmishes with rebels, both men and animals had come through the first leg of the journey in good shape.[19]

Confederate Borderlands

On April 15, 1862, the very day that Lieutenant James Barrett died in Picacho Pass, Brigadier General Henry Hopkins Sibley's Confederate Army of New Mexico fought its final battle. While Carleton's California Column regrouped in Tucson in May and June and began the final push to the Rio Grande, General E. R. S. Canby's Union forces in New Mexico were slowly pushing General Sibley's Texans south following a stunning Confederate reversal on the road to Fort Union, just east of Santa Fe.[20] The defeat of the Confederates, who appeared so close to capturing Fort Union's supply depot and conquering New Mexico, seemed all the more remarkable because of the rebels' nearly unbroken chain of victories, beginning with Lieutenant Colonel Baylor's capture of Lynde's regular troops at Fort Fillmore in the summer of 1861. Once Sibley, a West Point–educated career soldier, had taken over as commander of the Confederate Army of New Mexico, however, a change came over the invading Texans. With a brigade comprising infantry, cavalry, and artillery operating in desert country with hostile inhabitants, everything became more complicated, and the margin for error greatly diminished. There was no doubting the aggressiveness and spirit of the Texans, but their commander's inattention to logistical details doomed the expedition from the start.

While Baylor went through the motions of governing Confederate Arizona—a territory in name only—from his capital of Mesilla with almost no resources of any kind, Sibley had arrived with orders from

Richmond to commandeer all the rebel manpower in the territories and push up the Rio Grande with a force of more than 2,500 men. In truth, the roles of the two Confederate officers might have been better reversed. A Louisiana native, Sibley had exhibited courage with the Second Dragoons in the war with Mexico, but in 1861 he was still only a captain with the honorary rank of brevet major. He had been decorated for his war service in Mexico and had demonstrated physical endurance and fitness for command in his younger days, but it was well known in the small fraternity of the frontier army that Sibley drank heavily. His career seemed to have stalled. Believing that his regular army superiors, with whom he often quarreled, had not appropriately recognized his talent, he annoyed his brother officers with boasts of his accomplishments, which included several patented inventions adopted by the U.S. Army.[21]

Stationed at Fort Union and other posts in remote New Mexico, Sibley had been passed over in rank, and as the Southern states began seceding from the Union, the War Department seemed to have no good use for him. As with other regular army officers, including North Carolina–born department commander William W. Loring, he was endued with a martial spirit nurtured by his native South and felt compelled to fight for the side that would best appreciate his military skills. He resigned his U.S. commission on May 13, 1861, traveled to Richmond, and convinced Jefferson Davis that with his intimate knowledge of U.S. Army posts and resources in the Southwest, he could conquer not only New Mexico and Arizona but also the Colorado goldfields, Chihuahua and Sonora, and eventually California. Intelligent and loquacious, he talked his way into a brigadier's commission and received permission to recruit 3,500 men and equip them with captured supplies collected from abandoned U.S. posts and depots in Texas. Adding new territory to the Confederacy was not a priority for Davis, but Sibley's quest for empire in the Southwest and a pathway to the Pacific could further the administration's goal of foreign recognition. Though a long shot, this course provided undeniable opportunities for acquiring much-needed wealth, and at the very least, a campaign in the borderlands would tie up U.S. troops and worry the Lincoln administration. The extent of Sibley's grand plan was likely not known by even the Confederate high command, but the general's subordinates often heard him speak of it, and they appeared to be convinced that it could be carried out. Talking rather than fighting had always been Sibley's real talent. Perhaps he would have been better cast as a diplomatic emissary to Mexico or as a territorial governor, rather than a military strategist and field commander.[22]

Baylor, on the other hand, was a hard-charging combat officer with little talent for public relations. In his first months as governor of Arizona he had shot to death the editor of Mesilla's pro-Southern newspaper; invaded Mexico in pursuit of Mescalero Apache raiders, whom he successfully tracked and killed within sight of the town of Corralitos, Chihuahua; and drawn the attention and ire of Confederate officials in Richmond.[23] Jefferson Davis thought Baylor's Indian extermination policy uncivilized and morally repugnant. His character flaws were too deep to be corrected, and the Confederate president believed him a political liability. This assessment cost the Texan the Arizona governorship and his commission. He spent the rest of the war trying to restore his good name and his field command. In Baylor's view, all the controversies that dogged him involved honor and revenge. The editor had impugned Baylor's manhood by suggesting that he had lost his nerve and Arizona Territory when he failed to fight the federal columns approaching from the north and west. The Apaches had killed his men and other Anglos, and, according to Baylor's brand of frontier justice, the only fitting penalty for such crimes was death. He despised Sibley for usurping his authority in Confederate Arizona, and this hatred fueled his determination to go to Richmond to regain his honor. Baylor was a model of unrestrained martial manhood—brave, bold, quick to action—and he lived by the "code duello," as did most of his Texan countrymen with frontier roots in Kentucky and Tennessee. His own family viewed him as a crusader of old, and it is likely that he held the same opinion.[24]

Sibley had neither Baylor's energy nor his vengeful streak, but the more restrained man did command other subordinates cut from Baylor's same bolt. Most of the officers of the Fourth, Fifth, and Seventh Texas Mounted Volunteers had military experience in the regular army, volunteer service in Mexico, as Indian-fighting rangers, or as filibusters. Because of the animosity between Sibley and Baylor, Major Charles Pyron led Baylor's Second Texas Mounted Volunteers in the Confederate Army of New Mexico. Numbered among Sibley's other regimental and battalion commanders were William "Dirty Shirt" Scurry (Fourth TMV), Tom Green (Fifth TMV), and John Sutton (Seventh TMV). All were fighters, and their young soldiers from Texas and the Southwest

territories were eager to face the Union regulars and New Mexico militiamen who, Sibley had convinced them, were demoralized and would
put up little resistance. As the brigade commander, Sibley appointed the
officers above the rank of captain, but the enlisted men of each company
elected their own noncommissioned and commissioned officers. Most
of the enlisted Anglo and Hispano Texans were young (average age was
only twenty-three), and they were joined by a handful of enslaved African Americans, who were brought along to serve the officers.

Many of the Texans boasted of fighting for "independence" as had
their fathers at the Alamo and San Jacinto. But it was clear from their
letters home that the root cause of their hatred for the Union was
directed at Abraham Lincoln and the abolitionists they thought he represented. The young Texans did not believe in racial equality for blacks
and condemned "miscegenation," race mixing, as an abomination. They
sometimes referred to the U.S. soldiers as "federals," "federalists," or
"Union men," but more often as "abolitionists" or simply "abs." While
these sentiments were widespread in the ranks, many of the young men
who enlisted in the spring and summer of 1861 were simply caught up
in the war hysteria and a desire for adventure fueled by a culture steeped
in the traditions of martial manhood.[25]

Confederate morale was high, but esprit de corps could take the
Army of New Mexico only so far. Shortages of food and clothing already
plagued Sibley's command, but he assured the men that Colonel James
Reily's mission to Chihuahua and Sonora would soon begin the flow
of food and other needed supplies from Mexico. Most of the mounted
volunteers brought their own horses and equipment to the service, but
the arduous journey to New Mexico had taken its toll, and remounts
were in especially short supply. The best of the arms captured from government arsenals in Texas had already been distributed to other troops
before Sibley's men could muster in San Antonio, so many of his soldiers provided themselves with double barreled shotguns, squirrel rifles,
and antiquated muskets. Three companies of the Fifth Texas Mounted
Volunteers were issued nine-foot lances captured from the Mexicans
more than a decade earlier. Revolving pistols and bowie knives usually
rounded out the typical soldier's armament. The rebels also secured an
assortment of bronze field pieces and mountain howitzers, distributed
among the regiments, under the overall command of the able artillerist,
Major Trevanion T. Teel.[26]

Anglo Confederates versus Union Anglos and Hispanos

Preparing to face the Texans, Colonel E. R. S. Canby mustered a mixed force of 1,200 regulars—cavalry, infantry, and artillery—as well as 2,500 of New Mexico's Hispano militiamen and soldiers of the newly raised regiments of U.S. Volunteers. The predominantly Hispano New Mexico Volunteers, officered by regulars and experienced frontiersmen like Kit Carson, fell directly under Canby's control, while the militiamen reported to Henry Connelly, New Mexico's territorial governor. Added to this diverse array of troops were Captain Paddy Graydon's Independent Spy Company, composed of Anglo and Hispano recruits from New Mexico, and the men of Captain Theodore Dodd's independent company of Colorado Volunteers, who early responded to Connelly's and Canby's desperate pleas for assistance. These "Pike's Peakers" represented only the first contingent of Coloradans. More than six hundred miles to the north, an entire regiment recruited from Rocky Mountain mining camps now prepared to march from Denver City. In all, Canby had 3,800 men at his disposal, well armed and equipped but representing the full range of soldiery, from undisciplined and inexperienced recruits and militia to seasoned professionals and combat veterans. Not seen on Canby's muster roll but equally important to his success were the dry desert—inhospitably stingy with water, food, and forage—and the territory's Hispano civilians and Indian population.[27]

The New Mexicans feared and despised the Texans who, twice before in living memory, had invaded their homeland and arrogantly taken what they wanted. This time, the people would make it a point to deny the invaders sustenance and hinder them whenever possible. Uncertain of the cause of the strife now evident between the Anglo groups, New Mexico's Hispanos did not rush to join the militia companies that originally formed to fight Indian raiders or the U.S. Volunteer units called up to augment the regular army. The presence of the Texans, who were generally believed to be a distinctly different people than the Anglos originating in the other states, on their native soil, however, convinced many New Mexicans to set down their farm implements and corral their herds of sheep and goats to defend their homes, families, property, and honor from the hated Tejanos.[28]

Canby saw to it that Kit Carson received a colonel's commission and, so empowered, the frontiersman helped raise an entire regiment of New Mexico Volunteers. Four more regiments of infantry and additional companies of New Mexico cavalry would eventually be hurriedly recruited and rushed into service. Though uniformed and armed with the best equipment the U.S. Army had to offer, the Hispano soldiers received little or no training. Their field officers were largely regular army men like Colonel Gabriel Paul, a career soldier and hero of the Mexican-American War assigned to head the Fourth New Mexico Volunteer Infantry. The company officers were a mix of Hispanos and Anglos with varying degrees of military experience. Carson's men received the most thorough training and were considered the best disciplined of the New Mexico troops, but the colonel himself was not entirely certain that he was fit for command. Casting about, however, he could see few others better qualified. His wife's family was well-known and politically connected in New Mexico, and Carson had earned the respect of Hispanos and Indians across the territory. Though Carson spoke English with a Missouri drawl heavily inflected with frontierisms, he was fluent in Spanish and had mastered half a dozen Indian tongues as well, but to his embarrassment, he could neither read nor write a word in any language. Still, he was a proven fighter, his name was known even to the Texans, and he enjoyed the trust of superiors and subordinates alike.[29]

Sibley's campaign strategy was as simple as it was bold—he would march his brigade from Fort Bliss to Mesilla and up the Rio Grande, sweeping aside all armed resistance and capturing government forts and supplies as he went. Fort Craig, constructed on the high ground overlooking the west bank of the Rio Grande in southern New Mexico, would be his first great prize—if he could take it. With the munitions and food supplies stored there, he could advance northward to the territorial capital and then on to Fort Union, strategically situated only one hundred miles south of the Colorado border on the Santa Fe Trail. At this major depot, the stockpiles of food and ordnance, as well as the rolling stock and draft animals, would be vital for his army to successfully push on to Denver and the Rocky Mountain gold mines. By February 1862 Canby had rallied all his available manpower at Fort Craig, determined to prevent its capture. He prepared for the expected assault by strengthening the walls with adobe and stone and building new earthworks capable of resisting bombardment and accommodating his growing force, which far exceeded in number even the most optimistic estimates of the engineer officers who laid out the post in 1853.

Due to his uncertainty over the abilities of his hastily assembled command, especially his untried Hispano regiments, Canby assumed a defensive posture and remained cautiously entrenched at Fort Craig as Sibley's army approached. On February 16, 1862, the rebels demonstrated south of the fort, just out of artillery range, but could not lure the Union men from their secure defenses. Whipped by snow and sandstorms, Confederate Colonel Tom Green proposed to countermarch seven miles south to Paraje, cross the river, and then skirt around the fort by taking the waterless trail along the high mesa east of the Rio Grande to the Valverde fords located some six miles upstream. The maneuver forced Canby to meet the threat. Allowing the Confederates to bypass the fort would not only sever his supply line but also allow Sibley freedom to attack the now weakened garrisons at Albuquerque, Santa Fe, and Fort Union, the last bastion on the road to Colorado.[30]

On February 20, Canby's scouts detected the withdrawal of the Confederates arrayed south of the fort. The Texans made a show of battle with flags flying and regimental bands playing Dixie to cover the movement of the main body. Captain Graydon's Spy Company harassed the retreating rebel rear guard, and the captain himself procured two mules, loaded them with 24-pounder howitzer shells, and attempted to spook them into the night encampment of the Fourth Texas. The plan at first appeared to backfire when, after the fuses were lit, the mules dutifully followed the Union men rather than running away through the rebel camp. The shells exploded spectacularly in the darkness between the lines, but no blood was shed (save for the hapless mules). The bursting shells did serve to trigger a stampede. Nearly two hundred frightened and thirsty Texas mules and horses decamped for the Rio Grande where Canby's men found them watering in the morning. Though Graydon's suicide mules may not have had the intended effect, the result was devastating to Lieutenant Colonel William Scurry's Fourth Regiment. The loss of the draft animals forced the Texans to abandon or destroy thirty supply wagons and much of their precious contents.[31]

Now fully aware of the threating flanking movement, Canby sent a battalion to contest the three upstream fords at Valverde by throwing a line of battle across the river, hoping to deny Sibley's thirsty rebel vanguard access to the water. Just south of the fords on the east side of the river, the Mesa del Contadero stretched three miles long and two miles wide, looming more than three hundred feet over the valley. This massive basaltic obstacle anchored the right flank of Canby's line of infantry and cavalry, mostly New Mexico Volunteers and Militia, and two improvised batteries of artillery manned by regulars.[32] Confined to an ambulance as a result of illness, drunkenness, or both, Sibley relinquished command to Colonel Green and others who aggressively met the Union men deployed in the cottonwood thickets on the east bank, as artillery and infantry reinforcements rushed upriver the six miles from Fort Craig.

Valverde: Napoleonic Maneuver and Dash

The encounter at Valverde on February 21, 1862, would prove to be the pivotal battle of the Civil War in the Southwest. Though evenly matched numerically, the Union men had fewer but longer-range artillery pieces—including 12- and 24-pounder howitzers—opposing the rebels' mountain howitzers. Canby's small arms—.54-caliber Mississippi Rifles, .58-caliber model 1855 rifle muskets, and .69-caliber U.S. muskets of several models—also outdistanced the Texans' shotguns, carbines, revolvers, and lances. The rebels made up for their ordnance deficiencies with an inordinate belief in their own invincibility that gave them the morale advantage, which, in the end, carried the day. The most memorable events of the bloody action included a mounted charge on the Union left flank by two of the Fifth Texas lancer companies led by Captain Willis Lang. With their red pennons, each bearing a lone white star, snapping from the steel blades of their nine-foot lances, the rebels seemed irresistible as their charging horses bore down on the soldiers they took to be New Mexican militiamen. Dressed in dark blue frock coats and trousers, as were the other newly outfitted New Mexico Volunteers, the flank company was in fact composed of Captain Dodd's determined Colorado Volunteers, who formed square—the classic foot-soldier defense in the face of a mounted charge. With bayonets fixed, the Pike's Peakers fired two volleys from their muskets, loaded with buck-and-ball, mortally wounding Lang and slaughtering the Texans. The few lancers who actually reached the Coloradans were lifted from their saddles with bayoneted muskets. None of the horses survived the attack, and the men who were spared crawled back through the sand to the cover of an old, dry river channel.[33]

The Confederates set the tempo of the battle, and Canby's men maneuvered in response with charges and countercharges. Firing shell and spherical case shot, Robert H. Hall's battery of 24-pounders and Alexander McRae's 12-pounder field howitzers disabled several of the rebel guns commanded by Major Teel. The Union gunners set the time fuses on their shells to burst the iron balls directly over the Texans, showering with shrapnel the men sheltering in the sand hills and behind the banks of the dry river channel. The battle lines stretched nearly a mile, and the commanders found it difficult to coordinate the separated wings of their forces due to visual obstructions presented by the bend of the Rio Grande's channel, broken ground, and cottonwood bosques. Even mounted couriers moved slowly through the soft sand and dense scrub of the riverbanks. Canby shifted Carson's regiment and some of the regulars to support Captain Hall's battery on the extreme right of his overextended flank. All afternoon, the gunners under Captain Hall and Major Thomas Duncan had been creeping their pieces toward the dry river bed at the foot of the mesa. They hoped for a chance to wheel their guns into a position that would allow them enfilade the line of Texans hunkered behind the sandy banks on the Confederate left and possibly capture the vulnerable supply train parked nearby. Canby's shift, however, could not have come at a less opportune time.[34]

Colonel Green had had enough of the artillery barrage emanating from McRae's battery in the center of the Union line. Late in the afternoon of February 21, he ordered Lieutenant Colonel Scurry to lead Major Pyron, Major Samuel A. Lockridge, and Lieutenant Colonel Sutton in a charge intended to capture the guns. If the daring move succeeded, the demoralized Union men would be swept from the field and the Confederates could push on to the river. Bugles signaled the attack, and nearly one thousand rebels in a semicircular line stretching almost a half mile charged from their positions across the eight hundred yards of sandy bottoms straight for McRae's four 12-pounder field howitzers and two 6-pounder guns. At this long range the gunners cut the fuses on the shells to explode two and a half seconds after firing—enough time for the charging men to go to ground when they saw the muzzle flashes of the cannons—but as the rebel line converged within one hundred yards of the battery, they could no longer duck or dodge the hail of iron balls and lead bullets directed at them. Charged with double canister loads, the scattershot from the Union guns blasted holes in the closed ranks of the onrushing Texans. Sutton had a leg shot off, but Lockridge reached one of the cannons shouting, "This is mine!" A fierce filibuster famous for his braggadocio, Lockridge's men knew of his well-publicized boast to make his wife a "shimmy" from Fort Craig's colors. Now he seemed determined to make good on the promise or die trying. But Lockridge fell dead the moment he touched the howitzer's heated bronze barrel and his body slumped alongside the bloody corpse of McRae himself.[35]

The Texans had held their fire until they were within a stone's throw of the battery, then they let loose with their double-barreled shotguns and six-shot revolvers. Colonel Green reported, "Never were doubled-barreled shot-guns and rifles used to better effect." A hand-to-hand struggle ensued with clubbed guns and rammers, pistols, sabers, and bowie knives. Desperate and suicidal artillerymen threw lit fuses or fired pistols into the ammunition-filled limber chests and blew them up. The Union line collapsed and the panicked soldiers, volunteers and regulars alike, broke and ran for the river and the cover of the banks and trees on the far side. The rebels attempted to turn the six captured guns around, but due to their inexperience or lack of ammunition, did little damage to the retreating enemy.[36]

The Confederates clearly achieved a tactical victory, though both sides were appalled by the slaughter and agreed to a two-day truce to collect the dead and succor the wounded. The hate and violence seemed to break like a fever, and the burial details acted with uncommon compassion, considering the ferocity of the fighting just hours before. "The field was covered with blood, horses, torn and dismembered limbs, and heads separated from their bodies," observed New Mexican Captain Rafael Chacón following his duty with a burial detail. Chacón also expressed his belief that in the presence of the dead, "chivalry and courtesy" seemed to reign among the antagonists.[37] Just before nightfall on the evening of the battle, Major Charles Wesche's detachment of the Second New Mexico Militia discovered the train abandoned earlier by the Confederates for want of draft animals. The Hispano soldiers tightly corralled the rolling stock and baggage around the ammunition wagons and put them all to the torch—the sound of exploding shells, cooking-off in the intense heat, echoed against the mesas and lava rock canyons as darkness settled on the Rio Grande.[38]

The daylong struggle had been a set-piece, Napoleonic battle of maneuver and dash, which left more than five hundred men dead and wounded—nearly half of them Confederates.[39] Sibley had bypassed the fort but had not captured its vital supplies or whipped Canby's army, which now posed a threat to the rebel army's rear. Sibley sent Scurry with a surrender demand, but Canby, with his army secure within the fort's bastions and earthworks, was in no mood to treat with the Texans. Fort Craig was now a gigantic hospital, confused and congested with disorganized militiamen and other soldiers shocked and exhausted by the bloodbath at the river. The Union men had lost six officers killed or mortally wounded, including Captain George Bascom of Apache Pass fame and Captain Alexander McRae, the much-admired North Carolinian, who died trying to save his battery. Having lost six of his eight artillery pieces at Valverde, Canby set his men to fabricating and mounting intimidating but harmless "Quaker guns" from painted logs and awaited an attack that never came.[40]

The Battle of Valverde set a new benchmark for violent conflict in the Southwest Borderlands. More than five thousand Anglo and Hispano soldiers had faced off, and more than one in ten had been killed or wounded. Some companies suffered casualty rates of 70 percent. More than half of McRae's battery men died on the field defending their guns. Artillery fire resulted in casualties at up to one thousand yards, but most of the killing had been done at close range with cannon-fired canister balls and bullets from small arms. Some men had been stabbed with bayonets, swords, or bowie knives in hand-to-hand combat. Frontal assaults over open ground and flank attacks without cover characterized the linear tactics employed by both sides. And both the Union and Confederate Anglo troops manfully sacrificed themselves—for glory, honor, and country. The big mountaineers from Colorado, unwilling to back down in the hand-to-hand fighting, had distinguished themselves. For some Southerners, including the filibustering Lockridge and Sibley himself, the New Mexico campaign was just a step toward a larger Confederate empire that would encompass the American West and perhaps Northern Mexico as well. But when the day of battle actually came, most of the Anglo soldiers set aside patriotic or mercenary motives. As with most other Civil War–era soldiers, they fought for their comrades and to avoid the shame and lasting stigma associated with cowardice in the face of the enemy.[41]

The Hispano soldiers had generally acquitted themselves well, especially Carson's First Regiment, New Mexico Volunteers. They obeyed orders, fired disciplined volleys, and maneuvered under enemy small arms and artillery fire. The same could not be said of all the native New Mexican troops, especially the hastily recruited and poorly officered militiamen, many of whom remained at the fort or never made it into action at the fords. It is doubtful that any troops so organized and led would have done better. The untried Hispano soldiers had little notion of the formal warfare practiced by the Anglos. Although the New Mexicans were descended from Spanish colonists who had battled in massed ranks with muskets, generations had come and gone since that type of war had been seen in the borderlands. The Indians and Hispanos fought differently now, as "irregulars" or *guerrilleros*. They learned to attack by stealth, with decoys in ambush, or taking advantage of cover as skirmishers. Often a raid or counterattack in pursuit of raiders became a running fight, more akin to a mounted fox hunt than a military maneuver. In this sort of combat, personal risk was minimized—it was better to survive to fight another day than to charge headlong into almost certain death or enemies of unknown strength.

There was also the issue of motivation. The New Mexicans rallied to the U.S. flag not for national patriotic reasons but because joining the army seemed in their best interest at the time. They bore no great love for the Americans who had so recently moved into to their country and were now fighting among themselves in a "Revolution." Most who chose to join the Anglo army did so after the harvest and before planting season. Some were lured by the promise of good food, clothing, and pay. Others saw joining the army as an opportunity to acquire weapons with which to fight their longstanding Apache and Navajo enemies. Many of the New Mexican enlistees did not know what a "Confederate" was—but they knew Texans. Some remembered the previous Texan invasions and believed that any army that fought *Tejano* marauders was the right army to join. But when the bullets started kicking up the sand, shells burst overhead, and bloodied comrades fell by their side, all the inducements and rationales seemed insignificant. *Vergüenza*—the shame of dishonor—certainly motivated some to stay and fight, but for many, returning home to farms and families seemed the more prudent choice.[42]

As the smoke of battle cleared so did the fog that befuddled General Sibley. He emerged from his ambulance to resume command, though never again on a battlefield, having lost much of the esteem formerly evinced by his officers and men. With many officers killed or wounded, Sibley now had gaps in his command structure. Samuel Lockridge, John Sutton, Marinus van den Heuvel, and Willis Lang lay dead or dying, and Tom Green, Henry Raguet, Trevanion T. Teel, and others were wounded and temporarily out of action. The Confederates were now burdened with their wounded, a situation made worse by the shortage of wagons and draft animals. Sibley had little choice but to head north toward Albuquerque. The Confederates captured Colonel Nicolás Pino's two-hundred-man militia force at Socorro and established a brigade hospital there. Sibley's advance riders, hoping to forage and capture enemy supplies, found mostly uncooperative New Mexicans and burned or stripped government depots. Anglo Southern sympathizers bluffed a company of New Mexico militiamen into surrendering at Cubero, west of Albuquerque, capturing a small cache of medical supplies, arms, and ammunition, but no provender. A frustrated U.S. inspector general excoriated the Hispano soldiers as "worse than worthless; they are really aids to the enemy who catch them, take away their arms, and tell them to go home." Canby, only slightly more politic, "disembarrassed" himself of most of his militia and some of the New Mexico Volunteers, who he believed had let him down at Valverde. Carson's men had performed well enough, but others had indeed fled when the fighting began, though by the end of March a desertion amnesty had restored most of the volunteer companies to nearly full strength.[43]

Logistics were not Sibley's forte and, in the end, they would prove to be his downfall. Attempting to live off the land, he slowly moved his command north through Pueblo Indian and Hispano settlements, his two columns converging near Santa Fe. The Confederates stole what food they could from the locals, even ransacking Governor Connelly's home as well as the Albuquerque property of Colonel Carleton, whose California troops were then en route to Fort Yuma. With the exception of these private stocks and stores, Sibley's army found little to eat. They subsisted primarily on the dwindling herd of underfed beef cattle that had sustained them since leaving Fort Bliss. Just as Captain Herbert Enos fired the government stores stockpiled at Albuquerque before retreating north to Fort Union, other Union men stripped Santa Fe of government supplies. Pyron's companies of the Second Texas (Baylor's old Arizona Volunteers) reached the capital first, on March 10, led by men of the spy company officially enrolled as The Brigands but known to most of the Texans as the "Santa Fe Gamblers." Three days later, Pyron ran the Confederate stars and bars up the flagstaff at the Palace of the Governors. Proud of their victories and the achievement of surviving the almost one-thousand-mile trek from San Antonio to Santa Fe, the rebels were still confident, though most realized the campaign had already taken its toll. The men were hungry, ragged, and footsore—as many of the mounted volunteers were now, of necessity, infantrymen. Just when it seemed the invasion was losing momentum and would peter out, an unlucky U.S. supply train from the East bound for Fort Craig fell into Confederate hands east of Albuquerque. This bounty, combined with supplies rescued by the people of Albuquerque from the fires set by retreating federal troops, and other commissary stores confiscated from New Mexicans, led Sibley to once again entertain hope that a quick thrust to Fort Union might be successful.[44]

By late March, Canby's command of New Mexico Volunteers and regulars was still hunkered down at Fort Craig with the intention of cutting off Sibley's supplies from the south and harassing, if possible, the Confederate rear while the small garrison at Fort Union dug in and awaited reinforcements. Holding New Mexico would not be easy for the Union commander. The Confederates moved northward unopposed, and Apache and Navajo attacks increased daily.[45] He also discovered that not all the New Mexicans had chosen sides. Some, including natives of Sandia Pueblo, attacked Captain Herbert Enos's party as it moved north to destroy supplies ahead of the rebels and link up with the federal forces at Fort Union. Enos reported that he feared Albuquerque's citizens who, bent on plundering government stores, had threatened his command. Hispano deserters attacked his wagon train and made off with three wagons and part of the mule herd. Still other "Mexican robbers" attacked a U.S. Army train near Galisteo, fifteen miles from Santa Fe, capturing six more wagons and their teams. The remnants of Lieutenant Colonel Manuél Chaves's Second New Mexico Volunteers deserted en masse at Santa Fe as Major Donaldson attempted to destroy government stores that could not be transported to Fort Union. Some local Hispanos salvaged the stores left behind and gleefully watched Governor Connelly and his Anglo entourage, representatives and symbols of American occupation, flee the capital with Donaldson's troops. The governor wrote his superiors in Washington,

"The militia have all dispersed, and have gone to preparing their lands for the coming harvest, and this is by far the best use that can be made of them." The Hispano-Anglo divide was beginning to show, and it seemed that another civil war had erupted in New Mexico.[46]

The Civil War revealed the discontent that had been simmering ever since the American takeover of New Mexico in 1846. Believing that their enemy's enemy was a friend, longtime Hispano adversaries of the United States now made known their support for the Confederates. Rafael and Manuel Armijo and other New Mexico *ricos* pledged allegiance to the rebels and made available $200,000 worth of warehoused supplies in Albuquerque and Santa Fe. Sibley welcomed their "protests of sympathy for our cause," but he also recognized that "politically they have no distinct sentiment or opinion on the vital question at issue." He wrote his superiors in Richmond that for most New Mexicans, "power and interest alone control the expression of their sympathies." Sibley also noted in his report that Navajo raiders had in the last year driven off hundreds of thousands of sheep and that the best way to win the support of the Hispanos was to institute policy that would "encourage private enterprises against that tribe and the Apaches, and to legalize the enslaving of them."[47]

From his Albuquerque headquarters, Sibley directed the three Confederate columns—under Pyron, Scurry, and Green—moving slowly toward Fort Union. Pyron's men, joined by Major John S. Shropshire's battalion, gathered information about the strength of the Union garrison, especially the rumors of reinforcements from Colorado, and by March 25 began moving east on the Santa Fe Trail. Pyron's line of march took him through pine-forested canyon country, where the trail separated the Sangre De Cristo Mountains to the north from Glorieta Mesa on the south. The columns under Scurry and Green intended to bypass this pinch point, taking a more direct route toward the fort, and hoped to join forces on the trail somewhere east of Apache Canyon and Glorieta Pass. The arrival of Colonel John P. Slough and the 950 men of the First Colorado Regiment at Fort Union on March 11 dashed Confederate hopes of an easy victory and resupply in northern New Mexico.

In a little more than two weeks' time, Slough's Pike's Peakers had walked and run more than five hundred miles along the eastern flank of the Rocky Mountains through freezing rain and snow-choked passes—a feat that amazed both the War Department and the rebels—in order to reinforce Fort Union before Sibley's army arrived. The hardy miners marched more than fifty miles in a day during the last leg of the journey. As with the California Volunteers, then making their way across the Arizona desert, the Coloradans were physically bigger than their regular army counterparts. The volunteers also exhibited a readiness to take risks, a characteristic typical of the self-reliant migrants who had headed west in search of gold and adventure. Colonel Gabriel Paul's delight in the unprecedented march and timely arrival of the Coloradans quickly dissipated as he learned that Colonel Slough's volunteer commission predated his own.[48]

John Slough, a Denver lawyer without military experience but possessed of enormous ambition, chose to assume command of all the troops at Fort Union, volunteers and regulars alike, and leave Colonel Paul, the West Point professional, holding the fort, just as he had at Fort Craig during the Battle of Valverde just weeks before. By March 22, only eleven days after completing the grueling trek to Fort Union, the energetic Slough made certain that the quartermaster had outfitted the Coloradans in new, regulation uniforms, and that ordnance officers had issued the men new Springfield rifle muskets, accoutrements, and ammunition from the fort's well-stocked stores. Canby's cautious instructions to Paul had been to wait for reinforcements and to not give up the fort. The orders were vague enough, however, to permit someone with an active imagination to interpret them in a way that allowed for independent action, as long as the fort could be protected. Slough's imagination, combined with his lawyerly training, was indeed equal to the task, and he determined to meet the enemy in the narrow passes of the Santa Fe Trail some eighty-five miles southwest of the fort. Furious at being outranked by an amateur volunteer officer, Colonel Paul dashed off dispatches to Washington requesting a promotion to brigadier general to avoid such "mortification" in the future and to absolve himself of blame should Slough's impetuous movement prove disastrous.

Glorieta Pass: Broken Terrain, Logistics, and Morale

On March 26, Slough's lead battalion of cavalry and infantry under the command of Major John Milton Chivington met Major Pyron's advance astride the trail with two 6-pounders. A Methodist-minister-turned-soldier, well over six feet tall and powerfully built, Chivington inspired confidence in his men. He had gained a reputation for never backing down from a fight after preaching a sermon while wearing lion skins and armed with a brace of Colt revolvers. When Colorado's Governor Gilpin offered him the chaplaincy of the volunteer regiment, he turned it down in favor of what he called "a fighting commission." Surprised by the number and combativeness of the Colorado command, the overmatched Confederates retreated fighting. Chivington's mountaineers climbed the rocky heights of narrow Apache Canyon and repeatedly flanked the rebels, who were finally driven off by a charge led by Captain John Ford's mounted company of Colorado Volunteers. Throughout the melee, the towering, barrel-chested Chivington could be seen waving his pistols, bellowing commands, and conspicuously exposing himself to enemy fire, a fact not lost on his men or the Texans. In fact, when Colonel Scurry and the reinforcements from Galisteo arrived at Johnson's Ranch at the west end of Apache Canyon that evening, his men got an earful from Pyron's survivors, who had lost 25 percent of their number in killed, wounded, or captured, to the "Devils from Pike's Peak" and their larger-than-life leader.[49]

Chivington agreed to a truce to collect dead and wounded, mostly rebels, and then fell back to join Slough and the rest of the command at Kozlowski's Ranch, some thirteen miles to the east on the Santa Fe Trail. Both sides expected action on March 27, but none came as the opposing forces regrouped and probed each other's position. On the morning of March 28, however, both of the aggressive commanders made preparations to attack. Scurry moved his 1,300-man force, comprising elements of the Fourth, Fifth, and Seventh Texas, eastward on the trail. As they proceeded, they drew with malnourished mules or manhandled three pieces of artillery, two 12-pounder howitzers and one 6-pounder gun.

Hoping to hit the rebels in the rear somewhere near Johnson's ranch, Slough made the risky decision to split his command in the presence of the enemy and attempt a daring flank attack by crossing the rough terrain of uncharted Glorieta Mesa. Major Chivington led the 530-man flanking battalion, composed of regulars of the Fifth Infantry and Third Cavalry, Colorado Volunteers, and a detachment of the Fourth New Mexico Volunteers. Lieutenant Colonel Manuél Chaves of the Second

New Mexico Volunteers had no command authority, even though he outranked Chivington, but came along to guide the raiders across the broken Mesa. Before the war, Chaves had been a Santa Fe trader, and he knew the country well. Though unimpressed with the performance of Chaves's volunteer regiment at Valverde, the other officers knew he had a reputation as an Indian fighter and had seen combat during the Mexican-American War.

Slough warily moved his eight-hundred-man force of cavalry and infantry down the trail while towing behind the column two batteries of artillery. Captain John Ritter's "Light Battery" comprised two 12-pounder howitzers and two 6-pounder guns, while Lieutenant Ira Claflin commanded a battery of four 12-pounder mountain howitzers. By late morning, the mixed battalion of regulars and volunteers relaxed, filled canteens, and lounged behind the adobe walls of Pigeon's Ranch, a sprawling way station that straddled the trail and provided a year-round source of good water. Chivington had commandeered this place as a field hospital following the Apache Canyon fight two days earlier. Scouting the Union encampment, The Brigands alerted Scurry, who immediately unlimbered his artillery on a rise in the road a mile west of Pigeon's Ranch and prepared to attack. Slough sallied out to meet the Confederates as soon as the first shell burst. He placed his two batteries across the road and up the slopes of a hill just south of the ranch and detailed flanking parties to take the high ground on either side of the valley, as Chivington had done at Apache Canyon. The rebels were too strong, however, and their overlapping lines enfiladed the Coloradans on the left and pushed back those on the ridge north of the road as well.[50]

The incessant artillery fire echoed in the valley like rolling thunder, and clouds of pure white gun smoke filled the gullies and lingered in the tops of the pine trees that shaded the pass known to locals as La Glorieta. But after three hours of fighting, two of the three Confederate guns were silenced by Colorado sharpshooters posted on a rocky prominence. The Union infantrymen were armed with long-range rifle muskets, which could easily strike man-sized targets at two hundred yards. Though many of the Coloradans had never fired their newly issued weapons before this battle, they learned quickly. Many of the rebels had been re-armed with captured rifle muskets since Valverde, but others still carried their double-barreled shotguns, useful only at close range.[51]

Accurate counterbattery fire from the Union guns may have disabled the third gun, which also ceased firing, but Scurry pressed the attack, sending Majors Shropshire and Pyron up the hill occupied by Claflin's mountain guns, and personally led a frontal assault aimed directly at the adobe wall in the center of the Union line. But the Coloradans and regulars held. During the confused fighting in the wooded, rocky terrain on the crest of the hill, Shropshire fell with a bullet in his brain. Some Texans wearing captured federal overcoats escaped a similar fate when the Union men held their fire, believing that the blue-clad soldiers making their way through the trees were their own men. In the valley, Scurry himself was bloodied by minié balls that brushed his cheeks and perforated his uniform coat. Volleys of musketry from the Union men sheltering behind the adobes cut down the charging Texans before they could reach the wall. By five o'clock both sides were spent, and during the lull, Slough determined to withdraw five miles to Kozlowski's Ranch. Scurry's men were in no condition to continue the fight, so the rebel commander sent a white flag after the retreating Federals requesting a truce until noon the next day.

Just as the fighting at Pigeon's Ranch reached its fiercest, Chivington's men were scaling down the far side of Glorieta Mesa and descending on the corralled Confederate supply train, watched over by an unsuspecting corporal's guard lounging near a loaded 6-pounder gun. The surprise was complete, however, and the raiders swiftly torched the eighty wagons and slaughtered or ran off hundreds of horses and mules. The devastation finished, Chivington disabled the field piece and, with rebel prisoners and recaptured Federals in tow, used ropes and belts to climb back up the two-hundred-foot bluff to the mesa top. The twelve miles across the roadless pine- and cedar-forested mesa in complete darkness took all night, but when Chivington revealed the success of his exploit to Slough at Kozlowski's, the somber mood in the Union camp quickly cheered. The magnitude of the victory at Glorieta Pass became clear over the next few days when it was discovered that the Confederates had hastily buried their dead, abandoned their wounded at Pigeon's Ranch, and decamped. Without blankets, food, medicine, or ammunition, the rebels dragged themselves to Santa Fe a defeated army, whether or not they chose to believe it.[52]

Lieutenant Colonel Scurry issued a congratulatory order to the bloodied Texans: "Soldiers—You have added another victory to the long list of triumphs won by the Confederate armies."[33] The wounded and exhausted men of his command, now sheltering in every available adobe building in the New Mexican capital, felt little like victors. As Sibley attempted to make sense of the battle and his available options, Canby finally sallied forth from Fort Craig on April 1, 1862, taking his regulars to link up with Slough's troops while sending Carson and the volunteers to regarrison Fort Union.[54] Canby soon discovered that Slough's command was no longer his. The impetuous Coloradan believed that he would be censured for disobeying orders and unnecessarily jeopardizing Fort Union, so he hurriedly resigned and straightaway headed east to explain himself to superiors. In truth, there was more to the story. The Colonel had been engaged in a power struggle with Major Chivington for the affection and loyalty of the men ever since the march from Denver. Chivington supporters even threatened Colonel Slough's life, and during the fighting at Pigeon's Ranch, some of the Coloradans fired a volley that nearly killed him. Unnerved by the whole ordeal and seeing that the men clearly preferred the charismatic Chivington, Slough felt he had no choice but to get out while he still had a chance. The Colorado Volunteers' Lieutenant Colonel, Samuel Tappan, a newspaperman from a prominent New England abolitionist family, actually ranked Major Chivington, but he too saw the writing on the wall and decided to follow rather than confront the pugnacious preacher.

Now, Sibley's command headed south in two columns on either side of the Rio Grande, the men driven by the remote chance that they might yet capture Fort Craig's commissary and ordnance stores, the only hope for reviving Confederate fortunes. Canby consolidated his own forces and had a chance to size up the Coloradans and their newly promoted Colonel Chivington. The calm, cautious, and calculating Canby and the bombastic, bellicose Chivington were polar opposites, and the differences began to show almost immediately. Grumbling and dissent in the Union ranks began as Canby's pursuit of the rebels slowly progressed. In an Albuquerque corral on the night of April 11, Trevanion T. Teel surreptitiously buried eight of his mountain howitzers for want of ammunition to shoot and draft animals to pull the guns. The inhabitants of New Mexico's farms and pueblos provided little relief for the retreating rebels, who had so boldly stripped the countryside on their way north. Looking to administer the coup de grâce to the wounded but still dangerous Confederate Army of New Mexico, Chi[v]   [rec]-ommended a rush at Peralta before the rebels could unite their divided columns. Canby held back, however, and missed the opportunity, much to the disgust of the Coloradans. Long-range artillery fire and ineffectual exchanges of musketry characterized the final battle of the Civil War in New Mexico. The battle at Peralta, April 15, 1862, spent the last of Sibley's ammunition; still Canby contented himself with herding the Texans south and picking off straggling men, horses, and wagons as the rebels grew weaker and more disorganized by the day.

Colonel William Steele, Seventh Texas Cavalry, commanding the remnants of Sibley's army as it retreated, found the Texans' pitiable state of supply forced him to commandeer rolling stock and food from the New Mexican villages along the route of march. "This occasioned so much ill-feeling on the part of the Mexicans [sic]," Steele reported to Richmond, "that in many cases armed resistance was offered to forag-ing parties acting under my orders, and in the various skirmishes which took place one captain and several men of my regiment were killed by them. Besides this, the troops with me were so disgusted with the cam-paign and so anxious to return to Texas that in one or two instances they were on the point of mutiny, and threatened to take the matter in their own hands unless they were speedily marched back to San Antonio." As spring turned to summer, the soaring daytime tempera-tures and chilled nights further tormented the starving and half-naked Confederates who stumbled and dragged themselves through El Paso and across the parched desert to San Antonio.[55]

Canby's caution proved the right decision in the end. The goal of saving New Mexico for the Union and stopping the Confederate threat in the borderlands and the Pacific had been achieved—and with less loss of life than a more aggressive course would have offered. The Con-federates blustered that they had won every battle but somehow lost the campaign. Their pride would not allow them to admit that they were half-beaten before they began by the resistance of the people who resented their invasion, by the desert that could and did take their lives, and by their own logistical unpreparedness. Sibley was unfavorably compared to Baylor, who may not have been any better prepared but who acted decisively and struck his enemies quickly, winning victories before his logistical inadequacy became a factor. The editor of the *Santa Fe Gazette* called Baylor, "the fast man of Arizona." Trevanion T. Teel summed up Sibley's weakness when he observed that their leader "was too prone to let the morrow take care of itself."[56]

Carleton's California Column

In contrast to the Confederates in New Mexico, Surgeon James McNulty, the acting medical director of the California Column, attributed the excellent condition of these troops to good planning and the fact that the men composing the column were "inured to mountain life in California, pioneers and miners; self-reliant and enduring; men equal to any emergency, if guided by a firm hand and a clear head." Carleton marched his men at night, starting at four or five in the afternoon and ending before dawn the next day. The sandy roads and choking alkali dust made the march almost unbearable at times, but the men endured and pressed on.[57] Despite the disheartening news of McCleave's capture and the dismal outcome of the Picacho affair, the men were in good spirits. Most of the soldiers believed the expedition had been handled well, and they proudly wrote home of their remarkable record of marches from Los Angeles to Tucson—nearly six hundred miles—averaging about twenty miles a day.[58]

Carleton ensured that his officers made meticulous notes of all they observed, paying special attention to water (alkalinity, depth of wells, time it took for the wells to naturally replenish), grass, shade, game, and the condition of the road. He also required them to carefully record distances. Captain Shinn attached an odometer to one of the caissons of his artillery battery, enabling him to measure distances to the nearest hundredth of a mile. Infantry officers relied on the tried-and-true method of pace counting. A reliable soldier in each company was assigned the unenviable task of counting each step and reporting to the first sergeant at every halt. Of course the pace-counter had to have a regular stride and measured pace of twenty-eight inches from heel to heel. A knotted string helped him keep track of his count, but he had to forgo socializing on the march or doing anything that might break his concentration.[59]

The marching men seemed unaware that their route through the low desert country along the Gila to Tucson's Santa Catalina Mountains rose nearly a mile in elevation. The climb was gradual, nearly imperceptible, but the teamsters needed to urge their tired draft animals on and occasionally double-teamed the heavily loaded wagons over steep grades. Some observant soldiers noted the altitude change and its effect on the native flora—from creosote, sage, and prickly pear cactus in the low Colorado Desert to the mesquite, paloverde, and saguaros of the high desert.[60]

By the time the Californians regrouped and began the final push from the Pima Villages to Tucson on May 14, there was little chance they might overtake Hunter's men. In contrast to Carleton's attention to arms and ammunition, Hunter's company scrambled to find food in Tucson and hurriedly molded lead bullets and fabricated paper cartridges for various makes and models of firearms—a logistical disadvantage on the frontier where resupply was uncertain—before leaving Tucson. From the rebel prisoners taken at Picacho, Carleton learned that McCleave and Ammi White had been sent to the Rio Grande escorted by Lieutenant Jack Swilling. McCleave rejected an opportunity to be paroled because he refused to swear that he would not take up arms against the Confederacy. Knowing that it would now be impossible to rescue his friend, Carleton resumed his methodical preparations for subsisting his troops.

Before leaving Fort Yuma he ordered Colonel West to secure Tucson and establish a supply line to Sonora, Mexico, as soon as possible. Carleton impressed upon his subordinates that logistics mattered more than fighting on this campaign. He wrote to Sonora's liberal Republican governor, Ignacio Pesqueira, urging him to make supplies available to the California troops. As a gesture of goodwill, Carleton removed his earlier passport requirements and ban against Mexican migrants desiring to cross the border to work in the rich new mines on the lower Colorado River.[61]

Across the border in Mexico, Governor Pesqueira had his hands full. He fought Apaches who, it seemed, crossed the line with impunity, devastating unprotected Sonoran settlements. He also battled his conservative political rival, former governor and longtime *caudillo,* Manuel Gándara, who had allied himself with Ópata, Lower Pima, Papago, and Yaqui villagers. Pesqueira hoped that the increased American military presence might deter the Apache raiders and relieve some of the burden of garrisoning the border posts as a French army closed in on Mexico City. Given the internal and external threats, he had little choice but to accept Carleton's professions of friendship.[62]

Carleton saw Tucson as the key to Arizona, and his plan for its capture left nothing to chance. In accordance with orders, West did not take the Picacho route to Tucson but instead traveled the longer Fort Breckenridge trail by way of the Gila and San Pedro rivers.[63] The Picacho affair had been an embarrassment, and Carleton would not risk another failure. He cautioned West not to make any move against the town unless the chances for success were nearly all in his favor. Carleton also counseled his subordinate to make certain his cavalrymen kept their sabers very sharp and to not underrate the Confederates, who he now understood to be worthy opponents. "Pray teach your men," he instructed, "not to despise their enemy."[64] The Arizona rebels were tough and determined frontiersmen, expert in desert survival and warfare, but he believed that they could be overawed by bold action and "hand-to-hand" combat if the Californians were willing to close with them, mounted or on foot, with "cold steel" and pistols. The commander drew on his war experience in Mexico and offered advice on how to take the town if Hunter's men decided to fight it out on horseback, from entrenchments, or forted up in loopholed adobes. He explained how the California men might slash the reins of the rebels' horses, in order to disadvantage their better-mounted opponents. Carleton could imagine his men cutting through adobe walls and fighting house to house, lobbing by hand 12-pounder shells with lighted fuses in order to clear out hidden riflemen. These tactics, he reasoned, had worked during the Taos insurgency of 1847, and as his California soldiers closed on Tucson, Carleton's old confidence returned. Now he was so sure of victory, he warned West that Colonel Bowie's Fifth California Infantry, following close behind but not considered part of the original column, "must have equal chances" for glory with the First Infantry.[65]

On May 20, 1862, the men of Captain Emil Fritz's Company B, First California Cavalry, with drawn pistols at the ready, spurred their mounts into sleepy Tucson. One platoon entered from the east and another from the north, meeting without incident in the town's plaza, once the center of the Spanish presidio. Actually there was one embarrassing incident. As Fritz's men galloped through the dusty streets, they saw what appeared to be gun barrels projecting from the rooftops. According to Lieutenant George H. Pettis, Company K, First California Infantry, "Captain Fritz and his gallant troops, as they rode through the vacant streets of Tucson, threw themselves over on the sides of their horses when they saw the long water spouts [*canales*] protruding from the *casas* . . . pointing in their direction." The rattled California cavalrymen quickly regained their composure and secured the town. The following day the infantry marched down the narrow streets with flags snapping and fifes and drums echoing "Yankee Doodle" off the adobe buildings that crowded the pueblo. The Californians stacked arms in the plaza and slapped the dust from their blue uniforms. From sympathetic locals they learned that all but a handful of Hunter's men had cleared out a week earlier. Only five hundred people remained in town, a third of the former population, along with a surprisingly large number of cats and dogs.[66]

By the end of May, Colonel West had regarrisoned Fort Brecken-ridge—which he deemed proper to rename Fort Stanford in honor of the new governor of California, Leland Stanford—and then Fort Buchanan, forty-five miles southeast of Tucson. But West soon aban-doned these posts—the regulars had destroyed the buildings when they withdrew in 1861—and occupying forts had no place in Carleton's strategy to reach the Rio Grande and the real war in New Mexico.[67]

On June 6, Carleton himself arrived in Tucson. Lieutenant Shinn's four-gun battery boomed an impressive salute as the commander's entourage rode into the dusty adobe pueblo. Apparently Carleton had arranged for Shinn to arrive early to perform the ceremony by ordering his own escort to make a fatiguing detour that enabled the artillery contingent to travel straight through. Undeniably the nor-mally straight-laced Carleton had a flair for the dramatic. Just before leaving Fort Yuma on May 15, he issued General Order No. 1, which declared that his expedition would hereafter be known officially as the "Column from California." Although unorthodox, the name caught on immediately with the men, and soon all official correspondence reflected the change or clipped it to the more manageable "California Column."[68]

After Arizona City, on the banks of the Colorado River across from Fort Yuma, swollen with miners and military activity, Tucson was the largest permanent settlement in the territory. The people remain-ing in the town were a resilient lot—undeterred by Apache raids or the rebel occupation. Most had been born Mexican citizens, but the 1854 Gadsden Purchase had made Americans of them. The Hispanos seemed not to mind being recast as Americanos as long as the new government allowed them to practice their religion, tend their flocks, and till their fields as before. Some of the Mexican American population profited as merchants and freighters. Others offered important services such as blacksmithing, essential for the maintenance of army rolling stock. Captive Apaches (*mansos*) toiled alongside the Tucsonans, just as many Hispano captives had been adopted into Apache families. Pima, Maricopa, and Papago Indians could be found in the town as well. Some worked as farmers, teamsters, scouts, or domestic servants. Tucson's Anglo inhabitants, though a minority, dominated the political and economic life of the community. They were mostly young and middle-aged men—outnumbering the women five to one—who had emigrated from the "States" to seek fortunes as miners, tradesmen, and entrepreneurs. Some subsisted by gambling or some other illicit trade, and more than a few were fugitives from justice.[69]

Colonel Carleton had been feeling sorry for himself as he became aware that officers with less seniority had received promotions in other commands. But shortly before reaching Tucson, news reached him that President Lincoln had finally confirmed his appointment as brigadier general of volunteers. Though still unsure of the effective date of his new rank, Carleton moved forward with renewed self-assurance. Taking care not to overstep his authority (he still signed official documents as "Colonel"), he provisionally proclaimed Arizona a separate territory on June 8, 1862, and announced, "The Congress of the United States has set apart a portion of New Mexico, and organized it into a Territory complete by itself. This is known as the Territory of Arizona. It comprises within its limits all the country eastward from the Colorado River, which is now occupied by the forces of the United States, known as the 'Column from California.'" As the military governor of the new territory, Carleton quickly imposed martial law in Tucson.[70]

General Carleton also established a supply depot that could support the other posts in the territory and the column that would continue to New Mexico. While the rear guard filed into town, Governor Carleton set about rectifying civil matters in Arizona. Surgeon McNulty submitted a glowing account of Carleton's reign: "A number of notorious characters were arrested . . . and sent to Fort Yuma. Order sprang from disorder, and in a short time a den of thieves was converted into a peaceful village." Not everyone, however, was as well pleased with the new military government.[71]

Carleton sent a detachment under Colonel Eyre to arrest Sylvester Mowry, an ex-army officer turned mining entrepreneur and an avowed Confederate sympathizer, at his Patagonia Mine south of Tucson near the Mexican border. Eyre brought Mowry and the other occupants of the mining operation back to Tucson. A military commission tried the men and sent them in shackles to Fort Yuma for incarceration. Carleton extended his heavy-handed style of government to Tucson's gambling hall and saloon owners by imposing a monthly one hundred dollar tax on all tables used for monte or games of chance. He ordered that the tax revenue raised be used to benefit the sick and injured members of the California Column. He also instituted a military pass system, which monitored all citizens entering or leaving town. Although many Southern sympathizers had gone with Sherod Hunter, Carleton made it clear to any would-be secessionists that he would not tolerate any saboteurs or rebel spies.[72] Before leaving California, he revealed his no-nonsense side when he warned Eyre that he should be prepared to disobey a writ of habeas corpus, and "if any person fires into your camp, hang him."[73]

He directed that until the new territorial government could organize civil courts, martial law would prevail. Regulations for army courts-martial pertained to all public trials. A commission of not more than five and no fewer than three officers presided over the court. Only when the territorial government could establish civil courts would appeals be granted. A number of Tucson desperados, no doubt, breathed a sigh of relief when Carleton added, "No execution shall follow conviction" without orders from the president.[74]

Carleton had initially made public his intention to campaign against Western Apache raiders, though this "Tonto" ruse quickly gave way as his primary objective of linking up with the Union forces in New Mexico and driving the rebels back to Texas became obvious. While the contest for New Mexico raged, Carleton tried repeatedly to communicate with Canby. On June 15, he dispatched three expressmen in an attempt to reach Canby's command on the Rio Grande. John W. Jones, Sergeant William Wheeling of Company F, First Infantry, and an Hispano guide named Chavez left Tucson and rode their mules hard for three days until a large party of Chiricahuas attacked them just east of Apache Pass. Jones alone escaped with his life, but Confederate troops at another El Picacho, about six miles from Mesilla, captured him before he reached Canby. Incredibly, although imprisoned,

Jones somehow managed to get word to Canby that the California Column was on its way. Carleton's penchant for secrecy paid off. The expressman surrendered his false dispatch—intended for Confederate consumption in case of capture—and smuggled the tissue paper version to Canby.[75]

By June 21 the Californians began to move forward to the Rio Grande. Colonel Eyre pushed ahead with two companies of the First Cavalry on a "forced reconnaissance." This command met with no Confederate resistance, but it did encounter Cochise's Chiricahua Apaches, with whom Eyre had been admonished to "avoid collision." The advance companies encamped in Apache Pass, the narrow defile through the Chiricahua Mountains midway between Tucson and Mesilla. The Californians had ridden into the heart of Cochise's domain, hoping to treat with the chief while showing good faith by offering to share food and tobacco. Eyre little understood the enmity forged just the year before when Lieutenants Moore and Bascom hanged Chiricahua prisoners thought responsible for crimes actually committed by other Apaches from the White Mountains to the north. Cochise's own family members had been among those executed in the Bascom affair, and the Chiricahua leader still burned with a desire to settle his blood debt with the Americans.[76]

While Eyre offered a gift of canned pemmican and attempted to parley, Chiricahua warriors killed, stripped, and mutilated three of Captain Fritz's Company B troopers who strayed from the command after watering their horses. Furious that Eyre would not allow him to avenge the slaughtered men, Fritz threw down his saber and carbine and openly argued with his superior. The offending Chiricahuas could still be seen on the adjoining hills just out of rifle range, displaying contempt for the soldiers, and most of the Californians believed that honor demanded retaliation. But Eyre was determined the incident would not delay him. He tightened camp security and allowed the enraged Fritz to calm down. The Apaches fired a volley into the soldiers' camp that night, but the advance continued without further trouble. The pass had proven itself the bane of more than one expedition. At Dragoon Springs, just west of the pass, Sherod Hunter had lost four of his rangers and fifty-five animals as they retreated eastward from the California Column weeks earlier. The graves of the Union and Confederate dead now ominously marked the trail near the abandoned stage station.[77]

Just a month after Eyre's skirmish, these same Apaches ambushed Captain Thomas L. Roberts's command in the pass. This fight resulted in the largest armed conflict ever to take place between U.S. troops and the Apaches in Arizona. On July 15, 1862, Roberts's command, which included a company of infantry, a detachment of cavalry, and Lieutenant Thompson's two mountain howitzers, met several hundred Chiricahuas under the joint leadership of Cochise and Mangas Coloradas. The soldiers suffered two men killed and several seriously wounded after a four-hour fight for the spring in the pass. Only the effective deployment of the artillery and a bayonet charge saved the command. With but brief respite beside the cool water of the spring, the men of the strung-out California Column continued on toward the Rio Grande.[78]

The Anglo soldiers reduced the danger of attack in the pass after Major Theodore A. Coult and a company of the Fifth California Infantry established a post there on Carleton's orders. Coult named this strategic post Fort Bowie in honor of the regiment's colonel, George W. Bowie. Placing military posts in the heart of enemy country would become standard operating procedure for the U.S. troops in the borderlands during the Civil War years. Carleton also began to reorganize the command and communication network by creating the District of Western Arizona with headquarters at Tucson. He entrusted Major David Fergusson, chief commissary of the California Column, with the command of the district, which encompassed the region between Fort Yuma and Fort Bowie and provided for the protection of travelers, settlers, and miners. A detachment of Californians was already on the way to relieve the civilians at the Pinos Altos mines in southwestern New Mexico, where Apache attacks had killed so many of the miners that their families and others faced death by starvation.[79]

Carleton authorized a military mail, or "vedette service," to run from Tucson to Los Angeles, since Apache raiders and the rebel threat had shut down the Butterfield Overland Mail on the southern route in 1861. The U.S. mail contractor now ran stage coaches and Pony Express riders on the safer central route along the Platte River and across the high plains. Carleton recruited "first-rate men" and the best riders in the California Column for his elite corps of vedettes, and soon reestablished deliveries on the southern route. To lessen the fatigue of the horses and make certain the mail would get through, the general sought out small men with a good deal of grit. These mail carriers rode long distances, often without escorts, relying on their own survival instincts and the endurance of their picked animals to carry them safely through ambushes and an unforgiving desert. Although Carleton appealed to Postmaster General Montgomery Blair to restore regular mail service along the route, the U.S. Postal Service did not resume full operations until after the war. Arizona territorial governor John N. Goodwin later expressed appreciation to the Californians in his report to the first legislature, stating, "We have been indebted to the courtesy of the military authorities for the means of communication between the principal points in the territory and the mail routes in New Mexico and California."[80]

By August 1862 the California Column had reached the Rio Grande, with Carleton's men hot on the rebels' heels picking up the sick and wounded who were abandoned at the post hospitals in New Mexico and Texas and stragglers found along the trail. While awaiting the arrival of Chivington's Coloradans to continue the pursuit of the retreating Texans, Lieutenant Colonel Eyre's advance recovered the much-relieved Captain McCleave and his captured men in a tearful reunion near Fort Thorn. Almost immediately, Carleton succeeded Canby as commander of the Department of New Mexico. The War Department also saw fit to transfer permanent command of the California Column, which had previously reported to General Wright's Department of the Pacific, to Carleton's new department. Although supplies continued to pour into the depot at Tucson along the Yuma route, Carleton now commanded the whole operation from his headquarters at Santa Fe.[81]

In September Carleton redefined the District of Arizona as stretching from the Colorado River to the Rio Grande. The District of Western Arizona, now commanded by Major Coult, became a subdistrict, supporting the frontline troops then in pursuit of Sibley's retreating Texans. Carleton's change in command and the reorganization of the existing districts placed Coult and other officers in Arizona in a difficult position, receiving conflicting orders from both the Department of the Pacific and the Department of New Mexico. Washington finally resolved the problem by officially attaching the District of Western Arizona to Carleton's department in January 1863.[82]

Although the California Column had skirmished with rebel pickets and fought Apaches in Arizona, Carleton's men encountered no serious opposition from the Confederates retreating from New Mexico.

The half-starved and footsore rebels stole what provisions they could from the increasingly hostile locals; buried or abandoned their artillery, with the exception of McRae's "Valverde Battery"; and dodged the converging Union forces. Sibley's survivors then set out across a nearly waterless one-hundred-mile desert for Texas, leaving more than seven hundred of their comrades behind, either dead or captured. Nearly half these casualties had fallen victim to malnutrition, disease, or exposure to the elements. Sibley had been defeated by his inability to resupply his troops in the southwestern desert and the cautious but relentless pressure from Canby's troops from the north and Carleton's command from the west.[83]

Jefferson Davis never had great confidence in the scheme for a Confederate empire in the Far West. The Confederate government dedicated little financial support and manpower to the project, though the invasion of New Mexico and Arizona did serve to divert significant federal resources that relieved pressure in other theaters. Davis's administration had initially been intrigued by the possibility of securing foreign recognition for the Confederacy as Mexico's warring political factions and foreign intervention presented an opportunity to make a deal resulting in formal diplomatic relations. Though this international diplomacy did not achieve the desired ends, the aggressive Confederate high command viewed offensive operations into Northern territory— even in the remote borderlands—as opportunities to influence public opinion, North and South, and serve the Confederacy's overarching "let us alone" political strategy.

For Sibley and the Texans the invasion had been a quest for empire, pure and simple, premised on the racist belief that the Hispanos and Indians inhabiting the territories were incapable of developing the country. The campaign was a continuation of previous land grabs that had begun prior to the Mexican-American War. The invaders sought to extend their empire all the way to the Colorado gold mines and ultimately impose Texas-style Manifest Destiny on the northern states of Mexico, including the port of Guaymas, and possibly establishing permanent dominion over California. Realizing that his dream of empire was lost, Sibley harbored an "irreconcilable detestation of the country and the people." He summed up his disillusionment at the outcome of the campaign in his final report: "New Mexico is not worth a quarter of the blood and treasure expended in its conquest."[84]

As the California troops reoccupied abandoned forts in New Mexico and Texas, they dutifully ran the U.S. colors up the old flag poles—if only for a day—before worrying the Texas rebels back to San Antonio. "The retreat of Sibley," wrote a California soldier, "would appear to visibly diminish our chances for a fair stand up fight with the enemy; but it cannot be denied that we have traveled far to find one."[85] Carleton wrote with pride and sentimentality to superiors and reflected on the arduous journey his men had completed: "I send you a set of colors which have been borne by this Column. They were hoisted by Colonel West on Forts Breckenridge and Buchanan, and over Tucson, Ariz.; by Colonel Eyre over Forts Thorn, Fillmore, and over Mesilla, N. Mex., and over Fort Bliss, in Texas, and thus again have those places been consecrated to our beloved country." General in Chief Henry W. Halleck wrote in response from Washington on October 13, 1862, that the desert trek of the California Column was "one of the most creditable marches on record. I only wish our Army here had the mobility and endurance of the California troops." Though the Texas rebels were on the run, the volunteer soldiers remaining in the borderlands had only begun the task of wresting the territories from the indigenous peoples who were engaged in civil wars of their own.[86]

Chapter 4

Indians and Hispanos

By 1863 the borderlands were embroiled in civil strife. The Colorado River tribes still eyed the Pimas and Maricopas suspiciously, but because of the strong Anglo-American military presence, there was now little armed conflict between the tribes. South of the border, the French intervention in Mexico's civil war had escalated the violence, and Mexico City had fallen to the conservatives, driving Juaristas to the northern Mexican states or across the international boundary into the United States. Comanches, Kiowas, and Kiowa-Apaches fought Utes, Jicarilla Apaches, and Hispanos for survival and dominance on New Mexico's eastern border, and Cheyenne and Arapaho warriors, pressed by western-ing white settlers on the plains and in Colorado, pushed southward across the Santa Fe Trail and into the southern plains, which were fast becoming a flashpoint for violent interaction. New Mexico and the newly created Arizona Territory, however, became the main arenas for conflict spawned by the disruption and militarization resulting from the American Civil War. Anglos introduced the idea of total war, and Navajo and Apache warriors found themselves locked in a war to the death against an unprec-edented Anglo-Hispano-Indian alliance that would change everything.

Apacheans: Navajos and Mescaleros

As warfare intensified between Indians, Hispanos, and Anglos in the ter-ritories, the War Department expanded Carleton's authority to include all of New Mexico as well as most of Arizona. He wasted little time before launching expeditions against the Navajos and Apaches. Groups of warriors from these nations, operating independently, accounted for more than 90 percent of the raids and attacks reported by citizens and tribes considered "in amity" with the U.S. government.

Technically, all the tribes with peace treaties were in amity. This term of art in American statecraft meant that treaties supposedly guaranteed amicable and beneficial relations while making the tribes the responsibility of the federal government, which could, in turn, hold them accountable in the event of hostile acts against citizens, or other Indian tribes, resulting in the loss of property. In the borderlands during the 1860s, these "depredations," whether claimed or not, numbered more than one thousand, far more than the decade of the 1850s. Navajo and Apache raiders targeted the livestock of the sedentary Indian tribes as well as the herds of the Hispanos. The warriors also waylaid the wagon trains of Anglo merchants and occasionally even swept through mining camps and towns. In most cases, the attackers avoided armed conflict with their enemies, focusing their energies instead on driving off as many animals as they could.[1]

For decades after the end of the Civil War, the U.S. Court of Claims received depredation claims for civilian property taken or destroyed by Indians during the turbulent years of the 1860s. There were, of course, many more attacks for which claims were not filed. Military operations were not included, nor were killings that did not also involve the loss of property.[2] Only the claims involving property and meeting the strict guidelines for reporting were allowed. Still, the depredation claims provide both quantitative and qualitative evidence of the raiding and warfare that swept the borderlands during the 1860s. Some 84 percent of the claims were filed by Hispano farmers, ranchers, and businessmen residing in New Mexico and Arizona. Claimants attributed 70 percent of these depredations to Navajo raiders and 21 percent to Apaches. In nearly every case, the claimant lost livestock: horses, mules, donkeys, cattle, sheep, or goats. In addition, claimants lost provisions, firearms, camp equipage, and other goods.[3]

In most cases, the Apacheans armed themselves with a combination of bows and arrows, lances, and guns. The single-arc mulberry or willow bows were shaved half-round and strung with deer sinew. Men known for their skill as arrow makers crafted these missiles from *carrizo* (reed) and inserted a hard, ponil wood foreshaft into the end. They then affixed, with sinew and pitch, a white flint (chert) or iron point to the hardwood shaft. Some warriors applied to the arrowhead a potent poison made from deer spleen and fermented nettle root. Dogs and children had to be kept away as this concoction was prepared, and the user himself took precautions to avoid even a scratch that might result in swelling around the wound or even death. The thirty-inch-long *carrizo* arrows were fletched with three split hawk or turkey feathers. Ponil shafts, favored by Navajos, were necessarily shorter because of the difficulty in finding and straightening them by fire-shaping and scraping with broken pot shards or grooved stones. Longitudinal grooves, appearing as lightning or snakes, were often incised and painted for spiritual power and swiftness.

Each clan painted additional shaft markings to identify their arrows, which were carried in an animal skin quiver attached to a bow case. Men of proven ability crafted charms, war caps, and shields, which were painted, adorned, and imbued with medicine that might make enemy weapons break or misfire. Stone-headed clubs and rawhide slings for throwing stones were often found in an Apache man's kit, and these warriors might also carry seven-foot spears made of spruce or sotol stalk for combat on foot. Navajos preferred still longer lances for use on horseback. When stock raiding, the warriors often brandished their weapons, but only 9 percent of the depredation claimants indicated they were fired on or the weapons were wielded with intent to do bodily harm. More often than not firearms were discharged to frighten off herders or to drive cattle. Nearly one raid in five resulted in human casualties; of these, 62 percent were killed, 25 percent wounded, and 13 percent captured. As the civil wars in the borderlands dragged on, however, the incidence of deadly attacks increased.[4]

The Apaches and Navajos were linguistically and culturally related. After years of intermarriage and the exchange of captives, they were also related by blood. The diverse Apachean tribes and bands were at once trading partners and adversaries. As hunters and pastoralists, they competed for the same territory and resources, which often included the livestock of the sedentary agrarian Indians, Hispanos, and Anglos.[5] The semisedentary Navajos and seminomadic Apaches had much in common, but there were also significant cultural differences. The Apaches' supreme being (Yusn) contrasted with Navajo deities, but both groups believed in an afterlife, in spiritual helpers in nature, and in spirits of the departed. The "happy place," where people went when they died, existed under the ground, within the womb of mother earth. Here, the spirits of the dead had corporeal presence and enjoyed all the pleasures of the present world: love and children, family and friends, food and frolic, and hunting and raiding. Portals to this underworld remained well hidden from the living but were easily seen or revealed when death came. Once through the portal, mortals fell into the underworld, tumbling down an enormous cone of sand. Try as the recently deceased might, the soft sand gave way underfoot, and it was nearly impossible to scramble back up the slope and through the portal to the mortal world. The living only rarely spoke the names of the dead for fear that by so doing their ghosts would be called and disturbed.

Apachean tribes comprised bands made up of clans or groups of related families. Incest taboos were strong, and men generally married outside of their family group. Men who were good providers, especially warriors who had proven themselves to be good raiders and who possessed surplus horses and other stock, had the right to seek a wife. A married man would live with his wife's group and pledge to support her family, beginning with generous gifts of food and stock. Generosity was a virtue much admired by all the Apacheans. No man could aspire to a leadership position as a chief or band headman without demonstrating his ability and willingness to provide for people who were hungry or less fortunate. Chiefs were men of proven ability in war. They tended to be physically impressive—big and strong. Chiricahua Chief Mangas Coloradas was said to be six feet, five inches tall and his son-in-law, Cochise, stood six feet, exceptionally tall for an Apache. Mescalero Chief Santana, the son of a chief, was also unusually tall.[6] Theoretically, band and tribal leadership was not hereditary, but boys raised by chiefly fathers learned much about leadership, and the people of the tribe or band generally saw these young men of good families as potential candidates for chiefs and headmen. When the time came, leaders would be recognized by the people, rather than elected in a formal sense. The Navajo clans gathered around chiefs and *ricos,* wealthy men with many sheep and large followings.[7]

The Navajos had acquired and adopted much from the Pueblo peoples, who had been heavily influenced by their Hispano neighbors. The Navajos' hogans were usually made of earth, more substantial and permanent than the simple brush and grass wickiups of the Apaches. With regular crops and orchards and large flocks of sheep, goats, cattle, and horses acquired after centuries of interaction with European immigrants, the Navajos accumulated considerable wealth and developed a rich tradition of weaving colorful and intricately designed blankets from the yarn they spun from the wool of their sheep. Their ceramic, silversmithing, and sand painting traditions were also more sophisticated than those of the neighboring Apache tribes. In contrast, the more mobile Apaches perfected the use of tightly woven baskets, which when coated with pitch, served as lightweight, easily transported containers for water and food.[8]

Apaches lived a more Spartan and raid-dependent way of life, which had evolved over the centuries from their hunting and foraging traditions. The boys trained as warriors from a very young age. Parents and elders subjected the boys to "toughening" exercises and stressed that they must depend on their own wits and strength for survival. Obedience and teamwork were stressed, but a father would say to a *dikohe* (warrior in training), "My son, you know no one will help you in this world. You must do something. You run to that mountain and come back. That will make you strong. My son, you know no one is your friend, even your sister, father, mother. Your leg is your friend; your brain is your friend; your sight is your friend."[9] Even boys as young as ten or twelve were admonished: "You must have your arrows and your bow where you can grab them. You must have your knife right beside you. You must have your moccasins right beside you. Be on the alert in peace or in war. Don't spend all your time sleeping. Get up when the morning star comes out. Watch for the morning star. Don't let it get up before you do."[10]

When they had seen fourteen summers, the *dikohe* accompanied men on stock raids. On a raid, these "novices" did the drudgery of the camp, performing any task asked of them, from wood gathering to food preparation and horse care. They were required to use a special novice vocabulary of words reserved only for them, and to perform rituals that would ensure the success of the raid. Water was sipped only through a reed straw, which they carried with them along with a special stick to be used for scratching any itch. They could not risk touching blood, even their own, without jeopardizing the mission and the lives of their companions. During the first four raids, the boys were not to engage the enemy or directly capture stock, but they performed important support roles, holding horses or guarding supplies and enemy captives. They spoke as little as possible, made no noise, and learned much.[11]

By the time they were in their late teens, most Apache and Navajo youths could join a raiding party as a full-fledged member. They had become warriors, aspiring to return from a raid rich in horses, stock, captured goods, and perhaps even captives. The latter might be traded like livestock or turned over to families who had lost fathers or sons in combat. The captive then might be killed or adopted depending on the emotional state and need of the family who had suffered the loss. Though the Apaches and Navajos both feared displeasing the spirits of the dead—never speaking their names and burning the home and possessions of a dead family member or friend—they did take enemy scalps to pray and dance over. In taking a scalp, a warrior demonstrated his dominance over his foe, but great care had to be taken in the ritual handling of such a powerful and potentially dangerous talisman. If a raiding or war party suffered dead of its own, enemy scalps would be immediately discarded—there could be no celebration.

When the raid was successful, the scalp dance offered the band a rare social opportunity. Upon returning to the village, the warriors painted themselves as they had been in battle and reenacted their brave deeds in pantomime. As the people sang, the dancing men would brandish or fire their weapons whenever their names were called out by the singers. Bonfires lit the village during the nightlong celebration. Food was shared and captured goods were distributed, married women made much of their warrior husbands, and the strict prohibitions against contact between young unmarried men and women were temporarily relaxed. While the drumming and dancing continued, young people stood cloaked in blankets and whispered of love. It was a joyous time, and young men dreamed of being honored and feted at such events, which became powerful incentives for continued raiding.[12]

This warrior spirit fueled the culture of martial manhood that had long since become a way of life for the Apacheans of the borderlands. The Navajos fought their longtime Pueblo, Ute, Jicarilla, Mescalero, and Western Apache enemies, but they also stood guard against the bold incursions of the powerful Comanches and their allies, the Kiowas and Plains Apaches. Apache warriors raided deep into Mexico, whose people they despised, and against longtime enemies, Hispano and Indian, north of the border as well. The mines, ranches, unguarded herds in pasturage, and even well-populated settlements attracted young warriors in search of wealth and prestige. Their easiest targets were the corrals of the New Mexicans, Pueblo Indians, and O'odham farmers (Pimas and Papagos), and the Mexican villages of Chihuahua and Sonora, though increasingly the Anglo wagons loaded with supplies and trade goods traveling to Santa Fe and military forts and camps tempted the warriors.

As the war between the whites threw the borderlands into chaos in the 1860s, the Apacheans stepped up their raiding activities and the endemic warfare of the borderlands. When herders, freighters, or miners resisted or attempted pursuit of raiders, the encounters would inevitably turn deadly, and as soldiers responded to calls for help from citizens, Indian casualties mounted and retaliatory attacks increased. There developed a vicious cycle of raid, response, and reprisal. Among the Indian raiders, band members would be expected to avenge the death of a relative. The soldiers, too, recognized an unofficial code of honor requiring vengeance. The U.S. government, however, officially forbade soldiers and citizens from seeking "personal satisfaction or revenge," preferring that monetary restitution be made to aggrieved parties making formal claims of lost property. Property could be commodified, but the law made no compensation provisions for loss of life or pain and suffering. Faced with these conflicting ideologies and escalating violence, Carleton and the other army officers commanding troops in the territories believed that only swift retribution and, in some cases, extermination would stop the continuing raids and attacks.[13]

Whether the warriors were raiding for enemy property or waging war, Anglos and Hispanos expressed both wonder and terror at the phantomlike stealth of the Apaches. New Mexican *vaqueros* and herders believed that Apache raiding and war parties often deceived those tracking them by walking in the same moccasin tracks. It was said that fifty or even one hundred warriors traveling in this way could appear to be only a handful of men until an ambush in overwhelming strength revealed the truth to the unsuspecting pursuers. Though this perception may have exaggerated the stealth of the Apaches, the warriors did exhibit exceptional skills as raiders. They traveled as lightly as possible, living off the land and supplies captured from their enemies.[14]

Navajo and Apache stock raiders usually traveled on foot to ensure surprise.[15] A horse raiding party would set out with little more than heir weapons, water gourds, and pemmican or other dried food. They arried rawhide *reatas*, or horsehair ropes, with which to catch and bridle captured animals and, when necessary, to saw through the soft adobe of tall corral walls.[16] The Indian raiders' footsteps differed from those of their Anglo and Hispano adversaries. The white soldiers wore heavy leather brogans with built-up layers of hard leather on the heels. Sometimes the army shoe came equipped with iron heel plates or hobnails that allowed the wearer to walk with heavy loads by planting the heel first, even on rock-hard ground, while Indian men wore moccasins of uniform sole thickness. Mounted warriors preferred thin buckskin, but for walking moccasins they used thick buffalo or cattle hide. This sort of footgear allowed the wearer to walk more flat-footed, planting the ball of the foot first, causing footprints with toes pointing straight ahead or even slightly inward, "pigeon-toed." These tracks were easily discernible from those of the whites, whose heels always pressed deeper causing their toes to angle outward.[17]

Warriors determined to take enemy scalps in a war of revenge employed the same equipment, skills, and tactics used in successful raiding. When traveling mounted, they carried lances as well as bows. The Apaches and other indigenous peoples adapted a variety of weapons from metal scrap and weapons captured from or traded by whites. Arrow points were commonly fashioned from barrel hoop iron, and lance blades were made from broken knives, swords, and bayonets. As firearms became more readily available, these weapons either supplemented or replaced traditional arms.

By the 1860s, Chiricahua Apaches favored revolving pistols for close combat, but also carried a wide variety of indigenous and captured Anglo and Hispano arms. Ammunition resupply for firearms was a constant problem. Even when gunpowder could be secured or salvaged from captured cartridges of different calibers, finding the right-sized lead bullet presented real challenges. Some warriors scraped, hammered, and even chewed lead slugs to fit their firearms. Copper projectiles were sometimes pressed into service as well. Loading bullets that were too large or too small could jam or otherwise disable a gun and even result in explosions that might injure the shooter. At best, the mismatched ammunition would cause a gun to shoot wildly or inconsistently, reducing its effectiveness in either case. The inability to secure needed supplies of weapons and appropriate ammunition reflected the logistical disadvantage faced by the Apacheans when faced with sustained and concerted campaigning by the Anglos, Hispanos, and their Indian allies.[18]

The Navajos were the largest and most influential Indian nation inhabiting the mountainous southwestern territories in the 1860s. Raiding and killing had increased following a series of confrontations near Fort Defiance, located in the heart of Navajo country. Army posts were usually named for deserving officers or presidents, but here the name clearly reflected the adversarial approach the Anglo officers adopted in their relations with the Navajos. In 1858 Major William T. H. Brooks touched off vengeance warfare after he had Chief Manuelito's stock killed for grazing too close to the fort. One of Manuelito's men retaliated by shooting an arrow into Brooks's servant's back just a few feet from the officer's front door. Jim, an enslaved African American, died soon after, causing the infuriated Brooks to demand that Manuelito deliver up the killer. After much wrangling, the Navajos presented the body of the "killer," which turned out to be that of a captive New Mexican. Angered by the deception, the army officers prepared to press the issue by bringing Manuelito to justice.[19]

Neither side wanted to lose face. The young men in both camps seemed to be spoiling for a fight. Though they had the most to lose if it came to war, the wealthy Navajo headmen, including Manuelito, Barboncito, and Herrero, decided a bold show of strength might cause the Anglos to back down, and they determined to attack Fort Defiance itself. Ganado Mucho and other *na'taani* (band headmen) opposed this act of aggression and counseled restraint. Though the Navajo war faction invited other tribes—including traditional enemies among the Utes, Jicarilla Apaches, and Pueblos—to join them, few rallied to their cause.[20] Still there were warriors enough, and on April 30, 1860, nearly a thousand armed men stormed the fort. But the forewarned soldiers beat off the attack with artillery and musket fire. Many warriors were killed, and the rest retreated to their strongholds in the Chuska Mountains and mazelike canyon lands. Colonel Canby, then commanding in New Mexico, pursued them, but the Navajos eluded him in the many hiding places of Canyon de Chelly.

By 1861 Canby was making preparations for a campaign against the tribe in an effort to put a halt to the stock and slave raiding that he and most Anglo-Americans viewed as the principal obstacle to peaceful relations and prosperity in the territory. Canby proposed to the War Department that the Navajos be chastised and, once humbled, settled on a closely guarded reservation on their ancestral lands. This master plan was put on indefinite hold when the Civil War forced the withdrawal of U.S. troops. For the Pueblo Indians, Hispanos, and Anglos in New Mexico, the retreat of the soldiers could not have come at a worse time. Navajo raiders detected the weakness and exploited it in an unprecedented wave of stock raids along the Rio Grande settlements.[21]

The Navajos and Apaches excelled in the type of hit-and-run warfare that characterized the ramped-up raiding that followed the initial withdrawal of federal forces in the territories. Their war doctrine dictated that ambush and surprise was always to be preferred to an open encounter. Decoy traps that could lure an incautious enemy into a box canyon or hidden warriors offered the best chances for success at the least cost. Retreats rarely meant just running away; these were opportunities to regroup and counterattack when the enemy least suspected it. And the warriors would never head directly back to a base camp or *ranchería,* but would divide into smaller parties, covering the tracks that they did not want followed, and by circuitous routes find their way home undetected. The Anglos considered Apache caution and risk aversion as cowardly behavior. Apache stealth translated as "sneak attacks." Such tactics frustrated the military men who cried foul and demanded that their enemies offer them a "fair fight"—in broad daylight, face-to-face.[22]

In October 1862, under General Carleton's direction, Colonel Kit Carson launched a relentless campaign against the Mescalero Apaches and Navajos that eventually destroyed their ability to wage war and significantly diminished their fighting spirit—or at least their willingness to initiate raids and attacks. Carleton's campaign was no mere police action intended to put a stop to stock raids. The general gave Carson and other field commanders orders to kill all adult male Indians they encountered, if believed to be members of "hostile" tribes. No quarter would be given until chiefs or headmen sued for peace. Women and children would be spared if possible, but often the army turned these prisoners of war over to Hispano or Indian allies as slaves for their use or sale, along with other captured plunder. From Fort Stanton on the Rio Bonito, Fort Defiance in Arizona, and Fort Wingate in northwestern New Mexico, troops from California and New Mexico marched to strike the Indians. The general found in Kit Carson a man who not only expertly coordinated the efforts of the raw volunteer troops but also understood the ruthless brand of warfare thought to be required in order to subdue the raiding tribesmen. Carleton's orders were thorough and laced with menace:

> If the Indians send in a flag and desire to treat for peace, say to the bearer that when the people of New Mexico were attacked by the Texans, the Mescaleros broke their treaty of peace, and murdered innocent people, and ran off their stock; that now our hands are untied, and you have been sent to punish them for their treachery and their crimes; that you have no power to make peace; that you are there to kill them wherever you can find them; that if they beg for peace, their chiefs and twenty of their principal men must come to Santa Fe to have a talk here; but tell them fairly and frankly that you will keep after their people and slay them until you receive orders to desist from these headquarters; that this making of treaties for them to break whenever they have an interest in breaking them will not be done any more; . . . that we believe if we kill some of their men in fair, open war, they will be apt to remember that it will be better for them to remain at peace than to be at war.

Knowing that Carson might recoil from the harshness of the measures employed in bringing the Mescaleros to terms, Carleton explained that he believed "this severity, in the long run, will be the most humane course that could be pursued toward these Indians."[23]

Through the winter of 1862–63, Carson waged a war of attrition against first the Mescaleros of southern New Mexico, who soon sued for peace, and then the Navajos of northern Arizona and New Mexico, who had successfully defended their canyon land strongholds for two hundred years against attacks, in turn, by Spanish, Mexican, and regular U.S. soldiers. This new war was different. Now the Anglo and Hispano troops had the advantage of the War Department's vast logistical network, as broad as the continent itself, which provided them with food, clothing, weapons, and transportation. During the Civil War, the federal government fielded more soldiers in the borderlands than ever before, and these troops could launch their attacks at any time of year, even in the dead of winter when Indian ponies were low in flesh and the people subsisted on meager supplies of dried foods and lean mutton.

The tactics had changed too. The soldiers were not poorly trained local militia but U.S. volunteers, led by experienced regular officers and seasoned frontiersmen, who were not content to retaliate against raiders by stealing stray livestock and taking captives for slaves. These soldiers laid in wait for Apaches harvesting *maguey* (agave, known then as mescal), their dietary staple, and burned crops. The troops captured or killed entire herds and destroyed stored provisions, forcing the majority of the beleaguered bands to surrender.[24]

The Mescaleros gave up first. As if driving stock, Carson's men herded hundreds of dispirited Apache men, women and children to Fort Stanton. Some chiefs, including an elderly headman named Manuelito (Mescalero) and Jose Largo, agreed to come in and meet with Carleton and Carson. Before these Mescaleros could reach Santa Fe, they were intercepted by Paddy Graydon's freewheeling Spy Company. On October 12, 1862, while displaying a flag of truce on the pretense of peace negotiations, Graydon and his Hispano soldiers opened fire on the Apaches, killing eleven, including the two chiefs. Carson and Carleton both expressed extreme displeasure with this turn of events and made Graydon's men turn over the stock they captured and return the animals to the survivors of the massacre, who were then escorted to their new reservation on the Pecos.

It is likely that disciplinary action would have been severe for Graydon, but the situation spiraled out of control before any kind of military justice could be served. Dr. John M. Whitlock, a New Mexico Volunteer surgeon, openly criticized Graydon's conduct and the murder of the peace-seeking Mescaleros. The *Santa Fe Gazette* published Whitlock's remarks, and a duel ensued that left Graydon mortally wounded and the doctor, the apparent victor of the shootout, himself shot to pieces by Graydon's loyal troopers. Carson very nearly had the New Mexicans summarily executed on the spot, but cooler heads prevailed and the perpetrators were locked up—only to escape with the complicity of their jailers. Carson's men went after the doctor's killers—Hispanos and Anglos—who were eventually brought to justice.[25]

The Mescaleros may have surrendered, but many did not easily submit to confinement. Raiding parties, each composed of ten to thirty warriors, left Fort Stanton and swept through the Rio Grande settlements in search of cattle, as well as captives who could herd their stock in mountain hideaways. In February and March 1863, the warriors rounded up hundreds of cattle from the pastures surrounding the small villages near Socorro. In broad daylight they rode in and split into two groups—one to capture or kill the herders and the other to drive the stock toward the western mountains, away from forts and populated areas. In this attack, seven warriors rode down Francisco Baca and shot him to death with his own pistol then killed another herder and took thirteen-year-old Eulogio Sais captive. A hastily organized pursuit followed the raiders' trail. Sais deliberately dropped his shoes and distinctive black-handled knife along the trail to let would-be rescuers know which way he had been taken, but, in fact, the trail was not hard to follow. The warriors shot with arrows or lanced the cows and calves that could not keep pace with the fast-moving raiders and left the dying animals along the road. This tactic served two purposes: terrorizing the followers and denying them any hope of retrieving their abandoned stock—or the captive boy—alive. Julian Salazar remembered, "The road was strewn with the bodies of dead cows killed by the Indians. We saw before night that following the Indians was a dangerous and useless work." As night fell and without any sign of military relief, the rescue party gave up the chase, fearing to enter the canyons that offered the Mescaleros perfect ambush opportunities. The stolen cattle allowed some of the reservation holdouts to survive in the mountains for months and even years until starvation and relentless military pressure finally brought them in.[26]

The Navajos fared no better than the Mescaleros in the all-out campaign that left them no safe refuge and little choice but to capitulate to Carson. Carleton pitted likely allies against the Navajos, ordering Carson to take Zuni headmen hostage and warn the people that if they harbored Navajo raiders or held captured stock the soldiers would destroy the Zuni village "as sure as the sun shines." This punishment would be also be meted out if Carleton even suspected the Zunis of stealing stock from "white men, or injur[ing] the person of a white man."[27] With Ute guides in the lead, Carson's volunteer soldiers invaded the Navajo strongholds once thought to be impenetrable by troops. "The Utes," Carson said, "are very brave, and fine shots, fine trailers, and uncommonly energetic in the field." He believed that the Navajos' dread of their traditional enemies would make the Utes worth twice their number of white soldiers. In a closely coordinated campaign, Carson's columns closed off both the east and west portals to the Navajo canyon complex. The towering stone Fortress Rock in the heart of Canyon de Chelly offered only temporary refuge for the besieged Navajo clans of Barboncito and Manuelito. The soldiers even considered damming streams to shut off life-giving water while fields of corn and wheat burned and herds of horses, cattle, sheep, and goats were driven away. The troops discovered food caches, tore them open, and scattered the contents. So thorough was the destruction that even the pots and baskets were destroyed to prevent the Navajos from refilling them in preparation for the coming winter.[28]

By the time the first snow began to fall, the poorest of the Navajo people were beginning to starve. The army's adjutant general reported Carleton's campaign of "humane severity" to be an unqualified success. "The Navajos" he wrote, "soon found that they had no place of security from such determined adversaries, and being pressed on every hand by unexampled rigor, spirit of the tribe was soon broken." In contrast, the morale of Carson's men soared as their campaigning had the desired effect. They now sang as they rode: "Johnny Navajo, O Johnny Navajo. We'll first chastise, then civilize, bold Johnny Navajo!"[29]

Of the nearly fifteen thousand Navajo men, women, and children living in Arizona and New Mexico, nine thousand surrendered or were captured and placed on the newly established Bosque Redondo reservation on the Pecos River. Carleton instructed Carson to hold the *ricos* back and to send in the *pelados* (poorer class) of Navajos first. The stock-rich *ricos,* he reasoned, could subsist on their own sheep herds and were less inclined to fight while "among the poor are nearly or quite all the *ladrones* (thieves) and murderers, so that we have already in our hands the bad men of the tribe." There were some holdouts. Navajo chief Manuelito's band moved into unmapped Arizona, far to the northwest, but nearly all the other chiefs surrendered with their families, flocks, and herds.[30]

By the end of 1863 most of the Navajos had made the 250-mile "Long Walk" to Fort Sumner on the Pecos. During the forced march the people walked or rode twelve to fifteen miles a day with whatever belongings they could carry. The arduous trek took weeks, and many of the elderly and weak died along the trail. The Navajos knew this as the "fearing time" and the people feared nothing more than the hated *nacajalleses,* Pueblo and Hispano raiders who traded in Indian slaves and who now found the children and helpless women easy prey. Carson urged the commanders of the forts along to the route to provide the hungry travelers with "a sufficiency to eat," believing that "we must convince them of the kind intentions of the Government towards them, otherwise I fear that they will lose confidence in our promises, and desert."[31]

By 1864 the Mescaleros of New Mexico and most of the Navajos, including many of the holdouts in northeastern Arizona, had been defeated and relocated to the Pecos. In Santa Fe, Cadete, the Mescaleros' principal chief,[32] delivered a moving speech; in his characteristically "low, soft and rather musical" tone,[33] he directed at Carson and Carleton:

> You are stronger than we. We have fought you as long as we had rifles and powder but your weapons are better than ours. Give us like weapons and turn us loose; we will fight you again. But we are worn out; we have no more heart; we have no provisions, no means to live. Your troops are everywhere. Our springs and waterholes are either occupied or overlooked by your men. You have driven us from our last and best stronghold and we have no more heart.[34]

Carleton and Carson were feted as heroes by the Hispano and Pueblo peoples of New Mexico. The raiding Apachean tribes, it seemed, had finally been defeated and a new day of peace and security was dawning. Carleton accepted the accolades graciously and turned his considerable energy toward now winning a sustainable peace.

Carleton believed the Navajos and linguistically related Mescalero Apaches could and should be located on one reservation, Christianized, and trained to be full-time farmers. He little appreciated the enmity that existed between the tribes. The "hostile" Navajos and Mescaleros, he earnestly believed, once settled and acculturated, would never again pose a significant threat to one another or to settlements of agrarian Indians, Hispanos, and Anglos in Arizona and New Mexico.[35] But the tribes coexisted uneasily at Bosque Redondo, continually raiding each other's stock and joining the army in pursuit of renegades from the rival tribe. To make matters worse, Comanche raiders pressed ever closer to the Pecos. In large-scale dawn attacks, the warriors of the southern plains swooped in to drive off the remaining stock of their old Apachean enemies, who were now completely reliant on the army for protection. Without arms and under orders not to stray from the Bosque Redondo reservation, the Mescaleros and Navajos were virtually defenseless. The Comanches carried off women and children—for ransom, sale, or enslavement—along with the stock. The young men of the confined tribes felt impotent. When their frustration with the restrictive and sedentary life of the reservation reached a breaking point, they would bolt for the hills or ancestral hunting grounds, usually absconding with as many captured horses as they could drive.[36]

Pueblo Indians and Hispanos from the New Mexican settlements within a two hundred mile radius of the reservation accused the Bosque Redondo Indians of many "depredations." Cattlemen and government stock contractors cried foul as the young men of the interned tribes raided the herds of their neighbors. In many cases, the captured animals were sold to Comancheros or other unscrupulous traders and wound up back in Fort Sumner's pens and corrals, paid for with government gold or discounted greenbacks. Frustrated by these breakouts, Carleton instructed Captain Joseph Updegraff at Fort Sumner, "Should any of the men of those Mescaleros now at Bosque Redondo attempt to escape, after their promises to me to remain quietly there, you will cause them to be shot. If they give you much trouble in this respect, seize every animal they have and have all of them sent to Fort Union, and disarm all the men, even their bows and arrows." The commanding general even sent from his Santa Fe headquarters the men of Company B, Second California Cavalry—his personal body guard—to reinforce the soldiers at Sumner.[37]

In a precedent-setting move, Carleton ordered Captain John Cremony, Company B's commander, to hire Apache warriors at two dollars a day (four times the pay of Anglo and Hispano soldiers) to track and capture Navajo escapees. Cremony's men spent long days in the saddle, riding down Navajos, then turning around with Navajo guides in pursuit of Mescalero raiders who had bolted from the reservation. Carleton had learned from Carson that Indian auxiliaries "would render more service in this war than double their number of troops." The effectiveness of the Mescaleros against Navajos was not lost on the general, who reported to Washington that when Navajos left Bosque Redondo, the Apaches tracked down and killed twelve and captured one, along with nearly ten thousand sheep and other stock. He was forced to admit that "the Apaches who, one year ago, were our mortal enemies, did most all the work." The experiment with Indian scouts proved an unqualified success and would become, in later years, standard operating procedure in campaigns against indigenous peoples considered "hostile" or "renegade" by the government.[38]

Grumbling discontentment over affairs at the Bosque Redondo reservation found its way back to Carleton's Santa Fe headquarters and began to seep into his psyche. Behind his back, even once-admiring soldiers derisively referred to the dismal settlement on the sulfurous Pecos as "Fair Carletonia." Banishing ineffective Indian agents from the reservation and placing the loyal McCleave in command at Fort Sumner, Carleton hoped to stem the criticism and restore the confidence of the New Mexicans, who now read about Navajo "depredations" in nearly every issue of the influential *Santa Fe Gazette*. Carleton believed that harsh measures would be needed to convince the confined warriors that they must not leave the reservation, for any purpose, without a military pass. He ordered that McCleave shackle with a heavy iron ball and chain a Navajo man found off the reservation. The punishment would last for two months, during which time McCleave was to explain to the other Indians the reasons for the torture device and warn that future infractions would result in even more severe treatment.[39] At the same time, Carleton authorized a scorched earth policy for the center of the Navajo homeland in Canyon de Chelly. Captain John Thompson's First New Mexico Cavalry company destroyed corn crops and fruit orchards in the once impregnable stronghold in an effort to drive out the last of the holdouts and convince those already surrendered that there was nothing worth going home to.[40]

Manuelito defiantly refused to surrender his Navajo clans for internment at Bosque Redondo. In February 1865 Herrero and other Navajo chiefs were dispatched to Zuni and Fort Wingate in attempts to talk the holdouts into giving up, assuring their tribesmen that they would be well-treated and allowed to keep their stock and any other possessions they could carry. Though many of his followers begged him to give in, Manuelito told Herrero that he had committed no crimes and could never leave his native Chuska Mountains. Herrero parted saying, "I have done all I could for your benefit; have given you the best advice; I now leave you as if your grave were already made." Carleton's interpreters and officers assigned the task of bringing in the holdouts estimated that five additional bands still remained, from Colorado Chiquito, between Zuni and the Hopi villages, to Canyon de Chelly and Pueblo, Colorado. These small family groups—just over four hundred Navajo men, women, and children living on *piñon* nuts and roots—moved constantly, wary of attack by Utes, New Mexicans, and soldiers.[41]

Although Navajos and Apaches had slipped away from the reservation in small parties on stock raids, a major breakout led by Navajo headmen Barboncito and Ganado Blanco occurred on June 16, 1865, just as Senator James R. Doolittle's Special Joint Committee investigating the condition of the Indian tribes arrived in New Mexico. The committee members were especially interested in the Bosque Redondo experiment. Embarrassed by the situation, Carleton rallied all the support he could find, calling out every able-bodied man, "Mexicans and Americans," and diverting troops from every corner of the territory in order to stop the Navajo rush before it turned into a stampede. Within a week, Ganado Blanco and some of his followers were killed in a firefight while making a run for their ancestral homes in the Chuska Mountains. Pursuing cavalrymen rounded up the surviving renegades, with their stock and families, and returned them to Fort Sumner.[42]

Older headmen of both tribes used their influence to make the reservation economy work. Even Chief Cadete, the Mescaleros' most revered war leader, appeared resigned to his fate as a farmer. But the farming program was a disaster. Insect infestations, lack of water, and shortage of farming tools doomed the agricultural experiment. Waterborne and communicable diseases ranging from dysentery to smallpox killed hundreds and demoralized the rest of the internees. When government promises of clothing did not materialize, he requested that Carleton send his people looms with which they might make clothes to hide their nakedness. These woes, combined with the social tensions caused by being forced to live as neighbors with Navajo enemies while being guarded at gunpoint by soldiers, were too much to bear. For the adversarial tribes of Apacheans placed on the same reservation, the lure of the free life in the mountains or canyon lands was a powerful attraction.[43]

Lorenzo Labadie, the Hispano Indian agent to the Mescaleros, expressed his frustration over the fact that not all his wards had submitted themselves to the confinement of reservation life. Many New Mexican farmers and stock raisers living in the lower Rio Grande Valley complained of depredations committed by Mescalero bands that hovered near or had broken free from Bosque Redondo. Writing from his office at Fort Sumner, Labadie answered his critics, who believed he should exert more control over his charges. "Their nomadic style of life," he opined, "changing their camp almost every week, and wandering from place to place, is ill calculated to instill in them an idea of and love for home." Labadie could not have been more wrong, for it was home that the Mescaleros sought—their home in mountains and valleys that had sheltered them for generations and from which they derived strength.[44]

On the night of November 3, 1865, the disillusioned Cadete finally escaped the hated reservation, leading many of his people determined to hunt in the mountains and raid in the old ways. Some headed for Mexico in search of their Lipan Apache cousins while others joined their Comanche enemies on the Staked Plains. Cadete himself successfully eluded pursuers for five years, hunting and hiding out, though many of his followers were destitute and near starvation.[45] Before breaking out, the unreconstructed Cadete told Captain Cremony:

> You desire our children to learn from books, and say, that because you have done so, you are able to build all those big houses, and sail over the sea, and talk to each other at any distance, and do many wonderful things; now, let me tell you what we think. You begin when you are little to work hard, and work until you are men in order to begin fresh work. You say that you work hard in order to learn how to work well. After you get to be men, then you say, the labor of life commences; then too, you build big houses, big ships, big towns, and everything else in proportion. Then, after you have got them all, you die and leave them behind. Now, we call that slavery. You are slaves from the time you begin to talk until you die; but we are free as air. We never work, but the Mexicans and others work for us. Our wants are few and easily supplied. The river, the wood, and plain yield all that we require, and we will not be slaves; nor will we send our children to your schools, where they learn only to become like yourselves.[46]

Cadete understood the new order ushered in by the Americans only too well; the Anglos aimed to make Indian people dependent on rations of flour and beef, providing them with clothing and other annuities, and once reservationized, the people would no longer yearn for the free life.

Western Apaches, Chiricahuas, and Total War

To the west, other Apache tribes and bands dominated central Arizona and southern New Mexico, but their struggles to hold on to their home-lands and traditional ways while waging war against Indian enemies allied with Anglos and Hispanos proved nearly impossible during the turbulent 1860s. While many U.S. officials and military men thought of Apaches as a unified tribe, the various bands and local groups had their own leaders and operated quite independently, rarely cooperating for raiding or war. The Apache tribes included the Chiricahua bands—Bedonkohe, Chihenne, Chokonen, and Nednhi—centered in the Mimbres, Chiricahua, and Gila Mountains of southwestern New Mexico and southeastern Arizona but ranging for hundreds of miles southward into Mexico and in nearly every other direction as well.[47]

The Western Apaches to the north and west of the Chiricahuas included the Pinal, White Mountain, San Carlos, Cibecue, Tonto, Aravaipa, and other smaller bands, which occupied central New Mexico and Arizona from the Rio Grande to the Colorado. The westernmost Apacheans often interacted and intermarried with the Yuman-speaking Yavapais who hunted north of the Gila River and along the Salt River all the way to the Colorado,[48] where the western bands had close ties to the Yuman Mojaves, Hualapais, and Quechans. Even though they numbered in the thousands when taken as a whole, the independent and uncoordinated Western Apache tribes had little chance of successfully combating the coalition of allied warriors, soldiers, and civilians now assembled against them.

On July 1, 1852, the United States had entered into a treaty with chiefs or headmen representing Eastern and Western Apache tribes. Though the Anglos recognized the different tribes and bands as politically distinct, they chose for convenience to treat with all Apaches as a group and expected the chiefs and headmen to speak for their people, whether or not they actually had that authority. The treaty was formally approved by the Senate in March 1853, and in the minds of Anglo-Americans aware of such things, this sweeping agreement formally and permanently bound together the people of the United States and the "dependent domestic nation" known as Apache. The social contract proclaimed:

> Articles of a treaty made and entered into at Santa Fe, New Mexico, on the first day of July in the year of our Lord one thousand eight hundred and fifty-two, by and between Col. E.V. Sumner, U.S.A., commanding the 9th Department and in charge of the executive office of New Mexico, and acting superintendent of Indian affairs of said Territory, representing the United States, and Cuentas,

Azules, Blancito, Negrito, Capitan Simon, Capitan Vuelta, and Mangus Colorado, chiefs, acting on the part of the Apache Nation of Indians, situate and living within the limits of the United States.

[Article 1] Said nation or tribe of Indians through their authorized Chiefs aforesaid do hereby acknowledge and declare that they are lawfully and exclusively under the laws, jurisdiction, and government of the United States of America, and to its power and authority they do hereby submit.[49]

Though they little understood the larger political implications, when the Chiricahuas banished their Indian agent, renounced their allegiance to the United States, and declared war in 1861, they were engaged in an act of aggression tantamount to civil war. The Bascom affair had shed the first blood, but the subsequent withdrawal of federal troops from the borderlands had allowed the local conflict to erupt into full-blown civil war. The 1860s saw significant gold strikes along the lower Colorado River and in central Arizona, resulting in a flood of thousands of Anglo and Hispano miners from the East, California, and Mexico. These new arrivals nearly doubled the non-Indian population and contributed to a record number of deadly encounters with Apache people during 1863 and 1864.[50] Apache warriors raided and attacked Anglo and Hispano civilians, who, in turn, indiscriminately retaliated against Apaches and Yavapais, regardless of complicity. These attacks prompted Carleton to establish Fort Goodwin on the Gila River in the eastern part of Arizona Territory, and this outpost became the base of operations for an all-out campaign against the Western Apaches.[51] California Volunteer units stationed near the Mexican border at Tubac cooperated in the effort. From April to July 1864 the number of soldiers in Arizona increased from 233 to 1,076. Carleton's plans included a coordinated campaign against the Chiricahua bands. He ordered the troops to attack simultaneously from Fort Goodwin, Fort Whipple, Fort Bowie, Tubac, and Tucson, cooperating with soldiers from Fort McLane, Fort West, and other New Mexico garrisons along the Rio Grande.

In an unprecedented move to crush the warring Apaches once and for all, Carleton even requested the assistance of the pro-Juárez, Republican governors of Sonora and Chihuahua in an effort to cut off raiding and escape routes into Mexico. He received permission for "continuing the pursuit of hostile Apaches over the boundary line" and reciprocated the privilege by authorizing Mexican militia to "come over the line into our territory in pursuit of Apaches when, where, and as far as they please." Carleton requested that the Mexican forces stay "in hot pursuit of the Apaches of Sonora" for sixty to ninety days, until the warriors were "exterminated" or greatly "diminished." In this effort the U.S. troops found willing allies, for the people of the Mexican border states had suffered terribly from the escalation of raiding violence made possible by civil wars north and south of the international boundary.[52]

Mexicans took advantage of this opportunity to cross the border and retaliate against their Apache foes. In March 1864 Major Nelson H. Davis reported to Carleton that Governor Pesqueira "had a fight with the Apaches at Fronteras, Sonora, the other day, and killed 107 and took 6 prisoners; followed them within 40 miles of 'Apache Pass' (within our lines). This report comes by letter to a person here; it is generally believed true, except that the number killed may be too large; but Pesquiera [sic] has been trying to trap them there for some time." The Sonorans had pressed the attack almost to the gates of Fort Bowie, and Carleton knew the time was right for a concerted effort north of the border.[53]

He hounded his field commanders to make certain everything was in readiness for the all-out offensive against the Western Apaches. That spring, he rescinded his standing orders to conserve ammunition and ordered "systematic target practice to the extent of twenty rounds per man with musket and carbine and eighteen rounds with revolver" each day. For the first time, soldiers would be trained to fight as individuals, like their Indian adversaries, taking advantage of the broken desert and mountain terrain, instead of drilling on open ground in compact formations and firing volleys on command. Carleton believed that "the Apaches in Arizona are very hostile, and unless vigorous measures are pursued against them right away the miners will become panic-stricken and leave the country." He was convinced of the strategic importance of Arizona's gold mines and urged the War Department to send him another regiment of California infantry composed of "practical miners" who would at once exterminate the "hostile" Indians and develop the vast mineral wealth of the territories. Gold fever seems to have taken hold of the general, who authorized his soldiers to take time off to pan for the precious metal and carefully record the richness of their discoveries—information he enthusiastically shared with the War Department and promoted in the press.[54]

Yet even with the army's offensive, the Western Apache and related Yavapai bands of central Arizona and the southern bands along the Arizona–New Mexico border continued to attack the settlers and gold rushers flocking to the mines near Lynx Creek and the rich Walker diggings, as well as travelers on the southern overland road. The Apache bands who relied heavily on hunting, gathering, and raiding for survival found it increasingly difficult to find game and forage as the encroaching Hispanos and Anglos grazed their stock on hunting grounds and killed or frightened away wild animals. The allied invaders also attacked Indian *rancherías* without discriminating between warring and peaceful bands. Many of the newly elected Arizona territorial legislators (including some former army officers), as well as most of the citizens, were admitted exterminationists. They clamored for protection from the "savages."[35] Delegate Charles D. Poston's March 2, 1865, address to Congress urged the "extermination" or "subjugation" of the Apaches. "Their subjugation," he claimed, "would open to our hardy miners an unexplored gold field north of the Gila, which the Spaniards considered the true El Dorado. A sickly sympathy for a few beastly savages should not stand in the way of the development of our rich gold fields, or the protection of our enterprising frontiersmen."[36]

Yet as the three-year enlistments of many volunteer soldiers began to expire in late 1864, the military District of Arizona faced a critical manpower shortage. A company of New Mexico Volunteer Cavalry helped fill the vacant ranks of Fort Whipple's California garrison until reorganized companies of California Veteran Volunteers and the recently raised Arizona Volunteers, composed of Indians and Hispanos, arrived. The fact of the matter was Carleton and the subsequent commanders overseeing military affairs in Arizona simply did not have sufficient resources to protect the growing civilian population from the many bands of Western Apaches and Yavapais in central Arizona. Nor could they protect the Indians from vigilante-style reprisals and attacks by groups of armed citizens and their Indian allies. To make matters worse, Carleton was so eager to promote and develop the mineral resources of the territories that he made promises to mining entrepreneurs that he could not keep.

On July 11, 1864, he assured George Vickroy:

As to the safety of carrying on mining operations hereafter in Arizona, I will say I have already inaugurated a campaign against the Apache Indians that will result in their complete subjugation, and should you induce friends in the East to join you in erecting a quartz-mill in the newly discovered gold regions near Fort Whipple, the enterprise will be fully protected by the military. I am well assured that building a quartz-mill there, and developing some one of the rich mines, will result in such benefit to the Government as to amply compensate for the protection given.[57]

Vickroy did indeed find enough Philadelphia capitalists to bankroll the Walnut Grove Gold Mining Company and by September 1865 had reached Prescott with a twenty-stamp mill and a forty-horsepower steam engine along with thirty-five miners and mechanics. The subjugation of the Apaches, however, was not as complete as the miners had been led to believe.

With game increasingly scarce, small raiding parties of Apache warriors began picking off the mining company's mules, then the beef herds, and, growing increasingly bold, attacked the main operation at the Bully Bueno Mine, driving the men from their mill and shops. Time and again the miners called for help and for military escorts while transporting equipment and supplies, only to learn that the garrisons of soldiers were either already in the field or too understrength to be spared for guard detail at the mine. From 1865 to 1867, the Walnut Grove Company had eleven miners or herders killed and many more wounded. The surviving workers feared for their lives, and operations were repeatedly halted due to attacks that eventually led to a complete work stoppage resulting from insufficient manpower, food, and equipment. It soon became evident to the mining companies that Carleton had either deliberately overestimated or badly misjudged the reach and effectiveness of his far-flung command.[58]

The newly constituted Arizona legislature and the increasingly concerned citizenry agreed that something needed to be done to protect business interests. The legislators appropriated in the annual budget more funding ($250,000) for "Apache warfare" than for any other single purpose.[59] Nearly every Anglo and Hispano in the territory approved of arming native auxiliaries to augment the U.S. troops. The Pimas, Maricopas, and Papagos had repeatedly requested arms and ammunition to combat their long-standing Yavapai and Western Apache enemies. Legislators and citizens shared the opinion that the "friendly" tribes would perform well if given the opportunity. Every commander of the military District of Arizona endorsed the idea, as did a majority of rank-and-file soldiers. Army red tape, however, bogged down the implementation of the plan for nearly four years. Finally, between September and November 1865, long after the Civil War in the East had ended, the territorial legislature recruited five companies of Arizona Volunteers.

This battalion of 350 men comprised one company each of Pimas, Maricopas, and Papagos, and two of Hispanos. The army recruited many Mexican men in Bacuachi, Sonora, and other villages south of the border ravaged by incessant Apache raids. Recruiters found other willing Hispanos at the mines near Tubac in southern Arizona and around Prescott in the central part of the territory. In practice, most of the companies were mixed with Indians, Hispanos, and a few Anglos. White officers, some of whom had until recently served as enlisted men in the ranks of the California Volunteers, commanded the companies, but Hispanos, Pimas, and Maricopas were included among the junior commissioned officers and non-coms.[60]

With only one-year terms of enlistment, the Arizona Volunteers' orders were simple: scout central Arizona and kill Apaches. On several occasions they cooperated successfully with the few California companies still in the field. The native troops exceeded all expectations, and when their enlistments expired on November 7, 1866, the territorial legislature and the military district commander, Colonel Clarence E. Bennett, extolled their value and urged the War Department to extend their service. Bennett even suggested that the allied warriors be allowed to keep their weapons if orders came to disband. These native Arizonans, he reasoned, were highly motivated to kill their Apache enemies and carry on the war for their homes and farms, even without government assistance. But by this time, federal authorities focused their energies on demobilizing the tremendous war machine created during the rebellion and ignored pleas from Arizona for enlistment extensions and new regiments.[61]

Chiricahua Apaches

During the Civil War years, the united Chiricahua bands (Bedonkohe, Chokonen, Chihenne, and Nednhi) of southeastern Arizona and western New Mexico challenged the Anglo soldiers and their Hispano and Indian allies for power and dominance in the borderlands. These resilient people, living and fighting in small groups, continued their attacks along the main east-west road connecting Tucson and Mesilla and raided deep into Chihuahua and Sonora despite the army's best efforts to contain them. The resistance of the Bedonkohe and Chihenne bands of Chiricahuas (known as Mimbreños and Gileños to the Anglos and Hispanos because of their proximity to the Mimbres and Gila Rivers) abated only temporarily in Arizona after the capture of their charismatic chief and war leader, Mangas Coloradas, in January 1863. California Volunteer Cavalrymen cooperating with miners deceived the chief and then took him prisoner while negotiating under a flag of truce at the mining settlement of Pinos Altos near Fort West, New Mexico. The incident would prove to be another milestone on the path of bad relations between the Apaches and the Anglos.

Mangas had suffered a serious gunshot wound during the Battle of Apache Pass on July 15, 1862. While attempting to encircle Captain Thomas Roberts's California infantry company, the chief was hit by a bullet fired from the carbine of Private John Teal, one of six cavalry escorts sent back to Dragoon Springs for reinforcements.[62] Mangas survived the wound thanks to good treatment by a Mexican doctor in Janos, Chihuahua, who, under duress, tended the Bedonkohe leader. Unrelenting reprisal raids by Mangas's warriors made him the most feared Apache in the borderlands. On January 17, 1863, Jack Swilling, the former Confederate Arizona Guard now traveling with a party of gold prospectors while also working in concert with Captain E. D. Shirland's Company C, First California Cavalry, captured the Apache leader at Pinos Altos. Swilling hustled his prisoner off to nearby Fort McLane some twenty miles south.

Here, General J. R. West confronted Mangas with charges of murder and theft. The general specifically referenced the "bleached bones" of travelers that littered Cooke's Canyon on the wagon road. Mangas maintained that he had only fought in self-defense against whites who attacked his people while in search of "yellow iron."[63] The details of the chief's death will never be known with certainty, but most accounts agree that West made it known to his men that he wanted Mangas dead. The soldier guards tormented their captive with heated bayonets, and when he tried to make a run for his life, they shot him down with their rifle muskets and then fired their pistols into his head and chest as he lay dying. An imposing figure in life, standing well over six feet tall, Mangas's bullet-riddled body became a thing of curiosity to the Californians who, with the help of surgeon David B. Sturgeon, decapitated the corpse, boiled the head, and later shipped the defleshed skull to New York to be interpreted by Orson Squire Fowler, a prominent phrenologist. Other army units followed this murder with attacks on Mangas's Bedonkohe people near Pinos Altos. The Apaches, led by Victorio, Nana, and perhaps a young Geronimo responded with revenge raids of unrivaled boldness and ferocity.[64]

Twenty miles west, Anglo soldiers had strategically located Fort Bowie in Apache Pass, situated in the heart of Cochise's Chiricahua country. The pass, midway between Tucson and Mesilla, and the springs there offered the only reliable, year-round fresh water for miles in any direction. "Around this water," Carleton reported, "the Indians have been in the habit of lying in ambush, and shooting the troops and travelers as they come to drink." Since 1861 civilians and soldiers, Union and Confederate, had suffered ambush and death here at the hands of Mangas's and Cochise's warriors. Placing a fort in the middle of this trouble spot only made sense if there were enough troops to hold the place; but the garrison assigned could rarely muster sufficient strength to take the offensive against the Apaches. Protecting the fort's own livestock while attempting to safeguard overland travelers fully occupied the volunteer troops stationed there. In April 1863 a war party of nearly two hundred Apaches attacked the Fifth California Infantry company detailed to guard the pass. Outnumbered more than two to one, the soldiers managed to beat off the determined warriors after a two-hour fight.[65]

Meanwhile, General West continued to focus his intelligence-gathering efforts on Texas and Chihuahua, fully believing that the Confederates were stockpiling supplies at Fort Davis in preparation for another thrust up the Rio Grande. Though he understood the pressure New Mexico's Hispano leaders were applying on the military governor to stop Navajo and Apache livestock thefts and killings, West disagreed with Carleton's shift of focus toward containing the "hostile" tribesmen. From his Las Cruces headquarters West wrote on May 15, 1863, "The Indians will keep. The Texans are our immediate foes. To punish the Indians will contribute nothing toward suppressing the rebellion. That is the object of this war." He seemed obsessed with the Confederate threat and oblivious to the civil war raging all around him between Indian, Hispano, and Anglo peoples. But when the rebel offensive failed to materialize that summer, and the Chiricahua depredations that he himself had instigated with the killing of Mangas continued to take their toll on expressmen, outposts, and settlements, West finally began to change his tune.[66]

On June 21, 1863, General West authorized Major McCleave to hunt down the Chiricahua Apaches on the Mimbres River (Bedonkohe and Chihenne bands) who sought to avenge Mangas. Earlier that week about fifty warriors had killed the expressman from Fort Craig and destroyed all the mail and military dispatches he carried. At the same time the Bedonkohe men had also attacked a small party of New Mexico Volunteers on the Jornada del Muerto, east of the Rio Grande, and succeeded in killing the unit's popular commander, Lieutenant Ludam Bargie, mutilating his body and carrying off his head. It is likely that the warriors soon discarded the severed head as the Apache men would not have wanted to touch the grisly trophy for fear of the bad spirit and death it might bring to them.[67] The infuriated West ordered:

> This band of Mimbres River Indians must be exterminated to a man. At the earliest possible moment that the condition of your command will admit of it you will undertake this duty. Use every available man of your force; take rations sufficient for a campaign against them if necessary. Scour every foot of ground and beat up all their haunts. Do not hesitate to go yourself in person to conduct the affair, should you deem that your presence will contribute to the desired result.

The general promised whatever support he could offer in order to end the Mangas avengers' attacks and reopen the threatened interpost express routes.[68]

By May 1864 Carleton openly advocated civil war in the Southwest Borderlands, calling for a "general uprising" of Anglo, Hispano, and Indian people against the Apaches. The daunting size of the challenge soon sank in, however, and he came to believe that even if all the troops at his disposal in the territories actively campaigned, their efforts would be insufficient to subdue the elusive Apache bands. Now he advocated total war. Carleton called on Arizona's Governor Goodwin to get "every citizen of the Territory who has a rifle to take to the field," and encouraged armed bands of self-professed "Apache hunters," like King Woolsey, to step up their activities so that when "hostile" Indians attempted to escape, one group would inevitably run into another. If government-armed Papagos, Pimas, and Maricopas pushed from the west and Mexican allies in Sonora and Chihuahua pressured the Apache raiders from the south—even crossing the border if necessary—there would be no escape. This "general rising of both citizens and soldiers, on both sides of the line," Carleton explained, was the only way to quell the Apache uprising that threatened to destabilize the region.[69]

Carleton assured and admonished Goodwin: "You may count on my doing all that can be done to clear your Territory of the terrible savages; but it will take hard work and persistent work. Every man who has the development and prosperity of Arizona at heart must put his shoulder not only to the wheel, but to the rifle."[70] The people of Arizona did eventually respond to the call for an all-out war against the Apaches. The territorial legislature authorized a "war loan" that would support raising up to six companies of rangers composed of one hundred men each. These irregular units were to be compensated based of the success of their forays against the "savages." The people of New Mexico applauded the energetic efforts of their neighbor territory in eradicating the Apaches once and for all. Hoping to arm the New Mexican citizenry, the army offered to sell the people more than two thousand surplus muskets stored at Fort Union. Few citizens in the Southwest territories, however, were willing to buy arms and leave their homes, businesses, farms, ranches, or lucrative claims to devote their energies to killing Indians. Only a small number of unattached young men joined the Apache-fighting expeditions led by King Woolsey, who, conveniently, also served as the official "commissioner" delegated to oversee disbursements of Arizona's "Indian war fund."[71]

Violence Escalates: Martial Cultures and War to the Knife

Midway through their three-year enlistments, the Anglo soldiers who had so confidently marched into Arizona ready to do battle came to despise their Apache adversaries. "I abhor the idea of fighting Indians," wrote one volunteer. "Let me fight an enemy that is worthy of my steel." Fantastic rumors of terrible tortures, perpetrated by a "cowardly and inhuman" foe, circulated in the ranks. Captive children, it was said, had been found nailed to spiny cacti, and Apache warriors ornamented their bridles not only with the scalps of slain soldiers but with their severed mustachioed lips as well. Any lingering sympathy for "Lo, the poor Indian"[72] soon evaporated, and the soldiers set themselves to the task of extermination with hard hearts and grim determination. California and New Mexico newspapers printed soldiers' letters, many containing biased reports and wild rumors, fueling the growing race hatred and exterminationist sentiment directed toward Indians in the territories.[73]

During the Civil War years, officers in Arizona and New Mexico reported killing hundreds of "hostile" Indians, including men, women, and children, far more than at any other period in history. The Anglo soldiers from California reported losing nearly fifty officers and men in battles, skirmishes, or ambushes while traveling singly or in small parties. The Hispano New Mexico Volunteers suffered similar casualties. Carleton knew his soldiers to be better armed than his native enemies, and he placed his trust in "the gallantry of small parties against any number [of Indians]. Large parties move snail-like, are seen at once, and are avoided; generally are laughed at by these Apaches. Small parties move secretly, cover more ground, move with celerity, emulate to do better than all others, and in the end either destroy or worry the Indians into submission."[74]

In reality, the Anglo soldiers rarely matched their Indian adversaries in single combat, relying instead on superior firepower and well-coordinated assaults that often targeted not just warriors but entire villages. Apache men boasted that one of their own boys of fourteen was the equal of a soldier.[75] Inured from youth to hardship and privation, the warriors believed they drew strength and power from the very land. They knew well the welcoming desert environment that had been their home for generations and where the spirits of their ancestors still resided. Its game, flora, and water gave them life.[76] To the Anglo soldiers, this same desert landscape harbored death. Foreign and barren, it seemed devoid of water and comfort. The sun drove men mad and could kill those not prepared for its relentless power. Still, the soldiers believed themselves, man for man, better fighters than Apache warriors. One volunteer wrote, "The superiority of the Californians over the Apaches at their own style of fighting, was shown in the case of Corporal [Charles] Ellis of Company A [First Cavalry], who crawled to a rock behind which was an Indian, and, giving a short cough, the Indian raised his head to discover his course, when a bullet from Ellis's rifle dashed through his brain." The Apaches present at this fight remembered the warrior the soldiers shot in the head at long range but also recalled that the Apache men had killed three soldiers in close combat and captured and released one white man, whom they determined to be a holy man when he got down on his knees, begged for mercy, and "prayed to the sun." The warriors did not rejoice in their victory and threw away the one scalp they had taken after they discovered the body of their dead companion behind the rock.[77]

The soldiers relied heavily on their state-of-the-art small arms, including long-range rifle muskets, breech-loading carbines, and mul-tishot revolving pistols, as well as mountain artillery, to successfully contend with the frequently numerically superior Apaches. When an army officer later questioned an Apache war leader about the Battle of Apache Pass, where nearly two hundred Chiricahuas surrounded a California Volunteer command in July 1862, he replied that the Indians would have won the battle if the soldiers had not "fired wagons at us."[78] The wagons were, in fact, 12-pounder mountain howitzers that could blast scattershot canister loads at close range and throw exploding shells and spherical case shot up to one thousand yards. These weapons inflicted some casualties, but the psychological effect of the artillery had an even greater impact.[79]

The Anglos' technological advantages included rolling stock, which ensured essential logistical support—the key to success in desert war-fare—and made extended campaigning possible. With wheeled vehicles, the troops could travel longer distances, field larger bodies of fighting men, and maintain offensive operations for long periods of time in all seasons and conditions. Freight wagons, filled with ammunition and provisions, and rolling water wagons enabled the California Column to march nearly one thousand miles to the Rio Grande, fighting rebels and Indians as they went. The military supply chain allowed soldiers and civilians in the territories to establish towns, forts, and camps that supported bases from which attacks could be launched. Combined with alliances forged with Indians and Hispanos that concentrated forces for coordinated attacks, logistics gave the Anglo military its greatest advantage.[80]

The soldiers' technological superiority was no guarantee of success. In many instances desert conditions conspired to render arms and equip-ment useless. Desiccated soles of army shoes came apart when their shrunken wooden pegs fell out. Sand worked its way into dried felloes and spokes of the wagon wheels, and they, too, broke down. Rawhided saddles, wetted with sweat or rain, dried too quickly in the sun and split open, injuring horses and riders. During hard campaigning, fragile paper cartridges issued for cavalry carbines broke open in their leather boxes on the men's belts, spilling the powder. Even the mountain howitzers, which on several occasions gave the soldiers the edge in battle, were rendered ineffective after their oak carriages cracked under the strain of firing at extreme range and elevation.[81]

Captain T. T. Tidball's expedition against the Aravaipa Apaches in southern Arizona epitomized the type of warfare waged by the U.S. Army against bands within the territory. Tidball's command consisted of 25 picked men from Companies I and K of the Fifth California Infantry, 10 "American citizens," 32 "Mexicans," 20 Papagos from San Xavier, and 9 "tame Apaches [*mansos*] . . . as spies and guides." While the soldiers saw to their weapons and pack mules, the Hispanos and Apaches *mansos* celebrated mass at their respective churches in preparation for the attack. The allies left Tucson for the "Cajon de Arivaypa" in May 1863 to "chastise" Aravaipas accused of stock raiding. "All grown males are fair game," wrote the Tucson garrison commander, Colonel David Fergusson, "the women and children capture and bring here."[82] The troops headed northwest, marching only at night, in silence, and did not light a fire for five days. Tidball's caution enabled his command to completely surprise Eskiminzin's Aravaipa village of men, women, and children. The savage attack cut down more than fifty people and wounded as many more. Tidball lost control of his auxiliaries who indiscriminately killed men and women, including the wounded. Only the captain's personal intercession prevented a complete massacre. When the bloody affair was over, the soldiers, with sixty-nine head of captured stock, escorted only ten surviving women and children prisoners back to Tucson to become slaves in the homes of well-off Hispanos.[83]

Thomas C. McClelland, an Anglo civilian, was the only man attached to Tidball's command who was killed in the raid. A machinist from Pittsburgh seeking western adventure and working at Colonel Colt's silver mine south of Tucson, the twenty-three-year-old had written home to his mother, "I do not believe I was born to be shot by an Indian." McClelland volunteered to accompany the Aravaipa expedition several months after sharing his warrior wisdom in a letter to his brother serving in the Army of the Potomac, "I tell you in an Indian fight a man has to be lively and not give the enemy time to surround or come up on you." His prophetic warning came true when a wounded Apache man, playing dead, shot the mounted McClelland through the heart as he boldly rode by. Some of his overconfidence may have resulted from a false sense of security provided by the state-of-the-art, five-shot Colt revolving rifle he carried that day, and lost to the Aravaipa warrior.[84]

Colonel Fergusson praised the one-sided fight as a "brilliant little affair," regarding it as "something for emulation to others in future campaigns against Apaches." Carleton encouraged rivalry between field commanders and did indeed urge his subordinates to emulate the "zeal, energy, and gallantry" of Tidball's soldiers and civilians in order to even the score that had not been settled for the tortured death of the California cavalrymen in Apache Pass and the killing of Sergeant Wheeling and the courier Chavez the year before. Of course, the Aravaipas had nothing to do with these killings carried out by Chiricahuas under Cochise and Mangas Coloradas.[85]

In March 1864 Chiricahua raiders ran off with a herd of government mules corralled at Cow Springs, near the Arizona–New Mexico border. Captain James H. Whitlock's Company F, Fifth California Infantry, set out in pursuit with a mixed command of cavalry and foot soldiers, but the captain deliberately held his men back, allowing the raiders to get a good lead. When the Chiricahuas thought they had eluded the soldiers, they no longer attempted to mask their trail, which headed straight to a large village in the Sierra Bonita Mountains thirty-five miles northwest of Fort Bowie.

Breaking free of his pack animals, Whitlock struck out with a fast-moving force. To reduce the chance of reflected sunlight betraying his movements, he ordered his men to blacken the brightly burnished steel barrels of their rifle muskets. He allowed no fires for cooking or warmth and made his men hide out as much as possible during the day. Then he tracked the Chiricahuas by moonlight and attacked their sleeping camp at daybreak on April 7. Although outnumbered, the California soldiers killed twenty-one warriors, recaptured the stolen stock, and completely destroyed the Apaches' food supplies and camp equipage—all without loss to Whitlock's command. On the march home the soldiers tested the extreme range of their rifle muskets, and their sharpshooting kept the Apache warriors from getting closer than eight hundred yards from the column or camp. Carleton congratulated Colonel Bowie and Whitlock—and lost no time bragging about this rare victory in dispatches to the high command in Washington. "A dozen or two of pursuits like Captain Whitlock's," Carleton crowed, "would give our troops the *morale* over these Ishmaelites of our deserts."[86]

The Anglo and Hispano soldiers cooperated with civilian volunteers in hunting down Western Apache bands in the Pinal and White Mountains of the upper Gila country. Carleton's edict not to treat with Indians and to kill Apache men on sight led to tragic results in the total war climate that gripped the borderlands in the summer of 1864. In June, Major Thomas Blakeney's command of New Mexico and California Volunteers and a ranger company of Anglo citizens under King Woolsey set out north from Forts Bowie and Goodwin while Captain Julius Shaw's company of New Mexico cavalry departed Fort Wingate by way of the pueblo of Zuni and headed south. With mules packed with supplies sufficient for a sixty-day expedition into the heart of Apache country the columns moved out. Nearly everything that could go wrong did, beginning with some of Shaw's supply mules running away and falling over a cliff. The Apaches took Shaw's New Mexican soldiers for Hispano traders and even signaled for a parley in order to barter for powder, lead, and blankets. Shaw was incensed that the Zunis—who regularly traded with all sides from their neutral pueblo between Apachería, Navajo land, and the New Mexico settlements—had warned the Apaches of the coming expedition. Shaw reported to headquarters that the chances for successful negotiations had been nil from the start because the Zunis had panicked the Apaches by telling them, "After the Navajos had surrendered we had killed all the men, and left none alive but the women and children, of whom we made slaves."[87]

Though his men blackened their musket barrels and took other precautions to ensure stealth, Blakeney's column moved ponderously and took no one by surprise. Several Apaches, believing themselves to be under the protection of white flags, were captured by Blakeney's men. When a captive exchange did not occur, the major summarily hanged his prisoners, ending any hope of future negotiations and large-scale surrender as Carson had managed with the Mescaleros. The Gila Apaches would now fight until the last. At water holes, Blakeney's men endured the taunts of the warriors, who hurled epithets and stones with equal skill from positions of safety on the rocky ridges high above the soldiers. The troops contented themselves with long-range shooting and the destruction of more than 250 acres of Apache corn and wheat crops. Though he rarely got close to the warriors, Blakeney estimated that nearly half were armed with firearms—rifles or pistols—and most carried lances, bows, and "slung shots."[88]

The heaviest casualties inflicted during the expedition may have occurred after Blakeney received orders to return to Fort Goodwin to muster out some of the California troops whose enlistment terms had expired. Employing a ruse that Colonel Rigg had earlier taught him, the major hid twenty-four Hispano and Anglo soldiers and three of Woolsey's men in his apparently abandoned camp while making a show of pulling out with the rest of the command. When fifteen Apache men, intending to search the deserted camp for food and valuables, approached to within thirty yards, the soldiers and miners sprang the trap, killing or wounding five or more of the warriors. Altogether, the columns that converged in the Gila wilderness killed about twenty of their enemies, likely wounding as many more. The disruption of the *rancherías,* once thought safe from attack by outsiders, was even more devastating to the Apache families who now experienced firsthand the new brand of war-making introduced by the Anglos in the borderlands.[89]

In the civil wars that raged in the territories, Anglos, Hispanos, and Indians perpetrated atrocities without regard for sex, age, guilt, or innocence. Between 1864 and 1867, the war with the Apaches devolved into a blood feud in which noncombatants on all sides suffered the most. In June 1865 Captain Martin H. Calderwood had been in Arizona for only a month when his company of the Seventh California Infantry responded to a call for help from Rafael Saavedra's "Spanish Ranch" near Tubac. Calderwood described in grim detail the aftermath of the Chiricahua attack:

> Here I beheld one of the most sickening and cruel sights I ever witnessed during the whole of my campaign against the Apaches. The Indians had stripped naked the four women they had captured and after disemboweling them while still alive, had on the first sight of our approach lanced them through the heart. One of the lance heads had been pulled from its shaft and still remained in the woman's body. I pulled the lance from the woman and the still warm blood flowed from it. The two small children were lying dead near a mesquite log. The savages had taken them by

the feet and smashed their heads to a pulpy mass on the log which was besmeared with their blood and brains. Saavedra, who was as brave a man as ever lived and who was esteemed by all who knew him, had purportedly been shot through his kidneys with an arrow; we found him alive but in awful agony. He lived for two days and then died.[90]

The Anglo soldiers became hardened to the realities of war in the borderlands and soon matched the Hispano and Anglo citizens in their calls for revenge and extermination of the Apaches. In 1864 Colonel Oscar M. Brown wrote a poem that the men of his First California Cavalry soon adopted as their marching song:

> We'll whip the Apache
> We'll exterminate the race
> Of thieves and assassins
> Who the human form disgrace
> We'll travel over mountain
> And through the valley deep,
> We'll travel without eating,
> We'll travel without sleep.[91]

The most effective military forays against the Apaches were led by Merejildo Grijalva, a Mexican former captive of Cochise's Chiricahuas (Chokonens). In 1859 Grijalva had escaped ten years of captivity and soon became an interpreter and scout for the American soldiers determined to search out and destroy Apaches. In November 1865 Grijalva tracked Cochise's band by moonlight leading Major James Gorman's command of the First California Cavalry and several New Mexico Volunteer infantrymen from Fort Bowie to a *ranchería* hidden deep in the Chiricahua Mountains. The soldiers attacked "at the peep of day," and the surprise was complete. The Apaches lost seven killed and many more wounded. Cochise's people also lost weapons, camp equipage, clothing, and their entire winter supply of mescal (roasted agave), dried meat, and other food.[92]

Carleton's far-reaching Apache campaign was one of the largest and most sustained ever mounted in the territories, including the decades just before and after the Civil War, yet many citizens—Anglo and Hispano miners, freighters, farmers, and ranchers—complained that it was not enough.[93] Repeated military scouts, they contended, seemed only to antagonize the Indians, prompting bloody reprisals. In fact, only one in four expeditions resulted in any significant damage to the wary and very mobile Apache bands deemed hostile by the government. The soldiers measured their success in pounds of destroyed mescal, the essential food of the Western Apaches; the number of weapons and animals captured; and, of course, body counts.[94]

Some of the formally educated men among the California Volunteers recorded and attempted to preserve knowledge of Arizona's rapidly vanishing Indian cultures and artifacts. It is sadly ironic that the same troops who were engaged in vicious and relentless combat with the indigenous peoples also took the time and had the interest to study and carefully preserve evidence of their cultures. Some enlisted men kept daily journals and recorded detailed accounts of prehistoric sites, early Spanish *visitas*, churches, and landmarks. Many described Indian artifacts, noting with wonder the variety of polychrome shards found near Casa Grande and other ancient ruins. Private Thomas Keam became fascinated with the Navajo culture. He learned the language, married a member of that tribe, and lived near Fort Defiance where he collected ceramics and other objects, which he shipped to educational institutions in the East, including Harvard's venerable Peabody Museum.[95]

Raiding, Revenge, and War

During the war years, Apache warriors killed more Anglos, Hispanos, and enemy Indians than any other tribe, but the warriors of the powerful Navajo nation accounted for the largest number of raids and proportionately greater property loss. The *jinetes* (stock raiders) emerged from their canyon strongholds in well-organized parties and targeted the livestock of New Mexico's Hispano and Pueblo Indian herders, whose losses approached one million animals during the 1860s. Because of their scale and frequency, the Navajo attacks had even greater economic impact than those waged by Apache bands, but the Navajo stock raids resulted in significantly fewer deaths.[96]

Apache warriors were far more likely to engage in raids and reprisals that resulted in enemy casualties. They attacked Hispano herders, Anglo miners and freighters, and even well-armed military patrols and expeditions in Arizona and western New Mexico. The attacks peaked during the years 1862–64, corresponding with the Anglo military power vacuum followed by the period of increased military campaigning, and resulted in hundreds of casualties—killed, wounded, and captured.[97]

Apache bands responded to increased army patrols that resulted in the deaths of tribal members with avenging war parties of their own. All the Apache tribes recognized two fundamentally different kinds of warfare: the raid and the war of revenge.[98] Raiding was essentially an extension of the hunting and foraging tradition and required the same degree of stealth and skill with weapons. The avowed purpose of a raid was to bring home food for the family and band. War, on the other hand, involved a vengeance motive. It was localized and very personal. An Apache man would be expected to avenge the death of a family member when a widow or female relative approached him and implored him to mount a war party. Duty and honor bound, the men made their holy preparations with the help of spiritual leaders and elders and engaged in a war dance pre-enacting the deeds of revenge and bravery they planned to perform. The Apache word for this type of war translates literally as "to take death from the enemy." Vengeance attacks targeted people—either those responsible for the death of a family member or the same type of people (e.g., Pima, white man, Mexican, etc.). If successful, the men of the war party would present the aggrieved widow or female relatives with property—horses, clothing, weapons, food, tools—and scalps or captive men to be ritually slain by the women. Captive children, especially boys, might be adopted by a family to replace relatives lost to the enemy. In this way, *gegodza* (payback) might be achieved.[99]

Even in vengeance warfare, a secondary motive involved the capture of enemy property. During the preparatory war dance, before the war party departed, the men would attempt to gain as much "power" as possible. They smoked a pipe to the four cardinal directions and intoned a prayer: "May I kill an enemy. May I get food."[100] The warriors prayed to *Yusn*, the Great Spirit, and relied on spiritual helpers found in nature and preparations prescribed by holy men. Special shields, war paint, headgear, medicine pouches, and prayers would increase the chances for success. The men of a war party would speak a code-like sacred language reserved only for this purpose, and back at the band's camp the women would perform their daily chores as prescribed by holy men and ancient custom (e.g., stacking the firewood in neat rows, avoiding contact with men other than their husbands, not scratching their heads with their fingers) to ensure their men would return victoriously and with needed supplies.[101]

Hispanos also recognized a difference between raiding and war. A raid against Indians for the purpose of capturing livestock and people— usually women and children—who could be sold as property or kept as servants (*criadas*) was different than an attack intended to exact a measure of blood for blood spilled by the enemy. The Tidball expedition, cocaptained by Jesús Maria Elías and his Hispano company from Tucson, set out to exterminate the Aravaipa Apaches believed to have perpetrated murders and thefts. Months earlier, Elías's brother Ramón was killed by Aravaipas while attempting to recover stolen stock. He put up a good fight, evidently using his rifle so effectively that he killed one or more of the Apache raiders. When Ramón's attackers finally rushed his rocky position, the warriors used the stones to smash his hands to pulp, making certain that he would not be so formidable an enemy in the afterlife. He was the second of the Elías brothers to be killed by Apaches, and Jesús Maria vowed vengeance. With the support of Tidball's men, the attack by the allied Hispanos and Indians quickly turned into a killing frenzy in which Apache men, women, and children died without mercy.[102]

Hispano warriors were more likely to take scalps (*piezas*) as evidence of their kills than were Apaches or Anglos. As raids around Tucson increased, citizens took up a collection to offer one hundred dollar bounties for Apache scalps.[103] For nearly a century the governors of Sonora and Chihuahua had paid cash bounties for Indian scalps as positive proof of enemies killed. This practice spawned independent bands of mercenary scalp hunters who preyed on Apache and other borderlands tribes. Spanish and, later, Mexican soldiers and civilians also took ears and hands as irrefutable evidence of slain enemies. These grisly trophies were more difficult to subdivide and double-count, as was all-too-frequently the case with scalps.[104]

Both Navajo and Apache attacks on New Mexico's Hispano settlements escalated dramatically as the U.S. troops and local militia units were occupied fighting the rebel Texans. During the time of the Confederate invasion, old men and boys had to fight off the Indian stock raiders as best they could. On March 20, 1862, a large party of Navajos ran off cattle from the village of San Miguel. Most of the inexperienced *vecinos* (townsmen) who rode off in pursuit were teenagers, so the priest, Aniceto Lopez, went along to keep an eye on them. As usual, the raiders rode hard for the first twenty-four hours, knowing that they could push themselves and their animals through the night while the pursuers would have to wait until daylight to pick up the trail again. In this case, believing they had outdistanced their youthful trackers, the Navajos made camp at night and even built fires by which they could warm their feet and repair their worn-out moccasins. The Hispano boys crept to within fifty yards of the camp and opened fire, scattering the warriors. The blood trails in the snow the following morning led Francisco Sena to the body of a dead Navajo. The eighteen-year-old Sena victoriously scalped the warrior, took his ears, and cut off his "private parts" to show his friends, only to be severely chastised by the priest for this abhorrent behavior.[105]

An Apache war party on a successful revenge raid traditionally took a single scalp to dance over upon returning home. Generally, warriors wanted little to do with dead bodies or body parts, and handling such things required elaborate purification ceremonies. After the scalp dance, the trophy was usually discarded far from camp or thrown in a tree to decompose and return to nature. Still, the scalp dance became an important celebration of life for the families and bands of the successful warriors. Social restrictions limiting contact between unmarried men and women were relaxed at this time, and men who captured horses and other plunder demonstrated generosity and charity by giving away their goods to single women and others in need. Successful raiders might also use their wealth to acquire wives. In any case, a raider earned the honor and respect of his family and band.[106]

The Anglos, Hispanos, and Indians of the Southwest Borderlands each had a fundamentally different approach to warfare and military service. The Indian men, both allies and enemies of the Anglos and Hispanos, were hunters and providers first and warriors second. The Anglos brought a new kind of warrior to the fight in the borderlands. The U.S. troops, whether regulars or volunteers in federal service, were trained professionals contractually bound and paid for their service. In contrast to the Indians and Hispano civilians in the territories, the Anglo and Hispano soldiers in U.S. service were better armed and equipped, and they benefited from a seemingly inexhaustible supply of provisions. Though the army traditionally organized its soldiers in regiments of one thousand men, the difficulty of moving large bodies of troops in a desert environment, short on water and other subsistence, required that most of the campaigning and fighting in the Southwest be done by smaller units—usually no larger than one-hundred-man companies. Through effective use of written communication, carried by an elaborate network of military couriers or vedettes, and connected to the other states and territories by river and ocean transportation and by telegraph, military commanders in the Southwest could manage logistics and coordinate attacks on a large scale. Though the Apacheans were often numerically superior, the Anglos concentrated troops for coordinated attacks that offset their overall disadvantage in numbers. Whether animated by patriotic or mercenary motives, the troops sent to the borderlands during the Civil War years were, in fact, full-time soldiers.

The Hispano farmers and herders protected themselves and their families as best they could and occasionally joined militia companies for common defense, but these men received little or no training, were poorly armed, and seldom took the offensive. In 1861 many of the Hispano New Mexicans rallied around Kit Carson, who was considered a kinsman of sorts, having married into the influential Jaramillo family. Colonel Manuél Chaves also recruited Hispanos when the call came for U.S. Volunteer soldiers to fight the invading Confederates from Texas. Even these New Mexico Volunteers in federal service sometimes performed more like militiamen—part-time soldiers—whose roles as family men and providers came first. New Mexican officers were known to permit their men to return home for planting and other domestic duties, allowances never considered for Anglo soldiers. Even with the disparity in discipline and training, the Hispanos and Anglos cautiously joined forces to expel the Texans and put down the Southern rebellion. After succeeding in this strategic priority, they turned to face their common Navajo, Apache, and Comanche enemies. Often with Indian allies at their sides—and frequently leading the way—the Anglos, Hispanos, and Indians of the borderlands formed a powerful strategic alliance.[107]

Navajo and Apache chiefs and war leaders often achieved tactical success, but they rarely devised plans that might be considered strategic. The very idea of large-scale concerted effort by tribes and bands was foreign. Though warrior or "soldier" societies existed, they were in no way parallel to the Anglo and Hispano military systems. Because of the deeply rooted native tradition of warfare based on stock raiding or vengeance, the war for survival precipitated by the increased Anglo military presence brought about by the Civil War was something very difficult for Indian warriors to understand and effectively counter. Though the word "genocide" had not yet entered the lexicon, the idea of annihilating an enemy people was openly espoused by white exterminationists; the magnitude of such an extreme doctrine seems to have been beyond the ken of the indigenous people of the territories. Certainly they understood the concept of wiping out a wagon train or even a small settlement in response to a deadly attack. But the idea of the planned and systematic extermination of an entire people seems not to have occurred to them.[108]

As competition for food intensified during the Civil War years, and gathering and farming became less reliable, both Navajo and Apache economies depended increasingly on livestock raiding. These warriors often mounted raids in late winter, the time of year stores of food had been depleted and the people were hungry. Killing the Hispano, Anglo, or enemy Indian providers of this bounty would have been economically foolish and counterproductive. The Navajo tribesmen became expert horsemen and stock raisers themselves, which made them less dependent on raiding but also made them the target of Apache, Ute, and Hispano raiders. The Apaches never developed a sophisticated cattle- and horse-raising tradition. They often preferred butchering and eating captured animals immediately or drying and preserving the meat. Believing that they could always obtain more animals from neighboring tribes and pueblos, the Apaches did not keep large herds of cattle or horses.[109]

On a tactical level, only the Chiricahua Apache bands mounted large-scale offensive attacks aimed at killing or annihilating an enemy force or settlement. After U.S. troops temporarily abandoned their forts, Apache leaders Mangas Coloradas and Cochise gathered two hundred to three hundred warriors, numbers unheard of before or after the Civil War, for coordinated attacks against white civilians and soldiers. Though the Apaches achieved many small-scale tactical victories, they could not organize, coordinate, and sustain large-scale operations resulting in strategic success. Mangas and Cochise combined their Bedonkohe, Chihenne, and Chokonen bands in July 1862 and attempted to completely destroy Captain Roberts's California Volunteer infantry company in a well-planned ambush in Apache Pass. The fierce struggle for the springs lasted the better part of a day.

By nightfall, the Californians had driven the warriors from the water, using artillery followed by a desperate rush with fixed bayonets that cleared the surrounding hills of Apache marksmen positioned behind stone breastworks.[110]

Though this coordinated attack nearly succeeded, it was a rare occurrence due in part to the difficulty in communications and cooperation between disparate bands. Apaches used smoke for long distance signaling and left directional messages for friends by piling rocks with stick pointers, but detailed plans could only be communicated orally. Runners had remarkable memories, and, having grown up in a culture dependent on oral tradition, most Apache men and women demonstrated an ability to remember instructions with a high degree of accuracy. Still, the Anglo and Hispano soldiers employed detailed written communications and a well-organized express service, which enabled them to better coordinate their separated commands and allowed them to quickly unite and take the offensive.[111]

Apache raiding and war parties traditionally comprised only ten to twenty men, and the leaders of these tactical units had little experience in synchronizing closely timed attacks and maneuvering large bodies of fighting men. Smaller attacks usually took the form of a dawn surprise, an ambush, or a decoy trap. All required stealth and patience. Stock raids consisted of gathering grazing animals or running off entire herds or flocks in broad daylight and moving the captured stock as fast as possible before nightfall. Morning attacks allowed the raiders sufficient daylight to move the animals out of harm's way before darkness retarded their progress. A raiding party generally divided into two groups—one intent on chasing off the herders or guards and delaying pursuers while the other focused on rounding up and driving off as much stock as possible.

Pursuit might be thwarted by dividing herds or making false trails and reuniting at a predetermined rendezvous. The warriors often killed or wounded a small number of captured animals to discourage or distract pursuers. If the pursuers were Pueblo Indian or Hispano stock-raisers, they might well choose to butcher and return home with the meat from a slaughtered animal rather than continue the chase and risk coming back empty-handed.[112] Juan Cordova recalled a Navajo cattle raid in which the *jinetes* left dead cows in their wake. He believed that "this shows clearly that the Indians cared as much to do harm as to enrich themselves by stealing."[113] But the raiders also understood the psychological value of leaving a trail of death. Sometimes the warriors would shoot out the eyes or otherwise mutilate the sheep or cattle they left to be found on the trail—a warning to those who followed. For the raiders, moving as fast and as far as human endurance would allow was the key to success. They might stay in the saddle two or more days without stopping, riding captured horses to death if necessary. Unless they were out for revenge, Navajo and Apache raiders ambushed or fought pursuers only as a last resort. When strong and determined military patrols, citizens, or enemy tribesmen pursued, the raiders would turn and fight or prudently kill or abandon their captured animals and retreat.[114]

Hispanos

Hispano farmers, ranchers, and freighters suffered the most during the escalation of hostilities that characterized the civil wars in the territories from 1861 to 1867. Though accounting for less than 60 percent of the total population (Indian, Hispano, and Anglo), they suffered nearly 90 percent of the depredations reported to federal authorities.[115] They lived in small *pueblos* (villages), often clusters of adobe dwellings inhabited by related extended families, or isolated ranches, far from population centers and protecting forts. The stock herders, with their large flocks of sheep and goats, were especially vulnerable to attack, as they traveled to and from pasturages often located more than a day's ride from their homes.[116]

Typically, a Navajo or Mescalero Apache attack came in the early morning. In the predawn light, the animals would be stampeded by one party of raiders as a second group cut off and surrounded the herdsmen. The Navajos rode in large raiding parties of twenty-five to two hundred and almost always outnumbered the stockmen, who usually ran for their lives or hid out until the danger had passed. The isolated herders had always been the easiest prey for Indian stock raiders. During the Civil War years, when able-bodied Hispano men served with militia companies or U.S. Volunteers engaged in repelling the Confederate invasion in 1862, boy herders took charge of the flocks as Navajo and Apache raids increased in frequency and boldness.[117]

The boy herders were vulnerable on two counts: charged with protecting their animals, they were in harm's way, and the boys themselves were desired as captives and targeted by raiding parties. Pedro Padilla testified that two hundred Navajo and Apache warriors attacked Cañada Alamosa in January 1862. Most of the men eligible for military service had joined the army or were engaged by the government as freighters or civilian contractors. The Indians, he said, "were well aware of our small number and were bold in consequence. The whole population lost in this one raid, all the cattle, horses, goats, etc we had. The loss was heavy for everybody. It placed us all on one level. The rich ones lost by the thousand and the poor ones lost a few goats or a cow. The herder who was watching the sheep and goats got killed that day, the one herding the horses and cattle escaped."[118] Juan Jose Montolla, an eleven-year-old Hispano goat herder taken by Navajos rode blindfolded behind his captors for three days. When he finally arrived in Navajo canyon country, hundreds of miles from his home, he was immediately put to work herding the very animals that had been captured with him. Boy *pastores* (shepherds) were in demand by both the pastoral Indians and the Hispanos. The trained sheep dogs of the *pastores* were also highly valued by the Navajos and swept up with their flocks for the same reason the human herders were.[119]

The violence of the stock and captive-taking of the 1860s was not typical of the raiding exchange cycle that had evolved in the borderlands. Felix Tafoya, also from the village of Cañada Alamosa, remembered that prior to 1861 the neighboring tribes had been friendly, but suddenly, relations changed and "the Indians went to murdering."[120] The boldness of the raids shocked even the most seasoned residents of New Mexico. Hispano pueblos came under attack by warriors who entered houses, took captives, and seemingly plundered at will. The raiders broke into the corrals that held in common the villagers' best horses and mules. Twenty-five Mescalero Apache raiders swept through the village of Anton Chico, New Mexico, in October 1864, driving before them the horses and mules found grazing on the commons. Roman and Estípulo Lucero led six other men in a mounted pursuit covering fifty miles in three days. The Lucero brothers died of bullet and arrow wounds received when the Apaches finally stopped running and turned to fight. The surviving Hispanos returned empty-handed. More often than not, Hispano and Pueblo Indian pursuit parties turned back after confronting Navajo and Apache warriors ready to stand and fight rather than give up their plunder.[121]

As war raged along the roads in Arizona and the Rio Grande settlements in New Mexico, the level of violence escalated. Deadly encounters increased and reports of torture and rape began filtering in to federal authorities. Apache war parties waylaid freighters and burned the men alive, hanging them head down over slow fires or lashing them to wagon wheels before setting the vehicles ablaze.[122] Jose Chavez y Gallegos testified at a depredation hearing that his family party was attacked while traveling by ox cart to visit family at the village of Cubero, New Mexico, fifty miles away. Chavez, his young wife, a female servant, and a young man were on the road near Los Lunas, on the Río Puerco, when a lone Navajo man rode up and stopped them. Speaking Spanish, the man ordered Chavez to hand over the Navajo blanket he wore. Unwilling to surrender the garment without a fight, Chavez made a move for his pistol. The warrior leveled his carbine and shot him through the body, then signaled with his red head scarf to hidden associates. Chavez's terrified male servant leapt into the river and escaped just as twenty-four mounted warriors surrounded the wagon, stripped the three travelers, and repeatedly raped the women. The raiders smashed the cart to pieces, carried away everything of value, and rode off just as a heavy snow began to fall, leaving their naked and insensible victims to the elements.[123]

Attacks spurred retaliation and revenge. Often the people involved knew one another, if not by name, by family or general acquaintance. They also knew who had killed whom. When a large party of Navajos ran off Antonio Lucero's cattle near Socorro, the incensed stockman rode in pursuit with ten other men. When they caught up with the raiders, they found themselves hopelessly outnumbered. Lucero and several of his men were overwhelmed and killed, likely taking some of the warriors with them to the grave. Two weeks later, the surviving Navajos returned to Lucero's house seeking revenge. They rode into his dwelling, terrifying his widow, and destroyed everything—smashing furniture, slashing bedding, and making a shambles of the place.[124]

Augustín Montoya served with the New Mexico Volunteers in 1863 and 1864, but he knew virtually nothing of the war between North and South. His war was just as real, however, when Jicarilla Apaches attacked his village of Las Truchas in northern New Mexico, on July 5, 1865. Surviving four arrow wounds, he reported the Indians had killed two women and one man. Bent on destruction, the warriors lanced

Montoya's burros, smashed the boxes of eggs he intended to market, and scattered flour and grain to the wind.[125] Juan Manuel Lucero, a farmer from Cañon Largo summed up the state of affairs in New Mexico. He believed that since all the men from New Mexico's villages had "gone down the [Rio Grande] river to fight the Texanians [sic], the Indians broke out into a revolution and went to stealing and killing." This was civil war.[126]

When a raiding party of twenty-six Chiricahua Apaches overtook a freight wagon near Peñasco, New Mexico in the summer of 1866, the teamsters ran for their lives, believing the Apaches would be content with their booty. But the mounted warriors rode down one of the men, dragged him back to his wagon, and proceeded to shoot him full of arrows—then they climbed onto the wagon and cut open sugar sacks, pouring the contents over him and allowing his blood to soak into the mound of white crystals that covered him. Other warriors shot holes in the whiskey barrels and destroyed as much merchandise as they could before a relief party from San Antonio fortuitously arrived and interrupted the attack.[127]

After Anglo and Hispano U.S. forces and allied tribes subdued the Navajos and Mescalero Apaches, the people of Arizona and New Mexico engaged in a civil war that pitted raiding Western and Chiricahua Apache tribes against Hispano citizens and soldiers, agrarian Indian villagers and auxiliaries, and Anglo citizens and soldiers. The allied forces arrayed against the Apaches created an irresistible combination that doomed the roaming bands to the confinement of reservations by the late 1860s. While the Apache warriors surprised and in many cases outfought their adversaries on a tactical level, strategically they were no match for the powerful Anglo-Hispano-Indian alliance. The war of attrition drove the remaining Apache bands, and the few Navajo holdouts who escaped the Bosque Redondo roundup, to seek peace with the predominantly Anglo military and territorial officials.

Volunteer troops brought to the borderlands during the Civil War exceeded in number and hostility the prewar regular army and continued active campaigning in the territories until 1867. Anglos increasingly came to believe that the "wild Indians" either needed to be corralled and fed or exterminated.[128] Within a decade, all the Arizona and New Mexico tribes would be located on government-prescribed reservations receiving food, clothing, and other goods as annual allowances.[129]

Mexico

During the turbulent years from 1857 to 1867, President Benito Juárez's liberal Republicans competed for power with Mexico's parallel conservative government. Mexico struggled to survive its own civil wars, known to history as La Guerra de Reforma (Reform War, 1858–61) and its multinational continuation as the *intervención francesa* (French Intervention, 1861–67). Property-owning *hacendados* and Catholic Church officials, who controlled most of the nation's land and wealth, opposed Juárez's Republican reform laws supported by the poorer classes of the mixed race *casta*. The Indian peoples of Mexico's northern states, especially the Lower Pimas, Ópatas, and Yaquis were divided in their loyalties and engaged in intratribal civil war. When on July 17, 1861, Juárez placed a moratorium on the payment of foreign debts, Mexico's conservative elite took advantage of the opportunity to overthrow the Republican government by seeking assistance from European powers. On December 8, 1861, a tripartite coalition comprising Spain, Britain, and France arrived with an armada at the Mexican port city of Veracruz determined to seize assets and collect the overdue debts. Of course, Lincoln's divided states, engaged in their own civil war, were unable to enforce the 1823 Monroe Doctrine, which had discouraged European intervention in the Americas for more than a generation.

By the spring of 1862, Napoleon III made clear the extent of his imperialistic intentions in Mexico, and his reluctant Spanish and British allies soon departed. Within a year, Napoleon's expeditionary army captured Mexico City and kept Juárez's beleaguered government on the run. Determined to overthrow Juárez, Napoleon and the Mexican conservatives conspired to recruit Habsburg Prince Maximilian of Austria and install him as Mexico's puppet emperor, following a sham plebiscite in late 1863. Urged on by his ambitious young wife, Charlotte of the Belgians, Emperor Maximiliano I threw himself into his new role with a will. He and his empress, "Carlota," affected native dress with a European flair and redecorated Mexico City's Chapultepec Castle as befitted a monarch. Still, Maximilian struggled to establish his legitimacy. Unable to control the events that swept him into the international spotlight, he turned his attention to the trappings of empire and personally involved himself in the design of the uniforms of his gaily outfitted legions of lancers and riflemen and corps of voltigeurs and dragoons, merging brilliant Mexican colors and styles with the latest French and Austrian military fashion. He also saw fit to levy a fine of fifty pesos on any officer or enlisted soldier who wore outlawed Mexican medals, namely anything won during the years of Juárez's Reform War. Battle honors from the Texas rebellion and Mexican-American War, however, were allowed.[130]

The Franco-Mexican Imperial Army consisted of nearly thirty thousand conscripts and volunteers from the lower classes—many of the men were full-blooded Indians—while the officer corps comprised educated elites. This Mexican conservative force was augmented by French, Austrian, and Belgian regular and colonial troops, a force that by 1863 exceeded forty-five thousand men of all branches of the service—infantry, cavalry, and artillery. Splendidly armed and accoutered, the Imperial Army contrasted with the insufficiently armed, poorly attired, and underequipped Republicans.

Juárez's army was a mix of some twelve thousand well-led regulars and an uneven assemblage of auxiliary troops supplied from state National Guard and militia units. The regular infantrymen were distinguished in battle by their wool uniforms of dark blue wool, trimmed in red, and black leather shakos. British Enfield rifle muskets or obsolescent smoothbore muskets made up the armament of this professional establishment. Juárez's regular cavalrymen wore gray wool coatees edged in green and were armed with muzzle-loading carbines and sabers, when available. Mounted companies of *rurales,* originally intended as rural constabulary forces, soon proved to be excellent light cavalry, especially effective with their lances when employed in hit-and-run attacks against Imperial troops. The state troops, of varying quality and reliability, often went unarmed until weapons of any kind could be issued from captured enemy stores or from stockpiles of arms smuggled into the country from the United States or Britain.[131]

In the summer of 1861, District of Southern California commander General George Wright had proposed a plan for attacking Texas from California by way of the Mexican states of Sonora and Chihuahua. National boundaries, legalities, and politics aside, this invasion route was the most direct and easily supplied, but the War Department scuttled the notion of trespassing on Mexican soil while that nation was embroiled in its own civil war. The concerns were not limited to political squeamishness over trampling on Mexican sovereignty as had been

done during the bald-faced aggression of 1846–48. In 1861 the political
dangers were compounded by the fact that French, Spanish, and British
naval and land forces were poised for their own invasion of Mexico, to
collect the unpaid debts incurred during two decades of conflict with
the United States and incessant internecine fighting.

At the same time the United States fought to preserve its union,
Mexico found itself in a desperate struggle involving European
nations. The British and Spanish withdrew when it became evident
that Napoleon had imperialistic designs on Mexico. General Charles
de Lorencez's French army of six thousand seasoned veterans pushed
inland. On May 5, 1862—as Carleton's column closed in on Tucson
and Sherod Hunter's rebels rode east to the Rio Grande to join Sibley's
retreating army—the overconfident French army smashed itself against
the fortified mountain town of Puebla, on the main road between
Veracruz and Mexico City, held by General Ignacio Zaragoza's hastily
gathered force of Mexican regulars and ragtag militia men. While the
Mexican Republicans celebrated their *cinco de mayo* victory, which
inspired renewed hope by proving the French were not invincible,
Napoleon resolved to return with a larger force of men and siege guns
that would eventually batter their way through Puebla and on to the
Mexican capital in 1863.

The Lincoln administration feared the consequences of Juárez's or
Maximilian's recognition of the Southern Confederacy; either eventuality would add an international dimension to the American Civil War,
open other battle fronts, and complicate the U.S. blockade of rebel
ports of call. Though Lincoln secretly supported Juárez's liberal government, he could not risk more while the Southern rebellion still raged.
All the U.S. officials in the borderlands could openly do during the war
years was to tighten border security and enter into formal agreements
with local Mexican authorities in the border states regarding matters
of trade, pursuit of Indian raiders, and immigration related to gold
mining activities. The California Native Battalion, composed almost
entirely of Spanish-speaking Californios, joined the California Volunteer Cavalry in 1864 and 1865 for border duty in Arizona. But ethnicity
sometimes trumped allegiance to the U.S. Army. Many of the Hispano
cavalrymen, sympathetic to Juárez's liberal government, deserted their
companies to aid their countrymen in ousting Maximilian's French-
backed regime. U.S. troops pursued the deserters, who absconded with

large quantities of government equipment, risking confrontation with Mexican and French troops. Tense military and diplomatic standoffs resulted, and federal officers were repeatedly warned by the Lincoln administration and War Department not to engage the forces of Maximilian or Juárez on Mexican soil.

General John S. Mason followed Wright as commander of the Department of the Pacific in 1865 and inherited the challenge of securing the international border with Mexico while civil wars raged on both sides of the line. He recruited new California units, including the First Battalion of Native Cavalry, the Second California Infantry, and the Seventh California Infantry. Federal officials chose the Native Battalion, composed almost entirely of Californios, for service in Arizona because of the extraordinary horsemanship displayed by these *caballeros* whose fathers had come close to annihilating Kearny's First Dragoons in 1846. Mason, however, worried about using these troops so close to the border, fearing their sympathies for Benito Juárez's Republic of Mexico might result in conflicted loyalties. During the Civil War, American officers exercised diplomacy rather than military strength along the border in an effort to avoid open conflict with Maximilian's conservative government and its French allies. The pressing need for mounted troops for border patrol, however, soon overruled Mason's concerns about the loyalty of the Hispanos. The Native Battalion proudly rode into Arizona with red pennons waving from their nine-foot lances.[132]

Although Paragraph 1642 of the U.S. Army's 1861 *Revised Regulations* specifically stated that no volunteer "will be mustered into the service who is unable to speak the English language," most of the men of the Native Battalion spoke only Spanish. The *San Francisco Evening Bulletin* reported, "The battalion is truly a mixture of colors and tongues, the men very rugged and hearty—more than half being native Californians, and the remainder Mexicans, Chilenos, Sonorians, California and Yaqui Indians, Germans, Americans, etc. Those of them, however, who are not American speak more or less English, the English tongue crowd understanding Spanish—the officers being adept in both languages."[133]

Both the Hispano Native Battalion, commanded by Major Cremony, and parts of the Anglo-American Seventh California Infantry, commanded by Colonel Charles W. Lewis, served along the Arizona-Mexico border. Fort Mason, named in honor of the new district commander, became the principal post in southern Arizona in 1865–66. Its importance stemmed from its location near Calabasas on the main road from Arizona to Sonora. Union officers no longer feared Mexico as a possible route for a Confederate invasion, but they believed that French troops guarding Maximilian's puppet government posed an imminent danger. The presence of these foreign soldiers irritated American politicians and military men serving in the borderlands, but frontier commanders dutifully restrained their men and resorted to diplomacy.

In May 1862 Carleton had opened correspondence with Ignacio Pesqueira, the Republican governor of Sonora. Carleton acted on orders from the Department of the Pacific commander at the time, General George Wright, who wanted to stay on the Sonoran's good side and hoped to purchase supplies and gain trade concessions at the Mexican port of Guaymas. Carleton tactfully warned Pesqueira against recognizing or agreeing to supply the Confederates, whom he deemed "filibusters" ready to "usurp the power you yourself hold." The Mexican governor found himself in an embarrassing situation after his interpreter gave copies of his correspondence with Confederate ambassador Reily to a correspondent from the *San Francisco Bulletin*.[134]

In truth, Pesqueira never really trusted the Texans, and relations between the Sonoran government and the Californians remained cordial. Carleton lifted the stringent passport requirements that had amounted to a virtual ban against Mexican citizens attempting to cross the border into Arizona to work the rich Colorado River placer fields. Acutely aware of the Sonoran's suspicions of American imperialism, Carleton's conciliatory tone did much to defuse the tense situation on the border. He wrote of the passports, "No invidious distinction was made favoring Americans in preference to the people of Your Excellency. The people of Sonora," he added encouragingly, "are at liberty to come and work in our mines, or to sell their provisions, forage, fruits, &c., within our lines." These concessions were much to the beleaguered Pesqueira's benefit and satisfaction.[135]

By 1864 during the height of the French occupation of Mexico, California officers in Arizona and New Mexico had grown so friendly with the liberal Republicans in Sonora and Chihuahua that high-ranking officials in the War Department considered the relationship dangerous to the maintenance of France's neutrality in the American rebellion. In the fall of 1865, Franco-Mexican Imperial troops forced Sonoran Governor Pesqueira—with his family, servants, livestock, and valuables— to cross the border and take refuge with the Californians stationed at Fort Mason while pro-French Governor Don Manuel Gándara and Refugio Tánori's Ópata legion controlled much of Sonora and liberal forces engaged in dispersed guerilla attacks. At the same time that the French organized mounted *contra-guerilla* bands to combat the "insurgents," sympathetic American officers and men entertained Governor Pesqueira's entourage. The Americans had allowed Pesqueira to cross into Arizona in pursuit of Apaches a year earlier, and they respected the Sonoran's ability as an Indian fighter and his defiance of the French invaders.[136]

Major Nelson H. Davis wrote General Carleton on March 2, 1864:

"Pesqueira is friendly to the United States and says, *entre nous,* that in case of necessity or trouble in his State from the French, he will raise the United States flag and ask our assistance. If our Government will only allow our people to act in the matter, Sonora will soon be ours. Colonel Coult is anxious to go down with the troops here, when the proper opportunity arrives. I cautioned him to do nothing to complicate our international affairs with Mexico, or take any hasty steps in this matter. . . . Sonora must and is bound to be ours; it is well to have the question considered, and be prepared for whatever may turn up. It is essential to this Territory. We want the ports on the Gulf of California."[137]

Even the usually prudent Pacific Department commander, George Wright, believed the United States should possess Mexico's northern states.[138] Carleton agreed that the California troops ought to be ready to seize Guaymas. He wrote General Henry Halleck that "a naval station on the Gulf of California" would be the answer to the problems of developing Arizona's mineral resources. But the response from Washington quickly reined in the enthusiasm of the California officers. The Lincoln administration did not even want to discuss the possibility of conflict with French forces in Mexico while the Southern rebellion still raged. Carleton reluctantly cautioned his subordinates: "It is required by the War Department that no steps be taken by the military forces within this department [New Mexico] which will at all complicate us in the matter growing out of the occupation of any of the States of Mexico by the French. Our relations with France are of the most friendly character, and it is desirable that they remain so. You will be careful not to jeopardize those relations by act, or word, or letter." General Grant, while besieging Lee's army at Petersburg, Virginia, summed up the attitude prevailing in the army: "We want Napoleon out of Mexico, but we don't want any war over it; we have certainly had enough war."[139]

Lincoln and Secretary of State William Seward seethed at Napoleon's brazen disregard for the Monroe Doctrine, so they turned a blind eye to supplies of arms and ammunition sent from the United States to Juárez while publicly professing neutrality in the conflict. California Volunteers did, however, cross the international border on exploring and trade missions. Despite the official warnings to avoid contact with the French, U.S. troops also violated the border when the urgent necessity of hot pursuit of malefactors demanded it. On several occasions detachments pursued rebels, Apache raiders, and bandits into Mexico. The California soldiers conducted most of these forays quickly and without political incident. But rounding up Californio deserters from the Native Battalion in French-occupied Mexico proved more difficult.

In September 1865 Captain José Ramón Pico, with a mounted force of two junior officers and thirty men, crossed the Mexican border in pursuit of sixteen deserters from Companies A and B of the Native Battalion. The men bolted from Fort Mason with all their arms and equipment and thirty good army horses. Pico followed the deserters to Magdalena, Sonora, ninety miles south of Fort Mason. There his party encountered about 250 poorly armed Mexican soldiers fighting under Maximilian's Imperial flag. Wishing to avoid armed confrontation, Pico entered the town with only six soldiers and Lieutenant William Emery, Seventh California Infantry, sent by Colonel Lewis at Fort Mason to record any negotiations with Mexican or French officials.[140]

At Magdalena, Mexican prefect Jose Moreno refused Pico's demand for the return of the deserters unless the American officer agreed to recognize Maximilian's government. Of course, Pico understood that his recognition of the Imperialists could have international repercussions as great as the recognition of the Confederacy by a foreign power, so the captain replied that his government would recognize only President Juárez, Mexico's legitimate ruler. As tension mounted, Pico ordered the twenty-four troopers under Captain Porfírio Jimeno to return to Fort Mason while Moreno received instructions from the Imperial officials at Hermosillo. It took eight days for the orders to arrive from Hermosillo, during which time the Americans came to better understand the nature of Mexico's civil war as adherents of the two factions vying for control of the country alternately lauded and threatened them. Finally, Moreno sent word that he would not turn over the deserters and that the Californians had eight hours to leave Magdalena and forty-eight hours to get out of the country. Pico's party had no choice but to depart empty-handed.[141]

When Imperial commanders posted guards near the border, Colonel Lewis strengthened his own border sentinels. In late September six more Native Battalion deserters crossed into Mexico, taking fourteen pistols and fifteen horses with equipment. Lewis, fearing the consequences of another border crossing, mounted no pursuit. His men, however, chafed at this restraint. Lieutenant Emery wrote, "If we could only have a little fight with the French, it would be something worthwhile stopping here; but as it is, it is very dry. Fighting Indians is dangerous enough, but we do so little of that that the time drags." When rumors reached Fort Mason that Prefect Moreno was massing three hundred to four hundred men for an attack designed to capture Governor Pesqueira, the usually restrained Lewis exclaimed, "Let him come and try it."[142]

A Mexican Imperial force did attempt a raid across the border at San Gabriel, Arizona, opposite San Rafael, Sonora, about twelve miles north of the relatively large (population 3,000) city of Santa Cruz. On November 4, 1865, Colonel Refugio Tánori, an Ópata chief, attacked the border town with a force of nearly five hundred men while in pursuit of Republican forces under Garcia Morales. For more than two hundred years, the Spanish had considered the Ópata Indians of Sonora to be willing subjects and eager converts to Christianity. The Jesuit priests found these sedentary people susceptible to their "civilizing" efforts and established missions among their villages between 1628 and 1650. In the eighteenth and nineteenth centuries, the Spanish valued the Ópata men as warrior auxiliaries, and this esteem was reciprocated as the two peoples forged a strong alliance against their common Apache enemies, who raided through the Sonoran borderlands and deep into Mexico from their Arizona and New Mexico homelands in the north. Over time, the assimilated Ópatas became nearly indistinguishable culturally from other rural Mexicans, though they lived in their own *mestizo* mission villages. In 1858, Juárez's reforms abolished these distinct communities, and the ably led and well-organized Ópata soldiers were forced to side with either the liberal Juaristas or former Sonoran Governor Manuel Gándara's French-backed conservatives and, later, Maximilian's Imperial forces. Tánori had followed the latter course, and by 1865 he dominated the Sonoran theater, attacking Ures and, in his greatest victory, capturing the city of Nácori Grande.[143]

Now Tánori and his predominantly Ópata Indian command boldly crossed the border at San Rafael and fired on American citizens, wounding one or two in the skirmish. Major Cremony, who had recently arrived at Fort Mason with Company C of the Native Battalion, chased after the invaders, hoping to obtain a truce and a parley. Tánori retreated, however, easily outdistancing a detachment led by Lieutenant Edward Codington assigned to head off the Mexicans at Ures. Cremony later learned that the Imperial troops, most of whom were infantry, made the forty-three-mile retreat from Santa Cruz to the town of Ímuris in record time. Tánori's precipitous withdrawal was accomplished in nine hours, a remarkable feat that the best Anglo-American, Hispano, or French light infantry would have been hard-pressed to duplicate.[144]

The Yaquis and closely allied Mayos had resisted first the Spanish then the Mexican regimes in Sonora for hundreds of years. In September 1860 the Yaqui insurgents burned and leveled Mexican settlements between Guaymas and Hermosillo. Led by the stalwart Republican Governor Pesqueira, the heavily fortified cities held out against the rebels. But the local militias and regulars sustained heavy casualties in a fight at Jacalitos where the governor lost his entire command as well as the state seal, government documents, and baggage, only narrowly escaping with his life. There was no quit in Pesqueira, and in 1862 he invaded Mayo and Yaqui territory, forcing them to accept peace terms at Tórim, Sonora. Although the Indian leaders received pardons, a military post was established at Agua Caliente to watch over and control the Yaquis.

After the French defeated Pesqueira's Republicans at Guaymas in 1865, Mateo Marquín and a portion of the Yaquis joined Refugio Tánori's Ópatas and allied with the French-backed conservatives in fighting the Juaristas. These native forces took control of Álamos, Sonora, and drove Pesqueira from his headquarters at Ures in vicious fighting that pitted Yaqui against Yaqui and Ópata against Ópata. Following the withdrawal of European troops, Pesqueira regained control, but the bitterness caused by the civil war led to lasting resentment, assassinations, and continued conflict well into the twentieth century.[145]

The Native Battalion and the Seventh California Infantry served in the borderlands until the summer of 1866. The battalion spent almost its entire tour of duty in southeastern Arizona at the posts of Tubac, Revanton Ranch, and Fort Mason, the latter noted for its malarial fevers and high desertion rate. Companies of the Second and Seventh Infantry regiments were scattered about the territory, with detachments at Fort Goodwin, Fort Grant, Fort Mojave, Fort McDowell, Fort Whipple, Fort Yuma, Tucson, and Fort Mason. As expected when they were first recruited, their principal duties involved "Mexican frontier" and "Apache service," which meant constant patrolling, campaigning, and protecting the military mail. The Californians provided communication between Arizona and the "outside" until late 1865, when civil authorities once again accepted responsibility for the mail service.[146]

In February 1865 Juárez had commissioned an ex-Confederate to recruit a regiment of Americans for border service. This special unit was composed largely of former rebels and Union deserters enticed by high bounties, promises of rank, and generous payment for stolen U.S. government horses, arms, and equipment. Lieutenant Richard H. Orton, commanding a company of California cavalry stationed on the Rio Grande at San Elizario, Texas, made five raids into Mexico to break up the mercenary band. Twenty-five miles south of the border at Guadalupe, Chihuahua, Orton's troopers killed, wounded, or rounded up many of the Americans. As much as Juárez needed to equip and strengthen his northern army he could not afford to antagonize his generally sympathetic U.S. allies. After correspondence between Carleton and Juárez, the renegade regiment was officially disbanded, though unofficially weapons continued to flow across the border.[147]

By 1865 General Mariano Escobedo's Republican Army of the North had grown in strength and boldness. Cities on the American side of the border boomed as Juárez's forces sheltered near the border communities. El Paso and Brownsville saw steadily growing concentrations of U.S. troops under the command of General Phil Sheridan, Grant's most pugnacious combat officer. Stockpiles of arms, including artillery, now made their way across the Rio Grande on skiffs operated by Mexican civilians in broad daylight, much to the consternation of Maximilian's Imperial loyalists in the north, who complained about this state of affairs but remained powerless to prevent it. Juárez himself was safely ensconced at El Paso del Norte in the summer of 1865 as Escobedo rallied more and more recruits from the frontier to the Republican cause. Mexican relations with the Americans in the borderlands had never been better. Carleton urged his superiors to lend a "helping hand" to "the President of our sister Republic, who has been driven from his country by foreign bayonets and forced to take asylum on American soil."[148] Andrés S. Viesca, Coahuila's liberal governor, wrote expansively of the burgeoning alliance: "The United States, that great republic, the admiration of the world and terror of crowned heads, has already manifested in a very explicit manner its disapproval of the imported and ridiculous empire that has been pretended to be erected in Mexico. . . . Long live the national independence! Long live the legitimate government of the republic! Long life to the people of the frontier!"[149]

Receiving surplus Union Army uniforms and large supplies of weapons, including the latest Spencer and Henry repeating firearms, Juárez's northern forces were finally a match for the Franco-Mexican Imperial Army. General Tomás Mejía, Maximilian's able field commander in the north, sought to win the hearts of the Mexican people while keeping Juárez's organized armies corralled along the U.S. border. Marshal François Achille Bazaine ordered imperial forces in the remote northern states to suppress the wide-ranging guerilla bands with irregular French *contra-guerilla* forces. Bazaine's honor and career were on the line, but he had another more personal interest in continuing the French intervention. The flamboyant, somewhat corpulent general, age fifty-four, had married a well-connected yet Juárez-supporting seventeen-year-old Mexican girl and now announced that he desired to make Imperial Mexico his home.[150]

By mid-1865 Lincoln was dead, the victim of an assassin's bullet, and the American rebellion had been suppressed. Secretary of State Seward's hostility toward the French interventionists was at last unveiled, and President Andrew Johnson's most aggressive generals—Grant, Sherman, and Sheridan—who had already been covertly supporting Juárez's military efforts in northern Mexico, maneuvered their battle-hardened troops for action on the Texas border. The Americans, it seemed, were spoiling for a fight. Many officers and enlisted men who had gotten a taste of martial glory sought career and financial opportunities by serving with either of the warring Mexican factions.[151]

General Mejía brought to the attention of the American commander in Brownsville, General George Weitzel, that African American deserters from the Twenty-Third Infantry, U.S. Colored Troops, had been captured while fighting with the Juaristas at Matamoras. Weitzel appeared unfazed by this disclosure, knowing full well that many officers and men, both Union and Confederate, had been offered lucrative inducements to bring their military skills to the fighting in Mexico. The American brushed off the annoyed Mejía, writing, "If the three men of the twenty-third United States colored troops were captured in the lines of your enemies in arms against you, I have nothing more to say, of course. But for humanity's sake, I ask that, on their trial, your court may take into consideration their ignorance, their ignorance of your language, and the fact that officers and others from the other side induced these men to do what they did under promise of large sums of money."[152]

The brutal fighting along Mexico's main roadways and outside the population centers, especially near the northern frontier, devolved into bloody and vengeful small-unit actions and reprisals. Meanwhile, Juárez stepped up his diplomatic efforts. Margarita Maza de Juárez, the first lady of Mexico, visited Washington in the spring of 1866 and met with President Johnson, Secretary of State William Seward, and General in Chief U. S. Grant to plead for American support in ousting the French occupation forces. U.S. diplomats did indeed redouble their stern admonitions that Napoleon remove his troops. Under this pressure, the emperor could not continue backing Maximilian's regime and made preparations to withdraw the French soldiers as speedily as honor would allow.[153]

In the fall of 1865, Maximilian had issued the Ley de 3 Octubre 1865 in an attempt to finish off Juarista resistance before his French allies abandoned him. The emperor and members of his entourage later claimed, and many historians agree, that Marshal Bazaine had actually drafted the document.[154] However it came about, Maximilian accepted authorship and published it in his official *El Diario del Imperio*, a newspaper intended for the conservative Mexican intelligentsia and French allies. He also ordered the decree printed as a broadside in Spanish and Nahuatl, aimed at organized and irregular Juarista forces that now controlled the countryside. The *guerrilleros* attacked roadways, outposts, and towns at the edges of Maximilian's far-flung empire and then blended into the largely Republican population. When Maximilian learned that Juárez—whose presidential term had actually expired—might have crossed the U.S. border at El Paso to avoid capture, he jumped at the opportunity to declare victory and simultaneously offered an olive branch, or a threatening sword, to Republican forces still in the field.[155]

Maximilian's decree commended Juárez's followers for their valor and constancy ("*valor y constancia*") but insisted that no good could come of further resistance. The decree maintained that the insurgents, referred to as criminals and brigands ("*criminales y bandoleros*"), only endangered the people, and it threatened summary execution and other harsh penalties to ensure the restoration of order. The carefully written law enumerated all the punishments that would be meted out to *guerrilleros,* defined as any armed men loyal to Juárez, as well as citizens who offered the insurgents shelter or aid. Maximilian and his ministers of foreign affairs, commerce, interior, war, justice, and public instruction, as well as the treasury undersecretary, all signed the Ley de 3 Octubre 1865, which almost immediately became known as the "Black Decree."[156] Newspapers in the United States quickly picked up the story and trumpeted it on their front pages. "This decree is a novelty in the history of civil wars," declared the *San Francisco Daily Alta California,* which went on to criticize the presumption of Napoleon and Maximilian while supporting the rights of the Juaristas to rebel, since they, as citizens of Mexico, had a more legitimate claim to the country than did European interventionists.[157]

Although the civil wars in the Southwest Borderlands had been triggered or intensified by the American Civil War, each had its own peculiar history. The idea of sovereignty was at the heart of most of the conflicts, and in most instances one belligerent community considered itself to be an independent political or cultural entity while the other did not. The idea of state sovereignty was much discussed in the United States during the states' rights debate that preceded the secession crisis. Certainly, the Confederates considered themselves to be a sovereign nation, politically, culturally, and economically distinct from the United States. Not interested in dominating the more powerful North, the Southerners expressed their war aim as one of independence, though the acquisition of western territories and possibly parts of Mexico were not ruled out if the secession effort were successful.

New Mexico's Hispanos were either unaware of or ambivalent toward the underlying causes of the Anglo civil war. Most resigned themselves to the fact that they were no longer part of Mexico, and their loyalties centered on a self-interested maintenance of the status quo in their local communities. Some Hispanos were divided and found themselves fighting both Union and Confederate troops and, occasionally, one another. Navajos and Apaches fought to maintain their independence even though most of the Apachean tribes and bands had previously signed treaties subordinating themselves to the United States. However, Indian nations under congressionally recognized treaty obligations began to understand that the Anglos only loosely applied the term "sovereignty." The Americans believed that former Mexican citizens and other peoples occupying ceded or purchased lands were now either citizens or wards of the United States.

By the 1860s tribes fought for free access to their ancestral lands and a way of life that included raiding and captive-taking as a survival strategy. The Anglo military and civilian newcomers to the borderlands often found willing allies in the sedentary Indian and Hispano residents. Both north and south of the border, tribes were divided by civil war brought about by political and military alliances. The civil war in Mexico was a continuation of conflict that erupted between conservative and liberal political factions in the years following the Mexican-American War. Benito Juárez was elected president just as the North American power vacuum resulting from the American Civil War destabilized the already precarious political situation in Mexico. This led to renewed civil war, now with international dimensions, which led to open conflict among Mexico's borderland tribes. Ópata factions fought one another and the Yaquis were split as well, while southern Pimas and Papagos were forced to choose sides in Mexico's internecine war.

Christopher "Kit" Carson (pictured here as a colonel of volunteers)
served the U.S. government from 1847 to 1867
as a scout, Indian agent, and soldier.
(Palace of the Governors Photo Archives)

As an army officer, military governor, and social reformer, James H. Carleton (pictured as a brigadier general), more than any other man, transformed the Southwest Borderlands during the Civil War years.
(Arizona Historical Society)

John R. Baylor (pictured here as a Lieutenant Colonel) lived by the code duello and epitomized the hard-fighting and sometimes ruthless martial culture the Texas Confederates brought to the Civil War in the borderlands.
(Arizona Historical Society)

"Apache Hanging." In 1864 artist J. Ross Browne sketched his impression of an Apache or Yavapai warrior bristling with Pima arrows—a warning to raiders—suspended on the banks of the Gila River by self-professed "Apache hunter" King S. Woolsey.
(J. Ross Browne, *Adventures in the Apache Country*)

APACHE HANGING.

PIMO VILLAGE.

WHITE'S MILL.

EL PECACHO.

"Pimo Village," "White's Mill," and "El Pecacho." U.S. troops relied heavily
on the wheat and forage provided by the Pimas and Maricopas who, in turn,
received protection against Quechan, Yavapai, and Apache enemies.
The skirmish fought at Picacho Peak on April 15, 1862, is often
remembered as the westernmost engagement of the Civil War.
(J. Ross Browne, *Adventures in the Apache Country*)

Jack Swilling—miner, soldier, scout, entrepreneur—fought ably for the rebels, then joined U.S. government forces in warring against Apaches before becoming one of the founders of Phoenix.
(Arizona Historical Society)

Sonora governor Ignacio Pesqueira was a fierce foe of filibustering Americans, raiding Apaches, Mexican Imperialists, and invading Europeans—and a cautious ally of U.S. troops in the borderlands.
(Arizona Historical Society)

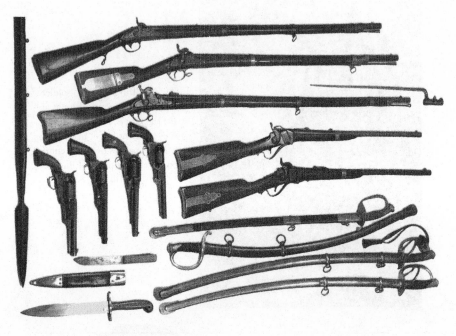

During the 1860s, U.S. troops in the borderlands maintained a logistical advantage and were far better equipped than their adversaries. Top to bottom, left to right: Benicia Arsenal lance; .54-caliber 1817 Common Rifle (marked "Native" on patchbox); .54-caliber 1841 Mississippi Rifle; .58-caliber 1855 Springfield rifle musket (Eli W. Hazen, Co. E, First California Infantry) with bayonet; .44-caliber 1847 Colt "Dragoon" revolver (ser. no. 13858, George W. Oaks, Co. I, First California Infantry); .44-caliber 1860 Colt New Model Army revolver (ser. no. 32281, George Hand, Co. G, First California Infantry); .44-caliber 1858 Remington New Model Army revolver (ser. no. 79296, Fritz Martin, Co. G, First California Infantry); .36-caliber 1851 Colt Navy revolver (ser. no. 63528, John H. Englebrecht, Co. F, First California Cavalry); .52-caliber 1853 Sharps "slanting breech" carbine (ser. no. 12976, William Tallman, Co. E, First California Cavalry); .52-caliber 1859 Sharps New Model carbine; "Green River" knife; 1849 Rifleman's knife and scabbard; 1840 light artillery saber; 1840 heavy cavalry saber; 1860 light cavalry saber. (Angela Bayardo/Arizona Historical Society)

A ferry linked the U.S. Quartermaster Depot in Arizona to Fort Yuma, California, on the Colorado River near its confluence with the Gila. As seen in this 1864 photograph, a rope stretched between tall masts on the banks allowed a flat-bottomed ferry to yaw across the swift river. The rope could be hoisted to permit steamboats, such as the *Mohave,* to carry supplies from the Gulf of California to forts and towns 300 miles above Yuma Crossing.
(Arizona Historical Society)

Captain Rafael Chacón defended Santa Fe against Americans in 1847 but led a company of U.S. New Mexico Volunteers to fight Confederate invaders from Texas during the Civil War. He placed a high value on martial honor and distinguished himself in combat against rebel soldiers and Indian warriors.
(Palace of the Governors Photo Archives)

Captain Charles Atchisson (right), Corporal Alonzo Davis (center), and the clerk (left) of Company I, Fourth California Volunteer Infantry, at Fort Mojave in 1863. French photographer Rudolph d'Heureuse captured some of the first images ever made of Arizona and its people, including this one—the earliest-known photograph of identified soldiers in the territory.
(Bancroft Library, University of California, Berkeley)

Mojave Indians fraternize with soldiers of Company I, Fourth California Infantry, on the banks of the Colorado River near Fort Mojave in 1863.
(Bancroft Library, University of California, Berkeley)

"John Moss and Piute Chief Tercherrum," photographed in El Dorado Canyon in 1863. Some considered "Johnny" Moss the "mining Kit Carson," after his gold discoveries on the Colorado River in 1861. Moss escorted Mojave Chief Iretaba and Pima Chief Antonio Azul to Washington, D.C. on a goodwill tour in 1864.
(Bancroft Library, University of California, Berkeley)

"Apache man with bow and arrows."
(Sharlot Hall Museum)

Manuelito (Hastiin Ch'il Haajiní), a Navajo chief of the Bít'aa'níí clan
(Folded Arms People), who resisted repeated attacks by U.S. troops and
offers to join the Navajo survivors of the "Long Walk" held captive at
the Bosque Redondo reservation on the Pecos River, New Mexico.

Navajo captives under guard at Fort Sumner on the Bosque Redondo reservation, New Mexico.
(Palace of the Governors Photo Archives)

Victorio (Bidu-ya), a Chihenne headman who, with Mangas Coloradas, Cochise, and other Chiricahua Apaches, waged war against Anglos who increased their incursions into Apache homelands during the 1860s. Eventually he succumbed to the pressure of relentless attacks and sued for "a lasting peace, one that will keep. We would like to live in our country, and will go onto a reservation where the government may put us, and those who do not come, we will go and help fight them."
(Huntington Library, San Marino, California)

"Indian Scouting in Arizona." Volunteer troops led by Indian scouts or former captives learned to surprise remote Apache *rancherías* with dawn attacks, though such "scouts" rarely succeeded when encumbered with the heavy pack train and mountain artillery pictured in this lithograph by George H. Baker. (Bancroft Library, University of California, Berkeley)

Merejildo Grijalva. Captured as a boy by Chiricahua Apaches raiding an Ópata village in Sonora, Grijalva spoke several Indian languages and, after his escape from Cochise's Chokonens in 1859, learned Spanish and English as well. He had lived with the Apaches for nine years and was intimately acquainted with their movements and tactics, knowledge that made him the most successful scout to work with the U.S. troops in the borderlands. (Buehman Photo Collection, Arizona Historical Society)

John M. Chivington was a Methodist minister turned soldier. The "fighting parson" was lauded for his 1862 victory over Confederates at Glorieta Pass, New Mexico, but was driven from the army in disgrace following the massacre of Black Kettle's village at Sand Creek, Colorado, in 1864. (History Colorado)

"Sand Creek Massacre," by Robert Lindneux. U.S. Volunteer cavalrymen encircle the peaceful Cheyenne and Arapaho village at Sand Creek as confused and frightened families flee up the dry riverbed and warriors attempt to resist the attackers determined to slay all—men, women, and children.
(History Colorado)

"A Running Fight." After lancing one soldier, Whirlwind,
a Cheyenne Dog Soldier, fires his pistol as he chases two others,
who return fire, in this 1865 Colorado encounter drawn by the warrior.
(Cheyenne Dog Soldier Ledger Book, History Colorado)

"Catching an Army Horse." A Cheyenne warrior captures a "US" branded army horse
after using an arrow to count coup on the animal. The U.S. model 1859 horse
equipments are depicted in detail, right down to the horseshoe nails.
(Cheyenne Dog Soldier Ledger Book, History Colorado)

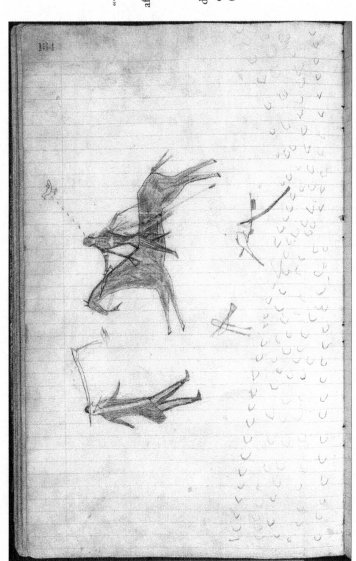

"Taps for a Bugler." White Bird shoots a dismounted bugler after counting coup with a saber during an encounter at Fort Rankin, Colorado, in 1865. The Cheyenne warrior artist displays the captured arms and equipment in the foreground. (Cheyenne Dog Soldier Ledger Book, History Colorado)

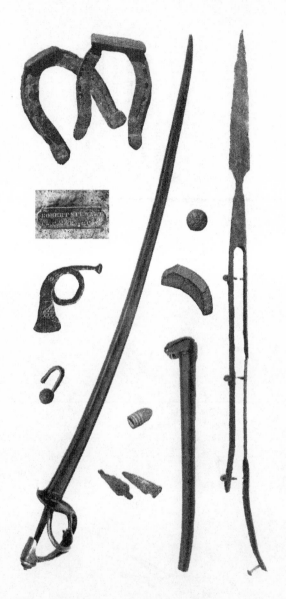

Archaeological evidence of war in the borderlands: shrapnel from an exploded 12-pounder case-shot round, .58-caliber minié ball, and iron arrowheads found in Apache Pass; steel-toed mule shoes, uniform button, infantry horn hat device, knapsack hook, and soldier's stencil ("Robert Stewart, Co. C, 2d Regt. CV" [California Volunteers]) found near Stanwix Station; Benicia Arsenal lance blade found at Tubac; M1855 Sharps carbine barrel, Papago Springs; 1840 pattern U.S. cavalry saber, Picacho Pass, Arizona.
(Arizona Historical Society)

A California Volunteer infantry regiment, with field musicians (left), company officers (front rank) in position, and the regimental colors unfurled, stands for a photographer in June 1865, prior to mustering out at the Presidio in San Francisco. (Huntington Library, San Marino, California.)

José Ramón Pico (pictured here as a colonel), First Battalion of Native California Cavalry. Displaying superb horsemanship and sometimes armed with lances, Hispano volunteers saw service along Arizona's border with Mexico during Maximilian's reign and French occupation in 1865.
(Security Pacific Collection, Los Angeles Public Library)

President Benito Juárez, as he appeared at El Paso del Norte, Mexico, in 1865 while eluding Maximilian's forces.
(Palace of the Governors Photo Archives)

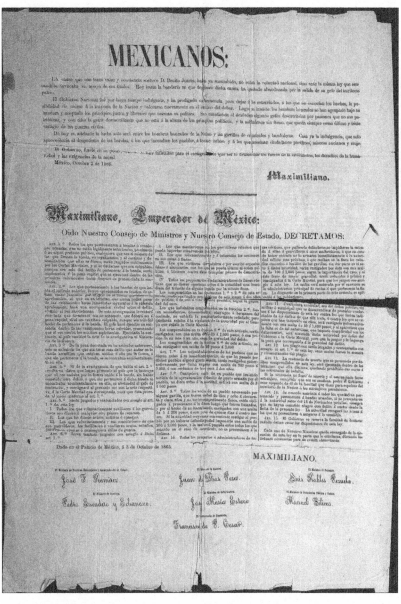

The "Black Decree." Maximilian authorized that the 1865 summary execution edict be printed in Spanish and Nahuatl in an effort to deter guerilla resistance during the civil war and French intervention in Mexico.

(Centro de Estudios de Historia de México)

Maximilian's Mexican Army firing squad, 1867, photographed by François Aubert.
(Metropolitan Museum of Art, Gilman Collection)

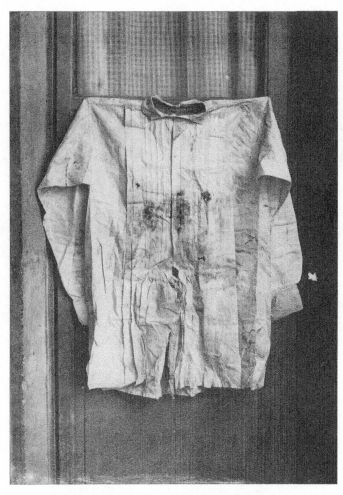

Maximilian's blood-stained and bullet-riddled death shirt,
as photographed by François Aubert only days
after the emperor's execution in 1867.
(Metropolitan Museum of Art, Gilman Collection)

Captain Richard H. Orton made this inscription on the sandstone of El Morro,
New Mexico, as his California Cavalry company left the territory in
October 1866. Orton began the Civil War as a lieutenant in 1861,
and in 1867 he was the last California Volunteer to be mustered out.
(Don Bufkin)

Chapter 5

The Balance of Power

The interruption and distraction of U.S. authority in 1861 had upset the fragile balance of power among the Indian, Hispano, and Anglo peoples of the Southwest and changed the nature of conflict in the borderlands. By 1865 the clashes over power and dominance among ethnic groups and nations had increased, and the level of violence had also risen. Starvation and the relentless war of attrition drove Apache bands, and the few Navajo holdouts who escaped reservations, to seek peace with Anglo military and territorial officials in New Mexico and Arizona. While intertribal fighting had existed since before the arrival of the Spanish, the Anglo-Americans introduced the concept of the war of extermination. The conflict in the territories had advanced far beyond the stock and slave raiding of the past, and the killing would continue long after Confederate armies had surrendered in the other theaters of what was already being referred to as the "War of the Rebellion."[1]

The peoples of Arizona and New Mexico were now engaged in violent conflicts that pitted raiding Navajos, Apaches, and Comanches against Hispano and Anglo citizens and soldiers and agrarian Indian villagers and auxiliaries. The allied forces arrayed against the pastoral, semisedentary mountain tribes forced their confinement on reservations by the late 1860s. The horse peoples of the southern plains moved into the power vacuum left by the subjugated tribes, and the fighting shifted eastward along the Santa Fe Trail and Staked Plains.

In Mexico, after the departure of French forces fearful of American military might, Juárez's restored Republican government turned its attention once again to Indian enemies along the northern border. On all fronts, clashing notions of manhood, honor, and warfare escalated the violence in the borderlands. It was now evident to most observers, however, that the Anglo-Americans from the United States would prevail and become the dominant power in the borderlands.[2]

Mexico's Civil War

South of the border, the nature of the civil war between Mexican liberals and conservatives had shifted as well. The French invasion in 1861 had temporarily tipped the scales in favor of Benito Juárez's conservative enemies, but Napoleon's puppet dictator Maximilian had been hard-pressed to control his vast empire, especially its northern borderlands where Republican forces and Indian raiders held sway. Some of the battles, such as the actions around Matamoros and Monterrey, were set-piece affairs involving entrenchment, flanking movements, and cannonades in preparation for infantry and cavalry charges. Sabers and lances were very much in evidence on both sides, but firearms and artillery ruled the battlefields and often determined the outcome. Early in the conflict, Republican troops carried arms deficient in both quantity and quality. Until 1865 many units still carried flintlock muskets that the men wrapped in their shirts in order to protect the priming powder from the rain. But as the American rebellion wound down and surplus weapons became available, the disparity in equipment became less of a factor. The violence escalated, however, as the armies in Mexico fought for survival rather than honor.[3]

Rumors of atrocities committed by the European troops in the interior states traveled quickly to the borderlands and to the United States, hardening public opinion against the invaders. The Belgian allies of the Imperialists were accused of using human shields and even baiting General Nicolás de Régules's troops to charge by displaying the general's captive wife "almost naked" on their earthworks at Tacámbaro. The Imperialists were also charged with showing a white flag and turning their muskets "breech uppermost" in a sign of surrender, then opening fire as the Republican soldiers approached the breastworks. One Republican officer wrote an open letter to "the Señor Marshal,

Commander-in-chief of the French Army in Mexico, (or wherever he may be)" upbraiding him for commanding "officers and soldiers [who] failed to keep their word of honor." Such infamous acts of perfidy, whether true or not, rippled indignation through the Republican ranks and caused the Juaristas to respond in kind. The "native imperialists" were dealt with most harshly, especially those "traitors" who "incited insurrection" or recruited Ópatas, Yaquis, and other Indians. Suspected traitors were subjected to the pretense of trials, but death by firing squad was invariably the sentence of the court.[4]

The desperate Maximilian had issued his infamous "Black Decree" in October 1865 at the urging of his allies, both foreign and domestic. The fighting had been bloody enough prior to the order, but now it took a savage new form. French-backed *contra-guerilla* units showed the black flag and summarily executed men and women suspected of Republican sympathies. The French and Imperial Mexican troops targeted non-combatants harboring Juaristas as well as enemy soldiers in the field and un-uniformed partisans. Republican forces, especially the unorthodox *guerrilleros*, retaliated in kind bringing about a frenzied orgy of killing and terror that escalated until Maximilian's own execution.[5]

The threat of U.S. intervention and Juárez's growing strength in the northern borderlands had forced Maximilian's hand. His Black Decree was a last-ditch effort to snuff out the "rebellion," but the ruthlessness of the order only stiffened Republican resolve and escalated the vio-lence, ultimately leading to the emperor's own death and the collapse of his empire. Without European support, the numerically inferior Mexican conservative forces and their Indian allies had little hope of continuing the war or prevailing in the internecine struggle. At the court-martial following Maximilian's capture by Juárez's Republican forces under General Escobedo at the siege of Querétaro, May 15, 1867, the court referenced the execution provisions of the Black Decree in the emperor's sentence. He would receive the same justice given Republican captives—death by firing squad.[6]

Maximilian's loyal generals, Miguel Miramón and Tomás Mejía, stayed by his side until the end. Most Europeans and Americans expressed sympathy for the plight of the misguided archduke who would be king of the Mexicans. Empress Charlotte went to Napoleon himself, only to be rejected and humiliated. Empress Eugenie attempted to intervene on Maximilian's behalf, but to no avail. Princess Agnes

Salm-Salm, the beautiful American wife of Prince Felix zu Salm-Salm, a Prussian mercenary serving as one of Maximilian's officers, begged Juárez for clemency in the final, desperate hours of the empire. Her tearful entreaties were rebuffed by Porfírio Díaz, Mariano Escobedo (in overall command of Republican forces), and Juárez himself. The President could only say to the distraught woman, "It causes me great pain, Madame, to see you like that on your knees; but even if every king and queen were in your place, I couldn't spare his life. It isn't me who takes it from him, it is the people and the law who claim his life."[7]

Maximilian's Black Decree played a significant role in bringing the emperor's reign to a close by alienating his own people and potential allies as well. Its harsh provisions and summary execution mandate went beyond the norms of acceptable warfare in Europe, the United States, and Mexico. Though Maximilian attempted to repeal the order one year after its issuance, the damage had been done. In effect, the Black Decree became the emperor's own death warrant.

Honor, Execution, and the End of Empire

On the morning of June 19, 1867, the sun rose on the cobble-strewn Cerro de las Campanas (the Hill of the Bells) overlooking the high desert city of Querétaro, some 125 miles northwest of Mexico City. Near the crest of the hill stood a wall of hastily stacked adobe bricks. Without ceremony, Maximiliano I stepped unaided from the donkey-drawn hackney that conveyed him the dusty mile from his prison, the convent of the Capuchins, near the city center. The emperor emerged from the carriage escorted by blue-uniformed Republican guards. His pale skin and wispy blond Dundreary side-whiskers made him instantly recognizable as the Austrian prince and emperor of Mexico. His fashionable Paris-made suit of the finest wool contrasted sharply with his broad-brimmed sombrero, much like those worn by the dark-skinned spectators that strained to get a glimpse of the condemned royal. All present—soldiers, clergy, and civilians—wondered at his calm. Only the priest who heard his confession and a few intimate friends understood that Maximilian was resigned to his fate. Honor would not allow him to abdicate and abandon the Mexico he had come to love.[8]

Three six-man squads detailed for the execution stood stiffly in two ranks. An officer and a noncommissioned officer flanked each of the squads. Many present still believed that somehow President Benito Juárez, pressured by world leaders—Napoleon III, Leopold of Belgium, Franz Joseph of Austria, Queen Victoria, President Andrew Johnson, even Pope Pius IX—might intervene at the last minute and stay the execution. Maximilian was, after all, a son of the house of Habsburg. But the reprieve did not come, and most understood that the emperor's own Black Decree had sealed his fate.

Two more dusty carriages rattled up the deeply rutted road, and armed escorts positioned General Miguel Miramón, once president of Mexico and now the emperor's ranking officer and field commander, placing him on Maximilian's left. General Tomás Mejía, an "*indio puro*" (full-blood Nahua Indian) and the loyal commander of the emperor's cavalry took his place on the right. Though Juárez's able General Escobedo was nominally in charge of the execution, he seemed detached and willing to let the scene unfold as if it had already been scripted by a higher authority and could not be altered by his command. Perhaps sensing this leadership vacuum, the condemned Maximilian appeared to take charge. Stepping from his place, he embraced Miramón and said, without bravado but loud enough for the Republican officers and poised riflemen to hear, "you deserve the place of honor" and motioned him to the middle position. The emperor then embraced Mejía saying that they would soon meet again in a better world.[9]

All eyes followed Maximilian as he approached the officer of the detail on the far right, opposite his own place, and presented him with a pouch containing a gold sovereign for each man of the firing squad. He asked them to aim for his heart, "*corazon*," he said, as he looked each man in the eye. Then the emperor handed his silver sombrero to his servant, returned to his place beside Miramón, and faced the firing line, less than ten paces away. Maximilian spoke his last words in a firm voice: "Mexicans! Men of my class and Race are created by God to be the happiness of nations or their martyrs. I forgive everybody. I pray that everyone may also forgive me, and I wish that my blood which is now to be shed may be for the good of the country. Long live Mexico! Long live independence!"[10]

He looked again at the firing squad, pointed to his heart and then held his arms out to his side, as if crucified. Then the orders were given: "*¡Preparen!*" "*¡Apunten!*" "*¡Fuego!*" The perfectly timed volley felled the three men at once. The one-ounce lead musket balls tore through their bodies and ricocheted up the hill to the adobe wall. But when the smoke cleared all could see the emperor writhing on the ground—his hands appeared to clutch his chest and, though his lips moved, he did not cry out. The officer in charge ran to the wounded man and pointed the tip of his sword at the emperor's heart; the corporal at his side aimed his musket at the spot indicated and, without waiting for further orders, pulled the trigger to administer the coup de grâce. The emperor's death struggle ended as his servant scrambled to his master's motionless body and snuffed out the smoldering embers ignited on the vest by the muzzle blast. At 7:00 A.M. on June 19, 1867, Maximilian lay still on the Cerro de las Campanas and the church bells of Querétaro tolled the end of an empire.[11]

As was customary in military executions, the men of the firing squad did not load their own firearms. One musket was secretly loaded with a blank powder charge, topped with a harmless wad but no bullet, so that when the volley was fired and the smoke cleared each man might imagine that he had not been the one to fire the fatal shot. This ritual allowed each man to plausibly deny the charge of murder when he met his maker and, thereby, improve his chance of gaining access to the kingdom of heaven. Maximilian's powder-burned and bloodied shirt itself was preserved by the emperor's private physician, Dr. Samuel Basch, who laundered the gory relic and allowed it to be photographed by the French artist François Aubert. Basch then smuggled the tattered and stained shirt out of Mexico and presented it to the emperor's grieving mother.[12]

Though Maximilian affected the dress of his adopted Mexico, often wearing a sombrero, bandana, and other tokens of native *"charro"* costume, he could not so easily change his preference for the finery of his homeland. With his dying words he uttered that his blood was now Mexican. This proved prophetic indeed for his life blood spilled on the Cerro de las Campanas, and ladies present at the execution, desirous of souvenirs, dipped the corners of their kerchiefs in the dark red pools before they soaked into the sunbaked earth. Two physicians drained what little blood remained in the emperor's body and discarded it, perhaps in a privy to discourage the ever vigilant curs and ubiquitous flies, before filling the corpse with an embalming fluid. The royal organs were carefully removed and mummified, and Maximilian's pale blue eyes were replaced with artificial glass orbs of brown, the only color kept on hand by doctors in Querétaro (or anywhere in Mexico for that matter).[13]

After months of indecision, a worried Juárez, fearing he might have made a martyr of Maximilian, finally authorized the shipment of the elegant glass-fronted royal coffin to the Habsburg crypt in Vienna. Aubert's photographs of the corpse and bloodstained shirt created an international sensation. Napoleon banned them, but thousands of bootlegged *cartes de visite* circulated in France and throughout Europe and the Americas—testaments to Napoleon's perfidy, Maximilian's vanity and naiveté, and the end of an empire in Mexico.

In Paris, French artist Edouard Manet had followed the news of Napoleon's invasion and occupation of Mexico with alarm. He and other French intellectuals saw the unfolding events for what they were: an imperialistic land grab intended to enhance the French emperor's prestige and power at the expense of a weaker nation. The installation of the Austrian archduke, some said "arch-dupe," as Napoleon's puppet did not surprise those watching France's "Mexican Adventure." Shocking, however, was the callousness with which Napoleon abandoned Maximilian once the occupation and counterinsurgency costs mounted and public opinion turned against the Mexican scheme.[14]

The French had pressured Maximilian to put an end to Juárez's Republican resistance as quickly and ruthlessly as possible while at the same time heavily taxing Maximilian's government and subjects to defray the expenses of the war. Manet's *Execution of Maximilian* was an oversized canvas (at eight by ten feet, larger than anything he had previously attempted) and a bold critique of Napoleon's greed and infidelity. It exposed the French emperor's betrayal of Maximilian and his Mexican allies while lauding General Mejía's loyalty and General Miramón's courage. Maximilian is depicted as an honorable character, refusing, as he did, Napoleon's entreaties that he abdicate his throne and abandon Mexico.[15]

As the United States ended its civil war, the Americans began exerting political and military pressure on France to begin the evacuation of its forces from Mexico. Prussia's rise as a European power may also have influenced Napoleon to reevaluate his priorities and focus his attention closer to home. In Sonora, the Imperialists' days were numbered, due in large measure to the fierce campaigning of Republican General Angel Martinez. He had joined the army at an early age, was quickly promoted, and, although only twenty-eight years old and illiterate, attained the rank of general by 1865. Motivated as much by plunder as political loyalties, Martinez and his machete-armed *mestizo* and Indian *macheteros* swept from Sinaloa into Sonora, killing and looting as they rode. By February 1866 Martinez had defeated the armies of Jose María Almada, once a loyal Republican who switched sides following the indiscriminate attacks of Juaristas that killed his father and other family members, desecrated churches, and looted the haciendas of Imperialists and Republicans alike. Almada became known as Chato and raised an Imperialist army composed of Yaqui and Mayo mercenaries. Now, Chato was dead and Martinez and the Republicans controlled the entire District of Álamos, Sonora, in northwestern Mexico.

Martinez publicly pledged Pesqueira his support and encouraged the governor to return from his Arizona sanctuary and rally his former supporters. From Calabasas, near the post of Tubac, Pesqueira cautiously viewed these developments. That same month he received a petition from General Jesús Garcia Morales and his officers asking that the governor resume command of the Sonoran troops, and in March the *caudillo* arrived at Bronces, near Arizpe, and accepted the leadership of a *guerrilla* band serving under Major Bernardo Zuniga. In April at Buenavista, Pesqueira resumed the offices of governor and commanding general of the state and with three hundred men marched to Álamos. Encouraged by Pesqueira's return, Martinez headed south and, with Garcia Morales, captured Magdalena.[16]

On June 20, 1867, the day after Maximilian's execution, Mexican conservatives and Imperialists sued for peace and surrendered Mexico City, bringing to a close the deadly reprisals and civil war that had destabilized the nation and decimated the population. Those who could flee the war-torn republic took ships to receptive European ports or traveled north to the United States. Beginning in 1865 the international border itself had become a very different thing. Large numbers of U.S. troops, many of them well-armed-and-led combat veterans, now massed on the previously porous boundary line along the Rio Grande in Texas. All along the border, from Texas to California, the Americans established checkpoints requiring passports on main traveled roads. From El Paso to Yuma, military patrols turned back emigrants and Indian raiders alike as the border became not just an imagined line but a boundary that denied access. In the process, Indian peoples were divided, especially the Papagos and Pimas. Though at first the new rules had little impact on traditional ways, over time families, bands, and cultures separated, and the people grappled with tribal and national issues of loyalty and identity.[17]

Clash of Martial Cultures

As the Navajo campaign came to a close in 1864 and Carleton transported the surviving Navajos and Mescalero Apaches to Fort Sumner and the Bosque Redondo reservation, other tribes began to feel the pressure of the increasingly aggressive U.S. military policy. The Western Apaches inhabiting the mountainous country along the upper Gila and the related Yavapais in central Arizona now went on the defensive, resisting the incessant forays by soldiers and their allied tribes.

On the Colorado River, Chief Iretaba of the Mojaves counseled his warriors against making war and kept them in check by recounting stories of the "white father's" might. From November 1863 until June 1864 the Mojave headman had traveled, at government expense, to San Francisco and then by sea to Washington accompanied by Pima chief Antonio Azul and Indian agent John Moss. The Arizona Indian leaders, once enemies, traveled together on steamships and railroad cars. They witnessed the firing of great cannons, participated in reviews of regiments of well-armed soldiers, and slept in fancy hotels in cities teeming with white men and women too numerous to count.

The goodwill tour and propaganda campaign worked where military action might have failed. Iretaba returned to his people gaudily outfitted in the dress uniform of a major general, convinced that resisting the whites would be futile. His people gathered about him as he compared the whites to the leaves of a cottonwood stand—beyond counting. For added emphasis he scooped a handful of sand representing the Mojaves and then pointed to a great sand bar in the river and dolefully intoned, "Americans." Antonio Azul needed little convincing, for the Pima and Maricopa Indian farmers already benefited from army contracts and the military alliance that protected their Gila River villages from Western Apache and Yavapai raiders. Still, Arizona civilians and soldiers considered such trips and gifts well worth the expense, reasoning that it was more cost effective in both lives and treasure to inspire awe and loyalty in native leaders than it was to fight them.[18]

The Paiutes, Hualapais, and Chemehuevis in northwestern Arizona, however, were another matter. Troops and miners consumed the meager crop yields of the Mojave Valley and killed or frightened away game animals, leaving the tribes in a state of starvation. Freighters' horses and mules were targeted as a source of food. The warriors then threatened Colorado River steamboat refueling stops and resisted incursions by Anglo and Hispano miners, teamsters, and travelers on the Mojave-Fort Whipple road across central Arizona. Mail carriers and freighters described the warriors as armed with bows and arrows, ready to "give battle to the settlers and the U.S. troops."[19] The soldiers retaliated, though with limited success. Unprepared for the hit-and-run style of warfare, one soldier commented that the Indians "were too fleet of foot for infantrymen and gave us wide berth when we got after them."[20] Men of the Fourth Infantry, California Volunteers, were issued horses and pressed into service as mounted infantry in order to chase Paiutes who had captured a boy from a Mexican immigrant train, but the soldiers turned back after their five-day supply of rations ran out.[21] Frustrated by their inability to track down elusive Chemehuevi warriors, the soldiers arrested innocent chiefs and held them hostage until depredations ceased or guilty raiders were apprehended.[22]

Colonel Thomas F. Wright, son of the former commander of the Department of the Pacific, led eight companies of the Second California Infantry to Arizona in the summer of 1865. Charged with hunting down Western Apaches on the upper Gila, the men of the Second had little stomach for combat once they learned that the Civil War was indeed over. Pressed by Carleton and Mason, however, the officers of the Second launched numerous scouts from Forts Goodwin and Grant. Corporal William A. Bushnell summed up the spirit of the men in a diary entry written on December 11, 1865, following a seventeen-day scout:

At this season of the year, carrying one blanket, your overcoat, half a shelter tent, your gun, accoutrements and 210 rounds of ammunition, is not a very desirable pastime, especially when you are out seventeen days without finding an Indian. If Jomini [author of The Art of War] could peruse a detailed account of our expedition, he would, no doubt, see fit to change his definition of military terms considerably. Thus the term Scouting (in an Indian country, at least) as our experience proves, is to start out and travel 8 or 10 miles a day, camping about noon and keeping good fires burning all night so as to warn all Indians of your whereabouts. In the morning a large fire should be built so as to make smoke so that the enemy can see it and flee your approach. It is also well to take precaution a few days before leaving the garrison to post all guides and interpreters so that they can easily go out into the mountains and intimate the coming danger to their savage brother. Thus you will easily avoid coming into collision with the noble red man. An appropriate report to send to Headquarters would be something like this: "Deserted Rancheria, December 1865 General: We are at the camp of the enemy and they are ours (hours ahead of us)."[23]

As Carleton focused the efforts of the New Mexico and California Volunteers on the Navajos, Mescaleros, Chiricahuas, and Western Apaches, the warriors of the southern plains stepped up their attacks on the Santa Fe Trail in Colorado south of the Arkansas and outlying Hispano and Pueblo Indian settlements in northeastern New Mexico. The young men of the Kiowa, Kiowa-Apache, Comanche, Cheyenne, and Arapaho tribes sought stock, goods, and other tradable commodities, including captive women and children.[24]

The Apacheans' warrior traditions bore remarkable similarities to those of the horse peoples of the southern plains. Though their mutually unintelligible tongues evolved from completely different language groups, the peoples of the mountains and plains shared beliefs in personal bravery and honor and understood the same distinctions between raiding and war. The Southern Cheyennes divided themselves into six warrior or "soldier" societies—Bowstrings, Crooked Lances, Dog Soldiers, Kit Fox Soldiers, Red Shields, and Chiefs. Each of these societies had its own dress, rituals, and songs. They recruited compatible young men who formed close male bonds. They danced, sang, hunted, raided, and went to war together. Holy men provided decorated shields, designed to protect the bearer in battle, to warriors willing to accept the weighty responsibilities associated with such a powerful war talisman. Weapons—bows and lances—were also carefully crafted and decorated to imbue them, when properly handled, with extraordinary power.[25]

As with the Apacheans, the Cheyennes and other peoples of the plains saw skills in raiding and war as virtuous and a sure way to achieve status. The different peoples also recognized similar taboos against touching blood and the importance of ritual purification after battle. Warriors handled scalps with great care and discarded these trophies immediately if members of their own raiding or war party were killed by the enemy. Women encouraged their men and gloried in their victories and exploits. Married women painted red lines on their faces to indicate the coups or brave deeds of their husbands, and the stringent restrictions on sexual contact between unmarried men and women were relaxed during scalp dances which celebrated victories over enemies and the well-being of the tribe or band. For men, success in raiding and war became the path to status within the tribe, access to women, and marriage. Martial prowess led to marital opportunity. Women recognized that successful warriors were both good providers and protectors against external threats.[26]

The horse peoples of the plains developed a ritualized mode of fighting that involved a kind of mock combat in which a warrior might demonstrate his superiority over an enemy by counting coup—touching or striking his adversary as if to say, "I touched you, and could have killed you, but I choose to give you your life." The blow might be delivered with a special coup stick or other nonlethal implement, but the bravest coups were made with the bare hand. With the proliferation of firearms resulting from increased contact with Anglo-Americans during the 1860s, the rules of war changed. Warriors would still count coups but then return to kill their white enemies, who failed to recognize the customs of warfare as understood by the Plains tribes. As with the Apacheans and other peoples of the borderlands, killings and war-related deaths reached an all-time high during and immediately following the Civil War, as reprisals and retaliatory wars of revenge escalated.

In the borderlands, a spirit of martial masculinity animated the Indian soldier societies, and elaborate preparations for war made fighting enemies, real and perceived, a foregone conclusion. As large numbers of Anglo-American military men entered the fray in the Southwest, a direct result of the Civil War troop buildup, the violence generated by the clashing martial traditions reached unprecedented levels. On the southern plains for over one hundred years the Comanches, with their Kiowa and Kiowa-Apache allies, had been the greatest military power. By the 1860s, this power hierarchy was about to change.[27]

During the spring and summer of 1864, attacks by Kiowas, Comanches, Cheyennes, and Arapahos nearly shut down the Santa Fe Trail. Wagon trains from Kansas joined in caravans for mutual protection. One such train included ten wagons owned by the Taos firm of Guttmann, Friedman & Company. At Cow Creek Crossing, Kansas, on July 12, 1864, four hundred Kiowa, Comanche, and Arapaho warriors surrounded the heavily laden wagons bound for Fort Union with uniforms, carbines, boots, shoes, and other government supplies, as well as general merchandise to be sold in Taos. The allied Indians first sent in a captive to ascertain whether this was a "Mexican" or an "American" train, the emissary indicating that if it were a Mexican train the wagoners would not be molested. As most of the teamsters were Hispanos and Juan Santistevan was a principal in the company, the captive reported back that they were Mexicans, and the warriors approached to parley and eat. But it soon became apparent that this was not to be a friendly encounter. The Indians drew their weapons and turned on the teamsters. The warriors appropriated axes and proceeded to chop to pieces the four wagons bearing government supplies. They slashed bundles of uniforms with knives and threw ransacked provisions onto the prairie. The raiders then ran off fifty-six yokes of oxen but spared the terrified Hispanos, who were left balancing on the tongues of their remaining wagons.[28]

The loss of vital supplies worried Carleton, but troubling him even more was the intelligence he received regarding the singling out of Anglo merchants and teamsters by the depredating Comanches. William Allison's train was attacked at the lower Cimarron Crossing of the Santa Fe Trail and the Hispano survivors testified that the five Americans among them were separated and "brutally murdered and scalped." The New Mexicans were allowed to return to their settlements unmolested, the raiders even furnishing them with transportation. "The discrimination which the Comanches have frequently made," Carleton explained to Superintendent of Indian Affairs Dr. Michael Steck, "in favor of the people, natives of this Territory, and against Anglo-Americans, cannot be regarded in any other light than as an insult to the government and to our people." It now seemed to Carleton that a race war was underway, and he was determined to put a stop to it. "I should be derelict of my duty," he wrote, "if I should refrain from making at least an attempt to avenge our slaughtered and plundered citizens." Short of troops because of the all-out campaign against the Apaches in Arizona, he dashed off messages to Carson and other officers in an attempt to recruit Navajo, Apache, and Ute auxiliaries that might be turned against the Kiowas and Comanches, as well as the Cheyennes and Arapahos that threatened the Santa Fe Trail.[29]

Vicente Otero's six freight wagons loaded with twenty-five thousand pounds of military supplies joined other Santa Fe traders on the 680-mile trek from Fort Leavenworth, Kansas, to Fort Union in the summer of 1864. With more than one hundred teamsters driving the heavily laden mule and ox-drawn wagons, the caravan appeared strong enough to protect itself from attack—so strong, in fact, that army officers at Leavenworth refused the escort promised by the military procurement officer. After suffering an attack near the Great Bend of the Arkansas on July 18, the freighters insisted on protection and appealed to the exasperated post commander at Fort Larned, who put his refusal in writing:

> Headquarters, Fort Larned, Kan.
> July 23, 1864
> Messrs. Otero, Luna and Jaramillo, Govt. Freighters,
> Fort Larned, Kansas.
>
> Gents: Yours of the 22nd inst. is received, and in reply I would say that on assuming command of this Post I found the force so small that I cannot with safety to the Government property at this Post spare any of the Troops for escort to freight trains, nor do I deem it necessary in your case. You have over one hundred men, all armed, and you will proceed immediately to select some one of your number to act as Captain and proceed on your way, keeping a vigilant watch night and day over your stock and wagons.
>
> Wm. H. Backus
> Capt. Co. L 1st Cav. of Colorado, Commanding Post

The freighters duly elected Jesús Luna "Captain" and pushed on. Luna directed the company to circle the wagons for the noon halt at Las Palomas on August 6 and cautioned the teamsters to be prepared to drive the grazing mules into the center of the corral if Indians were sighted. But the hundreds of Comanche and Kiowa warriors that swept into the train came without warning and too quickly for the herders to react. The freighters suffered the loss of nearly all their animals, and the partners were forced to rent the oxen of returning traders at ruinous rates in order to complete their journey to Fort Union.[30]

As winter approached, the attacks on the Santa Fe Trail and southern plains became more frequent and more violent. Soldiers hid in freight wagons and attempted to bait raiders with apparently easy pickings. But the warriors were wary and relied on carefully planned ambushes or hit-and-run attacks at river crossings. Watching from the few prominences on the prairie, they studied the movements of wagons and stayed ready to cut off hunters and outriders who strayed too far from the trains or their military escorts. The wagon masters learned to circle their wagons and corral the animals quickly, for the horses and mules remained the raiders' main objective, when they were not moved by vengeance. Atrocities committed by Anglos and Indians became commonplace. Finding teamsters with their feet chained to the wheels of their wagon and hoop iron driven into their eye sockets, the soldiers determined that warriors had first scalped the men then piled sacks of bacon on their legs and burned them alive. Colorado Volunteer Cavalry escorts adopted a fatalistic attitude as they hardened to their task and their enemies. Private Jesse Haire remembered, "If we go under, we get rubbed out. Game, you bet. For no quarters are given on either side fighting Indians."[31]

The callousness of the Anglo soldiers manifested itself in a kind of martial mob mentality. When a twelve-year-old Indian boy came into their camp with raised hands, the Colorado cavalrymen clamored for his immediate execution. Private Haire wrote in his journal, "Most every person in camp as is usually the case with a lot of unthoughtful men who is always ready to pitch in and kill somebody when there is no opposition against them hot headed with no reason they say he must die because he is an Indian. All want the boy to put up as a mark to shoot at for practice." Fortunately, a Spanish-speaking Anglo soldier among them discovered that the boy was a Ute who had just escaped his Comanche captors. Evidence of torture—his fingernails and toenails had been pulled out—corroborated his story, and the soldiers took him back to Fort Union and reunion with his family.[32]

The constant attacks by Comanche warriors on the flocks and herds of the Mescaleros and Navajos confined at Bosque Redondo threatened to undo Carleton's grand reservation experiment. Determined to put a stop to these and other raids by "the nomads of the plains,"[33] Carleton ordered Kit Carson to mobilize his newly organized regiment of New Mexico cavalry. This highly effective mounted force created expressly for Indian campaigning bore little resemblance to the hastily recruited

First New Mexico Infantry that he had rallied to repel the Texans and commanded at the Battle of Valverde in 1862. Having conquered the Navajos, considered by many to be the most powerful tribe in the borderlands, Carleton believed the reliable and resourceful Carson could take on the nomadic Plains warriors with similar success. "It is my desire," Carleton wrote, "that you give those Indians, especially the Kiowas, a severe drubbing." Having known and lived with the highly mobile and militarily well-organized Plains tribes, Carson knew this was a tall order, but he obeyed and set about training a command to get the job done.[34]

In October 1864 Carson began gathering his mixed battalion of Anglo and Hispano volunteer cavalry, infantry, artillery, and Indian auxiliaries on the Texas border some two hundred miles east of Santa Fe. Here Fort Bascom, named for the same George Bascom that touched off the Chiricahua Apache war in 1861 and then died fighting at Valverde the following year, served as one in a series of strong points Carleton established to protect settlements between the Staked Plains and the Rio Grande Valley. Located on the Canadian River along well-known, east-west trading and raiding trails, Fort Bascom was the logical place from which to launch a punishing expedition. Comancheros, Hispano and Indian traders from northern New Mexican pueblos, knew the way to the large villages of Kiowas, Kiowa-Apaches, and Comanches that gathered for mutual protection while wintering on the grassy plains along the Canadian. With the consent of the Comanches, the Comancheros lived by trading with the nomadic plains tribes, providing tools, cloth, flour, tobacco, and manufactured goods of all kinds—including firearms and ammunition—in exchange for hides, livestock, and slaves or ransomed captives.[35] Carson's artillery chief, Lieutenant George Pettis, remembered that the battalion comprised men selected for their proven ability as campaigners:

> Colonel Francisco P. Abreú, First New Mexico Infantry; Major William McCleave, First California Cavalry; Captain Emil Fritz, Company B, First California Cavalry, one officer and forty enlisted men; Lieutenant Sullivan Heath, Company K, First California Cavalry, one officer and forty men; Captain [John] Merriam, Company M [L], First California Cavalry, one officer and thirty-four men; Lieutenant George H. Pettis, Company K,

First California Infantry, one officer and twenty-six men, with two twelve pounder mountain howitzers mounted on prairie carriages; Captain Charles Deus, Company M, First New Mexico Cavalry, two officers and seventy men; Captain Joseph Berney, Company D, First New Mexico Cavalry, two officers and thirty-six men; Company A, First California Veteran Infantry, seventy-five men; Assistant Surgeon George S. Courtright . . . and an Assistant Quartermaster and Commissary—numbering, in all, fourteen officers and three hundred and twenty-one enlisted men.

Most important, the command also included seventy-two Ute and Jicarilla Apache warriors to whom Carson had promised all the plunder they could carry off. No friends of the Plains tribes, the mountain-dwelling, semisedentary peoples of northern New Mexico and southern Colorado respected Carson, who had once been their foe and then their Indian agent in the 1850s.[36]

Riding newly shod horses and supported with a supply train numbering twenty-seven wagons, an ambulance, and two mule-drawn mountain howitzers mounted on wide-tracking prairie carriages, the expedition set out from Fort Bascom on the frosty morning of November 6, 1864.[37] Directed by the mercenary Comancheros, Carson headed his men down the Canadian River across the northern Texas panhandle straight for the Bent brothers' ruined trading post known as Adobe Walls. Carson knew the Indian people who had frequented the place years before, and they knew him—the frontiersman and the Indians had hunted and traded together in the 1840s and 1850s. Now, under orders from Carleton, he was bound to kill them. "You know where to find the Indians," Carleton wrote, "you know what atrocities they have committed, you know how to punish them." The brutality of the Navajo war may have softened both men some, and knowing that Carson's command included Utes and Apaches sworn to kill their old enemies, Carleton stressed that only Indian men were to be targeted. "Of course," he added, "I know that in attacking a village women and children are liable to be killed, and this cannot, in the rush and confusion of a fight, particularly at night, be avoided, but let none be killed willfully or wantonly." The general had originally planned that a converging column under General James Blunt would strike from western Kansas, but these troops were diverted to attend to a rebel threat, and Carson was ordered to go it alone.[38]

The command marched more than one hundred miles through a rapidly changing weather system that brought a snow storm then bright sun and crisp, bracing air. The soldiers huddled together in blankets during the freezing nights as their Ute and Jicarilla allies danced, sang, and made their spiritual preparations for the coming battle. Their "war dance" involved singing and acting out in pantomime how they intended to slay their enemies. These rituals often went on until dawn, and the soldiers complained about losing sleep until they eventually "became accustomed to the groans and howlings incident to the dance." Carson prepared his Anglo and Hispano soldiers in his own way, regaling them with stories of daring deeds and deadly clashes that had occurred near Tucumcari Butte, the very ground on which they now slept. Here he told the story of Mrs. Ann White, a harrowing tale that quickened the men's hearts and inspired in them a lust for bloody vengeance, no doubt exactly the effect Carson desired.

Some fifteen years earlier he had guided a troop of dragoons in pursuit of Jicarillas who had attacked a Santa Fe–bound caravan led by James White. The men of the train, Carson recalled, had been killed in the initial rush, but Ann, a daughter, and a servant were taken prisoner. Carson tracked the raiders, finding bits of the Anglo woman's clothing she had purposely left behind as clues, and finally located the Apache camp on the Canadian. The soldiers failed to attack as soon as the enemy was sighted, a blunder, the scout believed, that resulted in Mrs. White's death from an arrow shot through her heart as she lay just two hundred yards from the charging scout. The incident still weighed heavily on him for, while searching the abandoned Jicarilla camp, a soldier had discovered a book, purporting to be history, featuring the heroic Carson and his exploits on the frontier. It was the first book of its kind he had ever seen, and after it was read to him he believed that he had failed Ann White, who surely must have been counting on him to come to her rescue. He now revealed to his men that the woman had been both physically and sexually abused, and he consoled himself that under these circumstances she was better off dead.[39]

By November 24, the day President Lincoln had recently proclaimed for the nation to observe Thanksgiving, the Indian scouts located a wide trail grooved by thousands of horses dragging lodge poles and followed by herds of cattle. Lieutenant Pettis reported that the scouts told Carson he "would have no difficulty in finding all the Indians that we desired."[40] As the command neared the enemy villages, Carson pushed on with his Indian, Hispano, and Anglo horsemen and the mountain howitzer battery, while the infantry escorting the wagons bought up the rear. The going was difficult in the bottoms near the river as the prairie grass grew to a height of eight feet in places, slowing the movement of the wheeled cannons and ammunition carts. The Utes and Jicarillas stripped off their buffalo robes and other impedimenta as soon as Kiowa outriders were discovered. Carson's warriors stopped only long enough to hurriedly paint their bodies for battle, don their feathered bonnets imbued with spiritual power, and pray to the four winds. The Utes and Jicarillas led the charge followed by Major McCleave and companies of California and New Mexico Volunteer Cavalry. The chase tore through a Kiowa village of 150 buffalo hide lodges, the tipi skins brain-tanned so white that Lieutenant Pettis and his gunners had believed from a distance that they approached an encampment of soldiers in their conical, bleached canvas, Sibley-patent tents. Four miles beyond the village lay the ruined adobe buildings and corrals of the old Bent trading post.

Around the Adobe Walls, Anglo and Hispano cavalrymen dismounted and deployed as skirmishers, kneeling or lying in the tall grass, keeping up a steady fire with their breech-loading carbines, while the Utes and Jicarillas shouted their war cries and charged forward toward a group of some two hundred Kiowa and Comanche warriors, who likewise made rushes toward the troops and their Indian allies. Both groups of mounted Indians would turn and rush back to their original positions when the opposing fire grew too hot or the momentum of an enemy charge seemed too great to resist. The main body of Kiowas and Comanches maintained their distance just out of rifle and howitzer range. Pettis set up his little mountain battery behind a twenty-five-foot sand hill and busily loaded the guns under cover, then manhandled them to the top of the hill and lobbed exploding shells, as Carson directed, into large groups of enemy warriors. The violent recoil of the little guns rolled or tumbled them back down the hill where they were reloaded and shoved back into battery. These "guns that shot twice" (the boom of the initial discharge followed by the explosion of the bursting shell seconds later) appeared to unnerve some of the warriors, while others continued to make bravery runs, riding close to the soldiers' lines at a full gallop, hanging precariously on the far sides of their ponies, while shooting guns or bows under their animals' necks. Chiefs in elaborate feathered bonnets exhorted their men while a mile east of the warriors' position, women and children could be seen abandoning a Comanche encampment of five hundred lodges.

The weathered mud buildings and corrals of Adobe Walls now became a field hospital and place of shelter for the soldiers' horses. Every fourth man detailed as a "horse-holder" led his four thirsty animals to drink from a stream of clear water that bubbled from the prairie nearby. Carson believed the Indians would break off the attack once the women and children abandoned the village, but the warriors seemed disinclined to withdraw and pressed forward as men of different bands arrived from more distant camp circles. The soldiers sounded bugle calls directing the several companies to advance then retreat toward the Adobe Walls. Some confusion followed during these maneuvers as a Kiowa warrior, whom some believed to be Chief Satanta himself, blew opposite signals from a captured army bugle. "When our bugles sounded 'advance,' he would blow 'retreat,'" Pettis remembered, "and when ours sounded the 'retreat,' he would follow with the 'advance'; ours would signal 'halt'; he would follow suit. So he kept it up all the day, blowing as shrill and clearly as our very best buglers."[41]

Outnumbered four to one, Carson now realized he had bitten off more than he could chew and ordered a general retreat. While he believed he could keep the Kiowa and Comanche warriors at bay, he could not advance and feared for the safety of the seventy-five men left behind with the wagon train. Satanta now redoubled his efforts, his dismounted warriors igniting grass fires that swept through the soldier skirmishers and threatened to break their line as mounted warriors darted in through the smoke. On Carson's left flank, a Comanche warrior rode up to the skirmish line screened by a cloud of smoke when a sudden gust of wind cleared the air for an instant leaving a young New Mexico Volunteer totally exposed, twenty feet from the charging warrior. Both men fired almost at once, but the dismounted soldier's aim was true and the Comanche man fell dead from his horse. Though the warrior's comrades attempted a mounted rescue, a scene that the soldiers witnessed repeatedly throughout the battle, the Hispano soldiers kept up a covering fire as the boy scalped his fallen foe. It turned out that this was to be the only scalp taken in combat during the whole bloody affair.

Carson's unhurried and well-organized retreat took the command back to the 150-lodge Kiowa camp the troops had earlier swept through. This time the soldiers, Jicarillas, and Utes had time to pick up beautifully tanned buffalo robes and other plunder. Two Ute women who had accompanied their warriors used an axe to kill the elderly and infirm Kiowas left behind. Then all the wonderfully painted and appointed lodges were put to the torch, lighting the night sky as the soldiers continued their retreat, covered by the fire of their mountain howitzers. Late that night the horse soldiers, with severely wounded men lashed to litters on the gun carriages and ammunition carts, reunited with the infantry reserve and supply train. The Kiowas and Comanches dogged the trail of the retreating column for days, keeping a respectful distance just beyond the range of the howitzers. The Utes purchased the scalp taken by the young New Mexican and used it in a nightlong "scalp dance" to celebrate their victory. Some of the California and New Mexico officers talked about renewing the attack and returning to destroy the five hundred Comanche lodges sighted near Adobe Walls, but this bold talk may have masked their genuine relief in having survived the ordeal.

The following day, November 26, the soldiers witnessed the ritualized warfare and martial display of the Indian warriors of the mountains and plains play out as the two sides sparred in a duel for honor and dominance. Pettis reported:

> Two of our Indians, mounted, rode out leisurely on the plains towards the Comanches; presently two of the enemy left their party and rode toward us, when another party of ten or a dozen left our camp, and then the same number left the camp of the enemy, like boys playing at goal, and then another from our camp, followed by a like party from the enemy, until there were over two hundred men of both sides moving at a walk towards each other in the centre of the plain. The leading parties of each side had approached each other until only about two hundred yards of space intervened, when shooting commenced, but before a dozen shots had been exchanged the entire body of the enemy turned their horses' heads towards their camp, and left on a run, followed by our people for a short distance, who afterwards returned to camp unharmed.[42]

Had the Utes and Jicarillas followed their adversaries over the next rise, they might well have fallen into a decoy trap, a time-honored technique of luring overbold enemies by appearing to run away.

When three weeks later the column of soldiers and their Indian allies rode into Fort Bascom, Carson initially reported the expedition to be a success. Carleton, elated by the news, wrote to Carson:

> I beg to express to you and to the gallant officers and soldiers whom you commanded on that occasion, as well as to our good auxiliaries, the Utes and Apaches, my thanks for the handsome manner in which you all met so formidable an enemy and defeated him. Please to publish an order to this effect. This brilliant affair adds another green leaf to the laurel wreath which you have so nobly won in the service of your country.

But Kit knew it was a very near thing. Years later he confessed that he had been lucky in extricating his command, which might just as easily have been wiped out, and confided these feelings to George Bent, the half-Cheyenne son of Owl Woman and trader William Bent, the builder of Adobe Walls. At the time, however, Carson bravely told the admiring Carleton that he would be willing to return to the Canadian to finish the job but admitted it would require one thousand men and heavier artillery, preferably long-range, rifled guns.[43]

While Carson's command had marched back to Fort Bascom, on November 29, 1864, two hundred miles to the north on a tributary of the Arkansas River known as Sand Creek, Colonel John Chivington attacked the peaceful Cheyenne and Arapaho village of 150 lodges sheltering 750 people gathered under the Chiefs Black Kettle and Left Hand.[44] The ambitious Chivington desperately wanted a brigadier's star and, eventually, a congressional seat. He believed a victory over the Colorado tribes would win him the fame needed to achieve these goals, but he needed to strike before the expiration of the hundred-day enlistments of Colonel George Shoup's Third Colorado Volunteer Cavalry. With companies of the battle-tested First Colorado Cavalry and a loaned company of Carson's First New Mexico Cavalry,[45] Chivington mustered nearly 750 men. He wasted little time, moving quickly to attack Black Kettle, whom army officers at Fort Lyon had recently instructed to camp nearby for protection. An American flag and a white flag of peace flew prominently over the chief's own tipi. Nearly two hundred confused and panicked Indian men, women, and children were cut down near their lodges or in the five-mile running pursuit that followed the initial attack. The soldiers fired small arms of all description and mountain howitzers loaded with exploding spherical case shot and canister rounds, each containing 148 lead balls, into the masses of fleeing people and pockets of frightened women and children huddled in hastily-dug pits along the banks of the dry creek bed.[46]

Chivington had previously scolded his officers and men, "Damn any man who sympathizes with Indians. . . . I have come to kill Indians, and believe it is right and honorable to use any means under God's heaven to kill Indians." The U.S. attorney for Colorado Territory reported the "Fighting Parson" had remarked, "kill and scalp all, big and little . . . nits make lice."[47] Invoking the memory of white women and children killed in Indian attacks, Chivington had aroused a killing frenzy that resulted in the wanton murder of innocents by the unruly and disorganized hundred-day men. Even some of the officers participated in the killing of children and the mutilation of corpses. Eyewitnesses among the First Colorado soldiers, some of whom refused to fire or take part in the massacre,[48] and Anglo traders present in the village reported seeing a Cheyenne child with a white flag on a stick deliberately shot down, a woman on her knees sabered while begging for her life, an unborn baby sliced from its mother's womb, and many other atrocities and acts of cruelty. Even the camp dogs were shot and their squealing pups thrown on the bonfires of burning lodges.

The destruction was complete, and the violence was unprecedented in the annals of U.S. military history. The returning volunteers openly displayed scalps and other body parts hacked from the Cheyenne and Arapaho men and women. Some of the grisly trophies were paraded by the triumphant troopers on their hats and saddle bows and still more exhibited in the Denver Theater.[49] Exterminationist sentiment ran high among Colorado's Anglo population; Jacob Downing, a New York lawyer before the war and a commissioned major of the First Colorado Cavalry, admitted, "[I] killed all I could; and I think that was the general feeling in the command. I think and earnestly believe the Indians to be an obstacle to civilization, and should be exterminated."[50] But the scale and level of violence perpetrated on the Cheyennes and Arapahos at Sand Creek were unusual, and detailed reports of the atrocities committed by the troops shocked the nation. When Carson learned of the massacre and received word that some of his own men had been used in the affair, he was disgusted and ashamed. Perhaps thinking of his own Cheyenne and Arapaho wives and children, he is reported to have said:

> Jist to think of that dog Chivington and his dirty hounds, up thar at Sand Creek! Whoever heerd of sich doings 'mong Christians! The pore Indians had the Stars and Stripes flying over them . . . they jist lit upon these Friendlies, and massacreed'em . . . that durned miscreant and his men shot down squaws, and blew the brains out of little innocent children. You call sich soldiers Christians, do ye? and pore Indians savages? . . . I don't like a hostile red skin any more than you do. And when they are hostile, I've fit'em—fout'em—and expect to fight'em—hard as any man. That's my business. But I never yet drew a bead on a squaw or papoose, and I despise the man who would.[51]

Though Chivington's and Carson's efforts had not destroyed the Santa Fe Trail raiders or swept them from the plains, the expeditions did have far-reaching consequences for Indian people in the Southwest. Survivors of the Sand Creek Massacre and warriors previously aligned with Black Kettle's peace faction now rode along the Platte with Cheyenne Dog Soldiers in a war of revenge. Other Cheyenne and Arapaho bands fled to the southern plains, seeking refuge from the whites even if it meant entering the territory of their traditional Indian enemies. At the same time, Carson's expedition sent a clear message that even the powerful united Kiowas, Comanches, and Plains Apaches were not invulnerable, and within a year they, along with the Cheyennes and Arapahos remaining in the south, sued for peace on the Little Arkansas River and signed a treaty with U.S. peace commissioners. The 1865 Treaty of the Little Arkansas recognized new reservation lands and made provisions for reparations to the families of the Sand Creek victims. Through the detailed investigative work of Senator Ben Wade's Joint Committee on the Conduct of the War, and Congressman Doolittle's Special Joint Committee on the Condition of the Indian Tribes, commissioned by Congress in 1865, the government and most of the American people came to understand that Chivington's massacre had been just plain murder. The army authorized its own tribunal which condemned the affair in no uncertain terms.

Most of the army's officer corps and high command abhorred the "Chivington massacre," yet they also recognized that the winter campaigns and coordinated pressure applied by several military departments in 1863 and 1864 had succeeded in punishing tribes considered hostile and forced them to surrender and treat. While the army's investigation of Sand Creek ingloriously hounded Chivington out of the service, the military men saw something worthy of emulation in Carson's campaign. His levelheaded leadership demonstrated what might be accomplished by a small force when the commander understood the enemy, could read the tactical situation, and knew when to aggressively attack and when to retreat. It was also clear that adequate support had made a difference when operating far from base camps—rolling stock with plenty of supplies, and, most importantly, artillery, which provided both long-range cover and the morale advantage over the more numerous tribesmen. Carson knew, and others were beginning to learn, that the key to successful campaigns against the indigenous peoples was to be found in employing native allies as trackers, scouts, and front-line fighting men.[52]

Strategic Alliances

Much of the army's success in reducing raiding attacks and subduing peoples considered hostile by the government resulted from alliances that pitted neighboring and related tribes and bands against one another, and by making common cause with the Mexicans in combatting the cross-border raiding. Dr. Michael Steck, Indian superintendent for all New Mexico tribes, criticized Carleton and Carson for recruiting his charges and encouraging intertribal rivalries and warfare. Steck had become Carleton's nemesis and the general believed him the embodiment of all that was wrong with the impractical and corrupt Department of Indian Affairs. Carleton acknowledged that he should have informed the agent prior to launching a campaign against people within his superintendency and promised, after the fact, to send him copies of his attack orders. Carleton was clearly on the defensive in this matter and condescendingly explained the patently obvious to Steck:

> I was not aware, until so informed by yourself, that it was expected that investigations, with reference to Indian hostilities on our people, were to be made through your office before a blow

could be struck. It is, however, acknowledged that you should be informed when hostile demonstrations are to be made against Indians within your superintendency, and, therefore, copies of orders in such cases have been sent to you. Utes and Apaches have had authority to go against the Comanches and Kiowas, with Colonel Carson, mainly because it was desirable, when so many coalitions are forming between the various Indian tribes against the whites, to have the savages of the mountains committed on our side as against the Indians of the plains. This subject seemed to be the peculiar province of the military department, which is charged with the protection of the people.[53]

Much of the conflict between Carleton, Steck, and the Indian agents was jurisdictional rather than philosophical. Nearly all the American civil and military officials agreed with the idea of concentrating and "civilizing" the "predatory tribes" of the "red race" in order to spare them from extermination or extinction in the face of competition with the "white race." The men agreed in principle that it was better to feed and care for the tribes than wage war against them, but Carleton, Steck, Labadie, and other agents would continue sniping at one another over matters of authority and control. Steck eventually lost his struggle with the strong-willed Carleton and resigned as superintendent in 1866, while Labadie was banned from the reservation that sheltered his charges. The feud was reflected in the Joint Special Committee's report which eventually influenced major changes in the conduct of Indian affairs; in the future, the army would be entrusted with greater control of tribal reservations and their increasingly dependent wards.[54]

American military men also found fast friends among the Pima and Papago warriors living along the Gila and Santa Cruz Rivers. These agrarian O'odham people welcomed the Anglos' weapons and manufactured goods and found the U.S. government to be a reliable trading partner. There had been some tension at the beginning of the Civil War when the commander of the troops at Fort Yuma called the Quechans and Cocopahs to meet with the Maricopas and Pimas as equals to discuss alliances and contracts. The Union officers, who focused entirely on their own pressing need to feed the troops gathering to suppress Confederate insurgents, had not considered the deep-seated animosities that existed between the Indian peoples of the borderlands. The allied Maricopa and Pima tribes of the Gila River threatened to resist the march of the California Column if the soldiers intended to treat the Colorado River Yumans as friends and allies. The Anglos quickly learned their lesson and engaged in separate negotiations that betrayed no favoritism. During the war years, a succession of Fort Yuma commanders kept a close watch on the Quechans and other Yumans while the Gila tribes became the staunchest of allies, supplying tons of forage for army teams and feeding the successive columns of hungry troops tramping up the Gila and stationed at military garrisons in the territories. The Pimas and Maricopas traded surplus stores of wheat and corn flour and fresh vegetables in exchange for bolts of manta and other manufactured clothing, tools, and goods. Importantly, the Gila tribes wanted weapons to keep the Yumans from attacking again and to fend off the ever-present Apache and Yavapai raiders from the north and east.[55]

In 1865 the War Department took the unprecedented step of authorizing the formation of a multiethnic battalion of Arizona Volunteers in order to combat increasingly aggressive Hualapai, Mojave Apache, Yavapais, and Western Apache warriors in central Arizona. The Maricopas, who had borne the brunt of the 1857 Quechan attack, discovered that the Yumans of the lower Colorado River no longer posed a serious threat once their young men joined the Arizona Volunteers composed primarily of Pimas, Papagos, and Hispanos from both sides of the border. Though chronically undersupplied, the integrated Indian-Hispano-Anglo volunteers were among the most effective troops ever to take the field against the raiding tribes. The Pima, Maricopa, and Hispano soldiers received little in the way of uniforms, other than blue wool blouses[56] and a yard of red flannel per man for headbands that distinguished them from enemy tribesmen. Food rations on campaign and in camp were often woefully inadequate, and the deficiencies forced the men to supplement their diet by fishing, hunting, and foraging when possible. The government supplied rawhide and buckskin for the native troops to make their own sandals and *teguas* (thick-soled, ankle-high moccasins), but oftentimes the men could be seen with their feet wrapped in rags—their only protection from rocky terrain and bitter cold while on mountain patrols in search of well-concealed Apache camps.

The allied warriors most valued, however, the government issues of new .58-caliber Springfield rifle muskets and, when those ran out, the older, second-class—but still deadly effective—.54-caliber Mississippi

Rifles and plentiful supplies of ammunition that enabled them to take the war to their enemies. The Anglo and Hispano recruits of Company A received triangular socket bayonets for their Springfields, while the companies that drew the shorter-barreled rifles made do without bayonets. Captain Hiram S. Washburn commanding Company E, composed of Sonorans, made repeated requests that his men also be issued lances for use when fighting in close quarters while mounted. His soldiers were familiar with and skilled in the use of this traditional weapon. Though formally designated as infantry, many of the Indian and Hispano volunteers chose to supply their own horses and fight as mounted rifle units.[57]

Anglos commanded the Arizona Volunteer companies, but the Indian and Hispano soldiers showed them the way to enemy camps, hideouts, and seasonal gathering and planting locations. As the winter of 1865–66 wore on, the seminomadic Western Apaches sheltered against the cold in mountain *rancherías* and retreats. Their horses were weak from want of forage at this time of year, and women gatherers did not stray far from their camps in search of roots and other edibles. Inevitably, they left telltale prints in the snow. In February, the native troops stationed at Camp Lincoln stepped up offensive operations. Company E located and attacked a large group of Apache families living in five caves at the South Fork of Beaver Creek. During a sunrise assault, Lieutenant Manuel Gallegos called out in an Apache dialect and attempted to convince the people to surrender. The response came in a storm of arrows, stones, and gunshots. At the end of a day of fighting the volunteers discovered thirty Apache bodies in the captured caves and took twelve women and children as prisoners of war to Fort Whipple. Seven of the Hispanos received wounds and nearly every man in the command had been struck by slung stones or rocks rolled from the heights. The combat toll in killed, wounded, and captured had been high that winter, but even more devastating to the people who managed to get away was the loss of stored food supplies and the destruction of the meager crops on which they depended for survival.[58]

By August starving bands of Indians began raiding the mining camps and roads of central Arizona. Lieutenant Oscar Hutton's Company F, Arizona Volunteers, operating from Fort Mason southwest of Prescott, came upon a large party of Hualapais, Mojaves, Yavapais, and Apaches while patrolling the wagon road to the mining camps at La Paz on the Colorado. The warriors had intercepted and hailed a freight-wagon train, which they now appeared ready to attack. Lieutenant Hutton questioned the Indian leaders, one of whom incautiously revealed that they intended to "clean out" the newcomers from the valley that had been robbed of its wood, water, and grass which rightfully belonged to the united tribes. More Indians, including women and children, joined the first group, and the standoff grew tense as some of the men drew closer to the wagons, holding aloft government identification papers, issued by army officers and Indian agents, attesting to peaceful relations. But when the warriors and some of the Indian women suddenly rushed the freighters and volunteers a melee ensued. When the tragic encounter came to an end and the gun smoke cleared, twenty-three Indians lay dead, including Hualapai Chief Hitachapitche.[59]

The intelligence-gathering and language skills of the Arizona Volunteers—combined with their familiarity with the land, tracking abilities, and ability to survive in the desert—made them especially effective when pitted against their longtime enemies. The Hispano and Indian soldiers repeatedly attacked with a vengeance-inspired determination not often seen in the Anglo volunteers and regulars. Arizona territorial officials lauded the native soldiers who, they believed, inflicted more casualties on the Apaches than "all other troops in the territory." The Arizona Volunteers demonstrated that Apache bands could be tracked and attacked successfully by lightly equipped troops that approached stealthily by night marches. These precedents were held up as models worthy of emulation for Anglo troops.[60] From their Indian allies the soldiers also learned how to better protect slow-moving freight wagons with military escorts and skirmish with warriors without being sucked into ambushes. By the end of 1866 the Colorado River tribes no longer posed a significant threat to Anglo and Hispano river men, miners, and settlers. The Western Apache and Yavapai tribes remained more cautious around and less likely to raid the Pima Villages, forts, and ever-growing central Arizona town sites—which now harbored more than 4,500 miners and settlers.[61]

By 1867 it had become apparent to all that the Anglos held the upper hand in the struggle for the southwestern territories. Strategic alliances and superior weapons kept the raiding tribes on the defensive. But as the violence escalated during the 1860s, it was not the superiority of the Anglo troops and their Hispano and Indian allies or even the military technology and battle tactics that really made the greatest difference. Logistics became the key to power and military success. Carleton convinced the War Department that the side that controlled the food supply would ultimately win the conflict. The Anglos and their allies were able to produce or import, store, and transport large quantities of subsistence stores all year round, while the Navajos' fields and livestock were destroyed and the Apaches' access to trading and raiding opportunities was cut off due to the increase in military pressure from all directions. The Apaches and Navajos were especially vulnerable during the lean winter months. In the winter, when the raiding tribes' horses were low in flesh and stored supplies had been consumed, the Anglos' wagons moved needed supplies from New Mexican granaries, Pima and Papago caches, army stockpiles at forts, and even from the eastern states, Mexico, and California.

Once the winter campaigns broke the fighting spirit of the besieged Navajo clans and starving Apache bands, surrender soon followed. Their crops and herds destroyed, thousands of hungry Navajos and Mescaleros were now herded by pitiless soldiers to Bosque Redondo to feed on army beef and flour rations. Indian agents also fed Western Apache bands who sought peace while some of the Chiricahua bands in southern Arizona preferred to cross the border into Mexico to seek food and supplies from the people of Chihuahua and Sonora. In time, however, even the most resistant of the Apache bands became dependent on government rations, blankets, manufactured goods, and shelter. Dr. David Wooster editorialized in the *San Francisco Daily Alta California* that, "the Apaches, and, indeed, all the wild Indians of Arizona and New Mexico, must either be fed or exterminated, and the sooner one policy or the other is adopted, and energetically carried out, the better it will be for both races."[62]

In 1866, entrepreneurial Texans saw the potential for making huge profits driving herds of longhorns and other beef cattle to New Mexican military posts and Indian reservations. At Bosque Redondo the government paid forty dollars a head for steers needed to feed nearly eight thousand interned Mescaleros and Navajos, as well as their army guards. Principal among these cattlemen were Charles Goodnight and Oliver Loving, who blazed a trail from Fort Belknap, Texas southwest along the old Butterfield route across central Texas then over the southern edge of the Staked Plains to Horsehead Crossing on the Pecos and on to Fort Sumner. The Comanches quickly saw the potential for raiding the herds on this cattle corridor. The warriors could trade captured cattle, and the remudas of horses that inevitably accompanied them, to Comancheros who would then sell them to the government.

One hundred and fifty Comanche and Kiowa warriors under Heap of Bears and Kicking Bird attacked four of cattleman Andy Adams' eight herds bound for Fort Sumner. Adams contracted with the army to supply five thousand beef cattle for the interned Mescaleros and Navajos at Bosque Redondo and had broken his herds into more manageable groups of four hundred to one thousand each. Perhaps the Comanches and Kiowas reasoned that since they were starving and the government intended the animals for the use of Indians, they would simply appropriate them at the Pecos River crossing. The warriors waited until the "grass began to rise" and their ponies were strong enough, then they launched their raids between April 23 and May 28, 1867, netting 2,449 cattle, as well as horses, mules, and oxen. Texas drovers fought for their lives as the attacks came in overwhelming force in broad daylight. The Indians burned the supply wagons and provisions they could not carry off.[63]

The raiders butchered many of the animals for their own use and traded the remaining stock to Comancheros or Mexicans for ammunition and other needed supplies. Jesse Leavenworth, the Comanche and Kiowa agent, reported that "a general guerilla warfare" had broken out and that much of his time was focused on securing the return of white captives held by the rebellious tribes. At the same time, he endeavored "to induce them to recognize their dependence upon the Government." The Comanche chiefs allowed that they had committed the depredations but had been forced to do it because of their starving condition resulting from raids on their herds by Navajos and Cheyennes who, pressured by the army, now invaded their territory from the west and north.[64]

About sixty miles above Horsehead Crossing on the night of July 15, 1867, sixty warriors stampeded the combined herds of Goodnight, Loving, and William J. Wilson. Nearly three thousand terrified animals thundered into the darkness, and at daybreak the cattlemen saw that they had lost more than a quarter of their stock. The Comanches cut out the biggest and strongest steers running at the head of the stampede, leaving the cows, yearlings, and weaker animals behind. Goodnight sent Wilson, Loving, and four drovers in pursuit of the raiders. "One-armed Bill" Wilson had lost his right arm years earlier but could still outride and outshoot most of the other men; Goodnight thought him the "clearest headed" man in the outfit. The searchers ended their pursuit two days later after a circuitous ninety-mile chase. They found the cattle all right, watering on the Pecos just south of where the original attack occurred, but they also found one hundred Comanches, loading their guns, stringing their bows, and ready to fight. Loving and Wilson sent the other cowboys galloping back to camp to tell Goodnight while they hurried on to Fort Sumner, nearly 150 miles, to alert the soldiers. The Comanche raiders, however, thought it best to intercept the two riders or risk military retaliation and the loss of their hard-won herd. On the third day out, Loving and Wilson made camp on a bank of the Pecos but soon found themselves surrounded and under attack. Arrows and bullets ripped through the tall *tules* and *carrizo* in which the men took shelter. A lead ball shattered Loving's wrist and lodged in his side while Wilson kept the warriors, creeping toward them through the dense cane, at bay with his five-shot Colt revolving rifle and the men's two pistols, which he dexterously managed with his one hand. When it got dark, he stripped down to his underwear, slipped into the water, and escaped downriver past the Comanche sentinels. After a four-day, eighty-mile trek, which included a wolf attack, he stumbled barefooted into Goodnight's camp. Riders set out in search of Loving only to discover that he had been found by New Mexican traders who conveyed him by wagon to Fort Sumner, where he died not long after the inexpert amputation of his arm.[65]

Such encounters did not deter the stockmen from Texas, many of whom had fought Comanches before and some of whom had been north with Sibley in 1862. The lure of great profit spurred the Texan cattle drives to New Mexico for as long as there were lucrative government beef contracts needed to feed hungry Indian captives and the garrison of soldiers assigned to guard them. The army had rounded up the Mescalero Apaches and Navajos and focused its attention on protecting Colorado's overland routes and the Santa Fe Trail against attack from the warriors of the southern plains. In the late 1860s the Goodnight-Loving Trail and other cattle trails from the southeast, however, remained vulnerable. The large herds funneling through Fort Sumner provided the most profitable targets for the Comanches, whose once endless domain seemed to shrink each year as more white immigrants and displaced tribes began to crowd the grasslands and the great buffalo herds rapidly diminished.[66]

More than any other man, James H. Carleton shaped and determined the course of the civil wars in the Southwest Borderlands. He
had known from the beginning that the outcome of the struggle in the
territories would be determined more by the commissary than combat.
By controlling the food supply he could starve enemies into submission
and win the hearts and minds of allies. The Navajos saw the near total
destruction of their orchards and annual crops as well as the slaughter or
confiscation of domesticated animals upon which they depended for survival. Similarly, the Western Apaches suffered from the loss of seasonal
crops and the shutting down of their traditional raiding routes through
military interdiction. The warring Mexican governments, liberal and
conservative, both understood the border Americans' need for food supplies and made efforts to prevent access unless political exigencies made
such concessions necessary or expedient. Carleton never gained what
he considered satisfactory control over Mexican supplies of fresh food,
but through persistent diplomacy he was able to bring some subsistence
stores of preserved food by way of the Gulf of California, either overland
through Guaymas and Sonora or up the Colorado to Fort Yuma. In the
end, Pima and Maricopa farmers in Arizona and Pueblo people in New
Mexico were the key to maintaining troops in the territories. Carleton
bartered manufactured goods for wheat and fresh produce while at the
same time offering the agrarian Indians the most valuable assistance he
could, protection from the raiding tribes.[67]

Anglo-American Power Shift in New Mexico and Arizona

By 1867 the raiding tribes no longer dominated the political and military landscape in New Mexico, Arizona, and northern Mexico, and
the Hispano population fit uneasily into the new order prescribed by
the Anglos. Though civil governments existed in the territories north of
the border, Carleton firmly held the reins of power as military governor
and the supreme authority in both army and civilian affairs. The stern
Maine Yankee had done much more than defeat those deemed hostile
to the federal government; he had reimagined the Southwest and begun
a transformation of the communities in the borderlands.

Though the Hispanos of New Mexico initially appeared to accept
Carleton's government and authority, they were worlds apart in temper-
ament and ideology. Adults residing in Arizona and New Mexico had

been born Mexican citizens; individuals in their forties came into the world when the Spanish still ruled the borderlands. The unrestricted war against the Mescalero Apaches and Navajos and the internment of these tribes on the vast Bosque Redondo reservation on the Pecos had broken the symbiotic cycle of raid, reprisal, and trade that for generations had fueled the economy and ethnic animosities along the Rio Grande in northern and central New Mexico. Then Anglo chaplains and teachers brought their brand of Christianity and taught the children English reading and writing in a concerted cultural assimilation effort focused on the interned tribes. Government contractors attempted to instruct adult Indians in new farming techniques and permanent home building on reservations. Cultures collided as the Anglos learned that the Apacheans felt compelled to destroy or abandon a house in which someone had died—or risk offending the ghost that inhabited the place. As the Civil War wound down, Carleton's reservation experiment drew even greater opposition in the form of political pressure from New Mexico Hispanos who hoped to put an end to the reservation system altogether and return to the antebellum status quo.

From the time he entered the territorial Southwest, Carleton maintained rigid military discipline wherever he went, but his heavy-handed authority made him many enemies. It was evident as early as the spring of 1862, when he closed most of Tucson's dram shops and gambling halls; those establishments that remained open he vexed and worried with regulations and heavy taxation. Desperados charged with crimes committed as many as four years earlier stood trial before his military commission composed entirely of California Volunteer officers. The commission sent the notorious criminals and secessionists to Fort Yuma for confinement.

Military authorities seized and sold at public auction property abandoned by southern Arizona secessionists who fled with Sherod Hunter's ranger company in 1862. In a controversial move, Carleton also ordered the seizure of Sylvester Mowry and his Patagonia Mine. Mowry, a former officer and an avowed rebel sympathizer, despised Carleton and filed a damage claim in December 1862 for the loss of the property associated with his southern Arizona silver mine valued at $1,029,000. Mowry's suit named Carleton and other officers involved in his arrest. Writing letters and planting defamatory newspaper stories, the well-connected Mowry did manage to get Arizona's first territorial legislature to pass a concurrent resolution condemning Carleton's actions, but even after a congressional investigation the government never paid damages.[68]

Most Anglo and Hispano citizens loyal to the Union considered Carleton's tough tactics justified. The presence of his troops encouraged the return of citizens that had earlier fled the territories and promoted the rapidly expanding mining industry. In Tucson, troops repaired William S. Grant's flour mill, which the departing regulars had disabled to deprive the rebels of its use. Law-abiding Anglo citizens and those who had escaped Carleton's justice generally believed that the law-and-order campaign served the interests of the territories. Fair elections continued only because of military supervision. Hispanos, too, benefited from the new order. In August 1862 the Tucson depot commander announced that Francisco S. Leon had been confirmed as "Commissioner of Streets, Roads, and Bridges" and Francisco Romero as "Mayordomo de Acequias," or head of Tucson's water department, under Carleton's authority as Arizona's military governor.[69]

Arizona residents had petitioned the U.S. government repeatedly for separation from New Mexico beginning in 1857. They believed that officials at distant Mesilla ignored the needs of the sparsely populated western portion of Doña Ana County. John R. Baylor recognized the need for separating Arizona from New Mexico Territory when his Texas command invaded in the winter of 1861, and Confederate president Jefferson Davis issued a proclamation in support of Baylor's plan in February 1862, the Confederate Arizona Territory Organic Act, which also confirmed Baylor as military governor.[70]

Carleton's proclamation on June 8, 1862, established Arizona as a U.S. territory, and as military governor he became the first federally recognized executive of Arizona. With congressional as well as military authority backing his actions, Governor Carleton moved quickly to define the new territorial boundaries and to establish mail, legal, and police services. He ordered a census taken, maps made, and property disputes settled. Accordingly, Major Fergusson commissioned Tucsonan William S. Oury to survey property in an attempt to settle land-ownership claims. This became no small task as irate citizens besieged the military government with requests for clear titles to contested properties. In September 1862, Fergusson wrote Governor Pesqueira requesting the Sonoran's aid in settling Tucson land claims based on old Spanish and Mexican grants. The frustrated major even asked that

Pesqueira forward to him the Mexican government documents taken when Mexican troops abandoned Tucson in 1856, two years after the United States ratified the Gadsden Purchase.[71]

Following the arrival of the newly appointed Arizona territorial officials in December 1863, military authorities gradually turned over the reins of government to these civilians. Although the military government was no longer needed, Governor Goodwin did rely on volunteer cavalrymen for protection and assistance in making his inspection tour of the territory, establishing a capital, and defining three temporary judicial districts. On July 18, 1864, citizens in Arizona held a general election, selecting Charles D. Poston as their delegate to Congress and voting in the twenty-seven members of the legislative assembly. Several of these legislators were California Volunteer officers who took leaves of absence to serve the new territory.[72]

During and immediately following the Civil War, Anglo-Americans began to dominate territorial politics, and a number of California soldiers became civil officials in the territories. Captain Converse W. C. Rowell,[73] Fourth Infantry; Colonel Charles W. Lewis, Seventh Infantry; Lieutenant Edward D. Tuttle, Fourth Infantry; and Sergeant Alonzo E. Davis, Fourth Infantry, all served in the Arizona legislature. Rowell also served as U.S. district attorney for Arizona and later became district attorney for Yuma County. Davis's commanding officer, Captain Charles Atchisson, had allowed him to "read law" in a darkened commissary building at Fort Mojave after taps. The ambitious sergeant later received an appointment as Mohave County attorney after serving several terms in the territorial legislature. Davis and Atchisson became business partners after the war, and the captain held public office as a Mohave County probate judge and postmaster. Discharged from the Second California Infantry at Fort Yuma in 1864, Private George E. Young received appointment as public administrator and examiner of schools for Mohave County. In short, California Volunteers provided the young territory with a corps of literate, formally educated, and energetic men to draw on for political leadership during and soon after the war. In 1861 Hispano legislators in New Mexico (which then included Arizona and southern Nevada) had outnumbered the Anglo-Americans more than ten to one. Now dominated by Anglos, the new Arizona legislature reflected and represented the rapidly growing population of newcomers to the territories.[74]

Occupied Borderlands

As the Civil War dragged on so, too, did the occupation duty for the thinly spread garrisons of volunteer soldiers. The troops provided protection and essential services for the civil government and the growing population, explored and improved roads, and prepared the first accurate maps of Arizona's interior. The Anglo and Hispano soldiers took advantage of their situation to mine, explore, and fraternize with the locals. The soldiers also provided the only reliable source of law and order in the territory, though occasionally they engaged in criminal activity themselves.[75] When not engaged in active campaigns against the Apaches and Navajos, the volunteer soldiers escorted journalists, politicians, and surveyors, as well as miners and other travelers. California cavalrymen escorted J. Ross Browne, the popular *Harper's* journalist, illustrator, and humorist, on a circuit of Arizona that resulted in widely read serialized articles in 1864 and 1865. In the fall of 1863, California and New Mexico Volunteers accompanied Arizona territorial governor John Goodwin's party from the East, by way of New Mexico, to the new territorial capital of Prescott. Volunteers also escorted those federal officials who traveled the long way from Washington by sea and entered Arizona from California. During the war years the army provided food, supplies, and protection for starving refugees from the Pinos Altos and Santa Rita mines on the Arizona–New Mexico border and other survivors of attacks by raiders.[76]

The soldiers also guarded the Colorado River steamers, the key to provisioning the Arizona Territory. Army officers considered the supply shipments from the Gulf of California to Fort Yuma and Fort Mojave especially vulnerable to attack or sabotage. Early in the war Carleton had ordered the commander at Fort Yuma to keep all boats secured on the California side of the river. Every vessel had a guard with instructions to be especially vigilant on downriver runs to the gulf. If the steamboat pilots were found to be in league with secessionists or even suspected of betrayal, the soldiers had orders to shoot them and disable or burn their boats. An attack on Fort Yuma by river would be disastrous for the entire District of Arizona, and possibly California as well.[77]

Some entrepreneurs accused Carleton of restricting business in the territories, when in fact he was an ardent booster. His troops enabled the resumption of commerce interrupted by war and the establishment of new enterprises. The general believed that only a firm hand would preserve military security, public health, and safety. Concern for private-property rights and individual liberties did not deter him. When Confederate attack seemed imminent in 1862, he had ordered his soldiers to destroy five Colorado River ferries, rope-hauled scows, including one in Mexico thirty miles below Yuma, and to move three others to the crossing near the fort. The Mexican ferry owner, a man named Gonzales, tried but never received compensation from the U.S. government for the loss of his boat.

Anglo and Hispano officials and citizens of Arizona and New Mexico agreed that the extermination or subjugation of the Apaches constituted the most important contribution the federal government could make to economic development. They firmly believed that the raiding tribes prevented the full exploitation of Arizona's mineral wealth by limiting the movement of miners, supplies, and ore. It mattered little that the Apacheans had occupied the borderlands for more than one hundred years prior to the arrival of the first U.S. citizens. Carleton turned his full attention to the Mescaleros, Navajos, Chiricahuas, and Western Apaches once he felt confident the Confederate threat had abated. His New Mexico and California troops responded to pleas for protection against Indian stock raiders, and miners petitioned to have soldiers stationed at their diggings and escort freight wagons hauling supplies and machinery. In 1864 Arizonans pressured Governor Goodwin to request permanent garrisons for the mines in the booming Lynx Creek and Randall districts of Yavapai County.[78]

California officers ordered their men to prospect in the borderlands. In April 1863 Major Fergusson instructed Captain James Whitlock, commanding Fort Bowie, to explore and prospect: "Take advantage of your own experience, and that of so many members of your company as possess it, to prospect the vicinity of Fort Bowie for minerals. I am under the impression that very rich deposits of gold and silver can be found in the Chiricahua Mountains in the vicinity of Fort Bowie. . . . When you can spare the men let them have leave to go hunting and prospecting in sufficient numbers to make it safe. . . . It is our duty to do all we can to develop the rich mineral resources of this country." In June Carleton ordered Captain Nathaniel Pishon's company of the First California Cavalry to the new diggings near Lynx Creek in central Arizona. He instructed Pishon to have his men "prospect and wash," record the time each soldier worked, and carefully note the amount of gold obtained. Carleton stressed that citizens relied upon such statistics, which would also determine whether the army would establish a post in that area. Carleton's tests proved that the diggings were indeed rich, and he ordered a fort built in the "heart of the gold region."[79] Major E. B. Willis established Fort Whipple in February 1864. The territorial governor and his entourage accompanied the soldiers, along with seventy-five miners. Willis reported, "we propose to afford them all facilities possible in prospecting the country over which we pass, and at the same time, if possible, to strike a blow at the Indians." When the major selected a site for Fort Whipple on Granite Creek, the governor and the miners established Prescott, the new capital, one and a half miles farther upstream.[80]

Carleton believed the discovery of new mineral wealth to be of strategic importance, not only for the development of the territory but also to aid the greater war effort. He thought it "providential that the practical miners of California should have come here to assist" in the finding and development of Arizona's riches and pleaded with superiors in Washington to sanction his prospecting plan: "I beg to ask authority to let, say, one-fourth of the command at a time have one month's furlough to work in the gold mines and the country will become developed, while the troops will become contented to remain in service where the temptation to leave is very great."[81] The War Department saw wisdom in Carleton's request, and the men prospected whenever they had the chance. Many soldiers whose enlistments expired in 1864 began successful placer operations in southern Arizona. California Volunteers in central Arizona filed 828 claims between 1864 and 1866. These men led the way for others who came with capital and equipment to work the rich gold and silver deposits. The entire Seventh California Infantry, raised in January 1865, became known as the "gold diggers" regiment of Arizona. Many had journeyed to California during the rush of 1849 and never lost hope that one day they might strike it rich in the Far West.[82] Mangas Coloradas's prophesy had come true—the men in search of the "yellow iron" were the same men who seemed determined to exterminate the Apache people.[83]

Two companies of the Fourth California Infantry had crossed the Colorado River two hundred miles above Yuma and reestablished Fort Mojave in May 1863. Captain Lewis Armistead's company of the Sixth U.S. Infantry abandoned the post two years earlier when the Civil War forced the withdrawal of the regulars, but miners drawn by the rich Colorado River gold deposits now coexisted uneasily with the Mojave Indians and their neighbors, prompting the Department of the Pacific to reoccupy the place.[84] The Mojaves remained peaceful, due in part to the intimidation campaign aimed at Iretaba and other headmen, and the hunger and disease that decimated the Colorado tribes. Measles and venereal disease took their toll, and Mojave doctors died at the hands of their tribesmen after being accused of losing too many patients to the new maladies.[85]

At the same time, the volunteer troops played a significant role in the economic development of the upper Colorado region. Glowing accounts of the richness of the area sent home by the soldiers encouraged many more Californians to prospect along the Colorado and its tributaries. The men of the Fourth California Infantry alone established several mining districts. In fact, they dominated the mining in the Cerbat Mountains near Fort Mojave to the extent that the citizen prospectors complained of a soldier monopoly. Alonzo Davis, then a corporal in Company I, Fourth California Infantry, understated the amount of soldier prospecting around Fort Mojave when he wrote, "a few of us boys went out on prospecting trips into the mountains. We would get a pass and, taking ten days rations of hardtack, pork and beans, we would explore the region for mining wealth." The volunteers controlled several of the mining districts, modeling their organizations on districts in northern California. In 1864 they filed 22 percent of the claims in Mohave County, Arizona's Sacramento and San Francisco mining districts.

When it came time for mustering out, many of the Fourth California Infantry soldiers stationed at Fort Mojave did not want to return to Drum Barracks, near Los Angeles. Some had purchased lots for homes and businesses in Mohave City, located on a bluff overlooking the river about a mile north of the fort, and hoped to remain with their profitable claims. After dutifully tramping back across the Mojave Desert to collect their discharge papers and pay, they quickly returned with grubstakes, mining equipment, and building supplies. When on active duty, the soldiers had somehow found time for prospecting and mining, recording their discoveries and working their claims. They had established the Iretaba District near Fort Mojave and competed with civilian miners, who continually criticized the soldiers in letters to newspapers for holding all the best claims. While few got rich, these veterans established new businesses and communities and were praised in the press and by boosters for leading the economic development of the territory. Heedless of the disruptive impact their presence had on the habitat, hunting traditions, and survival strategies of the indigenous peoples along the Colorado River and neighboring mountains, soldiers and contractors stripped the valleys of grass and timber, blasted mines from mountains, dammed streams, and carved roads through virgin desert and high country. The violence to the land was compounded by the soldier boosters who attracted new government, entrepreneurs, and settlers—who visited still more destruction on the land and disrupted the lifeways of the Mojaves, and their allies and enemies.[86]

The Anglo soldiers in the Southwest territories engaged in other non-military activities including hunting, fishing, sightseeing, and, on occasion, looting. Commanders occasionally sanctioned hunting parties for the subsistence of the troops; foragers ventured out in small detachments to hunt the bear and antelope that abounded in the rugged mountains and grassy river valleys. The men also hunted and fished individually for recreation and to vary their dismal diet of salted or dried meat and hard bread. The Anglo soldiers viewed the mountains and desert lowlands with the naïve delight of tourists. Unwary hunters and fishermen occasionally died at the hands of Indians, whose lands they had invaded. The soldiers seemed not to comprehend that the game they took to add variety to their diet might result in starvation for an Indian family. The taking of food without permission was akin to Indian raiders helping themselves to the stock in Anglo corrals. "The deer had been killed by the soldiers," an Apache man remembered, "and we killed some of their cattle to stay our hunger. What man can bear to hear his child crying for food and do nothing? And why was it any worse for us to kill the White Eyes' cattle than for them to kill our deer?"[87]

The soldiers wondered at not only the diversity and abundance of the game but also the incredible strength and tenacity of the desert's unusual flora and fauna. Wherever they went in the borderlands, the soldiers wrote of the sights they saw. They marveled at Arizona's towering saguaro cacti, gigantic agaves, and other exotic desert plants. Ancient Indian ruins, such as the abandoned city of Casa Grande north of Tucson with its massive multistoried mud structures, captured the imagination of many of the scholars in the ranks. Some of the volunteer officers demonstrated a talent for ethnography and included observations of native customs and lore in their reports and letters. Lieutenant E. D. Tuttle wrote a detailed description of the bark skirts worn by the women of the Colorado River tribes. Major John Cremony compiled a dictionary of Apache words, while other volunteers recorded Piman and Navajo dialects for the first time.[88]

With academic detachment, some of these educated observers lamented the plight of "Lo, the poor Indian," and recognized that the way of life for some of the indigenous peoples of the borderlands was about to change. Cremony had developed an especially close relationship with the Mescalero Apache warriors with whom he tracked and fought Navajos. The Major criticized the government's Indian strategy, noting, "we have entirely underrated their numbers, strength, mental capacity and indomitable spirit. We have haughtily and offensively approached them with expressions of superiority and disdain. We have failed to enquire into their natural instincts, training, language, habits or opinions." He decried the "stiff formality" and bureaucratic "red tape" that characterized all the Anglos' dealings with the admirably natural Indian people.[89] Looking back after his years of service in Arizona, Sergeant Alonzo Davis also mused ruefully, "I was always sorry for the Indians. Their side of the question was always so inadequately represented or considered." It seems he never fully understood the role he and other Arizona "pioneers"—who stripped the native habitat of its grass and timber, blasted mines from the mountains, and carved roads through virgin desert and high country—had played in the destruction of Indian communities.[90]

Most Anglos in the borderlands believed that the strange desert fauna and the Indian peoples were inevitably doomed, though few of the newcomers expressed feelings of remorse for their role in these "extinctions." A California officer traveling with Joseph R. Walker's mining and exploring party in 1863 asked superiors if he could send the cremated remains of an Indian, discovered in a cave, back to New York for analysis. The burial practices of the natives intrigued the men, who wrote home about them and published stories in their hometown newspapers. A number of soldiers noted in their journals that the Maricopas practiced cremation, as did the Colorado River Yumans, while the Pimas buried their dead. The Anglos considered the Indian people they encountered part of the natural environment—worthy of admiration perhaps but somehow disconnected from the human race. Mangas Coloradas had been feared and respected as one might a fierce animal. Few Anglos thought anything amiss when, following his murder at Fort McLane, his defleshed skull was sent to phrenologists and curators in the East for study.[91]

The racism born of ethnocentrism and a providential belief in Manifest Destiny was not confined to the enlisted ranks or lower grades of the officer corps. Many of the highest ranking officers in the western army subscribed to Darwin's new theories of natural selection. Others held that divine will would eventually dictate that Indian peoples should become extinct and Anglos would inherit the earth. Even the apparently hard-hearted Carleton lamented, "the red man of America is passing away!" He summarized views held by many in authority— in both Congress and the army—when he testified before the Doolittle Commission in 1865:

> As a general rule, the Indians alluded to are decreasing very rapidly in numbers, in my opinion. The causes for this have been many, and may be summed up as follows:
>
> 1st. Wars with our pioneers and our armed forces; change of climate and country among those who have been moved from east of the Mississippi to the far west.
>
> 2d. Intemperance, and the exposure consequent thereon.
>
> 3d. Venereal diseases, which they are unable, from the lack of medicines and skill, to eradicate from their systems, and which, among Indians who live nearest whites, is generally diffused either in scrofula or some other form of its taint.
>
> 4th. Small pox, measles, and cholera—diseases unknown to them in the early days of the country.
>
> 5th. The causes which the Almighty originates, when in their appointed time, He wills that one race of men—as in races of lower animals—shall disappear off the face of the earth and give place to another race, and so on, in the great cycle traced out by Himself, which may be seen, but has reasons too deep to be fathomed by us. The races of the mammoths and mastodons, and the great sloths, came and passed away.[92]

His deep religious convictions enabled him, without shame or regret, to dispassionately ascribe the extinction of American Indian people to the unfathomable design of a higher power. At the same time he thought it of paramount importance for a dictionary of Apache dialects to be made so that these tongues might not be lost to history.

Kit Carson held a much more pragmatic view of who was to blame for the destruction of the tribes of the borderlands. "As a general thing," he said, "the difficulties arise from aggressions on the part of whites." The Doolittle Commission supported Carson's thinking but acknowledged:

> From whatever cause wars may be brought on, either between different Indian tribes or between Indians and whites, they are very destructive, not only of the lives of the warriors engaged in it, but of the women and children also, often becoming a war of extermination. Such is the rule of savage warfare, and it is difficult if not impossible to restrain white men, especially white men upon the frontiers, from adopting the same mode of warfare against the Indians.[93]

The commission's findings also concluded that the loss of hunting grounds, the invasion of gold seekers, and the coming of the railroads would surely precipitate the decline of the tribes.[94] Carleton had presaged this event as early as 1863 when he wrote superiors in Washington, "As sure as the sun shines, [mineral treasures] will bring the great railroad over the 35th parallel, and thus unite the two extremes of the country by bars of steel, until, from the Atlantic to the Pacific, we become homogeneous in interest as in blood."[95]

It appeared inevitable to Anglo elites that the indigenous peoples of the borderlands were doomed to extinction, along with other "natural wonders." Placing the endangered Indians on reservations for their own protection and collecting evidence of their cultures, artifacts, and even human remains in natural history museums housing exotic species from around the world seemed to be the best chance for preserving the memory of a dying race. Even the best educated among the soldiers were too preoccupied with scientific discoveries and natural resources to bother about the impact the Anglo newcomers were having on the peoples of the borderlands. Carleton himself took time from his busy schedule to inspect a meteorite used as an anvil by Tucson blacksmith Ramón Pacheco. The "aerolite," a 632-pound meteor fragment of iron and nickel, so impressed the general that he succeeded in wresting it from the reluctant smithy. The "Carleton Meteorite" received a great deal of attention from geologists and others in San Francisco; eventually it became part of the Smithsonian's collections. Sergeant Alonzo Davis, stationed at Fort Mojave, also reported seeing meteors flash across Arizona's night sky and hunting for the meteorites that fell to earth.[96] While it might be expected that the officers would keep detailed journals, the enlisted men also recorded temperatures and made scientific observations. Whether driven by curiosity, scholarly zeal, or boredom, the soldiers continued to send specimens to academicians and museums. Seeds, flora, and fauna received much attention. Even the exorbitant freight rates did not deter them from shipping their discoveries back home to California or to the East.[97]

Borderlands Business, Boosterism, and Brides

The troops stationed in Arizona and New Mexico during the Civil War became ardent boosters, and their letters home were printed in newspapers that kept the territories on the front pages in California for five years. Soldier correspondents touted the rich mines and wrote descriptions of climate, natural curiosities, people, politics, towns, and events. The first accounts of Arizona sent back to California stressed the harshness of the land. Stories of "Plutonian" heat, rugged terrain, and gagging alkali dust riveted eager readers. But the soldiers developed a new appreciation for the territories after they settled into the routine of garrison life. California newspapers began featuring accounts of sparkling rivers, picturesque mountains, antelope herds, and abundant fish. Correspondents soon dispelled rumors of 142-degree temperatures as "humbug."[98]

The soldier correspondents and columnists attempted to lure capitalists and immigrants in order to develop the mines. Thousands of letters reached California postage due; unlike civilians, soldiers did not have to pay postage in advance. Proud families of volunteers willingly turned over their private correspondence for publication in local newspapers, which touted the efforts of the California soldiers in checking the "hostile" Indians, considered a necessary first step in exploiting mineral resources. The soldiers also submitted articles to mining journals praising the richness of the mines and encouraging investment by capitalists. Although it is difficult to accurately gauge the influence of these correspondents, Arizona's population exploded between 1863 and

1866. The territory also experienced an unprecedented boom in mining claims located and recorded during this same period.[99]

Many volunteer soldiers had previous newspaper experience, while others learned the trade during their enlistments. Alonzo Davis wrote under several pseudonyms during the war, including the thinly disguised "SIVAD" and even less imaginative "California Volunteer." Davis also contributed to J. Ross Browne's highly regarded book, *Resources of the Pacific Slope,* which excited great interest in the Southwest's mineral wealth. After mustering out of the service, Davis returned to Arizona and continued as an "occasional correspondent" for California's most popular daily, the *San Francisco Daily Alta California.* Invariably his articles cast Arizona in a favorable light, pointing out investment opportunities for capitalists and promising prospects for miners. In 1864 as many soldiers' enlistments expired, he wrote that most of the men "intend to stick to the country, for they feel confident they have got their 'golden-egged goose' cooped, sure." At the same time, the Anglo soldiers increased outside awareness of the territory, providing information-hungry Arizonans with news from the States by sharing their incoming letters and newspaper subscriptions.[100]

The military buildup and large occupation force in the borderlands of the 1860s resulted in increased business and profits for entrepreneurs. Lucrative army contracts encouraged new businesses and alleviated the chronic currency shortage in the territories. Government contractors stood to gain the most, but all the citizens of the rapidly growing territories reaped the benefits of access to commodities, currency, and improved transportation. A number of energetic men saw the profit potential in the contracts for delivering subsistence stores to the military garrisons; George F. Hooper, F. Hinton, Louis Jaeger, and José M. Redondo made small fortunes supplying cattle and other stores in Arizona. These men employed hundreds—teamsters, herders, butchers, farmers, smiths, mechanics, and laborers—to prepare food for men and animals and to haul massive quantities of supplies. The citizens of Arizona City, on the banks of the Colorado across from Fort Yuma, enjoyed a boom period as their town became the jumping-off point for freight destined for the interior.

The establishment of forts and sustained campaigns against the raiding tribes of the interior were only made possible by the introduction of commercial steamboating on the Colorado River. The Spanish had dreamed of water-borne support three hundred years earlier, when Captain Alarcón attempted to supply Coronado's overland expedition. But only with the advent of steam power was it possible for boats to beat against the strong currents of the western rivers. The urgent necessity of supplying armies during the war years enabled steam navigation to flourish. Entrepreneurs supplied the military posts and mines for nearly three hundred miles above Fort Yuma. George Alonzo Johnson, who began his career as a Colorado River ferryman in the early 1850s, monopolized the river trade until 1864. Johnson secured so many contracts that supplies stockpiled in Arizona City sat for months before he could ship them upriver on his overburdened boats.

When the Civil War began, George A. Johnson and Company had operated two sternwheelers, the *Colorado* and the *Cocopah*. The opportunities presented by large government contracts prompted Johnson to dismantle the *Colorado* under the protection of the guns of Fort Yuma in 1862 and to cannibalize its parts to construct a larger boat. By 1864 miners and officers upriver clamored for supplies, so Johnson built a third boat, the *Mohave*, a twin-engine vessel capable of beating against the mighty Colorado River even in flood stage. Before the *Mohave* launched, however, Thomas E. Trueworthy of San Francisco successfully established the Union Line to break Johnson's monopoly. Trueworthy commissioned Captain George B. Gorman to pilot the company's only boat, the *Esmeralda*, which towed a barge for increased capacity.

Alphonzo F. Tilden, managing director of the Philadelphia Silver and Copper Mining Company, entered the Colorado River trade competition in September 1864. His little boat, the *Nina Tilden*, soon found the current and competition too tough, and in the summer of 1865 he sold out to yet another new company that also bought Trueworthy's *Esmeralda*. The fierce rivalry for the river trade continued until the late 1860s, when Johnson and his newly organized Colorado Steam Navigation Company once again controlled river traffic. Reduced shipping rates and more frequent service made possible the development of many mining towns along the lower Colorado and as far as six hundred miles upriver from the mouth. The army, which was largely responsible for the boom, also benefited from the regular shipments and lower prices.[101]

The cost of provisioning the territories was prohibitively high due to the vast distances the goods had to be transported. As more miners swelled the population of soldiers, citizens, and Indians, the demand for food increased, and prices continued to rise during the war years. Starving Indians often saw no other course but to take what they needed from unguarded supplies at settlements or, even more frequently, from freight wagons laden with coffee, sugar, flour, bacon and all manner of comestibles and useful merchandise. Apaches waylaid one such wagon bound for the Walnut Grove Mine in Peebles Valley, Arizona, in 1865. The surviving children of the freighter later testified, "Everything was brought there [central Arizona] around by the Gulf of California, up the Colorado River, to La Paz, or Fort Mojave, and then packed across the Desert, on Spanish burros, 260 miles. It was very nearly worth its weight in gold when it got there." For the Anglo and Hispano entrepreneurs the profits outweighed the risks, so the boats kept steaming and the wagons kept rolling.[102]

Tribes dependent on foraging and raiding suffered from the American military occupation of the borderlands while other tribes found ways to benefit. Some developed accommodation strategies in order to survive the new Anglo order. Driven from their traditional hunting and raiding pathways and unable to cultivate crops as a result of constant attacks, hungry Apaches, Hualapais, Paiutes, and Yavapais frequently targeted freighters' mules as a source of food. Quechan and Mojave Indians gathered and stacked wood at designated points along the Colorado River for use by the steamboats carrying government supplies. Hualapais received contracts from freighters for cutting forage or herding draft animals to pasturage to feed on the grama and galleta grass. In Tucson, Major Fergusson issued a circular requiring citizens to reward Papagos who recovered stolen stock from the Apaches; the Papagos received four dollars per head for stock returned or one-third of the herd. The Pimas and Maricopas also profited directly by providing food crops and forage to the army.[103]

The Gila River tribes had provided wheat and corn for military consumption since the arrival of the California Column in 1862. The army, however, rarely paid the natives in cash. Carleton planned from the start to supply his command with the surplus crops produced by these farming tribes. Before the volunteer troops even entered the territory, the army commissioned Ammi White to trade for wheat. Later volunteer quartermaster and commissary officers dealt directly with the Pimas and Maricopas. In April 1863 James H. Toole, acting assistant quartermaster, with the assistance of Pima subagent Abraham Lyon, distributed fifty-eight "old pattern dragoon coats and jackets, and 415 pompons" to the Indians. Major Fergusson had suggested that Toole use these obsolete items for barter, adding that "two fanegas [1.56 bushels] of wheat can be got for each coat and jacket." Carleton also requested that the army ship ten thousand yards of manta (cheap cotton cloth) and five thousand pounds of other "presents" to trade for Pima and Maricopa grain and fodder.[104]

The complex economy of the Southwest territories was changing, and not necessarily for the better. Indians found negotiating with army purchasing agents difficult. Anglo businessmen and soldiers showed even less trust in the army than did the Indian and Hispano contractors. Most citizens disliked government scrip, but specie was in short supply. In the gold-based economy of the borderlands, lenders and merchants discounted paper money as much as 60 percent during the war years. General Wright requested that the army pay California troops in hard currency, for greenbacks "can only be converted at a ruinous discount." The soldiers accused the army of favoritism, particularly when rumors circulated that the few regulars still remaining in California received payment in specie. Whenever possible, the paymaster counted out hard cash to the volunteers in the territories.[105]

The army paymaster pumped a steady supply of money into the Southwest territories through the soldiers' payroll and contracts. In some of the placer mining settlements, gold bars, some as small as two dollars in value, served as currency. Volunteer officers repeatedly asked headquarters for hard money, insisting that beef contractors and Sonoran farmers would not accept paper money. They demanded U.S. gold dollars or Mexican silver *reales*. Lieutenant Colonel Davis wrote Carleton in 1864 that "coin is the currency which makes the mare go." Paydays were infrequent and unpredictable for the volunteers serving in Arizona and New Mexico. When the men did get their money, they often received six months or even a year in back pay, making them targets for unscrupulous merchants, crooks, and procurers.[106]

The disproportionate ratio of young men to women in the borderlands of the 1860s brought additional challenges for the communities of the Southwest. Large numbers of Anglo soldiers serving far from home were starved for female companionship. Officers' wives and laundresses who accompanied the troops often found themselves at the center of controversy in the all-male military environment during the war years.[107] The soldiers also sought the affections of local women. Major Edwin Rigg cautioned officers to "be careful of their men among the Pimas. They are, I understand, very sensitive about their squaws, and any outrage upon them would injure the command and might operate against them. They are now very much frightened, and until they are satisfied that we have the power to protect them, may not be disposed to be useful."[108]

Fraternization took many forms. Competition among Anglo soldiers for an attractive Hispana at a Tucson fandango resulted in a riot followed by arrests and a guardhouse full of bruised and battered men. Prostitutes could be found wherever soldiers were stationed. At Fort Sumner the First California Cavalry troopers suffered an unusually high incidence of syphilis. Starving Navajo women sold themselves to soldiers, and young girls were offered in exchange for food and supplies needed by the families confined on the Bosque Redondo reservation. Many unwanted pregnancies among the Navajos resulted in abortions and death.[109] Corporal Bushnell observed that a shooting at Fort Goodwin resulted from jealousy over a "mujere [woman] who holds forth in the lower part of the garrison." At many isolated military posts, however, even women of ill-fame were a rarity.[110]

Lasting liaisons frequently developed between Anglo soldiers and local women. The men met and married Hispanas and Indian girls, most of them still in their teens.[111] One of the express riders at Fort Mojave wed the youngest daughter of Bio-oo-hoot, a Mojave chief, in a service performed by the enlisted men in the presence of Captain Atchisson. Other volunteer soldiers married Indian women shortly after their enlistments expired. J. D. Walker married and settled with the Pimas at Sacaton after his discharge from the Fifth California Infantry; he later commanded a company of Pima Arizona Volunteers. Thomas V. Keam, a veteran of the First California Cavalry, married Astan Lipai (Gray Woman) and lived with the Salt Clan of the Navajo. These "squawmen" suffered discrimination from fellow Anglos, but army officers and government officials generally held them in high regard and employed them as interpreters and Indian agents.[112]

Anglo soldiers married youthful Hispanas at the Cathedral of San Agustín in Tucson between 1864 and 1867 and still more married New Mexican girls in Santa Fe and Albuquerque during and soon after the Civil War. Ninety percent of the Anglo veterans who legally married in the late 1860s wed Hispanas still in their teens, an age deemed respectable and appropriate by the marriage customs of the Southwest Borderlands. The enlisted men received permission to wed from their company commanders, who generally preferred that their men avoid local entanglements. The army had a longstanding tradition of non-commissioned officers marrying company laundresses, but marriages between California soldiers and the daughters of the most prominent Hispano families in the territories had the potential for creating political complications. Yet in many garrison towns, the opportunities for social contact increased the chances of meeting and marrying. Some of the soldiers eschewed convention, but it is difficult to determine the incidence of cohabitation or common-law marriages. In Yavapai County four volunteers married local women soon after discharge, and along the Colorado River Alonzo Davis married Emily W. Matthew, the teenage daughter of a Hardyville businessman, whom he had met at the Fort Mojave New Year's Eve Ball in 1864–65. Other veterans wed in later years, after returning to settle in the territories.[113]

Roads, Ports, and Maps

Logistics remained the U.S. government's greatest advantage and challenge in the struggle for dominance in the borderlands. Supply deficiencies continued at the Tucson depot throughout the war years. In the spring of 1864, army officials attempted to reroute the garrison's supply line through the Sonora towns of Libertad and Guaymas, on the Gulf of California, bypassing Fort Yuma entirely. As early as September 1862, Carleton had instructed Fergusson to survey a wagon road to these important coastal ports; the Guaymas route particularly offered advantages in freighting time and expense. The major reported that the route was "smooth or even all the way; and the largest stretch without water at any time is forty-five miles." But the French blockade of Mexican ports, mutual distrust between the United States and Mexico, and government red tape doomed the Sonora route to failure during the war years. Nevertheless, General Wright, commanding the Department of the Pacific, was so pleased with Fergusson's report that he recommended him for the colonelcy of the First California Cavalry. And Fergusson's map of the Tucson–Lobos Bay route became a standard source for cartographers and travelers in southern Arizona.[114]

The expanded U.S. military presence contributed to increased exploration and the mapping of the borderlands. A detailed map of Tucson commissioned by Fergusson in 1862 represented the layout of the "Old Pueblo" for the first time since the Spanish occupation nearly one hundred years earlier. Military surveyors also made a map of the District of Arizona, showing practical wagon roads. The most spectacular and useful chart of the Southwest ever produced to that time was drawn in 1864–65 by Captain Allen L. Anderson, on detached service from the Fifth U.S. Infantry. General Carleton ordered him to draft a map of Arizona and New Mexico that would identify transportation routes, facilitate mineral exploration, and serve field commanders in search of Indians "not in amity" with the government. With an escort of volunteer soldiers, Anderson explored Indian homelands considered "virgin territory" by the Anglo newcomers. He also relied upon the reports of officers who had made forays deep into uncharted country. The result, Carleton proudly proclaimed, was "much more correct than any other map of this country hitherto published." Volunteer officers also provided the miners flooding into the Arizona gold fields with reports of wells, grazing conditions, and intelligence regarding Indian tribes.[115]

During the Civil War years, the Anglo newcomers physically transformed the borderlands. Captain Cremony reported "the gigantic labors performed by the Column from California, in making roads; digging and restoring wells in desert places; constructing bridges; establishing depots; [and] escorting trains" as they occupied the territories.[116] During their years of service in the territory, the volunteer troops blazed or improved hundreds of miles of trails and wagon roads. For years, wagon masters had to double-team their wagons to haul loads up the steep riverbanks of the Colorado at Fort Yuma to reach the Gila Trail. Under Major Rigg's direction, soldiers cut through the sandy banks and regraded the approach, facilitating travel for military and civilian trains alike. Along the Gila route itself, troops removed obstacles, graded roads, and dug wells. The Mohave Trail across southern Nevada (then part of Arizona) to the Colorado River was made passable for wagons destined for central and northern Arizona. Volunteer soldiers built fortified way stations to guard against Indian attacks and blazed a new wagon road from Las Vegas to Fort Mojave. In October 1863 a detachment under Captain Herbert M. Enos established a practicable wagon road between Fort Whipple (near Prescott) and the Colorado

River. The Californians generally strengthened the lines of communication between the northern Arizona outposts, Las Cruces, and other points east.[117]

Military and civil officials worked to improve roads that facilitated movement through previously inaccessible regions, but their efforts brought destruction and death to many Apache bands whose remote mountain homes had once been places of refuge. In addition to improving the route from Fort Whipple to the La Paz placers along the Colorado, Major Thomas J. Blakeney opened a road between Fort Goodwin and the Salt River near the Pinal Mountains in the summer of 1864. In July 1865 Brigadier General John S. Mason directed Lieutenant Colonel Bennett to lead a small mounted force on a reconnaissance from Fort Bowie to Fort Barrett via old Fort Breckenridge. Bennett reported on the feasibility of a new, shorter wagon road. He also led a combined force of Arizona Volunteers and Californians to clear a road between Maricopa Wells, at the Gila, north to Fort McDowell, a new post in Tonto Apache territory at the Verde River. As a result of these efforts, a network of easily traveled roads now linked the forts and population centers of Arizona Territory. Traveling the primitive trails through the upper Gila country—some accessible only by pack mule—was still difficult, but soldiers and traders now penetrated previously inaccessible areas, making the Western Apaches' homeland vulnerable to appropriation and attack as never before.[118]

General Carleton believed that blazing trails, developing roads, making maps, and fort building would bolster the economies of the Southwest territories. The military occupation, he acknowledged, served to keep criminals and Indian raiders in check, encouraged Anglo and Hispano settlement, and made possible a population boom. Both officers and enlisted men publicized the mineral wealth of the borderlands and drew national attention to the region's climate, geography, and cultures. The Californians in particular took an active role in the establishment of the new Territory of Arizona, and many would return after their military service to settle there and to shape New Mexico's future as well.[119]

Carleton felt strongly that the volunteers should be mustered out in Arizona and New Mexico. Establishing a "military colony," he believed, would be an excellent way to populate the territories and provide a "good class of citizens" to develop the mines and establish the institutions required to "civilize" the borderlands. This social engineering experiment was entirely consistent with his belief in Anglo-Saxon dominance and manifest destiny. While populating the border territories with energetic and enlightened Anglos made perfect sense to him, he badly misjudged the desires and priorities of his men. Many veterans wanted to return home to California or "the States" when their enlistments expired. Believing that they ought to have a choice in the matter, some felt misused and cheated, even though Carleton believed he was being magnanimous by offering soldiers discharged in the territories a travel allowance that could be used if they chose to go home. The unhappy volunteers circulated petitions seeking redress, and Carleton, who had once been universally admired and respected by the men, became the principal target of their displeasure. California Volunteer newspaper columnists and letter writers now openly criticized him.[120]

Military Morale and Discipline

Introducing a military colony to the territories was one thing and permanently establishing it quite another. The volunteer regiments that served in Arizona from 1863 to 1866 suffered from poor morale, especially when contrasted with the high discipline and heady patriotism exhibited by Carleton's command at the beginning of the war. In 1861 the men of the California Column had marched to war with a will after enlisting to fight Confederates and save the Union. General Wright marveled at their martial appearance and discipline, declaring that he had never seen a finer body of troops. The First California Infantry earned an enviable record. Five companies of this regiment had not one desertion during their four years of service. In contrast the Fifth California Infantry and the Native Battalion which followed the California Column had some companies that suffered desertions totaling 30 to 40 percent of their total strength.[121] The war had already ended in the East when most of these soldiers arrived for garrison and patrol duty. Malarial fevers and poor living conditions at Fort Mason on the Mexican border frequently left only one-third of the command fit for duty. Sympathy for the Mexicans fighting against the French-backed Imperial forces precipitated some of the desertions, and many former volunteers, both officers and enlisted men, offered their services to the Republic of Mexico upon discharge.[122]

The Anglo soldiers from California and Colorado exhibited a high degree of independent and decidedly unmilitary thinking from the time they enlisted until their final discharge. Notable cases of dereliction of duty, absence without leave, desertion, and even mutiny began as early as 1862. Most of the men had emigrated to the western states and territories with the massive voluntary migration that followed the gold rushes of the 1850s. They were quick to seize initiative and thought and acted as their own best interests dictated. The course of some of these independent spirits occasionally took them beyond the bounds of law and authority. Many had participated in the vigilance committee violence that characterized the ad hoc justice systems in early California and Colorado towns and mining camps.

Resistance to military authority typically stemmed from poor communication by inexperienced volunteer officers and, at times, the arbitrary nature of military justice. The hard-charging Captain Henry Greene was one of Carleton's favorites because he pursued Apaches without letup. Some of Greene's men, however, despised him as a disciplinarian and unnecessary risk taker. They endeavored to undermine his authority and humiliate him whenever possible. The soldiers risked suffering harsh corporal punishment or even death for violating military law during wartime. A court-martial for a minor offense might result in disciplinary action ranging from a night in the guardhouse, carrying a heavy log around the parade ground for a day, or a month of hard duty. The *Articles of War*, however, prescribed a sentence of death for falling asleep on guard duty during time of war. Private Amos Taylor's conviction for this offense was commuted by President Lincoln, and the private was returned to duty and honorably served out his term of service. If the inflexibility of the Anglo-American code of martial honor and justice was difficult for the volunteer soldiers to accept, it often seemed incomprehensible to the Hispano and Indian allies that fell under its control.[123]

Officers remained vigilant and guarded against mutiny, the most dreaded threat to good order and military discipline. When the Californians converged on Fort Yuma in March 1862 in preparation for the invasion of Arizona, an entire company of the First California Infantry refused to drill with loaded knapsacks in the desert heat until the officers patiently explained the necessity of the rigorous exercises. On November 26, 1862, two months after Colonel Joseph R. West's command reached

Mesilla on the Rio Grande, the colonel ordered Corporal Charles Smith summarily executed by firing squad after speaking for the men of Company K, who refused to answer roll call in protest over the incarceration of some of their comrades accused of intentionally allowing deserters to escape from the guardhouse. The men of Company D selected for the execution detail believed the seemingly rash sentence unfair and deliberately aimed high to spare Corporal Smith's life. Their sympathy only compounded the tragedy, however, when their errant shots killed and wounded innocent bystanders. A second volley finally felled Smith and, indirectly, his distraught bunkmate who committed suicide shortly after the execution.[124]

Wronged enlisted men sometimes sought retribution from their officers. Some of the rough-and-ready Colorado Volunteer soldiers even threatened to kill their regimental commander. Colonel John Slough reported that he had been deliberately fired upon by his own men during the New Mexico campaign. Fearing for his life, he resigned and headed east in search of a safer war. Captain William H. Rossell of the Tenth U.S. Infantry embarrassed his company with his cowardly behavior and capture by the Texans at the Battle of Valverde. After his speedy parole, an around-the-clock guard watched over his tent to prevent his men from killing him. A few days later, he was seriously injured in a mysterious explosion near Hatch's Ranch, New Mexico. In San Elizario, Texas on December 29, 1863, a private in Company A, First California Cavalry used his pistol to shoot to death Samuel H. Allyne, who had risen through the ranks to be commissioned the company's first lieutenant only a month earlier.[125]

Desertions and cases of low morale increased during the last two years of the Civil War. By war's end, the desertion rate for all California troops reached 10 percent, slightly higher than the national average for volunteer soldiers but well below that of the regular army. Reduced rations, isolation, and the practice of mustering out soldiers in the territories may have caused men of the Fifth California Infantry to desert in larger numbers. Company D, which garrisoned Tucson—well known for its many opportunities for carousing and gambling—suffered an incredible 39 percent desertion rate. This hard-luck company, recruited primarily from Sacramento and Marysville, had three men die in post hospitals and a fourth shot to death by a noncommissioned officer of the provost guard. Ten other men received dishonorable discharges.[126]

Morale among the Anglo soldiers in Arizona and New Mexico reached a low point in late 1865 and early 1866. As the war wound down in the East so did the zeal of the volunteer troops in the West. Manning forts, guarding captive Indians, patrolling the Mexican border, and staying on the lookout for die-hard rebels became the inglorious tasks of the fresh regiments. But many of these men could not wait until the day came for their final discharge from service. In January 1865 Major General Irvin McDowell annexed Arizona Territory to his Department of the Pacific. Carleton had suffered much criticism from military men and civilians alike for neglecting Arizona during his administration. Actually the troops and transportation at his disposal allowed him to do little more than maintain the garrisons at only a few key forts in the territory.[127]

Due to its unusually high percentage of military-aged men, the state of California never conscripted soldiers to meet the wartime quotas imposed by the U.S. government, but patriotic fervor and enlistments declined sharply as the Southern rebellion began its fourth year. On April 4, 1864, the California legislature passed an act authorizing the payment of $160 for enlistment bounties, $40 payable at the time of enlistment and $20 at the end of each successive six-month period of service. In addition to these incentives, the U.S. government also began paying bounties to encourage reenlistment. Veterans received $50 for one-year extensions and $100 for two years. Of course these bounties also had time-payment provisions designed to discourage desertion. Some of the California soldiers wanted nothing more than a chance to fight the rebels. A few actually deserted in order to reenlist in eastern regiments and engage organized Confederate forces in the bloody battles that would determine the outcome of the war. One volunteer wrote, "There would be glory and honor in being a soldier if we were where we could distinguish ourselves in any way, but to be kept in this out of the way place doing nothing, there is but little fame in it that I can see."[128]

Most of the volunteer companies serving in the territories in 1865 and 1866 formally mustered out on the West Coast or at one of the military posts in New Mexico. Individual soldiers occasionally received their discharges in Arizona, but as a rule commanders sent troops to large military installations that made provisions for paying the men, issuing discharge papers, and recovering arms and accoutrements. The weapons were turned over to the ordnance officers for storage at forts and arsenals or sold at cost to the veterans, especially those choosing to remain in the borderlands. Although Carleton's decision to discharge troops in New Mexico angered many of the soldiers, the order had a positive influence on the economic development of the territories and was lauded by some public officials and business leaders.[129]

U.S. troops in the Southwest remained alert for Confederate reinvasion attempts until the Civil War ended. By 1865, however, the morale of the soldiers still on duty in the borderlands began to deteriorate. Newspapers brought reports of grand reviews of the victorious armies in Washington, D.C., following the surrender of the Confederates in the eastern and western theaters. The last spark of rebellion had been crushed, and the Anglo soldiers remaining in Arizona were eager for discharge and home. Since the beginning of the war, volunteer officers and men stationed in the borderlands felt their primary responsibility was to guard against another Confederate invasion of the territories. Rumors of rebel troop buildups and occasional confrontations with Southern sympathizers fueled their fears of attack from Texas or Mexico or even the "Red rebels" of the southern plains.[130]

Sympathy for the Confederate cause had been high in southern California in the months following the fall of Fort Sumter in 1861. Those first shots signaled an exodus of heavily armed secessionists, who traveled overland via Arizona or Mexico to the East. As soon as they could be mustered, federal authorities diverted California Volunteer units to quell civil unrest in Los Angeles and the southern counties. In November 1861 these troops surrounded and captured eighteen men traveling with the notorious secessionist Dan Showalter, on his way east by way of Fort Yuma and the Gila Trail. Other armed parties eluded the cavalry cordon. Rebel secret societies and unrest continued in southern California throughout the war, and the troops in the border territories remained constantly on alert for rumors of uprisings.[131]

Soon after arriving in the territories, Carleton clamped down on all Southern sympathizers bound to or from California on any of the overland routes near the Mexican border. During the war years, citizens and soldiers needed passes to enter or leave garrisoned towns and to travel the roads. When the California Column reached Tucson, Carleton had ordered suspected secessionists arrested and imprisoned at Fort Yuma. Most of these political prisoners were eventually released after they signed loyalty oaths, but one die-hard rebel, captured with the Showalter party, launched an attack in Arizona Territory that became the westernmost engagement of the Civil War.[132]

William "Frog" Edwards ambushed three soldiers belonging to the Fourth California Infantry near the steamboat landing at La Paz, Arizona, on May 20, 1863. Edwards seethed with resentment after nearly six months of imprisonment at Fort Yuma. After an escape attempt, Carleton had ordered him securely shackled. Edwards vowed revenge. After his release, he waited for an opportunity to get even and strike a blow for the Confederacy in the Far West. When news of General Robert E. Lee's victory at Chancellorsville, Virginia, reached the Colorado River, Edwards made his move. The escort soldiers aboard the steamer *Cocopah*, returning to Yuma after delivering military stores to the newly reestablished Fort Mojave one hundred miles upriver, disembarked to purchase supplies. The men had gathered in front of Cohn's Store when gunshots suddenly burst from the darkness, mortally wounding Privates Ferdinand Behn of Company H and Truston Wentworth of Company K. Two others, Private Thomas Gainor of Company H and a Mexican miner standing nearby, also received severe wounds. Lieutenant James A. Hale quickly organized a search of the town, but to no avail. A monthlong manhunt by a detachment of forty men from Fort Mojave under Captain Charles Atchisson failed to bring the "Frog" to justice, but soldiers later found a body that authorities identified as Edwards. On the run and alone, he had died of exposure in the desert between the Gila River and the Sonora border while attempting to elude his pursuers.[133]

The La Paz incident alerted federal authorities to other Confederate activity. Most believed Edwards had not acted alone. On May 28 Captain Joseph Tuttle received orders in Tucson to intercept a party of fifteen to twenty secessionists intending to join Confederate forces in Texas. Intelligence reports indicated that it might be possible to head off the rebels, along with the cattle and horses they had stolen in San Bernardino County, California, before they rode east. Tuttle commanded twenty men of the Fifth California Infantry and a "spy party," including Jackson H. Martin, deputy sheriff of San Bernardino County; Joseph Bridges; and a Mexican *vaquero* named Prefetto. The captain also had authority to enlist any other citizens deemed necessary to intercept the rebels. Tuttle tracked the raiders into Mexico and finally apprehended them in the Sonora village of Altar. The pursuers recovered the stolen livestock and prevented the California secessionists from uniting with Texas Confederates. Mission accomplished, Tuttle's exhausted command returned to Tucson nearly a month after the chase began.[134]

Loyal citizens and allies in the borderlands alerted federal authorities to rebel movements. On November 29, 1864, General McDowell, commanding the Department of the Pacific, which then included Arizona, received an alarming letter from Mathias O. Davidson, a mine superintendent:

> Dear Sir: Mr. Elihu Baker, a major-domo of the Arizona Mining Company, has just come down [to Guaymas] from Arizona to escort me to the Territory. He informs me that a band of Confederates are encamped in Sonora, between Magdalena and the boundary, awaiting re-enforcements from Texas, Chihuahua, and Durango, to make an attack upon the advanced military posts of Calaba[sas], Tubac, and Tucson. If they are successful in such a raid, for a while they will have the southern portion of Arizona at their mercy. Although you may not be the military commander of that department, I think it proper to give you this information, as it may be in your power to communicate with those who have the power to re-enforce speedily the limited garrisons of the posts so seriously threatened.[135]

While many of the rumors investigated by military authorities never panned out, some were based on solid evidence. On October 16, 1864, a Los Angeles "Government Detective" named Gustav Brown reported that a party of thirty-two heavily armed members of the Knights of the Golden Circle, an active Copperhead organization, had left San Diego for Texas on August 12. Brown cautioned that King Woolsey, the noted Arizona "Apache hunter," was waiting for a chance to spring into action with his armed band as soon as he could get assistance from Texas. The detective added that men were leaving "daily from Los Angeles by twos and threes who represent themselves as miners going to the Colorado." These California rebels believed that, in the event that Abraham Lincoln defeated General George McClellan in the November presidential election, they would be ready to grab Arizona.[136]

Judge Lansford W. Hastings had proposed this same plan to President Jefferson Davis in January 1864. Hastings outlined an elaborate scheme to capture "the most valuable agricultural and grazing lands, and the richest mineral region in the known world." He would send men disguised as miners to the Colorado mines above Fort Yuma and to Guaymas as well. These agents would then capture the vast quantities of military stores stockpiled at Yuma and use them to launch a campaign to recover the territories. Hastings believed the Knights of the Golden Circle and other secret societies would spring to the call and help carry out his plan.[137]

Though most high-ranking Confederates in Richmond had lost hope in retaking the border territories, in 1863 Major General John Bankhead Magruder still busied himself with the organization of an Arizona Brigade, "having been directed by the [Confederate] Secretary of War [James A. Seddon] to take steps to recover Arizona." Colonel Baylor's removal from command had stalled the planning effort, hampered from the start by President Davis's personal dislike for Baylor and his exterminationist Indian policy. Consequently the renewed Confederate campaign in the Southwest never got out of the planning stage, and Judge Hastings's clandestine approach received no official approval by the War Department. While Secretary of War Seddon conceded that "the overthrow of Federal domination in Arizona and the repossession of that country through the instrumentality of forces to be drawn from California [was] an end important to be accomplished," he had little confidence in Hastings. General E. Kirby Smith, commanding the Confederate Trans-Mississippi West, concurred, and so ended government-sanctioned Southern operations in Arizona. Unaware of the Confederate strategy shift and command difficulties, the troops in the territories remained vigilant for any renewal of the rebel threat.[138]

By 1866 the U.S. War Department began shifting the burden of military duties in the borderlands from the California Volunteers to other troops. The four companies of Hispano and Indian volunteers continued to wage a bloody campaign against defiant Apache raiders. These Pimas, Maricopas, Papagos, and Hispanos had endured decades of warfare with the Apaches, and they knew the ways, raiding paths, and places of refuge favored by their enemies. The native troops took to the field with a will. An enlisted man in the Second California Infantry noted that "the Pimas and Maricopas are allies against the Apaches, between which there seems to be a hereditary hatred," and conceded, "they fight the Apaches in their own way and in this respect are superior to our own soldiers." The army also began filtering regular troops back to the frontier after four years of hard service against the rebels in the East.[139]

Regulars of the Fourteenth U.S. Infantry and First U.S. Cavalry marched into the Southwest to relieve the volunteer soldiers in the spring of 1866. The professional army's return to the borderlands after a five-year hiatus resulted in a peculiar turnabout as the veteran volunteers returning home to California to be mustered out came to the rescue of the inexperienced regular soldiers unfamiliar with desert survival. John Spring, an enlisted man in Company E, Fourteenth Infantry, remembered that his company became lost in the desert east of Yuma, near El Camino del Diablo. Fortunately a homeward-bound company of the First California Cavalry saw their signal fire and came to their relief. The Californians buried one man, who had died of exposure, and provided the others with water and food. The regulars now marched the roads and trails blazed by the volunteers. The new companies often rested near the rain-filled *charcos* at Picacho Peak and may have wondered who lay buried beneath the bleached and nearly illegible headboards marking the graves of the first soldiers to fall in the struggle for Arizona. Reoccupying the camps and forts recently turned over by the Californians, the regulars appreciated the comfortable quarters at Fort Bowie and other posts, though they little understood the effort and sacrifice that had gone into building these places in the inhospitable desert.[140]

The men of the Second California Infantry turned over their quarters at Fort Goodwin to U.S. regulars on May 10, 1866. A seven-day march brought the volunteers to Tucson, where Corporal Bushnell observed "The boys indulged themselves to their heart's content drinking Tucson poison, Tarantula juice, Arizona lightening & & &. Many of the boys deprived for so long a time of the beverage they favored, got unconsciously drunk and in this state many were robbed of what few greenbacks they possessed by a set of harpies in the shape of regular soldiers belonging to the 14th U.S. Inf. stationed in the town." By the time the regiment reached Picacho Peak, most of the intoxicated men had rejoined the command, completing the 462-mile march from Fort Goodwin to Yuma in twenty-six days. A Colorado River steamer took the weary soldiers to the delta at Port Isabel to avoid contact with Mexican ports on the mainland. Here on the featureless tidal flats the muddy river joined the blue water of the Gulf of California, and in this international no-man's-land, the homesick men sang and cheered as they boarded an oceangoing vessel bound for San Francisco.[141]

Veteran Colonizers

The Anglo veterans discharged in or returning to the borderlands after the Civil War played prominent roles in the social, political, and economic development of the territories.[142] Carleton had tried to impress upon his superiors in Washington that the rich mines in the territories would bring on a population explosion, beginning with the troops posted there. Soon after the Confederates retreated, he predicted, "Every regiment you send here, whether from the east or from California, will stay. Thus, each one is a military colony to people the vast uninhabited region from the Rio Grande to the Pacific." Carleton's plan to muster out troops in the territories stirred controversy and heated debate in the ranks and in the press. Eventually, most of the veteran companies marched to the Presidio in San Francisco for their release from the service. By 1867, however, more than six thousand Californians had gotten a good look at the territories during the war and many vowed to return. Hundreds who were not mustered out in New Mexico reflected on the opportunities offered in the Southwest and soon found their way back to seek their fortunes. Most of these men returned to work in the mines or to prospect for new ones.[143]

Mining activity boomed from the lower Colorado River region to central Arizona and the mountains of southwestern New Mexico. At Pinos Altos, former California Volunteer Lieutenant Colonel and New Mexico legislator William L. Rynerson held five important gold claims and introduced the first steam-powered quartz mill to extract the precious metal. Other veterans found the more sedentary existence of hotelkeeper, shopkeeper, or military-post sutler to their liking. Still others raised cattle or worked on Colorado River steamers. A number of those returning were former officers and well-educated men. Several became prominent lawyers and territorial legislators, while others obtained government appointments. Energetic men willing to take risks accepted the dangerous duties of town marshal or sheriff. Two veterans worked as educators, one serving as Mohave County school superintendent. Some of the volunteer soldiers demonstrated an aptitude and liking for the military and accepted commissions in the regular army. Men who had married Indian women and had developed native language skills served as interpreters and guides for the postwar army. Overall, the returning soldiers equaled 10 percent of the population and civil officials lauded them for the boost they provided the economic growth of the Southwest territories.[144]

Strategically located to deter Yavapai and Western Apache raiders in central Arizona, Fort McDowell became the key to unlocking the riches of the Salt River valley for Anglo exploitation. In September 1865 Lieutenant Colonel Clarence E. Bennett, First California Cavalry, had established Fort McDowell along the Verde River, just above its junction with the Salt River. The fertile valley of the Salt lay uninhabited and fallow for centuries. Situated as it was between the sedentary Pimas and Maricopas of the Gila River and the raiding Yavapais and Western Apache bands to the north and east, the valley had become a no-man's-land between warring tribes. Hispano and Anglo miners and settlers also steered clear of the place until John Y. T. Smith discovered that the abundant native galleta grass in the river bottoms might be a path to wealth. Lieutenant Smith came to Arizona in 1863 with Company H, Fourth California Infantry. Soon after mustering out, the entrepreneurial officer secured the sutler contract at Fort McDowell. He then successfully bid on other lucrative government contracts to supply provisions for the hungry garrison, composed of three Seventh California Infantry companies, and hay for the horses and mules. The hay, it turned out, was the easy part. Seasonal rains caused the Salt to overflow its banks and flood the bottoms, yielding tons of grass—free for the taking.

Smith needed help to keep up with the demand for the fodder and produce needed to fill the army's contracts, so in 1867 he turned to former Confederate ranger, and later scout for the California Volunteers, Jack Swilling. Although Swilling had spent more time fighting Apaches than he ever invested in mining or ranching, he knew a good opportunity when he saw one and almost immediately organized his own Swilling Irrigation and Canal Company. Beneath the fields of grass Smith had found, the valley was crisscrossed with ancient canals abandoned by the Hohokam people nearly five hundred years earlier. The men took advantage of the well-engineered depressions and cut new connections to the river that flushed out the prehistoric ditches. Within months Swilling's crew had shoveled and scraped canals enough to flood fields of vegetables, corn, and grain. An agricultural boom resulted which provided the economic base for a thriving new settlement, appropriately dubbed Phoenix—as it had miraculously emerged from the ruins of an earlier civilization.[145]

Though the Colorado and New Mexico Volunteers had borne the brunt of battling the Confederates in the borderlands, Carleton's California Volunteers had marched across the desert and finished the job, securing California, Arizona, New Mexico, and western Texas. The Californians guarded the border against perceived threats by warring Mexican factions and foreign invaders. More than any others, the men from California spurred the growth of the Southwest territories by enabling settlers and prospectors from the United States and Mexico to open mines and build homes. Carleton's vision of establishing a military colony while improving the infrastructure to allow for further development and "civilization" seemed to be working. Prospecting boomed as the soldiers established military posts in mining districts and announced new discoveries of their own. After leaving the service, many soldiers returned to continue prospecting and worked the mining districts and related enterprises they had founded while serving in the territories. The volunteers also dealt the raiding tribes of the borderlands a devastating blow, particularly the Navajos and Mescaleros of New Mexico, who lost their ability to wage war. Establishing precedents for warfare against the Apaches in the borderlands, the volunteer soldiers systematically utilized Indian auxiliaries and inaugurated a system of international and military-civilian cooperation. The sedentary tribes flourished during the 1861–67 occupation; the agricultural Pimas, Maricopas, and Papagos as well as many of the Pueblo peoples benefited from army contracts and the military alliance against their traditional enemies. But the exigencies of the Civil War had allowed the introduction of a policy of total war against the more mobile foraging tribes, now considered hostile, and had marked them for subjugation or destruction.

Chapter 6

Dominance and the New Social Order

The American Civil War had triggered multiple wars in the Southwest Borderlands during the 1860s, a decade of violent interaction that transformed the region's communities. The preexisting tensions among the peoples of the borderlands lay at the root of these conflicts. Each group viewed its struggle for survival and dominance differently—some understanding it as local or intrastate warfare and others as transnational conflict. The antagonists' warrior traditions and cultures of martial masculinity contributed to the extraordinary levels of violence, and the struggles for power ultimately led to a reordered hierarchy in the region.

The disruption of federal influence, as tenuous as it had been in the western territories in 1861, upset the fragile balance of power among the peoples of the Southwest. Regrouping following the temporary distraction of the Civil War, the U.S. government, augmented by new alliances, brought overwhelming force to the borderlands, changing the nature of conflict and resulting in an escalation of violence among ethnic groups and nations. Driven nearly to starvation by a relentless war of attrition, most of the Apacheans sought peace with the Anglo military and territorial leaders in New Mexico and Arizona or with officials across the border in Mexico. Intertribal fighting had existed since before the arrival of Europeans, but Anglo-Americans introduced a grimly effective version of total war. When aimed at indigenous people standing in the way of the nation's Manifest Destiny, many frontier settlers believed a war of extermination to be morally justifiable.

By 1867 Anglos dominated the borderlands militarily, politically, and economically. The conflict in the territories had gone far beyond the stock and slave raiding of the past, and the killing would continue long after Confederate armies had surrendered. The civil wars in Arizona and New Mexico bore an indirect connection to the War of the Rebellion as the peoples of the borderlands engaged in fighting that pitted raiding Navajos, Apaches, and Indians of the southern plains against allied Hispanos, Anglos, and Indians. After the departure of French forces fearful of American military might, Juárez's restored Republican government turned its attention once again to Indian enemies along Mexico's northern border and worked to unify political factions by crushing dissent among indigenous peoples—all the while warily treating with the expansionist United States.

Rebellions, Civil Wars, and International Conflicts

More than three hundred years after the initial Spanish *entrada* into what became known as the American Southwest, Hispanos and Anglo-Americans interpreted Indian resistance to be rebellious behavior, tantamount to civil war. Most of the indigenous bands and tribes, however, would have characterized their struggles as wars against outside invaders. In truth, the conflicts of the borderlands were at once civil and international wars, depending on the perspectives of the belligerents. Some of the fighting is easier to categorize. When Ópatas fought Ópatas in Mexico, as the American Civil War created conditions that exacerbated the civil war south of the border, it was apparent that this was an intrastate conflict with international dimensions. The fighting between Yuman-speaking Colorado River tribes against the Yuman-speaking Maricopas and their allies, the Uto-Aztecan Pimas, was at once a civil war and a transnational conflict, since the Maricopas were River Yuman schismatics who sought the assistance (or intervention) of an outside nation. Similarly, the struggles between the U.S.-Anglo-Hispano alliance opposing the Apacheans—Navajos and Apaches—can be characterized as both civil wars and conflicts with international coalitions. The Athabaskan peoples were seminomadic (or semisedentary) and reliant on raiding-pastoral economies. Their wars amongst themselves and with their neighboring tribes, communities, and nations may appropriately be considered civil and international.[1]

In the Southwest Borderlands, nations existed within nations. The resulting struggles should be viewed and understood as civil wars and transnational conflicts. Communities perceiving themselves to be separate based on language, tradition, culture, religion, ethnicity, or race may, de facto, constitute a separate community or nation. In 1860 southern members of the U.S. Union declared themselves to be separate and sovereign states based on differences in culture (especially in regard to slavery), economy, interpretations of constitutional democracy, and definitions of freedom. The United States refused to recognize the separateness of the "rebelling" states even though the Confederacy exhibited all the traits of a nation—from culture to constitutional government. Throughout the nineteenth century, the U.S. government promulgated confused and inconsistent policies relative to Indian tribes. Since the 1830s the government referred to these indigenous groups as "domestic dependent nations," but individual Indian people were deemed wards or subjects of the federal government.[2] The tribes (and in some instances bands) may have seen themselves as sovereign, but when they resisted federal authority the government viewed the Indian insurgents as rebelling subjects. These rebellions were both civil wars and transnational conflicts.[3]

If "civil war" is interpreted to mean violent conflict between members of one nation, community, or polity over real or perceived political or ideological disagreements—from the U.S. government's perspective the wars of the southwestern territories *were* civil wars. This was, of course, the Union/Republican/Lincoln point of view of the sectional crisis during the American Civil War. But when civil war is examined as a clash between imagined communities (nations or ethnic groups), it is apparent that in most cases the resisting or rebelling communities do not recognize the boundaries drawn by larger nations attempting to control them—this was Jefferson Davis's secessionist argument. In the Southwest, claimed as both Union and Confederate states and territories during the 1860s, simultaneous wars occurred among ethnically related and unrelated communities occupying the same geographic territory. Depending on the motivation of the community in conflict, these wars may be interpreted as civil or international.[4]

Each of the antagonistic communities believed in its own cultural and, in some cases, racial superiority that allowed the warring parties to rationalize extreme measures and contributed to unusually high levels of violent interaction. By classifying enemies as those not sharing racial or cultural bonds, "war to the knife," "showing the black flag," "total war," and "war of extermination" all became possible and escalated the violence to unprecedented levels. Anglos racialized Indians and Hispanos. Hispanos also categorized races in an elaborate *sistema de castas* (caste-like system) based on *limpieza de sangre* (purity of blood), though by the 1860s the *mestizo* population was so predominant that the physical appearance of a mixed race person was only one factor in determining desirable family lineage and social rank (*calidad*). Indian peoples, though generally more open to adoption and inclusion, organized themselves in parochial tribes and bands that set clear bounds of culturally appropriate behavior and recognized purity of blood and heritage as important to full acceptance. The civil wars of the borderlands pitted ethnically unrelated and related people—including family members related by blood as a result of years of captive-taking, adoption, and slavery—against one another.[5]

Indians, Hispanos, and Anglos each brought distinct martial cultures and ways of war to the struggle for the borderlands, but in all cases a culturally rooted sense of manhood animated the warriors of the Southwest. Though all the warring peoples subscribed to long-established traditions regarding vengeance, honor, and compensation for wrongs inflicted by enemies, each acted on them differently. Even within each broad ethnic group there were significant differences in how subcultures acted and interacted. The Apacheans were both pastoralists and raiders whose willingness to fight balanced risk with the benefit derived from attacking those who possessed what the band or tribe needed to survive—livestock, useful tools and goods, and captives to replace their losses or for trade. The more acquisitive Navajos invested more energy in agricultural and domestic pursuits than their Apache cousins. Although both communities relied heavily on raiding, Apaches were far more likely to kill their enemies, while Navajos sought stock to augment their herds and captives to care for them. Navajo chiefs tended to be numbered among the *ricos* of the tribe, while Apache leaders owned little and often distributed their wealth among the poorer band members. Among both the Apaches and Navajos, chiefs only rarely coordinated the fighting efforts of tribes and bands, and in many cases were embarrassed by being unable to direct young men nominally under their control. Interband rivalries among the Apacheans also hindered cooperation and concerted action against common enemies.

Though Indian men were expected to care for their families as full-time providers, all men capable of being "warriors" were expected to fulfill their obligations to fight when necessary for raiding or in war. War and raiding activities often overlapped and to outsiders may have been difficult to distinguish. But war meant killing, usually in retaliation for a death taken by an enemy. *Gegodza* demanded revenge. But in a sense, all revenge was local and very personal. Band members, often related by blood or marriage, might feel duty- and honor-bound to avenge losses suffered by their family or band, but rarely was a war of revenge extended beyond the band level, and a tribal coalition was a short-lived and fragile union. Women encouraged the warriors to exact retribution in response to losses, and the men developed elaborate rituals, weapons, and tactics that enabled them to fulfill their martial responsibilities. The military doctrine or warrior traditions—including the treatment of enemy captives—of the communities in conflict played a major role in the causes and outcomes of the wars for the borderlands. The preparation and practice of warfare by men of the different ethnic groups set in motion actions that resulted in conflict.[6]

North of the Mexican border, Hispano martial traditions evolved and adapted to the needs of the sedentary pastoral and agricultural communities. The last of the presidios protecting Mexico's far northern frontier was abandoned in 1856 when the Mexican garrison finally left Tucson. Some of the professional soldiers willing to accept U.S. citizenship remained behind, and there were always men with a propensity for war—including those who participated at some level in local militias—but most of the men inhabiting the New Mexican pueblos were not trained, armed, or equipped for combat. Even the New Mexican Hispanos who enlisted as U.S. Volunteers in the 1860s did not see themselves as full-time soldiers, believing their duty to family and farm outweighed the demands of the service. These soldiers often returned home, with or without permission, for planting and harvesting—and when they perceived that the risks of soldiering were greater than the rewards. As with their Indian adversaries, Hispano men raided for livestock and captives. They were also motivated by revenge and displayed a highly developed notion of *vergüenza*—the shame brought about by the loss of personal and family honor—which demanded that an attack not go unanswered. Brave but unprepared men often pursued raiders only to become victims themselves.[7]

The Hispano lancers riding with the California Native Battalion stood in marked contrast to the New Mexico Volunteers. The Californios had entered the fight for reasons different than the men of New Mexico whose homes had been attacked by Texans and Indian raiders. Though the Native Battalion men proved themselves in active campaigning against Apaches along the Mexican border, their alliance with the ethnocentric Anglo-Americans was not easy. Border service tested the loyalty of the Hispano soldiers, many of whom deserted across the line to join the Juaristas fighting the French. Speaking Spanish, Captain José Ramón Pico had addressed the crowded plaza in San José hoping to recruit men for the Native cavalry battalion in 1863. Pico invoked with passion the Star Spangled Banner of the United States, but the loudest cheers came when he appealed to the Mexican pride of his *compadres:*

> Sons of California! Our country calls, and we must obey! This rebellion of the southern states must be crushed; they must come back into the union and pay obedience to the Stars and Stripes. United, we will, by the force of circumstances become the freest and mightiest republic on earth! Crowned monarchs must be driven away from the sacred continent of free America![8]

The Californios were skeptical and recruitment had been slow, but eventually the lure of martial distinction drew the young men in. Still, for the sons of the men who had lassoed and lanced General Kearny and the pride of the American army at San Pasqual in 1846, it was difficult to endure the racist sentiments frequently expressed by Anglo officers and citizens. A patronizing San Francisco newspaper announced that the Native Battalion men:

> make hardy and docile soldiers, exactly fitted, when commanded by officers who speak their language and understand their habits, for this very Mexican frontier or Apache service. The English have their Afghans and other Asiatic sepoys; the French, Algerians and Turcos; the Austrians, Slavs and Croats; and Maximilian his Austrians and Belgians; and out of the 10,000 or 12,000 Mexican Americans below San Jose it is singular if we could not get as many as we wanted for this kind of frontier and Indian service,

and mix them with Americans to increase their intelligence and fighting capabilities.[9]

South of the border, Mexico's stratified society influenced the alliances formed during Mexico's civil war. Though the liberal Republicans included the majority of the mixed-race, *mestizo*, population and the higher caste Mexicans of predominantly European descent generally supported conservative economics and the Catholic Church, both sides vied for the support of the indigenous Indian peoples, especially in the borderlands. The Mexican civil war became a struggle for ethnic survival and dominance. The people in Mexico City and in the southern states of the republic were generally more Europeanized than the Hispanos of the northern frontier and the southwestern United States, and at first the fighting in Mexico more closely resembled the stylized combat of Napoleonic armies. By the end of the French intervention and Maximilian's execution, the violence had devolved into guerilla warfare characterized by brutal combat with neither side offering quarter nor recognizing previously accepted rules of engagement.

The Anglo-Americans who fought in the borderlands in the 1860s had much in common with their allies and enemies, but there were significant differences as well. The Anglos from the United States and Confederate States waged a systematic and relentless brand of total war with armies composed of full-time, professional soldiers. Whether enlisted as regulars or volunteers, these soldiers were contractually bound to serve for specified periods—sometimes for the "duration of the war"—during which time they could not be released from duty without special authorization. The Confederates exhibited élan but neglected logistics, the key to success in the harsh and resource-poor desert Southwest. Even when outnumbered, the U.S. Anglos brought war to their enemies at any time of year and in all geographic and climatic conditions. They coordinated their campaigns using written communications that could be transported great distances by mail and telegraph. Their martial culture rewarded risk taking in concentrated frontal assaults calculated to awe and overwhelm enemies in a single blow, which they characterized by the French military term, coup de main. Technological superiority in weapons, transportation, and food preservation and storage gave the Anglos the upper hand tactically and logistically. They did not launch expeditions for the sole purpose of raiding for plunder, though the appropriation of enemy territory was deemed a legitimate spoil of war. The soldiers were motivated by a spirit of martial masculinity, honor, and vengeance. With some notable exceptions, military discipline generally prevailed—a decided advantage in coordinating attacks and extended campaigns. Anglo commanders also recognized the strategic advantage of controlling food supplies and water. By mobilizing Hispano and Indian allies while controlling the means of subsistence, the numerically inferior Anglos prevailed in a war of attrition that eventually broke the fighting spirit of their enemies.

The reasons men joined a band of fighters and went to war in the borderlands varied. For most, the risks attendant to war also brought offsetting rewards, but for some, war was simply the only option for survival. Sometimes war hysteria resulted from an enemy attack or the perception that such an attack was imminent. Men rallied to protect their communities: nations, tribes, bands, clans, families, warrior societies, or comrades-in-arms. This retaliation response was a powerful motivator for all the fighting men of the borderlands, though leaders found it difficult to sustain the high level of emotional intensity needed to keep combatants in the field for extended periods. As conflict dragged on, men and women questioned their leaders and their own willingness to sacrifice themselves for the community's generally understood war aims. Discouragement resulting from martial failure and losses of comrades from combat, accident, discipline, and desertion took their toll on morale. When fear and war weariness caused men to reconsider their continued participation in armed conflict, peer pressure, shame, and a powerful desire to support comrades kept men fighting even when their morale flagged.

The more abstract the original motivation for joining in martial violence, the more discipline was required to keep men in the field. Those who fought for their families, villages, and comrades tended to fight with a tenacity born of do-or-die purpose. This devotion to a cause and good morale contributed significantly to low desertion rates. Confidence in leaders and esprit de corps kept men fighting, but one's willingness to fight also related to self-serving motives—usually personal gain in wealth and status. Whether this involved acquiring horses, property, land, captives, bounties, gold, greenbacks, rank, or martial glory, war provided opportunities for improving one's condition in ways not often available during peacetime. With war honors and wealth came status that could be leveraged to acquire mates and power within a community.

In 1865 Senator James Doolittle distributed hundreds of "circulars" to Americans with experience in Indian affairs—public officials, military men, Indian agents, and chiefs—asking twenty-three questions aimed at better understanding the causes for the decline and apparent degradation of the Indian peoples in the United States. The survey responses augmented a massive 532-page report titled *The Condition of the Indian Tribes; A Report of the Joint Special Committee,* which delved into military and civilian affairs across the continent, though more than two-thirds of the document focused on the Southwest Borderlands. Through written responses and oral testimony, the respondents (all of whom were men) confirmed that as a result of war, disease, physical dislocation, and moral decline, the tribes were, in fact, diminishing at an alarming rate. A good deal of the questioning targeted gender issues and sexual mores, including prostitution and related venereal diseases, as well as the roles of men and women relative to work.

The Anglo investigators saw Indian women as enablers in perpetuating their male-dominated culture that resulted in the unbalanced workloads and status accorded the sexes. The men of the more nomadic tribes in particular were criticized for "laziness" and abuse of women, who, it seemed, did most of the remunerative labor and provided for the family to a far greater extent than did the men. The men, it was generally believed, spent an inordinate amount of time preparing for or engaging in war, raiding, hunting, and "idling about." The experts believed that if the idle men were put to work, conflict resulting from warrior cultures could be avoided or sublimated. Some military men and religious leaders believed that farming or wage labor in mines and industry could eventually mitigate the dangers attendant to large numbers of unemployed and unproductive young men. However biased and culturally insensitive the study was, it did accurately reflect the beliefs of many Indian, Hispano, and Anglo military, political, and cultural leaders in the borderlands. The influential report would have a profound impact on public opinion and government policy relative to the Indian peoples of the borderlands.[10]

The agrarian Pueblos and other sedentary peoples were generally seen as models for behavior that would lead to sustainable Indian communities in the rapidly changing world of the vanishing frontier. In the most successful agrarian pueblos and villages, men more often shared with women the labors associated with farming, activities considered unmanly by the warriors of the pastoral and nomadic raiding tribes. The asymmetrical gendered work roles contributed to the continuous raiding for captives and wealth that for generations had characterized the relations between the Hispano and Indian communities of the borderlands. Often at the behest of Navajo *ricos, ladrones* stole stock and captured boy herders from the New Mexicans in order to accumulate enough wealth and status to take a wife. Similarly, Hispano *nacajalleses* took stock and captured children and women for *criadas* and concubines. The Anglos sought to break the violent exchange cycle with still more violence—on an unprecedented scale—while at the same time disrupting centuries of culturally rooted tradition.[11]

Each group brought to the conflict in the borderlands its own means of fighting, and each adapted to the evolving political and social landscape. Martial traditions were tied to cultural beliefs. The peoples in conflict actively prepared for war, made war a priority, and fostered warrior cultures. The men of the different groups shared some aspects of their martial societies. Each valued personal bravery and skill with weapons, and all the men saw themselves as the protectors of their communities and lifeways. In the end, each fought not only for the physical survival of community, family, and comrades but for ethnic identity and the preservation of their culture. At the beginning of the Civil War, the numerous and militarily powerful Navajos, Apaches, and southern plains tribes held the reins of power in the borderlands, while sedentary tribes, Hispanos, and Anglos struggled to maintain strongholds in fortified communities, pueblos, outposts, and mining settlements. The national conflict spawned or reignited regional civil wars, and the level of violence reached new heights as the Anglos introduced to the borderlands the concept of extermination.[12]

Most Anglo-Americans were culturally endued with an ethic of restrained martial manhood and, therefore, recognized moral limits even in a "war of extermination." Only individual Anglos and some Hispano civilians and soldiers advanced the idea of genocidal extinction of all Indian people—no government, Union or Confederate, ever adopted such a policy. It is true that some army officers believed "extermination" to be an unwritten policy, but extermination talk by civilians and military men was often just so much rhetoric intended to spur government action and protection from Indians they considered hostile. Neither Baylor nor Carleton, among the most influential extermination exponents, ever advocated the slaughter of women and children. They focused their wrath and resources on adult male "warriors" who were "hunted" and shown no quarter until their tribes or bands surrendered unconditionally. Though both commanders believed collateral casualties among noncombatants inevitable and morally acceptable, they exhibited a measure of restraint. It appears that both would have preferred either confinement or slavery to the indiscriminate slaughter of an entire race.[13]

Individual officers espousing exterminationist policies were usually reined in by superiors before they could do too much damage. Colonel John M. Chivington is perhaps the exemplar of the rogue commander, ready and willing to massacre innocents. Major Edward McGarry also earned a reputation as a "no prisoners" leader of the Second California Cavalry in campaigns against Chief Bear Hunter's Shoshones in Idaho and Utah. In late 1862, he executed male prisoners when Shoshone emissaries failed to comply with the conditions of a truce. But superiors saw promise in this officer who had seen combat in Mexico with the Tenth U.S. Infantry in 1847–48 and followed orders with uncommon zeal while campaigning against Indians in the West during the Civil War. Under Colonel Patrick Edward Connor he won accolades at the battle of Bear River, Idaho, in 1863. Following this crushing defeat of the Shoshones that left Bear Hunter and more than 250 of his people dead, Connor won his brigadier's star and McGarry became a lieutenant colonel. The action, however, drew "massacre" allegations and the attention of the Doolittle Commission, though both Connor and McGarry were eventually exonerated.[14]

After serving in Nevada Territory, the southern portion of which was ceded from Arizona in 1866, McGarry was posted to Tubac in 1867, having been commissioned a lieutenant colonel in the newly created Thirty-Second U.S. Infantry. With characteristic energy he set out after Cochise's Chiricahua warriors, then raiding virtually unchecked back and forth across the international border. The Anglo officers and men thought the Apaches ghost-like, and the frustration level quickly rose among the soldiers, one of whom wrote of "Apache hunting": "Chase them and they sink into the ground or somehow vanish, look behind and they are peeping over a hill at you."[15] McGarry ordered that "no prisoners will be brought back" from punitive expeditions against the Apaches, and he instructed his officers to hang all Indians they captured. This harsh order brought a reprimand from the Pacific Department commander, Irvin McDowell, who informed the Arizona officers that "no killing in cold blood will be authorized. If the Indians are captured they will *not* be put to death. This is due to the character of civilized warriors."[16]

The peoples of the Far West followed somewhat different rules of war during the Civil War years, but for most Anglo-Americans—even in the violent borderlands—restrained martial manhood was still seen as a virtue. Perhaps Kit Carson came closest to epitomizing that masculine ideal. He was a self-confident man of action, but he possessed a conscience. While he could be driven to violent action when duty or necessity demanded it, he did not enjoy killing, nor did he boastfully celebrate the conquest of an enemy. Carson quickly sprang to the defense of women, children, and even vanquished enemies, earning a reputation among friends and foes alike for his honorable conduct in war.[17]

All the antagonists in the civil wars of the 1860s engaged in acts of violence that were previously uncommon or unknown. Vengeance torture and summary execution were most likely to occur among Apaches, Anglos, Mexicans, and Plains Indians, though even the agrarian and semisedentary peoples occasionally engaged in these practices. The incidence of captivity, forced servitude, and concubinage reached an all-time high during this period. Women and children were often victimized. Documented acts of rape were uncommon, but examples of this form of violence exist for each of the warring groups. The warring peoples even resorted to poisoning their enemies.[18] Atrocities extended even to animals, as pets, work dogs, and livestock became victims of torture, killing, and post mortem mutilation. The martial traditions that characterized the peoples of the borderlands contributed to the outbreak of civil wars, and the warfare resulted in unprecedented violence in the region.[19]

The war footing in the American West brought about by the War of the Rebellion allowed even rational and normally restrained men to entertain radical ideas that would never have gained popular support in peacetime. A martial frenzy gripped the predominantly young, male population of Colorado's mining districts during the war years. This fostered an environment in which martial masculinity prevailed and enabled John Chivington, with his peculiar brand of muscular Christianity, to manipulate his followers and rationalize his Indian extermination crusade. Though he boasted of nearly annihilating an entire "tribe," even he limited his mad agenda to the massacre of a single village of "hostile Cheyennes and Arapahos" in order to blood his command of hundred-day volunteers in an effort to advance his political ambitions. It appears that even Chivington, described as an "inhuman monster" by a fellow officer, fell short of advocating the complete extermination an entire race. Indian people also perpetrated what might be termed "massacres," in which all enemies were slain, but these, too, were isolated incidents and in most cases women and children were spared when identified as suitable for adoption, enslavement, or trade.[20]

John N. Ward, a former army officer and longtime special agent to the Pueblos, had the Indians' interests at heart. He feared that contact with whites endangered all the indigenous peoples and urged the government to establish protective reservations and "resist encroachments at all hazards." But Ward was savvy enough to know that true "exterminationists" were rare, even on the wild frontier. He went on the record and gave Senator Doolittle his unvarnished opinion:

> It is no use to dodge the question any longer. Too much time has already been lost. The fact is, we have the Indians on our lands, and the government is duty bound to take care of and protect them regardless of all [the] newspaper scribblers and bombast about "wiping them out," and the like and all other outside pressure, which has no other effect than to keep up bad feelings and to prejudice the minds of many against the Indian service and everyone connected therewith. There should be strong barriers between the citizens and the Indians, and both should be made to know their place. It behooves the government to take strong measures in regard to its Indian policy, and the sooner this is done the better it will be for all concerned. Otherwise, we may expect nothing else but the continuance of trouble and confusion in the management of our Indian affairs on the frontiers, particularly in this portion, where so much enmity exists between the two races.[21]

W. H. Waterman, another respondent to Doolittle's circular, summed up the indifference of most Americans toward the indigenous peoples, stating disgustedly that Indian testimony was not admissible in the American judicial system and that "the heresy is so common in the minds of the people, that 'the Indian has no rights that the white men are bound to respect'—that he is doomed to extermination and the faster he disappears the better—that it is impossible to obtain justice in our ordinary courts."[22]

The persistence of slavery in the borderlands, however, remained a major obstacle to bringing about peace between the races. Slavery in the Southwest differed from that practiced elsewhere in the United States, but it figured prominently as both a cause and a product of the civil wars of the 1860s. Carleton discovered—as had Stephen Watts Kearny, his mentor and predecessor as military conqueror and governor of New Mexico—that the Anglos, both army and civilian, were not ideologically aligned with the Hispano residents of the territories. Slavery based on ethnicity was endemic and central to the cultural economics of the Southwest. The slave system practiced by Indians and Hispanos bore some resemblance to the South's peculiar institution and yet there were significant differences that evolved as a result of the conditions and cultures of the borderlands.

The laws governing the racialized system of chattel slavery in the Southern states were very explicit about the fungible nature of human commodities. Chief Justice Roger B. Tanney's Supreme Court had ruled that "the Negro had no rights that white men were bound to respect," yet before the Civil War slaves were considered both persons and property. Under the law, killing a slave was considered murder, unlike the slaughter of other property, and slaves were enumerated as part of the human population of the states when calculating congressional representation. Slavery in the borderlands was different, yet it still involved the captivity of ethnically dissimilar people and involuntary servitude. In the Southwest, both law and custom dictated that conquered peoples might be treated as prisoners of war, subject to forced labor and ransom. As with the Southern system, slaves were compelled to submit to corporal punishment, sexual intercourse, and subservient behavior in the presence of hegemonic authority. The system of servitude in the Hispanic Southwest Borderlands permitted assimilation of *cautivos* (captives) through religious conversion (including baptism), adoption, legal marriage, childbearing, and godparenthood—all expressly forbidden and taboo in the Southern chattel system.

The fact remains that the Anglo, Hispano, and Indian peoples of the borderlands all engaged in some form of slavery before and during the Civil War. Carleton himself, a Maine Yankee married to a Southern woman, sold the first African American slave in New Mexico while stationed there with the regular army in the 1850s. When the war began, he brought his black "servant," Jim, along with the California Column as it marched to recapture the territories from Texas Confederates, who also brought their black slaves with them. But in the Southwest territories, enslaved African Americans never exceeded one hundred in any given year, and Southern-style chattel slavery did not figure significantly in the mining and agricultural economies. Shortly after the Mexican-American War and the acquisition of New Mexico, territorial Governor James Calhoun advocated the exclusion of all free blacks, and in 1857 the territorial legislature passed the Act Restricting the Movement of Free Negroes to the Territory. The racist sentiments expressed toward African Americans by southwest border Anglos from the North and South cannot be denied, but the rights of blacks and the wrongs of slavery were not generally considered the reason for the war. The majority of western volunteer soldiers would not have admitted to fighting for or against slavery, professing instead patriotic "Union Forever" or "States Rights" motives.[23]

Arizona and New Mexico Hispanos had come to depend on the labor of enslaved Indian captives, primarily Apaches and Navajos, for domestic servants and workers. This paternalistic *crianza* system of slavery was not unlike that espoused, but not necessarily practiced, by Southern plantation owners. In the minds of the practitioners of the evil, slavery and peonage served to civilize, educate, and improve the lives of those enslaved. Of course, Southern slave owners asserted this same argument, and, as in the South, many southwestern slaves and peons resisted their captivity and resented their mistreatment at the hands of even the best-intentioned master. As in Southern slavery, captive women in the Southwest satisfied the sexual appetites of well-off, landowning men and were sometimes taken into households as concubines or second wives. The fact that the enslaved *cautivos* were objectified can be seen in the Spanish word *pieza* (slave), the same word used for an enemy scalp taken as a trophy.[24]

In contrast to the South, the condition of slavery in the borderlands was not hereditary. The offspring of enslaved Indians could and often did merge into the general population within a generation or two. The *compadrazgo* (Catholic godparenthood) customs enabled children to be baptized and watched over by their owner who was also their *padrino* (godfather, or, in some cases, biological father). In the hierarchical but socially flexible Spanish-Mexican *castas* system, the stigma of race or color did not prevent socioeconomic integration in the same way the "one drop rule" in the American South limited upward mobility for people of African ancestry. In the early days of the transatlantic trade, children descended from African captives had been categorized as "colored" if the mother was phenotypically "black," but by the nineteenth century most Anglo-Americans believed black racial identity to be tied to any African blood quantum, whether provided by the father or mother.[25]

For the Indian peoples of the Southwest, the practice of capturing enemies to replace losses due to war and natural attrition was both ancient and practical. Enforced servitude in an Apache band or Navajo *rancheria* may not have been benign at first; the captors inflicted beatings and physical coercion to force compliance with band rules and family needs. Like the chattel slavery of the South, rape and the threat of physical punishment ensured control of the enslaved people. Apache war parties that returned with captives often bartered them in Mexico or to other bands or tribes for needed supplies or stock. The plight of these captives was terrifying and abusive but as with Southern chattel slavery, commodification also meant that human property had monetary value that often protected captives from the harshest forms of torture or summary execution.

In Apache bands, however, captives might be turned over to families that required revenge for a relative killed by that enemy's people. While death might be exacted, often the aggrieved family would be "paid back" by adopting the captive—a form of retribution consistent with Apache *gegodza*. Once incorporated into the tribe, the newcomer soon enjoyed the rights and privileges of the people, though to some degree the captives would always be considered outsiders, and when disputes arose, the purity of one's blood might be called into question. As in the Hispano tradition and unlike the Atlantic slave trade and Southern chattel slavery, adult male captives or slaves were rarely taken. Considered more tractable than men, women and children were preferred for domestic service, marriage, and adoption.[26] Wealthy Navajo *ricos* became so dependent upon their enslaved Hispano and captive Indian servants and herders that even the best efforts of army officers and Indian agents of the new, post–Civil War, Anglo regime did not completely eliminate the practice until a generation had passed.[27]

Civil leaders in the territories clamored for more army protection from Indian raiders. But Hispanos and their Indian allies cried foul when the military campaigns launched against the Navajos and Mescalero Apaches resulted in the wholesale destruction of Indian crops and herds and relocation of the defeated tribes to reservations protected by U.S. troops from civilians and sedentary tribesmen seeking to raid stock and capture slaves.[28] New Mexico's Hispanos often masked slave raids as attempts to recover livestock taken by Indians, but the real object was the acquisition of slaves or concubines. The roots of this system are found in Iberian slave practices in which the enslaved would gradually shed their status as war captives and *piezas* to become full, though subordinate, family members.[29]

Carleton and Carson both used their positions to protect their Indian charges, and both were forced to publicly defend their actions, testifying in 1865 that New Mexicans still held more than three thousand Navajo captives as slaves. Even with New Mexico governor Henry Connelly's May 4, 1864, proclamation prohibiting "traffic in captive Indians" and the Thirteenth Amendment to the U.S. Constitution (signed by Lincoln on February 1, 1865, and ratified December 6, 1865) declaring that "neither slavery nor involuntary servitude . . . shall exist within the United States," chattel slavery and peonage still thrived in the territories. Carleton bluntly stated that the Hispanos rejected his Bosque Redondo reservation experiment simply because they would have "no more tribes from which they can capture servants." Defending Carleton's grand plan for peace and prosperity, Carson simply reckoned, "some New Mexicans now object to the settlement of the Navajos at the Bosque because they cannot prey on them as formerly."[30]

Governor Connelly attempted to summarize the peculiar relationship that existed between the citizens of the territory and the Navajos: "The Navajos made forays to take sheep and stock, killing all who made resistance, their object seeming rather to plunder, especially flocks and herds, than a desire to take life by attacking towns and villages. The Mexicans generally have been on the defensive. But sometimes they go after them to make reprisals, to get back their own, and to get what more they could. They mutually also captured and held as slaves the women and children of each other. I believe the Mexicans captured the most children, the Indians the most herds." The editor of the *Santa Fe Gazette* opined that allowing incursions by citizens into Indian country "meant nothing more or less than a license to steal women and children and reduce them to slavery."[31]

Indian captives of Hispanos in the 1860s would have discerned little difference between a life of peonage and slavery, and for most inhabitants of the borderlands, the terms were interchangeable. Peonage was often defined as debt bondage, but the "debt" to be paid with a lifetime of servitude might simply be the captive's status as an enemy Indian. Though the Thirteenth Amendment prohibited involuntary servitude for all but convicted criminals, peonage remained widespread in New Mexico after the Civil War. As late as 1866, U.S. Army officers in New Mexico expressed their confusion over the status of peons; some officers believed the practice to be involuntary servitude equivalent to slavery and others believed it to be a voluntary contractual arrangement. Complicating matters still further, Hispanos often "adopted" their peons. Because New Mexico laws supported peonage, the U.S. Congress passed an anti-peonage law on March 2, 1867. Section 1990 of the Peonage Act proclaimed, "The holding of any person to service or labor under the system known as peonage is abolished and forever prohibited in the territory of New Mexico, or in any other territory or state of the United States; and all acts, laws . . . made to establish, maintain, or enforce, directly or indirectly, the voluntary or involuntary service or labor of any persons as peons, in liquidation of any debt or obligation, or otherwise, are declared null and void." The Peonage Act finally closed any loopholes, lingering doubt, or chances for misunderstanding related to the abolition of slavery in the Southwest.[32]

The process of detribalizing the Apacheans began in earnest at Bosque Redondo, but Carleton had not invented the idea of "civilizing" the "savages" of the borderlands. Indian removal and relocation to reservations had been experimented with sporadically by Hispano and Anglo leaders for a century or more. By the 1860s, however, Carleton had become the most aggressive and able advocate of this form of control over ethnic groups deemed hostile to or incompatible with the general population. He was at the vanguard of those who believed that individualizing Indians and turning them from wards or subjects into citizens would be in the best interests of both the nation and its dependent peoples. New Mexico's agrarian and partially Christianized and Hispanicized Pueblo Indians were viewed as already on the path to citizenship. Consequently, the lands of most of these people would not be confiscated and reapportioned in the same manner the Apacheans saw their homelands taken. But confinement at Bosque Redondo crushed the fighting spirit of the thousands of Mescalero and Navajo people interned there. The reservation system also forced their dependency on the federal government for subsistence and other basic needs. Though by 1867 most Indians, Hispanos, and Anglos considered the Bosque Redondo experiment to be a failure, it nevertheless became the model for future reservations and for the treatment of indigenous peoples who did not readily assimilate.[33]

Carleton had been the lead actor in the culture-clash drama that unfolded in the Southwest Borderlands. He was unwavering in his conviction that the white race and the "powerful Christian nation" that the United States had become had a moral obligation to civilize the Indian tribes. For Carleton, this missionary cause was in itself sufficient justification for subjugating the indigenous peoples, but he needed more to convince Congress, the War Department, and the Bureau of Indian Affairs. During the Civil War years, the government deemed the military necessity of suppressing the rebellion as reason enough for seizing control of the territories and their peoples. The fierce resistance offered by the warriors of mountains and plains in response to increased military campaigning fueled the fires of civil war in the Southwest. Carleton made the economic argument, insisting to the War Department and all who would listen that *we can feed them cheaper than we can fight them.* By 1864, however, Carleton relied on the apparent urgent necessity of securing the mineral wealth of the region—against threats foreign and domestic—to support the national war effort. In the end, it was evident that Carleton and others believed in their hearts that "our race" was destined to inherit the continent. Dispossessing the native peoples of their lands and their cultures was a necessary step in this process.[34]

Carleton viewed the brutal military campaigns and harsh subjugation process as "humane" in the long run. Though he lamented the hardships of the Navajo "exodus" as regrettable, he saw the "colonization" effort on the Pecos as a necessary step in detribalizing, homogenizing, and civilizing the Mescaleros and Navajos, whom he considered to be one tribe of Apaches. He believed that these peoples had to "give way to the insatiable progress of our race" and that the government was now duty-bound to protect its subjects who had nobly "sacrificed to us their beautiful country, their homes, the associations of their lives, [and] the scenes rendered classic in their traditions." Senator Doolittle had asked Carleton for his opinion on "the best policy, as white settlements advance and surround Indian reservations—to maintain the Indians upon them, and endeavor to resist encroachments, or to remove them to new reserves, remote from settlements." The general answered with eloquent brevity and self-righteous conviction:

> Maintain the Indians upon such reservations, and resist the encroachments of the whites. It must come to this sooner or later; because, from the rapid spread over the unoccupied lands of the tidal wave or "bore" of the great and advancing ocean of pale-faces, you will soon have no places suited by climate and extent to which to remove them, so that they can be remote from the settlements. Therefore, place them upon reservations now, and hold those reservations inviolate. In the great and rising sea here prefigured, those reservations will be islands; and, as time elapses and the race dies out, these islands may become less and less, until, finally, the great sea will ingulf them one after another, until they become known only in history, and at length are blotted out of even that, forever.

Though he feared they were doomed to extinction unless protected on reservations, which would serve much like game preserves, he thought that with proper schooling and aggressive Catholic-style Christianization efforts, the Indian peoples could one day own property in severalty and become citizens of the United States. His romantic notions of an idyllic Indian community on the Pecos were dashed, however, by the reality of bureaucratic red tape and partisan politics, but also by his fundamentally flawed notions of race, ethnicity, and the superiority of his own culture.[35]

Carleton himself eventually became disenchanted with the territories he had helped save for the Union and then transform into the Anglo-American vision of civilization. At first he had exercised supreme control, making war and peace as he saw fit.[36] He built forts, roads, and oversaw all government activities, military and civil. He colonized the Navajos and Apaches and even envisioned a colony of Anglo-American soldiers that would "civilize" the territories. Now, stung by criticism from his own California soldiers and hounded mercilessly by Anglo and Hispano political opponents—including territorial leaders, newspaper editors, and businessmen—opposed to his "military despotism," the general seemed incapable of making new friends and political allies. Most felt him unapproachable and imperious in his dealings with soldiers and citizens alike. "Behold him!" wrote the editor of the *Santa Fe New Mexican,* "his martial cloak thrown gracefully around him like a Roman toga." Carleton's efficiency and self-reliance had made him a favorite of his superiors, up to and including General U. S. Grant, who saw fit to bestow upon him the brevet rank of major general of volunteers in October 1865. But during the months following the end of the war, Carleton's Bosque Redondo reservation had proved a disaster as the emotionally devastated Navajo and Mescalero internees died by the hundreds of disease and malnutrition.[37]

The 1866 election of Carleton's one-time subordinate and now chief political adversary, J. Francisco Chavez, as congressional delegate from New Mexico territory sent the War Department a clear message—the people had lost confidence in the general's leadership. Secretary of War Edwin M. Stanton informed the beleaguered Carleton that as of April 30, 1866, he would be relieved of his duties in New Mexico. After a furlough and much-needed rest with family and friends in the East, the War Department saw fit to assign Carleton to serve as Lieutenant Colonel of the Fourth U.S. Cavalry and military oblivion in Texas. While Carleton stewed in self-righteous indignation, Anglo politicians and many of the traditional *jefes politicos,* such as Chavez, took advantage of their new freedom to woo and consolidate the support of New Mexicans. Even though the majority of Hispanos resisted political and social Americanization, many took an accommodationist stance. In some ways, New Mexican politics continued as before. American political parties—Republican, Democrat, and Whig—had little meaning. Allegiances were based on family and church ties. New Mexicans joined the "Chavez Party," "Gallegos Party," or "Perea Party."[38]

As Hispanos struggled to find their place in the increasingly Anglo territories, the newcomers jockeyed for power and dominance in a fast-changing world of wild-west politics and frontier justice. In 1867

John P. Slough, the Colorado Volunteer regimental commander who had won victory at Glorieta Pass in 1862, was shot down in the lobby of a Santa Fe hotel in a political dispute with a former California Volunteer officer, William Rynerson. Rynerson and other Anglo power brokers backed the Chavez faction. Slough was anti-peonage and determined to break up the alliance between Hispano elites and Anglos that flouted the justice system. He had become the chief justice of the New Mexico Supreme Court, yet his widow could get no justice for his murder in the volatile, partisan environment that characterized the territory's politics in the postwar years.[39]

With the end of the Civil War, the nomadic horse tribes of the southern plains saw their traditional way of life coming to an end. By 1867 Anglo immigrant trails and transcontinental railroad tracks divided the buffalo, once numbering in the tens of millions, into northern and southern herds. Eastern businessmen discovered buffalo hides were a commercially viable substitute for leather, formerly produced from domesticated cattle, for industrial drive belts and other applications. Railroad workers, soldiers and westering Americans—white and black—displaced by the War of the Rebellion created a demand for buffalo meat as well. The slaughter of the herds disrupted the lifeways of the southern plains peoples. In response to this invasion, Comanche, Kiowa, Cheyenne, and Arapaho buffalo hunters turned increasingly to raiding for subsistence and, inevitably, to wars of revenge. The destruction of the buffalo economy doomed the nomadic hunters who were eventually resettled on reservations and became truly "dependent nations"—an enforced dependency that made them wholly reliant on the federal government. By the end of the decade, the disintegration of the Indian communities of the southern plains and borderlands was well underway.[40]

By 1867 the Republic of Mexico emerged from its civil war financially and militarily exhausted but more united politically than at any time since its creation as a nation. Mexico's civil war also brought great social change, especially for Indian peoples. In the Sonoran borderlands, the conflict had spawned internecine fighting between Ópata factions. Most of the Ópatas sided with Manuel Gándara, Mexican conservatives, and Maximilian's Imperial regime, and had counted on the restoration of their autonomy and lands, wrested from them first by the Spanish and then by Mexican reformers. But General Refugio Tánori's Ópata army

suffered defeat by Republican forces aided by their own Ópata auxiliaries at the battle of Mátape in 1865.⁴¹ Tánori himself boarded ship at
Guaymas en route for Baja California, but Republican forces stopped
the vessel before it reached the peninsula and executed the general.⁴²
Many of the remaining Ópatas were either killed or dispersed by Juárez's
supporters. A similar fate befell the Yaquis and their Mayo allies. The
Juaristas colonized many in settlements in Sonora and Chihuahua or
assimilated them into the general *mestizo* population, but others continued to resist until destroyed or driven north across the border into
southern Arizona, where the surviving refugees eventually established a
separate Yaqui community near Tucson.⁴³

After Juárez's victory, Mexico's conservative party was so thoroughly
discredited by its alliance with the invading French troops that it
effectively ceased to exist, and the liberals went almost unchallenged
as a political force during the first years of the restored republic. U.S.
support of Mexico's Republicans fostered less hostile though still
mutually suspicious international relations, but the border itself was
more regulated than ever before, complicating the continuing struggle
with Apache raiders who took advantage of the lack of cooperation that
resulted from the hardened borderline. O'odham people (Pimas and
Papagos) also found that families and bands were now separated by an
international boundary that interfered with their freedom of movement
and disrupted communication and community cohesion.⁴⁴

During the period of filibustering and political instability in Central
America in the late 1850s, the idea of Manifest Destiny came of age
and the concept of "Latin America" also emerged. Nearly one in four
Americans were European-born and the United States struggled with
its own national identity as it aggressively attacked other peoples in the
path of territorial expansion. The conquest of Mexico in the late 1840s,
led by the unashamedly imperialistic Polk administration, had been
little more than a filibustering expedition on a grand scale, exacerbated
by the Manifest Destiny fever fueled by Anglo-American belief in
ethnic superiority.⁴⁵ The economic opportunities presented by the vast
land and mineral wealth of the Southwest were powerful attractions
to Americans, most of whom believed that racially and culturally inferior Mexicans were incapable of governing themselves and that Indian
people had demonstrated their incapacity for making productive use of
the territory they controlled. First imagined by Mexican elites and then

adopted popularly north and south of the U.S.-Mexico border after the French Invasion of 1862, "Latin America" became racially identified as the home of the people of *mestizaje* (those of mixed European and Indian ancestry). Similarly, American Indians had not thought of themselves as a united group, even at the tribal level, until Hispanos and Anglos began categorizing them in this way. Then, for mutual protection and survival, Indian people began to band together against the newcomers, albeit too late to stem the tidal wave of Euro-American invasion.[46]

The Civil War years saw the largest engagements and the most war-related deaths in the history of the borderlands. Although the violence abated somewhat by 1867, the struggle for physical and cultural survival continued for many communities, especially the Chiricahua and Western Apache bands. Isolated instances of raiding, warfare, and retaliation between Apaches and their Hispano and Anglo adversaries, both military and civilian, can be documented through military reports, petitions to congress, depredation claims, and newspaper accounts through the 1870s. Even so, the scale, frequency of attacks, and death toll related to this fighting during the postwar years did not come close to equaling the violence seen between 1861 and 1867.[47] The Anglo-dominated U.S. military exploited the use of Hispano and Indian auxiliaries, sometimes resulting in conflicted loyalties and leading to civil strife. The Chiricahua Apache leader Victorio, under intense pressure from constant campaigns by U.S. troops and their Indian allies, promised federal authorities, "We want a lasting peace, one that will keep. We would like to live in our country, and will go onto a reservation where the government may put us, and those who do not come, we will go and help fight them."[48] South of the border internecine conflict saw a marked decline after the death of Maximilian in 1867, the departure of his European allies, and the triumph of Juárez's Republican government; but for many Indian communities, such as the Yaquis, determined to maintain their tribal traditions, the struggle for cultural survival continued.[49]

The Civil War years ushered in a new age of increased federal control and involvement in the lives of the American people. Slavery was constitutionally abolished, an income tax had been instituted for the first time, and millions of veterans became eligible for pensions and other public assistance not previously recognized as the responsibility of the

U.S. government. Congress empowered federal agencies to compensate both citizens and subject peoples for war losses and "depredations." Hispanos, Anglos, and Indians alike made claims for property destroyed by opposing armies and by tribes recognized by treaty as being "in amity" with the U.S. government. Officers and agents placed tribes on reservations and made provisions for housing, provisioning, educating, and retraining Indians as farmers and stock-raisers in the Anglo-American tradition. The expanded role of the federal government resulted in an inflated bureaucracy, including a massive Indian Bureau, an enlarged Interior Department, and a new Court of Claims. The regular army, far larger than its prewar counterpart, now mustered for duty in the Reconstruction South and the western territories in order to keep the peace and prevent a renewal of civil war.[50]

The American Civil War had created conditions that expanded the long-simmering conflict between peoples of different communities and led to civil war on a scale that had never been seen before in the Southwest Borderlands. The causes of civil wars are often so deeply rooted that such conflicts never really end—they just subside for a time until triggered again. The Indian, Hispano, and Anglo peoples of the borderlands had each evolved unique cultures based on martial masculinity that became precursors of deadly conflict. Combined with the intense competition for resources—water, food, minerals, and land—this predisposition for war ignited the combat of the 1860s. Equally important was the desire of competing societies, especially seminomadic raiders and sedentary agriculturalists, to dominate and enslave one another. The American Civil War was not the root cause of the multiple civil wars of the Southwest Borderlands, but it did fan the smoldering embers of cultural and economic insecurity into flames of war.

Ethnocentrism characterized all the cultures that clashed in the Southwest Borderlands during the Civil War. Each group was willing to share the gift of its culture with deserving outsiders, who did not naturally inherit it as their birthright. So certain were they in the superiority of their life ways that the morality of compelling assimilation was only rarely questioned. The Spanish had attempted compulsory acculturation by mass missionization and religious conversion of *"gente sin razón,"* while the Mexicans selected individual captives to convert and incorporate into their communities. The Indian peoples of the borderlands had been doing this for generations, adopting enemy captives and teaching them the ways of their tribe until the captives' original culture was subordinated or erased from memory. The Anglo brand of ethnocer   ered little. As with the other cultures, there were those amon   es who advocated putting all the "barba- rous" peoples to   , but the belief in sharing the benefits of Anglo-American   dominated among the soldiers and govern- ment officials repr   he most recent arrivals to the borderlands. The real differenc   e scale and ruthless efficiency with which the Americans ap   the challenge of capturing and converting those "benighted'   vho did not already enjoy the benefits of "civilization."

Ethnic groups   for survival and dominance in ways that reflected their unique cultures and traditions. Before the Civil War, there existed a hostile but interdependent raid-and-reprisal relationship between the Indian, Hispano, and Anglo peoples characterized by raid- ing and captive-taking but not "war to the death" resulting in the total domination or extermination of the enemy. The numerically superior and militarily powerful Indian peoples of the borderlands set the terms of engagement. The concurrent rise of militaristic societies in which young men—Indian, Hispano, and Anglo—glorified and prepared for war and the arrival of large numbers of Anglo newcomers advo- cating total war contributed significantly to the escalation of violence that made the 1860s the deadliest decade the region had ever seen. The peoples of the borderlands struggled not just for the physical safety of their communities but for their cultural survival as well. These conflicts resulted in new military, political, and social alliances and hierarchies.

The initial withdrawal of Anglo soldiers in 1861 and redirection of federal priorities had led to a temporary power vacuum filled by Indian raiders who outnumbered their Hispano, Anglo, and Indian adversaries and contributed to the conditions that enabled civil wars and even for- eign intervention south of the border. The invasion of the borderlands by Anglos, Union and Confederate, further disrupted local authority and traditional power hierarchies. The Anglo invasion resulted in alliances among Anglos, Hispanos, and Indian tribes allowing them, collectively, to wage relentless war on raiding Navajo, Apache, and Plains tribesmen. New transnational alliances and relationships also emerged between the United States and Mexico. During the Civil War and its aftermath, the peoples of the region, north and south of the border, struggled for survival and dominance in wars that required that they adapt to the changing conditions in the Southwest. The diverse peoples of the region fought civil wars quite apart from the Civil War of the Southern rebellion that raged in the East. The culturally distinct peoples occupying the same territory were disposed to fight to ensure preservation of their communities and identities. While the dominant or militarily stronger parties viewed the conflict as "civil war," the insurgent factions usually considered the struggle to be international or interethnic. Survival in the Southwest required accommodation, compromise, and alliances as much as it did violent confrontation, martial prowess, and war-making capacity.[51]

The Civil War triggered cataclysmic change in the borderlands. By 1867 peonage and slavery—as economic and social systems—were dying, and a new social, political, and economic order existed with Anglos, Hispanos, and assimilated tribes at the top of the hierarchy and the raiding tribes at the bottom. Racial and ethnic distinctions were institutionalized, and the federal government exerted control over reservation-restricted Indians and defined new territorial boundaries.[52] Hispano and Anglo citizens adopted and uneasily shared the Anglo-American political and economic model for survival in the Southwest, while struggling for cultural identity. Transnational relations had also changed, and a better-defined and more controlled border between Mexico and the United States—a border that divided some Indian and Hispano communities—characterized the new world that emerged from the war-torn borderlands.[53]

Epilogue

In October 1866, Captain Richard H. Orton, First California Cavalry, passed by the sandstone cliffs near the Arizona border just west of Albuquerque. Known since Spanish times as El Morro, the place was not far from Hawikuh, where in 1540 Coronado met such fierce resistance as he searched for the mythical Golden Cities of Cíbola. Over time, the bluffs became a prominent landmark, and the Spanish newcomers inscribed their names over the centuries-old pictographs left by the first peoples.[1] Now, as Orton led one of the last groups of U.S. Volunteer soldiers serving in the territories as they rode back to California for their final discharge, he was inspired by the graffiti he found cut into the soft stone of El Morro. Determined to make his own mark near the inscription *"Paso por aquí"* (he came this way), left by New Mexico governor Juan de Oñate in 1605, Orton used a knife to neatly incise his name, unit, and date. The captain mustered out of U.S. service at the Presidio in San Francisco on January 4, 1867, the last of the California Volunteers enlisted for the Civil War.

More than twenty years later, Orton, now serving as adjutant general of California, rode a Southern Pacific Railroad passenger train across southern New Mexico and Arizona. As the steam locomotive chugged through the desert north of Tucson, he discerned the familiar jagged silhouette of Picacho Peak standing alone in the broad, flat valley of the dry Santa Cruz River. At the narrowest point in the pass the line began a gradual turn to the northwest and into the setting sun. The general glimpsed the remains of the overgrown Butterfield stage road as it meandered through saguaro and mesquite thickets parallel to the railroad tracks.

Then he saw what he was looking for—Lieutenant James Barrett's grave. The marker, on the right side only twenty feet from the tracks, flashed past his window in an instant and was gone. Orton had last seen this place as a youthful captain of volunteers. He wondered why Barrett's sister had never claimed her brother's remains or had them properly buried in California. Even the two enlisted men, Johnson and Leonard, shoveled into the desert sand beside their lieutenant in 1862, had been reinterred at the military cemetery in Tucson and, when Fort Lowell was later deactivated, moved again to the national cemetery at the Presidio in San Francisco. But Barrett, the first California soldier to fall in the Southwest Borderlands during the Civil War, had been forgotten.[2]

Orton often thought of the war and the role played by the young volunteers from California in the mountains and plains of the Far West. Many of his old comrades participated in the activities of the Grand Army of the Republic—GAR posts had sprung up everywhere, from coast to coast—but the western men usually sat silently as the veterans of the Army of the Potomac recounted great battles of the eastern theater.[3] The westerners found it difficult to share stories of desert marches, Indian fights, border skirmishes, and saving the gold-rich territories for the Union. The memories, it seemed, were buried and forgotten with Barrett. But some survivors of the border wars—Californians, Coloradans, and New Mexicans—did remember. These veterans, with grandchildren on their knees, would eagerly scan new history texts and encyclopedias for even a mention of the war in the borderlands, only to be disappointed.[4]

Kit Carson, bearing the rank of brevet brigadier general, also mustered out of U.S. service in 1867—he was the last of the New Mexico Volunteers. The next year, though physically exhausted and ailing, Carson went to Washington with a delegation of Utes in an effort to ensure government compliance with their new treaty. The years of hardship and campaigning had taken their toll on the frontiersman, and while in the East doctors confirmed he was dying of an aortic aneurysm. He hurried home to Colorado to be with Josefa and soon after died at Fort Lyon on May 23, 1868. At Fort Sumner, five days later, General

William T. Sherman declared the internment of the Mescalero Apaches and Navajos at the Bosque Redondo reservation to be a dismal failure. Sherman signed an agreement delivering the people from exile and authorized the surviving families to return to reservations near their traditional lands. A month later, New Mexico was finally connected to the rest of the world by telegraph. Two hundred miles east on November 27 of that same year, George Armstrong Custer's Seventh Cavalry rode through Chief Black Kettle's camp on the Washita River—almost four years to the day that this Cheyenne peace chief had survived the infamous Sand Creek massacre. Hopes for peace on the plains died with Black Kettle.[5]

On April 30, 1871, a heavily armed group of Papagos, Hispanos, and Anglos attacked a village of Aravaipa and Pinal Apaches under the protection of the army at Camp Grant, fifty miles northeast of Tucson. The expedition was almost a carbon copy of Captain T. T. Tidball's 1863 attack. As then, more than one hundred Apaches, mostly women and children, were slain and twenty-nine more taken captive and kept as *criadas* or sold into slavery in Mexico. President Grant called it "purely murder" and threatened to declare martial law in Arizona, but even so, the sensational trial in Tucson failed to bring the perpetrators of the Camp Grant Massacre to justice.[6] Members of other Apache bands, the Chiricahuas in particular, broke free of confining reservations in the 1870s and 1880s escalating raiding activities north and south of the border and prompting strong military responses from the governments of the United States and Mexico. The violence continued until the renegades under Geronimo finally surrendered in 1886 to army officers working with Apache scouts enlisted to hunt down their fellow tribesmen. The railroad trains that crisscrossed the nation following the Civil War had by this time found their way to the territories, so the "hostile" Apaches, their families, and the scouts were loaded into boxcars pulled by steam locomotives and deported far from the borderlands to be held as "prisoners of war."[7]

In 1871, the same year as the Camp Grant Massacre, Congress finally recognized in the annual appropriations bill that the confusing idea of a "domestic dependent nation" being a "sovereign tribe" was at best oxymoronic and at worst an unworkable sham. The Indian tribes, it was argued, had been for some time wholly dependent upon and subordinate to the United States and could not be treated with the same "nation-to-nation" status reserved for international relations with European powers. No Indian treaties would be approved by the Senate after this time.[8] As the nation celebrated its centennial, Colorado finally joined the Union in 1876, the same year the Cheyennes and their Lakota allies exacted a measure of revenge by nearly wiping out General Custer's command at the Little Big Horn. By 1887 the government stepped up its efforts to assimilate Indian peoples. Following the passage of the Dawes Act, which recognized the right of individual Indians to own land, reservations in Oklahoma were broken up and allotted "in severalty" to Apache, Cheyenne, Kiowa, and Comanche heads of households. "Surplus land" was then made available to whites, who snapped up the cheap acres in frenzied "land runs."[9]

In 1889 Major Trevanion T. Teel, the artillery commander of General Sibley's Confederate Army of New Mexico, traveled from Texas to Albuquerque at the request of a New Mexico veterans' group. Though it had been more than twenty-five years, Teel pointed out the exact spot in the plaza where his men had hurriedly buried eight bronze mountain howitzers as the rebels retreated down the Rio Grande in the spring of 1862. Much fanfare followed the discovery, and veterans from New Mexico and Colorado squabbled over ownership of the trophy cannons, which were finally divvied up equitably and placed on display in Albuquerque and Denver.

That same year, as federal reeducation programs worked to detribalize Indians, Wovoka, a Paiute holy man in Nevada, began spreading word of a "spirit dance" that united Indian people through a religious revival that promised to hasten the return of the old free way of life—the way it had been before the whites came. Soon Indians from the Mexican border to Canada were dancing and wearing bullet proof "ghost shirts." Many began questioning federal authority, and to some military men, a dangerous resistance movement appeared to be taking shape. The Ghost Dance ended tragically with the massacre of Big Foot's band of Minneconjou (Teton Lakota Sioux) by the Seventh Cavalry at Wounded Knee in 1890—the very year the U.S. Census Bureau declared the western frontier to be closed, inspiring a young historian, Frederick Jackson Turner, to propose his frontier thesis just in time for the four hundredth anniversary of Columbus's discovery of the "New World."[10]

As time passed and the veteran ranks began to thin, interest in the Civil War grew, as if the nation recognized that something precious would soon be lost. Congress published the Official Records of the War of the Rebellion (128 volumes in all), and in 1890 the State of California commissioned a war record of its own. General Orton compiled and published in a single volume the extant records of the California Volunteers. GAR members and widows making military pension claims, along with civilians demanding compensation for "depredations" committed by tribes, put enormous strain on the federal budget and marked the beginning of what some Americans viewed as a welfare state. The depredation claims also kept the civil wars of the Southwest in the news and public eye until the claimants and their heirs died or finally gave up any hope of compensation in the face of endless bureaucratic red tape.[11]

John Milton Chivington died on October 4, 1894, just weeks before the thirtieth anniversary of the Sand Creek Massacre that had shocked the nation with its brutality and delayed Colorado statehood. Chivington insisted, "I stand by Sand Creek" until his dying day, and unrepentant Colorado Volunteer veterans turned out by the hundreds to ensure that the "Fighting Parson" had the largest funeral ever seen in Denver.[12]

As this historical activity passed in the early twentieth century, only rare mentions of the Civil War in the borderlands could be found in print. Arizona and New Mexico both achieved statehood in 1912—the first U.S. states with majority minority populations[13]—and in 1913 exiled Apaches were allowed to return to New Mexico as the nation turned its attention to the more than fifty thousand Union and Confederate veterans that gathered for a reunion at Gettysburg for the fiftieth anniversary of the battle. References to the Texan invasion, Indian wars, the march of the Colorado Volunteers, and the Column from California now appeared only rarely in newspaper obituaries. Hundreds of soldiers had stayed in or returned to the Southwest after the war. They had built homes and businesses, raised families, and become community leaders. Newspapermen in the prosperous cities of Phoenix, Prescott, Tucson, Yuma, Albuquerque, Las Cruces, and Santa Fe now wrote sentimentally of the passing pioneers—"the boys of '63." They also lamented the passing of the Indians of the borderlands. Though the indigenous peoples were now remembered nostalgically as noble primitives and memorialized in the nation's finest natural history museums, most Anglo and Hispano citizens approved of the government-funded Indian schools established to speed up the "civilization" process by targeting the youth of the tribes now located on confining reservations. "Kill the Indian to save the man," the Anglo teachers preached, believing assimilation meant salvation. Apaches and Navajos in Arizona and New Mexico were granted U.S. citizenship under the Indian Citizenship Act of 1924.[14]

In 1910 the civil unrest in Mexico that had continued to simmer since Benito Juárez first took power in 1861 broke out anew in a violent revolution that devastated the economy and drove many Mexicans north across the border in search of jobs and safety in the United States. The immediate trigger for renewed fighting had been the election of Francisco Madero, who rallied insurgents in the northern border states and wrested power from perennial president Porfírio Díaz, who, under the Juárez administration, had fought the French at the Battle of Puebla on *cinco de mayo*, 1862.[15]

In 1928 Southern Pacific Railroad workers in Arizona improving the road bed near Picacho Peak found bones, scraps of cloth, and the rotted remains of a headboard. Believing they had uncovered Lieutenant Barrett's lost grave, the Arizona Pioneers Historical Society participated in erecting a large stone obelisk as a tribute to the Civil War generation. Subsequent investigation, however, revealed the bones were likely those of a Mexican migrant laborer who died while laying railroad tracks in the 1880s. The discovery deflated the patriotic spirit of some Anglo "Pioneers" who considered Mexican Americans to be second class citizens— they seemed not to remember that the forebears of most Hispanos in the territories had not crossed the border, the border had crossed them.[16]

In 1940 Columbia Pictures released *Arizona*. This major Hollywood production, starring movie box office magnet Jean Arthur and debuting young William Holden, dramatized the Civil War origins of the state, but by the time of the Second World War the last GAR post had closed its doors forever—the records of its members lost or dispersed.[17] Young Indian men from Arizona, New Mexico, and Oklahoma endued with warrior tradition joined the army and Marine Corps in large numbers. During the Pacific island-hopping campaign of 1944, Navajo and Comanche Code Talkers ensured the security of U.S. combat communications, and on February 23, 1945, Pima Marine PFC Ira Hays helped raise the American flag on Mount Suribachi at Iwo Jima, an act immortalized by the iconic photograph of the war.[18] In 1948 the Indian people of Arizona and New Mexico were finally granted the right to vote as citizens of the United States.[19]

By the 1960s, as the nation commemorated the centennial of the Civil War, the U.S. Census Bureau determined that Anglos had become a majority of the population in the American Southwest. Fifty years later, as the nation commemorated the Civil War sesquicentennial, the Census Bureau announced that California, New Mexico, and Texas were once again "majority minority," with Hispanos being the reigning plurality, and predicted that Arizona would soon follow suit . . . as the civil wars of the borderlands, fought 150 years earlier, fade from memory.[20]

Appendix

Arizona and New Mexico Indian Depredation Claims
at the National Archives

The largely unorganized and unresearched group of documents known as "Indian Depredation Claims" are housed with related U.S. Court of Claims records at the National Archives in Washington, D.C. Researchers will find more than ten thousand depredation claim cases filed between 1796 and 1920, many still bundled and securely tied with their original red tape. Of these claims, nearly seven hundred relate to Arizona and New Mexico during the period 1861–67. The case files in Record Groups 75, 123, and 205 contain depositions, testimony, cross-examinations, and other evidence—a wealth of information detailing the nature of raids and warfare in the Southwest that provides historians with answers to questions about the groups initiating the attacks; the number, extent, and violence of depredations over time; and the patterns of conflict and tactics employed. The claims represent only a fraction of the raids, attacks, and skirmishes that occurred during this period, but when examined with other primary sources, a complex picture emerges of culturally distinctive methods of conflict, accommodation, cooperation, and other survival strategies employed by Indian, Hispano, and Anglo peoples of the Southwest during the Civil War.[1]

The Indian Depredation Claim files found in record groups 75, 123, and 205 at the National Archives are records relating to claims made against American Indian tribes by individuals seeking compensation for lost property or productivity as a result of thefts or attacks while the defendant tribe was "in amity" (under treaty and considered at peace) with the federal government. Thousands of claims were adjudicated between 1796 and 1920. The problem for historians wishing to access these records is the lack of accurate finding aids and consistent cataloging. The disorganized state of the collection resulted from changes in the depredation claim process and jurisdiction of the records. Though the Department of the Interior was nominally responsible for the records, at one time or another the U.S. Army, Office of Indian Affairs, Congress, and U.S. Court of Claims became directly involved in the review of the case files and recommendations for awarding payment for losses. When administrative jurisdiction changed, the records would be bundled and moved. New numbering systems were created and indexes made. Over the years, most of the indexes have been lost, and the only remaining finding aid is a partial name index, relating to Court of Claims records in RG 123, created by the Forty-Ninth Congress in 1887.[2] I used this index, and a supplement made in 1896, to locate the names of claimants believed to be located in Arizona or New Mexico. These names could then be matched by NARA staff, who had access to a master name index prepared in 1955, to case files stored in RG 123, yielding about one hundred claims made for depredations occurring in the territories between 1860 and 1867.

Suspecting that there were more claims to be found, I systematically examined nearly ten thousand depredation claim file "jackets" located in RG 75. These mostly empty folders had once contained claims, depositions, testimony and correspondence relating to each claim. In most cases, the contents were missing but handwritten on each jacket cover was the name of the claimant, the tribe involved, the date of the alleged depredation, and a summary of what was lost and its value. These jackets served as an index, of sorts, from which I identified additional Civil War–era Arizona and New Mexico claimants. Knowing the date, place, and name of a depredation, I used the 1955 RG 123 name index to locate hundreds of additional claims. While sorting through each box of numerically filed claims, I discovered hundreds of additional claims not previously identified in RG 75 or in the RG 123 index. Department of Justice case files in RG 205 yielded additional claims revealed when searching for appeals and additional testimony related to previously identified claimants. In total I found nearly seven hundred claims relating to Arizona and New Mexico from 1860–67 and examined each folder in detail. I made photocopies or digital photographs of claim statements, depositions by claimants and witnesses, testimony and cross-examinations generated by attorneys for the claimant and defendant, relevant correspondence, printed documents from appeals, and evidence (including brand books, watercolor paintings, and sketches). A worksheet was created for each claim, organized by the name of the claimant. Excel spreadsheets enabled me to classify and quantify specific details of the depredations and permitted analysis and graphing, providing insights into the difference between raiding and warfare, tactics, and motivations for civil wars in the Southwest Borderlands. More work remains to be done. Careful examination of depredation claim case files will provide scholars with insights into:

- Human casualties (dead, wounded, tortured, and sexually assaulted), property losses (horses, cattle, goods, etc.), and which group was responsible
- Patterns of raiding/warfare by group and what they reveal about the martial traditions and cultures of the combatants
- Violent attacks (war, revenge, and raid) before, during, and after the Civil War years
- The relationship of revenge attacks to Union and Confederate conflict
- The frequency of attacks (war, revenge, and raid) over time
- The most frequent attackers
- The most frequent victims
- The types of property most often taken or destroyed
- The value of the property loss
- Which group suffered the most killed or wounded, captured, sexually assaulted, or tortured, and which group was responsible
- Motives for attacks: "war" (retaliation) or "raid" (for property)
- The "anatomy" of an attack by different groups and its relationship to different cultures
- Years (or months, days, or hours) that saw the greatest number of raids
- Whether the attackers came mounted or on foot
- Whether the attackers used firearms
- The average size of a war/raiding/pursuit party
- The tactics most frequently employed

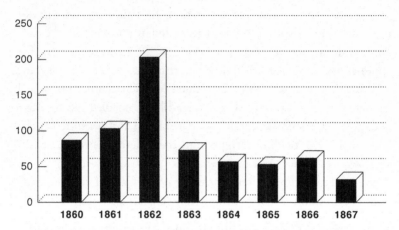

New Mexico and Arizona Indian depredation claims, 1860–67. The number of armed combats and "depredations" during the period 1861–67 far exceeded the period preceding and following it. For comparison see *Reports of the Secretary of War, 1851–1860* and *Record of Engagements With Hostile Indians Within the Military Division of the Missouri, from 1868 to 1882, Lieutenant General P. H. Sheridan, commanding. Compiled from Official Records.*

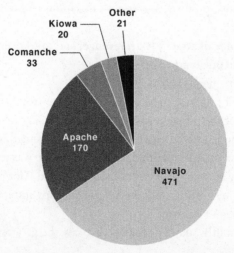

Depredations attributed to New Mexico and Arizona tribes, 1860–67.

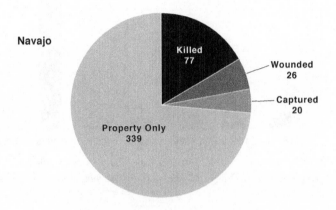

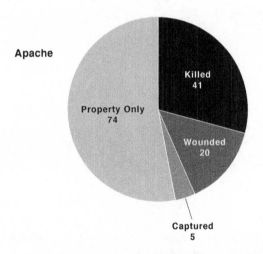

Depredation casualties attributed to Navajos and Apaches
in New Mexico and Arizona, 1860–67.

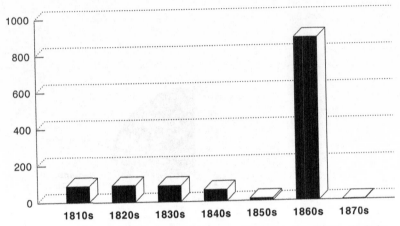

New Mexico citizens or subjects killed in Indian attacks as recorded in Catholic Church records, 1810–70. Brugge, *Navajos in Catholic Church Records of New Mexico, 1694–1875*, 30–31, 156.

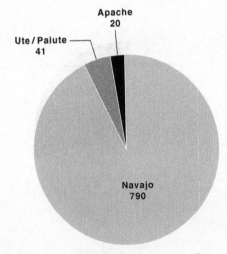

Captives recorded in New Mexico church records, 1860–69. Brugge, *Navajos in Catholic Church Records of New Mexico, 1694–1875*, 22–23.

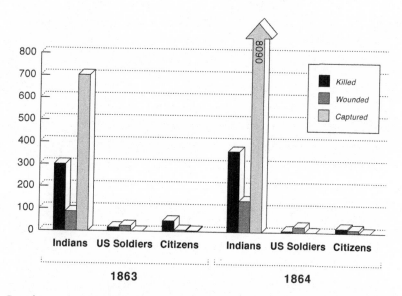

Casualties reported by U.S. Army in New Mexico and Arizona, 1863–64. Doolittle, *Condition of the Indian Tribes,* 256–57, 267–68; Lorenzo Labadie *v.* Navajo, Case 3259, RG 123, NARA.

Glossary

American A citizen of the United States of America. Though this shorthand term is problematic from a number of perspectives, most especially from the viewpoint of the other inhabitants of the Americas, it was generally understood in the Southwest Borderlands of the 1860s, and is still in common usage around the world today, to denote North Americans and, more specifically, U.S. citizens. Mexicans and Mexican Americans of the Civil War era referred to these people as *norteamericanos*, *americanos*, *gringos*, or Yankees. Indian peoples of the Southwest often adopted Spanish/Mexican names when referring to Anglo-Americans (e.g., Navajo: *bilagáana* is derived from Spanish *americano*, a cognate of English "American," as is O'odham: *milga:n*) or employed descriptive terms in their native tongues (e.g., Cheyenne: *ve'hoe*, literally, "spider"; Apache: *n'daa*, "eye" or "pale eye"; Comanche: *taibo*, literally, "list-checker").

Anglo English-speaking, non-Hispanic, Euro-American citizen of the United States or Confederate States.

Apache (Zuni, enemy). The Athabaskan-speaking peoples of the Southwest Borderlands who refer to themselves as *Nnee*, *Ndee*, or *Indé*, meaning "the people" or "human beings." The Zuni first called these people 'a·pacu 'Navajos' (meaning "enemies"), and the shortened term "Apache" was borrowed in turn by Hispanos and Anglos. Other Apacheans, including the Navajos, shared a linguistic heritage and many cultural traditions. Anthropologists and ethnologists often identify the largest divisions of Apacheans as Eastern (Mescalero, Jicarilla, Lipan), Western (Warm Springs, White Mountain), and Southern (Chiricahua) Apaches. By the 1860s, the seasonally mobile Apache bands included within these broad groupings identified themselves without reference to the larger affiliations, though they may have acknowledged some kinship. Western Apaches refer to themselves as *Nnee*, including the group known in the 1860s as Aravaipas. Southern Apaches, who had become known to Hispanos and Anglos as Chiricahuas, Gileños, and Mimbreños referred to their bands as *Bidánku, Chukunende, Chíhénde*, and *Ndé ndaí*. By the time of the Civil War, the U.S. government referred to Eastern Apaches as Mescaleros, Jicarillas, and Lipans[1] while still more bands inhabiting the borderlands of New Mexico, Texas, and Indian Territory (Oklahoma) were known as Plains or Prairie Apaches (e.g., Kiowa-Apaches).

Arapaho (a name possibly inspired by Pawnee or Crow words for traders or tattooed people). *Hinono'eino* people are Algonquian speakers who, in the 1860s, organized in nomadic, horseback-hunting bands, often allied with Cheyennes. Some southern Arapaho bands cooperated with their former enemies, Kiowas and Comanches, south of the Arkansas River.

band A subset of an American Indian tribe or nation usually made up of one or more smaller groups of related individuals (e.g., Bedonkohe, a Chiricahua or Southern Apache band) and led by a chief or headman.[2]

borderlands The territory on both sides of the U.S-Mexico border in the American Southwest, including all or parts of (but not limited to) the states of Arizona, California, Chihuahua, Colorado, Nevada, New Mexico, Sonora, Texas, and Utah that became the middle ground in the inter-national and civil wars of the 1860s. In American historiography, the term originally applied to the northern frontier of the Spanish holdings of New Spain in the Americas, from Florida to California. Today, scholars broadly apply the term in reference to places of interaction between diverse groups around the globe.

captive A person taken in a raid or attack. During the colonial period, the Spanish sought male captives from American Indian tribes for work in mines and other hard slave labor, but by the 1860s

Anglos, Indians, and Hispanos in the borderlands generally preferred women and children captives, who could be kept or sold as slaves. The less tractable men and older boys were not deemed suitable for this purpose. Most Apaches preferred boy children captives; their rules of war allowed that captive men might be returned to the band for final disposition by members of grieving families who required compensation for a man lost to the enemy. Such a debt could be paid with an enslaved enemy, an adoptive replacement or, in some cases, blood. Hispanos and all the southwestern tribes often adopted captives. Anglos might adopt, intern, or enslave captives depending on circumstances and the state of war recognized at the time of capture.[3] See ***cautivo***.

casta (Spanish, race or mixed-race people). The term *castas* is also used in reference to a type of caste system[4] (*sistema de castas*) based on the degree of acculturation to Hispanic culture as distinguished between *gente de razón* (Hispanos) and *gente sin razón* (nonacculturated natives). The system of *castas* was based on the Spanish belief in racial superiority and that the character and quality of people varied according to their birth, color, and race. In this fluid yet still hierarchical society, socioeconomic status, including taxation, often depended on skin color and apparent *limpieza de sangre* (purity of blood) or *calidad* (quality). In colonial Mexico, one's status generally correlated with the racial categories as identified by observable characteristics and family history, but generally, lighter-skinned people enjoyed higher status. The broadest classifications were *peninsulares* (European- or Spanish-born), *criollos* (Creole descendants of Europeans born in the Americas), *mestizos* (American Indian and white), and *Indio puro* (pure blood Indian). At least sixteen mixed-race combinations are documented in *casta* paintings from the eighteenth century, including *Español con India, Mestizo; Mestizo con Española, Castizo; Castizo con Española, Español; Español con Negra, Mulato; Mulato con Española, Morisco; Morisco con Española, Chino; Chino con India, Salta atrás; Salta atrás con Mulata, Lobo; Lobo con China, Gíbaro; Gíbaro con Mulata, Albarazado; Albarazado con Negra, Cambujo; Cambujo con India, Sambiago; Sambiago con Loba, Calpamulato; Calpamulato con Cambuja, Tente en el aire; Tente en el aire con Mulata, No te entiendo; No te entiendo con India, Torna atrás.* With the rapid growth of the *mestizo* population in the borderlands of the 1860s, the system of racial categorization became less important in determining social status as people of mixed ancestry possessed of wealth, political position, and military rank moved much more easily between social categories.[5]

cautivo (Spanish, captive). An Indian captive might also be referred to as *pieza*, the word used for slave and scalp.

Cheyenne (Lakota, literally, red talkers, the people whose language we cannot understand). *Tsistsistas*, an Algonquian-speaking American Indian tribe whose nomadic, horseback hunting bands, by the 1860s, followed the buffalo herds and inhabited the Great Plains from south of the Arkansas River to the Black Hills.

Chiricahua (Ópata, literally, Turkey Mountain people). A Southern Apache tribe comprising the Bedonkohe (*Bidánku*), Chokonen (*Chukunende*), Chihenne (*Chíhénde*), and Nednhi (*Ndé ndaí*) bands.

civil war Violent conflict between parties, factions, or inhabitants of different communities within the same country or occupying the same geographic region. Such deadly conflict usually occurs within a polity or region considered unified by one or both antagonists.[6]

civilized By the 1860s, Anglos often referred to Indian people in the borderlands as either "wild" or "civilized." The latter distinction was usually determined by whether an agricultural and sedentary lifestyle (including permanent dwellings) predominated and taxes were paid. The federal government and Anglos in general did not believe Christianization and literacy were requirements for an Indian to be considered "civilized."[7] For the Hispano point of view, see **gente de razón**.

clan A kinship group that extended beyond the local group, served as an affinity network, and tied people of different bands together even when separated by great distance. Navajo and Apache clans are related as both groups are Southern Athabaskan-speaking Apacheans who became physically isolated and socially segmented by the seventeenth century. Anthropologists refer to an exogamous subdivision of a tribe constituting two or more related clans as a phratry.[8]

Comanche (from Ute *komántica*, literally, enemy who fights all the time). *Numunuu*, a buffalo-hunting, horse culture comprising more than thirty distinct bands. The Uto-Aztecan-speaking Comanches split from the Shoshones soon after acquiring horses in 1705 and were responsible for driving the Athabaskan Apaches and Navajos from the plains and stopping Spanish conquest on the Texas plains and *provincias internas*. The Comanches became the most powerful Indian nation on the southern plains by the late eighteenth century. By the nineteenth century, James Wilkinson, American general and envoy to Mexico, considered them to be "the most powerful nation of savages on this continent."[9]

Comanchería The Comanche Empire's sphere of influence on the southern plains in the nineteenth century, including western Texas, eastern New Mexico, and portions of the present states of Colorado, Kansas, and Oklahoma, as well as Mexico's northeastern frontier.

community A group of people with common interests, real or imagined.

compadrazgo (Spanish). Catholic godparenthood; *padrino/padrina*: godfather/godmother.

criada (Spanish). A female servant, especially a female Indian captive placed in servitude and adopted by Hispano families within the *compadrazgo* system of godparenthood. The system of adoptive servitude is *crianza*.

depredation Generally considered an unlawful and unprovoked attack, during the nineteenth century "depredation" became a term of art in the American justice system for claims made by victims of Indian attacks who sued the U.S. government for compensation for losses incurred. Depredation claims could only be adjudicated if the depredators were members of a treaty tribe considered to be "in amity with" the government.

dragoon A specialized mounted soldier trained and equipped to fight on horseback as heavy cavalry as well as on foot, like infantry. Dragoons evolved from the European military tradition, and the U.S. Army raised two regiments of these mounted troops in the 1830s as it became evident that foot soldiers could not effectively fight highly mobile equestrian Indians and guard the overland trails of the vast western frontier. By 1861, however, the War Department determined that all mounted units—dragoons, mounted rifles, and cavalry—would be redesignated as "cavalry," as these specialized units all came to function as light cavalry, only rarely fighting in massed formations and most often deployed in small mobile units and as skirmishers. As a result of this change, the First and Second Dragoons became the First and Second Cavalry, the First Mounted Rifles became the Third Cavalry, and the First and Second Cavalry became the Fourth and Fifth Cavalry. During the 1860s, many mounted volunteer units in U.S and C.S. service adopted fanciful names such as "Lancers," "Mounted Rifles," and "Dragoons," but all these horse soldiers were considered to be cavalry by their respective military establishments.

ethnicity   Refers to a self-identified, linguistically related group whose members may share physical characteristics as well as religious and other cultural connections.

extermination   The belief that an enemy people, tribe, or band that cannot be coerced into submission or assimilated must be wiped out in order to achieve peace and full access to land and other resources. Westering Anglo-Americans believing in Manifest Destiny and the superiority of the "white race" often espoused a platform of extermination for "savage" Indian peoples deemed hostile to "civilized" peoples. Though this policy was never officially endorsed by the United States or any state or territorial government, during the 1860s political debate in the Southwest often centered on the subject. Armed groups of civilians, soldiers, and Indians attempted to implement this practice on a small scale in a number of raids and engagements. See **genocide**.

filibuster (Spanish: *filibustero*)   A freebooter who engages in an unauthorized military expedition into a foreign country to foment or support a revolution with the aim of acquiring wealth and power. The term is usually used to describe U.S. adventurers who invaded Central and South America in the mid-nineteenth century.

gegodza   (Apache, literally, to be paid back). Revenge or compensation for a killing perpetrated by an enemy. Once the family, clan, or band had exacted revenge they felt satisfied that the debt had been paid back.[10]

genocide   The deliberate killing of a large group of people, especially those of a particular ethnic group or nation. Genocide is related to the idea of "ethnic cleansing." Both terms were coined in the twentieth century, and are roughly equivalent to the nineteenth century concept of extermination as understood in the Southwest Borderlands. The indigenous peoples of the Americas no doubt understood the idea prior to the Spanish *conquista*, and the killing of male foemen and captives was common practice. American Indians rarely slaughtered enemy women and children, who might serve as slaves or adoptive replacements for lost family members, in the borderlands of the 1860s. See **extermination**.

genízaro Detribalized Indians reduced to slavery or peonage, resettled in Hispano villages, and often used as military auxiliaries or janissaries.[11]

gente de razón Indians considered by Hispanos to be "people of reason" once Christianized and schooled in Spanish. In the 1860s Anglos used the term "civilized" to connote Indian people willing to assimilate by living and working as Americans. By the second half of the nineteenth century, the U.S. Census Bureau defined civilized Indians as "self-supporting" and enumerated them separately as "taxable Indians."[12]

guerilla (Spanish: **guerrilla, guerrillero**, French: **guerillero**) Partisan warfare characterized by small independent units operating against conventional forces. During the Civil War era, the U.S. Army defined a partisan party as a guerilla and an individual partisan as a *guerillero*. Scott's *Military Dictionary* warned that guerillas "annoyed the flanks and rear of columns, they intercept convoys, cut off communications, attack detachments, and endeavor to spread terror everywhere. This kind of warfare is advantageously pursued only in mountainous or thickly-wooded districts. In an open country, cavalry very readily destroys partisans. The Spanish race make active partisans."[13] French forces in Mexico formed special mounted units known as *contra-guerillas* to combat Juarista partisans.

hacendado An *hacienda* (large landed estate) owner who employed hired help, Christianized captives, or *peones* for a labor force. The Spanish crown made grants of Indian labor to *encomendados* in return for their commitment to provide religious instruction and physical safety for their wards/vassals. This system fell into disuse because it could not be used to subjugate *mestizos*. Over time *encomendados* became *hacendados*, finding more economic advantage in land ownership and peonage than in ownership of labor that could through race-mixing become unbound.

Hispano Spanish-speaking Mexican or American of Spanish ancestry, most often of mixed Spanish and Indian heritage.

Indian Indigenous people descended from the first inhabitants of the Americas. During the Civil War years, the U.S. government defined Indians as "the red man of America," and Scott's *Military Dictionary* lamented the "disappearance of the race" while advocating their recruitment because "no men would make better light cavalry and light infantry than the Indians of our western frontier."[14] While the federal government and most present-day American Indian tribes in the United States use this term, rather than the more ambiguous "Native American," referring to people by their specific tribe and band names is nearly always preferred. Many anthropologists have adopted Amerindian, First Peoples or, especially in Canada, First Nations.[15] See **Mexican.**

jinetes (Spanish). Originally referred to horsemen or light cavalry, but in New Mexico during the 1860s *jinetes* were usually raiding Indian horsemen.

ladrones (Spanish, thieves). Navajo and Apache livestock raiders. Among the Navajos, the *ladrones* were often young men without considerable wealth in livestock, as opposed to the stock-rich *ricos.*

lancer During the Civil War era, a number of U.S. and C.S. mounted volunteer units carried lances into battle in the far western theater of war—the only theater in which troops actually engaged enemy forces with these obsolescent weapons. The Fifth Texas Mounted Volunteers' lancer companies fought U.S. regular and volunteer troops at the Battle of Valverde in 1862. Mexican regular soldiers and militia had a long tradition of mounted warfare which evolved on the Iberian Peninsula. These mounted troops carried lances well into the nineteenth century, as did the Hispano soldiers of the California Native Battalion who carried lances in Arizona as late as 1865. Anglos of the South Dakota Volunteers were also issued lances, but there is no record of their use in combat. Throughout the 1860s, all the Plains tribes as well as Apaches and Navajos carried and effectively used lances, it being the weapon of choice for most mounted warriors of the borderlands.[16]

manso (Spanish). A "tame" Indian. In the borderlands during the 1860s, the term *Apaches mansos* was most often used in reference to captive Apaches who had been assimilated into the Mexican American population and served as auxiliaries in campaigns against "wild" Apaches (*Apaches bárbaros*).[17]

Maricopa *Piipaash*, Yuman-speaking people who split from the Colorado River tribes in the late eighteenth or early nineteenth century to live and farm alongside their Pima (*Akimel O'odham*) allies on the Gila River.

mestizo (Spanish, literally, mixed). A person of mixed Spanish and Indian descent resulting from *mestizaje*—the process of racial and ethnic mixing.

Mexican A citizen of the Republic of Mexico. By the middle of the nineteenth century most Mexicans were of mixed Spanish and Indian blood—*mestizos*. In Mexico today, citizens of American Indian ancestry are referred to as "indigenous peoples," the identifier recognized in the second article of the 1917 Constitution and preferred by scholars as well. Mexico defines itself as a "pluricultural" nation in recognition of the diverse ethnic groups that constitute it. The Mexican census only reports cultural ethnicity, not racial ethnicity, of indigenous communities who preserve their native languages, traditions, beliefs, and cultures. Mexico's indigenous peoples have the right of free determination under the second article of the Law of Linguistic Rights of the Indigenous Languages, which recognizes sixty-two "national languages" having the same validity as Spanish in all territories in which they are spoken. According to Mexico's National Institute of Statistics, Geography and Data Processing (INEGI), approximately 5.4 percent of the population speaks one of these languages. This represents approximately half of those identified as indigenous.[18] See **Indian**.

militia Nonprofessional troops commanded by the governors of the states or territories for service within those political units in time of war or emergency. In the United States "every free, able-bodied, white male citizen . . . of the age of 18 years and under 45 years" was to be enrolled in the militia. The federal government provided arms and assistance for the maintenance of militias, which often served as cadres for professional volunteer units authorized in times of war to augment the regular army. The Anglo-American militia tradition traces its heritage to the feudal military service introduced in England at the time of William the Conqueror, which required every freeman to arm himself and serve in defense of the country. In Mexico and New Mexico, *milicias activas* were volunteers activated for short periods (forty-five days).[19] See **volunteer**.

nacajalleses (Navajo). New Mexican livestock and slave raiders.

nation A people, community, or tribe with geographic boundaries, imagined or defined, whose common identity creates a unifying bond. The nation's political identity usually comprises such characteristics as a common language, culture, ethnicity, traditions, and history. Though more than one nation may constitute a state, the terms nation, state, and country are often used interchangeably.[20]

Navajo (from Tewa-puebloan *nava hu*, literally, place of large planted fields). *Diné*, an Apachean people known to the Spanish as *Apaches del Navahu*, who, beginning in the eighteenth century, became pastoralists, farmers, and raiders in northern New Mexico after being forced westward by the expanding horse cultures of the plains. Sharing the Athabaskan linguistic tradition, the Navajos traded and fought with neighboring Apaches and developed reciprocal raid-trade relationships with Pueblo peoples and Hispanos on the upper Rio Grande in New Mexico. By the time of the Civil War, the Navajos were the most numerous and powerful Indian nation in the desert and mountain Southwest.

nomadism A survival strategy characterized by foraging, hunting, and/or pastoralism wherein a community moves for the purpose of seasonal gathering, hunting herds of migrating animals (e.g., buffalo), or searching pasturage for domesticated animals. The lodges (tipis) of the tribes of the southern plains were highly mobile to accommodate this lifestyle. Anthropologists have recognized a shift in human subsistence strategies over time depending on prevailing local conditions and resources. The change from nomadic hunting and foraging to sedentism is coupled with the adoption of agriculture and animal domestication. Seminomadic people (e.g., Chiricahua Apaches) tended to seasonally gather and harvest in locations of known natural abundance and fertility while continuing to raid for stock and moving to find good pasturage. Semisedentary people (e.g., Navajo) were less mobile and relied on the same locations to plant and harvest seasonal crops but supplemented their needs by hunting and gathering strategies, including opportunistic raiding. Sedentary people (e.g., *O'odham* Pima and Papagos) were primarily agriculturalists with domesticated animals and fixed villages and homes.[21]

Papago (Piman, literally, bean eaters). *Tohono O'odham*, desert dwelling people inhabiting southern Arizona and northern Sonora for hundreds of years. Hispanos and Anglos of the 1860s adopted the Pima word Papago when referring to these agrarian people of southern Arizona and Sonora. All *O'odham* people, including the Piman *Akimel O'odham*, speak a Uto-Aztecan language.

pastores (Spanish, sheepherders).

***peón*, peonage** (Spanish). A form of debt bondage in which involuntary servants or laborers (*peones*) have little control over employment and living conditions. For Indian captives of Hispanos, peonage and slavery were often interchangeable terms. The "debt" to be paid with a lifetime of servitude was simply the captive's status as an enemy Indian. Though the Thirteenth Amendment (adopted December 1865) prohibited involuntary servitude such as peonage for all but convicted criminals, peonage was still widespread in New Mexico after the U.S. Civil War. U.S. Army officers expressed their confusion over the status of peons; some officers believed the practice to be involuntary servitude equivalent to slavery and others believed it to be a voluntary contractual arrangement. Confusing matters further, Hispanos often "adopted" their peons. Because New Mexico laws supported peonage, the U.S. Congress passed an anti-peonage law on March 2, 1867. Section 1990 of the Peonage Act proclaims: "The holding of any person to service or labor under the system known as peonage is abolished and forever prohibited in the territory of New Mexico, or in any other territory or state of the United States; and all acts, laws . . . made to establish, maintain, or enforce, directly or indirectly, the voluntary or involuntary service or labor of any persons as peons, in liquidation of any debt or obligation, or otherwise, are declared null and void."[22]

pieza (Spanish, literally, piece). A slave, especially a captured Indian child. Pieza may also refer to a scalp taken from an enemy as a trophy or proof of a kill.

Pima, Piman *Akimel O'odham*, an agrarian tribe of Uto-Aztecan speakers living in partnership with the Yuman-speaking Maricopas (*Piipaash*) in sedentary villages along the Gila River of southern Arizona. The name Pimo (the most common form used by Anglos in the 1860s) or Pima is believed to have been derived from the phrase *pi mac*, meaning "I don't know," which tribesmen on the southern fringe of Pimería may have uttered in response to Spanish interrogatories.[23]

race Though not based on scientific or empirical evidence, the concept of "race" is an artificial or social construct often used in the nineteenth and twentieth centuries for political purposes to identify peoples or "nations," especially "others"—those seen as different from the dominant group based on perceived physical differences or physiognomy. During the eighteenth and nineteenth centuries the term, as used by Europeans and Americans, experienced a gradual shift in meaning from "nation" to a pseudoscientific classification of peoples. See *casta*.

raid An extension of hunting traditions based on resource acquisition for survival. Hispano and Indian raiders most often sought women and children captives, livestock, and other useful or fungible commodities. Apaches defined "raiding" as "to search out enemy property."[24] Anglo military doctrine defined raids as attacks seeking tactical advantage such as destroying crops, homes, and food supplies, and killing enemy combatants. See **war**.

ranchería (Spanish). Extended family group or band encampment serving as a base for seasonal hunting, gathering, or agricultural activities.

rebellion Open and armed defiance of or resistance to an established power or government. Such a revolution or civil war often results from ideological change or a desire to maintain traditionally held values. The U.S. government officially termed the American Civil War the War of the Rebellion.

rebel A Southern Confederate in rebellion against the United States.

regular A member of the professional, standing army of a nation. See **militia**, **volunteer**.

revolution A civil war which attempts to overthrow a government or ruler stemming from ideological change or a desire to maintain traditionally held values, depending on the perspective of the antagonists.

slave A person bound in servitude to another person, family, or household. Several systems of slavery and forced servitude coexisted in the borderlands during the 1860s, including Indian and Hispano chattel and adoptive captivity, Spanish-Mexican peonage, and the Anglo-American variety of African chattel bondage. See *pieza*.

Tejano (Spanish). An Anglo-American Texan. Conventions regarding the use of this term have changed over time. Some writers prefer using *Tejano* to refer to Hispano Texans, especially during the period of the 1830s–40s, and cast Anglo Texans owing fealty to the Mexican government as Texians. In the borderlands during and after the 1860s, however, these terms were used interchangeably, and New Mexican Hispanos and Indians almost universally referred to Anglo-American Texans as *Tejanos*.[25]

territory A part of the United States not included within any state but organized with a separate governing body. Territorial expansion during the mid-nineteenth century reflected a national policy of colonialism not unlike that practiced by Spain, Great Britain, and France a century earlier. Settlement followed land claims and the conquest of indigenous peoples, who were then either summarily destroyed or subjugated and assimilated. While the American form of colonization differed in its democratic rationalizations, treaties, and other political particulars, the process was essentially the same. As far as the U.S. government was concerned, once the inhabitants of a frontier region determined themselves capable of self-government, or Congress determined them so, territorial status was conferred. Territories with federally appointed governors and popularly elected legislators were viewed as prospective states in training. Once populated with a sufficient number of citizens, a territory might be granted statehood. The most confusing aspect of U.S. territorial colonialism involved the status of citizens. Former Mexican citizens were adopted as U.S. citizens, whatever their "race," but for Indian peoples living in tribal communities citizenship was conferred based on their perceived level of "civilization," which often translated as house-dwelling agriculturists. If the government determined them to be "taxable," they usually passed the citizenship test.

total war A war in which the belligerents mobilize all available resources and population. In the mid-nineteenth century, military men influenced by Clausewitz's widely read, *On War*, construed total war ("*absoluter Krieg*") somewhat differently. At that time, this term referred to a separate class of warfare in which little or no distinction was made between combatants and civilians, as both could be seen as supporting an enemy's war effort. Clausewitz also advocated the use of terror tactics as an essential ingredient in successful warfare.[26]

tradition The terms "tradition" and "custom" are often used interchangeably, but anthropologists and sociologists, and some historians, discern subtle distinctions. Eric Hobsbawm and others see "customs" as the actions derived from long-standing conventions, and "traditions" as the trappings or physical manifestations of the customs. In a military sense, war customs, traditions, tactics, and strategies may in time become doctrine.[27]

tribe   An Indian nation or linguistically and culturally related group whose bands or subdivisions are inclined to cooperate, especially when faced with an external threat. Led by one or more chiefs or headmen, tribes in the borderlands valued social ties and recognized geographical boundaries. They tended to be homogeneous, parochial, stable, and offered organizing links between families (including clans and lineages), providing social and ideological solidarity more limited than that of an ethnic group. During the 1860s, the U.S. government used the terms "tribe" and "nation" interchangeably, and "tribe" is still officially used by the federal government, tribal governments, tribal elders, and generally by American Indian people today.[28]

vergüenza   A deep and personal shame, especially that related to failure to comply with the Spanish code of honor.

volunteer   A U.S. or C.S. soldier mustered into national service. Volunteer troops were raised by the states and territories when authorized by the president in times of national emergency. These soldiers were armed, equipped, paid, and trained the same as regular troops. Officers were often veterans with professional training or experience in prewar militias. During the Civil War, volunteers generally served for three years but terms of service could be as short as one hundred days or as long as the duration of the war. By 1863 eastern states implemented compulsory drafts (even conscripts were officially considered "volunteers"), but this was not necessary in California, New Mexico, and Colorado, which enrolled more than enough able-bodied men to fill the quotas established by the War Department. See **regular, militia**.

war   Socially or politically motivated organized violence on a relatively large scale. Clausewitz, the principal European military theorist of the nineteenth century, defined war as "an act of violence to compel our opponent to fulfil our will." The principal motives for war in the Southwest Borderlands during the 1860s were social security and defense, ethnic rivalry, conquest and economic gain, and vengeance. Apacheans made a sharp distinction between raiding—for property and other spoils—and war. They defined war as "taking death from an enemy" for vengeance and justice.[29] See **raid**.

warrior   An Indian man or boy willing and able to fight enemies. Indian men were not full-time soldiers but were expected by their band to take up arms for the purpose of raiding, retaliating, exacting revenge, or a preemptive attack against an enemy. Some tribes had warrior societies ("soldier society") with distinctive weapons and rituals, but even in these instances the members of the society were family providers first and warriors when necessary.

Yavapai (literally, people of the sun). Comprised four bands who considered themselves separate peoples: the *Tolkepayas*, or Western Yavapai; the *Yavapés*, or Northwestern Yavapai; the *Kwevkepayas*, or Southeastern Yavapai; and *Wipukepas*, or Northeastern Yavapai. The Yuman-speaking Yavapais were sometimes identified by whites as Tontos as well as Yuma Apaches or Mohave Apaches as a result of mixing with the Western Apache bands and Colorado River tribes.

Yuman A language family of Hokan stock or the tribes located on the Colorado River and its tributaries who speak such a language. By the 1860s Anglos and Hispanos referred to the Quechans living near the confluence of the Colorado and Gila Rivers as Yumas. Other Yuman tribes living in California, Arizona, Baja California, and Sonora include the Cocopahs, Maricopas, Halchidomas, Mojaves, Hualapais, Havasupais, and Yavapais.

Notes

Introduction

1. Extensive testimony found in the Indian Depredation Claims demonstrates that the withdrawal of federal troops at the beginning of the Civil War and their subsequent distraction in fighting Confederates created a situation that led to increased stock raiding by Apaches and Navajos and then to war. For examples, see Rafael Chavez *v.* Navajo, Case 4097; Peter Kitchen *v.* Apache, Case 6845; Tomas Montoya *v.* Apache, Case 4101; Pedro Padilla *v.* Apache and Navajo, Case 5957; Abraham Peeples *v.* Mimbres Apache, Case 6253, all in National Archives and Records Administration (NARA), Record Group (RG) 123; Lorenzo Ortero *v.* Navajo, Claim 4048; Mariano Pino *v.* Navajo, Claim 6141, both in RG 75, NARA. Evidence of increased attacks and violence on the main traveled roads across Arizona, New Mexico, and Texas is corroborated by voluminous correspondence between army officers, Union and Confederate, found in *War of the Rebellion: Official Records of the Union and Confederate Armies* (cited hereafter as *OR*), especially vols. 50 (1 & 2), 4, and 9, as well as newspaper accounts from California and the territories. See, for example, *San Francisco Daily Alta California,* Aug. 10, 1862; *Tucson Weekly Arizonian,* Aug. 10, 1861.

2. James F. Brooks, in *Captives and Cousins: Slavery, Kinship and Community in the Southwest Borderlands,* carefully and quantitatively examines the cultural interaction and institutionalized slavery based on raiding for and trading in Indian and Hispano captives. New Mexico Hispanos often masked slave raids as attempts to recover livestock taken by Indians, but the real object was captives to be used as laborers or concubines. The roots of this system are found in Iberian slave practices in which the enslaved would gradually shed their status as war captives to become full, though subordinate, family members. Brooks's groundbreaking work also demonstrates that the raid-and-reprisal system was not unilateral.

3. Amy Greenberg, in *Manifest Manhood and the Antebellum American Empire*, addresses the Anglo-American filibustering phenomenon that reached its peak that same year, 1857, arguing that economic stress and a form of "martial masculinity" led ambitious young men such as William Walker to seek opportunity and empire south of the U.S. border while becoming a "race hero" to his Anglo-American countrymen. Greenberg, *Manifest Manhood*, 12–14, 42, 168–69. See also Smith-Rosenberg, *This Violent Empire*.

4. In the 1930s, ethnographer Grenville Goodwin lived and worked with Apaches in Arizona to better understand the underlying causes of the violent conflict of the 1860s. This work remained inaccessible to historians until 1971, when anthropologist Keith Basso published Goodwin's field notes and extraordinary insights in *Western Apache Raiding and Warfare*. Key among the conclusions is that Apaches made a sharp distinction between "raiding" for property and going to "war" for revenge (*gegodza*). Clifton Kroeber and Bernard Fontana, in *Massacre on the Gila*, trace the origin of war between Indian peoples of the Southwest Borderlands to a shift in subsistence strategies and the transfer of the burden of agriculture and food production to women, giving rise to a male tendency to make war in order to demonstrate their masculinity and essential service to their families and communities. The rise of this martial culture led to conflict with neighboring tribes.

5. See Novick, *That Noble Dream*, 74–82, 234–38, 354–59, for a survey of Civil War historiography to 1980 and, for more recent scholarship, Couvares, *Interpretations of American History*, 339–64. Eminent historians in this field include James Ford Rhodes (*History of the United States*), Charles Beard (*The Rise of American Civilization*), W. E. B. DuBois (*Black Reconstruction in America, 1860–1880*), Arthur M. Schlesinger Jr. ("The Causes of the Civil War: A Note on Historical Sentimentalism"), Alan Nevins (*Ordeal of the Union*, 8 Vols.), and Eric Foner (*Free Soil, Free Labor, Free Men*).

6. Alvin Josephy's *The Civil War in the American West* provided a sweeping look at the Civil War in the far western states and territories by focusing attention on the war's impact on the native populations of the Trans-Mississippi West. Richard White wrote in *"It's Your Misfortune and None of My Own"* that "the Civil War is critically important in this history of western origins . . . it created the conditions in which the West arose." European domination was not a foregone conclusion in encounters with powerful American Indian empires and tribal domains. Whether motivated by their quests for empire, cultural supremacy, or defense of their homeland, Indian people demonstrated political savvy, military might, and the ability to accommodate and compromise when necessary as a survival strategy. Whereas Roger Nichols, in *Warrior Nations*, examines violence between Indians and Anglo-Americans that devolved into "an all-out race war," Gary Anderson (*Conquest of Texas*) argues that the actions of white American "exterminationists" in Texas resulted in "deliberate ethnic cleansing" of Indian peoples. Karl Jacoby takes a decidedly microhistorical turn with his *Shadows at Dawn*, exploring in detail the motives for the massacre of Apache people at Camp Grant, Arizona, in the aftermath of the Civil War from a multicultural—Indian, Hispano, Anglo—perspective. Jacoby follows the plight of Apache slaves distributed among Tucson's Hispano citizens who desired the women and

children as household servants and domestic laborers. Captivity and slavery did, in fact, play a significant role in conflicts in the Southwest Borderlands. For an overview of the origins of conflict and the value of studying war, see Keegan, *History of Warfare.*

7. For the purpose of this study I endeavor to abide by terminological conventions generally accepted in borderlands and western history scholarship today. Still evolving are terms such as "Anglo" and "Hispano," but the use of "(American) Indian" rather than "Native American" and of "tribes" and "bands" in conjunction with the names preferred by the descendants of those historical communities are now accepted practice. For an excellent discussion of these terms in modern scholarship, see Mann, *1491*, 2–5, 339–43.

8. Tribal and band names for the indigenous peoples of the Southwest have been subject to change over the years and vary even today with the historian, anthropologist, or native speaker. For consistency with quoted primary sources, I have used the following names for Yuman- and Uto-Aztecan–speaking tribes: Quechans (Yumas), Mojaves ('Aha Makhav), Chemehuevis (Nüwüwü), Maricopas (Piipaash), Pimas (Akimel O'odham), and Papagos (Tohono O'odham). In recent years historians have adopted new names and orthography for many Athabaskan-speaking tribes and bands, usually to reflect the preference of present-day tribal members for the traditional spoken names for their people, rather than names adopted by Spanish- and English-speaking newcomers. These Apacheans include Navajo (Diné), Western Apaches (Nnee, including the Aravaipas), Chiricahua Apaches (including the allied Bedonkohe, Chokonen, Chihenne, and Nednhi; a.k.a. Bidánku, Chukunende, Chíhénde, and Ndé ndaí), and Eastern Apaches (including Jicarilla, Mescalero, and Lipan). It was their traditional Pueblo Indian adversaries who first used the name Apache, from the Zuni word 'a·pac̆u 'Navajos,' meaning "enemies." Juan de Oñate, the Spanish governor of New Mexico, used it as early as 1598. In Oñate's time no distinction was drawn between Apaches and Navajos. The agrarian Pueblo Indians of northern New Mexico were culturally and linguistically diverse. By the 1860s many Pueblo communities (including Ácoma, Cohiti, Hopi, Isleta, Jemez, Kewa, Laguna, Nambe, Ohkay, Picuris, Pojoaque, San Felipe, San Ildefonso, Sandia, Santa Ana, Santa Clara, Tesuque, Taos, Zia, and Zuni) had been significantly influenced after centuries of acculturation by New Mexico's Spanish-speaking population.

9. Edward Spicer, David Weber, Alfred Kroeber, Bernard Fontana, James F. Brooks, Amy Greenberg, and Karl Jacoby have been especially influential. See Brooks, DeCorse, and Walton, *Small Worlds.*

10. Though the term "Southwest" is culturally skewed toward the American perspective—depending on a people's vantage point, the region might be considered a "northern frontier" or "homeland"—it has been generally adopted by borderlands scholars and the people of the U.S.

11. Spickard, *Almost All Aliens,* 18–19; Meeks, *Border Citizens,* 4–5, 241–42. Meeks expresses a debt of gratitude to Jean and John Comaroff's *Ethnography and the Historical Imagination,* which he credits for first articulating this distinction between race and ethnicity. Meeks argues that Yaqui and O'odham people still fight for unrestricted U.S.-Mexico border crossing.

European-model nations "imagined" boundaries that split Indian homelands and families.

12. RG 123, Records of the U.S. Court of Claims, Indian Depredation Case
Records; RG 75, Evidence Concerning Depredation Claims; RG 205,
Records of the Court of Claims Section of the Department of Justice, Indian
Depredation Case Records, NARA. By themselves, these documents do
not present a complete record of conflict during the Civil War. The U.S.
government had little interest in human casualties, for which there would
be no compensation. Victims of deadly attacks could, of course, make no
claims, though family members sometimes chose to seek compensation for
property lost. Most of the claims report losses of Hispano and Anglo civilians to Indians considered to be at peace with and under the protection of
the U.S. There are also a small number of Indian versus Indian claims, as
well as claims by Indians against "White Persons." Army reports and War
Department records, Office of Indian Affairs reports, newspaper accounts,
reminiscences (letters, diaries, oral interviews, memoirs), and church and
cemetery records must be consulted to complete the picture raiding and
warfare in the borderlands.

Prologue

1. The Zuni pueblo of Hawikuh was situated west of present-day Albuquerque
near the Arizona–New Mexico border. Díaz set out on his journey to the
west with twenty-five men chosen for their experience and hardiness. The
exact location of Díaz's grave is unknown, but it is somewhere in the Ópata
Indian territory between the Yuma crossing of the Colorado River and the
village that later became the Spanish outpost of Caborca in northern Sonora,
on the present U.S.-Mexico border. Ives, "Grave of Melchior Díaz," 31–40;
Bolton, *Coronado*, 175. See also Farish, *History of Arizona*, 1:20–21; Castañeda
de Nájera, *Expedition to Cíbola*, passim.

Chapter 1

1. For the best articulation of the origin of and motives for war as it relates to
indigenous peoples of the Southwest, see Kroeber and Fontana, *Massacre on
the Gila*, 165–74.

2. There is little research on how African Americans' earlier warrior traditions
might have influenced warfare in the Southwest. Blacks accounted for less
than 1 percent of the population of the Southwest when the Civil War began.
Indian peoples of the borderlands had limited contact with black people,
but when first encountered during the fur trade era and through the 1860s,
Cheyennes referred to them as "black whitemen" (*mok-ta-veho*) because they
exhibited most of the usual characteristics of the whites (they wore hats, had
heels on their shoes, spoke the same language, and generally behaved like
whites); the only noticeable difference was the color of their skin. George
Bent remembered, "My father [William Bent] had a slave at the fort, a very
black Negro, and as the Cheyennes had seen few if any Negroes before, they
thought this slave was very wonderful. They called him the black whiteman."
George Bent to George Hyde, Aug. 10, 1910, and Feb. 5, 1913, Bent Letters,
Beinecke Library. See also Afton, Halaas, and Masich, *Cheyenne Dog Sol-*

diers, 108–9. The term "Buffalo Soldier" is of obscure origin, but the earliest usage may be attributed to Comanches, referring to the buffalo-like hair of troopers of the black Tenth U.S. Cavalry in Texas in the late 1860s. See Leckie, *Buffalo Soldiers,* 27; Alt and Alt, *Black Soldiers, White Wars,* 56–58; Taylor, *Racial Frontier,* 167–77. African "cultural survivals" as viewed by indigenous people (as well as African Americans) in the borderlands is a promising area of research virtually unexplored by scholars.

3. For the origins of western military culture and the rise of Napoleonic strategy and tactics, see Keegan, *A History of Warfare;* Bell, *The First Total War;* and Black, *America as a Military Power.*

4. There are no truly "native" peoples in the Southwest Borderlands—no humans originated in North America—scholars now believe that the indigenous peoples of the Americas arrived after the great ice sheets that covered the continent began retreating twenty to thirty thousand years ago. Most of the diverse peoples inhabiting the borderlands by the 1860s began their migration to the Southwest at the same time as the arrival of Spanish conquistadors in the middle of the sixteenth century. Dillehay, *Settlement of the Americas,* passim.

5. The terms "tradition" and "custom" are often used interchangeably. Hobsbawm and others see customs as the actions derived from long-term conventions and traditions or as the trappings or physical manifestations of the customs. British judges and barristers, for example, *customarily* argue and pass judgment while the robes and wigs they wear are *traditional.* Hobsbawm and Ranger, *The Invention of Tradition,* 2–3. Among the Uto-Aztecan Pueblo peoples are several groups of Tanoan-speakers.

6. In an attempt to lessen confusion, I have adopted the following names for Yuman- and Uto-Aztecan–speaking tribes: Quechans (Yumas), Mojaves, Chemehuevis (Nüwüwü), Maricopas (Piipaash), Pimas (Akimel O'odham), Papagos (Tohono O'odham), and Ópatas. Yavapais were divided into four geographical bands that considered themselves separate peoples: the Tolkepayas, or Western Yavapai; the Yavapés, or Northwestern Yavapai; the Kwevkepayas, or Southeastern Yavapai; and Wipukepas, or Northeastern Yavapai. The Maḏqwadabaya or "Desert People" were another Yavapai band believed to have mixed with Mojaves and Quechans and who no longer exist as a separate people. The Yavapai have much in common with their linguistic relatives to the north, the Havasupai and the Hualapai. Though closely related to the Mojaves, the Yavapai were often mistaken as Apache by Anglo settlers, who variously referred to them as "Mohave-Apache," "Yuma-Apache," or "Tonto-Apache." These names are generally, though not universally, preferred by present-day tribal members: Navajo (Diné); Western Apaches (Nnee), including the Aravaipas (Tsé Binesti'é); Chiricahua Apaches (including Bidánku, Chukunende, Chíhénde and Ndé ndaí bands); and Eastern Apaches (including Mescalero, Jicarilla, and Lipans). The agrarian Pueblo Indians of northern New Mexico were culturally and linguistically diverse, including Uto-Aztecan-, Keresan-, Tanoan-, Tewa-, and Zuni-speaking peoples. By the time of the Civil War, many of the twenty Pueblo groups (e.g., Ácoma, Isleta, Jemez, Laguna, and Taos) in Arizona and New Mexico had been heavily influenced or partially assimilated by the

Spanish and Mexicans. Utley, *Frontiersmen in Blue*, 255; Gifford, *Yavapai*, 249–50. For more on bands and terminology related to the Yavapai people, see Braatz, *Surviving Conquest*, ix, 1–13.

7. The Comanches (N₩m₩n₩₩) split from the Shoshones soon after acquiring horses from Pueblo Indians, who had captured many animals from the Spanish during the revolt centered in northern New Mexico in 1680. The Comanche language is Uto-Aztecan. The Kiowas speak a Tanoan language as do some of the Pueblo Indians. The Cheyenne (Tsistsistas) language has Algonquian roots. These people migrated from the Great Lakes region after acquiring horses through trade with Comanches about 1750.

8. Linguists have identified seven distinct southwestern Athabaskan (sometimes called Apachean) dialects: Navajo, Western Apache, Chiricahua, Mescalero, Jicarilla, Lipan, and Kiowa-Apache. http://www.everyculture.com/multi/A-Br/Apaches.html#ixzz2ycXHrKg2

9. Kroeber and Fontana, *Massacre on the Gila*, 63–65.

10. See DeLay, *War of a Thousand Deserts*, for an excellent survey of the near-continuous skirmishing and reprisals that characterized the Hispano-Indian conflict in the Southwest prior to the Civil War.

11. Santiago, *Massacre at the Yuma Crossing*, 170–75 and passim; Salmón, "A Marginal Man," 61–77. For a better understanding of the complex relationships between the people (*vecinos*) of frontier Hispano communities and *indios bárbaros and mansos*, see also Valerio-Jiménez, *River of Hope*, 50; and Officer, *Hispanic Arizona*, 309, 328–30.

12. DeLay, *War of a Thousand Deserts*, 10, 15–16; for a summary of the Spanish losses on the northern frontier see 11–12.

13. Hämäläinen, *Comanche Empire*, 179; Manchaca, *Recovering History, Constructing Race*, 201, 172; Barr, *Black Texans*, 17.

14. Hämäläinen, *Comanche Empire*, 202–16. Hämäläinen's work compels scholars to reexamine indigenous imperialism as seen in Comanchería where the Comanche Empire stopped European conquest in its tracks on the Texas plains.

15. Santa Anna's army killed all the Alamo's defenders, some of whom had refused to surrender even after the Mexicans warned that they would not be shown quarter if they continued to resist. Following the assault, the few male survivors were executed. Some scholars consider the Alamo an overwhelming tactical victory for Santa Anna, but his actions at Goliad the following week can only be interpreted as a massacre—some 350 Texans were executed after surrendering. Houston's subsequent rout of Santa Anna's army at San Jacinto ended in a massacre as well (630 Mexicans died, while the Texans lost only nine killed); though not under orders, many of the enraged Texans showed no quarter as they shouted "Remember the Alamo!" and cut down enemy soldiers attempting to surrender.

16. Hyslop, *Bound for Santa Fe*, 275–83, 289–99.

17. "Proclamation of S. W. Kearny, Brigadier General of the U.S. Army," issued at Las Vegas on Aug. 15, 1846, in Emory, *Lieutenant Emory Reports*, 49–50. Another proclamation dated Aug. 22, 1846, substitutes Eutaws (Utes) for Apaches but otherwise conveys the same assurances ("henceforth look to me for protection") while proclaiming that the Territory of New Mexico had

been taken by and annexed to the United States. Original copy of Kearny's "Proclamation," handwritten in Spanish, Arizona Historical Society, Tucson.

18. Keleher, *Turmoil in New Mexico*, 7, 16, 18–19, 34; Weber, *Foreigners in Their Native Land*, 161.

19. DeLay, *War of a Thousand Deserts*, 194–96, 198–99.

20. Kit Carson, *Autobiography*, 108–10; Remley, *Kit Carson*, 166. Carson later learned that his wife, Josefa Jaramillo, and her sister, Ignacia Bent (the governor's wife), had miraculously survived the Taos uprising.

21. Mangas was related by birth and marriage to both the Chihenne and Bedonkohe bands of the Chiricahua Apaches. Sweeney, *Mangas Coloradas*, 141–44.

22. Woodward, "Lances at San Pasqual," 32. Kearny's dragoons carried the army's most advanced firearm, the Hall breechloader, the first U.S. military arm designed to use a percussion ignition. However, the men complained that the cold and rain-dampened gunpowder made the weapons difficult to load and fire at San Pasqual. Pico's Californios cut and thrust with their swords (*espadas*) and used their *reatas* to good effect, lassoing the dragoons and dragging them from their saddles. Hyslop, *Contest for California*, 391–93. In the Southwest, the word *caballero* (knight, cavalier) is often used to connote a horseman. The word *jinete* referred to a horseman or cavalryman, but in the borderlands this term was often used to refer to mounted Indian raiders.

23. DeLay, *War of a Thousand Deserts*, 214–16, 270–73, 297.

24. Charles Bent had gone west with his brothers William and George, teaming up with partner Cerán St. Vrain and trapper Kit Carson. The enterprising brothers established good working relations with Arapahos, Cheyennes, Comanches, and Kiowas, as well as the New Mexicans, and built a Rocky Mountain trapping-and-trading empire that included a string of tributary forts that fed the Santa Fe Trail trade from St. Louis through Bent's Fort on the Arkansas River to Santa Fe. Halaas and Masich, *Halfbreed*, 48–49. For the only eyewitness account of the Taos rebels see Garrard, *Wah-to-yah and the Taos Trail*.

25. General Scott chose the same path—from Veracruz on the coast, through the mountains at Puebla, and on to Mexico City—taken by Hernán Cortés's Spanish conquistadors nearly three hundred years earlier.

26. While it can be argued that the acquisition of Texas in 1845 was a consensual annexation between two nations, the Republic of Texas and the United States, all the dealings with Republic of Mexico were characterized by coercive political and military tactics that left that nation little choice in the cession of nearly half its territory—915,000 square miles—to its more powerful northern neighbor. Mexico relinquished an additional 29,640 square miles in the Gadsden Purchase of 1854.

27. Greenberg, *A Wicked War*, 3 and passim. This tradition of compensation for property loss but not for human suffering would become official U.S. government policy in the years following the wars for the borderlands, codified in the legislation authorizing the payment of depredation and war claims following the Civil War. See Skogen's *Indian Depredation Claims* for the evolution of the federal government's thinking regarding compensation for property losses in order to maintain peace between American peoples. The Anglo-Celtic legal tradition recognizes the concept of "solatium," a form of

compensation for emotional rather than physical or financial harm. In Scots Law, reparations can be awarded for pain and suffering in personal injury cases (although it can also be awarded in other types of cases)—similar, but not identical, to the English Law concept of general damages. Scots Law damages are divided into pecuniary and nonpecuniary losses, rather than general and special damages. In the Apachean tradition, compensation for pain and suffering often meant taking a life for a life (*gegodza*)—in some cases, torture might be administered as well—but a captive substitute for a lost family member or property might satisfy the blood debt.

28. Blyth, *Chiricahuas and Janos*, 21; DeLay, *War of a Thousand Deserts*, xiii, xv, xix and passim.

29. Kroeber and Fontana, *Massacre on the Gila*, 12.

30. Kroeber and Fontana, *Massacre on the Gila*, 35, 45–50, 58, 68, 79, 80–88. The Quechans' allies included the Yuman-speaking Mojaves, Chemehuevis, and Cocopahs (whose loyalty the Mojaves and some Quechans questioned) as well as Yavapais. Some of the Western Apache bands were then known to Hispanos and Anglos as Tontos (Dilzhe'e), though some today find this Spanish word meaning "foolish" offensive. The Spanish most likely were influenced by the other tribes encountered before meeting the Tontos. The Chiricahua and other Apache groups referred to the Tontos as *binii?e'dine'*, the "wild or crazy people" or "people whose tongue we do not understand." The Maricopa (Piipaash) and Pimas (Akimel O'odham—"Pima" or "Pimo" is believed to have been derived from a Uto-Aztecan phrase *pi mac*, meaning "I don't know," which neighboring tribesmen may have used in response to Spanish queries) may have had some of their Papago (Tohono O'odham) allies present as well. Sturtevant, *Handbook of North American Indians*, 13:488. For an excellent description of the Pimas and Maricopas and their numerous subdivisions at this time see Report of the Commissioner of Indian Affairs, 1858, 555–60.

31. Greenberg, *Manifest Manhood*, 12–14 and passim. Greenberg explores the social and economic origins of what she has termed "martial manhood," a root cause of the filibustering expeditions launched from the United States into Latin America between 1848 and 1860. Martial manhood celebrates bravery, physical strength, and the ability to dominate both men and women. "Martial men," Greenberg writes, "believed that the masculine qualities of strength, aggression, and even violence, better defined a true man than did the firm and upright manliness of restrained men." For other views of American and European masculinity paradigms, see Kimmel, *Manhood in America*; Connell, *Masculinities*; Smith-Rosenberg, *This Violent Empire*, x, 21, 41, 466; Pinker, *Better Angels*, 518, 524–26, 686–87, Nye, *Masculinity and Male Codes of Honor*; and Gilmore, *Manhood in the Making*.

32. The decreasing importance of men's labor is well documented by anthropologists, see Kroeber and Fontana, *Massacre on the Gila*, passim. For an Anglo soldier's perspective see Carlson, "Martial Experiences." For current scholarship on the correlation of affluence and the rise of warrior cultures and violence, see Pinker, *Better Angels*, 31–56, 675.

33. By 1857, the Maricopas (Piipaash) comprised at least four separate tribes—Halchidoma, Kohuana, Kaveltcadom, Halyikwamai—that had been driven

from their Colorado River homes by the more powerful Quechans and Mojaves in the late eighteenth century. Kroeber and Fontana, *Massacre on the Gila*, 23, 34.

34. Kroeber and Fontana, *Massacre on the Gila*, 35–39, 151, 165.

35. For an Apache perspective on preservation of race, see Daklugie's reminiscence in Ball, *Indeh*, 19. Blyth, *Chiricahua and Janos*, 5–7. For additional views of Apache manhood see Opler, *Apache Life-way*, 396; Goodwin, *Western Apache Raiding*; and Lahti, *Cultural Construction of Empire*, 148, 221, 243, 303. For views on motives for violence and the origins of war, see Kroeber and Fontana, *Massacre on the Gila*, 165–74; Greenberg, *Manifest Manhood*, 14 and passim; White, *The Middle Ground*, xxv–xxvi; Aron, "Frontiers, Borderlands, Wests," in *American History Now*, 270–71; Anderson, *Imagined Communities*, 5–8. See also Pinker, *Better Angels*, 44, 517–18, 523–26, 675.

36. In 1860 Walker finally met his death in Honduras by a firing squad assembled by a coalition of Central American armies. John E. Norvell, "How Tennessee Adventurer William Walker Became Dictator."

37. Greenberg, *Manifest Manhood*, 15, 42, 168; Wyllys, "Henry A. Crabb," 187.

38. Lindsay, "Henry A. Crabb, Filibuster," 1–2.

39. U.S. Congress, *Execution of Colonel Crabb*, 31, 33, 40, 44, 63; *San Francisco Alta California*, May 14, 1857; *Sacramento Daily Union*, May 14, 1857.

40. Charles E. Evans affidavit, Sept. 27, 1857, U.S. Congress, *Execution of Colonel Crabb*, 64–68. Filibuster Camp was located on the Gila 35 miles east of Fort Yuma and 140 miles west of the Pima Villages. Special Order 15, Hdqrs. Column from California, June 16, 1862, *OR* 50(1):138–42; General Order 6, Hdqrs. Dist. of Southern Calif., May 7, 1862, *OR* 50(1):1056.

41. Henry A. Crabb to Jose Maria Redondo, Prefect of Altar, Mar. 26, 1857, U.S. Congress, *Execution of Colonel Crabb*, 31.

42. Ignacio Pesqueira, Substitute Governor, to the People of Sonora, Mar. 30, 1857, U.S. Congress, *Execution of Colonel Crabb*, 33. See also John Forsyth to Juan Antonio de la Fuente, May 30, 1857, 39–44, 63–68, 74; Farish, *History of Arizona*, 3:27–29.

43. Charles E. Evans affidavit, Sept. 27, 1857, U.S. Congress, *Execution of Colonel Crabb*, 63–74.

44. Latin American scholars caution against using the word "caste" because, in some contexts (e.g., Hindu India), it implies a rigidly hierarchical system while in the system of *castas* (the word from which caste was derived) evident in nineteenth century Central America, *limpieza de sangre* (purity of blood) was not the sole determiner of social status. As the *mestizo* population increased in the late colonial period, social ranking, though still based largely on physiognomy, became much more fluid. See Restall, *The Black Middle*, 90–91, and Bakewell, *History of Latin America*, 173, 303–4. See also Mora, *Border Dilemmas*, 5, 9, 33.

45. Brooks, *Captives and Cousins*, 364.

46. Over time, Mexican *espadas anchas* became shorter and heavier, evolving into a machete-like, all-purpose weapon and tool. A common variant of the engraved inscription is "*No me saques sin razón, ni me guardes sin honor.*" Numerous inscribed specimens may be found in museum collections, including the Arizona Historical Society, New Mexico History Museum, and Museo de Historia Mexicana.

47. For the best overview of the reciprocal raiding traditions of the peoples of the Southwest prior to the Civil War, see Brooks, *Captives and Cousins*, passim.

48. For a clear expression of the race-based argument for Manifest Destiny and Anglo hegemony over the indigenous peoples of the Southwest, see *San Francisco Daily Alta California*, July 4, 1864, in which a correspondent of the *Santa Fe Gazette* opines that from Atlantic to Pacific the country should be populated "with a thriving, resolute, intelligent people" and "the Great Republic [should] be knitted [with rails] into one complete whole, and become homogeneous in interests as in blood." For a view of "white mythologies" and racism in the U.S. Army of the borderlands, see also Lahti, *Cultural Construction of Empire*, 4, 9, 69. For the Mexican viewpoint in regard to "savage" Apaches thwarting progress and mineral exploitation, see "The Apaches—Eighty Murders in One Week," *San Francisco Alta California*, Sept. 15, 1853, reprinted from the August 22, 1853, edition of *El Nacionál*, the government newspaper in the Sonoran capital, Ures. The article succinctly captures the sentiment of Mexicans in the borderlands: "The Apaches! The Apaches are the cancerous sore which threatens the State with death—the enemy which exhausts our blood and destroys our power, and deprives us of hope for the future." For Chiricahua Apache warrior Daklugie's viewpoint on race and Apache superiority over other peoples, see Ball, *Indeh*, 19, 23, 81.

49. In 1857 much of the nation was already preoccupied with news of the outbreak of civil war as John Brown's Kansas "Free Soilers" battled proslavery "Border Ruffians" from Missouri. Bagley, *Blood of the Prophets*, 162–72, 225–28. Carleton, *Special Report*, 1–8.

50. The U.S. government did not consistently enumerate Indians until after 1870. Extrapolating from later census data and combining reports from Indian agents, the aggregated population of Arizona and New Mexico in 1861 is estimated to have been about 140,000: Indians 60,000, Hispanos 78,000, Anglos (including military) 3,000, and African Americans 100. These numbers do not reflect the influence of the "nomadic" peoples (e.g., Comanches, Cheyennes, Arapahos, Utes, Paiutes, Lipans, Cocopahs, Lower Pimas, Papagos, etc.) who lived primarily outside or on the periphery of the territorial boundaries. *U.S. Census*, 1850, 1860, 1870; *Annual Report of the Commissioner of Indian Affairs*, 1861, 1862, 1863, 1863, 1865, 1866; *San Francisco Daily Alta California*, May 6, 1866.

Chapter 2

1. While civil wars are as old as human societies, scholars still dispute the definition and causes of civil war. Most agree, however, that civil war is violent conflict between parties, factions, or inhabitants of communities within the same nation or living in the same geographic region. Such deadly violence usually occurs within a polity or region considered unified by one or both antagonists. For perspectives on the problem of identifying and defining civil wars, see Wong, "A Matter of Definition." Much debate centers on whether ethnicity or economics is the primary cause of civil war. See Berdal and Malone, *Greed and Grievance*, passim; Collier and Hoeffler, "On Economic Causes," 563–73; and Collier and Hoeffler, "Greed and Grievance in Civil War," 563–95. Some scholars have attempted to quantify the point at which

civil unrest or an uprising becomes "civil war"—death tolls of 100 to 1000 are often cited as the threshold indicating civil war. Though scholars do not agree on the definition or causes of civil wars, most agree that civil wars since 1945 have resulted in more than 20 million deaths and have replaced international war as the most common type of conflict in the world today. See Collier and Sambanis, *Understanding Civil War*, 2–8.

2. The rebels sought the mineral wealth of the territories, political recognition from Mexico, and the geographic integrity that would provide the Confederate states with a link to the Pacific. See Finch, *Confederate Pathway*, passim.

3. Spanish, British, and French naval forces entered Veracruz in December 1861 after signing the "Convention of London," ostensibly to collect debts after Mexico's Congress suspended some interest payments due to the nation's growing fiscal crisis. Raymond, "The History of Foreign Intervention in Mexico."

4. *Annual Report of the Commissioner of Indian Affairs, 1862,* 388.

5. The total Hispanic population of New Mexico Territory, including some "civilized" Pueblo Indians and other assimilated tribes, enumerated in the *Eighth and Ninth U.S. Census* (1860 and 1870), was about 80,000. Semi-nomadic and nomadic tribes on the periphery of the territory had a direct impact on the peoples of New Mexico. The twenty thousand members of the dispersed Comanche empire dominated the southern plains of Texas, Oklahoma, and New Mexico for more than a century, by raids and attacks against Apache and Pueblo villages east of the Rio Grande and on Hispano and Anglo traders on the Santa Fe Trail. See Hämäläinen, *Comanche Empire*, for the best account of the far-reaching influence of the Comanche empire north and south of the border with Mexico.

6. A series of three Supreme Court decisions rendered under chief justice John Marshall between 1821 and 1832, now known as the Marshall Trilogy, clarified the constitutional basis for the federal government's relationship with Indian tribes. Marshall's decision in the Cherokee Nation *v.* State of Georgia (1831) ruled, "They are in a state of pupilage. Their relation to the United States resembles that of a ward to his guardian." Macklem, "Distributing Sovereignty," 1311.

7. Félix, who as an adult became a scout known as Mickey Free, was actually taken by Aravaipas and later traded to Tontos (Western White Mountain Apaches). Radbourne, *Mickey Free*, 9–16.

8. Lieutenant George N. Bascom graduated from West Point in 1858, twenty-sixth out of a class of twenty-seven. He was killed on the Rio Grande at the Battle of Valverde on February 21, 1862, just a year after the infamous Bascom affair at Apache Pass. Established in 1863, Fort Bascom, New Mexico, was named in his honor. Heitman, *Historical Register*, 2:14.

9. While Bascom is usually credited with starting the conflict with the Chokonens and other Chiricahua Apaches, it was Moore's order for hanging the captives that actually led to warfare and heightened violence between this band and some of their allies during the 1860s. Sweeney, *Cochise, Firsthand Accounts*, 14–18; Sweeney, *Cochise*, 163.

10. Chiricahua sources consistently point to February 1861 as the beginning of Cochise's war. Sweeney, *Cochise*, 168.

11. This reconstruction of the attack on the Ake party in Cooke's Canyon, New Mexico, Aug. 1, 1861, is based on detailed depositions and testimony found in Indian Depredation Case 3112, Felix Grundy Ake *v.* U.S. and Apaches, RG 123, NARA, as well as an eyewitness account by Ake's son, Jeff, in O'Neil, *They Die But Once,* 38–48. See also U.S. Census 1860, New Mexico, Sonoita Creek, Felix G. Ake and family, 30. Additional information from the Apache perspective may be found in Sweeney, *Mangas Coloradas,* 416–22.

12. Sweeney, *Cochise,* 178; *Annual Report of the Commissioner of Indian Affairs, 1861,* 636, 732.

13. Carleton, Camp Latham, Dec. 23, 1861, Orton, *California Men,* 42; *Annual Report of the Commissioner of Indian Affairs, 1861,* 636, 732–33.

14. *Tucson Weekly Arizonian,* Aug. 10, 1861.

15. The attack at Punta de Agua, twelve miles south of Tucson, occurred October 20, 1861. Many depredation claims and a great deal of testimony resulted from the raid. Nearly all the claimants and deponents cited the fact that the Civil War had resulted in the withdrawal of federal troops which, in turn, emboldened the Apaches to attack settlements from Tucson to Hermosillo, Mexico. Fritz Contzen *v.* Apache, Case 3358; Ventura Curriel *v.* Apache, Case 6843; Peter Kitchen *v.* Apache, Case 6845, RG 123, NARA.

16. *Annual Report of the Commissioner of Indian Affairs, 1861,* 636–46, 733; Orton, *California Men,* 42; Lynde to AAAG, July 21, 1861, *OR* 4:60–61; Canby, Santa Fe, to A.A.G, St. Louis, Dec. 1, 1861, *OR* 4:77–78.

17. See General Wright's report to AAAG Colonel E. D. Townsend in Washington, Oct. 31, 1861, Orton, *California Men,* 29–31. "Northern Mexico: Civil War in Sonora," *New York Times,* dateline Tubac, Sept. 26, 1860, published Oct. 18, 1860.

18. Pani, "Between Reform."

19. Capt. S. Hunter to Col. John R. Baylor, Apr. 5, 1862, *OR* 9:708; *San Francisco Daily Alta California,* Jan. 9, 1873. James H. Carleton's obituary reported "the Apaches and Navajoes . . . were then [1862] virtually rulers of Arizona and New Mexico."

20. Morris, *Address Delivered Before the Society of California Volunteers,* 3–25. During the nineteenth century, the federal government recognized three types of military organizations: regulars (the professional standing army), militia (unpaid volunteers organized by each state and territory for local emergencies as determined by the respective governor), and volunteers (troops raised by the states, at the request of the president in times of national emergencies, but paid, armed, equipped, and controlled by the federal government). Scott, *Military Dictionary;* Col. J. H. Carleton to R. Drum, Dec. 21, 1861, *OR* 50(2):773–80; Capt. B. Cutler to Col. J. R. West, Mar. 31, 1862, *OR* 50(1):970.

21. *Congressional Globe,* 37th Congress, 1st session, 1861, 209–19.

22. Orton, *California Men,* 12; Wright, *Civil War in the Southwest,* 10.

23. The peacetime regular army of the United States mustered approximately fifteen thousand men in all branches of the service. By the end of the war, California had raised eight regiments of infantry, a battalion of "Native California Cavalry," and a "Battalion of Mountaineers." When enlistment terms began to expire in 1864, state authorities organized a battalion of "Veteran

Volunteers" for continued service in New Mexico and Arizona. Third and Sixth California Infantry and the unusual Battalion of Mountaineers were the only California Volunteer units that did not serve in Arizona. Orton, *California Men*, 5. By July 1861 the War Department's abandonment of military posts in the Southwest and consolidation of forces in New Mexico under the experienced and capable Colonel Canby were already under way. I. Lynde to AAG, Hdqrs. Dept. of New Mexico, Aug. 7, 1861, *OR* 4:5–6.

24. The son of a U.S. Army surgeon, Baylor was born in Paris, Kentucky, but raised in Texas. Many of his men were also descended from Anglo-Americans with Kentucky and Tennessee roots. See Thompson, *Colonel John Robert Baylor*.

25. There is some debate over the significance of the medicinal whiskey that may have replaced water in some canteens—in any event, Lynde's troops suffered terribly from dehydration. See Wilson, "Whiskey at Fort Fillmore," 109–32. The Texans drew full rations from the supposedly destroyed Fort Fillmore. The men enjoyed bacon, beef, onions, and flour, making dough from the latter, which they cooked over open fires on the iron ramrods of their muskets. Noel, *Campaign from Santa Fe*, 21.

26. Baylor, *John Robert Baylor*, 6; *OR* 4:1–20. See especially the statement of Captain Alfred Gibbs for an understanding of the dissension and frustration among Lynde's officers regarding the necessity and terms of surrender, *OR* 4:11–13; and Baylor's report of the engagement, Sept. 21, 1861, *OR* 4:17–20. Abraham Lincoln personally approved that Lynde's name be stricken from the army's rolls for "abandoning his post" and "surrendering his command to an inferior force of insurgents." GO 102, Nov. 25, 1861, HQ of the Army, Lorenzo Thomas, AG, *OR* 4:16. The disgraced officer was not restored to the service until after the Civil War when he was placed on the "retired list of the Army" in November 1866. Orton, *California Men*, 43.

27. Comanche society also transformed in the warlike environment of Texas; bands reorganized themselves around leaders who had proven themselves in battle with the Texans. Hämäläinen, *Comanche Empire*, 311.

28. J. R. Baylor, Proclamation, Aug. 1, 1861, *OR* 4:20–21.

29. Baylor, *John Robert Baylor*, 12; *OR* 50(1):1108.

30. Wilbarger, *Indian Depredations in Texas*, 338–39; *Indian Depredations, Hearings before the United States Congress*, 46. For additional details on the number of Comanche raids in Texas in 1860–67 see Evidence of Indian Depredations, entry 700, boxes 1–62, RG 75, NARA. Comanche attacks and raids fall off sharply in 1861 and then rise sharply again in late 1865 and continue to increase through 1867.

31. "War to the knife" was a common expression during the 1860s referring to total war in which no quarter was given. Wellman, *Indian Wars*, 294.

32. Wilbarger, *Indian Depredations in Texas*, 548–49. See also Hämäläinen, *Comanche Empire*, 311–12.

33. Col. J. R. Baylor to Capt. Thomas Helm, Mar. 20, 1862. *OR* 50(1):942.

34. Felix Grundy Ake *v.* Apache, Case 3112, RG 123, NARA. For Felix Ake's son Jeff's account of the Cooke's Canyon attack see O'Neil, *They Die But Once*.

35. As the six- to twelve-month enlistments of Confederate territorial units such as the Arizona Rangers and Arizona Guards began to expire, men wishing

to reenlist were merged into Hunter's company, which Baylor and Sibley hoped would become the nucleus of an entire regiment dedicated for service in Arizona. Hall and Long, *Confederate Army of New Mexico,* 21.

36. The portion of the Gadsden Purchase south of the Gila River had been known since the Spanish entrada as "Arizonae," probably a Basque word meaning "the good oak tree." Garate, *Juan Bautista de Anza,* 164. For other theories on the origin of Arizona, see Barnes, *Arizona Place Names,* xv. See also Finch, "William Claude Jones," 405–24. From 1854, when the Senate ratified the Gadsden Purchase, to 1860, no fewer than ten bills were introduced in Congress calling for the creation of an Arizona separate from New Mexico Territory. The proponents of these bills all imagined an east-west division of New Mexico from the Colorado River to the Rio Grande. In February 1863 Abraham Lincoln finally signed into law the bill that created Arizona Territory divided on a north-south line in order to separate what was thought to be a voting block sympathetic to the Confederacy. Walker and Bufkin, *Historical Atlas of Arizona,* 25; J. R. Baylor, "Proclamation to the People of the Territory of Arizona," Aug. 1, 1861, *OR* 4:20–21; Sherod Hunter to Col. J. R. Baylor, Apr. 5, 1862, *OR* 9:707–8; H. H. Sibley to Pesqueira, Fort Bliss, Texas, Dec. 16, 1861, *OR* 50(1):668–70; Villa, *Compendio de Historia de Sonora,* 280; Hall, "Colonel James Reily's Diplomatic Missions," 232–42.

37. Edwin A. Rigg to James H. Carleton, Mar. 25, 1862, *OR* 50(1):950–52; Carleton to Wright, Mar. 22, 1862, *OR* 50(1):944–45. Writing on July 10, 1862, following a trip through Apache Pass, James Newcomb noted the increase in "murders" by Apaches on the road between Tucson and the Rio Grande, estimating that between July 1861 and July 1862 more than "one hundred white persons have been killed." *San Francisco Alta California,* Aug. 10, 1862.

38. The term "Apache" is frustratingly vague and inadequate for historians attempting to identify specific tribes and bands, but it is necessarily used here because it is often how Hispanos and Anglos referred to the seminomadic bands of Apachean (Southern Athabaskan) speakers they encountered in Arizona and New Mexico in the 1860s. The U.S. and C.S. soldiers applied "Apache" to Chiricahuas, Mescaleros, Jicarillas, Lipans, Western Apaches, Plains Apaches, and even Yavapais. If their identities were known with certainty, it would be more appropriate to refer to specific bands. The Chiricahuas, for example, comprised the Bidánku, Chíhénde, Chukunende, and Ndé ndaí bands. Yet it is often nearly impossible to identify Apache bands with any sort of precision based on contemporary accounts, so period terminology has been retained in most cases to avoid confusing the issue with speculative identifications.

39. Wright to Pesqueira, May 3, 1862, *OR* 50(1):1047–48; Carleton to Pesqueira, May 2, 1862, *OR* 50(1):1044–45.

40. Wright to E. D. Townsend, AAAG, Oct. 31, 1861 and GO 28, HQ Dept. of the Pacific, Oct. 21, 1861, Orton, *California Men,* 19, 23.

41. Sumner expressed his fear that the presence of an organized Confederate force in California would "inevitably inaugurate civil war here immediately." Sumner to AAAG Townsend, Sept. 7, 1861, Orton, *California Men,* 24, 28–32; George Wright to Lorenzo Thomas, Dec. 9, 1861, *OR* 50(1):752–53.

Although Wright preferred Yuma as the base of operations for the recapture of the Southwest territories, he also believed that the capture of the Mexican port of Guaymas was important, both to deny the rebels and as a supply depot on the Gulf of California. Orton, *California Men*, 29–31.

42. Carleton modeled much of his behavior on his mentor, Kearny, under whom he served as commissary on the much admired South Pass Expedition of 1845. Major Carleton dedicated himself to exposing the 1857 atrocity at Mountain Meadows in Southern Utah, where 120 men, women, and children were massacred by Mormon zealots and their Paiute allies. For the most thorough biography of Carleton, see Hunt, *James Henry Carleton*, 57, 82–92 and passim. The Utah expedition was reassigned to Colonel Patrick Edward Connor and his Third California Infantry, which arrived in Salt Lake City in the summer of 1862. Brigham Young had overseen the destruction of Carleton's cairn at Mountain Meadows, but the massacre monument was reconstructed by California Volunteers in 1864. Long, *Saints and the Union*, 96–97, 225.

43. Report of James M. McNulty, Oct. 1863, *OR* 50(1):137; Wright to Thomas, ibid., 752–53; Even the hard-bitten regular General Edwin V. Sumner found the "great and unaccountable success [of the Confederates] in Arizona and New Mexico" cause for alarm and moved to take precautions in the event that they did indeed reach the Pacific coast—an eventuality that seemed possible in the first year of the war. Sumner to E. D. Townsend, AAAG, Sept. 7, 1861, Orton, *California Men*, 24.

44. Richard C. Drum, AAG, to Carleton, Dec. 19, 1861, *OR* 50(1):772 and passim; Pettis, *California Column*, 8, 11.

45. Hunt, *Army of the Pacific*, 24; Altshuler, *Cavalry Yellow*, 94; Orton, *California Men*, 68, 87. The forty-niners, and those who followed, exhibited the characteristics of many populations that voluntarily migrate, including greater height, weight, and intelligence as well as the more difficult to quantify trait of risk taking. Several studies demonstrate this, including examinations of Mexican migrants to the United States in the mid-twentieth century. Hulse, "Migration and Cultural Selection in Human Genetics," 1–21. For comparisons of "migrantes" and "sedentes," see Goldstein, *Demographic and Bodily Changes in Descendants of Mexican Immigrants*, passim, and Lord, *They Fought for the Union*, 227. A survey of "descriptive lists" for California regiments shows that the height of the average western soldier was more than an inch taller than his eastern counterpart. Quartermaster records indicate that the hat, coat, and shoe sizes were also larger. Lieutenant Colonel George H. Crosman, commanding the Philadelphia Depot, noted, "The tariff for boots and bootees has been in operation for twenty years, with slight variations, but I have discovered that it does not suit the men of the West and those of the East equally well. In the western departments larger sizes are needed than in the East. The men are generally larger and have larger feet in the West." *OR* 19(2):505. See California Volunteer Descriptive Lists and Clothing Accounts, RG 94, NARA.

46. Orton, *California Men*, 5; Davis, "Pioneer Days in Arizona by One Who Was There," 34; Utley, *Frontiersmen in Blue*, 12–18; Utley, *Frontier Regulars*, 23–24.

47. Dayton, "California Militia, 1850–66," 398. California had the third largest militia prior to the Civil War, exceeded only by New York and Illinois. Scott, *Military Dictionary*, 419; Altshuler, *Chains of Command*, 24.
48. Even the rigid Carleton could be swayed by political favoritism and friendship. Nathaniel J. Pishon, related by marriage and a former sergeant in the First Dragoons, landed the captaincy of Company D, First Cavalry CV after the Pacific Department ordered that unit to accompany the Arizona expedition. Carleton kept his relationship quiet but later confided to McCleave that he had secured Pishon's appointment. Carleton to William McCleave, Mar. 15, 1862, *OR* 50(1):931–32; Wallace, "Fort Whipple," 114; Hunt, *Army of the Pacific*, 94; Altshuler, *Cavalry Yellow*, 209; Mullin, *Fulton's History*, 46.
49. This holds true for Anglo volunteers from California, Colorado, and Texas. Colorado Volunteer officers John P. Slough and John M. Chivington were 6 ft., 3 in. and 6 ft., 4 in. respectively. William L. Rynerson, who entered the California Volunteers as a sergeant and mustered out a Lieutenant Colonel, stood well over 6 ft., 6 in. (Slough called him a "seven foot son of a bitch" the night before Rynerson shot him to death). Texas officers John R. Baylor and John S. Shropshire measured 6 ft., 3 in. and 6 ft., 5 in. None of these officers still served with their original commands when the rebellion ended in 1865. The average height of a Civil War soldier was 5 ft., 8 in. For stature and weight comparisons see Regimental Descriptive Lists, RG 94, NARA; Haire, Journals; Hunt, *Kirby Benedict*, 193. For description of Colorado troops, see Allyne, *West By Southwest*, 84. See also Lukaszewski et al., "Role of Physical Formidability," 385–406.
50. Dayton, "California Militia, 1850–66," 400–401; Wallace, "Fort Whipple," 114; Altshuler, *Chains of Command*, 24. Late in the war enlisted men competed fiercely for commissions. Cpl. Aaron Cory Hitchcock, First California Cavalry, wrote home asking, "If you can fit in a word for me with the Governor in any shape I shall by much obliged. The Lieutenant Governor has promised me his influence for a position when ever an opportunity offers. . . . I would rather not let any person know that I have any promise or that I want anything for the reason that there are a great many old volunteers that think they are first on the list and if they know of any one attempting to get promoted they will throw everything in the way that they can." C. A. Hitchcock to W. M. Smyth [brother-in-law], Oct. 7, 1863, Aaron Cory Hitchcock Letters.
51. George Wright to Thomas, Dec. 9, 1861, *OR* 50(1):752–53.
52. General Sumner supported Carleton's appointment to command the expedition. The general, an experienced campaigner, revealed his concerns about marching large bodies of troops across the desert, noting he had outfitted "Kearny's command of one hundred men on the Rio Grande in the fall of 1846. I gave him the best of everything in the regiment, and yet when he arrived on this coast this small force was completely broken down and unable to contend successfully with the Californians who attacked him." Sumner to AAAG Townsend, Sept. 7, 1861, Orton, *California Men*, 24; Hunt, *James H. Carleton*, 165–70.
53. Sharps breech-loading .52-caliber Model 1853 and a few Model 1855 (with Maynard tape primers) carbines were replaced with newer Sharps models as supplies became available. While most of the cavalry with the California

Column carried "slanting breech" M1853 Sharps carbines, the units that followed were also issued the "straight breech" 1859 and 1863 models. The longer paper cartridges designed for the earlier model would function in the later models (with some difficulties related to powder spillage and misfires), which employed a shorter, linen cartridge. When the supply of carbines ran out, ordnance officers issued "3rd class" Common Rifles of the 1817 pattern, recently altered from flintlock to the new percussion system. The heavy 1840 pattern saber and the old Model 1847 .44-caliber Colt "Dragoon" revolver were initially issued. In 1865 and 1866 some California units received .44-caliber Colt and Remington New Model Army revolvers and brass-cartridge Maynard carbines. These improved arms introduced additional ammunition problems as the Colt and Remington pistol balls were not interchangeable and the specialized metallic cartridge for the Maynard could not be easily manufactured in the field. J. McAllister to Drum, Nov. 20, 1861, Benicia Arsenal Letters Sent, 1861–63, p. 65, RG 156, NARA; Carleton to Drum, Dec. 21, 1861, *OR* 50(1):775; Ordnance Returns, California Cavalry, Office of the Chief of Ordnance, 1861–66, RG 156, NARA. *Appendix to the Journals of the 16th Session of the Legislature of the State of California,* 1:459; Wright to Drum, Mar. 23, 1865, *OR* 50(2):1169. Even after Carleton took up his duties as department commander in New Mexico, subsequent commanders of the California Volunteers in Arizona followed his guidelines.

54. Carleton to Drum, Dec. 21, 1861, *OR* 50(1):775. Ordnance testing in the 1850s demonstrated that the Sharps carbine was very accurate up to 150 yards and that the new .58-caliber rifle muskets were effective at twice that distance. For a summary of these tests see Lewis, *Small Arms and Ammunition,* 101–5.
55. Carleton to Drum, Dec. 21, 1861, *OR* 50(1):775.
56. Late in the war some of the horse soldiers would receive cartridge boxes for their pistol ammunition, but when Carleton's Arizona expedition set out, he did not deem this item essential. Carleton to Drum, Dec. 21, 1861, *OR* 50(1):775.
57. Carleton to West, May 2, 1862, *OR* 50(1):1045.
58. Carleton to R. W. Kirkham, Apr. 11, 1862, *OR* 50(1):1000. The first regiments carried the Model 1855 Springfield; later regiments received Model 1861 or 1863 rifle muskets, which no longer employed the unreliable Maynard tape system.
59. McAllister to Carleton, Sept. 10, 1861, *OR* 50(1):616.
60. Carleton to Canby, May 3, 1862, *OR* 50(1):95; Carleton to Rigg, Mar. 25, 1862, ibid., 950–51; *Ordnance Manual,* 20, 74.
61. McAllister to H. M. Judah, Oct. 3, 1861, Benicia Arsenal Letters Sent, 41, RG 156, NARA.
62. Carleton to Drum, Dec. 21, 1861, *OR* 50(1):777; Ordnance Returns, California Cavalry, Office of the Chief of Ordnance, RG 156, NARA. In 1865, when many Sharps carbines became unserviceable through hard use, ordnance officers issued Mississippi Rifles to cavalry companies in Arizona. Single-shot Maynard carbines, designed to use brass cartridges, replaced these obsolete rifles in 1866.
63. Ordnance Returns, California Cavalry, Office of the Chief of Ordnance, RG 156, NARA.

64. Carleton prescribed what each man would carry on the march:

> I. Each soldier will carry one greatcoat, one blanket, one forage cap, one woolen shirt, one pair of drawers, one pair of stockings, one towel, two handkerchiefs, one fine [louse comb] and one coarse comb, one sewing kit, one piece of soap, one toothbrush.
>
> II. Each soldier will wear his uniform hat without trimmings, one blouse, one pair trousers, one pair stockings, one woolen shirt, one pair drawers, and may wear a cravat in lieu of the leather [neck] stock.
>
> III. Each soldier, whether of cavalry or infantry, will have one canteen, one haversack, and one tin cup. In his haversack he will carry one fork, spoon, and plate. He will wear a good sheath knife.
>
> IV. Each company, whether of cavalry or infantry, will have only enough mess pans and camp kettles (in nests) for absolute requirements; also a few short-handed frying pans, some large tin pans in which to mix bread, one or two strong coffee-mills, a 6-gallon keg for vinegar [to prevent scurvy], a few pounds of black-grained pepper, four axes, four camp hatchets, six spades, six shovels.
>
> V. Officers will not take mess-chests, or trunks, or mattresses on the march. It is suggested that each mess of officers of not less than three be provided with two champagne baskets covered with painted canvas for their mess furniture. These can be packed upon a mule. Their necessary clothing can be carried in a small hand-valise, or pair of saddlebags.
>
> GO 3, HQ Dist. of Southern Calif., Feb. 11, 1862, *OR* 50(2):858–59.

65. Ibid.

66. Wright to Thomas, Oct. 21, 1861, *OR* 50(1):668; Clothing Account Books of CV Regiments, 1861–66; *San Francisco Alta California*, 1863.

67. Carleton to Drum, May 10, 1862, *OR* 50(1):1060; Carleton to Drum, May 24, 1862, Orton, *California Men*, 50–51; An inspection report from Capt. A. W. Evans at Fort West from June 1863 indicates that while most of the shoes and boots on hand were of good quality with sewn soles, he had discovered several boxes "of a very inferior quality of pegged, the shoes being filled in with wood under the soles. These shoes were found to stand but a very short wear." Thompson, *New Mexico Territory*, 162.

68. *Downieville (California) Sierra Democrat*, Nov. 30, 1861; GO 3, Hdqrs. Dist. of Southern Calif., Feb. 11, 1862, *OR* 50(2):858. For Rifleman's knives issued to teamsters, see Hutchins, "The United States Mounted Rifleman's Knife," 20–21.

69. Carleton to Thomas, Dec. 19, 1861, *OR* 50(1):777; Carleton to Drum, Dec. 21, 1861, "Memorandum of supplies needed for 1600 Men," *OR* 50(1):778–80. The Anglos and, to a lesser degree, Hispanos developed a sophisticated animal husbandry culture that systematically crossed jackasses with horses to produce sterile mules. Old mule skinners quipped that this hardy hybrid had "neither pride of ancestry nor hope of posterity."

70. McAllister to Carleton, Sept. 10, 1861, *OR* 50(1):616; Drum to McAllister, Sept. 9, 1861, Dept. of the Pacific Letters Sent, 381, RG 393, NARA; Carleton

to H. K. Craig, Oct. 18, 1861, First California Infantry Letter Book, RG 94, NARA.

71. Carleton to Drum, Dec. 21, 1861, "Memorandum B," *OR* 50(1):780.

72. Most of the Californians would have been familiar with the doggerel verse popularized by Benjamin Franklin in *Poor Richard's Almanack:*

> For the want of a nail the shoe was lost
> For the want of a shoe the horse was lost
> For the want of a horse the rider was lost
> For the want of a rider the battle was lost
> For the want of a battle the kingdom was lost—
> And all for the want of a horse-shoe nail.

Franklin, *Poor Richard's Almanack*; Carleton to Drum, Dec. 17, 1861, *OR* 50(1):769; GO 10, HQ California Column, Cutler to Drum, July 17, 1862, *OR* 50(1):90–91.

73. For a discussion of the advantages of shod versus unshod horses and mules for carrying or pulling heavy loads, see testimony of William Warford in William G. Poindexter *v.* Hualapai and Chemehuevi, Case 2271, RG 123, NARA.

74. Opler, *Apache Life-way*, 396; Goodwin, *Western Apache Raiding*, 32, 301; Ferg, *Western Apache Material Culture*, 81. For a description of Apache rawhide horseshoes see Juan Analla testimony (p. 12), Juan Analla *v.* Navajo, Case 5426, RG 123, NARA. Colorado Volunteer Jesse Haire described how Plains warriors removed horse and mule shoes from captured animals in Fort Lyon, Oct. 1, 1864, Haire, Journals. See also Halaas and Masich, "You Could Hear the Drums," 4–5. For Plains warrior traditions see also Afton, Halaas, and Masich, *Cheyenne Dog Soldiers*. See also Masich, "Cheyennes and Horses," 10–13.

75. The tipi-inspired army tent and its conical sheet iron stove were patented in 1856 by Henry Hopkins Sibley, commander of the Confederate Army of New Mexico. Carleton discovered the utility of the Sibley Tent on the Utah expedition of 1857–58. Scott, *Military Dictionary*, 142.

76. Carleton to George Bowie, Apr. 28, 1862, *OR* 50(1):1036–37; Benjamin C. Cutler to Rigg, Mar. 15, 1862, ibid., 930; Rigg to Carleton, Feb. 14, 1862, ibid., 866; Carleton to West, Oct. 22, 1861, ibid., 672. Weight (in pounds) of equipment carried by a California infantryman, under arms, in heavy marching order: clothing: 0.25 hat (without trimmings other than worsted cord), 2.50 blouse (lined), 2.50 trousers, 4.00 bootees, 1.00 drawers (2), 1.00 shirts (2 woolen), 0.50 stockings (2 pairs), 0.05 cravat, 5.25 greatcoat, 0.25 forage cap; arms and accoutrements: 9.25 1855 rifle musket, 0.50 musket sling, 0.75 bayonet, 0.75 bayonet scabbard, 1.74 waist belt and plate, 4.00 cartridge box with shoulder belt and plates, 3.20 forty cartridges (.58-caliber elongated ball), 0.50 percussion cap box (with caps); other equipment: 2.00 knapsack, 5.25 blanket, 0.50 haversack, 5.25 ten days' rations, 4.00 canteen (w/3 pints water), 0.25 plate, 0.50 cup, 0.20 fork and spoon, 0.25 towel, 0.05 handkerchiefs (2), 0.05 combs (2, fine and coarse), 0.20 sewing kit, 0.20 soap, 0.05 toothbrush, 1.00 sheath knife. Total: 57.75 pounds. Only items specifically mentioned in orders or known to have been carried by California Column companies are included.

77. McNulty's Report, *OR* 50(1):138.
78. Ibid.; Rigg to Carleton, Jan. 23, 1862, *OR* 50(1):815–18. Rigg wrote in exasperation, "I have the honor to report to you that Fort Yuma is now an island." For flood details, see *San Francisco Alta California*, Feb. 17 and Mar. 5, 1862.
79. Carleton to Joseph R. West, Oct. 22 and Nov. 5, 1861, *OR* 50(1):672, 704–5.
80. Carleton to Rigg, Nov. 4, 1861, *OR* 50(1):700; Rigg to Carleton, Feb. 15, 1862, ibid., 870; Carleton to E. E. Eyre, Oct. 26, 1861, ibid., 681. Though Carleton was an old friend and collaborator of Philip St. George Cooke, the latter's new book of cavalry tactics, published in November 1861, was not yet available when the California Volunteers departed for the territories. Inspection reports for the first quarter of 1863 indicate that the First Cavalry, CV, was still using the old manual. Thompson, *New Mexico Territory During the Civil War*, 158–59.
81. Carleton to Rigg, Feb. 9, 1862, *OR* 50(1):854; Rigg to Carleton, Mar. 27, 1862, ibid., 958; P. R. Brady to Rigg, Mar. 4, 1862, ibid., 911–12; Brady, "Portrait of a Pioneer," 171–94; S. Warner to F. Hinton, Jan. 31, 1862, *OR* 50(1):867.
82. Rigg to Carleton, Feb. 14, 1862, *OR* 50(1):865.
83. Fort Yuma may have brought back painful memories for McCleave. Elizabeth, his bride of only a year, had died there three years earlier as he and the First Dragoons rode from Fort Buchanan, Arizona, to California. Altshuler, *Cavalry Yellow*, 209.
84. Carleton to McCleave, Mar. 15, 1862, *OR* 50(1):932.
85. Julius C. Hall, "Wild West," *National Tribune*, Oct. 20, 1887; George H. Pettis to Annie (wife), Apr. 30, 1862, Pettis Papers, Beinecke Library; Browne, *Adventures in the Apache Country*, 99–102.
86. Rigg to Carleton, Mar. 20, 1862, 940, *OR* 50(1); S. Hunter to J. R. Baylor, Apr. 5, 1862, *OR* 9:707–8. McCleave did not know that the resourceful Jones opted to take the more circuitous and nearly waterless Camino del Diablo route back to Yuma from Tucson to avoid suspicion. The Confederates in Tucson had actually arrested the spy but released him after he signed a loyalty oath. Mahan, "John W. Jones," 228–30.
87. James B. Whittemore's "Report to the Society of California Volunteers," Apr. 25, 1895, McCleave Papers, Bancroft Library.
88. *San Francisco Alta California*, June 23, 1862; Carleton to Henry W. Halleck, Nov. 14, 1862, *OR* 50(2):222–23; Rigg to Carleton, Mar. 20 and Mar. 30, 1862, *OR* 50(1):939–40, 965–66.
89. *San Francisco Alta California*, June 8, 23, and 29, 1862; Hunter to Baylor, Apr. 5, 1862, *OR* 9:708; Rigg to Carleton Mar. 30, 1862, *OR* 50(1):965–66; *Sacramento Daily Union*, May 23, 1862.
90. Hunter to Baylor, Apr. 5, 1862, *OR* 9:708; Rigg to Carleton, Mar. 30, 1862, *OR* 50(1):965–66. There is considerable confusion over how many men were captured with McCleave. After the war McCleave himself remembered nine (1894) and ten (1897); Major E. A. Rigg and Colonel Carleton reported eight men taken with McCleave, plus the miller, Ammi White. Sherod Hunter reported nine men captured with McCleave; the *San Francisco Daily Alta California* reported nine and ten in addition to McCleave. See Finch, *Confederate Pathway*, 129. For variations on the composition of the nine-man squad, see *Alta*, June 8, 23, 29, 1862. William McCleave, "Recollections of

a California Volunteer," McCleave Papers, Bancroft Library; Carleton to
Halleck, Nov. 14, 1862, *OR* 50(2):222–23.

91. Hunter to Baylor, Apr. 5, 1862, *OR* 9:708; Rigg to Carleton, Apr. 12, 1862, *OR*
50(1):978–79; Orton, *California Men*, 69. *Sacramento Daily Union*, May 23,
1862. Private Semmelrogge recovered sufficiently from the bullet wound to
his right shoulder to return to light duty within a month. William Semmelrogge, Charlotte Semmelrogge Dependent Pension 490423, RG 15, NARA.

Chapter 3

1. For the European roots of American military tactics and strategy, see Griffith, *Battle Tactics of the Civil War* and Hagerman, *The American Civil War
and the Origins of Modern Warfare*.

2. Newcomb, Diary, May 15, 1862; Orton, *California*, 333.

3. Carleton to McCleave, Mar. 15, 1862, *OR* 50(1):932; Cutler to Rigg, Mar. 15,
1862, ibid., 930. See also Goodwin, *Social Organization*. The Tonto Apaches
(Dilzhe'e) are one of the groups of Western Apache people. Tonto also refers
to their dialect, one of the three dialects of Western Apache (a Southern
Athabaskan language). The Chiricahuas living to the south called them
Ben-et-dine or biniiʔe'dine' ("brainless people" or "people without minds,"
"wild," "crazy," "those who you don't understand"). The neighboring Western Apache name for them was Koun'nde ("wild rough people"), from which
the Spanish derived their use of Tonto ("loose," "foolish"). The related but
enemy Navajo to the north called both the Tonto Apache and their allies,
the Yavapai, Dilzh'i' diné'i' ("People with high-pitched voices"). Goodwin
divided the Tontos into two groups: the Northern Tonto and Southern
Tonto, though many Western Apaches reject such classification, preferring
identification based on bands and clans.

4. All the tribes of the borderlands used mineral and vegetal body paints for
ceremonial purposes and warfare. For examples of Apache face paint rendered in color by Grenville Goodwin, see Ferg, *Western Apache Material Culture*, 86. Other Apacheans also used war paint; Navajos painted themselves
black with red lines during an 1862 attack on Hispano *pastores*. José Luna *v.*
Navajo, Case 2567, RG 123, NARA.

5. *San Francisco Alta California*, June 11, 1862.

6. Lockwood, *Life in Old Tucson*, 212–13.

7. Carleton to Joseph R. West, Oct. 22, Nov. 4, and Nov. 5, 1861, *OR* 50(1):672,
698–99, 704–5.

8. West to Carleton, Nov. 4, 1861, *OR* 50(1):698–99; Rigg to Carleton, Mar. 25,
1862, ibid., 950–52. The Tennessee-born, half-Cherokee Powell Weaver was
known to Spanish-speaking Arizonans as Paulino. Others called him Pauline. He apparently answered to all these variants with good humor. While
fighting alongside the Maricopas, he and his constant companion known
only as "Moore" had survived many skirmishes with Apaches. Weaver died
June 21, 1867, and was buried at Camp Lincoln with full military honors in
recognition of his service as a scout and as an influential intermediary with
Indian peoples. *Arizona Miner*, July 13, 1867.

9. Richard, et al., *Geologic Map of the Picacho Mountains*, 5–6.

10. Hunter to Baylor, Apr. 5, 1862, *OR* 9:707–8.

11. Barrett's Co. A cavalrymen were described as "pawing for the advance," while Captain Pishon's Co. D men were said to be "full of fight." Rigg to Carleton, Mar. 25, 1862, *OR* 50(1):951.

12. When James Barrett enlisted in 1854, he was 5 ft., 9 in. tall, with brown hair and gray eyes. James Barrett, CMSR, RG 94, NARA; Altshuler, *Cavalry Yellow*, 21; Clothing Account Books of CV Regiments; J. H. Carleton, GO 3, Hdqrs. Dist. of Southern Calif., Feb. 11, 1862, *OR* 50(2):858–59; N. J. Pishon and B. F. Harvey to J. R. West, Pimos Villages, May 1, 1862; William P. Calloway to J. R. West, Pimos Villages, May 9, 1862; and J. R. West to Ben C. Cutler, Hdqrs. Advance Guard, CV, Pimos Villages, May 11, 1862, William P. Calloway CMSR, RG 94, NARA; E. A. Rigg to J. H. Carleton, Mar. 25 and 30, 1862, *OR* 50(1):950–52, 965–66; Hall, "Wild West"; Sherod Hunter Jacket, Compiled Service Records of Confederate Soldiers, Microcopy 323, Roll 182, NARA, cited in Finch, "Sherod Hunter," 203; *Sacramento Union*, May 23, 1862; J. H. Carleton, SO 15, June 15, 1862, Hdqrs. Column from Calif., *OR* 50(1):142; *San Francisco Alta California*, May 14, 1862; E. E. Eyre to R. C. Drum, May 14, 1862, *OR* 50(1):120; "Knapsack" (James P. Newcomb), untitled clipping, *San Francisco Herald and Mirror*, May 9, 1862, in James P. Newcomb Papers; Finch, *Confederate Pathway*, 141–44; J. H. Carleton to J. R. West, May 3, 1862, *OR* 50(1):1048–49.

13. *Sacramento Union*, May 23, 1862. The rebel rangers fired at close range and with deadly accuracy. Barrett and his men were all shot in the head or upper body. Two men, Corporal James Botsford and Private Peter Glann, suffered gunshot wounds to their left shoulders. Botsford soon returned to duty and earned his sergeant stripes, while Glann never fully recovered; he was discharged at Camp Drum for disability on January 6, 1863. Private William C. Tobin was a lucky man. A bullet had smashed into the brass crossed sabers pinned to the front of his uniform hat, then raked across the top of his head, fracturing and exposing his skull, resulting in an ugly wound. Temporarily paralyzed on one side, Tobin convalesced at Forts Barrett and Yuma before being discharged for disability on January 6, 1863. George H. Pettis to Annie [wife], Apr. 30, 1862, George H. Pettis Papers, Beinecke Library; Orton, *California Men*, 69, 90, 98, 107, 109, 120; William C. Tobin, CMSR, RG 94, NARA.

14. Report of the Battle of Picacho Pass, Sherod Hunter Jacket, Compiled Service Records of Confederate Soldiers, Microcopy 323, Roll 182, NARA, cited in Finch, "Sherod Hunter," 139–206.

15. The grave markers read: "Lieut. Jas Barrett, 1st Cav. Cal. Vols, Killed in action, April 15th 1862, aged 28 years; Geo. Johnson, Co. A 1st Cav. Cal. Vols Killed April 15th 1862, aged 25 years; W. S. Leonard, Co. D 1st Cav. Cal. Vols died of wounds April 16, 1862," from Newcomb, Diary, Oct. 19, 1862; Hall, "Wild West," *National Tribune*, Oct. 20, 1887; William S. Leonard, Hayden Arizona Pioneer Biography Files, Arizona State University. James Tevis, a former Overland Mail agent turned Confederate lieutenant, saw Calloway's retreating column and reported the names on the graves to Capt. Sherod Hunter in Tucson. See Tevis, *Arizona in the '50s*, 12–13 and Finch, "Sherod Hunter," 194–97.

16. Orton, *California Men*, 47; Col. J. H. Carleton to Col. J. R. West, May 3, 1862, *OR* 50(1):1048–49. The best account of the skirmish at Picacho may be

found in Finch, *Confederate Pathway,* 139–48. All who passed the graves of the fallen California cavalrymen paid homage. See "Mr. Greeley's Letters from Arizona," *San Francisco Alta California,* Mar. 15, 1864; and *Calaveras (Calif.) Chronicle,* July 1, 1865. In June 1862 Carleton and Captain Shinn noted that the graves were on the left of the road to Tucson near a mesquite thicket and dry *charcos* (water holes) on the right of the road. He recorded the distance as 13.9 miles from Blue Water Station, south of the Pima Villages, and 1 mile from Picacho Station. J. H. Carleton, SO 15, June 15, 1862, Hdqrs. Column from California, *OR* 50(1):142; *Alta,* Mar. 15, 1864. Privates Johnson and Leonard were reinterred at the post cemetery in Tucson but were moved again when Fort Lowell was relocated northeast of the growing town in 1884. When the post was deactivated in 1892, the remains were dug up yet again and moved to the national cemetery in San Francisco. Barrett's remains were never reinterred and they remained in the mesquite thicket near Picacho. E. E. Eyre to R. C. Drum, May 14, 1862, *OR* 50(1):120; *Arizona Daily Star,* Apr. 27, 1959; Edith C. Tompkins Manuscript; Hunt, *James Henry Carleton,* 214; *Oakland Tribune,* Apr. 16, 1961; J. C. Hall, a member of the "Jackass Battery," reported that when traveling west the graves were on the *right* side of the railroad tracks. Hall, "Wild West," *National Tribune,* Oct. 20, 1887.

17. George Oakes Reminiscence, Arizona Historical Society.

18. Though many expressed displeasure with Calloway, and his actions were investigated, it had always been Carleton's intention to construct a "redoubt" and "sub-depot" at the Pimas and not to attempt an attack on Tucson unless all the conditions for success were in his favor. Carleton to McCleave, Mar. 15, 1862, *OR* 50(1):932.

19. GO 8, Hdqrs. Dist. of Southern Calif., May 10, 1862, *OR* 50(1):1061. Carleton's pemmican was specially produced in San Francisco and packed in large tin cans. Carleton to Drum, Dec. 31, 1861, *OR* 50(1):774. Intended to be a nonperishable campaign ration, one soldier described the unpalatable pemmican concoction as, "rotten old dried beef and the refuse of a soap factory." Carleton to Drum, Dec. 21 1861, Memorandum of Supplies "B," *OR* 50(1); 779; *San Francisco Alta California,* Aug. 10, 1862. Los Angeles entrepreneur Phineas Banning may also have supplied pemmican. Bennett, Diary.

20. Orton, *California Men,* 44–45. The best account of the service of the Colorado Volunteers in New Mexico is found in Whitlock's *Distant Bugles, Distant Drums.*

21. Though the holder of U.S. patents since 1856, Sibley did not request Confederate patents for his innovative tipi-shaped tent, fly, and stove, which he hoped would aid the war effort. *New Orleans Picayune,* July 16, 1861; Thompson, *Henry Hopkins Sibley,* 102–7.

22. Hall, *Sibley's New Mexico Campaign,* 23, 38, 85; Thompson, *Westward the Texans,* 2–3; Thompson, *Henry Hopkins Sibley,* 209.

23. Baylor shot Robert P. Kelley, one of Mesilla's leading citizens and editor of the *Mesilla Times.* Hall, "The Mesilla Times; A Journal of Confederate Arizona," 337. Sibley and his aides despised Baylor and made sure the Confederate high command saw Baylor's extermination orders. Thompson, *Henry Hopkins Sibley,* 314–16. Baylor personally led the dogged pursuit of Apache raiders (there is uncertainty over whether they were Chiricahuas

or Mescaleros) who ran off more than one hundred horses and mules from Mesilla. The showdown may have occurred at Corralitos on the northeastern flank of the Sierra Madres. Thompson, *Henry Hopkins Sibley*, 315; Sweeney, *Mangas Coloradas*, 426–27; Sweeney, *Cochise*, 194.

24. Baylor, *John Robert Baylor*, 13–16, 33, 35–36. He used political influence to get to Davis and others, sending an Apache shield adorned with the "fair tresses" of a murdered white woman. Baylor to J. B. Magruder, Dec. 29, 1862, *OR* 15:914–18; Thompson, *Colonel John Robert Baylor*, 76–77; Frazier, *Blood and Treasure*, 190–91. By March 1865 Baylor had succeeded in securing a colonel's commission and permission to raise a regiment of mounted volunteers for the recapture of Arizona. This was, of course, an impossible dream at this point in the war, and had he been successful in securing one thousand men, arms, horses, and supplies, his efforts would have been only a temporary diversion as the Confederacy collapsed. Still, the appointment provided Baylor with a measure of vindication and helped restore his honor. Baylor fits the nineteenth-century model of the unrestrained martial male as defined by Greenberg in *Manifest Manhood*, 13–14.

25. Alberts, *Rebels on the Rio Grande*, 10, 43, and passim. Prior to enlisting, many young Texans were members of the Knights of the Golden Circle, an organization that advocated the conquest of Mexico, Central America, and portions of South America and the Caribbean in order to establish a slave empire. See Thompson, *From Desert to Bayou*, iv.

26. Hall and Long, *Confederate Army of New Mexico*, 13–23; Teel, "Sibley's New Mexican Campaign," 700.

27. In his official report of the Battle of Valverde, Canby described his troops as consisting of "five companies of the Fifth, three of the Seventh, and three of the Tenth Infantry, two companies of the First and five of the Third Cavalry, McRae's battery (G of the Second and I of the Third Cavalry), and a company of Colorado volunteers. The New Mexican troops consisted of the First Regiment (Carson's), seven companies of the Second, seven of the Third, one of the Fourth, two of the Fifth, Graydon's Spy Company, and about 1,000 hastily collected and unorganized militia, making on the morning of [February] 21st an aggregate present of 3,810." *OR* 9:488.

28. The New Mexicans risked much by joining the U.S. government to fight the rebels. Not only would the Texans exact revenge, but the Hispano soldiers left their homes and livestock unguarded against Navajo and Apache raids, which increased dramatically in 1862. Vicente Tafoya *v.* Navajo, Case 4085 and Nestor Armijo *v.* Navajo, Case 425, RG 123, NARA.

29. See Taylor, *Bloody Valverde*, 130–31, for an excellent breakdown of the New Mexico Volunteers' order of battle and officer corps.

30. See Josephy, *Civil War in the American West*, 63–68, for an excellent recapitulation of the New Mexico campaign.

31. Estimates of the Confederate horses and mules lost range from 162 to 300. See Canby's Report, Mar. 1, 1862, *OR* 9:489; Ickis, *Bloody Trails*, 75. Sibley reported only one hundred mules lost through "careless herding." Sibley to S. Cooper, *OR* 9:508.

32. Canby's Report, Mar. 1, 1862, *OR* 9:488.

33. Ickis, *Bloody Trails*, 62–63; Whitford, *Colorado Volunteers in the Civil War*,

64. Nine days after the battle, an African American slave brought Lang his pistol and the captain shot himself, ending his suffering. Taylor, *Bloody Valverde*, 69–70.

34. Lt. Col. Scurry's Report, Feb. 22, 1862, *OR* 9:513–15; Major Raguet's Report, ibid., 516–18.

35. Samuel Lockridge filibustered in Nicaragua with William Walker before the two hotheads fought and parted company. Thompson, *Civil War in the Southwest*, 153.

36. Green's Report, Feb. 22, 1862, *OR* 9:520; Canby's Report, Mar. 1, 1862, *OR* 9:491.

37. Meketa, *Legacy of Honor*, 170–71

38. Taylor, *Bloody Valverde*, 84, 103.

39. See Taylor's summary of casualties in *Bloody Valverde*, 132–44.

40. Sibley to Canby, Feb. 22, 1862, *OR* 9:632; McRae epitomized the ideals of Anglo martial masculinity. Canby reported that the brave "Captain McRae died, as he had lived, an example of the best and highest qualities that a man can possess." Canby's Report, Mar. 1, 1862, *OR* 9:489–92; Whitford, *Colorado Volunteers*, 68.

41. There is a great body of scholarship related to why soldiers fought the Civil War. For a sampling of literature relevant to the Civil War in the borderlands see McPherson, *For Cause and Comrades*; Grear, *Why Texans Fought*; Thompson, *Westward the Texans*; Taylor, *Bloody Valverde*; Josephy, *Civil War in the American West*; Utley, *Frontiersmen in Blue*; and Meketa, *Legacy of Honor*.

42. The New Mexicans who joined the Union Army had little idea of the larger Civil War or its causes. The Battle of Valverde, however, became an event so memorable that it served as a temporal marker—people remembered their own history by whether it occurred before or after Valverde or when the Texans came. For examples and additional Hispanic soldiers' experiences see "Revolution" in Casimorio Lujan y Sandoval testimony in Altagracia Garcia Zamora *v.* Navajos Case 1363, RG 123, NARA; Valverde references in Jose Gallegos y Rivali *v.* Navajos, Case 5453, RG 123, NARA; and "Confederates" in Jose Abran Candelario testimony in Vicente Lujan *v.* Navajos, Case 5456, RG 123, NARA.

43. Captain Gurdin Chapin, AIG, to Halleck, Feb. 28, 1862, *OR* 9:634–35; Canby to Adjutant General of the Army, Feb. 23, 1862, *OR* 9:633. An Anglo correspondent from Maxwell's Ranch on the Cimarron in Mora County wrote on March 11, 1862, "The Mexicans are not to be depended upon. They run as soon as they see the enemy, and many go before." However exaggerated and biased, this view became the prevailing sentiment among army officers and Anglo New Mexicans. *New York Times*, Apr. 13, 1862.

44. Capt. Herbert Enos's Report, Mar. 11, 1862, *OR* 9:527–28; Capt. A. S. Sutton's Report, Mar. 19, 1862, *OR* 9:528–29; *New York Times*, Fort Union (Mar. 20, 1862), Apr. 13, 1862; Josephy, *Civil War in the American West*, 75.

45. The year 1862 saw an unprecedented increase in Navajo and Apache raids on New Mexican herds. Depredation claims bear out the perception of the Hispanos and Anglos in the territories that the Indians had stepped up their attacks as a direct result of the military-aged men ("valid men") being enlisted to fight the Confederates, leaving pastures, corrals, and villages

without adequate protection. Vicente Tafoya *v.* Navajo, Case 4085, RG 123, NARA. Hundreds of raids were reported. For examples, see Jose Luna *v.* Navajo, Case 2567 and 2568; Fritz Contzen, *v.* Apache, Case 3358; Ventura Curriel *v.* Apache, Case 6843; Peter Kitchen *v.* Apache, Case 6845; Rafael Chavez *v.* Navajo, Case 4097; Tomas Montoya *v.* Apache, Case 4101; Pedro Padilla *v.* Apache and Navajo, Case 5957; Abraham Peeples *v.* Apache, Case 6253, RG 123, NARA; Lorenzo Ortero *v.* Navajo, Claim 4048; Mariano Pino *v.* Navajo, Claim 6141, RG 75, NARA.

46. Enos to Donaldson, Mar. 11, 1862, *OR* 9:528; Donaldson to Paul, Mar. 11, 1862, *OR* 9:527; Connelly to Seward, Mar. 11, 1862, *OR* 9:645.

47. Sibley to S. Cooper, AIG, May 4, 1862, *OR* 9:511–12.

48. Arizona Territorial Justice Joseph Pratt Allyn on October 26, 1863, as he made his way to Arizona from Missouri via the Santa Fe Trail wrote, "The Colorado troops are certainly the finest troops physically I have seen, and their courage and endurance have been tested by a campaign as grand for distance marched as the famous one of Xenophon and the 10,000 Greeks, and battles the most bloody in proportion to the number of men engaged of this war; and yet whose very names are unknown to eastern ones. It is difficult for you to realize the grandeur of our empire and the magnitude of this war. You cherish the battle standards inscribed with names utterly forgotten if not unknown here. Kansas and Missouri hold dearest the achievements of the army of the frontier, and a list of engagements I never heard of. Here on the plains you meet soldiers bronzed by the tropic sun and powder grime of battles on the frontiers of Chihuahua." Allyn, *West By Southwest*, 84.

49. For excellent recapitulations of the Apache Canyon fight and impressions of the Texans, see Alberts, *The Battle of Glorieta*, 64–67; and Edrington and Taylor, *The Battle of Glorieta Pass*, 41–51.

50. Report of Capt. John F. Ritter, May 16, 1862, *OR* 9:539.

51. Thirty-two Confederate bodies discovered in a burial trench near Pigeon's Ranch in 1987 revealed that some of the Texans carried in their pockets buckshot and slug loads for their shotguns. Don Alberts to Masich, personal communication, May 21, 1998. Alberts was the consulting historian on the excavation of the Confederate graves.

52. Though historians continue to debate many of the details (including the slaughter of the Confederate livestock) of Chivington's daring flank attack, excellent accounts may be found in Alberts, *The Battle of Glorieta;* Edrington and Taylor, *Battle of Glorieta Pass;* and Whitlock, *Distant Bugles, Distant Drums.*

53. Alberts, *Rebels on the Rio Grande*, 90.

54. By all accounts, Louisa Canby, Colonel Canby's wife, and other Union officers' wives who had stayed behind in Santa Fe, tended the Confederate wounded, saved lives, and earned the admiration of friends and foes alike. *Santa Fe Gazette*, May 21, 1862.

55. Col. William Steele to Gen. S. Cooper, AIG, Richmond, July 12, 1862, *OR* 50(2):22.

56. *Santa Fe Gazette*, Aug. 17, 1861. See also Teel, *Sibley's New Mexican Campaign.*

57. McNulty's Report, *OR* 50(1):136; John C. Cremony, *Life Among the Apaches*, 181. One soldier wrote from Tucson on July 7, 1862, that every man lost from

eight to ten pounds on the march, but aside from some fevers, the California Volunteers enjoyed remarkably good health. See *San Francisco Evening Bulletin,* July 30, 1862. A soldier correspondent with the First Infantry, CV, noted that before each day's march, "the Colonel orders out the sick, sore and sorry, in front of each company, and a man must be either clearly broken down or tell a very plausible story" in order to earn himself a wagon ride. *San Francisco Evening Bulletin,* Oct. 29, 1861.

58. Camps/Miles: Camp Latham (Los Angeles) /18, Reed's Ranch/15, Chino/18, Temescal/17, Laguna Grande/13, Temecula/21, Giftaler's/13.5, Camp Wright (Warner's Ranch, San Diego)/25, San Felipe/13, Vallecito/17, Carrizo Creek/16.5, Sackett's Well/17.5, Indian Wells/15, New River Station/15, Alamo Station/14, Salt or Seven Wells/18, Pilot Knob/25, Fort Yuma, Colorado River/10, Gila City/17.5, Mission Camp/11.5, Filibuster Camp/6, Antelope Peak/9.25, Mohawk Station/13, Texas Hill/11, Lagoon Camp/5, Grinnel's Ranch/11.25, Grassy Camp/3, Burkes Station/6.5, Oatman Flat/11.25, Kenyon Station/13.5, Shady Camp/10, Gila Bend/4, Desert Station/22, The Tanks, 7.5, Maricopa Wells/11.25, Pima Villages/11.25, Sacaton Station/12, Oneida Station/11, Blue Water Station/10, Barrett's Grave/13.9, Picacho Station/1, Point of Mountain/25, Tucson/15. SO 15, Hdqrs. Column from California, June 16, 1862, *OR* 50(1):138–42; GO 6, Hdqrs. Dist. of Southern Calif., May 7, 1862, ibid., 1056; J. R. West to B. C. Cutler, Fort Yuma, Nov. 7, 1861, ibid., 709–14.

59. Scott, *Military Dictionary,* 451; Bowman, "Diary of Corporal A. Bowman." One soldier wrote home that when marching in "route step" the men were able to "crack our jokes and sing our songs, and thus enliven the way." Officers had to ensure that rival companies (e.g., "city boys" vs. "mountaineers") did not quicken the pace in order to demonstrate their marching prowess. *San Francisco Evening Bulletin,* Oct. 29, 1861.

60. Yuma is just above sea level, and the road from Fort Breckinridge to Tucson passes along the base of the Santa Catalina Mountains, nearly a mile high. McNulty's Report, *OR* 50(1):140.

61. Carleton to Drum, Mar. 22, 1862, *OR* 50(1):944–45; Carleton to Pesqueira, May 2, 1862, *OR* 50(1):1044–45; HQ Fort Yuma, Orders No. 80, May 2, 1862, Maj. E. A. Rigg, ibid., 1045.

62. Carleton to Pesqueira, Tucson, July 12, 1862, *OR* 50(2), 17–18; Acuña. "Ignacio Pesqueira" 157–59. Dabbs, *The French Army in Mexico,* 99–100; Martin, *Maximilian in Mexico,* 206; Armand de Castagny to François-Achille Bazaine, Mazatlán, Feb. 16, 1865, in Garcia and Pereyra. *Colección de Documentos Ineditos,* Segunda Parte, Tomo XXIV, 228–35.

63. McNulty's Report, *OR* 50(1):140; S. Hunter to J. R. Baylor, Apr. 5, 1862, *OR* 9:707–8; E. A. Rigg to J. H. Carleton, Mar. 30, 1862, *OR* 50(1):965–66.

64. Carleton to West, May 2, 1862, *OR* 50(1):1046. Carleton frequently used the word "despise" in his dispatches. He most often employed the term not to mean "hate" but, rather, in its now archaic sense of looking down on or underestimating the strength or positive attributes of a people or place. For example, he believed that the territories were not just military backwaters but had war-winning potential due to their great mineral wealth. He urged his superiors in Washington not to "despise New Mexico as a drain on the general government. The money will all come back again." Carleton to Halleck, May 10, 1863, Doolittle, *Condition of the Indian Tribes,* 110.

65. Carleton to West, May 2, 1862, *OR* 50(1):1046.
66. Pettis, *The California Column*, 11; *Tucson Arizona Citizen*, May 19, 1883, Sept. 27, 1884. Lieutenant Pettis contends that the *canales* that frightened Fritz's men became a standing joke with the California Column. Bowman, Diary, May 21, 1862. The Californians surprised Lieutenant James Tevis and a few Confederate sentinels who rode out from the opposite end of town. Finch, *Confederate Pathway*, 153; Lt. George H. Pettis to Annie (wife), May 26, 1862, Pettis Papers.
67. Carleton to Drum, Tucson, June 10, 1862, *OR* 50(1):1128–29. Fort Breckinridge had been named to honor Vice President John C. Breckinridge, who later lost the 1860 presidential election to Lincoln and was appointed a Confederate major general on April 14, 1862, for conspicuous service at the Battle of Shiloh. The fort was renamed Stanton, for California's governor, Leland Stanford, in 1862. In 1863 it was again named Breckenridge, the incorrect variant spelling evidently preferred by loyal Union men. By war's end the fort would be again renamed; on November 1, 1865, it became Fort Grant. See Masich, *The Civil War in Arizona*, 185n86.
68. *San Francisco Alta California*, June 10, 1862; GO 1, Hdqrs. Column from California, May 15, 1862, *OR* 50(1):1075.
69. U.S. Census, *Federal Census—Territory of New Mexico and Territory of Arizona*. Carleton's proclamation may be found in *OR* 50(1):96–97. The United States acquired present Arizona north of the Gila River with the Mexican Cession of 1848. Gadsden's treaty, which included Tucson and the land south of the Gila, was amended and ratified by the Senate in June 1854—though this new territory was not occupied by U.S. troops until November 1856. See Sonnichsen, *Tucson*, 40.
70. *OR* 50(1):96–97. From Dept. of the Pacific Headquarters, Gen. Wright "approved and confirmed" Carleton's actions and rank as "Brigadier-General of Volunteers" on June 28, 1862, Orton, *California Men*, 56. Congress and President Lincoln ratified Carleton's action by officially establishing Arizona as a U.S. territory on February 24, 1863.
71. Carleton to E. R. S. Canby, June 15, 1862, *OR* 50(1):96–97; McNulty's Report, ibid., 142.
72. Orton, *California Men*, 44–45; SO 142, Sept. 10, 1863, Tucson, Commands of J. R. West, Special, General and Post Orders, 1861–66, Records of the U.S. Army Continental Commands, RG 393, NARA; E. E. Eyre to Benjamin C. Cutler, acting AAG, Column from California, June 16, 1862, *OR* 50(1):1142–43; Proclamation, Executive Dept., Ariz. Terr., by Order of General Carleton, June 17, 1862, *OR* 9:693.
73. Carleton to Eyre, Nov. 4, 1861, *OR* 50(1):700–701.
74. Carleton to Canby, June 15, 1862, *OR* 50(1):97.
75. "Jones call[ed] to the sergeant to mount his mule, as flight was their only chance. Jones mounted and put spurs to his mule; but the sergeant never followed. Jones ran the gauntlet for several miles, with Indians running alongside him, and shooting at him. He shot three of his pursuers, who gradually dwindled down to one Indian, who brushed by him on a swift horse, and wheeled and took deliberate aim at Jones, cutting the rim of his hat with the ball. Jones drew up and fired at him. They then parted, the Indian

exclaiming, '*Mucho wano [bueno] mula, bravo Americano.*' [You have a good mule, brave American.] The Indians dogged Jones for sixty miles, and then gave him up." *San Francisco Alta California,* Aug. 10, 1862; Carleton included Jones's testimony in his own report of the expedition's march, noting that the Chiricahuas shouted "now let's have a race" when the chase began. Jones's statement, July 22, 1862, *OR* 50(1):119–20.

76. The Chiricahuas reported that the Coyotero Apaches were responsible for the stock raid and capture of the Ward boy. See Bascom's own Feb. 14 and 24, 1861, reports of the affair in Sweeney, *Cochise; Firsthand Accounts,* 16–18. See also Sweeney, *Mangas Coloradas,* 391–412; Sweeney, *Cochise,* 142–60; Mulligan, "Apache Pass and Old Fort Bowie," 5–10.

77. Carleton to Eyre, June 17, 1862, *OR* 50(1):98; McChristian and Ludwig, "Eyewitness to the Bascom Affair," 277–300.

78. Report of Thomas L. Roberts, July 19, 1862, *OR* 50(1):128–29.

79. Carleton to West, Aug. 6, 1862, *OR* 50(1):105; Shirland to West, Aug. 10, 1862, *OR* 50(1):105–6.

80. Carleton to Coult, May 20, 1862, *OR* 50(1), 1082–83; Carleton to Postmaster-General Montgomery Blair, Santa Fe, Oct. 18, 1862, *OR* 50(2):181–82; ibid., May 2, 1863, *OR* 50(2):419–20; GO 11, Order of Brigadier General Carleton, July 21, 1862, *OR* 50(1):92; GO 9, Order of Brigadier General Carleton, May 15, 1862, *OR* 50(1):1075; John N. Goodwin, Report to the First Arizona Territorial Legislature, Prescott, Sept. 1864, cited in Hunt, *Army of the Pacific,* 133–34.

81. Carleton to Wright, Mar. 7, 1864, *OR* 50(2):783–84; Eyre to Cutler, July 8, 1862, *OR* 50(1):124–26. McCleave's highly developed sense of honor forbade him from accepting his pay ($582.50) for the period he had been a captive of the rebels. Altshuler, *Cavalry Yellow,* 209.

82. Pettis, *California Column,* 18–19; Orton, *California Men,* 669–70.

83. Sibley was forced to abandon all his sick and wounded men in hospitals at Santa Fe, Albuquerque, Socorro, and Franklin. Sibley to S. Cooper, AIG, May 4, 1862, *OR* 9:511.

84. Sibley made a point of reminding the Confederate high command that the "entire campaign has been prosecuted without a dollar from the quartermaster's department" and that his men were better armed and equipped than when the expedition began. Sibley to S. Cooper, AIG, May 4, 1862, *OR* 9:511–12.

85. *San Francisco Alta California,* June 7, 1862.

86. Carleton to R. C. Drum, Sept. 20, 1862, Orton, *California Men,* 64–67; Henry W. Halleck, Oct. 13, 1862, quoted in Hunt, *James Henry Carleton,* 236. Though the Californians controlled Forts Bliss, Quitman and Davis in west Texas, some of the California soldiers rode all the way to San Antonio, escorting wounded rebels.

Chapter 4

1. Records of the U.S. Court of Claims, Indian Depredation Case Records, RG 123, NARA; Evidence Concerning Depredation Claims, 1835–96, RG 75, NARA. After 1834, depredation claimants had to prove, by means of a treaty or other evidence, that the tribe responsible for the loss was "in amity with"

NOTES TO PAGES 113–15

the United States at the time of the crime. Records for the years prior to the Civil War indicate not only were there fewer attacks, but the number of deaths per attack was also lower, revealing that the nature of war had also changed. See also Skogen, *Indian Depredation Claims,* passim.

2. Claims were filed between 1865 and 1893. Depredation Case Records, RG 123, NARA; Evidence Concerning Depredation Claims, RG 75, NARA. A chronological list of military actions with Indians, with a tabular statement showing that in 1863–64 alone there were 143 encounters resulting in 604 Indians killed, 227 wounded, and 8,793 captured; officers and men killed: 24 and 50 wounded. Doolittle, *Condition of the Indian Tribes,* 93, 247–57.

3. Based on hundreds of cases describing attacks between 1861–67, claimants lost provisions 10 percent of the time, camp equipage 17 percent, firearms 9 percent, saddles and horse equipage 9 percent, and other goods 23 percent. The percentage of killings may not represent an accurate proportion of all deaths resulting from fighting during this period. There were many attacks and combats that were not reported as depredations but were recorded in military, church, newspaper, correspondence, oral, and other sources. The purpose of making a depredation claim was to petition for compensation for property lost. The record of killings and wounds resulting from attacks is incidental, since the government disallowed compensation for death, injury, and suffering. Depredation Case Records, RG 123, NARA; Evidence Concerning Depredation Claims, RG 75, NARA.

4. Goodwin, *Western Apache Raiding,* 227–45; Opler, *Apache Life-way,* 286, 311, 386–93. Apacheans preferred mountain lion skins for quivers and bow cases but also used horse, steer, *javelina,* deer, wolf, coyote, fox, and deer. Ferg, *Western Apache Material Culture,* 50–53. Hundreds of depredation cases reference the types of weapons employed by the Apacheans. Generally, informants believed that Apaches preferred arrows made of *carrizo* (cane) while Navajos more often used ponil (made from *fallugia paradoxa,* a hard woody shrub). This distinction became an important point of evidence in assigning blame for a raid. In New Mexico, Hispanos reported that in the summer of 1862, Apaches usually tipped their arrows with flint while Navajos generally relied on iron points. Juan Domingo Sanchez *v.* Navajo, Case 3841, RG 123, NARA. See also Ferg, *Western Apache Material Culture,* 50–53, 86. Evidence used to determine the percentages of killed, wounded, and captured may be found in Depredation Case Records, RG 123, NARA; Evidence Concerning Depredation Claims, RG 75, NARA.

5. Intergroup raiding appears to be a nearly universal feature and survival strategy of foraging-pastoral societies. For the most recent scholarship on this and adaptive advantages of raiding by stealth versus open combat, see Glowacki and Wrangham, "Warfare and Reproductive Success" *PNAS,* 348.

6. Mangas is frequently reported to have stood 6 ft., 5 in. tall, but one eyewitness among the California Volunteers described him as, "Six feet four inches in his moccasins." Gwyther (Co. K, First Infantry), "Our Scout to Black Canyon." An army officer described fifty-year-old Cochise as 6 ft., 2 in. tall and "strongly muscled." *Arizona Weekly Miner,* Mar. 20, 1869. Of the Apacheans, the mountain dwelling peoples were typically shorter in stature than their buffalo-hunting Kiowa-Apache cousins of the Plains. The Cheyennes were the tallest of the southern plains tribes and their contemporaries

generally thought them to be the most physically impressive. The Colorado River Yumans were known for their stature and strength. Mojave Chief Ireteba stood well over six feet, and the Quechan's best-known chief, Pascual, was unusually tall, standing between 6 ft., 3 in. and 6 ft., 7 in. *San Francisco Daily Alta California*, May 23, 1859. Pauline Pascual, descendant of Chief Pascual, personal communication, Feb. 14, 1985. For historical observations on the correlation of power, dominance, and stature see Pinker, *Better Angels*, 517–18.

7. Ball, *Indeh*, 9, 23, 56–57. For a brief overview of Navajo leadership, religion, marriage, and death customs, see Capt. H. B. Bristol's testimony, Doolittle, *Condition of the Indian Tribes*, 357–58. Descended from Chief Barranquito, Santana and his brothers/cousins (Apache kinship does not differentiate the terms brother and cousin), Cadete and Roman all became chiefs. Sonnichsen, *Mescalero*, 142. The indigenous peoples of the Plains and the Southwest all valued the virtue of generosity, especially toward those in need.

8. Ferg, *Western Apache Material Culture*, 8, 66, 69–73.

9. Opler and Hoijer, "Raid and War-Path Language," 618.

10. Chiricahuas believed that by the age of fourteen, Apache boys were "as well trained and dangerous as a soldier." Ibid.

11. Ibid., 619–22.

12. Ibid., 619; Opler, *Apache Life-way*, 349–54. For more on scalping from the Apache point of view, see Ball, *Indeh*, 4, 11–12, 20, 35; Goodwin, *Western Apache Raiding*, 276–78; Bourke, *On the Border*, 26.

13. For chronological lists of raids gleaned from army reports, newspapers, and other sources see *U.S. Army, Chronological List of Actions &c, with the Indians* and Kuhn, *Chronicles of War*, 73–161. The compensation system instituted by the federal government was intended to discourage citizens and subject peoples from seeking revenge. Claimants in Indian Depredation claims submitted to the U.S. government were required to swear "I have never sought any private revenge or redress against said Indians on account of said depredations." See, for example, Trinidad Romero de Jaramillo *v.* Navajo, Claim 5977, RG 75, NARA; John H. Dixon *v.* Tonto Apaches, Case 7958, RG 123, NARA; Skogen, *Indian Depredation Claims*, xv, 141; Opler, *Apache Life-way*, 336; Goodwin, *Western Apache Raiding*, 16.

14. Lummis, *Land of Poco Tiempo*, 118–19.

15. Horse raiders often traveled on foot for stealth, carrying only the most minimal equipment—a braided horsehair rope or rawhide *reata* was sufficient to fashion a war bridle by putting a loop around the horse's lower jaw. For an example of a Navajo horse raid see Carleton to Maj. Joseph Smith, Commanding Ft. Stanton, Nov. 15, 1863, Doolittle, *Condition of the Indian Tribes*, 143.

16. Apache raiders made off with a Lemitar, New Mexico, horse and mule herd after scaling a twelve-foot corral wall and sawing through the adobe with a woolen or horsehair rope to create an opening. Josefa Lujan de Gonzales (Venceslado Lujan) *v.* Gila Apaches, Case 3849, RG 123, NARA.

17. Juan Analla testified that Apache trails could easily be distinguished from those of white men—citing the distinctive tracks made by Apache moccasins and "raw hide horse shoes." He also believed Apache warriors, when traveling,

often walked in the footprints of the man ahead to deceive enemies. Juan Analla *v.* Navajo, Case 5426, RG 123, NARA. Chiricahua and Western Apache moccasins were made with a distinctive toe guard of tough hide and were much narrower than moccasins worn by New Mexican Hispanos and Pueblo Indians. See especially testimony by Jojola and Porfírio Pajilla in Ciriaco Jojola *v.* Apaches, Case 2932, RG 123, NARA. Pablo Padilla detailed a February 1862 attack and described the difference between Navajo and Apache (turned-up toe) moccasins in Luciano Chavez *v.* Navajos Case 3840, RG 123, NARA. Cayetano Tafoya testified that Apache tracks differed from Navajo because of the Apache moccasin's toe and the fact that Navajos made a more uniform footprint in soft sand while Apaches pushed the dirt forward. Tafoya also believed Navajos stepped more pigeon-toed than Apaches. Juan Domingo Sanchez *v.* Navajo, Case 3841, RG 123, NARA. Another Hispano tracker observed, "Indians walk pegeon-toed [*sic*] while the Mexican walks with the toes square to the front . . . the Indians bears more on the outside of the foot than the inside, while the Mexican stands square on his feet." Agapito Lucero *v.* Navajo, Case 4177, RG 123, NARA. Apaches could identify enemy Yavapais by their distinctive tracks as this tribe typically sewed the rawhide sole of their moccasins to the buckskin upper with thin strips of hide that could be clearly seen in a footprint. Goodwin, *Western Apache Raiding*, 32. See also Farrow, *Mountain Scouting*, 230.

18. Capt. James Whitlock to Capt. C. A. Smith, Apr. 13, 1864, *OR* 50(2):829; Lt. Col. E. E. Eyre to Lt. Ben Cutler, July 6, 1862, Orton, *California Men*, 58–59. Chiricahua informants reported that stone points found on the ground or near anthills made by earlier peoples, "ancient ones," were reused when available, but by the 1860s most of the tribes in the borderlands were manufacturing iron arrowheads. Opler, *Apache Life-way*, 311, 340–41, 386–90. Examples of mismatched, Apache-fired bullets may be found in the Arizona and New Mexico archaeological record. While working on Fort Bowie artifacts in the conservation lab of the Western Archaeological Center in Tucson, the author identified a .54- or .58-caliber minié ball, designed for a rifle musket, that was determined to have been fired from a Sharps carbine, based on the distinctive rifling marks imparted to the soft lead bullet. Additional archaeological bullet specimens in the collection of the Fort Bowie National Historic Site show modifications by scraping, hammering, and chewing that would have enabled a shooter, most likely Apache, to fire the projectiles from a mismatched gun. One scraped (.58 to .50) French minié ball would indicate traded or captured ammunition from Mexico during the French intervention. Ludwig, *Archaeological Findings of the Battle of Apache Pass*, 53–55. Sergeant Daniel Robinson remembered that Apaches cut lead bars into slugs and "rounded the corners with their teeth so as to fit the bore." McChristian and Ludwig, "Eyewitness to the Bascom Affair," 289. See also Watt and Hook, *Apache Tactics*, 54–56; Watt and Hook, *Apache Warrior*, 29–32. For additional illustrations and descriptions of Civil War–era bullets excavated at Fort Bowie, see Herskovitz, *Fort Bowie Material Culture*, 46, 52.

19. For Major Brooks's interpretation of the start of hostilities between the Anglos and Navajos see Brooks's reply to the Doolittle "circular" in *Condition of the Indian Tribes*, 491.

20. It is not surprising that the Utes and Jicarillas did not support the Navajos, their traditional enemies. Bancroft, *History of Arizona and New Mexico*, 660–67.

21. In the 1860s, Pueblo Indians from San Ildefonso suffered from Navajo stock raiders. For example, see Ramon Medina *v.* Navajo, Case 993, RG 123, NARA.

22. Goodwin, *Myths and Tales of the White Mountain Apache*, 9; Opler, *Apache Life-way*, 345–46. See also Goodwin, *Western Apache Raiding*, 16 and passim.

23. Gen. J. H. Carleton to Col. Christopher Carson, Oct. 12, 1862, Doolittle, *Condition of the Indian Tribes*, 100. Carleton ordered, "All Indian men of that tribe [Mescalero] are to be killed whenever and wherever you can find them." In 1862 Confederate Colonel John R. Baylor lost his command and governorship of Arizona when Jefferson Davis learned of his Indian extermination policy, which called for the killing of adult Apaches, by poison or other means, and capturing the children who were to be sold into slavery in Mexico or New Mexico to defray the expenses of the campaign. Baylor falsely represented this scheme to subordinates as the official policy of the Confederate Congress: "The Congress of the Confederate States has passed a law declaring extermination to all hostile Indians. You will therefore use all means to persuade the Apaches or any tribe to come in for the purpose of making peace, and when you get them together kill all the grown Indians and take the children prisoners and sell them to defray the expense of killing the Indians. Buy whisky and such other goods as may be necessary for the Indians and I will order vouchers given to cover the amount expended. Leave nothing undone to insure success, and have a sufficient number of men around to allow no Indian to escape." Col. J. R. Baylor to Capt. Thomas Helm, Mar. 20, 1862. *OR* 50(1):942. For Baylor's point of view regarding Indian extermination, see Baylor, *John Robert Baylor*, 14–15, 32.

24. Carleton to West, Mar. 16, 1863, Doolittle, *Condition of the Indian Tribes*, 105–6.

25. Sabin, *Kit Carson Days*, 2:704–6; Dunlay, *Kit Carson and the Indians*, 244–46; Sonnichsen, *Mescalero*, 112. Thompson, *New Mexico Volunteers*, 272–76; Meketa, *Legacy of Honor*, 269–73.

26. Young Sais lived with his captors and worked as a herder for six months in the Mimbres and San Andres Mountains. His description of life with the renegade Mescaleros offers insight into their existence while raiding and on the run. Eventually, Sais escaped and returned home. See Sais's testimony in Jose Antonio Baca y Pino *v.* Apaches, Case 2931, RG 123, NARA.

27. Carleton to Carson, Sept. 19, 1863, Doolittle, *Condition of the Indian Tribes*, 137. This hostage strategy continued during the Civil War years. Both Zuni and Hopi headmen were targeted on the suspicion of harboring Navajos. Cyrus H. De Forrest to Capt. Asa B. Carey, May 3, 1865, Doolittle, *Condition of the Indian Tribes*, 183.

28. At Carson's urging, Carleton requested permission to recruit one hundred Utes to be used against the Navajos in their canyon land strongholds. Carleton to Lorenzo Thomas, AG, June 17, 1863, Doolittle, *Condition of the Indian Tribes*, 114; Sides, *Blood and Thunder*, 423.

29. Other verses of the song include praise for Carleton and Carson:

> Here's health to Gen'l Carleton that wise and brave hero
> His arrival was a blessing great, to speed New Mexico;
> May he win unfading laurels and sorrow never know
> And live to see the country free from Johnny Navajo.
> [refrain]

> Here's a health to Col. Carson whose swift and crushing blow
> Brought terror to the Savage, and reduced the Navajo,
> May promotion raise him to the stars and may his country show
> She holds him as the conqueror of Johnny Navajo.

    Santa Fe Gazette, Dec. 8, 1863.
30. Martin Saiz & Son *v.* the Navajo. Case 2597, RG 123, NARA; Gen. J. H. Carleton to Col. Christopher Carson, Oct. 12, 1862 and Apr. 8, 1864, in Doolittle, *Condition of the Indian Tribes,* 100, 174; Carleton to Lorenzo Thomas, AG, Mar. 12, 1864, ibid., 166.
31. It is difficult to know how many Navajos perished on the 250-mile "Long Walk," though scholars estimate 100 to 150 died. Navajo tradition holds that women and children were snatched from among the refugees to be enslaved by Pueblo Indians and Hispanos as the column moved slowly southeastward past pueblos to Bosque Redondo on the Pecos. Sides, *Blood and Thunder,* 444; Bailey, *The Long Walk,* passim. For an understanding of the New Mexico slave trade, *ladrones,* and *nacajalleses,* see Brooks's *Captives and Cousins,* 366–67.
32. Cadete (Zhee-ah-nat-tsa or Gianatah) took over as chief soon after the death of his father, Barranquito, in 1857. Sonnichsen, *Mescalero,* 91. Cremony, "Some Savages," 207.
33. Captain Cremony admiringly described Cadete (Gianatah) in some detail, including his melodic voice, and believed the chief to be "possessed of great foresight and mental calibre." Cremony, "Some Savages," 207.
34. Cremony, *Life Among the Apaches,* 201; Sonnichsen, *Mescalero,* 113.
35. Carleton to Lorenzo Thomas, Mar. 19, 1864, Doolittle, *Condition of the Indian Tribes,* 169. For details on the Navajo war and the Bosque Redondo experiment, see McNitt, *Navajo Wars;* Thompson, *Army and the Navajo,* passim; and Dunlay, *Kit Carson and the Indians,* 228–342.
36. Carleton to Lorenzo Thomas, AG, Dec. 23, 1863, Doolittle, *Condition of the Indian Tribes,* 151; Thompson, *Army and the Navajo,* 88, 140–41; Sides, *Blood and Thunder,* 457.
37. Cremony, *Life Among the Apaches,* 254–60; Carleton to J. Updegraff, Apr. 10, 1863, Doolittle, *Condition of the Indian Tribes,* 107.
38. Carleton had previously requested permission to recruit one hundred Utes to be used against the Navajos in their canyon land strongholds. Carleton to Updegraff, Aug. 19, 1863, ibid., 129; Carleton to Lorenzo Thomas, AG, June 17, 1863, ibid., 114, and Dec. 23, 1863.
39. As cruel as fettering with an iron ball and chain may have been for Navajos caught without a pass, army regulations allowed such punishments, which

were frequently meted out to soldiers as well. See "legal punishments," article 895, *United States Army Regulations of 1861* [Revised 1863], 126.

40. Carleton to Lorenzo Thomas, AG, Feb. 7, 1864, Doolittle, *Condition of the Indian Tribes*, 157; Thompson, *Army and the Navajo*, 27, 76–77; Jett, "Destruction of Navajo Orchards," 365–78.

41. Carleton to Steck, HQ Dept. of New Mexico, Mar. 21, 1865, Doolittle, *Condition of the Indian Tribes*, 221–22. Manuelito and Ganado Mucho finally brought their destitute people to the reservation in the spring of 1866. Within weeks they were victimized by Comanche raiders, who killed Ganado Mucho's son and other herders while running off most of the Navajos' remaining stock.

42. Carleton to Maj. William H. Lewis, June 19, 1865, Doolittle, *Condition of the Indian Tribes*, 227–28; Cutler to Lewis, June 25, 1865, ibid., 228–29; Carleton to Lorenzo Thomas, AG, July 20, 1865, ibid., 230.

43. For details of diseases and shortages that plagued the Bosque Redondo reservation from 1863 to 1868, see Thompson, *Army and the Navajo*, 46–68.

44. Labadie letter dated Oct. 10, 1863 found in Jose Antonio Baca y Pino v. Mescaleros, Case 2931, RG 123, NARA, 13–14. Carleton later accused Labadie of corruption and ordered him banished from Bosque Redondo, a controversial move that incurred the displeasure of the powerful Baca and Chaves families to whom the agent was related by marriage.

45. Thompson, *Army and the Navajo*, 84, 98–99.

46. Cremony, "The Apache Race," 208. The 5 ft., 10 in. tall Cadete was noted by Cremony to be physically impressive though deeply scarred by smallpox. Cremony, "Some Savages," 207.

47. Some Apache people and scholars today refer to the Chiricahua bands as allied tribes. Whether they are called bands (as Goodwin, Opler and other anthropologists believed) or tribes, they are independent communities sharing a common language and many other traditions.

48. Yavapai bands comprised four separate groups: the Tolkepayas, or Western Yavapai, the Yavapés, or Northwestern Yavapai, the Kwevkepayas, or Southeastern Yavapai, and Wipukepas, or Northeastern Yavapai (Verde Valley Yavapai). Gifford, *Northeastern and Western Yavapai*, 249–50. For more on bands and terminology related to the Yavapai people, see Braatz, *Surviving Conquest*, ix, 1–13.

49. Treaty With The Apache, July 1, 1852, ratified Mar. 23, 1853, proclaimed Mar. 25, 1853, http://digital.library.okstate.edu/kappler/vol2/treaties/apa0598 .htm#mn14. Bailey, *A Diplomatic History*, 15. For Mangas Coloradas's view of the Americans and their international boundary, see St. John, *Line in the Sand*, 34.

50. Maj. Edward B. Willis to Capt. B. Cutler, May 27, 1864, *OR* 50(2):868–69; *OR* 15:227–32.

51. Col. E. A. Rigg to Capt. B. C. Cutler, Sept. 14, 1864, *OR* 50(1):360–70.

52. GO 12, May 1, 1864, Hdqrs. Dept. of New Mexico, *OR* 34(1):387; abstract of troop returns, *OR* 34(3):372; *OR* 41(2):495; Col. J. R. West to Sonoran Governor Ignacio Pesqueira, Jan. 30, 1863, *OR* 50(2):299–300. Carleton coordinated his attacks north of the border with Mexican pressure timed to begin on June 10, 1864. Carleton to Pesqueira, Apr. 20, 1864, and Carleton to Governor of

Chihuahua, Luis Terrazas, Apr. 20, 1864, Doolittle, *Condition of the Indian Tribes,* 177. U.S. officers dealt only with the Republican governors of Mexico's border states, as French-backed conservatives waged civil war against Benito Juárez's liberal government, and Napoleon III installed Austrian Archduke Maximilian as the puppet emperor of Mexico in July 1864.

53. N. H. Davis to Carleton, Mar. 2, 1864, *OR* 34(2):591–93.

54. Carleton to George W. Bowie, Apr. 15, 1864, *OR* 50(2):820; GO 8, Tucson, June 13, 1862, Dept. of the Pacific, general, Special, and Post Orders, Vol. 1, RG 393, NARA. In 1862, the California troops had been ordered to draw and preserve the loads from their muzzle-loading rifle muskets rather than wasting ammunition by firing at a target following guard duty shifts, as was the custom. Carleton to Nathaniel Pishon, June 22, 1863, Orton, *California Men,* 72; Hdqrs. Dept. of New Mexico, GO 27, Oct. 23, 1863, *OR* 50(2):54; Fergusson to James Whitlock, Apr. 23, 1863, ibid., 413; Carleton to Halleck, May 10, 1863, Doolittle, *Condition of the Indian Tribes,* 110.

55. *Arizona Miner,* Oct. 26, 1864; Orders No. 8, HQ, Tucson, May 12, 1863, *OR* 50(2):431–32.

56. Farish, *History of Arizona,* 3:159.

57. Walnut Grove Mining Company *v.* Apaches, Case 4715, RG 123, NARA.

58. The first attack was reported by the Walnut Grove Mining Company wagon train while camped at Navajo Springs on August 1, 1865, while en route to Prescott. By 1867 the entire operation was idled, and in 1869 the Apaches completely burned or otherwise destroyed the mill, storehouse, sawmill, superintendent's house, boarding house, blacksmith and carpenter's shops, and stables, along with all the tools, machinery, books, papers, and supplies. The shareholders claimed that since the territory was under martial law and Carleton "exercised supreme control," his assurances should have the weight of a guaranty. They therefore held the U.S government liable for the $292,800 in losses incurred. Walnut Grove Mining Company *v.* Apaches, Claim 1144, RG 75, NARA; Case 7397 and Case 4715, RG 123, NARA.

59. The first session of the Arizona legislature in 1864 also allocated funds for the establishment of a reservation for the Colorado River Indian tribes ($150,000) and navigation improvements on the Colorado ($150,000). Fearing the history of the territory would be lost, along with the vanishing tribes, the legislators also incorporated the Arizona Historical Society. Bancroft, *History of Arizona and New Mexico,* 539.

60. Carleton to R. H. Drum, May 24, 1862, Orton, *California Men,* 51; Underhill, *First Arizona Volunteer Infantry,* 2, 20.

61. C. E. Bennett to Jonathan Green, May 1, 1866, in Underhill, *First Arizona Volunteer Infantry,* 5, 76; Gen. J. S. Mason to Col. R. C. Drum, May 30, 1865, *OR* 50(2):1247–48; Braatz, *Surviving Conquest,* 95–98.

62. After shooting Mangas, Private Teal stripped his equipment from his dead horse and walked the remaining eight miles to the stage station at Dragoon Springs where his wounded and scared comrades (Sgt. Mitchell and Pvts King, Keim, Young, and Maynard) and Captain Cremony expressed amazement over his survival. Walker, "Soldier in the California Column," 41; Cremony, *Life Among the Apaches,* 158–60; Cremony to Roberts, July 16, 1862, *OR* 50(1):133; *San Francisco Daily Alta California,* Aug. 16, 1862. Private

Eli Hazen, who inspected the scene of the fight that same day recorded in his diary that Teal had propped his blouse and hat on a bush and heard the Apaches "blaze away at the decoy" as he crawled away to safety. Schreier, "Hazen's Civil War Diary," 43-44. For additional details of Teal's fight and flight, see also Masich, *Civil War in Arizona*, 68, 239.

63. Sweeney, *Mangas Coloradas*, 454.

64. Conner, *Joseph Reddeford*, 179; McCleave, "Our Scout to Black Canyon," 7–9; Capt. Benjamin Cutler to Brig. Gen. J. R. West, Jan. 28, 1863, *OR* 50(2):296; Colton, *The Civil War in the Western Territories*, 133; Sweeney, *Mangas Coloradas*, 441-49, 457. Orton, *California Men*, 71; Conner, *Joseph Reddeford Walker*, 39–41. No charges were leveled against Mangas's murderers, and General West evaded censure for his role in the affair. *OR* 50(2):296–97; Josephy, *Civil War in the American West*, 279–81. See also St. Hoyme, "Skull of Mangas Coloradas." Some Chiricahuas remembered that the violence of their attacks escalated after Mangas's brutal murder at the hands of Carletons's soldiers and that Apache warriors scalped and mutilated their white enemies with greater frequency. Ball, *Indeh*, 83.

65. Carleton to R. C. Drum, Santa Fe, Sept. 20, 1862, Orton, *California Men*, 64; Colton, *Civil War in the Western Territories*, 133.

66. West to Bennett, Headquarters District of Arizona, May 15, 1863, *OR* 50(2):433–34.

67. Touching a dead person or even a body part required elaborate purification rituals and burning "ghost medicine" to ward off the spirit of the deceased. Opler, *Apache Life-Way*, 349–50.

68. Gen. J. R. West to Maj. William McCleave, Hart's Mill Texas, June 21, 1863, *OR* 50(2):490; For details of the attack on Lieutenant Bargie and his party see Rigg to Cutler, June 24, 1863, Dept. NM Letters Received, RG 98, NARA.

69. Carleton to Governor John Goodwin, Apr. 20, 1864, Doolittle, *Condition of the Indian Tribes*, 178–79. See also ibid., 156, 172, 177. While historians debate the definition of "total war," it appears that this call for civilian mobilization combined with evidence of genocidal attacks—massacres and the willingness to treat women and children as combatants or targets of an extermination policy—clearly constitutes total war by any definition. However, the question of genocide, a term that does not enter the lexicon until after WWII, is more difficult to answer; there is no clear evidence that total extermination of all the men, women, and children of a people was ever made policy by any recognized government or tribe in the borderlands during the 1860s. Neely, *"Was the Civil War a Total War?"* 434–58. See also Dwyer and Ryan, *Theatres of Violence:* 128–29.

70. Carleton to Goodwin, Apr. 20, 1864, Doolittle, *Condition of the Indian Tribes*, 179.

71. The $100,000 Indian War Fund was authorized Jan. 1, 1865. *Santa Fe Weekly Gazette*, Feb. 11, 1865. Military Storekeeper William R. Shoemaker offered New Mexicans 2,390 surplus French muskets at auction on Sept. 12, 1864. Fisher, *The Western Territories*, 96.

72. Anglo soldiers in the borderlands commonly referred to native people as "Lo, the poor Indian" or simply, "Lo," a reference to the popular Alexander Pope poem, "An Essay on Man" (1734), sympathetic to the plight of Indians ("*Lo!*

The poor Indian, whose untutored mind sees God in clouds, or hears him in the wind.") and Horace Greeley's satirical response, "Lo, the Poor Indian," in *New York to San Francisco, in the Summer of 1859.*

73. San Francisco *Evening Bulletin,* Mar. 11, 1863. The author of this letter is most likely Manson A. Mesenheimer, a saddler in Company B, Second California Cavalry. See also "Dispatches from the California Volunteers," soldiers' letters home published in the *San Francisco Daily Alta California* in Masich, *Civil War in Arizona,* 143–331; Colorado Volunteers expressed similar sentiments: "We would rather go under fighting Sesech in the States than fighting Indians on the plains for they are the worst of the two." Jesse S. Haire Journals, Jan. 18, 1865, Ohio Historical Society. Citing more than one hundred "murders" since the initial withdrawal of federal troops, James Newcomb, a civilian interpreter traveling with the California Column, confessed that, "I am an advocate for the extermination of the Apaches." *San Francisco Alta California,* Aug. 10, 1862.

74. Carleton to Lorenzo Thomas, AG, USA, Washington, Apr. 17, 1864, *OR* 34(3):200; Martin Saiz *v.* Navajo, Case 2597, RG 123, NARA. See also Michno, *Encyclopedia of Indian Wars,* 367–68; Kuhn, *Chronicles of War,* 319, 331, 335. Though the actual numbers cannot be known, many more members of the indigenous Apachean and other borderlands tribes considered "hostile" died of starvation or disease while on the run or in captivity during this same period, 1861–67.

75. Chiricahuas believed their fourteen-year-old boys were "as well trained and dangerous as a soldier." Opler and Hoijer, "Raid and War-Path Language," 618.

76. Goodwin, *Western Apache Raiding,* 15; Kaut, "Western Apache Clan and Phratry Organization," 63–64.

77. Orton, *California Men,* 72; McCleave, "Our Scout to Black Canyon," 20; Morris, *Address Delivered Before the Society of California Volunteers,* 34; Goodwin, *Western Apache Raiding,* 84.

78. Cremony, *Life Among the Apaches,* 164.

79. Capt. Cremony attributed Capt. Roberts's success at the Apache Pass battle to the effective use of his mountain howitzer battery. Ibid., 160.

80. Walker, "Freighting from Guaymas to Tucson, 1850–1880," 291–304; Altshuler, "Military Administration in Arizona, 1854–1865," 215–38. See also Miller, *Military Supply in the Southwest, 1861–1865.*

81. Carleton to Roberts, Dec. 19, 1861, *OR* 50(1):773; Post Returns, Tubac, Ariz. Terr., June 1865, reel 1297, M1652, RG 393 NARA; Report of W. S. R. Taylor, Sept. 19, 1863, *OR* 50(1):237. Report of Nelson H. Davis, acting inspector general, Dept. of New Mexico, Feb. 1865, Office of the Inspector General, Extracts of Inspection Reports, 1864–65, RG 156, NARA, 575–76. Carleton to Drum, June 18, 1862, *OR* 50(1):1146–47. C. E. Bennett to Greene, July 6, 1865, *OR* 50(1):418. J. L. Merriam to J. Green, June 10, 1865, Regimental Letter Book, First California Cavalry, Co. L, RG 94, NARA. Cremony, *Life Among the Apaches,* 164; W. A. Thompson to West, July 18, 1862, *OR* 50(2):26–27.

82. Fergusson to T. T. Tidball, May 2, 1863, *OR* 50(2):422–23.

83. GO 3, Feb. 24, 1864, HQ Dept. of New Mexico, Santa Fe, Doolittle, *Condition of the Indian Tribes,* 249.

84. McClelland had worked at the Cerro Colorado Mine south of Tucson until Apache raiders forced the workers to take refuge in Tucson. On September 16, 1861, he wrote to his mother, "I do not believe I was born to be shot by an Indian." Tom McClelland to James McClelland, Mar. 11, 1863. McClelland Papers, Senator John Heinz History Center, Pittsburgh.

85. GO 8, May 12, 1863, Tucson, *OR* 50(2):432–33; Orton, *California Men*, 671; *San Francisco Daily Alta California*, Sept. 11, 1863; *Los Angeles Star*, Aug. 30, 1864; Carleton to West, May 30, 1863, *Condition of the Indian Tribes*, 111. Others followed Tidball's example during the war years, and as late as 1871, men who had accompanied Tidball instigated the infamous Camp Grant Massacre. Their route, method of attack, and results were almost identical; the main difference was that, in 1871, Chief Eskiminzin's Aravaipa Apaches had surrendered to the officer commanding Camp Grant and supposedly enjoyed his protection. For precedent of the Tidball attack for the Camp Grant Massacre, see Juan Elias *v.* Apache, Case 7550, RG 205, NARA.

86. Carleton to Lorenzo Thomas, Apr. 24, 1864, *OR* 50(2):826; Bowie to Carleton, Apr. 15, 1864, ibid., 826–27; James H. Whitlock to Capt. C. A. Smith, Apr. 13, 1864, ibid., 827–29.

87. Capt. Julius Shaw to Maj. E. W. Eaton, First New Mexico Cavalry, July 14, 1864, *OR* 50(1):370–73, 377.

88. Rigg to Cutler, Sept 14, 1864, *OR* 50(1):368; Report of Capt. Julius Shaw to Maj. E. W. Eaton, First New Mexico Cavalry, July 14, 1864, ibid., 370–77.

89. For an excellent account of this expedition see Meketa and Meketa, *One Blanket*, 50–58. Corporal Alexander Bowman, Fifth Infantry, CV, reported in his diary a similar ambush on Apaches intent on butchering dead horses left behind as bait at a soldier camp: "a Squad concealed in the brush, six Indians came in camp soon after the com left to devour their game, the men raised up & let them have a volley killing one & wounding others, they escaped, the men brought in one scalp, gun &c, we marched down the river the Indians followed us on the opposite side of the River on the Table land, making all kind of jesters [gestures]." Bowman, Diary, Nov. 5, 1863.

90. *Arizona Enterprise*, June 13, 1891; Capt. H. M. Calderwood to J. F. Calderwood, June 27, 1865, in *Dutch Flat Enquirer*, Aug. 12, 1865. The killings, especially the braining of the children (girls aged three and five), at Saavedra's ranch outraged both soldiers and civilians in Arizona. Farish, *History of Arizona*, 6:130–31; Sweeney, *Firsthand Accounts*, 84n13. After Mangas Coloradas's death in 1863 at the hands of the California Volunteers, Cochise became the most aggressive Apache leader and the most pursued by the army. See Report of Lt. Col. C. E Bennett, July 6, 1865, *OR* 50(1):415–19.

91. *Santa Fe Gazette*, Dec. 17, 1864.

92. Gorman reported that his thirty-three-man force routed about sixty Chokonens eighteen miles from Fort Bowie. For Gorman's report and more on the career of Merejildo Grijalva, see Sweeney, *Firsthand Accounts*, 94–97. For Grijalva's escape from Cochise with the help of James Tevis, Overland Mail employee and later Confederate lieutenant, and subsequent partnership with Apache agent Michael Steck, see Tevis, *Arizona in the '50s*, 168–69.

93. Walnut Grove Gold Mining Company *v.* Apaches, Case 4715 and Case 7397, RG 123, NARA.

94. Morris, *Address Delivered Before the Society of California Volunteers,* 34; Utley, *Frontiersmen in Blue,* 259.
95. A soldier in the Seventh California Infantry's Co. E wrote that his unit stopped to admire the Spanish mission San Xavier, "the inside of which beggars all description. It contains some fine paintings and some of the most beautiful plaster statues I have ever seen." *Calaveras* (Calif.) *Chronicle,* July 1, 1865; Bailey, "Thomas Varker Keam," 15–19.
96. Martin Saiz *v.* Navajo, Case 2597, RG 123, NARA. *U.S. Army, Chronological List of Actions; Arizona Superintendency and New Mexico Superintendency, 1861–1866.* More than 300,000 sheep and goats were reported stolen between 1861 and 1866. *Annual Report of the Commissioner of Indian Affairs, 1861, 1862, 1863, 1864, 1865, 1866, 1867;* Records of the U.S. Court of Claims, Indian Depredation Case Records, RG 123, NARA; Evidence Concerning Depredation Claims, RG 75, NARA. See also Michno, *Encyclopedia,* 83–189, 367–68.
97. Evidence Concerning Depredation Claims, RG 75, NARA; *U.S. Army, Chronological List of Actions;* Adjutant Generals Reports, 1861–66. See also evidence from Catholic Church burial records, which clearly show that Apache attacks were more likely to result in death, especially among "non-combatants," Brugge, *Navajos in Catholic Church Records,* 149–52.
98. Opler, *Apache Life-way,* 334.
99. Goodwin, *Western Apache Raiding,* 16, 284–85.
100. Opler, *Apache Life-way,* 338.
101. Ibid., 340–45.
102. Jacoby, *Shadows at Dawn,* 84; Record, *Big Sycamore Stands Alone,* 124, 203.
103. Ventura Curriel *v.* Apache, Case 6843, Reply to Defendant's Brief, RG 205, NARA.
104. *San Francisco Daily Alta California,* Sept. 11, 1863; David Fergusson to T. T. Tidball, May 2, 1863, *OR* 50(2):422–23; Sweeney, *Mangas Coloradas,* 261. It was widely rumored during the late 1850s and early 1860s that the Mexican government had placed a bounty of five thousand pesos on the scalp of Mangas Coloradas. For a firsthand account of borderlands scalp hunting see Chamberlain, *My Confession.* Arizona Territory authorized scalp hunting in 1865, see Record, *Big Sycamore Stands Alone,* 319 n156. Hispanos took other body parts as evidence or trophies, see Santiago, *Jar of Severed Hands,* 7, 81–86, 162–65; Officer, *Hispanic Arizona,* 308–9.
105. All present agreed that scalping was common practice but admitted that this sort of mutilation was not considered appropriate behavior. In this instance the perpetrator, Francisco Sena, was reprimanded by the priest and later attempted to deny the mutilation, beyond taking the scalp. See the testimony of witnesses in Miguel Gonzales y Baca *v.* Navajo, Case 6564, RG 123, NARA. In a stock raid at the foot of the Picacho Mountains near Mesilla in 1861, one boy and one "old man" herder were killed and an eleven-year-old was captured. Jose Trujillo y Baca *v.* Navajo, Case 4083, RG 123, NARA. Vicente Lujan's 1862 depredation claim provides a case study in tracking Navajo raiders, pointing out that the raiders almost always had the advantage because they did not have to stop at dark, while the trackers did, and, therefore, outdistanced their pursuers. Vicente Lujan *v.* Navajos, Case 5456, RG 123, NARA.

106. Goodwin, *Western Apache Raiding*, 84, 276–78, Apache warriors might discard a scalp before returning home if they had lost comrades to the enemy, believing the cost to the war party had been too high to allow rejoicing. Some Chiricahua Apache bands may not have practiced scalping or did so only rarely. Opler, *Apache Life-way*, 349–50. For comparison to similar Plains Indian traditions related to scalp dances see Halaas and Masich, *Halfbreed*, 179, 185–86, 216. Pueblo Indians also scalped their Apachean enemies. See, for example, Ramon Medina *v.* Navajo, Case 993, RG 123, NARA.

107. In this case, the claimant's attorneys made the point that "killing by Indians was incident, not object, whilst as against the Indians both Mexicans and soldiers made personal slaughter the object." Lorenzo Labadie *v.* Navajo, Case 3252, 5–9, RG 123, NARA; Stanley, *The Civil War in New Mexico*, 387–94.

108. The increase in violence beginning in 1861 caused many non-Indians, even those in Indian Affairs, to believe the Apaches and Navajos were combining for a "war of extermination" aimed at the "white race." This thinking allowed martial men to rationalize preemptive attacks and exterminationist sentiment. J. F. Collins to W. P. Dole, Oct. 8, 1861, in *Annual Report of the Commissioner of Indian Affairs 1861*, 733.

109. Depredation Claims indicate that raids by mountain tribes were more likely to occur in the months of February and March. The warriors of the Plains became more active in the spring and summer when their ponies were well fed. See Depredation Case Files, RG 123, NARA.

110. For a description of the bayonet charge (a rare occurrence) and other details of the battle of Apache Pass, see Sgt. Albert J. Fountain's reminiscence: *Rio Grande Republican*, Jan. 2, 1891. For more on the battle and career of Fountain, see Fountain, *The Life and Death of Colonel Albert Jennings Fountain*.

111. When Apache raids shut down the southern Overland Mail, California Volunteer troops established a vedette service of mounted couriers. GO 11, July 21, 1862, *OR* 50(1):92. Written communications allowed coordinated attacks from the U.S. territories and the Mexican states of Sonora and Chihuahua, Carleton to Gov. Ignacio Pesqueira, Apr. 20, 1864, Doolittle, *Condition of the Indian Tribes*, 177. Mounted warriors of the mountainous Southwest and southern plains signaled basic information (e.g., "enemies coming") by riding their horses back and forth in patterns that could be discerned at great distances. Blankets were also waved for long-distance signaling of simple communications. Allied tribes could understand these generally recognized signals just as sign language and stylized drawing (e.g., tipi liners and ledger books) were comprehensible to Indian peoples of different linguistic traditions. George Bent to George Hyde, Dec. 11, 1905, Coe Collection, Beineke Library, Yale.

112. Navajos ran off a herd of twenty-four oxen near Fort Craig on January 20, 1863. The raiders cut the hamstrings of several fat oxen in hope the Hispano teamsters pursuing them would give up the chase and stop to butcher the wounded animals. Estanislao Montoya *v.* Navajos, Case 1593, RG 123, NARA.

113. See Cordova's testimony regarding a June 1862 stock raid in Socorro Co. in Julian Torres *v.* Navajos, Case 5455, RG 123, NARA.

114. Evidence Concerning Depredation Claims, NARA, RG 123, see, for example, Martin Saiz & Son *v.* Navajo, Case 2597; Lorenzo Labadie *v.* Navajo, Case 3529; Juan Elias *v.* Apache, Case 7550; Diego Montoya *v.* Navajo, Case 5954 and Juan Cristobal Armijo *v.* Navajo, Case 447; also NARA, RG 75 Evidence Concerning Depredation Claims, Lorenzo Otero *v.* Navajo, Claim 4048; Opler, *Apache Life-way*, 345; Goodwin, *Western Apache Raiding*, 67.

115. Approximately 60,000 Indians of all tribes and conditions could call Arizona and New Mexico home in 1860. Hispanos accounted for about 80,000 inhabitants. Anglos, including soldiers, only added another 2,000 to the total. *U.S. Eighth Census* (1860), 596–98 and *U.S. Ninth Census* (1870), xii, xvii.

116. Tucson rancher Juan Elias lost stock to Apache raids in 1858 and 1871, but during the 1860s he suffered six devastating raids that peaked in frequency and violence in 1863. Juan Elías *v.* Apache, Case 7550, RG 205, NARA.

117. For examples of increased raiding and violent attacks as a result of Hispanos serving in the militia or volunteer force during the Confederate invasion in New Mexico, see Mariano Pino *v.* Navajo, Claim 6141; Pilar Cordova *v.* Navajo, Claim 5620; Lorenzo Otero *v.* Navajo, Claim 4048, RG 75, NARA; Juan Cristobal Armijo *v.* Navajo, Claim 4193, RG 75 and Case 447, RG 123, NARA; Rafael Chavez *v.* Navajo, Case 4097 and Case 3044; Tomas Montoya *v.* Apache, Case 4101, RG 123, NARA. In Arizona see Juan Elias *v.* Apache, Case 7550; Charles Poston *v.* Apache, Case 6845, RG 123, NARA, and Abraham Peoples *v.* Mimbres Apache, Claim 5216, RG 75 and Case 6253, RG 123, NARA. See also Opler, *Apache Life-way*, 343–45. Reports of raids and warfare in Arizona and New Mexico during the 1860s are more than twice as numerous as in the decade preceding or following. Kuhn, *Chronicle of War*, 73–161.

118. Pedro Padilla *v.* Navajo and Apache, Case 5957, RG 123, NARA.

119. An older boy herder had been killed the day Montolla was taken. Young Montolla finally found a way to escape "Navajo country" and returned home three years later, though his patron never thought him mentally competent after his ordeal. See Montolla's testimony in Victoria Gonzales de Candelario *v.* Navajos, Case 5421, RG 123, NARA. Sheep dogs were valued at $25. Manuel Barela *v.* Navajos, Case 4109, RG 123, NARA.

120. Felix Tafoya *v.* Apache and Navajo, Case 5958, RG 123, NARA.

121. Rafael Chávez *v.* Navajo, Case 4097, RG 123, NARA; Julian Aragón *v.* Navajo, Claim 1408, RG 75 and Case 2391, RG 123, NARA.

122. Baylor to J. B. Magruder, Dec. 29, 1862, *OR* 15:914–15.

123. José Chávez y Gallegos *v.* Navajos, Claim 6149, RG 75 and Case 7549, RG 123, NARA.

124. Miguela Chaves de Lucero *v.* Navajos, Case 396, RG 123, NARA. Jose Gallegos testified that he knew the Navajos who took stock from Sabinal in Socorro County in November and December 1861. See Victoriana Padilla *v.* Navajos, Case 3962, RG 123, NARA.

125. Augustín Montoya (a.k.a. Montalla) *v.* Apaches, Case 1530, RG 123, NARA. Some Hispano New Mexican depredation claimants were not aware there had been a nationwide Civil War and, when being deposed, could not say what year the war had ended or when Lincoln had been assassinated.

126. See Juan Manuel Lucero testimony in Nestor Armijo *v.* Navajo, Case 425, RG 123, NARA.

127. Incredibly, teamster Luis Torres survived this attack. See his testimony in Jose Trujillo y Baca *v.* Apaches, Case 408, RG 123, NARA.

128. Orton, *California Men*, 2–14; Morris, "Combats With Indians of Arizona and New Mexico," 1–2, 7–21. At the beginning of the Civil War, the entire regular army of the United States did not exceed 15,000 men. From 1861–66, California, New Mexico, and Arizona mustered more than 21,000 soldiers for service in the Far West. During this time, the number of armed confrontations between military units and Indians increased by a factor of ten.

129. Morris, *Address Delivered Before the Society of California Volunteers*, 25–34; *San Francisco Daily Alta California*, July 4, 1864 and May 6, 1866.

130. See *Decreto, Palacio de México*, Nov. 7, 1864, AGN, *Segundo Imperio, caja*, 44 in Duncan, "Political Legitimation and Maximilian's Second Empire in Mexico, 1864–67," 43–44. Bailey, *A Diplomatic History*, 350–51. For descriptions of uniforms, see Chartrand and Hook, *The Mexican Adventure*, 23–38.

131. Chartrand and Hook, *The Mexican Adventure*, 8–9, 14–18. For additional detail on Republican Army order of battle and arms and equipage, see de León Toral, et al., *El ejército Mexicano*, 216–53.

132. French, Spanish, and British warships anchored at Veracruz to collect on loans incurred by Antonio López de Santa Anna and other past presidents, but Juárez's beleaguered government could not pay the bill. Although the liberal Juárez had been duly elected president in 1861, Mexico's conservative landed aristocracy, backed by Napoleon III, installed Maximilian as emperor of Imperial Mexico in 1864. Anderson and Cayton, *Dominion of War*, 305–7. Brinckerhoff, "Last of the Lancers," 6–7; and Prezelski, "Lives of the Californio Lancers," 29–52.

133. Paragraph 1642, *Revised U.S. Army Regulations of 1861*, 496; *San Francisco Evening Bulletin*, July 8, 1865.

134. Carleton to Pesqueira, May 2, 1862, *OR* 50(1):1044–45. In April 1857, during the Reform War, Henry A. Crabb's force of American filibusters was defeated by Ignacio Pesqueira's militia, which included O'odham warriors. Pesqueira had initially invited the Americans to settle in northern Sonora, to help the fight his political enemies, but before Crabb's expedition arrived in Sonora, Pesqueira defeated the federal troops and took control of the state. When the Crabb party arrived, Pesqueira ordered his men to attack the invaders. Over the course of eight days, from April 1 to April 8, about 25 Americans and a reported 200 Mexicans and O'odham people were killed in battle, at the end of which some 55 captured filibusters, including Crabb, were executed by firing squad. In honor of the victory, in April 1948 the city officially changed its name to Heróica Caborca. Hunt, *Army of the Pacific*, 58.

135. Carleton, Report 2, May 25, 1862, *OR* 50(1):89; Carleton to Pesqueira, May 2, 1862, ibid., 1044–45; Wright to Pesqueira, May 3, 1862, ibid., 1047–48.

136. Bancroft, et al., *History of the North Mexican States*, 696–97; Davis to Carleton, Mar. 2, 1864, *OR* 34(2):593.

137. Miller, "Californians against the Emperor," 193–214; Davis to Carleton, Mar. 2, 1864, *OR* 34(2):593. See also Acuña, "Ignacio Pesqueira: Sonoran Caudillo," 159–60.

138. Wright to Col. E. D. Townsend, AAG, HQ of the Army, Mar. 14, 1864, *OR* 50(2):788–89.

139. Carleton to Halleck, Mar. 13, 1864, *OR* 34(2):591–92; Carleton to Coult, May 10, 1864, *OR* 50(2):842; Carleton to Halleck, Mar. 13, 1864, *OR* 34(2):591–92; Carleton to Coult, May 10, 1864, *OR* 50(2):842; Porter, *Campaigning with Grant*, 256. The army officers assigned to guard the border received mixed signals from the East regarding the official U.S. attitude toward the French occupation of Mexico. Andrew Johnson, Lincoln's vice presidential running mate during the election of 1864, warned Napoleon in an impassioned public address: "You cannot found a monarchy on this continent." Bailey, *A Diplomatic History*, 353.

140. Pico was the nephew of Andrés Pico and may have accompanied his famous uncle at the battle of San Pasqual in 1846. The younger Pico was famous for his horsemanship. *San Francisco Alta California*, Oct. 7 and Nov. 2, 1860; *San Francisco Bulletin*, Oct. 23, 1865.

141. *San Francisco Bulletin*, Oct. 20, 1865; Orton, *California Men*, 5. See also Duncan, "Political Legitimation," 64–66.

142. *San Francisco Bulletin*, Oct. 20 and 23, 1865; Prezelski, "California Lancers," 43–45.

143. Sturtevant, *Handbook of North American Indians*, 10:320–21; Spicer, *Cycles of Conquest*, 103–5; Bancroft et al., *History of the North Mexican States*, 697.

144. Brinckerhoff, "Last of the Lancers," 11–12. Cremony claims that he had encouraged Morales to shelter near the border crossing so that California Native Battalion lancers might support him in the event of such an attack. In this scenario, the pursuit of Tánori by the Californios was part of a plan to force a showdown with the Imperialists. Cremony took credit for the capture of Santa Cruz and driving the Franco-Mexican Imperialists from northern Mexico, which "emboldened [Morales and] other leaders, and animated the people generally," allowing Pesqueira's return and beginning the collapse of Maximilian's empire. Cremony, "How and Why We Took Santa Cruz," 335–40.

145. Not all the Yaquis sided with the French; Cajemé (a.k.a. José María Bonifacio Leiva Perez), the best known of the Yaqui military leaders, sided with Pesqueira and the Juaristas. At Pesqueira's direction Garcia Morales led a successful campaign against the Yaquis in 1868, interning captives in a church at Cócorit. When surrender negotiations broke down, Morales's artillery blasted the church, and in the ensuing fire 120 people died. The massacre convinced other Yaqui holdouts to sue for peace. Spicer, *Cycles of Conquest*, 61–67.

146. Orton, *California Men*, 763–65; SO 12, Jan. 31, 1864, Hdqrs. Tucson, Commands of J. R. West, RG 393, NARA; Fergusson to J. F. Bennett, Apr. 14, 1863, *OR* 50(2):396–97; Hunt, *Army of the Pacific*, 143; *Calaveras (Calif.) Chronicle*, Aug. 12, 1865; *San Francisco Bulletin*, July 18, 1865.

147. Though the elusive ex-Confederate "Col. Leaton" was never captured, Lieutenant Orton's aggressive campaigning won him his captaincy. Orton, *California Men*, 76. Not only deserters made their way across the border. More than two hundred former California Volunteers offered their services to Juárez's government. Miller, "Californians against the Emperor," 193, 212.

148. Carleton to E. D. Townsend, AG, Aug. 14, 1865, *OR* 48(2):1182–83.
149. A. S. Viesca to the Inhabitants of Moncolva and Rio Grande, Aug. 13, 1865, *Message of the President of the United States, of March 20, 1866, Relating to the Condition of Affairs in Mexico, in Answer to a Resolution of the House of December 11, 1865*, 331–32; G. Weitzel to Tomás Mejía, Dec. 4, 1865, ibid., 353. See also Miller, *Arms Across the Border*, 6–7.
150. Bazaine's marriage to "Pepita" de la Peña y Azcárate took place June 26, 1865. The general's first wife had committed suicide in 1863. Maximilian thought the Frenchman "perfectly infatuated and in love like a ninny," though the emperor may have seen positive political implications for the marriage of the star-crossed lovers in civil-war-divided Mexico. McAllen, *Maximilian and Carlota*, 188.
151. Custer and others sought commissions in Mexico. Utley, *Cavalier in Buckskin*, 39.
152. Approximately 180,000 black soldiers served in the United States Colored Troops (USCT) during the Civil War. The 23rd Infantry, USCT, suffered the heaviest losses of any unit engaged in the disastrous Battle of the Crater at Petersburg, Virginia, on July 30, 1864. African American troops captured by the Confederates ran the risk of execution or enslavement. After Appomattox, the 23rd USCT was assigned to the 3rd Brigade, 1st Division of the XXV Corps in the Department of Texas. The three men referred to may have been James McElrath, Bartley Quinn, and James Smith. *Message of the President of the United States, of March 20, 1866, Relating to the Condition of Affairs in Mexico*; Tomás Mejía to G. Weitzel, Dec. 1, 1865, ibid., 351; G. Weitzel to Tomás Mejía, Dec. 4, 1865, ibid., 353. See also Ridley, *Maximilian and Juárez*, 223. Though the use of black troops was still controversial due to the endemic racism in the army and general population, in 1866 the War Department authorized four regular black regiments: 9th and 10th Cavalry and 24th and 25th Infantry, which eventually became known as the "Buffalo Soldiers." See Leckie, *Buffalo Soldiers*, passim.
153. After more than thirty years in the service, Bazaine achieved the rank of Marshal of France in 1864, an extraordinary feat considering he had enlisted as a legionnaire and, by dint of hard work and personal bravery, had risen through the ranks. Napoleon devised a three-phase pull-out over the course of a year. Bazaine oversaw the departure of the last troop transport in March 1867.
154. Only four months earlier, Bazaine had married a Mexican (17-year-old Josefa de la Peña y Azcárate) and redoubled his determination to defeat Juárez's government—it is not certain whether Napoleon, who already contemplated his Mexican exit strategy, approved of the drastic measures of the Black Decree, but Maximilian himself said that Bazaine had dictated portions of it. Basch, *Recollections of Mexico*, 260.
155. *El Diario del Imperio*. Oct. 3, 1865, 1–4. The decree was originally published in several forms—in both Spanish and Nahuatl. Centro de Estudios de Historia de México CARSO. Some historians believe that the Black Decree was not an act of desperation, but rather a calculated policy to end the civil war. See Neely, *Limits of Destruction*, 72–89.

156. For a full text transcription of the Ley de 3 Octubre 1865, a.k.a. "Bando Negro" and "Decreto Negro" ("Black Decree"), see http://www.bibliojuridica.org/libros/4/1669/6.pdf, 246–50.
157. *San Francisco Alta California*, Dec. 29, 1865.

Chapter 5

1. By the end of the Civil War, the U.S. government officially named the four-year conflict as the "War of the Rebellion," though it was referred to then, and still is today, by other names depending on one's cultural and geographical perspective: War Between the States, War of Northern Aggression, War for Southern Independence, Second American Revolution, Freedom War, and War of Secession. President Andrew Johnson finally declared the Rebellion to be at an end on August 20, 1866. After Texas established a new state government, he proclaimed: "The insurrection in the State of Texas has been completely and everywhere suppressed and ended, and the authority of the United States has been successfully and completely established . . . the said insurrection is at an end and that peace, order, tranquility, and civil authority now exist in and throughout the whole United States of America." Presidential Proclamation, August 20, 1866, Acts of the Thirty-Ninth Congress, Sanger, *Treaties and Proclamations*, 814–17.
2. Hämäläinen, *Comanche Empire*, 315. Maximilian's personal physician and confidant reported in 1868, "The Union Government of the United States, which had been victorious against the Secessionists, wanted to settle accounts with the French Emperor because of his support of the South. The tough notes of the Washington Government were effective and successful. Caesar (Napoleon III) apparently did not feel strong enough to pick a fight with the American colossus and eagerly avoided any possible conflict." Basch, *Recollections of Mexico*, 14.
3. M. Escobedo to I. Mariscal, Dec. 1, 1865 and M. Saavedra to I. Mariscal, Dec. 8, 1865, *Message of the President of the United States, of March 20, 1866, Relating to the Condition of Affairs in Mexico*, 354–55. Damp gunpowder would not ignite when showered with sparks from a flintlock, hence the admonition to "keep your powder dry."
4. José Maria Arteaga to Señor Marshal, HQ Tacámbaro de Codallos. Apr. 24, 1865, ibid., 396–97; José Maria Patoni to Pesqueira, HQ, Fuerte, ibid., 371.
5. *San Francisco Alta California*. July 26 and Aug. 7, 1867.
6. On April 4, 1864, the U.S. Congress unanimously passed a resolution that opposed the establishment of the Mexican monarchy. On February 12, 1866, in accordance with the Monroe Doctrine, the U.S. asked the French to withdraw their forces from Mexico. At the same time, General U. S. Grant moved soldiers to positions along the Rio Grande and ordered a naval blockade to prevent French reinforcements from landing. The U.S. officially protested to Austria about its troops in Mexico on May 6. Choosing Franco-American relations over his Mexican monarchy ambitions, Napoleon III announced the withdrawal of French forces beginning May 31. Taking advantage of the end of French military support to the Imperial troops, the Republicans won a series of victories and by July had occupied Chihuahua, taken Guadalajara, and captured Matamoros, Tampico and Acapulco. Napoleon urged Maxi-

milian to abandon Mexico and evacuate with the French troops. The French evacuated Monterrey on July 26, Saltillo on August 5, and the whole state of Sonora in September. Maximilian's French cabinet members resigned on September 18. The Republicans defeated Imperial troops in the Battle of Miahuatlán in Oaxaca in October, occupying the whole of Oaxaca in November, as well as parts of Zacatecas, San Luis Potosí, and Guanajuato. The French evacuated Mexico City on February 5, 1867. On February 13, Maximilian withdrew north to Querétaro. The Republicans began a siege of the city on March 9, and Mexico City on April 12. An Imperial sortie from Querétaro failed on April 27. On May 11, Maximilian resolved to attempt an escape through the enemy lines but was apprehended before he could carry out this plan. On May 15, following a court-martial, he was sentenced to death. Many of the crowned heads of Europe and other prominent figures sent telegrams and letters to Mexico pleading for Maximilian's life to be spared, but Juárez refused to commute the sentence, believing that it was necessary to send a message that Mexico would not tolerate any government imposed by foreign powers. *San Francisco Alta California,* Aug. 26, 1867; "The Execution of Maximilian," *Boston Daily Advertiser,* July 6, 1867; "Mexico and the Mexicans," *New York Times,* July 26, 1867; "The Military Execution of Maximilian Confirmed," *Washington Daily National Intelligencer,* July 2, 1867.

7. Moreno, El sitio de Querétaro; *El Diario del Imperio,* Oct. 3, 1865: 1–4. See also Salm-Salm, *My Diary in Mexico*; Bailey, *A Diplomatic History,* 349–54.

8. This reconstruction of the scene at Cerro de las Campanas is based on eyewitness accounts and photographic evidence. The emperor received credible, but erroneous, news of his wife's death as the Empress pleaded with Napoleon and the Pope to intercede and save Maximilian's empire. This news according to Samuel Basch broke his will to live, "one less tie that binds me to life." Though the reports turned out to be unfounded, Maximilian confided to friends that he now welcomed death. *San Francisco Alta California,* May 18, 1867, July 8, 1867, July 26, 1867, Aug. 7, 1867; *New York Tribune,* June 28, 1867; Basch, *Recollections of Mexico,* 244–47. For photographs taken soon after the execution by François Aubert, Noriega, and Agustín Peraire see Elderfield, *Manet and the Execution of Emperor Maximilian,* 14, 83, 90, 98, 188, 190.

9. Stevenson, *A Woman's Reminiscences,* 274; Hanna and Hanna, *Napoleon III and Mexico,* 262–63.

10. There are several versions of Maximilian's last words. Prussian minister Baron Magnus, an eyewitness, is generally considered reliable, though the "men of my race" portion is not entirely consistent with Maximilian's egalitarianism and accounts left by others. *San Francisco Alta California,* July 26, 1867; Ridley, *Maximilian and Juárez* 277.

11. *San Francisco Alta California,* July 26, 1867; Basch, *Recollections of Mexico,* 244, 247, 250–54.

12. *San Francisco Alta California,* July 26, 1867. Dr. Basch's autopsy described in detail the six perforating bullet wounds in Maximilian's corpse. Maximilian's photographed shirt appears powder-charred, bullet-riddled, and visibly blood soaked. Six musket balls passed through it—three fatal shots

tore through his chest and three through his abdomen. Basch, *Recollections of Mexico*, 251.

13. Bailey, *A Diplomatic History*, 357. The embalming and organ mummification process took 8 days. For details regarding disposition of the body see Basch, *Recollections of Mexico*, 245–56.

14. *Littell's Living Age*, Jan.–March 1865, vol. 84, 472. See also Case, *French Opinion*, 327–30 and passim.

15. Art historians debate the significance of the symbolism, especially the Christian allusions (including Christ between the thieves and the halo-like sombrero of the martyred king), but all agree that Manet intended to expose Napoleon's Mexico propaganda for what it was. The painting is today considered one of Manet's masterworks, yet it was never exhibited in France during the artist's lifetime. Napoleon's ministers censored the painting and all lithographic reproductions, and the work was banned from exhibition in the prestigious salon in 1868 and 1869. *The Execution of Maximilian* was first exhibited in the United States nearly fifteen years after the event. In creating the piece, Manet struggled to obtain accurate newspaper and eyewitness accounts. He pored over Aubert's photographs of the Mexican firing squad and even enlisted the help of soldier models from a local French garrison to pose for him. Art historians have x-rayed the finished work and analyzed it in detail, determining that the artist revised the work four or more times. Wilson-Bareau, *Manet, The Execution of Maximilian*, 107. See also Murphy, "New Information," 288–89. Additional images of the firing squad and execution scene at Querétaro may be found at the Museo Nacional de las Intervenciones, Mexico City.

16. Acuña, *Sonoran Strongman*, 160; See correspondence from Martinez, Romero, Seward, and Garcia Morales, Military Operations of the Western Division reports, in *Message of the President of the United States, of January 29, 1867, Relating to the Present Condition of Mexico*.

17. For the best recent work on the reimagining of national borders overlaid on traditional peoples and the influence of race and ethnicity see Meeks, *Border Citizens*, 5–6 and passim; for the economic influences on lifeways in the Southwest, see Reséndez, *Changing National Identities at the Frontier*, 3–6, and Truett, *Fugitive Landscapes*, 7–9; for the impact of cultures of violence, see Blyth, *Chiricahuas and Janos*, 5–6. See also Adelman and Aron, "From Borderlands to Borders." For a fuller understanding of the evolution of the U.S.-Mexico border line, see St. John, *Line in the Sand*, 54–55 and passim.

18. Davis, "Pioneer Days in Arizona," 132–34; *San Francisco Alta California*, June 12, 1864. Throughout the 1860s the government sponsored many such goodwill tours including chiefs and headmen from some of the tribes most resistant to government diplomatic and coercion efforts, including Apaches, Comanches, Kiowas, and Cheyennes. Viola, *Diplomats in Buckskins*, 1–16.

19. For descriptions of Hualapai and Chemehuevi attacks on mail carriers and freighters resulting in the loss of horses and mules on the Mojave-to-Prescott road in 1866, see testimony of William Warford, David Burrow (who freighted out of Fort Yuma with former cameleer Hi Jolly), Lyman Smith, and Rosa Poindexter in William G. Poindexter *v.* Hualapai and Chemehuevi, Case 2271, RG 123, NARA.

20. Tuttle, "River Colorado," 60–61; Davis, "Pioneer Days in Arizona," 52. "Johnny" Moss, "the mining Kit Carson," discovered gold and started a rush to El Dorado Canyon on the Colorado River in 1861. Lingenfelter, *Steamboats on the Colorado*, 32–33.

21. Davis, "Pioneer Days in Arizona," 78–81.

22. GO 4, Feb. 18, 1865, Hdqrs. Dept. of New Mexico, *OR* 48(1):909; Browne, *Adventures in the Apache Country*, 29; *San Francisco Daily Alta California*, July 4, 1864 and Apr. 5, 1865; Col. James F. Curtis to Capt. Charles Atchison, Feb. 22, 1865, *OR* 50(2):1152.

23. Bushnell, Diary, Dec. 11, 1865. Antoine-Henri Jomini (1779–1869) served as a general in the French and later in the Russian service and was one of the nineteenth century's most influential writers on the Napoleonic art of war. His theories were taught at West Point prior to the Civil War, and some military historians consider him the father of modern strategy.

24. Calloway, *Pen and Ink Witchcraft*, 206.

25. Grinnell, *Cheyenne Indians*, 2:48–78.

26. For Cheyenne marital customs and war, see Halaas and Masich, *Halfbreed*, 210–12. For an Apache example of the relationship between war and marriage, see Blyth, *Chiricahua and Janos*, 79–80.

27. In addition to those listed, the Northern Cheyennes included the powerful Crazy Dogs among their warrior societies. Grinnell, *Cheyenne Indians*, 2:48, 124; Hyde, *Life of George Bent*, 200–201, 213, 296; Halaas and Masich, *Halfbreed*, 32. See also Afton, Halaas, and Masich, *Cheyenne Dog Soldiers*, passim; Hämäläinen, *Comanche Empire*, 11, 71, 314–16.

28. Teamster Elias Trujillo testified that the Plains warriors had made positive assurances that the "Mexicans" would not be harmed, implying that they were at war only with the "Americans." Adolph Guttmann *v.* Comanche, Kiowa, and Arapaho, Case 1898, RG 123, NARA. See also Louise Barry, "The Ranch at Cow Creek Crossing," 416–44.

29. Dr. Steck arrived in the territory as an army doctor in 1849 and served as agent for a number of tribes before being appointed superintendent for New Mexico on Jan. 22, 1864. Carleton to Michael Steck, Oct. 29, 1864, Doolittle, *Condition of the Indian Tribes*, 205–6; Carleton to Carson, Aug. 15, 1864, ibid., 190; Carleton confided in Brigadier General Marcellus Crocker, commanding at Fort Sumner, "If the Navajos had the spirit with reference to the Comanches which they ought to have toward their hereditary enemies, a war party of five hundred of the former could go out and get all the stock they wanted. It would add to the punishment which the Comanches deserve for their depredations and butcheries of this year." Carleton to Marcellus Crocker, Oct. 31, 1864, ibid., 209.

30. Otero and his partners were Hispano traders subcontracting with Anglo businessmen incorporated as Stewart, Slemmens & Co., which secured the government contract for supplying the New Mexico forts. See Otero's testimony and "Exhibit A" in Vicente A. Otero *v.* Kiowa and Comanche, Case 88, RG 123, NARA.

31. Haire, *Journals*, 45–47, 60–61, 91–97, Jan. 18, 19, 20, and 25, 1865.

32. The incident involving the Ute boy occurred on Sept. 16, 1864, about twenty miles west of Point of Rocks. Private Haire, Company D, First Colorado

Cavalry, expressed relief that his hotheaded comrades had not touched off a war with their Ute allies. Haire, *Journals,* Sept. 16, 1864.

33. Carleton to Lorenzo Thomas, AG, Mar. 12, 1864, Doolittle, *Condition of the Indian Tribes,* 168.

34. Pettis, *Kit Carson's Fight,* 5–6. Carson had married an Arapaho woman, Waa-Nibe ("Singing Grass"), and then a Cheyenne, "Making-Out-Road," in the 1840s, prior to marrying Josefa Jaramillo. Simmons, *Kit Carson and His Three Wives,* 35–36.

35. Carleton attempted to control trading with the Kiowas and Comanches by issuing passes and regulating the goods sold. After the Adobe Walls battle he stepped up efforts to suppress those trading powder, shot, and military intelligence with enemy warriors. GO 2, HQ Dept. of New Mexico, Jan. 31, 1865, Doolittle, *Condition of the Indian Tribes,* 268.

36. He knew that he risked losing the Apaches and Navajos then corralled at Bosque Redondo, but Carleton was so eager to defeat the Comanche and Kiowa raiders that he ordered both McCleave and Carson—his most trusted officers—on this expedition. Pettis, *Kit Carson's Fight,* 8–9; Orton, *California Men,* 75, 156.

37. The prairie carriage's axle was 16 inches wider than the version employed for packing the Model 1835 mountain howitzer; when towed the prairie carriage's track was 42.5 inches and the pack carriage was 30.2 inches. Still Pettis considered the prairie carriage to be too narrow and discovered that it was prone to tipping over in the tall grass and rough terrain of the southern plains. Pettis, *Kit Carson's Fight,* 18; *Ordnance Manual,* 74–75.

38. Carleton to James Blunt, Oct. 22, 1864, *OR* 41(1):939; Carleton to Carson, Oct. 23, 1864, *OR* 41(4):214; Pettis, *Kit Carson's Fight,* 9–10.

39. Carson, *Kit Carson's Autobiography,* 131–34; Dunlay, *Kit Carson and the Indians,* 138–40. The book discovered in the Apache camp was likely Charles Averill's *Kit Carson, Prince of the Gold Hunters,* published in 1849, the first of many novellas featuring Carson, ibid., 154, 181, 391–92, 455.

40. Pettis, *Kit Carson's Fight,* 14.

41. Ibid., 29; Col. Ford's sworn testimony, May 31, 1865, in *Condition of the Indian Tribes,* 64–65.

42. Pettis, *Kit Carson's Fight,* 40.

43. Carleton to Carson, Dec. 15, 1864, Doolittle, *Condition of the Indian Tribes,* 213–14. Too costly in terms of men and matériel, Carleton never mounted the second campaign. Pettis, *Kit Carson's Fight,* 32–36.

44. Eyewitnesses interviewed by the investigative committee headed by Senator James R. Doolittle in 1865 estimated the number of people in the Cheyenne/Arapaho village to be between 500 and 800. Robert Bent thought 600 to be the most accurate number. Recent research sponsored by the National Park Service at the Sand Creek National Historic site, which incorporates Cheyenne and Arapaho oral history and a reconstruction of the bands and families present at the time of the attack, puts the number at 750. Eighteen of the 33 chiefs present were killed as were 212 others—150 women, children, and elderly people and 62 men—along with some 200 wounded.

45. Though Carleton was desperately short of manpower as his Apache campaign ramped up in the summer of 1864, Colorado Governor Evans pressured him for troops to fight Indians, real and imagined. The Coloradan believed

Cheyennes and Arapahos threatened Denver itself. Carleton eventually dispatched some of Carson's men but lectured the panicked Evans on the folly of starting an unnecessary war and urged him to negotiate first. If war is unavoidable, he wrote, "it should be commenced because they have been the aggressors and are clearly in the wrong." Carleton to Evans, June 26, 1864, Doolittle, *Condition of the Indian Tribes,* 186.

46. John Smith sworn testimony, Jan. 16, 1865, Doolittle, *Condition of the Indian Tribes,* 60; Lt. C. M. Cossitt sworn testimony, ibid., 74; Robert Bent testimony, ibid., 95–96; Halaas and Masich, *Halfbreed,* 145–50.

47. Lt. Cramer sworn testimony, Doolittle, *Condition of the Indian Tribes,* 73–74; S. E. Brown sworn testimony, ibid., 71; Hyde, "Manuscript based on the letters of George Bent (working copy)," *George Bent Collection,* Western History Department, Denver Public Library. See also Roberts and Halaas, "Written in Blood," 22–32.

48. It is estimated that one hundred of the First Colorado men, including Captain Soule's company and Lieutenant Baldwin's battery, refused to participate in the butchery. Some of these men later provided damning testimony against Chivington and the Third Colorado men. Soule was murdered on the streets of Denver following his testimony. Haire, *Journals,* Nov. 28 and Dec. 1, 1864. Private Haire wrote dispassionately in his journal, "No quarters are given on either side fighting Indians." Ibid., Jan. 18, 1865. See also Milavec, "Jesse Haire," 1–7; Rein, "'Our First Duty,'" 217–38; Roberts and Halaas, "Written in Blood," 22–32. Massacres are not an aberration in human history. For insight into the psychology of massacre from both victim and perpetrator perspective, see Dwyer and Ryan, *Theatres of Violence,* xvi–xxii.

49. Robert Bent sworn testimony, Doolittle, *Condition of the Indian Tribes,* 95–96. The body parts and other trophies were exhibited at the Denver Theatre on three occasions. *Daily Rocky Mountain News* (Denver), Dec. 28, 29, and 30, 1864.

50. Jacob Downing sworn testimony, July 21, 1865, Doolittle, *Condition of the Indian Tribes,* 68–70.

51. Dunlay, *Kit Carson,* 391–93; Ellis, *The Life of Kit Carson,* 258–59. For graphic testimony of the Sand Creek Massacre see Wade, *Report on the Conduct of the War,* I–V and testimony in "Massacre of Cheyenne Indians"; Doolittle, "The Chivington Massacre," *Condition of the Indian Tribes,* 26–96; Capt. Silas Soule to Maj. Edward Wynkoop, Dec. 14, 1864 and Lt. Joseph Cramer to Wynkoop, Dec. 19, 1864, Colorado Historical Society; Halaas and Masich, *Halfbreed,* 147, 160. For the massacre and its aftermath, see also Kelman, *A Misplaced Massacre.*

52. Halaas and Masich, *Halfbreed,* 250–51; Pettis, *Kit Carson's Fight,* 41–42. See also eyewitness testimony recorded by the two Joint Special Committees of Congress in 1865: Wade's *Report of the Joint Committee on the Conduct of the War* (1865) and Doolittle's Joint Special Committee report, *The Condition of the Indian Tribes.* For convenient reference to these reports see Carroll, *The Sand Creek Massacre,* passim. Col. Patrick E. Connor, Third California Volunteer Infantry, commanding the District of Utah, assigned to protect the Overland Mail route and telegraph, attacked and defeated chief Bear Hunter's Shoshone encampment on the Bear River in southeastern Washington Territory (present Utah) on January 29, 1863. This battle, also considered by

many to be a massacre, resulted in 67 soldier casualties and at least 250 among the Indians, including more than 50 women and children. In the Bear River fight, well-armed Shoshone warriors mounted significant resistance from prepared defensive positions. Women and children were taken prisoner and, in some cases, provided with medical care. Snow and freezing temperatures worsened the horrors and death rates for both sides. This winter campaign had a profound impact on the Shoshones and was held up by many military men as a model worthy of emulation. Connor was promoted brigadier soon after the battle. *OR* 50(1):185–87; Hunt, *Army of the Pacific*, 194–96; *San Francisco Alta California*, Feb. 19, 1863. In many ways, the Chivington massacre at Sand Creek is more similar to the Mountain Meadows Massacre of 1857. Both events were set in motion by territorial governors (Colorado Gov. John Evans and Utah Gov. Brigham Young) who fostered an environment of war hysteria and were supported by crusading lieutenants (John Chivington and John D. Lee) in the role of avenging angels intent on killing all—men, women, and children. The ambitious and zealous Chivington and Lee used their religious convictions to rationalize their actions. In both cases, the press and the nation were shocked and appalled by the massacres. This was not the case at Bear River. See Bagley, *Blood of the Prophets*, 84, 280, 298, 382; and Wetherington and Levine, *Battles and Massacres*, 113–34, 153–90.

53. Carleton to Steck, Nov. 8, 1864, Doolittle, *Condition of the Indian Tribes,* 210–11.

54. *Annual Report of the Commissioner of Indian Affairs 1861*:634–37; ibid., *1863*:5–6.

55. Carleton to Governor John Goodwin, Apr. 20, 1864, Doolittle, *Condition of the Indian Tribes,* 178. Prior to the Civil War, U.S. authorities recognized the strategic importance of maintaining friendly relations with the Pimas and Maricopas. George Bailey to C. E. Mix, Nov. 4, 1858, *Report of the Commissioner of Indian Affairs 1858,* 557.

56. Underhill, *First Arizona Volunteer Infantry,* 24, 35. The blue uniforms of the Company B Maricopas were trimmed in red while the Pimas of Company C wore blouses with blue trim. The Arizona Volunteers also drew sky blue wool trousers, which were worn as issued or were adapted for leggings, breech clouts, or other garments as preferred by the soldier. When supplies of shoes ran out, worn-out army brogan scraps were recycled and adapted as sandals.

57. Ibid., 3, 24, 27.

58. Ibid., 36, 50, 57; Prescott *Weekly Miner*, June 13, 1866.

59. Underhill, *First Arizona Volunteer Infantry,* 38. For a more nuanced interpretation of this fight and the confusion caused, in part, by the mixed motives of the members of the several tribes and bands involved, see Braatz, *Surviving Conquest,* 32, 105–6. Though army officers typically wrote identification letters for "friendly" Indians, Pauline Weaver and other sympathetic whites occasionally provided such safe conduct passes for Yavapais. Ibid., 88.

60. Underhill, *First Arizona Volunteer Infantry,* 58; Prescott *Weekly Miner*, April 25 and May 9, 1866.

61. In 1860 there had been only a few hundred non-Indian people in Central Arizona. *Arizona Territory Special U.S. Census,* 1864; Braatz, *Surviving Conquest,* 45–48.

62. D. Wooster, "Indian Affairs in California, Arizona and New Mexico," *San Francisco Alta California*, May 6, 1866. Dr. David Wooster advocated either feeding or exterminating the Indians in order to develop the territories. The doctor accompanied the California Column to Arizona in 1862 and later became one of California's most prominent physicians. This position predominated among educated Americans. Even Kit Carson and William Bent who believed the "Indian troubles" to be the fault of whites encroaching on Indian lands and rights believed that protective reservations and feeding at government expense were the only alternatives to extermination. See also Senator Doolittle's report, *Condition of the Indian Tribes*, 3–8 and passim.

63. Speaking for the Kiowas and Comanches at Medicine Lodge in 1867, Chief Satank said of the increased raiding and fighting during the Civil War, "We thought the Great Father would not be offended for the Texans had gone out from among his people, and became his enemies." Calloway, *Pen and Ink Witchcraft*, 206, 209.

64. Horsehead Crossing, some 75 miles from the New Mexico border and 250 miles from Fort Sumner, became a favorite place for attacking the Texas cattle herds. Some of the tribes and bands, then under treaty, admitting responsibility for these attacks were: Comanche—Qua-ha-das (Kwaha-das), Co-che-ta-kyas, Penne-tag-ka (Peatekas), Noconee (Nokonis)—and Kiowa—Lone Wolf, Satanta, Timber Mountain. When the chiefs gave their depositions for the Andy Adams depredation claim, Horse Back (Ter-yer-quoiss) of the Noconee appeared to be assigning blame to the Qua-ha-da band of Comanches; Kiowa chief Lone Wolf interjected, "Why not tell the whole story, as it was, as we were all in it." The total amount of the compensation paid from Comanche and Kiowa annuities was $107,560. Andy M. Adams *v.* Comanche and Kiowa, Case 7803, RG 123 and Claim 237, RG 75, NARA. See also Hämäläinen, *Comanche Empire*, 314.

65. Wilson detailed the Comanche attacks in his depredation claim. He noted that the warriors drove the stampeded cattle due east for 25 miles, then south for 25 miles, then—once they thought they were no longer being followed—turned the cattle westward toward the New Mexico settlements. Wm. J. Wilson *v.* Comanche, Claim 784 (24559), RG 75, NARA; Hunter, *Trail Drivers of Texas*, 904; Cox, *Record of the Cattle*, 306, 477.

66. Hämäläinen, *Comanche Empire*, 315.

67. Typical of the missions assigned the volunteer troops, Captain William Ffrench was ordered to destroy a ten-acre crop of Apache wheat spotted by scouts in Aravaipa Canyon north of Tucson. The fifteen soldiers dispatched on the raid were instructed to feed the wheat to their stock and destroy the rest to prevent the Indians from harvesting it. N. H. Davis to T. A. Coult, Commanding Tucson, June 5, 1864, *OR* 50(2):860–61; Stanley, *Civil War in New Mexico*, 367–85.

68. Mowry, a Second lieutenant in the Third U.S. Artillery, and Carleton had locked horns in California before the war. In 1859, Mowry famously fought a duel with the editor of the *Weekly Arizonan* in Tubac. Altshuler, "The Case of Sylvester Mowry," 149–52. Lockwood, *Life in Old Tucson*, 132–33; Hunt, *James Henry Carleton*, 265–67; Colton, *Civil War in the Western Territories*, 110. Carleton took advantage of the opportunity to relieve his command of

dead wood and made certain that the escort ordered to Fort Yuma with the Tucson prisoners was made up of hard cases and outcasts from the California Column. See Pettis, *The California Column*, 15.

69. Pedersen, "A Yankee in Arizona," 127–44; Proclamation, Aug. 2, 1862, Hdqrs. Tucson, Commands of J. R. West, RG 393, NARA.

70. "Executive Dept., Ariz. Terr., Proclamation," June 11, 1862, *OR* 9:692.

71. James H. Carleton, Proclamation, June 8, 1862, *OR* 50(1):96–97; Hunt, *James Henry Carleton*, 220–21; Fergusson to Ignacio Pesqueira, Sept. 15, 1862, Sonora, in "Fergusson," Hayden Arizona Pioneer Biography Files, Arizona Historical Society. Fergusson commissioned John B. Mills to make an accurate map of Tucson. Sonnichsen, *Tucson*, 66.

72. Capt. John H. Butcher, Eleventh Missouri Cavalry, escorted Governor Goodwin's party from Los Pinos, New Mexico, to Arizona. Carleton cautioned the troops new to the territory that once crossing the Rio Grande into Chiricahua country the men must be more than usually vigilant, keeping advance men and flankers out to foil ambushes—especially near water holes—the men sleeping in their clothes with their weapons at their sides, and the trooper to dismounting and walking most of the time to spare the horses and ensure that they are rested and "ready for fighting." "If . . . you lose a hoof of stock," he warned, "you and your men will be forever disgraced." Carleton to Butcher, Nov. 23, 1864, Doolittle, *Condition of the Indian Tribes*, 145; Bancroft, *History of Arizona and New Mexico*, 522, 539.

73. C. W. C. Rowell served as captain of Co. A, 4th Infantry, CV, but spent a good deal of time "under arrest" after demonstrating insubordinate behavior toward the regiment's Lieutenant Colonel Harvey Lee. He was ultimately ordered dismissed for "mutinous conduct" on April 27, 1863. Lee resigned on May 31. Converse W. C. Rowell CMSR, RG 94, NARA. Orton, *California Men*, 599. Not only did Rowell serve political office but he is also credited with founding the Arizona Pioneer Society, formed late in 1865, which later merged with the Arizona Historical Society, incorporated by the first territorial legislature in November 1864.

74. Davis, "Pioneer Days in Arizona," 53, 93; *San Francisco Alta California*, June 12, July 19, and Sept. 10, 1864; "Alonzo E. Davis," and "Charles Atchisson" Hayden Arizona Pioneer Biography Files, Arizona State University; Bancroft, *History of Arizona and New Mexico*, 539, 634–36; By the end of the war, Arizona's Anglo legislators outnumbered Hispanos nearly ten to one. New Mexico legislatures included more Anglos, but Hispanos predominated—all the governors, attorneys, clerks, and other appointees were Anglos, ibid., 704–7. See also Masich, *Civil War in Arizona*, 265, 269, 272.

75. Illegal trade in army goods plagued all the posts situated near population centers in Arizona. Corrupt soldiers in the Quartermaster Department sold civilians everything from government mules, wrongfully branded "C" for condemned, to army clothing. Inspector General Davis informed Carleton that "grave and discreditable accusations . . . of fraudulent and unauthorized transactions [had surfaced at Fort Yuma and elsewhere] with regard to supplies purchases of horses, etc." Davis to Carleton, Apr. 4, 1864, *OR* 34(3):207; SO 14, June 13, 1862, Hdqrs. Tucson, Commands of J. R. West, RG 393; Conner, *Joseph Reddeford*, 307–8. Browne, *Adventures in the Apache Country*, 139.

76. GO 27, Hdqrs. Dept. of New Mexico, Oct. 23, 1863, *OR* 50(2):653–64. J. Ross Browne's illustrated articles did much to promote the mineral wealth and opportunities in Arizona Territory. His two books, *Adventures in the Apache Country* and *Resources of the Pacific Slope,* also gained wide readership.

77. SO 9, Jan. 17, 1864; and SO 16, Feb. 16, 1864, HQ, Tucson, Commands of J. R. West, Special, General and Post Orders, RG 393, NARA; Davis to Carleton, Apr. 5, 1864, *OR* 24(3):209–10. Drum to Commanding Officer, Fort Yuma, Apr. 11, 1863, *OR* 50(2):390; Carleton to West, Nov. 5, 1861, *OR* 50(1):704–5; Carleton to Rigg, Feb. 5, 1862, ibid., 847–48.

78. Davis to Carleton, Mar. 2, 1864, *OR* 34(2):595; Underhill, "History of the Regiment of Arizona Volunteers," 7–8.

79. Carleton to Nathaniel Pishon, June 22, 1863, Orton, *California Men,* 72; Hdqrs. Dept. of New Mexico, GO 27, Oct. 23, 1863, *OR* 50(2):654; Fergusson to James Whitlock, Apr. 23, 1863, ibid., 413. See also Carleton's correspondence in *Condition of the Indian Tribes,* 98, 110, 115–16, 121, 135.

80. E. B. Willis to Cutler, Feb. 11, 1864, *OR* 34(1):121–22.

81. Carleton to Lorenzo Thomas, Feb. 1, 1863, Doolittle, *Condition of the Indian Tribes,* 105.

82. Ibid., 110, 114–15, 135–37, 140; Farish, *History of Arizona* 3:153.

83. Carleton strongly advocated the use of California soldiers to exploit mining opportunities in the territories. See his correspondence related to the importance of developing the mineral wealth of the borderlands (including Sonora, Chihuahua, and Sinaloa) with political leaders, army superiors, and subordinates in Doolittle, *Condition of the Indian Tribes,* 98, 110, 115–16, 121, and 135. William P. Dole, Commissioner of Indian Affairs, correctly predicted as early as November 27, 1861, that "the recent discovery of gold within this Territory has drawn thither a rapid tide of emigration, which being precipitated amongst the tribes occupying the gold bearing regions of the Territory, thus mingling the white and red races . . . has greatly increased the difficulties." *Annual Report of the Commissioner of Indian Affairs, 1861,* 634.

84. Armistead had established Fort Mojave in April 1859 and successfully combatted the Mojaves, forcing them to negotiate a treaty in August that ended organized hostilities with the U.S. government. Armistead was killed in Picket's Charge at Gettysburg on July 3, 1863, just two weeks after Fort Mojave was reestablished. Altshuler, *Cavalry Yellow,* 11.

85. *San Francisco Alta California,* May 14, July 4, and Dec. 24, 1864.

86. Davis, "Pioneer Days in Arizona," 53; *San Francisco Alta California,* Jan. 26, Mar. 26, 1864, Jan. 15, Apr. 3, 1865; Mohave County Book of Claims, 1864–66, Office of the Mohave County Historian, Kingman.

87. Ball, *Indeh,* 202. Soldiers often wrote home of their desire to supplement the monotonous government fare with local game to satisfy "pemmican-sick palates." *San Francisco Alta California,* Aug. 10, 1862.

88. One volunteer private swore on his honor as a gentleman that "he had shot a hare four times and carried away a leg every time, so that the body of the poor animal had nothing left on it but the ears and the tail; yet with even such limited means of locomotion it actually escaped by whirling over on its ears and tail, though he ran after it as fast as he could." Browne, *Adventures in the Apache Country,* 280; Tuttle, "River Colorado," 59.

89. Cremony, "The Apache Race," 209.
90. A respected lawyer and community leader, Davis died in Pasadena, California, on January 19, 1915, at the age of 75, proud of his service and role as a "pioneer." Alonzo E. Davis, Widow's Pension no. 794743, RG 15, NARA. His daughters, Louise and Jesse, typed the memoirs he had meticulously reconstructed from diaries he kept during the Civil War years. *Los Angeles Times*, January 20, 1915; Davis, "Pioneer Days in Arizona," 171, 186–88.
91. Conner, *Joseph Reddeford Walker*, 47; Cremony, *Life Among the Apaches*, 102–3; *San Francisco Alta California*, June 29, July 9, 1862, July 4, 1864.
92. J. H. Carleton testimony, Doolittle, *Condition of the Indian Tribes*, 4–6. See also testimony by General George Wright and General Sprague.
93. Kit Carson testimony, ibid., 5. William Bent also condemned whites for their aggressions against the tribes.
94. Ibid., 6.
95. Carleton to Lorenzo Thomas, AG, Sept. 13, 1863, Doolittle, *Condition of the Indian Tribes*, 136.
96. The Carleton Meteorite may be seen on exhibit at the Smithsonian National Museum of Natural History. Hunt, *James Henry Carleton*, 326; *San Francisco Alta California*, Apr. 3, 1865.
97. One item particularly treasured by the Smithsonian was the skull of a two-headed rattlesnake found by a California soldier. Farish, *History of Arizona*, 3:153; Bushnell, Diary, Oct. 11, 1865.
98. For the best treatment of the post-Civil War impact of the California Volunteer soldiers in the territories, see Miller, *California Column in New Mexico*, passim. See also *San Francisco Daily Alta* and other California newspapers for letters written home by soldier-correspondents, many of which are compiled in Masich, *Civil War in Arizona*, 143–331.
99. There were more claims filed in central Arizona between 1864 and 1866 than during the next two decades combined. Yavapai County Book of Claims No. 1.
100. Browne, *Resources*, 443–81; *San Francisco Alta California*, July 19, 1864. In May 1862 some of the printers among the California Volunteers attempted to publish their own newspaper in Tucson and cranked the old Washington hand press that had once issued the *Arizonian*. After the war, California Volunteer officer Sidney R. DeLong purchased the press and started a new paper in Tucson. Soon after, DeLong became the city's first elected mayor. See *Arizona Daily Star*, Nov. 29, 1879; Sonnichsen, *Tucson*, 82, 91.
101. For the steamboat industry in Arizona and on the Colorado River in the 1860s, see Lingenfelter, *Steamboats on the Colorado*, passim.
102. Abiel Lord McCloud testimony, William Abiel McCloud *v.* Apache, Case 8047, RG 123, NARA; Braatz, *Surviving Conquest*, 85.
103. Circular, July 27, 1862, Hdqrs. Dist. of Western Arizona, Tucson, Commands of J. R. West, RG 393, NARA; Tuttle, "River Colorado," 57; Yavapais occasionally got government contacts for wood to fuel forts. They were more often attacked by the Anglos and their allies: Pimas, Maricopas, Papagos, and Mojaves. Braatz, *Surviving Conquest*, 34–35, 110–11. When Hualapai chief Hitche Hitche's hungry followers were accused of stealing one of the animals in their charge, an Anglo freighter killed the chief and touched off a

war with that tribe in 1865. Davis, "Pioneer Days in Arizona," 64–65.

104. Fergusson to George A. Burkett, Apr. 17, 1863, *OR* 50(2):405–6; Cutler to West, Mar. 31, 1862, *OR* 50(1):970; Carleton to Drum, Dec. 21, 1861, ibid., 773–80.

105. Young, *Journalism in California,* 61; Wright to Thomas, adjutant general, Feb. 4, 1863, *OR* 50(2):303.

106. Altshuler, "Case of Sylvester Mowry," 160; Davis to Carleton, Mar. 2, 1864, *OR* 34(2):595.

107. Lieutenant William J. Perkins of the Seventh California Infantry had gotten disgracefully drunk while in charge of a wagon train en route to Fort Yuma during the final days of the war in April 1865. The lieutenant's wife had accompanied the train, and Perkins accused her of dallying with an enlisted man. The enraged officer threatened to "shoot any damned son of a bitch" who attempted to interfere and then aimed his cocked pistol at the head of Private Henry A. Howard of Company K while screaming at his wife, "if you want some beef, I'll shoot it for you." Mrs. Perkins and Private Howard both survived the assault, which took place in front of the entire command. Lieutenant Perkins was cashiered for drunkenness and conduct unbecoming an officer. Perkins clearly violated Article of War 45 ("Any commissioned officer who shall be found drunk on his guard, party, or other duty, shall be cashiered"), for he admitted at his court-martial to being "so drunk that he did not know his ass from a hole in the ground." William J. Perkins Court-Martial, GO 2, Jan. 5, 1866, Hdqrs. Dept. of California, C. E. Bennett Papers, Arizona Historical Society; Orton, *California Men,* 767; *Revised U.S. Army Regulations of 1861,* 494; *San Francisco Alta California,* Jan. 16, 1866.

108. Rigg to Carleton, Mar. 25, 1862, *OR* 50(1):952.

109. M. Hillary to Theodore Dodd, Sept. 6, 1866, *Annual Report of the Commissioner of Indian Affairs 1866,* 150–51; Erastus Wood to Marcellus Crocker, Jan. 5, 1865, Doolittle, *Condition of the Indian Tribes,* 214; testimony of Navajo chiefs, ibid., 356; Thompson, *Army and the Navajo,* 81; Sides, *Blood and Thunder,* 456.

110. Bushnell, Diary, Feb. 19 and Feb. 24, 1865; Hand, Diary, Oct. 26 and Nov. 2, 1862. Women rarely accompanied the California soldiers to Arizona, but occasionally exceptions were made for the wives of surgeons and officers. The army frowned on such arrangements, however, because the practice undermined morale and discipline. See Perkins Court-Martial, GO 2, Jan. 5, 1866, Hdqrs. Dept. of California, C. E. Bennett Papers, Arizona Historical Society and *San Francisco Alta California,* Jan. 16, 1866. Many California soldiers wrote home with titillating tales of licentious local women. Some disparaged the virtue of Hispanic and Indian women who fraternized with the volunteers, though in truth the camp followers who inevitably hovered around army posts—from California to Washington, D.C.—were not representative of the general population. A deep-seated racism pervaded the ranks, and while contact with people of the territories enlightened some soldiers, others continued to harbor prejudices: "The whole race of natives of this country are no better [than "*peones* (slaves)"] neither do they look any more enlightened than the dirty Greasers of Cal. The women here are nearly

all prostitutes, never work but all smoke, drink, and gamble. There is some exceptions but they are few and far between. The diggers [Diegueño Indians] of Cal. will compare better with the natives of Mexico than anything I know of." Cpl. Aaron Cory Hitchcock to Thomas and Naomi Hitchcock, July 20, 1864, Hitchcock Letters.

111. The Arizona "Howell Code" of 1864 codified practices related to interracial sex and the age of consent—ten years for females. The Code set the age of marriage at sixteen. Jagodinsky, "Territorial Bonds:," 257.

112. Farish, *History of Arizona,* 4:117–18; Bailey, "Thomas Varker Keam," 15–19; *San Francisco Alta California,* July 15, 1864.

113. Marriage Registry, San Augustín Cathedral, Tucson; Yavapai County Marriage Records; Davis, "Pioneer Days in Arizona," 83, 114; Alonzo E. Davis, Dependent's Pension (Emily W. Davis) 794743, RG 15, NARA. Some of the Californians expressed revulsion at the thought of marrying outside their race. Soon after leaving Tucson for New Mexico, Corporal Aaron Hitchcock wrote his parents, "Once and awhile we hear of a Soldier marrying a Spanish Girl. I tell you what it is I will die single before I will disgrace the whites so much as to marry one of those that live in this country." Hitchcock to Thomas and Naomi Hitchcock, July 20, 1864, Hitchcock Letters. Miller, *California Column,* 25, 196–99. In the colonial period, one in four New Mexican Hispanas were married before age fifteen and canon law allowed marriage as young as eleven; Simmons, *Kit Carson,* 60. See also Gutiérrez, *When Jesus Came,* 249–53, 271, 295.

114. Walker, "Freighting from Guaymas to Tucson," 291–304," 294; GO 20, Sept. 5, 1862, Hdqrs. Las Cruces, *OR* 50(1):115.

115. Wheat, *Mapping the Trans-Mississippi West,* 5:127–28, 381; Carleton to Drum, Sept. 15, 1865, *OR* 48(2):1230.

116. Cremony's newspaper stories, articles, and books should be read with a critical eye for he was prone to self-promotion and exaggeration; in this case, however, his claims can be substantiated. Cremony, *Life Among the Apaches,* 145.

117. Poston, "Military Roads in Arizona," 54.

118. Report of Thomas J. Blakeney, Aug. 8, 1865, *OR* 41(1):81–86; Clarence E. Bennett to Green, AAG, Hdqrs. District of Arizona, July 21, 1865, *OR* 50(1):421–23; Underhill, "History of the Regiment of Arizona Volunteers," 38.

119. For the best treatment of the post–Civil War impact of the volunteer soldiers in the territories, see Miller, *California Column in New Mexico.* See also Masich, *Civil War in Arizona.*

120. Carleton to Lorenzo Thomas, AG, Sept. 13, 1863, Doolittle, *Condition of the Indian Tribes,* 135–36; *San Francisco Alta California,* July 4 and Oct. 17, 1864; Cremony, *Life Among the Apaches,* 198.

121. Hunt, *James Henry Carleton,* 202; Orton, *California Men,* 5, 304–20, 668–719.

122. *Santa Fe New Mexican,* Apr. 7, 1865; *San Francisco Alta California,* Sept. 26, 1866; Orton, *California Men,* 76, 151. See also Hunt, *Army of the Pacific,* 182–83; Miller, *California Column,* 43; and *OR* 50(2):788–89. Leadership at both the regimental and company level made a big difference in troop morale. The Seventh California Infantry served at various posts in Arizona at the

same time the Native Battalion patrolled the border. The "hungry Seventh" experienced only a 5 percent desertion rate, and most occurred at the Presidio in San Francisco just prior to discharge. Once home many volunteers could not understand the delay in formal mustering out, especially when the war was over and their job done. Orton, *California Men,* 776–87.

123. Morale and discipline suffered most during extended periods of tedious garrison duty. Charges at courts-martial ranged from sitting down on guard to outright insubordination. The judges found most offenders guilty of minor infractions, such as refusing to police the camp or straying from the post boundaries. Many of the enlisted men believed themselves to be their officers' equals. Sergeant Hand commented that Captain H. A. "Humpy" Greene of Company G, First California Infantry was not an effective commander because he had not won the respect of the men. They mocked him and called him "Right Face" and "Shoulder Arms" behind his back, see Hand, Diary, Sept. 30, 1862; Results of Garrison Court-Martial, May 12, 1862, Tucson, Commands of J. R. West, RG 393; Results of Garrison Court-Martial, June 19, 1862, ibid.; Orton, *California Men,* 363. A Tucson court-martial convicted one private of "conduct to the prejudice of good order and military discipline." He received a sentence of thirty days at hard labor and forfeited ten dollars of his pay for addressing a second lieutenant "with words too obscene to repeat." Private Frederick Franklin of Company D, Fifth California Infantry allegedly remarked while on duty at the Tucson depot on January 21, 1864, that "he would be damned if he would turn out the Guard for Coult or French." The court sentenced the defiant soldier to carry a forty-pound log on his shoulder in front of the guardhouse for three days. GO 4, Jan. 21, 1864, Hdqrs. Tucson, Commands of J. R. West, RG 393; E. D. Townsend, *Court Martial and Courts of Inquiry, 1817–93,* War Dept., GO 197, Washington, June 30, 1863, vol. 6, 382.

124. Orton, *California Men,* 124, 377, 871; *Mesilla Valley Independent,* Oct. 6, 1877; Pettis, *Personal Narratives,* 34–37; Kiser, *Turmoil on the Rio Grande,* 198.

125. Canby saw fit to recommend Rossell for promotion to major by brevet for "distinguished and meritorious service" at Valverde, but by 1863 he was retired from the service. *Journal of the Executive Proceedings of the Senate,* 216, 518; Whitford, *Colorado Volunteers in the Civil War,* 101–2; J. P. Slough to Samuel Tappan, Feb. 6, 1863, letter, Colorado Historical Society; Whitlock, *Distant Bugles, Distant Drums,* 157, 222; Ickis, *Bloody Trails,* 67. New Mexico Chief Justice John Slough was eventually gunned down in 1867 by William Rynerson, a former California Volunteer officer, in Santa Fe in an affair of honor. See Roberts, *Death Comes for the Chief Justice,* 155 and passim. See also Miller, "William Logan Rynerson in New Mexico," 89, 94; Orton, *California Men,* 335, 342, 346.

126. Lonn, *Desertion During the Civil War,* 219.

127. GO 9, AGO, Jan. 10, 1865, *OR* 50(2):1121; GO 10, Hdqrs. Dept. of the Pacific, Feb. 20, 1865, ibid., 1137. McDowell believed simultaneous attack from posts established near Apache homelands to be the only way to suppress the warriors' "murdering and marauding forays." See his own pessimistic assessment of the undermanned and undersupplied department and its war against

Western and "Sonoran" (Chokonen) Apache bands, in Ventura Curriel *v.* Apache, Case 6843, RG 205, NARA.

128. Hunt, *Army of the Pacific,* 140–41; Davis, "Pioneer Days in Arizona," 52; Ryan, *News from Fort Craig,* 65.

129. Carleton had to rethink his policy of disarming at Fort Union those troops determined to be mustered out in California. The military storekeeper and Chief of Ordnance at Fort Union pointed out the men of the First Infantry, CV, would need their arms for self-defense while traveling "in the wilderness surrounded by hostile Indians." He convinced Carleton and others up the chain of command to allow the men to purchase their arms at cost. Capt. W. R. Shoemaker to Carleton, May 27, 1864, Office of the Chief of Ordnance, RG 156, NARA; Miller, *California Column in New Mexico,* 33–36.

130. Pettis, *California Column,* 18; Orton, *California Men,* 669–70.

131. Rigg to Carleton, Nov. 30, 1861, *OR* 50(1):33. See also Finch, "Arizona in Exile," 57–84; Chandler, "California's 1863 Loyalty Oaths," 215–34; and Chandler, "The Velvet Glove: The Army during the Secession Crisis in California, 1860–1865," 35–42.

132. Theodore A. Coult, HQ Tucson, Sept. 10, 1863, SO No. 142, Commands of J. R. West, RG 393, NARA.

133. This skirmish is considered by some historians to be the farthest west action of the Civil War. Fireman, "Extending the Civil War." Edwards may have acted alone, but there is evidence he was acting in concert with other Confederates. C. E. Bennett to Drum, May 28, 1863, *OR* 50(2):459–61; William Ffrench to Joseph Tuttle, May 28, 1863, ibid., 461; *Tri-Weekly News* (Los Angeles), June 1 and July 29, 1863. The first shot shattered the knee of Private Thomas Gainor of Company H. Before he knew what hit him, Private Truston Wentworth of Company K fell over with a mortal chest wound. Edwards's next bullet passed completely through Private Ferdinand Behn's abdomen and struck a nearby Mexican miner in the head. Wentworth died aboard the *Cocopah* the following day while Behn succumbed to his wounds by the time the boat reached Yuma on May 22. Orton, *California Men,* 652–53, 667, 872, 883; Tuttle, "River Colorado," 57. The pistol ball that hit twenty-six-year-old Thomas Gainor in the back of the left leg broke his femur. He survived the wound but spent more than a year in the hospital at Fort Yuma and never returned to active duty. Gainor's healed but shortened leg caused him to walk with a limp for the rest of his life, and the lead bullet remained lodged just above his kneecap. Thomas Gainor, Pension 480975, RG 15, NARA and Service Record, RG 94, NARA.

134. Orton, *California Men,* 669–70; Pettis, *California Column,* 18; French to Joseph Tuttle, May 28, 1863, *OR* 50(2):461.

135. M. O. Davidson to Irvin McDowell, Nov. 29, 1864, *OR* 50(2):1080.

136. Gustav Brown to A. Jones Jackson, Oct. 16, 1864, ibid., 1018–19.

137. Lansford W. Hasting to Jefferson Davis, Dec. 16, 1863, ibid., 700–701.

138. John B. Magruder to S. Cooper, Mar. 2, 1863, ibid., 332; Baylor to Thomas Helm, Mar. 20, 1862, *OR* 50(1):942; Colton, *Civil War in Western Territories,* 123; James A. Seddon to E. Kirby Smith, Oct. 15, 1863, *OR* 50(2):648–49; Smith to Seddon, Nov. 22, 1863, ibid., 681. Hastings was a schemer and opportunist of the first rank; he plotted the overthrow of California in 1844

and his ill-advised "Hastings Cut-off" doomed the Donner Party in 1846. Bagley, "Lansford Warren Hastings," 12–26.

139. Carleton to Drum, June 10, 1862, *OR* 50(1):52–53; Hunt, *James Henry Carleton*, 222.

140. *San Francisco Evening Bulletin*, Mar. 11, 1863, July 9, 1864; Coult to Drum, Dec. 31, 1862, *OR* 50(2):270–71.

141. GO 5, Apr. 18, 1863, Hdqrs. Tucson, Commands of J. R. West, R 393; SO 2, Jan. 1, 1864, ibid.

142. Browne, *Adventures in the Apache Country*, 134–35; Hand, Diary, Sept. 30–Oct. 4, 1862; Fergusson to J. F. Bennett, Apr. 14, 1863, *OR* 50(2):396. See also Bushnell, Diary, Nov. 10, 1865.

143. Carleton to Lorenzo Thomas, AG, Sept. 13, 1863, Doolittle, *Condition of the Indian Tribes*, 136.

144. GO 35, Sept. 14, 1862, Hdqrs. Tucson, Commands of J. R. West, RG 393; GO 13, June 28, 1862, ibid. More than five hundred California Volunteers settled in Arizona after the Civil War. See U.S. censuses for Arizona and New Mexico territories, 1864, 1870, 1880, 1890, 1900, 1910; Hayden Arizona Pioneer Biography Files; Miller, *California Column in New Mexico*, 35, 43–59; Davis, "Pioneer Days in Arizona," 101.

145. Early in the twentieth century, Phoenix took its place as Arizona's largest and most prosperous city. The three men most often honored with the title "Father of Phoenix" all have California Volunteer connections. William A. Hancock, Seventh California Infantry, built the first store, served in every imaginable elected office including first sheriff, and surveyed the canals that provided the desert town with its vital water supply. In 1866 John Y. T. Smith, Fourth California Infantry, established his hay camp and recognized the agricultural potential of what became the Phoenix town site. Jack Swilling served the Confederacy for only eleven months before defecting and working as a scout and government contractor with the California Volunteers. To Swilling goes the credit for renewing the ancient Hohokam canals and beginning large-scale irrigation in the Salt River Valley. Farish, *History of Arizona*, 6:70–74; Finch, "Sherod Hunter,"194–97; Orton, *California Men*, 651, 794.

Chapter 6

1. Nationalism and nation-state building began in the Americas, and the newly declared nations defined boundaries that physically delineated their territories. Anderson, *Imagined Communities*, 5–8; and St. John, *Line in the Sand*, 5–7, 34. For examples of indigenous "nationalism," see Fontana and Kroeber, *Massacre on the Gila*, 128–29.

2. Chief Justice John Marshall himself recognized the peculiar nature of the relationship between American Indians and the rest of the nation, writing in 1831, "The condition of the Indians in relation to the United States is perhaps unlike that of any other two people in existence." Skogen, *Indian Depredation Claims*, xx.

3. The fact that the federal government saw warfare involving Indian tribes with treaties as domestic conflicts rather than international wars is abundantly illustrated in the thousands of depredation claims that the United

States received and paid. Evidence Concerning Depredation Claims, RG 75, NARA; and Depredation Case Records, RG 123, NARA. Skogen, *Indian Depredation Claims*, 91–92, 206.

4. For recent scholarship with a borderlands perspective on this subject, see Kearny, "Transnationalism in California and Mexico." See also *The Journal of American History: Rethinking History and the Nation-State: Mexico and the United States as a Case Study*. See also Lempérière, "Transnationalizing."

5. Bakewell. *A History of Latin America*, 303–4; Restall, *The Black Middle*, 90, 92; Brooks, *Captives and Cousins*, passim; Mora, *Border Dilemmas*, 33–35.

6. Grenville Goodwin lived and worked with Apaches in Arizona to better understand the underlying causes of the violent conflict of the 1860s. Apacheans made a sharp distinction between "raiding" for property and "warring" for revenge (*gegodza*), Goodwin, *Western Apache Raiding*, passim. Kroeber and Fontana attribute the origin of war between Yuman peoples of the Southwest Borderlands to be the result of a shift in subsistence strategies and the transfer of the burden of agriculture and food production to women, giving rise to a male tendency to make war in order to demonstrate their masculinity and essential service to their families and communities. The rise of this martial culture led to conflict with neighboring tribes. Kroeber and Fontana, *Massacre on the Gila*, passim.

7. Citing the uprising of the Navajos and Apaches when the Texas rebels invaded, Hispanos in New Mexico characterized the early 1860s as a time of "revolution." See Juan Manuel Lucero testimony in Nestor Armijo *v.* Navajo, Case 425, RG 123, NARA.

8. *San Francisco Alta California*, Mar. 11, 1863. Pico was only a teenager when he accompanied his famous uncle, Andrés Pico, at the battle of San Pasqual. Many California Hispanos supported the Union war effort only because they believed it would help the Republican cause in Mexico. Rosenus, *General Vallejo*, 227–28.

9. San Francisco *Bulletin*, July 18, 1865.

10. More than two hundred leaders (Anglo, Indian, and Hispano) provided oral testimony or responses to queries made by the Joint Special Committee in 1865. Doolittle, *Condition of the Indian Tribes*, 3–10, 424. See also Fontana and Kroeber, *Massacre on the Gila*, 155–56, 165, 169, 173; Brooks, *Captives and Cousins*, 349, 368.

11. Brooks, *Captives and Cousins*, 366–68; Blyth, *Chiricahua and Janos*, 79. For the advantages of raiding by stealth versus open combat, see Glowacki and Wrangham, "Warfare and Reproductive Success," 348–49.

12. Greenberg addresses the Anglo-American filibustering phenomenon that reached its peak in 1857, arguing that economic stress and a form of "martial manhood" led ambitious young men like William Walker to seek opportunity and empire south of the United States border. Greenberg, *Manifest Manhood*, passim. For perspective on military readiness as a cause of war among indigenous peoples, see Fontana and Kroeber, *Massacre on the Gila*, 128, 163. The peoples of the borderlands, though ethnically distinct, have much in common. In 1982 David Weber furthered the evolution of borderlands history by looking northward at the United States from the vantage point of post-Spanish Mexico. Where some historians focused on difference,

Weber saw commonalities; his transnational approach in *The Mexican Frontier* helped bring about a better understanding of how interconnected the peoples of the United States and Mexico were and are.

13. Colonel Carroll H. Potter of the Sixth U.S. Volunteer Infantry ("Galvanized Yankees"), commanding the South Sub-District of the Plains, believed "as far as I know the policy of the military department here, is to exterminate the Indians." Some 5,600 captured Confederate soldiers enlisted as "United States Volunteers" and organized into six regiments between January 1864 and November 1866 for service along the Overland Mail routes and on the frontier. Col. Potter sworn testimony, July 27, 1865, Doolittle, *Condition of the Indian Tribes,* 71. For an overview of massacre history and the concept of genocide, see Dwyer and Ryan, *Theatres of Violence,* xi–xii, 5.

14. Rogers, *Soldiers of the Overland,* 33; Long, *Saints and the Union,* 141; *OR* 50(1):178–79.

15. *Army and Navy Journal,* Sept. 28, 1867.

16. Shortly after this reprimand, McGarry was removed from command in Arizona after being disgracefully drunk on parade at Tubac. Transferred to San Francisco, he committed suicide in his hotel room by using a knife to cut his own throat. Altshuler, *Chains of Command,* 78–81, 256–58; McDowell quoted in Thrapp, *Frontier Biography,* 903–4. Army policy on the appropriate level of violence was still evolving at this time. Commanders issued conflicting orders, and in 1867–68 both General William T. Sherman and Phil Sheridan believed that total war should be the policy and encouraged Lieutenant Colonel George Custer and other field commanders to hang Indian depredators in order to put an end to the fighting on the southern plains. Utley, *Frontier Regulars,* 144. See also Donovan, *A Terrible Glory,* 62–63.

17. Keefer, *Muster Roll, Kit Carson Post, No. 2,* 3–4.

18. Military commanders searched for bodies and animal carcasses used to poison wells, and Confederate Colonel J. R. Baylor advocated poisoning Apaches. Baylor, *John Robert Baylor,* 14–15, 32. Apaches had long used poisoned arrows for deer hunting but during the 1860s applied the same deadly formula to arrowheads and musket balls intended for men. Goodwin, *Western Apache Raiding,* 232. Alonzo Davis reported that strychnine-laced sugar was left at camps along the road between Fort Mojave and Prescott for unwary Paiutes who had been waylaying travelers. Davis, "Pioneer Days in Arizona," 106–8.

19. Depredation case files detail many cases of stock killing and/or mutilation by raiders to prevent recapture and deter pursuit. See, for example, Estanislao Montoya *v.* Navajo, Case 1593, RG 123, NARA. Herd dogs were also killed at attack sites or along the escape trail. See Victoria Garule de Chavez *v.* Navajo, Case 3846, RG 123, NARA.

20. Chivington to Charles Wheeler, Nov. 29, 1864, Doolittle, *Condition of the Indian Tribes,* 92–93; Wynkoop sworn testimony, Jan. 16, 1865, ibid., 62–64; Halaas and Masich, *Halfbreed,* 120–25; Roberts, "Sand Creek: Tragedy and Symbol," 2–3, 295–99.

21. After serving under Stephen Watts Kearny, John Ward spent more than twenty years as an interpreter (he spoke several Indian languages, including

Apache) and Indian agent. Ward fought against the alienation of Indian lands, believing that if Indians were given the right to own land in severalty, unscrupulous New Mexicans, "by hook or by crook," would get it. J. Ward, reply to the Doolittle "circular," in *Condition of the Indian Tribes*, 457.

22. W. H. Waterman, Supt. of Indian Affairs, Washington Territory, Doolittle, *Condition of the Indian Tribes*, 452–53.

23. Brooks, *Captives and Cousins*, 309. For examples of Anglo ethnocentrism and discrimination directed at both African Americans and Hispanos see Hand, Diary, Oct. 26 and Nov. 2, 1862; Hunt, *James Henry Carleton*, 48–50, 120 and *Kirby Benedict*, 112–22; Thompson, *From Desert to Bayou*, 38. Indian peoples of the borderlands had limited contact with African Americans prior to the Civil War; Cheyennes referred to them as "black whitemen" (*mok-ta-veho*). George Bent to George Hyde, Aug. 10, 1910 and Feb. 5, 1913, Bent Letters, Coe Collection, Beinecke Library. See also Afton, Halaas, and Masich, *Cheyenne Dog Soldiers*, 108–9.

24. Jagodinsky, "Territorial Bonds," 256–59.

25. Opler, *Apache Life-way*, 336–37; Goodwin, *Western Apache Raiding*, 77; Brooks, *Captives and Cousins*, 236–37; Restall, *The Black Middle*, 90–96. See also Wright, "One Drop of Blood," *The New Yorker*, July 24, 1994; Phillips, *American Negro Slavery*; Stampp, *The Peculiar Institution*; Genovese, *Political Economy of Slavery*; Brown, *Good Wives*, passim.

26. Goodwin, *Western Apache Raiding*, 77; Opler, *Apache Life-Way*, 335–36, 350–51.

27. For the best treatment of Navajo captivity and slave practices see Brooks, *Captives and Cousins*, 349–60.

28. Carleton and Carson are quoted at length in several depredation claim defense arguments. See Martin Saiz v. Navajo, Case 2597, "Supplemental Testimony," pages 11–13, RG 123, NARA, for their ideas concerning Hispano slave practices. Brooks, *Captives and Cousins*, 327–30, 351–52.

29. Brooks carefully and quantitatively examined the cultural interaction and institutionalized slavery based on raiding and trading Indian and Hispano captives. Brooks, *Captives and Cousins*, 364, and passim.

30. Martin Saiz v. Navajo, Case 2597, pp. 11–13, RG 123, NARA; *Report of the Joint Special Committee Appointed under Joint Resolution, March 3, 1865*, 333. Brooks, *Captives and Cousins*, 309, 329–30. Fewer than 100 African Americans appear in the *1860 U.S. Census* for New Mexico and Arizona *Special Census of 1864* combined. In 1859 the New Mexico legislature (composed of 34 Hispanos and 3 Anglos) passed the "Otero Slave Code," which made a distinction between the existing system of peonage, Indian slavery, and African American slavery. The purpose of the code was to enable the continuation of the trade in Indian captives. Curiously, one of the first to sell African American slaves in New Mexico (1851) was none other than James H. Carleton, who, though a staunch Union man, kept an enslaved black servant throughout the war.

31. From *Report on the Condition of the Indian Tribes*, testimony of Gov. Henry Connelly, in Lorenzo Labadie v. Navajo, Case 3259, RG 123, NARA; "Peonage in New Mexico," *Santa Fe Gazette*, Feb. 2, 1867. See also Thompson, *Army and the Navajo*, 100–130.

32. Soifer, "Federal Protection, Paternalism, and the Virtually Forgotten Prohi-
bition of Voluntary Peonage," 1617; Goluboff, "The Thirteenth Amendment
and the Lost Origins of Civil Rights," 1609, 1638. See also Roberts, *Death
Comes for the Chief Justice*, 36–38. For examples of Anglo confusion over the
status of peons, see J. H. Whitlock to Nelson H. Davis Aug. 22, 1866 and
Davis to Whitlock, Sept. 1, 1866, *Annual Report of the Commissioner of Indian
Affairs*, House Exec. Doc. No. 1, Thirty-Ninth Congress, Second Session,
Serial No. 1284, 137. See also Correll, *Through White Men's Eyes*, 360–66.
Many Hispanic New Mexicans refused to admit that peonage was a form of
slavery, e.g., Antonio José Martinez testimony, Taos, July 26, 1865: "There is
an idea that the Indians captive and bought from their fathers, similar to the
Yutas [Utes], who sell their sons and daughters in exchange for horses and
other objects, are held as slaves. No, they are servants, and are well treated;
if they marry, they are free to live in their master's house and pass their life
as they please, the same as with the sons of Indians, who, if not married
when attaining their majority, become free after their marriage." Doolittle,
Condition of the Indian Tribes, 490. Well into the late nineteenth century,
Anglo elites, including King Woolsey and Jack Swilling, also took advantage
of racial ambiguity and the vestigial peonage system supported by territorial
law, such as Arizona's Howell Code, to keep physical and sexual control of
subordinate women and their mixed-blood children. Jagodinsky, "Territorial
Bonds," 256–73.
33. For an excellent discussion of the disintegration of Apachean local groups,
social and political impacts on tribes, and the nationalization of the Navajos
under Anglo-American rule, see Spicer, *Cycles of Conquest*, 406–21.
34. Carleton to Lorenzo Thomas, AG, Feb. 7, Mar. 6, and Mar. 12, 1864, Doolittle, *Condition of the Indian Tribes*, 157, 162–63, 166–68. See also Spicer, *Cycles
of Conquest*, 406–8.
35. Carleton to Lorenzo Thomas, AG, Mar. 12, 1864 and Mar. 19, 1864, Doolittle, *Condition of the Indian Tribes*, 166–69; Carleton's reply to questions
presented by Sen. J. R. Doolittle's Joint Special Committee, July 25, 1865,
ibid., 432–35.
36. Carleton brought his military governorship and control of civil affairs in
New Mexico to an end on July 4, 1865, the same day the Doolittle Committee began its hearings in Santa Fe. Sonnichsen, *Mescalero*, 131.
37. Select Committee on Indian Depredation Claims Report No. 1701, Fiftieth
Congress, First Session, House of Representatives, Report to Accompany
bill H. R. 9383, 3–7. The congressional committee accepted the depredation
claim of J. G. Fell and other trustees of the Walnut Grove Gold Mining
Company, which concisely summarized Carleton's "supreme control" in
the territories and also implied culpability for failing to protect the lives of
citizens and property in his domain. Walnut Grove Gold Mining Company
v. Apaches, Case 4715, RG 123, NARA.
38. Carleton died in 1873, still on active duty but embittered by the treatment he
received from the country he had served for more than thirty years. News
of his death was received with expressions of sorrow in the territories. Even
his critics seemed willing to recognize his accomplishments. The citizens of
Santa Fe drew up resolutions honoring Carleton's memory, which they asked

to be published in territorial newspapers, the San Antonio *Herald*, the *Army and Navy Journal*, and the *San Francisco Daily Alta California. Santa Fe New Mexican*, Sept. 23, Dec. 16, 1864, Feb. 4, 11, 1873; Hunt, *James Henry Carleton*, 348–49; Miller, *The California Column in New Mexico*, 210; Thompson, *Army and the Navajo*, 121–28; Gibson, "James H. Carleton," 59–74.

39. Miller, *California Column in New Mexico*, 174–75. Carleton assumed duties as lieutenant colonel of the Fourth U.S. Cavalry at San Antonio, where he died of pneumonia at the age of 58 on January 7, 1873. His obituary noted, "During the Rebellion his duties lay not only in suppressing the rebels in Texas and New Mexico, which he successfully did, but in subduing the Apaches and Navajoes, who were then virtually the rulers of those Territories." *San Francisco Alta California*, Jan. 9, 1873. See also Roberts, *Death Comes for the Chief Justice*, 6–7, 37, 103, 156–57.

40. Edward Spicer noted that while local communities began to disintegrate and became more dependent on the government, the reservation system created a sense of tribal identity and encouraged Anglo-style politics by collecting in close proximity people who once lived in small tribal units or isolated bands. Spicer, *Cycles of Conquest*, 406, 420.

41. Sturtevant, *Handbook of North American Indians*, 10:321.

42. Tension between the Spanish, Mexicans, and Ópatas manifested itself in numerous revolts in the nineteenth century. In 1820, 300 Ópata warriors defeated a Spanish force of 1,000 soldiers and destroyed a mining town near Tonichi. Later, the Ópatas won another battle at Arivechi, killing more than 30 soldiers. A Spanish force of 2,000 soldiers finally defeated the Ópatas, forcing the survivors to surrender. The Spanish executed the Ópata leaders, including Dorame, whose surname is still common in the Opatería region of Sonora. Revolts continued after Mexico gained its independence from Spain in 1821. Another Ópata leader, Dolores Gutierrez, was executed in 1833 by the Mexicans for his involvement in a revolt. Although the Ópatas had reputations as formidable warriors, they were never able to unite as a single people to oppose the Spanish and Mexicans. Most Ópatas supported the French during their brief rule of Mexico from 1864 to 1867, as did many other Sonoran Indians. Republican retribution following the expulsion of the French resulted in the loss of nearly all the Ópatas' remaining lands and the end of their resistance to Mexican rule. Spicer, *Cycles of Conquest*, 62; Yetman, *The Ópatas*, 243–45. See also Forbes, "Historical Survey of the Indians of Sonora," 335–49. For the early war practices of the Ópatas and other Sonoran Indians see Nentvig, *Rudo Ensayo Sonora*, 64–66, 84–92; *Message of the President of the United States, Jan. 29, 1867, Relating to the Present Condition of Mexico*.

43. In the twentieth century, the Yaquis' economic survival strategy changed radically in Arizona, but many rituals and traditions were maintained or adapted. Spicer, *Pascua*, passim.

44. Meeks, *Border Citizens*, 241–47.

45. May, *Manifest Destiny's Underworld*, xiv and passim; Smith-Rosenberg, *This Violent Empire*, x, 22, 41.

46. The term Latin America (l'Amérique latine) is believed to have originated in Napoleon III's France as that regime attempted to legitimize its intervention

in Mexican affairs. Gobat, "The Invention of Latin America," 1345–75; Mora, *Border Dilemmas*, 5–6, 19, 61.

47. The number of armed combats and "depredations" during the period 1861–67 far exceeded the period preceding and following it. For comparison see *Record of Engagements With Hostile Indians Within the Military Division of the Missouri, from 1868 to 1882*. See also Evidence Concerning Depredation Claims, RG 75, and Court of Claims Depredation Case Records, RG 123, NARA for evidence of the relative frequency and destructiveness of attacks from the 1850–70s. Geronimo's Chiricahua insurgency of the 1870–80s resulted in a renewal of large-scale military operations against Apaches. For an excellent quantitative analysis of violence during this period see Kuhn, *Chronicles of War*.

48. Victorio made this statement in 1865. He found the enforced dependence of the U.S. reservation system humiliating for his Chihenne people and continued warfare. He was killed by Mexican troops in the Tres Castillos Massacre of 1880. Palmer, *Apache Peoples*, 279.

49. For perspective on the Chiricahua experience, which differed from that of other Apaches and Navajo people, see Nichols's summary in *Warrior Nations*, 146–65; Spicer, *Cycles of Conquest*, 64–67, 83–85; and Spicer, *Pascua*, passim.

50. Gutierrez argues that the Pueblo Revolt against the Spaniards in 1680 was in fact a civil war with terrible consequences. The losses in dead alone are difficult to estimate for the Pueblo insurgents, but 422 Spanish citizens died in the 1680 uprising in New Mexico. By 1700 the "rebellion" was quashed and Spanish rule prevailed until the Mexican Revolution of 1821. Gutiérrez, *When Jesus Came*, xxvii–xxix, 107.

51. The vacuum resulting from inept governance or the withdrawal of power (the "Leviathan," as Hobbs termed it), is one of the most common causes of civil wars. The American West and Southwest saw violent aggression peak in the decade of the 1860s. Pinker, *Better Angels*, 102–4, 681. In the twentieth century, the rapid loss of authority in European nation-states led to civil wars, massacres, and genocide. See also Snyder, *Black Earth*, 9–12 and passim.

52. Arizona and New Mexico's Indian people did not gain full citizenship until long after the civil wars of the 1860s. The Fourteenth Amendment defined as citizens any person born in the United States, but only if "subject to the jurisdiction thereof," a clause thought by some to exclude certain indigenous peoples. Non-reservation Indians were declared citizens by the 1924 Indian Citizen Act ("Snyder Act"), signed into law by President Calvin Coolidge on June 2, 1924, partially in recognition of the thousands of Indian men who served in the U.S. armed forces during WWI. However, the states of Arizona and New Mexico (admitted to the Union in 1912) refused to grant full citizenship, with voting privileges, to all Indian people until forced to by their states' supreme courts in 1948. Bruyneel, "Challenging American Boundaries: Indigenous People and the "Gift" of U.S. Citizenship," 30–43. On July 15, 1948, the Arizona Supreme Court unanimously reversed earlier courts' rulings. Justice Levi S. Udall quoted noted Indian law scholar Felix Cohen in his decision: "In a democracy suffrage is the most basic civil right, since its exercise is the chief means whereby other rights may be safeguarded. To deny the right to vote where one is legally entitled to do so, is to do

violence to the principles of freedom and equality." After the 1948 decision, legal and cultural barriers remained. Potential voters had to prove they could read and write English, a provision that excluded many Indians. In 1976, the Arizona Legislature passed a law that allowed a voter to bring someone of his or her own choosing to help in voting. http://www.azcentral.com/arizonarepublic/arizonaliving/articles/2008/06/23/20080623azjournal0623 .html#ixzz2inodTD11.

53. Newspapers and government documents provide abundant evidence that the withdrawal of federal troops at the beginning of the Civil War and the distraction of fighting Confederates created a situation that led to increased stock raiding by Apaches and Navajos and then to increased violence and revenge warfare; testimony found in Indian Depredation Claims provides some of the most convincing and quantifiable data to support this conclusion. See, for example, Rafael Chavez *v.* Navajo, Case 4097; Fritz Contzen *v.* Apache, Case 3358; Peter Kitchen *v.* Apache, Case 6845; Tomas Montoya *v.* Apache, Case 4101; Pedro Padilla *v.* Navajo, 5957; Abraham Peeples *v.* Mimbres Apache, Case 6253; Martin Saiz *v.* Navajo, Case 2597; Felix Tafoya *v.* Navajo and Apache, Case 5958; Vivian Tafoya *v.* Navajo and Apache, Case 3470, RG 123, NARA; Lorenzo Ortero *v.* Navajo, Claim 4048; and Mariano Pino *v.* Navajo, Claim 6141, RG 75, NARA.

Epilogue

1. El Morro is a sandstone promontory, faced with cliffs, some fifty miles southeast of Gallup, New Mexico. Lying on an ancient east-west trail, the bluffs have been a popular campsite over the centuries as there is a reliable waterhole at its base, one of the few in the region. Ancestral Puebloans in the late thirteenth and fourteenth centuries established a large village on the top of El Morro. Over time, the natives carved petroglyphs into the bluffs, most likely religious symbols. Their descendants, the Zuni, refer to the village as Atsinna, or "writing upon the rocks." The Spaniards' first recording of El Morro was in 1583, with Juan de Oñate in 1605 the first to carve his name. Americans continued the tradition, calling the promontory Inscription Rock. El Morro became a national monument in 1906.

2. Orton, *California Men,* 5, 47, 83. In 1887 Julius Hall, a member of the "Jack-ass Battery," reported that when traveling *west* the graves were on the *right* side of the railroad tracks. Julius Hall, "Wild West," *National Tribune,* Oct. 20, 1887; Pettis, *California Column,* 10–24. Barrett's remains were never reinterred following his 1862 burial at Picacho. The army tried to locate next of kin, but his only known relative, Ellen Brady of Albany, New York, never claimed the body, and it remained in the mesquite thicket near Picacho until all traces of the grave were lost. Lt. Col. E. E. Eyre to Major R.C Drum, May 14, 1862, *OR* 50(1):120; Masich, *Civil War in Arizona,* 42. The last of the New Mexico Volunteers also mustered out in 1867, Compiled Service Records of New Mexico Volunteers, 1861–67, RG 94, NARA.

3. By 1890, some 5,000 GAR posts across the U.S. hosted over 400,000 Union army veteran members.

4. Franklin, "In Memory of Alexander G. Bowman [Co. B, Fifth California Infantry]," Special Collections, University of Arizona Library, Tucson.

Franklin remembered her uncle, Colonel Bowman, "sat silent in groups of Civil War veterans discussing the battles of Gettysburg and Appomattox."

5. Carson mustered out November 22, 1867. He was fifty-nine years old when he died. Josefa Jaramillo tragically preceded him in death (age forty) following the birth of their eighth child just two days after his return from Washington. Keefer, *Muster Roll, Kit Carson Post, No. 2*, 2–4; Dunlay, *Kit Carson and the Indians*, 405–15. Former California Volunteer, Ben C. Cutler inaugurated the first telegraph in New Mexico on July 10, 1868. Miller, *The California Column in New Mexico*, 138–39. Black Kettle's people had camped near other Cheyenne, Comanche, Kiowa, and Apache bands, some of which harbored young warriors recently returned from raids against Kansas settlements. Lieutenant Colonel Custer's controversial attack killed nearly fifty Cheyenne, Comanche, and Arapaho men and women. The retreating cavalrymen used fifty-three captured women and children as human shields to affect their retreat from the Indian villages. Utley, *Frontier Regulars*, 150–52. In 1866 Custer attempted to join Benito Juárez's forces in their struggle against Napoleon III and Maximilian's Mexican regime but Sheridan denied him leave of absence from the U.S. Army for that purpose. Utley, *Cavalier in Buckskin*, 39.

6. Thrapp, *Conquest of Apachería*, 92.

7. After imprisonment in Florida, Alabama, and Oklahoma, Geronimo died at Fort Sill in 1909, still a prisoner of war. In 1913 Chiricahua Apache POWs were permitted to return to the Mescalero Reservation in New Mexico, though about a third of these survivors and their families elected to remain on allotments in Oklahoma, and by 1914 they were no longer designated POWs by the federal government. Sweeney, *From Cochise to Geronimo*, 576–81. The Atchison Topeka & Santa Fe RR reached Raton Pass on New Mexico's northern border by 1878 and the first Southern Pacific RR train steamed into Tucson in 1881. Beck and Haase, *Historical Atlas of New Mexico*, 58; Walker and Bufkin, *Historical Atlas of Arizona*, 46.

8. After the Treaty of the Little Arkansas negotiations of 1867, army officers, Indian Commission members, and members of Congress had criticized the treaty system, pointing out that Indian tribes were not really being treated as sovereign nations, whether or not they deserved to be. In 1869, Eli Parker, a Seneca Indian and President Grant's Commissioner of Indian Affairs, called the treaty system a "cruel farce" and advocated for doing away with it. Calloway, *Pen and Ink Witchcraft*, 231.

9. The 1887 Dawes Severalty Act sought to break up tribes as social units, further the progress of Indian farmers, reduce the cost of Indian administration, secure parts of the reservations as Indian land, and open the remainder of the land to white settlers. Carlson, *Indians, Bureaucrats, and Land*, 79. By 1934, Indian lands had been reduced from 138 million acres to only 48 million acres. Only the "Indian New Deal" of the 1940s stopped this depletion of Indian-controlled land. See also Washburn, *The Assault on Indian Tribalism*.

10. Turner's "The Significance of the Frontier in American History," was presented to the annual meeting of the American Historical Association in Chicago during the World's Columbian Exposition in 1893.

11. By 1890 military pension payments accounted for 40 percent of the federal budget, see Neu, "Worthy Comrades All." Nearly $6 million was awarded by

the U.S. Court of Claims for Indian depredations, 82 percent of all the depredation claims filed were for incidents that occurred 1861–70. Skogen, *Indian Depredation Claims,* 91–92, 206. Depredation claims and other government document bundles were routinely tied with red twill cotton tape—the term "red tape" and the desire to cut through it to hurry things along also emerged from the Civil War years.

12. For the best understanding of Chivington's legacy and the contested memory of Sand Creek, see Kelman, *A Misplaced Massacre.*

13. New Mexico became the first state to be admitted with a majority non-Euro-American population and the first to elect an Hispano governor (1917) and senator (1928). Mora, *Border Dilemmas,* 274.

14. Other important rights, and some attributes of sovereignty, have been restored to tribes by legislation such as the Indian Civil Rights Act of 1966 (25 U.S.C. 1301), the Indian Self-Determination and Educational Assistance Act of 1975 (25 U.S.C. 451a), and the Indian Child Welfare Act of 1978 (25 U.S.C. 1901). http://www.everyculture.com/multi/A-Br/Apaches.html#ixzz2ycYdH8Qb

15. After Juárez's death in 1872, Díaz ruled Mexico until the Mexican Revolution ended his reign (*"Porfiriato"*) in 1911. The Revolution and political power struggle became a multisided civil war that continued until 1920.

16. In 1928 the Arizona Historical Society and the Southern Pacific Railroad erected a fifteen-foot stone obelisk in the railroad right of way between the tracks and the peak on a spot a railroad signal superintendent believed to be Barrett's burial site. The original bronze plaque on the monument was stolen, prompting the Arizona State Parks Department to move the marker nearer to the entrance of Picacho Peak State Park in 1975. E. E. Eyre to R. C. Drum, May 14, 1862, *OR* 50(1):120; *Arizona Daily Star,* Apr. 27, 1959; Edith C. Tompkins Manuscript; Hunt, *James Henry Carleton,* 214; *Oakland Tribune,* Apr. 16, 1961.

17. More than 400,000 Anglo men joined the GAR during its heyday in the 1890s. Nearly 300 GAR posts were active in California, Arizona, New Mexico, Texas, and Colorado. Except for some of the Native Battalion men in California, very few of the more than 5,000 eligible Hispanos joined and no posts were named for Hispanos. The GAR held its last encampment in 1949 and the last member died in 1956, when the organization was dissolved. See http://www.loc.gov/rr/main/gar/.

18. Warrior traditions remain strong among most American Indian tribes, and their young men serve in the U.S. Armed Forces in greater proportions than the general population. The story of the Navajo Code Talkers of WWII is well known; Comanches and others were also employed to confound enemies with their unique and impossible-to-decode native tongues. See Fort Sill Museum exhibit, "Comanche Code Talkers."

19. On July 15, 1948, the Arizona Supreme Court unanimously reversed earlier courts' rulings regarding suffrage for native peoples, but even after the 1948 decision, legal and cultural barriers remained. Voters still had to prove they could read and write English, and many Indians could not. In 1976 the Arizona Legislature passed a law that allowed a voter to bring someone of his or her own choosing to help in voting. Apache POWs were granted permission to return to New Mexico in 1913. In 1986, one hundred years after

Geronimo's deportation, surviving Chiricahua POWs returned to Arizona for the first time to participate in a commemoration of Geronimo's surrender held at Fort Bowie National Monument. Mildred Imach Cleghorn (*Eh-Ohn*, 1910–97), Chiricahua POW and first chair of the Fort Sill Oklahoma Apache Tribe, personal communication, July 10, 1986.

20. U.S. Census, 2010. See also "Historical Racial and Ethnic Demographics of the United States," http://en.wikipedia.org/wiki/Historical_racial_and_ethnic_demographics_of_the_United_States#Mexican_.281910.E2.80.931930.29_and_Hispanic.2FLatino_.281940.E2.80.932010.29_Population_as_a_Percentage_of_the_Total_Population_by_U.S._Region_and_State.

Appendix

1. Court of Claims Depredation Case Records, RG 123, NARA; Evidence Concerning Depredation Claims, RG 75, NARA; and Records of the Court of Claims Section of the Department of Justice, Indian Depredation Case Records, RG 205. Taken alone, these documents do not represent a complete record of conflict during the 1860s. The successful claims report losses of civilian property to Indians considered to be at peace with and under the protection of the U.S. government. Army reports and War Department records, Office of Indian Affairs reports, newspaper accounts, reminiscences (letters, diaries, oral interviews, memoirs), and church and cemetery records should also be consulted to complete the picture. Depredation claims must also be scrutinized for indications of fraud. During the late nineteenth century, unscrupulous lawyers preyed on victims of Indian attacks in an effort to cash in on the federal government's depredation payment program. The U.S. Court of Claims received a flood of claims in the 1880s and 1890s. Chicago and Washington attorneys sought out potential claimants and promised windfall payments for losses suffered at the hands of Indian depredators. Many of the claimants were Mexican Americans in their fifties or sixties at the time they testified or provided depositions. Most spoke Spanish as their primary language and were either illiterate or poorly educated. See Skogen, *Indian Depredation Claims* for an overview of the depredation claims process.

2. *Indian Depredation Records All Claims filed to 1887*, House Ex Docket 125, 49th Cong. 1st Sess., Congressional Serial Set 2399, No. 125, Vol. 31.

Glossary

1. Following concerted efforts by Mexican troops to exterminate the Lipans, this tribe moved north of the border and by 1869 merged with the Mescaleros or were otherwise assimilated.

2. There has been and still is considerable disagreement over the terms band and tribe. Are the Bedonkohe, for example, a band of Chiricahua Apaches or are they a tribe? For a discussion of the definition of bands, tribes, and nations relative to the U.S. government's view of American Indian social organization, see William H. Robeson testimony in *Indian Depredations, Hearings Before the United States Congress*. See also Goodwin, *Western Apache Raiding*, 15, and Opler, *Apache Life-way*, 1–3, 463.

3. Opler, *Apache Life-Way*, 350–51. See also Bailey, *Indian Slave Trade in the Southwest*.

4. The word "caste" is a cognate of *casta*, from which it was derived. In English, caste has taken on the sense of a rigid hierarchy unlike the more flexible sociocial categories that existed in Spanish colonial America. See Bakewell, *History of Latin America*, 303–4; and Restall, *The Black Middle*, 90, 95.

5. One of the best examples of these *casta* paintings (titled *Las castas*, anonymous) may be found at the Museo Nacional del Virreinato, Tepotzotlán, Mexico. Some scholars believe that historians have placed too much emphasis on their significance and that the racial categories and stereotypes depicted in such paintings were not generally recognized at the time and served only to exotify colonial peoples. Restall, *The Black Middle*, 94. For differences in notions of *calidad* and *casta* in New Mexico, see Mora, *Border Dilemmas*, 33, 61.

6. For perspectives on the problem of identifying and defining civil wars, see Wong, "A Matter of Definition." Wong writes, "The common scholarly definition has two main criteria. The first says that the warring groups must be from the same country and fighting for control of the political center, control over a separatist state or to force a major change in policy. The second says that at least 1,000 people must have been killed in total, with at least 100 from each side." Much debate centers on whether ethnicity or economics is the primary cause of civil war. See Berdal and Malone, *Greed and Grievance*; and Collier and Hoeffler, "On Economic Causes," 563–73, and "Greed and Grievance in Civil War," 563–95. Though scholars do not agree on the definition or causes of civil wars, most agree that civil wars since 1945 have resulted in more than twenty million deaths and have replaced international war as the most common type of conflict in the world today. Collier and Sambanis, *Understanding Civil War*, 2–8.

7. Another term Anglos used in contrast to "civilized" was "barbarous." See examples of all these terms in play by an educated writer, Dr. David Wooster, in "Indian Affairs in California, Arizona, and New Mexico," *San Francisco Daily Alta California*, May 6, 1866.

8. Goodwin, *Western Apache Raiding*, 15–16; Kaut, "Western Apache Clan and Phratry Organization," 140–46.

9. DeLay, *War of a Thousand Deserts*, 11, 15. See also Hämäläinen, *Comanche Empire*.

10. Goodwin, *Western Apache Raiding*, 77.

11. Indian captives sold to Spaniards became household servants and/or *genízaros* (military auxiliaries). In the seventeenth century, many *genízaros* in the borderlands were Plains Indians sold to individual Hispanos or Pueblo Indians. The Recopilacíon de Leyes de Reynos de las Indias in 1681 sanctioned the purchase of captives citing the Christian obligation to ransom captives. The practice was further codified in 1694 after a group of Navajos attempted to sell Pawnee children captives to the Spanish. When the Spaniards refused the offer, the Navajos executed the children. Spanish King Charles II ordered that royal funds be allocated to purchase Indian captives in order to prevent further tragedies of this kind. See http://newmexicohistory.org/people/genizaros.

12. *Report on Indians Taxed and Indians Not Taxed in the United States*, 133. For a convoluted explanation of "Indians taxed" (non-reservation Indians) see also U.S. Ninth Census, 1870, xii.
13. Scott, *Military Dictionary*, 453.
14. Ibid., 346; Mann, *1491: New Revelations*, 339–43.
15. After consultation with tribes and much public debate, the Smithsonian Institution in 2004 opened the National Museum of the American Indian.
16. Thiele, "Some Notes on the Lance and Lancers," 31–37.
17. The terms "Apaches mansos" and "tame Apaches" are seen less often in U.S. government documents after the 1860s. Officer, *Hispanic Arizona*, 309, 328–30, 403n87.
18. According to the National Commission for the Development of Indigenous Peoples (Comisión Nacional para el Desarrollo de los Pueblos Indígenas, or CDI) and the INEGI (official census institute), there are 15.7 million indigenous people in Mexico, of many different ethnic groups, who constitute 14.9 percent of the population in the country. The number of indigenous Mexicans is judged using the political criteria found in the second article of the Mexican constitution. Some scholars believe that Euro-Americans, especially Anglos, hardened the distinction between "Mexicans" (*mestizos*) and Indians in the borderlands. Mora, *Border Dilemmas*, 61, 276.
19. Scott, *Military Dictionary*, 419–21.
20. Benedict Anderson considers nation-state building as imitative action, in which new political entities "pirate" the model of the nation-state. As Anderson sees it, the populations of the political entities that sprang up in the Americas between 1778 and 1838 all self-consciously defined themselves as nations and were historically the first such states ever to do so. He concluded that these nations provided the first real models for what such states should look like and that nationalism, as an instrument of nation-state building, began in the Americas. In all these cases the newly declared nations defined boundaries that physically delineated their territory. Anderson, *Imagined Communities*, 5–8.
21. Evolutionary anthropologists recognize raiding as a common survival strategy of foraging-pastoral societies. Warriors are more likely to reproduce their genes, but there are adaptive advantages of raiding by stealth as opposed to open combat. Glowacki and Wrangham, "Warfare and Reproductive Success."
22. Anglo officers expressed conflicting opinions on the status of peons. See J. H. Whitlock to Nelson H. Davis, Aug. 22, 1866, and Davis to Whitlock, Sept. 1, 1866, in House Exec. Doc. No. 1, 39th Congress, 2nd Session, Serial No. 1284, 137. The Peonage Act of 1867 abolished "the holding of any person to service or labor under the system known as peonage," specifically banning "the voluntary or involuntary service or labor of any persons as peons, in liquidation of any debt or obligation." Soifer, "Federal Protection," 1617; Goluboff, "Thirteenth Amendment," 1609, 1638.
23. Sturtevant, *Handbook of North American Indians*, 13:488.
24. Goodwin, *Western Apache Raiding*, 16; Opler, *Apache Life-Way*, 322. General Phil Sheridan categorized the seminomadic southwestern tribes as "roving and predatory bands." *Record of Engagements With Hostile Indians*, 7.

25. O'Neil, *They Die But Once*, 155. Comanches and Kiowas also used the term Tejano or Tehanna for Anglo Texans. Wilbarger, *Indian Depredations in Texas*, 600–601. Camped beside the Rio Grande, First California Infantry Private Eli Hazen referred to Texans as "Texicans" and "Texians" in the same sentence in the notes accompanying his August 8, 1862, diary entry. Schreier, "Hazen's Civil War Diary," 45. Hispanos also referred to Texans as "Texians" or "Texanians" in depredation claims. See, for examples, José Luna v. Navajo, Case 2567 and Nestor Armijo v. Navajo, Case 425, RG 123, NARA.
26. See Neely, "Was the Civil War a Total War?" 434–58. See also Bell, *The First Total War*.
27. Using British barristers and judges as an illustration, the people *customarily* argue and pass judgment while the robes and wigs they wear are *traditional*. Hobsbawm and Ranger, *Invention of Tradition*, 2–3.
28. There is considerable debate over this term, and anthropologists are now wary of it due to the perceived differences between pre-state tribes and contemporary tribes. There is controversy, especially in African studies, over the cultural evolution of tribes and colonialism. In the popular imagination and common usage today, the term "tribe" usually reflects a way of life predating and more natural than that of modern states.
29. Clausewitz, *On War*; Goodwin, *Western Apache Raiding*, 16.

Bibliography

Primary Sources

Akers, Thomas. Diary, October 8, 1861–December 6, 1865. University of Arizona Library Special Collections, Tucson.

Allyn, Joseph P. *The Arizona of Joseph Pratt Allyn.* Edited by John Nicholson. Tucson: University of Arizona Press, 1974.

———. *West By Southwest: Letters of Joseph Pratt Allyn, A Traveler Along the Santa Fe Trail, 1863.* Edited by David K. Strate. Dodge City: Kansas Heritage Center, 1984.

Annual Report of the Commissioner of Indian Affairs, 1861, 1862, 1863, 1864, 1865, 1866, 1867. Washington, D.C.: Government Printing Office, 1861–67.

Appendix to the Journals of the Senate and Assembly of the 16th Session of the Legislature of the State of California. Vol. 1. Sacramento: O. M. Clayes, State Printer, 1866.

Archivo Histórico de APAN, Centro Cultural, Mexico City, México.

Archivo Histórico Genaro Estrada, Mexico City, Mexico.

Ayer, Edward E. "Reminiscences of Edward E. Ayer, 1860–1918." Arizona Historical Society, Tucson.

———. "Reminiscences of the Far West and Other Trips, 1861–1918." Bancroft Library, University of California, Berkeley.

Basch, Samuel. *Recollections of Mexico: The Last Ten Months of Maximilian's Empire.* 1868. Reprint, Wilmington, DE: Scholarly Resources, 2001.

Bennett, Clarence E. Diary and Papers. Arizona Historical Society, Tucson.

Bent, George. Letters. Coe Collection. Beinecke Library, Yale University, New Haven, Connecticut.

Bourke, John G. *On the Border with Crook.* New York: Charles Scribner's Sons, 1891.

Bowman, A. "Diary of Corporal A. Bowman, Pace-counter, Co. B., 5th Infantry, California Volunteers." University of Arizona Library Special Collections, Tucson.

Bowman, Alexander Grayson. Diary, December 20, 1861–February 22, 1865. Typescript. University of Arizona Library Special Collections, Tucson.

Brinckerhoff, Sidney B. "Last of the Lancers: The Native California Cavalry Volunteers, 1863–1866." Arizona Historical Society, Tucson.

Browne, J. Ross. *Adventures in the Apache Country.* New York: Harper and Brothers, 1869.

———. *Resources of the Pacific Slope.* New York: D. Appleton, 1869.

Bushnell, William Addison. Diary, 1865. Typescript in author's possession.

Carleton, James H. "Papers Relating to Service in Arizona and New Mexico, 1851–1865." Stanford University Libraries, Palo Alto, California.

———. *Correspondence between Carleton and Governor F. F. Low Concerning Complaints of California Volunteers Discharged in Arizona.* Sacramento: O. M. Clayes, State Printer, 1865.

Carlson, Edward. "Martial Experiences of the California Volunteers." *Overland Monthly,* May 1886, 480–90.

Carson, Kit. *Kit Carson's Autobiography.* Edited by Milo Milton Quaife. Lincoln: University of Nebraska Press, 1966.

Castañeda de Nájera, Pedro de. *Narrative of the Expedition to Cíbola, Undertaken in 1540.* In *Narratives of the Coronado Expedition.* Edited by George P. Hammond and Agapito Rey. Vol. 2, Coronado Cuarto Centennial Publications. Albuquerque: University of New Mexico Press, 1940.

Centro de Estudios de Historia de México CARSO

Chamberlain, Samuel E. *My Confession: Recollections of a Rogue.* New York: Harper and Brothers, 1956.

Clausewitz, Carl von. *On War.* Translated by J. J. Graham. London: Kegan Paul, Trench, Trübner, 1908.

Cleghorn, Mildred Imach. (Eh-Ohn, 1910–97), Chiricahua POW and first chair of the Fort Sill Apache Tribe. Personal communication, July 10, 1986. Fort Sill Apache Tribe, Apache, Oklahoma.

Clothing Account Books of California Volunteer Regiments, 1861–66. California State Library, Sacramento.

Comisión Pesquisidora de la Frontera del Norte. Informé de la Comisión Pesquisidora de la frontera del Norte al Ejecutivo de la Unión en cumplimiento del artículo 30 de la ley de 30 de Septiembre de 1872, Monterey, Mayo de 1873. México: Imprenta de Díaz de Leóny White, 1877.

Congressional Globe. 37th Congress, 1st Session, 1861.

Conner, Daniel E. *Joseph Reddeford Walker and the Arizona Adventure.* Edited by Donald Berthrong and Odessa Davenport. Norman: University of Oklahoma Press, 1956.

Cooke, Philip St. George. *Cavalry Tactics, or Regulations for the Instruction, Formulations, and Movements of the Cavalry of the Army and Volunteers of the United States.* Philadelphia: J. B. Lippincott, 1862.

Cremony, John C. *Life Among the Apaches.* New York: A. Roman, 1868.

———. "The Apache Race." *Overland Monthly* 1, no. 3 (September 1868): 201–9.

———. "How and Why We Took Santa Cruz." *Overland Monthly* 6, no. 1 (April 1871): 335–40.

————. "Some Savages." *Overland Monthly* 8, no. 3 (March 1872): 201–10.

Davis, Alonzo E. "Pioneer Days in Arizona by One Who Was There." Typescript. Arizona Historical Society, Tucson.

————. "Pioneer Days in Arizona by One Who Was There." Edited by Louise Van Cleve, Jessie White, and Rae Van Cleve (1916). Arizona State University Library, Tempe.

De la Guerra Papers. Owen Coy Room. University of Southern California Library, Los Angeles.

de las Casas, Bartolomé. *Short Account of the Destruction of the Indies.* 1552. Reprint, London: Penguin, 1999.

D'Heureuse Photograph Collection. Bancroft Library, University of California, Berkeley.

Doolittle, J. R. *Condition of the Indian Tribes: Joint Special Committee Report; Appointed under Joint Resolution of March 3, 1865.* U.S. Congress, Washington, D.C.: Government Printing Office, 1867.

Elías, Amelia. "Reminiscences of Amelia Elías." Arizona Historical Society, Tucson.

Emory, William Hemsley and U.S. Army Corps of Topographical Engineers. *Lieutenant Emory Reports: A Reprint of Lieutenant William H. Emory's Notes of a Military Reconnaissance.* Edited by Ross Calvin. Albuquerque: University of New Mexico Press, 1951.

Evans, George S. *List of Electors Resident of California in the Military Service of the United States.* Sacramento: State Printing Office, 1865.

Farrow, Edward S. *Mountain Scouting; A Handbook for Officers and Soldiers on the Frontiers.* Reprint, Norman: University of Oklahoma Press, 2000. First published 1881.

Fergusson, David. Biographical File. Arizona Historical Society, Tucson.

Fireman, Bert. "Jack Swilling, the New Father of Arizona." Arizona Collection. Arizona Historical Foundation, Tempe.

Fort Sill National Historic Landmark and Museum, Lawton, Oklahoma.

Franklin, Louise Estes. "In Memory of Alexander G. Bowman [Co. B, 5th California Infantry]." University of Arizona Library Special Collections, Tucson.

Gilman Collection, The Metropolitan Museum of Art.

Grace, Joanne. Private Collection.

Gwyther, George [Co. K, 1st Infantry, C.V.] "Our Scout to Black Canyon." *Overland Monthly,* September 1870.

Haire, Jesse S. Journals, 1859–97. Ohio Historical Society.

Hand, George. Diary, 1861–63. Arizona Historical Society, Tucson.

Hayden Arizona Pioneer Biography Files. Arizona Historical Society, Tucson.

Hitchcock Collection. Photograph Collections. El Dorado County Museum, Placerville, California.

Hitchcock, Aaron Cory. Letters, 1864–66. Copies in author's possession.

Hughes, T. "Anonymous Journalism." *MacMillan's Magazine* 5 (December 1861): 157–68.

Ickis, Alonzo Ferdinand. *Bloody Trails Along the Rio Grande—A Day-by-Day Diary of Alonzo Ferdinand Ickis.* Edited by Nolie Mumey. Denver: Old West Publishing, 1958.

Indian Depredation Records, All Claims Filed to 1887. House Ex Docket 125, 49th Congress, 1st Session, Congressional Serial Set 2399, No. 125, Vol. 31.

Indian Depredations, Hearings Before the United States Congress, House Committee on Indian Affairs. Washington, D.C.: Government Printing Office, 1908.

Journal of the Executive Proceedings of the Senate. Wilmington, DE: M. Glazier, 1887.

Littell, E. *Littell's Living Age.* Boston: Littell, Son and Company, 1865.

Lummis, Charles F. *The Land of Poco Tiempo.* New York: Charles Scribners, 1893.

Marriage Registry, 1864–67. San Augustin Cathedral, Tucson.

McCleave, William A. "Our Scout to Black Canyon." BANC MSS, C-B 300, William McCleave Papers. Bancroft Library, University of California, Berkeley.

———. William McCleave Papers. Bancroft Library, University of California, Berkeley.

McClelland Papers, Library and Archives. Senator John Heinz History Center, Pittsburgh, Pennsylvania.

Memorial and Affidavits Showing Outrages Perpetrated by the Apache Indians in the Territory of Arizona for the Years 1869 and 1870. San Francisco: Arizona Territorial Legislature, 1871.

Message of the President of the United States, of March 20, 1866, Relating to the Condition of Affairs in Mexico, in Answer to a Resolution of the House of December 11, 1865. U.S. Department of State, Washington, D.C.: Government Printing Office, 1866.

Message of the President of the United States, of January 29, 1867, Relating to the Present Condition of Mexico, 39th Congress, 2nd session, House Executive Documents. Washington, D.C.: Government Printing Office, 1867.

Mohave County Book of Claims, 1864–66. Mohave County Courthouse, Kingman, Arizona.

Morris, William G. *Address Delivered Before the Society of California Volunteers.* "Combats with the Indians of Arizona and New Mexico." San Francisco: Society of California Volunteers, 1866.

Mowry, Sylvester. *Arizona and Sonora: The Geography, History, and Resources of the Silver Region of North America.* 3rd ed., 1864. Reprint, New York: Arno, 1973.

———. *The Geography and Resources of Arizona and Sonora.* San Francisco, 1863.

Museo del Virreinato, Tepotzotlán.

Museo Nacional de las Intervenciones, Instituto Nacional de Antropología e Historia, Mexico City.

National Archives Records Administration, Washington, D.C.

Record Group 15: Pension Files, Records of the Department of Veterans Affairs

Record Group 75: Evidence Concerning Depredation Cases, entry 700, 1835–1896; Records of the New Mexico Superintendency of Indian Affairs 1849–80

Record Group 92: Records of the Office of the Quartermaster General

Record Group 94: Records of the Office of the Adjutant General, Letters Received; California Volunteers, Regimental Letter Books, 1861–66; California Volunteers Clothing Accounts; California Volunteers Descriptive Lists; Compiled Military Service Records of California, Colorado, and New Mexico Volunteers 1861–67

Record Group 98: U.S. Army Commands, Fort Bowie Letters Received, 1862–71

Record Group 109: Records of Organizations from the Territory of Arizona; War Department Collection of Confederate Records

Record Group 123: Records of the U.S. Court of Claims, Indian Depredation Case Records

Record Group 156: Benicia Arsenal Letters Sent, 1846–1923; Office of the Chief of Ordnance, Returns, 1861–65; Office of the Inspector General, Extracts of Inspection Reports, 1864–65; Records of the Chief of Ordnance, "Records of Arsenals and Armories, 1794–1944

Record Group 205: Records of the Court of Claims Section of the Department of Justice, Indian Depredation Case Records, entries 71–80.

Record Group 393: Department of the Pacific, General, Special, and Post Orders, 1861–66; Department of California, Letters Sent, 1861–62; Department of the Pacific, Letters Sent, 1861–66; Records of the U.S. Army Continental Commands, Commands of J. R. West, Special, General, and Post Orders, 1861–65

Nentvig, Juan. *Rudo Ensayo Sonora; tentativa de una prevencional descripcion geographica de la provincia de Sonora, sus terminos y confines; ó mejor, Coleccion de materiales para hacerla quien lo supiere mejor. Compilada así de noticias adquiridas por el colector en sus viajes por casi toda ella, como subministradas por los padres missioneros y practicos de la tierra.* San Augustin de la Florida: Albany, Munsell Printer, 1863.

Newcomb, James P. Papers, Journals, and Diaries, 1857–71. Center for American History, University of Texas at Austin.

Newton, Irene. "Column from California." California State Library, Sacramento.

Noel, Theophilus. *A Campaign from Santa Fe to the Mississippi: Being a History of the Old Sibley Brigade, 1861–1864.* Originally published 1865, Shreveport, Louisiana. Houston: Stagecoach Press, 1961.

Oakes, George. Reminiscence. Arizona Historical Society, Tucson.

O'Neil, James B., with Jeff Ake. *They Die But Once: The Story of a Tejano.* New York: Knight Publications, 1935.

Ordnance Manual for the Use of the Officers of the United States Army. 3rd ed. Philadelphia: J. B. Lippincott, 1861.

Orton, Richard H. *Records of California Men in the War of the Rebellion 1861 to 1867.* Sacramento: State Printing Office, 1890.

Oury Family Papers. University of Arizona Library Special Collections, Tucson.

Patterson, Moses. Diary, December 1863–April 1866. California State Library, Sacramento.

Peticolas, A. B. Diary. Arizona Historical Society, Tucson.

———. *Rebels on the Rio Grande: The Civil War Journal of A. B. Peticolas.* Edited by Don E. Alberts. Albuquerque: University of New Mexico Press, 1984.

Pettis, George H. *The California Column.* Monograph 11. Santa Fe: Historical Society, 1908.

———. *Frontier Service during the Rebellion, or a History of Co. K, First Infantry, California Volunteers.* Providence: Rhode Island Soldiers and Sailors Historical Society, 1885.

———. *Kit Carson's Fight with the Comanche and Kiowa Indians.* Providence: Sidney S. Ryder, 1878.

———. Papers. Western Americana Collection. Beinecke Library, Yale University, New Haven, Connecticut.

———. *Personal Narratives of Events in the War of the Rebellion, Frontier Service.* Providence: Soldiers' and Sailors' Historical Society of Rhode Island, 1885.

Porter, Horace. *Campaigning with Grant.* New York: Century Company, 1897.

Poston, Charles D. "History of the Apaches." 1886. University of Arizona Library Special Collections, Tucson.

———. "Military Roads in Arizona." *American Railroad Journal* 38 (January 14, 1865): 54.

Poston, Ida Louis Estes. Untitled reminiscences of Alexander G. Bowman (uncle), 1957. University of Arizona Library Special Collections, Tucson.

Record of Engagements with Hostile Indians within the Military Division of the Missouri, from 1868 to 1882, Lieutenant General P. H. Sheridan, Commanding. Compiled from Official Records. Chicago: Headquarters Military Division of the Missouri, 1882.

Report of the Commissioner of Indian Affairs. U.S. Senate. Exec. Doc. 1, part 1. Serial 974. 35th Congress, 2nd Session, 1858.

Report on Indians Taxed and Indians Not Taxed in the United States (except Alaska). Department of the Interior, Eleventh Census 1890. Washington, D.C.: Government Printing Office, 1894.

Revised Regulations for the Army of the United States, 1861. Philadelphia: J. G. L. Brown, 1861.

Revised U.S. Army Regulations of 1861. Washington, D.C.: Government Printing Office, 1863.

Ryan, Andrew. *News from Fort Craig, New Mexico, 1863: Civil War Letters of Andrew Ryan with the First California Volunteers.* Edited by Ernest Marchand. Santa Fe: Stagecoach, 1966.

Salm-Salm, Prince Felix Constantine Alexander Johan Nepomak. *My Diary in Mexico 1867: Including the Last Days of the Emperor Maximilian.* London: R. Bentley, 1868.

Scott, Henry L. *Military Dictionary: Comprising Technical Definitions; Information on Raising and Keeping Troops; Actual Service, Including Makeshifts and Improved Matériel; and Law, Government, Regulation, and Administration Relating to Land Forces.* New York: Van Nostrand, 1864.

Select Committee on Indian Depredation Claims Report No. 1701. 50th Congress, 1st Session, House of Representatives, Report to Accompany Bill H. R. 9383.

St. Hoyme, L. E. "The Skull of Mangas Coloradas." Report. Smithsonian Institution, National Museum of Natural History.

Stevenson, Sara Yorke. *A Woman's Reminiscences of the French Intervention in Mexico, 1862–7.* New York: Century Company, 1897.

Stone, Charles P. *Notes on the State of Sonora.* Washington, D.C.: Henry Polkinhorn, printer, 1861.

Stratton, Royal B. *Life Among the Indians: Being an Interesting Narrative of the Captivity of the Oatman Girls, Among the Apache and Mohave Indians.* San Francisco: Whitton, Townet, 1857.

Tappan, Samuel. Samuel Forster Tappan Collection. MSS 617. History Colorado, Denver, Colorado.

Teel, Trevanion T. "Sibley's New Mexican Campaign: Its Objects and the Causes of its Failure." *Battles and Leaders of the Civil War*. Vol. 2. New York: Yoseloff, 1956.

Tidball, Thomas T. Diary. Huntington Library, San Marino, California.

Tompkins, Edith C. Manuscript. Small Collection, John Spring Papers 1850–1921. Arizona Historical Society, Tucson.

Tuttle, Edward D. Diary. University of Arizona Library Special Collections, Tucson.

Tuttle, Edward D. Letters. Huntington Library, San Marino, California.

U.S. Army Charges and Specifications, Courts-Martial and Courts of Inquiry, 1817–93. E. D. Townsend, AAG. Washington, D.C.: Government Printing Office, 1893.

U.S. Army, Chronological List of Actions &c, with the Indians from January 15, 1837 to January, 1891. Adjutant General's Office, Washington, D.C.: Government Printing Office, 1891.

U.S. Army, Chronological List of Actions; Report of the Secretary of the Interior, Commissioner of Indian Affairs, Arizona Superintendency and New Mexico Superintendency, 1861–1866.

U.S. Census. *Federal Census—Territory of New Mexico and Territory of Arizona (1860, 1864, 1870)*. 89th Congress, 1st Session, S. Doc. 13. 1965.

U.S. Census. *Seventh Census of the United States: 1850*. Washington: Robert Armstrong, Public Printer, 1853.

U.S. Congress. *Execution of Colonel Crabb and Associates, Message from the President of the United States*. House of Representatives, 35th Congress, 1st Session, Exec. Doc. 64, 1858.

U.S. Congress. *Special Report*, James H. Carleton, 57th Congress, 1st Session, House Exec. Doc. 605, Serial 4377.

U.S. Infantry Tactics. Philadelphia: J. B. Lippincott, 1863.

U.S. War Department. *Annual Report of the Secretary of War, 1860, 1861, 1862, 1863, 1864, 1865, 1866, 1867*. Washington, D.C.: Government Printing Office, 1860–67.

Wade, Benjamin. *Report of the Joint Committee on the Conduct of the War*. U.S. Senate Report No. 142, 38th Congress, 2nd Session. 3 vols. Washington, D.C.: Government Printing Office, 1865.

War of the Rebellion: The Official Records of the Union and Confederate Armies. 139 vols. Washington, D.C.: Government Printing Office, 1880–1901. [All references cited are from Series I and are cited as *OR*.]

Watts, John S. *Indian Depredations in New Mexico*. Washington, D.C.: Gideon, 1858.

Wyckoff, Charles A. "Journal of Company C, Seventh Infantry, California Volunteers, May 20, 1865, to March 26, 1866." Typescript by Aurora Hunt of original at Sutter's Fort Museum, Sacramento, California. Sharlot Hall Museum, Prescott, Arizona.

Wynkoop, Edward. Edward Wanshear Wynkoop Collection. MSS 695. History Colorado, Denver, Colorado.

Yavapai County Book of Deeds and Claims No. 1, Yavapai County Courthouse, Prescott, Arizona.

Yavapai County Marriage Register. Typescript. Arizona Historical Society, Tucson.

Dissertations, Theses, and Papers

Dayton, Dello G. "California Militia, 1850–66." PhD dissertation, University of California, Berkeley, 1959.

Edwards, Glenn Thomas, Jr. "The Department of the Pacific in the Civil War." PhD dissertation, University of Oregon, 1963.

Fireman, Bert M. "Extending the Civil War Westward to the Bloodied Banks of the Colorado River." Paper presented at the Arizona Historical Convention, Tucson, March 16, 1962.

Hastings, Virginia. "A History of Arizona during the Civil War." Master's thesis, University of Arizona, 1943.

Jagodinsky, Katrina. "Intimate Obscurity: American Indian Women in Arizona Households and Histories, 1854–1935." PhD dissertation, University of Arizona, 2011.

Jewell, James Robbins. "Left Arm of the Republic: The Department of the Pacific during the Civil War." PhD dissertation, West Virginia University, 2006.

Killin, Hugh E. "The Texans and the California Column." Master's thesis, Texas Technological College, 1931.

Lewis, Albert L. "Los Angeles in the Civil War Decades, 1851–1868." PhD dissertation, University of Southern California, 1970.

Murray, Richard Y. "The History of Fort Bowie." Master's thesis, University of Arizona, 1951.

Pani, Erika. "Between Reform, an 'Ungodly Constitution,' and National Defense: Mexico's Civil War, 1858–67." a paper delivered at the American Historical Association Conference, Washington, D.C., January 2, 2014.

Roberts, Gary L. "Sand Creek: Tragedy and Symbol." PhD dissertation, University of Oklahoma, 1984.

Rogan, Francis Edward. "Military History of New Mexico Territory during the Civil War." PhD dissertation, University of Utah, 1961.

Underhill, Lonnie. "A History of the Regiment of Arizona Volunteers." Master's thesis, University of Arizona, 1979.

Yoder, Phillip D. "The History of Fort Whipple." Master's thesis, University of Arizona, 1951.

Newspapers

Arizona Daily Star (Tucson)
Arizona Enterprise
Arizona Miner (Prescott)
Army and Navy Journal
Boston Daily Advertiser
　　"The Execution of Maximilian." July 6, 1867.
Calaveras (California) Chronicle
Daily Rocky Mountain News (Denver)
Downieville (California) Sierra Democrat

Dutch Flat (California) Enquirer
El Diario del Imperio
Los Angeles News
Los Angeles Tri-Weekly News
Los Angeles Weekly Star
Mesilla Valley Independent
Oakland (California) Tribune
National Tribune
> Hall, Julius C. "In the Wild West: Arizona at the Outbreak of the Rebellion . . . Campaigning across the Arid Plains in 1862." October 20, 1887.

New Orleans Picayune
New York Times
> "Mexico and the Mexicans." July 26, 1867.

> "Northern Mexico: Civil War in Sonora, Invasion of the State from the North, Indian Depredations, Miscellaneous." October 18, 1860.

> Raymond, Henry Jarvis [H. J. R.]. "The History of Foreign Intervention in Mexico." July 9 and July 12, 1867.

> Wong, Edward. "A Matter of Definition: What Makes a Civil War, and Who Declares It So?" November 26, 2006.

New York Tribune
Prescott (Arizona) Courier
Sacramento Record Union
Sacramento Union
San Francisco Call
San Francisco Daily Alta California
San Francisco Evening Bulletin
San Francisco Herald and Mirror
San Francisco Weekly Alta California
Santa Fe Gazette
Santa Fe New Mexican
Tucson Arizona Citizen
Washington Daily National Intelligencer
> "The Franco-Mexican Question." January 6, 1866.

> "The Military Execution of Maximilian Confirmed." July 2, 1867.

Wilmington (California) Journal

Published Books and Articles

Acuña, Rodolfo F. *Sonoran Strongman: Ignacio Pesqueira and His Times*. Tucson: University of Arizona Press, 1974.

Acuña, Rudolph F. "Ignacio Pesqueira: Sonoran Caudillo." *Arizona and the West* 12, no. 2 (Summer 1970).

Adelman, Jeremy and Stephen Aron. "From Borderlands to Borders: Empires, Nation-States, and the Peoples in Between in North American History." *American Historical Review* 104 (June 1999): 814–41.

Afton, Jean, David F. Halaas, and Andrew E. Masich. *Cheyenne Dog Soldiers, A Ledgerbook History of Coups and Combat*. Niwot: University Press of Colorado, 1997.

Agnew, S. C. *Garrisons of the Regular US Army, 1851–1899*. Arlington: Council on Abandoned Military Posts, 1974.

Ahnert, Gerald T. *Retracing the Butterfield Overland Trail through Arizona: A Guide to the Route of 1857–1861*. Los Angeles: Westernlore, 1973.

Alberts, Don E. *The Battle of Glorieta: Union Victory in the West*. 1998. Reprint, College Station: Texas A&M University Press, 2001.

Almada, Francisco R. *Diccionario de Historia, Geografía, y Biografía Sonorenses*. Chihuahua, Mexico, 1952.

Alt, William E. and Betty S. Alt. *Black Soldiers, White Wars: Black Warriors from Antiquity*. Westport, CT: Praeger, 2002.

Altshuler, Constance Wynn. "Camp Moore and Fort Mason." *Council on Abandoned Military Posts Periodical* 26 (Winter 1976): 34–37.

———. "The Case of Sylvester Mowry, the Charge Treason." *Arizona and the West* 15 (Spring 1973): 63–82.

———. "The Case of Sylvester Mowry, the Mowry Mine." *Arizona and the West* 15 (Summer 1973): 149–74.

———. *Cavalry Yellow and Infantry Blue: Army Officers in Arizona between 1851 and 1886*. Tucson: Arizona Historical Society, 1991.

———. *Chains of Command: Arizona and the Army, 1856–1875*. Tucson: Arizona Historical Society, 1981.

———. *Latest from Arizona!: The Hesperian Letters, 1859–61*. Tucson: Arizona Historical Society, 1969.

———. "Military Administration in Arizona, 1854–1865." *Journal of Arizona History* 10 (Winter 1969): 215–38.

———. "Poston and the Pimas: The 'Father of Arizona' as Indian Superintendent." *Journal of Arizona History* 18 (Spring 1977): 23–42.

———. *Starting with Defiance: Nineteenth Century Arizona Military Posts*. Tucson: Arizona Historical Society, 1983.

Anderson, Benedict R. *Imagined Communities: Reflections on the Origin and Spread of Nationalism*. London: Verso, 1991, revised 2006.

Anderson, Fred, and Andrew Cayton. *The Dominion of War: Empire and Liberty in North America, 1500–2000*. New York: Viking, 2005.

Anderson, Gary C. *Conquest of Texas: Ethnic Cleansing in the Promised Land*. Norman: University of Oklahoma Press, 2005.

Archambeau, Ernest R. "The New Mexico Campaign of 1861–1862." *Panhandle Plains Historical Review* 37 (1964): 3–32.

Arenson, Adam and Andrew Graybill, eds. *Civil War Wests: Testing the Limits of the United States*. Oakland: University of California Press, 2015.

Armstrong, A. F. "The Case of Major Isaac Lynde." *New Mexico Historical Review* 36 (January 1961): 1–35.

Aron, Stephen. "Frontiers, Borderlands, Wests." In *American History Now*, edited by Eric Foner and Lisa McGirr. Philadelphia: Temple University Press, 2011.

Arrington, Leonard J. *Great Basin Kingdom: An Economic History of the Latter Day Saints, 1830–1900*. Salt Lake City: University of Utah Press, 2000.

Athearn, Robert G. "West of Appomattox: An Interpretive Look at the Civil War and Its Impact beyond the Great River." *Montana: The Magazine of Western History* 12 (April 1962): 2–12.

Ávila, Velasco. *En manos de los bárbaros. Testimonios de la Guerra india en el noreste*. Mexico: Breve Fondo Editorial, 1996.

Avillo, Phillip V. "Fort Mojave: Outpost on the Upper Colorado." *Journal of Arizona History* 2 (Summer 1970): 77–100.

Bagley, Will. *Blood of the Prophets: Brigham Young and the Massacre at Mountain Meadows.* Norman: University of Oklahoma Press, 2002.

———. "Lansford Warren Hastings: Scoundrel or Visionary?" *Overland Journal* 12, no. 1 (Spring 1994): 12–26.

Bailey, Lynn R. *If You Take My Sheep: the Evolution and Conflicts of Navajo Pastoralism, 1630–1868.* Pasadena: Westernlore Publications, 1980.

———. *Indian Slave Trade in the Southwest: A Study of Slavetaking and the Traffic of Indian Captives.* Los Angeles: Westernlore Press, 1966.

———. *The Long Walk. A History of the Navajo Wars, 1846–68.* Pasadena: Westernlore Publications, 1978.

———. "Thomas Varker Keam: Tusayan Trader." *Arizoniana* 2 (Winter 1960): 15–19.

Bailey, Thomas. *A Diplomatic History of the American People.* Englewood Cliffs, NJ: Prentice-Hall, 1974.

Bakewell, Peter. *A History of Latin America c.1450 to the Present.* 2nd ed. Oxford: Blackwell, 2004.

Ball, Eve. *In the Days of Victorio: Recollections of a Warm Springs Apache.* Tucson: University of Arizona Press, 1970.

———. *Indeh, An Apache Odyssey.* Norman: University of Oklahoma Press, 1988.

Bancroft, Hubert H. *History of Arizona and New Mexico, 1530–1888.* 1889. Reprint, Albuquerque: Horn and Wallace, 1962.

———. *History of Mexico.* 6 vols. San Francisco: History Company, 1888.

Bancroft, Hubert H., with J. J. Peatfield, H. L. Oak and W. Nemos. *History of the North Mexican States.* San Francisco: A. L. Bancroft, 1889.

Bandel, Eugene. *Frontier Life in the Army, 1854–1861.* Glendale, CA: Arthur H. Clark, 1932.

Barnes, William C. *Arizona Place Names.* Revised and edited by Byrd H. Granger. Tucson: University of Arizona Press, 1985.

Barney, James M. "Battle of Apache Pass." *Arizona Highways,* January–February 1936.

———. "Colonel Edward E. Eyre." *Sheriff Magazine,* March 1952.

Barr, Alwyn. *Black Texans: A History of African Americans in Texas, 1528–1995.* 2nd ed. Norman: University of Oklahoma Press, 1996.

———. "Texas Civil War Historiography." *Texas Libraries* 26 (Winter 1964): 160–69.

Barr, Juliana. *Peace Came in the Form of a Woman: Indians and Spaniards in the Texas Borderlands.* Chapel Hill: University of North Carolina Press, 2007.

Barry, Louise. "The Ranch at Cow Creek Crossing." *Kansas Historical Quarterly* 38, no. 4 (Winter 1972): 416–44.

Baylor, George Wythe. *John Robert Baylor: Confederate Governor of Arizona.* Edited by Odie B. Faulk. Tucson: Arizona Pioneers Historical Society, 1966.

Beard, Charles A. *The Rise of American Civilization.* New York: Macmillan, 1927.

Beck, Warren A., and Ynez D. Haase. *Historical Atlas of New Mexico.* Norman: University of Oklahoma Press, 1976.

Bell, David A. *The First Total War: Napoleon's Europe and the Birth of Warfare as We Know It.* Boston and New York: Houghton Mifflin, 2007.

Bellah, James Warner. "The Desert Campaign." *Civil War Times,* April 1961.

Bender, Thomas, ed. *The Antislavery Debate: Capitalism and Abolitionism as a Problem of Historical Interpretation.* Berkeley: University of California Press, 1992.

Benet, William Rose. *Reader's Encyclopedia.* New York: Crowell, 1969.

Bensell, Royal A. *All Quiet on the Yamhill: The Civil War in Oregon.* Edited by Gunther Barth. Eugene: University of Oregon Books, 1969.

Berdal, Mats, and David M. Malone. *Greed and Grievance: Economic Agendas in Civil Wars.* Boulder, CO: Lynne Rienner Publishers, 2000.

Berthrong, Donald J. *The Southern Cheyennes.* Norman: University of Oklahoma Press, 1963.

Black, Jeremy. *America as a Military Power 1775–1882.* Santa Barbara: Greenwood, 2002.

Blackhawk, Ned. *Violence over the Land: Indians and Empires in the Early American West.* Cambridge: Harvard University Press, 2006.

Blyth, Lance R. *Chiricahuas and Janos: Communities of Violence in the Southwestern Borderlands, 1680–1880.* Lincoln: University of Nebraska Press, 2012.

Boatner, Mark M. *The Civil War Dictionary.* New York: David McKay, 1966.

Bolton, Herbert E. *Coronado, Knight of Pueblos and Plains.* New York: McGraw Hill, 1949.

———. *The Spanish Borderlands: A Chronicle of Old Florida and The Southwest.* New Haven: Yale University Press, 1921. Reprint, introduction by Albert L. Hurtado, Albuquerque: University of New Mexico Press, 1996.

Braatz, Timothy. *Surviving Conquest: A History of the Yavapai Peoples.* Lincoln: University of Nebraska Press, 2003.

Brady, Francis P. "Portrait of a Pioneer, Peter R. Brady, 1825–1902." *Journal of Arizona History* 16 (Summer 1975): 171–94.

Brandes, Ray. *Frontier Military Posts of Arizona.* Globe, AZ: Dale Stuart King, 1960.

Brennan, Irene J., ed. *Fort Mojave, 1859–1890: Letters of the Commanding Officers.* Manhattan: MA/AH, Kansas State University, 1980.

Brinckerhoff, Sidney B. *Boots and Shoes of the Frontier Soldier, 1865–1893.* Museum Monograph 7. Tucson: Arizona Historical Society, 1976.

———. "Soldiers Came, Fought, and Stayed." *Arizona* 15 (1975): 76–81.

Brooks, James F. *Captives and Cousins: Slavery, Kinship and Community in the Southwest Borderlands.* Chapel Hill: University of North Carolina Press, 2002.

Brooks, James F., Christopher R. N. DeCorse, and John Walton, eds. *Small Worlds: Method, Meaning and Narrative in Microhistory.* Santa Fe: SAR Press, 2008.

Brown, Kathleen. *Good Wives, Nasty Wenches, and Anxious Patriarchs: Gender, Race, and Power in Colonial Virginia.* Chapel Hill: University of North Carolina Press, 1996.

Brugge, David M. *Navajos in the Catholic Church Records of New Mexico, 1694–1875.* Santa Fe: SAR Press, 2010.

Bruyneel, Kevin. "Challenging American Boundaries: Indigenous People and the 'Gift' of U.S. Citizenship." Cambridge University Press, *Studies in American Political Development* 18 (April 2004): 30–43.

Buckwald, V. F. *Handbook of Meteorites.* Berkeley: University of California Press, 1975.

Byars, Charles. "Documents of Arizona History: The First Map of Tucson." *Journal of Arizona History* 7 (Winter 1966): 188–200.

Byrne, Henry L. "Early Journalism in California." *Society of California Pioneers Quarterly* 3 (1926): 108–44.

Calloway, Colin G. *Pen and Ink Witchcraft: Treaties and Treaty Making in American Indian History.* New York: Oxford University Press, 2013.

Carlson, Leonard A. *Indians, Bureaucrats, and Land: The Dawes Act and the Decline of Indian Farming.* Westport, CT: Greenwood Press, 1981.

Carmony, Neil B., ed. *The Civil War in Apacheland: Sergeant George Hand's Diary, California, Arizona, West Texas, New Mexico, 1861–1864.* Silver City, NM: High-Lonesome Books, 1996.

Carroll, John M. ed. *The Sand Creek Massacre: A Documentary History.* New York: Sol Lewis, 1973.

Carroll, Thomas F. "Freedom of Speech and of the Press during the Civil War." *Virginia Law Review* 9 (1923): 516–51.

Case, Lynne M., ed. *French Opinion on the United States and Mexico, 1860–1867; Extracts from the Reports of the Procureurs Généraux.* New York: D. Appleton-Century Company, 1937.

Casebier, Dennis G. *Camp El Dorado, Arizona Territory.* Tempe: Arizona Historical Foundation, 1970.

———. *Carleton's Pa-Ute Campaign.* Norco, California: Tales of the Mojave Road, 1972.

———. *Fort Pa-Ute.* Norco, California: Tales of the Mojave Road, 1974.

———. *Mojave Road.* Norco, California: Tales of the Mojave Road, 1975.

———. *The Mojave Road in Newspapers.* Norco, California: Tales of the Mojave Road, 1976.

Chandler, Robert J. "California's 1863 Loyalty Oaths: Another Look." *Arizona and the West* 21 (Autumn 1979): 215–34.

———. "A Confederate Spy in California: A Curious Incident of the Civil War." *Southern California Quarterly* 45 (September 1963): 219–34.

———. "Dan Showalter—California Secessionist." *California Historical Quarterly* 40 (December 1961): 309–25.

———. "General James Henry Carleton." *New Mexico Historical Review* 30 (January 1955): 23–43.

———. "Southwestern Chronicle: A Little More on Sylvester Mowry." *Arizona Quarterly* 10 (Winter 1954): 358–60.

———. "Southwestern Chronicle: Was Sylvester Mowry a Secessionist?" *Arizona Quarterly* 10 (Winter 1954): 260–66.

———. "An Unknown Chapter in Western History." *Westerners Brand Book, New York Posse* 1 (Summer 1954).

———. "The Velvet Glove: The Army during the Secession Crisis in California, 1860–1865." *Journal of the West* 20 (October 1981): 35–42.

Chartrand, René, and Richard Hook. *The Mexican Adventure 1861–67.* London: Osprey, 1994.

Collier, Paul, and Anke Hoeffler. "On Economic Causes of Civil War." *Oxford Economic Papers.* (50) 4, (1998): 563–73.

———. "Greed and Grievance in Civil War." *Oxford Economic Papers.* (56) 4, (2004): 563–95.

Collier, Paul, and Nicholas Sambanis, eds. *Understanding Civil War: Evidence and Analysis.* Vol. 2, *Europe, Central Asia, and Other Regions.* Washington, D.C.: The World Bank, 2005.

Colton, Ray Charles. *The Civil War in the Western Territories: Arizona, Colorado, New Mexico and Utah.* Norman: University of Oklahoma Press, 1959, reprinted 1984.

Colwell-Chanthaphonh, Chip. "The 'Camp Grant Massacre' in the Historical Imagination." Paper read at the Arizona History Convention, Tempe, Arizona, April 25, 2003.

Comaroff, John, and Jean Comaroff. *Ethnography and the Historical Imagination.* Boulder, CO: Westview Press, 1992.

Conkling, Roscoe P., and Margaret B. Conkling. *The Butterfield Overland Mail, 1857–1869.* 3 vols. Glendale, CA: Arthur H. Clarke, 1947.

Connell, F. S. "The Confederate Territory of Arizona as Compiled from the Official Records." *New Mexico Historical Review* 17 (April 1942): 148–63.

Connell, R. W. *Masculinities.* Berkeley: University of California Press, 2005.

Cook, F. A. "War and Peace: Two Arizona Diaries." *New Mexico Historical Review* 24 (April 1949): 95–129.

Correll, J. Lee. *Through White Men's Eyes: A Contribution to Navajo History: A Chronological Record of the Navajo People from Earliest Times to the Treaty of June 1, 1868.* Window Rock, AZ: Navajo Heritage Center, 1979.

Couvares, Francis G., Martha Saxton, Gerald N. Grob, and George Athan Billias, eds. *Interpretations of American History: Patterns and Perspectives.* Boston: Bedford/St. Martins, 2009.

Cox, James. *Historical and Biographical Record of the Cattle Industry and the Cattlemen of Texas and Adjacent Territory.* St. Louis: Woodward and Tiernan, 1895.

Cullum, George W. *Biographical Register of the Officers and Graduates of the U.S. Military Academy.* New York: Houghton, Mifflin, 1891.

Dabbs, Jack Autrey. *The French Army in Mexico, 1861–1867.* The Hague: Mouton, 1963.

Dary, David. *Red Blood and Black Ink: Journalism in the Old West.* Lawrence: University Press of Kansas, 1998.

Davis, David Brion, Peter Kolchin, Rebecca J. Scott, and Stanley L. Engerman. "AHR Forum: Crossing Slavery's Boundaries." *The American Historical Review* 105, no. 2 (April 2000): 452–79.

DeGraff, Lawrence B., Kevin Mulroy, and Quintard Taylor. *Seeking El Dorado: African Americans in California.* Seattle: University of Washington Press, 2001.

DeLay, Brian. *War of a Thousand Deserts: Indian Raids and the U.S.-Mexican War.* New Haven: Yale University Press, 2008.

de León Toral, Jesús, et al. El ejército Mexicano: historia desde los orígenes hasta nuestros días. México, DF: Secretaría de la Defensa Nacional, 1979.

DeLong, Sidney R. *History of Arizona.* San Francisco: Whitaker and Ray, 1905.

Dickson, Paul. *War Slang: Fighting Words and Phrases of Americans from the Civil War to the Gulf War.* New York: Pocket Books, 1994.

Dillehay, Tom D. *The Settlement of the Americas: A New Prehistory.* New York: Basic Books, 2000.

Donovan, James. *A Terrible Glory: Custer and the Little Bighorn—the Last Great Battle of the American West.* New York: Little, Brown, 2008.

DuBois, W. E. B. *Black Reconstruction in America, 1860–1880.* New York: Harcourt, Brace, 1935.

Duffen, William A. "Overland Via 'Jackass Mail' in 1858: The Diary of Phocion R. Way." *Arizona and the West* 2 (Spring, Summer, Autumn 1960): 35–53.

Duncan, Robert H. "Political Legitimation and Maximilian's Second Empire in Mexico, 1864–67." *Estudios Mexicanos* 12, no. 1 (Winter 1996): 27–66.

Dunlay, Tom. *Kit Carson and the Indians.* Lincoln: University of Nebraska Press, 2000.

Dunning, Charles, and Edward H. Peplow. *Rock to Riches.* Phoenix: Southwest, 1959.

Dutton, Bertha P. *Indians of the American Southwest.* Englewood Cliffs, NJ: Prentice-Hall, 1975.

Dwyer, Philip G., and Lyndall Ryan, eds. *Theatres of Violence: Massacre, Mass Killing and Atrocity throughout History.* New York: Berghahn Books, 2012.

Edrington, Thomas S., and John Taylor. *The Battle of Glorieta Pass: A Gettysburg in the West, March 26–28, 1862.* Albuquerque: University of New Mexico Press, 1998.

Elderfield, John. *Manet and the Execution of Emperor Maximilian.* New York: Museum of Modern Art, 2006.

Elkins, Stanley. *Slavery: A Problem in American Institutional and Intellectual Life.* Chicago: University of Chicago Press, 1959.

Ellis, Edward S. *The Life of Kit Carson: Hunter, Trapper, Guide, Indian Agent and Colonel U.S.A.* New York: Grosset and Dunlap, 1889.

Elson, Mark D., and William H. Doelle. *Archaeological Survey in Catalina State Park with a Focus on the Romero Ruin, Technical Report No. 87–4.* Tucson: Institute for American Research, 1987.

Farish, Thomas E. *History of Arizona.* 8 vols. San Francisco: Filmer Brothers Electrotype, 1915–18.

Ferg, Alan, ed. *Western Apache Material Culture: The Goodwin and Guenther Collections.* Tucson: University of Arizona Press, 1987.

Fields, Barbara. "Ideology and Race." In *Region, Race, and Reconstruction: Essays in Honor of C. Vann Woodward,* edited by J. Morgan Kousser and James McPherson. New York: Oxford University Press, 1982.

Finch, L. Boyd. "Arizona in Exile: Confederate Schemes to Recapture the Far Southwest." *Journal of Arizona History* 33 (Spring 1992): 57–84.

———. "Arizona's Governors without Portfolio: A Wonderfully Diverse Lot." *Journal of Arizona History* 26 (Spring 1985): 77–99.

———. "The Civil War in Arizona: The Confederates Occupy Tucson." *Arizona Highways* 65 (January 1989): 14–17.

———. *Confederate Pathway to the Pacific: Major Sherod Hunter and Arizona Territory, C.S.A.* Tucson: Arizona Historical Society, 1996.

———. "Sanctified by Myth: The Battle of Picacho Pass." *Journal of Arizona History* 36 (Autumn 1995): 251–66.

———. "Sherod Hunter and the Confederates in Arizona." *Journal of Arizona History* 10 (August 1969): 139–206.

———. "William Claude Jones: The Rogue Who Named Arizona." *Journal of Arizona History* 31 (Winter 1990): 405–24.

Fireman, Bert M. "What Comprises Treason? Testimony of Proceedings against Sylvester Mowry." *Arizoniana* 1 (Winter 1960): 5–10.

Fisher, LeRoy H., ed. *The Western Territories in the Civil War*. Manhattan, KS: Sunflower University Press, 1977.

Foner, Eric. *Free Soil, Free Labor, Free Men: The Ideology of the Republican Party before the Civil War*. New York: Oxford University Press, 1970.

———. "The Meaning of Freedom in the Age of Emancipation." *The Journal of American History* 81, no. 2 (1994): 435–60.

Forbes, Jack D. *Apache, Navajo and Spaniard*. Norman: University of Oklahoma Press, 1960.

———. "Historical Survey of the Indians of Sonora, 1821–1910." *Ethnohistory* 4, no. 4 (Autumn 1957): 335–68.

———. *Warriors of the Colorado: The Yumas of the Quechan Nation and Their Neighbors*. Norman: University of Oklahoma Press, 1965.

Forbes, Robert H. *Crabb's Filibustering Expedition into Sonora, 1857*. Tucson: Arizona Silhouettes, 1952.

Fountain, Albert J. *The Life and Death of Colonel Albert Jennings Fountain*. Edited by A. M. Gibson. Norman: University of Oklahoma Press, 1965.

Franklin, Benjamin. *Poor Richard's Almanack*. Philadelphia: B. Franklin, 1758.

Frazier, Donald S. *Blood and Treasure: Confederate Empire in the Southwest*. College Station: Texas A&M University Press, 1995.

Garate, Donald T. *Juan Bautista de Anza: Basque Explorer in the New World, 1698–1740*. Reno: University of Nevada Press, 2003.

Garcia, Genaro, and Carlos Pereyra. *Colección de Documentos Ineditos*. 35 vols. Mexico, D.F., 1905–11.

Garrard, Lewis H. *Wah-to-yah and the Taos Trail; or Prairie Travel and Scalp Dances, with a Look at Los Rancheros from Muleback and the Rocky Mountain Camp-fire*. Norman: University of Oklahoma Press, 1955.

Genovese, Eugene. *The Political Economy of Slavery: Studies in the Economy and Society of the Slave South*. New York: Pantheon, 1965.

———. *Roll, Jordan, Roll: The World the Slaves Made*. New York: Pantheon, 1974.

Gibson, Arrell Morgan. "James H. Carleton." In *Soldiers West: Biographies from the Military Frontier,* edited by Paul A. Hutton, 59–74. Lincoln: University of Nebraska Press, 1987.

Gifford, Edward. *Northeastern and Western Yavapai*. Berkeley: University of California Press, 1936.

Gilbert, Benjamin F. "California and the Civil War: A Bibliographic Essay." *California Historical Society Quarterly* 40 (December 1961): 289–307.

———. "The Confederate Minority in California." *California Historical Society Quarterly* 20 (1941): 154–70.

Gilmore, David. *Manhood in the Making*. New Haven: Yale University Press, 1990.

Glowacki, Luke, and Richard Wrangham, "Warfare and Reproductive Success in a Tribal Population." *Proceedings of the National Academy of Sciences* [PNAS] 112, no. 2 (January 13, 2015): 348–53.

Gobat, Michael. "The Invention of Latin America: A Transnational History of Anti-Imperialism, Democracy, and Race." *American Historical Review* 118, no. 5 (December 2013): 1345–75.

Goldstein, Marcus S. *Demographic and Bodily Changes in Descendants of Mexican Immigrants, with Comparable Data on Parents and Children in Mexico*. Austin: Institute of Latin-American studies, the University of Texas, 1943.

Goluboff, Risa L. "The Thirteenth Amendment and the Lost Origins of Civil Rights." *Duke Law Journal* 50 (2001): 1609.

Goodwin, Grenville, ed. *Myths and Tales of the White Mountain Apache.* 1939. Reprint, Tucson: University of Arizona Press, 1994.

———. *The Social Organization of the Western Apaches.* Tucson: University of Arizona Press, 1942.

Goodwin, Grenville. *Western Apache Raiding and Warfare, from the Notes of Grenville Goodwin.* Edited by Keith H. Basso. Tucson: University of Arizona Press, 1971.

Gorley, Hugh A. *The Loyal Californians of 1861.* Commandery of California, Military Order of the Loyal Legion, War Paper 12. San Francisco, 1893.

Granger, Byrd H. *Arizona Place Names.* Tucson: University of Arizona Press, 1960.

Grear, Charles David. *Why Texans Fought in the Civil War.* College Station: Texas A&M University Press, 2010.

Greeley, Horace. *An Overland Journey from New York to San Francisco, in the Summer of 1859.* New York: C. M. Saxton, Barker, 1860.

Greenberg, Amy S. *Manifest Manhood and the Antebellum American Empire.* New York: Cambridge University Press, 2005.

———. *A Wicked War: Polk, Clay, Lincoln, and the 1846 U.S. Invasion of Mexico.* New York: Alfred A. Knopf, 2012.

Greene, Laurence. *The Filibuster: The Career of William Walker.* New York: Bobbs-Merrill, 1937.

Griffen, William B. *Apaches at War and Peace: The Janos Presidio, 1750–1858.* Norman: University of Oklahoma Press, 1998.

———. *Utmost Good Faith: Patterns of Apache-Mexican Hostilities in Northern Chihuahua Border Warfare, 1821–1848.* Albuquerque: University of New Mexico Press, 1988.

Griffith, Paddy. *Battle Tactics of the Civil War.* New Haven: Yale University Press, 1989.

Grinnell, George Bird. *The Cheyenne Indians.* 1928. Reprint, Lincoln: University of Nebraska Press, 1972.

———. *The Fighting Cheyennes.* 1915. Reprint, Norman: University of Oklahoma Press, 1956.

Grinstead, Marion C. *Life and Death of a Frontier Fort: Fort Craig, New Mexico, 1854–1884.* Socorro, NM: Socorro County Historical Society, 1973.

Gustafson, A. M., ed. *John Spring's Arizona.* Tucson: University of Arizona Press, 1966.

Guth, Jerry. "The Battle of Picacho Pass: The Turning Point for the Southwest in the War of the Rebellion." *American West,* 1969.

Gutiérrez, Ramón A. *When Jesus Came, the Corn Mothers Went Away: Marriage, Sexuality, and Power in New Mexico, 1500–1846.* Stanford: Stanford University Press, 1991.

Hadley, Diana, Peter Warshall, and Don Bufkin. *Environmental Change in Aravaipa, 1870–1970: An Ethnoecological Survey.* Phoenix: Arizona State Office of the Bureau of Land Management, 1991.

Hageman, E. R., ed. *Fighting Rebels and Redskins.* Norman: University of Oklahoma Press, 1969.

Hagerman, Edward. *The American Civil War and the Origins of Modern Warfare:*

Ideas, Organization, and Field Command. Bloomington: Indiana University Press, 1988.

Halaas, David Fridtjof. "'All the Camp Was Weeping': George Bent and the Sand Creek Massacre." *Colorado Heritage,* Summer 1995, 2–17.

———. *Boom Town Newspapers: Journalism on the Rocky Mountain Mining Frontier, 1859–1881.* Albuquerque: University of New Mexico Press, 1981.

Halaas, David Fridtjof, and Andrew E. Masich. "'You Could Hear the Drums for Miles': A Cheyenne Ledgerbook History." *Colorado Heritage.* (Autumn 1996): 2–44.

———. *Halfbreed: The Remarkable True Story of George Bent—Caught between the Worlds of the Indian and the White Man.* Cambridge, MA: Da Capo, 2004.

Hall, Martin H. "Colonel James Reily's Diplomatic Missions to Chihuahua and Sonora." *New Mexico Historical Review* 31 (July 1956): 232–44.

———. "The Mesilla Times, a Journal of Confederate Arizona." *Arizona and the West* 5 (Winter 1963): 337–51.

———. "Native Mexican Relations in Confederate Arizona, 1861–1862." *Journal of Arizona History* 8 (Autumn 1967): 171–80.

———. *Sibley's New Mexico Campaign.* Austin: University of Texas Press, 1960.

———. "The Skirmish at Mesilla." *Arizona and the West* 1 (Winter 1959): 343–51.

———. "The Skirmish of Picacho." *Civil War History* 4 (March 1958): 27–35.

Hall, Martin H., and Sam Long. *The Confederate Army of New Mexico.* Austin: Presidial, 1978.

Hämäläinen, Pekka. *The Comanche Empire.* New Haven: Yale University Press, 2008.

Hamilton, Patrick. *The Resources of Arizona.* 1881. Reprint, Tucson: Pinon, 1966.

Hanna, Alfred, and Kathryn Hanna. *Napoleon III and Mexico: American Triumph over Monarchy.* Chapel Hill: University of North Carolina Press, 1971.

Hart, Herbert M. *Old Forts of the Far West.* Seattle: Superior, 1965.

Haslip, Joan. *The Crown of Mexico; Maximilian and His Empress Carlota.* New York: Holt, Rinehart and Winston, 1971.

Heitman, Francis B. *Historical Register and Dictionary of the U.S. Army, 1789–1903.* 2 vols. Washington, D.C.: Government Printing Office, 1903.

Herskovitz, Robert M. *Fort Bowie Material Culture.* Anthropological Papers of the University of Arizona, no. 31, Tucson, 1978.

Hess, Earl. *The Rifle Musket in Civil War Combat: Reality and Myth.* Lawrence: University of Kansas Press, 2008.

Heyman, Max. *Prudent Soldier; A Biography of Major General E. R. S. Canby, 1817–1873: His Military Service in the Indian Campaigns, in the Mexican War, in California, New Mexico, Utah, and Oregon; in the Civil War in the Trans-Mississippi West, and as Military Governor in the Post-war South.* Glendale, CA: Arthur H. Clark, 1959.

Hicks, James E. *Notes on United States Ordnance.* 2 vols. Mount Vernon, NY.: privately printed, 1940.

Hinton, Richard J. *Handbook to Arizona: Its Resources, History, Towns, Mines, Ruins, and Scenery.* San Francisco: Payot, Upham, 1878.

Henson, H. Keith. "Evolutionary Psychology, Memes and the Origin of War." http://www.kuro5hin.org/story/2006/4/17/194059/296

Hobsbawm, Eric, and Terence Ranger, eds. *The Invention of Tradition*. Cambridge: Cambridge University Press, 1983.

Hoig, Stan. *The Sand Creek Massacre*. Norman: University of Oklahoma Press, 1961.

Holt, Ronald L. *Beneath the Red Cliff: An Ethnohistory of the Utah Paiutes*. Albuquerque: University of New Mexico Press, 1992.

Holton, Woody. *Unruly Americans and the Origins of the Constitution*. New York: Hill and Wang, 2007.

Hulse, F. S. "Migration and Cultural Selection in Human Genetics." In *The Anthropologist*, 1–21. Delhi, India: University of Delhi, 1969.

Hunsaker, William J. "Lansford W. Hastings' Project for the Invasion and Conquest of Arizona and New Mexico for the Southern Confederacy." *Arizona Historical Review* 4 (July 1931): 5–12.

Hunt, Aurora. *The Army of the Pacific: Its Operations in California, Texas, Arizona, New Mexico, Utah, Nevada, Oregon, Washington, Plains Region, Mexico, etc., 1860–1866*. Glendale, CA: Arthur H. Clark, 1951.

———. "California Volunteers." *Historical Society of Southern California Quarterly* 36 (June 1954): 146–54.

———. "California Volunteers on Border Patrol, Texas and Mexico, 1862–1866." *Historical Society of California Quarterly* 30 (December 1948): 265–76.

———. "The Far West Volunteers." *Montana: The Magazine of Western History* 12 (April 1962): 49–61.

———. *Kirby Benedict, Frontier Federal Judge*. Glendale, CA: Arthur H. Clark, 1961.

———. *Major General James Henry Carleton, 1814–1873: Western Frontier Dragoon*. Glendale, CA: Arthur H. Clark, 1958.

Hunter, J. Marvin. *The Trail Drivers of Texas: Interesting Sketches of Early Cowboys and Their Experiences on the Range and on the Trail during the Days that Tried Men's Souls—True Narratives Related by Real Cow-Punchers and Men Who Fathered the Cattle Industry in Texas*. Nashville: Cokesbury Press, 1924.

Hutchins, James S. "The United States Mounted Rifleman's Knife." *Man at Arms* 13 (March/April 1991): 10–21.

Hutton, Paul A., ed. *Soldiers West: Biographies from the Military Frontier*. Lincoln: University of Nebraska Press, 1987.

Hurtado, Albert. *Intimate Frontiers: Sex, Gender, and Culture in California*. Albuquerque: University of New Mexico Press, 1999.

Hyde, George E. *Life of George Bent Written from His Letters*. Edited by Savoie Lottinville. Norman: University of Oklahoma Press, 1968.

Hyslop, Stephen G. *Bound for Santa Fe: The Road to New Mexico and the American Conquest, 1806–1848*. Norman: University of Oklahoma Press, 2002.

———. *Contest for California: From Spanish Colonization to the American Conquest*. Norman, OK: Arthur H. Clark, 2012.

Illsley, G. W., A. Finlayson, and B. Thompson. "The Motivation and Characteristics of Internal Migrants." *Milbank Memorial Fund Quarterly* 41 (1963): 217–48.

Irwin, Bernard. "The Apache Pass Fight." *Infantry Journal* 22 (1928): 1–8.

Ives, Ronald L. "The Grave of Melchior Diaz: A Problem in Historical Sleuthing." *Kiva* 25, no. 2 (December 1959).

Jacoby, Karl. "'The Broad Platform of Extermination': Nature and Violence in the Nineteenth Century North American Borderlands." *Journal of Genocide Research* 10, no. 2, 2008: 249–67.

———. *Shadows at Dawn: A Borderlands Massacre and the Violence of History.* New York: Penguin Press, 2008.

Jagodinsky, Katrina. "Territorial Bonds: Indenture and Affection in Intercultural Arizona, 1864–1894." In *On the Borders of Love and Power: Families and Kinship in the Intercultural American Southwest,* edited by David W. Adams and Crista DeLuzio, 255–77. Berkeley: University of California Press, 2012.

Jett, Stephen C., ed. "The Destruction of Navajo Orchards in 1864: Captain John Thompson's Report." *Arizona and the West* 16, no. 4 (Winter 1974): 365–78.

Johnson, Allen, and Dumas Malone, eds. *Dictionary of American Biography.* Vol. 17. New York: Scribner's, 1937.

Johnston, William P. *The Life of General Albert Sidney Johnston.* New York: D. Appleton, 1878.

Josephy, Alvin M. *The Civil War in the American West.* New York: Alfred A. Knopf, 1991.

Julyan, Robert. *The Place Names of New Mexico.* Albuquerque: University of New Mexico Press, 2001.

The Journal of American History: Rethinking History and the Nation-State: Mexico and the United States as a Case Study: A Special Issue. (September 1999).

Karolevitz, Robert F. *Newspapering in the Old West.* Seattle: Superior, 1965.

Kaut, Charles. "Western Apache Clan and Phratry Organization." *American Anthropologist* 58:1 (February 1956).

———. *The Western Apache Clan System: Its Origins and Development.* University of New Mexico Publications in Anthropology, no. 9. Albuquerque, 1957.

Kearney, Michael. "Transnationalism in California and Mexico at the End of Empire." In *Border Identities: Nation and State at International Frontiers,* edited by Thomas M. Wilson and Hastings Donnan. Cambridge: Cambridge University Press, 1998.

Keefer, Charles F. *Muster Roll, Kit Carson Post, No. 2.* Washington, D.C.: GAR Department of the Potomac, 1889.

Keegan, John. *A History of Warfare.* New York: Alfred A. Knopf, 1993.

Keleher, William A. *Turmoil in New Mexico, 1846–1868.* Santa Fe: Rydal, 1952.

Kelman, Ari. *A Misplaced Massacre: Struggling over the Memory of Sand Creek.* Cambridge: Harvard University Press, 2013.

Kemble, Edward C., and Helen H. Bretnor, eds. *A History of California Newspapers, 1846–1858.* Los Gatos, CA: Talisman, 1962.

Kemble, John H. *The Panama Route, 1848–1869.* Berkeley: University of California Press, 1943.

Kennedy, Elijah R. *The Contest for California in 1861: How Colonel E. D. Baker Saved the Pacific States to the Union.* Boston: Houghton, Mifflin, 1912.

Kerby, Robert L. *The Confederate Invasion of New Mexico and Arizona, 1861–1862.* Los Angeles: Westernlore, 1958.

———. *Kirby Smith's Confederacy: The Trans-Mississippi South, 1863–1865.* New York: Columbia University Press, 1972.

Kerner, Gaiselle. Preliminary Inventories, No. 58, Records of the United States Court of Claims, Southern Claims Commission Washington, D.C.: NARA, 1953, RG 123, Entry 22, 16E3 Row 8.

Kibby, Leo P. "California, the Civil War, and the Indian Problem: An Account of California's Participation in the Great Conflict." *Journal of the West* 4 (April, June 1965): 183–209, 377–410.

———. "California Soldiers in the Civil War." *California Historical Society Quarterly* 40 (December 1961): 343–50.

———. "A Civil War Episode in California—Arizona History." *Arizoniana* 2 (Spring 1961): 20–22.

———. "Some Aspects of California's Military Problems during the Civil War." *Civil War History* 5 (September 1959): 25–62.

———. "With Colonel Carleton and the California Column." *Historical Society of Southern California Quarterly* 41 (December 1959): 337–44.

Kimmel, Michael. *Manhood in America: A Cultural History.* New York: Oxford University Press, 2012.

Kiser, William S. *Turmoil on the Rio Grande: History of the Mesilla Valley, 1846–1865.* College Station: Texas A&M University Press, 2011.

Knight, Oliver. *Following the Indian Wars: The Story of the Newspaper Correspondents Among the Indian Campaigners.* Norman: University of Oklahoma Press, 1960.

Knightley, Phillip. *The First Casualty: From the Crimea to Vietnam, the War Correspondent as Hero, Propagandist, and Myth Maker.* New York: Harcourt Brace Jovanovich, 1975.

Kroeber, A. L. *Handbook of the Indians of California.* Berkeley: California Book, 1953.

Kroeber, Clifton B., and Bernard L. Fontana. *Massacre on the Gila: An Account of the Last Major Battle Between American Indians, With Reflections on the Origin of War.* Tucson: University of Arizona Press, 1986.

Kuhn, Berndt. *Chronicles of War: Apache and Yavapai Resistance in the Southwestern United States and Northern Mexico, 1821–1937.* Tucson: Arizona Historical Society, 2014.

Lahti, Janne. *Cultural Construction of Empire: The U.S. Army in Arizona and New Mexico.* Lincoln: University of Nebraska Press, 2012.

Lasker, G. W. "The Question of Physical Selection of Mexican Migrants to the U.S.A." *Human Biology* 26 (1954): 52–58.

Leckie, William H. *The Buffalo Soldiers: A Narrative of the Black Cavalry in the West.* Norman: University of Oklahoma Press, 2003.

Lempérière, Annick. "Transnationalizing the Nation-Building History of Mexico from the VIIIth to the XXth Century." *Nuevo Mundo Mundos Nuevos* (Online debates since March 27, 2010). Accessed June 28, 2014. http://nuevomundo. revues.org/59401; DOI: 10.4000/nuevomundo.59401

Lepore, Jill. *The Name of War: King Phillip's War and the Origins of American Identity.* New York: Knopf, 1999.

Lewis, Berkeley R. *Small Arms and Ammunition in the United States Service, 1776–1865.* Washington, D.C.: Smithsonian Institution Press, 1968.

Lewis, Oscar. *The War in the Far West: 1861–1865.* Garden City, NJ: Doubleday, 1961.

Limerick, Patricia N. *Legacy of Conquest: The Unbroken Past of the American West.* New York: Norton, 1987.

Lindsay, Diana, ed. "Henry A. Crabb, Filibuster, and the San Diego Herald." *The Journal of San Diego History* 19, no. 1 (Winter 1973).

Lingenfelter, Richard E. *Steamboats on the Colorado River, 1852–1916.* Tucson: University of Arizona Press, 1978.

Lockwood, Frank C. *Arizona Characters.* Los Angeles: Times-Mirror Press, 1928.

———. "John C. Cremony, Soldier of Fortune." *Westways* 41 (March 1946): 18–19.

———. *Life in Old Tucson, 1854–1864.* Tucson: Tucson Civic Committee, 1943.

Long, E. B. *The Saints and the Union: Utah Territory during the Civil War.* Urbana: University of Illinois Press, 1981.

Lonn, Ella. *Desertion during the Civil War.* Gloucester, MA: Peter Smith, 1966.

Lord, Francis A. *They Fought for the Union.* New York: Bonanza Books, 1960.

Ludwig, Larry. *Archaeological Findings of the Battle of Apache Pass.* Fort Bowie National Historic Site, Southeast Arizona Group Resource Report NPS/FOBO/SRR-2015/001. Tucson: National Park Service, 2015.

Lukaszewski, Aaron W., Zachary L. Simmons, Cameron Anderson, and James R. Roney. "The Role of Physical Formidability in Human Social Status Allocation." *Journal of Personality and Social Psychology* 110, no. 3 (March 2016): 385–406.

Macklem, Patrick. "Distributing Sovereignty: Indian Nations and Equality of Peoples." *Stanford Law Review* 45, no. 5 (May 1993): 1311–67.

Mahan, Don M. "John W. Jones: The Southwest's Unsung Hero." *The Journal of Arizona History* 51, no. 3 (Autumn 2010): 223–40.

Manchaca, Martha. *Recovering History, Constructing Race: The Indian, Black, and White Roots of Mexican Americans.* Austin: University of Texas Press, 2001.

Mann, Charles C. *1491: New Revelations About the Americas Before Columbus.* New York: Alfred A. Knopf, 2005.

Manning, Chandra. *What This Cruel War Was Over: Soldiers, Slavery, and the Civil War.* New York: Vintage Books, 2007.

Martin, Douglas. "The California Column and the Washington Press." *Arizoniana* 1 (Winter 1960): 10–11.

Martin, Percy F. *Maximilian in Mexico.* London: Constable, 1914.

Masich, Andrew E. *The Civil War in Arizona: The Story of the California Volunteers, 1861–1865.* Norman: University of Oklahoma Press, 2006.

———. "Cheyennes and Horses: A Transportation Revolution on the Great Plains." *History News* 52 (Autumn 1997): 10–13.

Mathews, Mitford M., ed. *A Dictionary of Americanisms on Historical Principles.* Chicago: University of Chicago Press, 1966.

May, Robert E. *Manifest Destiny's Underworld: Filibustering in Antebellum America.* Chapel Hill: University of North Carolina Press, 2002.

McAllen, M. M. *Maximilian and Carlota: Europe's Last Empire in Mexico.* San Antonio: Trinity University Press, 2014.

McChristian, Douglas C. *Fort Bowie, Arizona: Combat Post of the Southwest, 1858–1894.* Norman: University of Oklahoma Press, 2005.

McChristian, Douglas C., and Larry L. Ludwig. "Eyewitness to the Bascom Affair: An Account by Sergeant Daniel Robinson, Seventh Infantry." *Journal of Arizona History* 42 (Autumn 2001): 277–300.

McClintock, J. H. *Arizona: Prehistoric, Aboriginal, Pioneer, Modern.* 3 vols. Chicago: S. J. Clark, 1916.

McGinty, Brian. *The Oatman Massacre: A Tale of Desert Captivity and Survival.* Norman: University of Oklahoma Press, 2005.

McNitt, Frank. *Navajo Wars: Military Campaigns, Slave Raids, and Reprisals.* Albuquerque: University of New Mexico Press, 1972.

McPherson, James. *Battle Cry of Freedom: The Civil War Era.* New York: Oxford University Press, 1989.

———. *For Cause and Comrades: Why Men Fought in the Civil War.* New York: Oxford University Press, 1997.

———. *Tried By War: Abraham Lincoln As Commander in Chief.* New York: Penguin Press, 2008.

Meeks, Eric V. *Border Citizens: The Making of Indians, Mexicans, and Anglos in Arizona.* Austin: University of Texas Press, 2007.

Meketa, Charles, and Jacqueline Meketa. *One Blanket and Ten Days Rations.* Globe, AZ: Southwest Parks and Monuments Association, 1980.

Meketa, Jacqueline D., ed. *Legacy of Honor: The Life of Rafaél Chacón.* Albuquerque: University of New Mexico Press, 1986.

Michno, Gregory F. *Encyclopedia of Indian Wars: Western Battles and Skirmishes, 1850–1890.* Missoula, MT: Mountain Press, 2003.

Milavec, Pam. "Jesse Haire: Unwilling Indian Fighter." NARA, *Prologue Magazine* 43, no. 2 (Summer 2011).

Miller, Darlis A. *The California Column in New Mexico.* Albuquerque: University of New Mexico Press, 1982.

———. "Carleton's California Column: A Chapter in New Mexico's Mining History." *New Mexico Historical Review* 53 (1978): 5–38.

———. "Historian for the California Column: George H. Pettis of New Mexico and Rhode Island." *Red River Valley Historical Review* 5 (Winter 1980): 74–92.

———. *Military Supply in the Southwest, 1861–1865.* Albuquerque: University of New Mexico Press, 1989.

———. *Soldiers and Settlers: Military Supply in the Southwest, 1861–1885.* Albuquerque: University of New Mexico Press, 1989.

———. "William Logan Rynerson in New Mexico, 1862–1893." New Mexico Historical Review, 48 (April 1973).

Miller, Robert R. *Arms Across the Border: United States Aid to Juárez during the French Intervention in Mexico; Transactions of the American Philosophical Society,* new series, vol. 63, no. 6. Philadelphia: American Philosophical Society, 1973.

———. "Californians against the Emperor." *California Historical Society Quarterly* 37 (September 1958): 193–214.

Mora, Anthony. *Border Dilemmas; Racial and National Uncertainties in New Mexico, 1848–1912.* Durham: Duke University Press, 2011.

Moreno, Daniel. El sitio de Querétaro: Según protagonistas y testigos, 3rd Edición. México: Editorial Porrúa, 1982.

Morrow, Robert E. *Mohave County Lawmakers.* Kingman, AZ: Mohave County Miner, 1968.

Mulligan, R. A. "Apache Pass and Old Fort Bowie." *The Smoke Signal* 11 (Spring 1965).

———. "Sixteen Days in Apache Pass." *Kiva* 24 (1958): 1–13.

Mullin, Robert N., ed. *Maurice Garland Fulton's History of the Lincoln County War*. Tucson: University of Arizona Press, 1968.

Murphy, Kevin D. "New Information Concerning Edouard Manet's 'Execution of Maximilian.'" *The Burlington Magazine* 31, no. 1033 (April 1989): 288–89.

Myers, Lee. "The Enigma of Mangas Coloradas' Death." *New Mexico Historical Review* 41 (October 1966): 287–304.

Myers, R. D. "The Confederate Intrusion into Arizona Territory, 1862." *Cochise Quarterly* 2 (Spring 1972): 1–27.

Neeley, James L. "The Desert Dream of the South." *The Smoke Signal* 4, Tucson Corral of the Westerners, 1961.

Neely, Mark E. *The Civil War and the Limits of Destruction*. Harvard University Press, 2007.

———. "Was the Civil War a Total War?" *Civil War History* 50, no. 4 (December 2004): 434–58.

Neu, Jonathan. "Worthy Comrades All: The Grand Army of the Republic and the Campaign for Union Veterans' Pensions, 1880–1910." Paper delivered to the 2014 Carnegie Mellon University Graduate Research Forum, Pittsburgh, April 10, 2014.

Nevins, Alan. *Ordeal of the Union*, 8 vols. New York: Scribner, 1947.

Newmark, Harris. *Sixty Years in Southern California 1853–1913*. 4th ed. Edited by M. H. and W. R. Newmark. Los Angeles: Zeitlin and VerBrugge, 1970.

Nichols, Roger L. *Warrior Nations: The United States and Indian Peoples*. Norman: Oklahoma Press, 2013.

Nicholson. John, ed. *The Arizona of Joseph Pratt Allyn. Letters from a Pioneer Judge: Observations and Travels, 1863–1866*. Tucson: University of Arizona Press, 1974.

Nielsen, Axel E., and William H. Walker, eds. *Warfare in Cultural Context: Practice, Agency, and the Archaeology of Violence*. Tucson: University of Arizona Press, 2014.

North, Diane M. T. *Samuel Peter Heintzelman and the Sonora Exploring and Mining Company*. Tucson: University of Arizona Press, 1980.

Norvell, John E. "How Tennessee Adventurer William Walker Became Dictator of Nicaragua in 1857; The Norvell Family Origins of *The Grey Eyed Man of Destiny*." *Middle Tennessee Journal of Genealogy and History* 25, no. 4 (Spring 2012).

Novick, Peter. *That Noble Dream: The 'Objectivity Question' and the American Historical Profession*. New York: Cambridge University Press, 1988.

Nye, Robert A. *Masculinity and Male Codes of Honor in Modern France*. Berkeley: University of California Press, 1998.

Oakes, James. *The Ruling Race: A History of American Slaveholders*. New York: Alfred A. Knopf, 1982.

Officer, James. *Hispanic Arizona 1536–1856*. Tucson: University of Arizona Press, 1984.

O'Meara, James. "Early Editors of California." *Overland Monthly*, new series, 14 (1889).

Opler, Morris Edward. *An Apache Life-way: The Economic, Social, and Religious Institutions of the Chiricahua Indians*. 1941. Reprint, Lincoln: University of Nebraska Press, 1996.

Opler, Morris Edward, and Harry Hoijer. "The Raid and War-Path Language of the Chiricahua Apache." *American Anthropologist*, new series, 42, no. 4, part 1. (October–December 1940): 617–34.

Orozco, Víctor. Las guerras indias en la historia de Chihuahua. Primeras fases, Mexico, Consejo General de la Cultura y las Artes, 1992.

———. Las guerras indias en la historia de Chihuahua; antología, Ciudad Juárez, Universidad Autónoma de Ciudad Juárez, 1992.

Painter, Nell Irvin. *The History of White People*. New York: W. W. Norton, 2010.

Palmer, Jessica Dawn. *The Apache Peoples: A History of all Bands and Tribes through the 1880s*. Jefferson, NC: McFarland, 2013.

Paulding, James K. *The Diverting History of John Bull and Brother Jonathan*. New York: Innskeep and Bradford, 1812.

Pearce, T. M., ed. *New Mexico Place Names: A Geographical Dictionary*. Albuquerque: University of New Mexico Press, 1965.

Pedersen, Gilbert J. "A Yankee in Arizona: The Misfortunes of William S. Grant, 1860–61." *Journal of Arizona History* 16 (Summer 1975): 127–44.

Perry, James M. *A Bohemian Brigade: The Civil War Correspondents Mostly Rough, Sometimes Ready*. New York: John Wiley and Sons, 2000.

Phelps, Robert. "On Comic Opera Revolutions: Maneuver Theory and the Art of War in Mexican California, 1821–1845." *California History* 84, no. 1 (Fall 2006).

Phillips, Ulrich B. *American Negro Slavery: A Survey of the Supply, Employment and Control of Negro Labor as Determined by the Plantation Regime*. New York: D. Appleton, 1918.

Pierce, Gilbert A., with additions by William A. Wheeler. *The Dickens Dictionary*. New York: Kraus Reprint, 1965.

Pinker, Steven. *The Better Angels of Our Nature: Why Violence Has Declined*. New York: Viking, 2011.

Pitt, Leonard. *The Decline of the Californios: A Social History of the Spanish-Speaking Californians, 1846–1890*. Berkeley: University of California Press, 1966.

Pomeroy, Earl S. "Military Roads in Arizona." *American Railroad Journal* 38 (January 1965).

———. *The Territories and the United States, 1861–1890*. Philadelphia: University of Pennsylvania Press, 1947.

Potter, David Morris, and Don E. Fehrenbacher. *The Impending Crisis, 1848–1861*. New York: Harper and Row, 1976.

Prezelski, Tom. "Lives of the Californio Lancers: The First Battalion of Native California Cavalry, 1863–1866." *Journal of Arizona History* 40 (Spring 1999): 29–52.

Prucha, Francis P. *Guide to the Military Posts of the United States, 1789–1895*. Madison: State Historical Society of Wisconsin, 1964.

Quebbeman, Francis E. *Medicine in Territorial Arizona*. Phoenix: Arizona Historical Foundation, 1966.

Radbourne, Allan. *Mickey Free: Apache Captive, Interpreter and Indian Scout*. Tucson: Arizona Historical Society, 2005.

Randall, James G. "The Newspaper Problem in Its Bearing upon Military Secrecy during the Civil War." *American History Review* 23 (1918): 303–23.

Rathbun, Daniel, and David V. Alexander. *New Mexico Frontier Military Place Names*. Las Cruces, NM: Yucca Tree, 2003.

Record, Ian W. *Big Sycamore Stands Alone: The Western Apaches, Aravaipa, and the Struggle for Place.* Norman: University of Oklahoma Press, 2008.

Rein, Christopher. "'Our First Duty Was to God and Our Next to Our Country': Religion, Violence, and the Sand Creek Massacre." *Great Plains Quarterly* 34, no. 3 (Summer 2014): 217–38.

Remley, David. *Kit Carson: The Life of an American Border Man.* Norman: University of Oklahoma Press, 2011.

Reséndez, Andrés. *Changing National Identities at the Frontier: Texas and New Mexico, 1800–1850.* New York: Cambridge University Press, 2005.

Restall, Matthew. *The Black Middle: Africans, Mayas, and Spaniards in Colonial Yucatan.* Stanford: Stanford University Press, 2009.

Rhodes, James Ford. *History of the United States from the Compromise of 1850 to the Final Restoration of Home Rule at the South in 1877.* New York: Macmillan, 1909.

Rice, William B., and John Walton Caughey, eds. *The Los Angeles Star, 1851–1864: The Beginnings of Journalism in Southern California.* Berkeley: University of California Press, 1947.

Richard, Stephen M., Jon E. Spencer, Charles A. Ferguson, and P. A. Pearthree. *Geologic Map of the Picacho Mountains and Picacho Peak, Pinal County, Southern Arizona.* Arizona Geological Survey Open-File Report 99–18, September 1999.

Rickey, Don. *Forty Miles a Day on Beans and Hay.* Norman: University of Oklahoma Press, 1963.

Ridley, Jasper. *Maximilian and Juárez.* New York: Ticknor and Fields, 1992.

Riggs, John L. "William H. Hardy, Merchant of the Upper Colorado." Edited by Kenneth Hufford. *Journal of Arizona History* 6 (Winter 1966): 177–87.

Roberts, Gary L. *Death Comes for the Chief Justice: The Slough-Rynerson Quarrel and Political Violence in New Mexico.* Niwot: University Press of Colorado, 1990.

Roberts, Gary L., and David Fridtjof Halaas. "Written in Blood: The Soule-Cramer Sand Creek Massacre Letters." *Colorado Heritage* (Winter 2001): 22–32.

Robinson, John W. *Los Angeles in Civil War Days.* Los Angeles: Dawson's Book Shop, 1977.

Robinson, Sherry. *Apache Voices: Their Stories of Survival as Told to Eve Ball.* Albuquerque: University of New Mexico Press, 2003.

Robrock, David P. "Edward D. Tuttle: Soldier, Pioneer, Historian." *Journal of Arizona History* 30 (Spring 1989): 27–50.

Rodenbaugh, T. F. *Army of the United States.* New York: Maynard, Merril, 1896.

Rogers, Fred B. *Soldiers of the Overland.* San Francisco: Grabhorn, 1938.

Rosenus, Alan. *General Vallejo and the Advent of the Americans.* Albuquerque: University of New Mexico Press, 1995.

Royster, Charles. *The Destructive War: William Tecumseh Sherman, Stonewall Jackson, and the Americans.* New York: Vintage Books, 1993.

Ruhlen, George. "San Diego in the Civil War." *San Diego Historical Society Quarterly* 7 (April 1961): 17–22.

Sabin, Edwin Legrand. *Kit Carson Days, 1809–1868: Adventures in the Path of Empire.* Vol. 2. New York: Press of the Pioneers, 1935.

Sacks, Benjamin. *Be It Enacted: The Creation of the Territory of Arizona.* Phoenix: Arizona Historical Foundation, 1964.

Salmon, Lucy Maynard. *The Newspaper and the Historian*. New York: Oxford University Press, 1923.

Salmón, Roberto Mario. "A Marginal Man: Luis of Saric and the Pima Revolt of 1751." *The Americas* 45, no. 1 (July 1988): 61–77.

Sanger, George P., ed. *Treaties and Proclamations of the United States of America from December, 1865, to March, 1867*. Vol. 14. Boston: Little, Brown, 1868.

Santiago, Mark. *Massacre at the Yuma Crossing; Spanish Relations with the Quechans, 1779–1782*. Tucson: University of Arizona Press, 1998.

———. *The Jar of Severed Hands: Spanish Deportation of Apache Prisoners of War, 1770–1810*. Norman: University of Oklahoma Press, 2011.

Scheiber, Harry N. "The Pay of Troops and Confederate Morale in the Trans-Mississippi West." *Arizona Historical Quarterly* 18 (Winter 1959): 350–65.

Schellie, Don. *Vast Domain of Blood*. Los Angeles: Westernlore, 1968.

Schlesinger, Arthur M., Jr. "The Causes of the Civil War: A Note on Historical Sentimentalism." *Partisan Review* 16 (October 1949): 969–81.

Schreier, Konrad F., ed. "The California Column in the Civil War, Hazen's Civil War Diary." *San Diego Journal of History* 22 (Spring 1976): 31–47.

Sides, Hampton. *Blood and Thunder: The Epic Story of Kit Carson and the American West*. New York: Anchor Books, 2006.

Simmons, Marc. *Kit Carson and His Three Wives*. Albuquerque: University of New Mexico Press, 2011.

Skinner, Woodward B. *The Apache Rock Crumbles: The Captivity of Geronimo's People*. Pensacola, FL: Skinner Publications, 1987.

Skogen, Larry C. *Indian Depredation Claims, 1796–1920*. Norman: University of Oklahoma Press, 1996.

Sloan, Richard E., and Ward R. Adams. *History of Arizona*. 4 vols. Phoenix: Record, 1930.

Smith-Rosenberg, Carroll. *This Violent Empire: The Birth of an American National Identity*. Chapel Hill: University of North Carolina Press, 2012.

Snyder, Timothy. *Black Earth: The Holocaust as History and Warning*. New York: Tim Duggan Books, 2015.

Soifer, Aviam. "Federal Protection, Paternalism, and the Virtually Forgotten Prohibition of Voluntary Peonage." *Columbia Law Review* 112:1607 (2012).

Sonnichsen, C. L. *The Mescalero Apaches*. Norman: University of Oklahoma Press, 1958.

———. *Tucson: The Life and Times of an American City*. Norman: University of Oklahoma Press, 1982.

Spaulding, Imogene. "The Attitude of California toward the Civil War." *Historical Society of Southern California Publication* 9 (1912–13): 104–31.

Spicer, Edward H. *Cycles of Conquest: The Impact of Spain, Mexico, and the United States on the Indians of the Southwest, 1533–1960*. 1962. Reprint, Tucson: University of Arizona, Press, 1976.

———. *Pascua: A Yaqui Village in Arizona*. Chicago: University of Chicago Press, 1940.

———. *The Yaquis: A Cultural History*. Tucson: University of Arizona Press, 1980.

Spickard, Paul R. *Almost All Aliens: Immigration, Race, and Colonialism in American History and Identity*. New York: Routledge, 2007.

Splitter, Henry Winfred. "The Adventures of an Editor, in Search of an Author." *Journal of the West* 1 (October 1962): 1–10.

————. "Newspapers of Los Angeles: The First Fifty Years, 1851–1900." *Journal of the West* 2 (October 1963): 435–58.

Splitter, Henry Winfred, ed. "Tour in Arizona: Footprints of an Army Officer by 'Sabre.'" *Journal of the West* 1 (October 1962): 74–97.

Spring, John A. "A March to Arizona from California in 1866, or: Lost in the Yuma Desert." *Journal of Arizona History* 3 (1962): 1–6.

Stampp, Kenneth M. *The Peculiar Institution: Slavery in the Ante-Bellum South.* New York: Knopf, 1956.

Stanley, F. *The Civil War in New Mexico.* Denver: World Press, 1960.

St. John, Rachel. *Line in the Sand: A History of the Western U.S.-Mexico Border.* Princeton: Princeton University Press, 2011.

Sturtevant, William C. *Handbook of North American Indians.* Washington, D.C.: Smithsonian Institution, 1978.

Swanton, John R. *The Indian Tribes of North America.* Washington, D.C.: Government Printing Office, 1952.

Swartz, Deborah L., and William H. Doelle. *Archaeology in the Mountain Shadows: Exploring the Romero Ruin.* Tucson: Center for Desert Archaeology, 1996.

Sweeney, Edwin R. *Cochise: Chiricahua Apache Chief.* Norman: University of Oklahoma Press, 1991.

————. *Cochise: Firsthand Accounts of the Chiricahua Apache Chief.* Norman: University of Oklahoma Press, 2014.

————. *From Cochise to Geronimo: The Chiricahua Apaches, 1874–1886.* Norman: University of Oklahoma Press, 2010.

————. *Mangas Coloradas: Chief of the Chiricahua Apaches.* Norman: University of Oklahoma Press, 1998.

Tap, Bruce. *Over Lincoln's Shoulder: The Committee on the Conduct of the War.* Lawrence: University Press of Kansas, 1998.

Taylor, John. *Bloody Valverde: A Civil War Battle on the Rio Grande, February 21, 1862.* Albuquerque: University of New Mexico Press, 1999.

Taylor, Quintard. *In Search of the Racial Frontier: African Americans in the American West, 1528–1990.* New York: W. W. Norton, 1998.

Taylor, Quintard, and Shirley Ann Wilson Moore, eds. *African American Women Confront the West, 1600–2000.* Norman: University of Oklahoma Press, 2003.

Tevis, James H. *Arizona in the 50s.* Albuquerque: University of New Mexico Press, 1954.

Thelen, David. "Rethinking History and the Nation-State: Mexico and the United States." *Journal of American History,* 86 (1999): 438–52.

Thian, Raphael P. *Notes Illustrating the Military Geography of the United States, 1813–1880.* Austin: University of Texas Press, 1979.

Thiele, Thomas F. "Some Notes on the Lance and Lancers in the United States Cavalry." *Military Collector and Historian, Journal of the Company of Military Historians* (Summer 1955): 31–37.

Thompson, Major Dewitt C. *California in the Rebellion.* Commandery of California, Military Order of the Loyal Legion, War Paper 8. San Francisco, 1891.

Thompson, Gerald. *The Army and the Navajo: The Bosque Redondo Reservation Experiment, 1863–1868.* Tucson: University of Arizona Press, 1976.

————. "'Is There a Gold Field East of the Colorado?': The La Paz Rush of 1862." *Quarterly of the Southern California Historical Society* 67 (Winter 1985): 345–63.

Thompson, Jerry D. *A Civil War History of the New Mexico Volunteers and Militia.* Albuquerque: University of New Mexico Press, 2015.

———. *The Civil War in the Southwest: Recollections of the Sibley Brigade.* College Station: Texas A&M University Press, 2001.

———. *Colonel John Robert Baylor: Texas Indian Fighter and Confederate Soldier.* Hillsboro, Texas: Hill Junior College Press, 1971.

———. *From Desert to Bayou: The Civil War Journal and Sketches of Morgan Wolfe Merrick.* El Paso: Texas Western Press, 1991.

———. *Henry Hopkins Sibley, Confederate General of the West.* Natchitoches, LA: Northwestern State University Press, 1987.

Thompson, Jerry D., ed. *New Mexico Territory during the Civil War: Wallen and Evans Inspection Reports, 1862–1863.* Albuquerque: University of New Mexico Press, 2008.

———. *Westward the Texans: The Civil War Journal of Private William Randolph Howell.* El Paso: Texas Western Press, 1990.

Thrapp, Dan L. *The Conquest of Apacheria.* Norman: University of Oklahoma Press, 1975.

———. *Encyclopedia of Frontier Biography.* 3 vols. Lincoln: University of Nebraska Press, 1988.

Todd, Frederick P. *American Military Equipage, 1851–1872.* 3 vols. Westbrook, CT: Company of Military Historians, 1978.

Truett, Samuel. "Epics of Greater America: Herbert Eugene Bolton's Quest for a Transnational American History." In *Interpreting Spanish Colonialism: Empires, Nations, and Legends,* edited by Christopher Schmidt-Nowara and John M. Nieto-Phillips, 213–47. Albuquerque: University of New Mexico Press, 2005.

———. *Fugitive Landscapes: The Forgotten History of the U.S.-Mexico Borderlands.* New Haven: Yale University Press, 2005.

Tuttle, Edward D. "The River Colorado." *Arizona Historical Review* 1 (July 1928): 50–68.

Twitchell, Ralph E. "The Confederate Invasion of New Mexico, 1861–62." *Old Santa Fe* 3 (January 1916): 5–43.

Underhill, Lonnie. *First Arizona Volunteer Infantry, 1865–1866.* Tucson: Roan Horse Press, 1983.

———. *Index to the Federal Census of Arizona for 1860, 1864, and 1870.* Tucson: Roan Horse, 1981.

Utley, Robert M. *Cavalier in Buckskin: George Armstrong Custer and the Western Military Frontier.* Rev. ed. Norman: University of Oklahoma Press, 2001.

———. *Frontier Regulars: The U.S. Army and the Indian, 1866–1891.* New York: Macmillan, 1973.

———. *Frontiersmen in Blue: The U.S. Army and the Indian, 1848–1865.* New York: Macmillan, 1967.

———. *Historical Report on Fort Bowie.* Santa Fe: National Park Service, 1958.

Valerio-Jiménez, Omar. *River of Hope: Forging Identity and Nation in the Rio Grande Borderlands.* Durham: Duke University Press, 2013.

Villa, Eduardo. Compendio de historia del estado de Sonora. Mexico, DF: 1938.

Viola, Herman J. *Diplomats in Buckskins: A History of Indian Delegations in Washington City.* Norman: University of Oklahoma Press, 1995.

Virden, Bill. "The Affair at Minter's Ranch." *San Diego Historical Society Quarterly* 7 (April 1961): 23–25.

Wagoner, Jay J. *Arizona Territory, 1863–1912*. Tucson: University of Arizona Press, 1970.

Walker, Franklin. "Bohemian No. 1." *Westways* 29 (September 1937).

———. *San Francisco's Literary Frontier*. New York: Alfred A. Knopf, 1943.

Walker, Henry P. "Freighting from Guaymas to Tucson, 1850–1880." *Western Historical Quarterly* 1 (July 1970): 291–304.

Walker, Henry P., ed. "Soldier in the California Column: The Diary of John W. Teal." *Arizona and the West* 13 (Spring 1971): 33–82.

Walker, Henry P., and Don Bufkin. *Historical Atlas of Arizona*. Norman: University of Oklahoma Press, 1986.

Wallace, Andrew. "Fort Whipple in the Days of the Empire." *The Smoke Signal* 26 (Fall 1972).

Washburn, H. S. "Echoes of the Apache Wars." *The Arizona Graphic* 1 (March 24, 1900): 6–7.

Washburn, Wilcomb E. *The Assault on Indian Tribalism: The General Allotment Law (Dawes Act) of 1887*. Philadelphia: Lippincott, 1975.

Watford, W. H. "The Far-Western Wing of the Rebellion, 1861–1865." *California Historical Society Quarterly* 39 (June 1955): 125–48.

Watt, Robert N., and Adam Hook. *Apache Tactics, 1830–1886*. Oxford: Osprey, 2012.

———. *Apache Warrior, 1860–1886*. Oxford: Osprey, 2014.

Webb, George E., ed. "The Mines in Northwestern Arizona in 1864: A Report by Benjamin Silliman Jr." *Arizona and the West* 16 (Autumn 1974): 247–70.

Weber, David. *Bárbaros: Spaniards and Their Savages in the Age of Enlightenment*. New Haven: Yale University Press, 2005.

———. *Foreigners in Their Native Land: Historical Roots of the Mexican Americans*. Albuquerque: University of New Mexico Press, 2003.

———. *The Mexican Frontier, 1821–45: The American Southwest Under Mexico*. Albuquerque: University of New Mexico, 1982.

Webster's American Military Biographies. Springfield, MA: Merriam, 1978.

Wellman, Paul I. *Death in the Desert*. New York: Macmillan, 1935.

———. *Indian Wars of the West*. Garden City, NY: Doubleday, 1947.

West, Elliott. *The Contested Plains: Indians, Goldseekers, and the Rush to Colorado*. Lawrence: University of Kansas Press, 1998.

Wetherington, Ronald K., and Frances Levine, eds. *Battles and Massacres on the Southwestern Frontier; Historical and Archaeological Perspectives*. Norman: University of Oklahoma Press, 2014.

Wheat, Carl I. *Mapping the Trans-Mississippi West, 1540–1861*. 5 vols. San Francisco: Institute of Historical Cartography, 1963.

White, Richard. *"It's Your Misfortune and None of My Own": A New History of the American West*. Norman: University of Oklahoma Press, 1991.

———. *The Middle Ground: Indians, Empires and Republics in the Great Lakes Region, 1650–1815*. New York: Cambridge University Press, 1991.

———. "Western History." In *The New American History*, edited by Eric Foner. Philadelphia: Temple University, 1997.

Whitford, William Clark. *Colorado Volunteers in the Civil War: The New Mexico Campaign in 1862.* Denver: State Historical and Natural History Society of Colorado, 1906.

Whitlock, Flint. *Distant Bugles, Distant Drums: The Union Response to the Confederate Invasion of New Mexico.* Boulder: University Press of Colorado, 2006.

Wilbarger, J. W. *Indian Depredations in Texas.* Austin: Hutchings Printing House, 1889.

Willis, Edward B. "Volunteer Soldiers in New Mexico and Their Conflicts with Indians in 1862 63." *Old Santa Fe* (April 1914).

Wilson, John P. *When the Texans Came: Missing Records from the Civil War in the Southwest, 1861–1862.* Albuquerque: University of New Mexico Press, 2001.

———. "Whiskey at Fort Fillmore: A Story of the Civil War." *New Mexico Historical Review* 68 (April 1993): 109–32.

Wilson, Thomas M., and Hastings Donnan, eds. *Border Identities: Nation and State at International Frontiers.* Cambridge: Cambridge University Presss, 1998.

Wilson-Bareau, Juliet. *Manet, The Execution of Maximilian: Painting, Politics and Censorship.* London: National Gallery/Prince University Press, 1992.

Woodruff, Charles A. *The Work of the California Volunteers as Seen by an Eastern Volunteer.* Commandery of California, Military Order of the Loyal Legion, War Paper 13. San Francisco, 1893.

Woodward, Arthur. "Irataba, Big Injun of the Mohaves." *Desert* 1 (January 1938): 10–11.

———. "Lances at San Pasqual." *California Historical Society Quarterly* 26, no. 1 (March 1947): 32.

Woodward, Arthur, ed. *Man of the West: Reminiscences of George W. Oaks.* Tucson: Arizona Pioneers Historical Society, 1956.

Woodworth, Steven E. *Jefferson Davis and His Generals: The Failure of Confederate Command in the West.* Lawrence: University Press of Kansas, 1990.

Wright, Arthur A. *The Civil War in the Southwest.* Denver: Big Mountain, 1964.

Wright, Lawrence. "One Drop of Blood." *The New Yorker,* July 24, 1994.

Wyllys, Rufus K. *Arizona: The History of a Frontier State.* Phoenix: Hobson and Herr, 1950.

———. "Henry A. Crabb—A Tragedy of the Sonora Frontier." *The Pacific Historical Review* 9 (June 1940): 183–94, 187.

Yetman, David A. *The Ópatas: In Search of a Sonoran People.* Tucson: University of Arizona Press, 2010.

Young, John Phillip. *Journalism in California.* San Francisco: Chronicle, 1915.

Zabriskie, James A. *Address to Arizona Pioneers.* Report of the Board of Regents, University of Arizona. Tucson, 1902.

Index

Chiricahua Apaches, 24–25, 285,
306, 328n30, 334n38, 341n3; attack
on Ake party, 42–43, 52; bands
included in, 131, 306, 355n47; and
Bascom Affair, 41, 331n9, 349n76;
campaigns against, 132–33, 144,
158, 207, 234, 272–73; and conflicts with California Volunteers,
107–8, 142; leaders, 115, 147; raids
and attacks by, 51, 53, 106, 136–39,
144, 146–47, 343–44n23, 374n72;
raids in Mexico, 226; relocation as
prisoners of war, 389n7, 391–92n19;
waging of war, 51, 53, 132, 153–54,
158, 212, 291, 357n64, 387n46;
warrior traditions, 351n10, 358n73,
361n106; weapons used by, 119,
352n18; and withdrawal of troops,
43–44. *See also* Gileño Apaches;
Mimbreño Apaches; Southern
Apaches; *names of individual
bands*
Chiricahua Mountains (Ariz.), 131,
147, 234
Chivington, John Milton, 96, 100,
336n49; at Battle of Glorieta Pass,
97–98, 346n52; as commander of
Colorado Volunteers battalion,
95, 109; death, 293; power struggle
with Slough, 99; and Sand Creek
Massacre, 218–21, 272, 274,
371n48, 372n52
Chokonen Apaches, 40–41, 52, 147,
153, 323n8, 331n9, 359n92; as band
of Chiricahuas, 136–37. *See also*
Chiricahua Apaches
Chukunende (Chiricahua Apache
band), 306, 323n8, 325n6, 334n38
Chuska Mountains (Ariz. and
N.Mex.), 120, 128–29
Cibecue Apaches, 131
Civil War, U.S., 3, 48, 87, 136,
161–62, 294, 365n152, 366n1; end
of, 206, 230; factors, 264; impact
on increased violence in and
militarization of Southwest, 4–6,
37–38, 42, 94, 112, 122, 153, 155, 171,
208, 235–36, 263, 285–86, 321n1,

332n15, 388n52; preservation of
memory of in Southwest, 292–94;
westernmost engagement, 255,
380n128
Claflin, Ira, 97–98
Clay, Henry, 28
Cleghorn, Mildred Imach, 391n19
Coahuila y Tejas, Mexico, 20–21
Coahuila, Mexico, 20, 169
Cochise (Chiricahua chief), 138,
350n6, 359n90; attack on Ake
party, 42, 52; and Bascom Affair,
40–42; conflicts with California
Volunteers, 107–8, 144, 153; as
leader of Chokonen Apaches, 147;
U.S. Army's pursuit of, 272; and
war on Anglos, 40, 43–44
Cocopah (steamboat), 243, 255, 380n133
Cocopah Indians, 12, 14, 319, 330n50;
as allies of military, 222–23; as
allies of Quechan, 112, 328n30
Codington, Edward, 167
Cohn's Store (La Paz, Ariz.), 255
Colorado, 256, 370n45, 390n17; Carson's death in, 290; Confederate
desire for goldfields in, 57, 81,
85–86, 110; Indian attacks in, 207,
228; Indians of, 112, 213, 273–74;
Sand Creek Massacre, 218–19;
statehood, 292–93; volunteer
troops from, 47–48, 54, 96, 251, 318
Colorado (steamboat), 243
Colorado Chiquito (Ariz.), 128
Colorado River, 24, 52, 79, 223, 229,
247, 319, 324n1; as boundary of
Arizona Territory, 105, 334n36; as
boundary of California peninsula,
12; as boundary of District of
Arizona, 109; and California
Volunteers, 53, 56, 68, 70–71,
74, 104, 259; commercial steamboating, 242–43, 258; economic
development of mines in upper
regions of, 236; Edwards attack on
La Paz, 255; Fort Yuma overview,
68; increase in gold strikes along,
132; Indian attacks on settlements,
225; Indian tribes of, 112, 205, 223,

Pueblo Indians, 19, 23, 26, 92–93, 115, 126, 274, 323n8, 352n17; alliance with Hispanos and Anglos, 54, 152; Anglo view of culture, 270–71, 280; Apaches and Navajos raids on, 46, 113–14, 117–18, 121, 127, 148, 154, 156, 353n21; campaigns against Apaches, 35, 120, 125, 263; Comanches and Kiowas as enemies, 18, 207, 331n4; language and culture, 325n6, 326n7; trade in captives, 121, 354n31, 392n11; as traders, 212, 229, 314; as volunteer troops, 47; warfare traditions, 151
Pueblo Revolt of 1680, 19, 26, 326n7, 387n49
Pyron, Charles, 82, 88, 92–94; as commander during Battle of Glorieta Pass, 95–96, 98

Qua-ha-da Indians. See Comanche Indians
Quechan Indians, 12, 19, 24–25, 131, 319, 325n6, 328n30, 351n6; as allies of California Volunteers, 222–23; Arizona Volunteers, members of, 223; army supply contracts, 244; Maricopas, Pimas, Papagos as enemies, 29–30, 35, 112, 329n33; warrior traditions and weapons, 14, 29–3. See also Colorado River Yuman Indians
Quechan-Maricopa-Pima Indian War, 29–30
Querétaro, Mexico, 199–200, 202, 367n6, 368n15

Raguet, Henry, 92
Randall Mining District (Ariz.), 234
Raton Pass (N.Mex.), 23, 389n7
Redondo, José M., 242
Reform War. See La Guerra de Reforma (1858–61)
Régules, Nicolás de, 198
Reily, James, 52–53, 71, 83, 163
Republic of Texas, 21–22. See also Texas
Republicans (Mexico), 132, 161, 163,

169, 171, 204, 268, 356, 382n8, 386n41; government, 159, 362, 285; victory against Imperialists, 198–99, 203, 284, 366–67n6. See also Army of the Mexican Republic
Resources of the Pacific Slope (Browne), 242
Rigg, Edwin A., 59, 69–70, 146, 245–46, 248, 340n90
Rio Grande, 18, 23–24, 26, 30, 42, 102, 131, 139, 158, 168, 204, 252, 259, 331n4, 334n36, 336n52, 366n6, 394n25; Apache raids along, 121, 123, 157, 334n37; Battle of Valverde on, 86, 88–89, 106, 331n8; California Volunteers garrisons along, 109, 132; California Volunteers march to, 57, 75–76, 80, 104, 107–8, 142; Confederate Army along, 44, 51, 53, 57, 77, 81, 85, 99, 138, 161, 292; consolidation of Union troops on, 38, 43–44, 47; settlements, 17, 24–25, 35, 314
Rio Grande Valley, 129, 212
Rio Puerco (N.Mex.), 157
Ritter, John, 97
Robert, Thomas L., 108, 153, 358n73
Roberts, Thomas, 137
Robinson, Daniel, 352n18
Romero, Francisco, 231
Rossell, William H., 252, 379n125
Rowell, Converse W. C., 232, 374n73
Rynerson, William L., 283, 259, 336n49, 379n125

Saavedra, Rafael, 146–47, 359n90
Sabinal, N.Mex., 362n119
Sais, Eulogio, 124, 353n26
Salazar, Julian, 124
Salm-Salm, Agnes, 199–200
Salm-Salm, Felix zu, 200
Salt Clan (Navajo), 246
Salt River (Ariz.), 131, 249, 260
Salt River Valley (Ariz.), 260, 381n145
San Agustín Cathedral (Tucson), 246
San Andres Mountains (N.Mex.), 353n26

CPSIA information can be obtained
at www.ICGtesting.com
Printed in the USA
LVOW03s1102170118
562929LV00007B/9/P